9780714614533

LORD PALMERSTON
VOL. I

[1840]

LORD PALMERSTON

BY
HERBERT C. F. BELL

IN TWO VOLUMES
VOLUME ONE

WITH ILLUSTRATIONS

ARCHON BOOKS
HAMDEN CONNECTICUT
1966

FIRST PUBLISHED 1936
LONGMANS, GREEN AND CO., LTD.

REPRINTED WITH PERMISSION 1966
IN AN UNABRIDGED AND UNALTERED EDITION

LIBRARY OF CONGRESS CATALOG CARD NUMBER: 66-14604
PRINTED IN THE UNITED STATES OF AMERICA

TO MY MOTHER
EMILY ROGERS BELL
MY UNFAILING INSPIRATION AND MY
GAYEST COMPANION

R. J. P.

FOREWORD

In what Palmerston called 'the stagnant pool of history' his own figure takes up almost undue space. He was unconscionably long in dying, and unconscionably active in living. He was born before the American constitution saw the light, yet survived the Civil War. He was a minister five years before Napoleon laid down his power at Fontainebleau, a minister for three years after Bismarck came into power at Berlin, and a minister for all but about ten of the years that lay between. During those years his attitude was a factor in almost every political issue of real importance which sought solution in England ; his pen and voice influenced a remarkable number of developments in five continents. His pen especially. He shed letters and memoranda, official and private, until even now there seems to be no end to them.

These things doubtless explain why so few lives of Palmerston have been written. Mr. Guedalla's beautifully executed and quite indispensable portrait has so far shared the field with almost nothing save a brief biographical sketch in *The Queen's Prime Ministers* series, and a five-volume example of the mid-Victorian 'official' type of biography, a running commentary on such letters as two admiring co-workers and friends were minded to publish. It seemed to me, then, that there was room for a new study, traversing matters for which Mr. Guedalla had no space, and of which the 'official' biographers could not or would not speak. And I decided that I should try in particular to find out how Palmerston regarded the issues which he faced, rather than how he handled them. There was fresh material to be had on every side.

One of my troubles has been that there is far too much

of it. Only a man of Palmerston's industry and vitality, I have felt sometimes, could write a proper life of such a man as Palmerston. It is not only that he himself, both as an individual and a statesman, has left so much material behind; but that the letters, diaries and speeches of the men and women of his time, to say nothing of a recent flood of books and articles on the period, are full of him. And, though I have had no ambition to write a 'Life and Times,' I have used some of this incidental material a good deal. For who can so well understand and judge a public man, in respect to issues of the moment, as those who live among the same ideas, and in general act under the same limitations or with the same advantages, as he himself? And I have had other reasons for basing my study on a rather broad range of material. It was well enough for 'official' biographers to let their subjects 'tell their own stories'; but readers do not often have the time or opportunity to ascertain the essential truth or falsehood of the solemn affirmations of injured innocence and high purpose with which so many letters and diaries are sprinkled. A little history is a great corrective to impressions given by autobiographical material; and so are the statements and comments of contemporaries. With so wide a field of investigation and so inexhaustible a supply of 'authorities,' the selection of matters to be treated, and still more of materials to be employed, has been somewhat arbitrary. One really cannot pretend to what is known as 'exact scholarship' in a somewhat extended life of Palmerston. Partly for this reason, perhaps, I have found even more pleasure than difficulty in the work.

I should like to explain a little further what I have had in view. What I wish to emphasise again is that I have not attempted to show what Palmerston did, so much as what he thought and what he therefore wished to do. This seems to me the essential task of a biographer, or at any rate a limitation which he must place upon himself when his subject's life is entwined with much of the history of a long period. What the ministries in which Palmerston served did or did not do, has been related, or soon will be, by historians with time to make special studies of special aspects or episodes. So, in deference to the limitations of space and of special knowledge under which I have written, I have often contented myself with showing how Palmerston bore himself at certain critical junctures, without following the general story to its issue. I am quite aware that this procedure has great disadvantages ; but the only alternative was to offer more generalized and therefore less personal accounts of his conduct throughout the great sequences of events of which these episodes formed a part. And for the same reasons I have omitted any reference whatever to many of the things he did. There are already histories enough to fill out the tale.

So many people have been more than kind. Mr. Guedalla has contributed a quantity of valuable transcripts, an inspiring interest, and some criticisms that erred only in being too merciful. Dr. G. P. Gooch and Professor Carlton J. H. Hayes have given me every possible assistance and encouragement. Professors Basil Williams, Conyers Read, B. E. Schmitt, Chester New and J. P. Baxter, 3rd, have read various chapters of the manuscript and offered valuable comments. And my colleagues here at Wesleyan (I cannot enumerate) have always been ready with their help. Professor Baxter and Professor L. D. Steefel furnished me with advance copies of their books on the ironclads and Schleswig-Holstein (how slowly I have worked is sadly obvious), and bits of material besides. Professor F. S. Rodkey, Professor N. C. Kendrick and Mr. C. F. Strong were good enough to permit my use of unpublished monographs. Professor J. H. Hollander generously advised me on economic theory. Professors Carl Becker and Wallace Notestein did me a great service, years ago, by criticising a first draft of the earliest chapters. Mr. A. T. Milne transcribed some manuscripts with rare judgment and skill. And I should have got nowhere without the librarians. Dr. J. F. Jameson has taken a personal and active interest for which I cannot sufficiently thank him. Messrs. Ellis of the British Museum, Buckland and Ratcliffe of the Public Record Office, Wilder of Bowdoin, the Reverend Albert Lee of Windsor Castle, and Miss Eugenia Henry at Wesleyan have placed me under deep obligations by contributing without stint their time and their knowledge.

And in still other ways I have been greatly favoured. His late Majesty King George V, thanks to the kind offices of the late the Hon. Sir John Fortescue, graciously permitted me to use the Windsor archives. The Earl Grey gave me complete access to the papers at Howick House, and assistance in searching them. The Earl of Clarendon allowed me to copy many of his family records, and the Marquess of Lansdowne to use Mr. Guedalla's transcripts of letters at Bowood Park. Mr. Guedalla made it unnecessary for me to avail myself of Lord Gladstone's kind permission to inspect his father's papers when they were still at Hawarden. On this side of the water, Mr. Albert W. Johnston of Greenwich, Connecticut, lent me his very valuable collection of Palmerston's correspondence with Adair and Bagot.

Even time and money have been given me. The Social Science Research Council and the president and trustees of Wesleyan University have helped me to defray the cost of the secretarial assistance which I have required ; while the presidents and trustees both of Bowdoin College and of Wesleyan have given me special leaves of absence. To all these persons and institutions I offer my most grateful thanks. And so I do to Miss Madelyn Sullivan, whose skill and watchful interest have saved me many a slip, and whose patience in the midst of a disorderliness on my part which would have brought instant dismissal to the humblest clerk who served Lord Palmerston, has been remarkable.

So let this book, endowed by the kindness of many, but all too burdened with limitations and imperfections by its author, now fall into ' the stagnant pool of history.' The author, a little tired of trying to improve the book, and always inclined to mix his metaphors, feels that he is himself following the ancient injunction ' to jump into a pond in order to escape the rain.'

HERBERT C. F. BELL.

MIDDLETOWN, CONNECTICUT,
July, 1935.

CONTENTS OF THE FIRST VOLUME

CHAPTER I
THE CHILD OF FORTUNE, 1784–1809

The gifts of fortune; the era of change; the Anglo-Irish Temples in politics and society; the model youth at Harrow, Edinburgh and Cambridge; his early impression of the danger of a Bonapartist landing; young Viscount Palmerston and the world of politics in 1806–1807; how fortune and the rotten borough system served him in securing a place in the Admiralty and a seat in parliament; his first connection with Canning; how modesty and caution led him to refuse the Exchequer and a seat in the cabinet; his acceptance of the War Office; Palmerston as a Tory, a man of the world and a landlord . . . 1

CHAPTER II
THE WAR OFFICE, 1809–1828

The duties of a secretary for War, 'as ascertained by law, by His Majesty's warrant or by established practice'; the upper and nether millstones; conflicts with the 'crabbed and austere' Sir David Dundas; instructing the duke of York; industry, economy and system at the War Office; army reforms; the emergence of the Palmerstonian temperament . . 26

CHAPTER III
THE BREACH WITH THE TORIES, 1826–1828

Sport, business and patriotism; Palmerston's dislike of tyranny and revolution; his failure to secure advancement, and his increasing connection with the liberal Tories; the election at Cambridge in 1826, and his repudiation of 'the stupid old Tory party'; the Canning ministry; first lessons in Canningite foreign policy; the Goderich fiasco; Wellington recruits the Canningites; 'Ministers blackguard each other like draymen'; Palmerston mutinies in defence of Canning and the Canningites receive dishonourable discharge 44

CHAPTER IV

The Junction with the Whigs, 1828–1830

The Canningites in the wilderness; Wellington meets mutiny on the right wing; Palmerston turns to diplomacy, and secures useful information at Paris; his emergence as an orator, a religious liberal, a patriot and an interventionist; his discovery of the discontent of the French with their frontiers; fortune returns to him through the death of George IV and the glorious revolution at Paris; his inability to share Wellington's forgetfulness of their past differences; his decision to act with men he cannot 'think with' about parliamentary reform 73

CHAPTER V

Parliamentary Reform and Settlement in Greece, 1830–1832

'Cupid' and 'Lord Pumicestone' at the Foreign Office; Grey's moderating influence; Palmerston's policy of 'intermeddling' in order that England might have 'constitutional states' for 'natural allies'; his difficulty of 'thinking with' Lord John Russell about reform; his futile attempts to make the reform bill less liberal and arrange a compromise with the 'Waverers'; his submission to the public will; the European crisis, with London and Palmerston as the centre; Louis Philippe's dependence on England, and the origins of the first *entente cordiale*; how Greece secured a good frontier, a 'constitutional' king and more 'protection' than she wanted 96

CHAPTER VI

The Birth of Belgium, 1830–1832

Palmerston's alleged paternity; he leads England to the defence of the Netherlands against a political counter-reformation and the desire of France to alter her frontiers; the difficulty of dealing with two or three French policies, of checking the three eastern Powers, and keeping the Dutch and Belgians in order all at once; the usefulness of activity in the navy yards; the selection of fortresses to protect neutralized Belgium against the French; Louis Philippe learns that the victories of the first French republic 'cannot serve as a bugbear to all Europe' . 116

CHAPTER VII

Palmerston's first 'Intermeddling' in Spain, Portugal, Germany and Italy, 1830–1834

The political counter-reformation in other parts of Europe; Palmerston's Elizabethan touch in dealing with affairs in Spain and Portugal; his

CONTENTS

'powerful counterpoise to the Holy Alliance of the East'; his debated 'liberalism' in foreign policy; his dislike of reaction and revolution, and his interest in commerce, as displayed in his relations with the German Bund; his care for 'the maintenance of peace and the preservation of the balance of power,' as shown in his first dealings with the Italian question 139

CHAPTER VIII

PALMERSTON AND EASTERN EUROPE, 1830–1834

Palmerston decides that the use of gentle persuasion with the Tsar offers the only practicable means of helping the Poles; distrust and amiability in Anglo-Russian relations; Durham's 'perfectly successful' mission; Durham and the Princess Lieven interfere in the dispute over Stratford Canning's appointment as British ambassador at St. Petersburg; the Princess is punished; Mehemet Ali's first war with the Porte puts Palmerston in a dilemma; Russia 'rescues' Turkey and exacts the treaty of Unkiar Skelessi; England and Russia, avoiding war, indulge in 'snarls' 165

CHAPTER IX

PALMERSTON, THE WHIGS AND THE ENTENTE CORDIALE, 1834–1835

Palmerston, disliking 'extreme parties,' and finding the reformed House of Commons 'wonderfully like all its predecessors,' is not disturbed by the liberalization of the cabinet and its 'dismissal' by King William; his disagreement with Aberdeen on foreign policy in general; the decline of the *entente cordiale*; Palmerston and Talleyrand; Palmerston loses favour with the Whigs, gains favour with the public, and is heartily disliked by most of his subordinates; the first Whig attempt to prevent his return to the Foreign Office, 1835; his election at Tiverton, in 1837, shows some of the sources of his strength 187

CHAPTER X

THE FADING-OUT OF THE ENTENTE AND THE DECLINE OF BRITISH INFLUENCE IN SPAIN, PORTUGAL AND GREECE, 1835–1841

Palmerston's return to the Foreign Office; Louis Philippe becomes more Bourbon at home and abroad; fresh intervention in Spain, Portugal and Greece, for the benefit of constitutional government and British prestige, proves discouraging, and hastens the decline of the entente; the 'Holy Alliance' Powers threaten Belgium and get a taste of real Palmerstonian treatment; Palmerston tutors Queen Victoria in foreign policy and even convinces her that King Leopold is wrong regarding the settlement of the Belgian question 208

CHAPTER XI

Palmerston's War against the Slave Trade and First Relations with the United States, 1830–1841

His resolve that England shall have the glory of extinguishing the 'diabolical' slave trade; his pursuit of the slavers from flag to flag until they reach that of the United States; how he showed his sincerity in dealing with Texas; his plans for robbing the slave-traders of American and all other protection; his pleasant relations with the American government survive the boundary dispute, the 'battle of the maps,' some irritability, and a series of border incidents; Stevenson's doubts concerning the effects of a change of government 231

CHAPTER XII

Palmerston as a Seasoned Diplomat and Cabinet Minister, 1835–1841

His relations with the press; his resemblance to 'river-gods' and dray horses; good fortune comes again to him, and also to the party through his marriage; his need for 'varnish' in dealing with envoys and Foreign Office clerks; his anxieties in the east, from Canton to Cairo, and from Constantinople to the Baltic; his duel with Russia; his inability, arising from 'local and geographical circumstances,' to put an end to the occupation of Cracow 256

CHAPTER XIII

Further Problems in the East, 1835–1841

'The Chinese at Canton,' the 'Opium' War, and the commercial opening of China; 'flirtation' and watchfulness between London and St. Petersburg; Palmerston gratifies the radicals by appointing Urquhart, and Urquhart shocks Europe by publishing the *Portfolio*; the voyage of the *Vixen* and Urquhart's recall; Palmerston and the first Afghan War; Bright and the mutilation of the Burnes despatches . . . 272

CHAPTER XIV

The Near Eastern Crisis, 1839–1841

Palmerston's desire to defend and reinvigorate Turkey; his surprise at finding in France an opponent instead of a partner, and in Russia a partner instead of an opponent; the convention of July, 1840, the *furia francese*, and Palmerston's determination to 'stand fast'; 'unprincipled intrigue' in his 'own camp,' and the advantages it offered to Louis

Philippe; shrewd calculation and 'standing fast' give him his greatest diplomatic triumph; but his ungenerous and sometimes insulting attitude creates bitter and lasting enmity at the Tuileries; King Leopold commences to get the upper hand at Windsor . . . 291

CHAPTER XV

Palmerston's Longest 'Holiday,' 1841–1846

Palmerston's insistence on standing fast in parliament fails to save the Whigs; the kindly landlord and acquisitive traveller reappears; foreign affairs as managed by Aberdeen seem to him 'upon a sliding scale,' especially with regard to the Maine boundary, British influence in Spain, and the war on the slave trade; the new entente with France, ministerial and royal; the Whigs once more find Palmerston dangerous and refractory; Palmerston as a free-trader who advocates a fixed duty on corn, and a defender of the 'establishment' in Ireland who wishes government support for Catholic clergy 322

CHAPTER XVI

Palmerston's Second Return to the Foreign Office, 1845–1846

Victoria and Aberdeen, visiting Louis Philippe, come to a verbal agreement about the marriage of the Spanish princesses; discontent with Aberdeen's yielding policy to France and the United States increases in England; Palmerston points out that 'influence abroad is to be maintained only . . . by hope and fear'; in the cabinet crisis of December, 1845, some of the Whigs again try to keep him from returning to the Foreign Office, giving Russell the opportunity to hand the 'poisoned chalice' back to Peel, and producing a strong reaction in Palmerston's favour; the Anglo-French 'clique' at Paris; Louis Philippe prepares to face the 'ennemi de ma maison' at the Foreign Office once more, while 'Palmerston House' dreams of greater things; Palmerston, visiting Paris, proves less expert in acting than the French; his return to the Foreign Office, his enthusiasm for 'constitutions everywhere,' and his possible influence on Prussia worry Nesselrode . . . 349

CHAPTER XVII

The Spanish Marriages, The Death of the Entente, and the Effect on Continental Politics, 1846–1847

The aftermath of the Aberdeen-Guizot bargain about the Spanish princesses; Palmerston's apparent over-trustfulness gives Guizot the opportunity to play a 'little trick'; the Queen, finding the French government's conduct 'infamous,' speaks her mind to Louis Philippe and joins the country in supporting Palmerston; the 'little trick' produces unforeseen results for the French king and Guizot; Palmerston co-operates with the French government in settling affairs in Portugal, but makes Louis Philippe and Guizot pay the price of their trickery when Austria annexes Cracow 373

CHAPTER XVIII
The Prelude to the Revolutions of 1848

Palmerston points out the new 'steam bridge' between England and the continent, and becomes the great apostle of 'preparedness'; he helps to bring out 'the bankruptcy of the Metternich system,' and 'makes game of' all the Powers in connection with the war of the *Sonderbund*; Palmerston in his early sixties; he suggests the fixing of compensation for expelled Irish tenants at will; he tries to satisfy his anxiety concerning developments in Ireland and Italy at one stroke by sending Minto on mission; the Queen's increasing resistance to his foreign policy; he desires regular diplomatic relations with the Vatican but refuses to receive an ecclesiastical envoy; his task of carrying England through the revolutions of 1848-1849 398

CHAPTER XIX
The Revolutions of 1848, and Palmerston's Conflict with the Queen—I

Palmerston meets his greatest continental foes as exiles in London; his mixed feelings toward the second French republic; his fears, his aims and policies regarding northern Italy; his struggle against the Queen's efforts to hold England to an eighteenth-century policy; he gambles on Sardinia's success, and allows the one opportunity of helping the Lombards and Venetians to escape him; the Court, the exiles, King Leopold and the Aberdeen circle combine to make his progress difficult; what real success he had in his North Italian policy; the conflict with the Queen grows personal; her first vain effort to get rid of him; the suppressed correspondence with Prince Schwarzenberg; the cabinet, noting all the hostility which he creates, becomes restive . . . 422

Guide to Citations 448

Notes 457

ILLUSTRATIONS IN THE FIRST VOLUME

PALMERSTON IN 1840	*Frontispiece*
	To face p.
A MEETING OF THE BOARD OF ADMIRALTY	16
THE ADMIRALTY, THE WAR OFFICE AND THE TREASURY	28
THE COUNTESS COWPER	56
INTERIOR OF THE OLD HOUSE OF COMMONS	78
'BLOWING UP THE FIRE'	108
DOWNING STREET	148
THE PRINCESS LIEVEN	174
'THE RUSSELL PURGE BEGINNING TO WORK'	204
'SCENE IN THE NEW POLITICAL PANTOMIME'	226
METTERNICH	268
LOUIS PHILIPPE	298
THE FOURTH EARL OF ABERDEEN	330
'I'M AFRAID YOU'RE NOT STRONG ENOUGH FOR THE PLACE, JOHN'	364
'THE JOHN-BULL FIGHT OF LOUIS PHILIPPE'	384
QUEEN VICTORIA IN 1846	432

LORD PALMERSTON

CHAPTER I

THE CHILD OF FORTUNE, 1784–1809

THE fairies were very kind to Henry John Temple as he lay in his cradle in October 1784. One wished him brains and another zest for using them ; a third added optimism and kindliness, a fourth bestowed a powerful constitution in a powerful physique. Yet another came forward to endow him with ancient lineage and an assured position in society—the more assured in being backed by a title and sufficient, if not superabundant, wealth. Again, early initiation into a world where gaiety ran hand in hand with intellectual and artistic achievement was assured the infant through a father who enjoyed a comfortable footing there ; while wise guidance in his early years was guaranteed through a mother in whom sense and maternal affection were combined. Nor was this all that the fairies brought by any means. For extraordinary opportunity was laid before this child of fortune in the very time chosen by Providence for his birth. Before him stretched a great period of experiment and discovery in politics. English statesmen and their parties, shaken already in some of their traditional convictions by events that had transpired in India, Ireland, and America, awakening gradually to the presence of new ideas in the air, and commencing to adjust themselves to a changing economic world, were about to find their beliefs and policies subjected to the still more searching tests produced by the era of the French Revolution and the first Napoleon. Already there were new

Tories in the making, new Whigs, and, more disturbing still, persons whose demands for fundamental change were branding them as 'radicals.' New theories of democratic government, of economic freedom, of greater social equality and of liberal nationalism, were taking shape in men's minds, and would soon have to be considered and dealt with. In short, a new Europe and a new England were gradually to appear as decade after decade of the nineteenth century would roll by. Since the fairies had not forgotten to add long life to Henry John Temple's other gifts, he would have full chance to try his powers.

Looked at more closely, his endowments seem even to gain in impressiveness.[1] The Temples were a mighty and widely-connected family in eighteenth-century England; and, while the Irish Temples had been separated from the English branch since Elizabethan times, even their remote connection with some of the greatest Whig houses was not to be despised. Moreover, the Irish Temples could, on their own account, offer a good deal of distinguished ancestry to the infant now born to be their head. The new heir-apparent could pride himself on being descended from a provost of Trinity, Dublin, an Irish master of the Rolls, and a speaker of the Irish House. A more suitable progenitor, though merely a collateral one, was the great Sir William Temple of the late seventeenth century. For he, establishing himself in England, had achieved eminence in statecraft and diplomacy as well as in the literary world. With him and with his brother's son, the first Viscount Palmerston (in the Irish peerage), the Irish Temples had ceased to be Irish in any sense other than that of being Irish absentees. In fact, it seemed that the first viscount could not do too much to consolidate his position in Walpole's England, where society, politics and trade were forming the amalgam that was to endure so long. He improved the family seat at Broadlands, near Southampton, and the great suburban residence of the Temples at East Sheen; he acted as chairman of a committee (containing four dukes no less!) formed to watch over that social sanctuary, St. James's Square. He married a daughter of the governor of the Bank of England (setting a precedent of alliance with Threadneedle Street and the Guildhall adhered to for two generations after him) ; and he sat for twenty years as 'little Broadbottom Palmerston' in parliament. His grandson, the second viscount, not only entered the House of Commons in his early twenties, but occupied minor ministerial posts under Rockingham, Grafton and North. With North's resignation in 1782, the second Lord Palmerston's office-holding came to an end. He was known after that mainly as a man of fashion, a poetaster, and a patron of the arts. But he held a seat in the Commons to the end. He made, indeed, vain efforts to exchange it for one in the British House of Lords. But his failure to attain the splendour of a British peerage was another piece of great good fortune for his heir. Never would the heir be forced, as would several of his contemporaries and rivals in politics, to accept the political handicap of sitting in the upper House. On the other hand, an Irish peerage offered its holder distinct political advantages in a day of aristocratic cabinets. The boy would be able to have his cake and eat it, too.

Just because this child was so very fortunate, his earliest experiences were not of a sort calculated to mould, or even to reveal, character. 'Harry' Temple had no real sorrows to endure nor obstacles to overcome. Yet it seems altogether probable that certain tastes and views were nurtured in him by glimpses of the gay and talented circle in which his parents moved. At their town house, and at the 'prodigious great magnificent' edifice at East Sheen, Lord and Lady Palmerston made a 'toil of pleasure,' wearing themselves out with incessant 'junketings,' dashing from sailing parties to dinners and assemblies, from plays and operas to balls and masquerades. But it would be unjust to think of them merely as seekers of pleasure in the most shallow sense. Perhaps the second viscount was no more than a ' dilettante of rank with brains enough to admire brains, but not enough to be distinguished for them.' Still, the fact remains that he received a D.C.L. from Oxford, and words of mild commendation for his literary accomplishments from Boswell and Horace Walpole. More significant still appears the circumstance that he was welcomed by Samuel Johnson into the famous Literary

Club, to sit with Sheridan and Garrick, Burke and Fox, Gibbon, Sir Joshua Reynolds and Adam Smith. And among these olympians he made actual friends. How else would he have served as a pall-bearer to both Garrick and Reynolds, and received through Sir Joshua's will a second choice of all the pictures that remained in the master's studio ? How much the heir knew of junketings and olympians is largely a matter of surmise. In all probability Lord and Lady Palmerston saw to it that he spent most of his time at Broadlands, where he acquired the rudiments of his education from a French governess, played with his brother and two young sisters, and impressed visitors with his sturdiness, good temper and good looks. Yet he must have had sufficient touch with the sparkling life that went on at East Sheen and Hanover Square to make it certain that he and the great world would not be complete strangers to one another when his own time came. Neither in that day would he find himself entirely a stranger on the continent. For in 1792 the family went to Italy for a stay that covered between one year and two. One can no more than guess at the effects of this experience. Old enough and observant enough to notice many things, he lacked both age and temperament to understand the turmoil that was going on in the Italian states. The stirrings of romanticism and liberalism, which heralded the appearance of so many nineteenth-century problems with which he would have to deal, must almost certainly have passed him by. Yet he was tutored by a political exile ; and the impressions of a boy of eight are not easily effaced. Hence speculation, pleasant if unprofitable, must deal with the fruits of his first visit to the continent. All that one can assert with assurance is that the visit failed to correct his tendency toward excessive insularity.

Taken all in all, the impressions received in his impressionable nursery years must have predisposed him to an attitude of tolerance, especially where morals and politics were concerned. English society, with the example of the corpulent ' first gentleman of Europe ' before it, was not over-particular as to its amusements, or as to the private lives of those whom it received ; and the Palmerstons seem to have been less particular than some of their friends. The viscount was censured for allowing his guests at Naples to play *rouge-et-noir*—'an example which every other person had discountenanced'; and his lady accused of making herself 'a great protectress of the class of demireps' in order to attract 'gay young men' to her house. Their elder son, who must have sensed the absence of Mrs. Grundy from gatherings which could attract attention even in those gay days, was not growing up in an atmosphere best fitted for the upbringing of a prime minister of Queen Victoria. As for political tolerance in at least the party sense, that was no very rare commodity at a time when many a man had trouble in deciding whether to call himself a Tory or a Whig. And the Palmerstons, who were never prone to take things too seriously, and who had the will and ability to make friends everywhere, were the last people to be impressed with party principles or party tags. There was no reason to assume that the heir would grow up with deeply rooted political attachments of any sort.

The boy, mercifully oblivious as yet to considerations such as these, went up to Harrow in his eleventh year. The school, though still comfortably small, was at this time in particular favour with the nobility. Young Temple found himself surrounded by youths whose fathers helped to rule the land, and who would themselves rank among the most powerful of his political associates and opponents in later times. In this illustrious company 'Temple's frame of iron,' which Harrow song still celebrates, was truly welded in cricket, football and hunt-the-hare. Like every schoolboy hero, it was his to thrash a young Goliath, 'twice his size' and be brought home 'with black eyes and a bloody nose'; to express his soul's desires in terms of cricket bats; and to bear his part stoutly when his school-fellows went on strike. We find him even in the time-honoured pillow fight; and, most prophetically, driving before him a discomfited youth who was to become the fourth and most famous earl of Aberdeen. His, too, the fame of being kind to fags, of finding swearing most 'ungentlemanlike,' and failing to discover pleasure (this at fourteen years) in getting drunk. But through his letters ran a vein of gaiety and independence that model schoolboy heroes lack. A pun on Holy Trinidad, made more *holy* still by British guns; a pagan interest in the stage; and, alas ! the blasphemous comment, made after a holiday in town, that 'the Queen gives me the idea of a housemaid.' Whether he showed equal zest and nonchalance in finding his way through the prescribed Greek and Latin texts is not disclosed; but he professed to enjoy reading *Don Quixote* in the original, and to be content enough to keep up his Italian in the holidays. He had apparently gone beyond the necessity of 'keeping up' his French. But his talents were linguistic rather than literary: and he had not yet been called upon to think. Four years at Harrow seem, as was perhaps natural, to have developed without awakening him. In July of 1800 'Mr. Temple Sen.' (his brother had joined him at the school) gave proof of his high attainments by declaiming *Ger. Caesar ad Legiones, In Catilinam,* and 'The Bard,' and was ready to go elsewhere.

It seems impossible to exaggerate the importance of his next move; for it carried him to Edinburgh, where he received his intellectual awakening. Indeed, according to his much-quoted statement of a later time, his three years at the Scotch capital gave him 'whatever useful knowledge and habits of mind' he possessed. The very exaggeration in this statement makes it the more significant. For Harrow and Cambridge, to which he went on leaving Edinburgh, offered as good conventional education as was available at this time and helped to form a strikingly large proportion of early nineteenth-century England's greatest men. Why then did Palmerston, who acquitted himself well at both, and showed to Harrow at least a sentimental loyalty, more than once speak of the contributions they had made to his own development with scorn? What did Edinburgh offer which a famous school and a more famous university withheld? For one thing it allowed and encouraged him to think for himself; for another it gave him, as the basis of his thinking, ideas not only fresh but revolutionary. For the first time he came into intimate personal contact with the new and moving forces of his age.

In enjoying such opportunities at Edinburgh he was

the child of fortune still. In ordinary times he would, no doubt, have made a grand tour of the continent—picking up, perhaps, something of continental thought, but without necessity or opportunity of mastering it. But Napoleon and his armies had made grand tours for the time being impossible ; and English parents who desired to broaden their sons' minds were sending them beyond the Tweed to imbibe some of the famous Scotch philosophy. Yet not all English parents, by any means, were willing to do this. For some of the new ideas expounded from Edinburgh chairs were regarded with grave suspicion by the more conservative elements in British society. Most notably the doctrines of Adam Smith, which had been quoted freely in parliament and warmly endorsed by Pitt himself, had come, during the 'nineties, to be associated with those subversive French theories which constituted the bolshevism of that day. Hence the great majority of young men who went to Edinburgh were, and were always to be, Whigs. And not a few of these would develop in the Scotch air views which would make ' new ' or liberal Whigs—the kind of Whigs who launched the *Edinburgh Review* and stood out stoutly for reform. It says something for the broadmindedness of Lord and Lady Palmerston that they were among the few Tories (albeit Pittite ones) who sent their sons to join this group. Moreover, being anxious that their heir should have the very best, they placed him in the household of Dugald Stewart, a professor who ranked at once as the leading philosopher in the British Islands and the leading commentator on Adam Smith. Stewart, a man of amazing eloquence and great fertility of mind, had made something of a sensation in the preceding winter by daring to offer a ' separate course ' on political economy. It was considered shocking that ' the gospel of Mammon ' should appear in the curriculum of a great university, and very doubtful whether public discussion of matters which might bring under consideration ' questions touching the constitution of government ' should be allowed.

Young Temple experienced no doubts or questionings of this sort. Instead, he devoured his opportunities. His mornings seem to have been spent in taking copious notes on Stewart's lectures (notes so copious that they were drawn upon for the publication of these lectures in 1855), and in dabbling happily with drawing and chemistry. The rest of his time was apparently given to reading, to exercise on the water and on the hills, and to conversation with as interesting a company of people as could have been desired. At the Stewarts' he met the great of Edinburgh's intellectual and social world : at the house of his parents' Whig friends, Lord and Lady Minto, living temporarily in Edinburgh to watch over and share in the education of their children, he must have encountered members of the French *émigré* court of Holyrood as well. Perhaps, in spite of all his application, he failed to plumb the depths about him ; for his name never graced the rolls of the Speculative Society, 'joined by every man of mark in the University.' But neither speculation nor conformity to what others did was ever to his taste. He spent his time to suit himself, and spent it well. Lord Minto was a ready witness to the fact:

> Harry is as charming and as perfect as he ought to be. I do declare that I never saw anything more delightful. On this subject I do not speak on my own judgment alone. I have sought opportunities of conversing with Mr. and also with Mrs. Stewart on the subject, and they have made to me the report which you have already heard from others, that he is the only young man they ever knew in whom it is impossible to find any fault. Diligence, capacity, total freedom from vice of every sort, gentle and kind disposition, cheerfulness, pleasantness, and perfect sweetness, are in the catalogue of properties by which we may advertise him if he should be lost.[2]

Curiously enough, the one fault Lord Minto found in the boy was ' a want of the spirits belonging to his age.' Perhaps the atmosphere of Stewart's house was a little sombre for a youth so high spirited. But occasional flashes of his old boisterous nature showed that the Palmerston of Harrow days was not yet dead.

A really sobering influence came to him, however, at Edinburgh, through the death of his father, who closed a graceful and not undistinguished life in April 1802. The youth's loss was in some respects severe ; but, all things considered, it probably contributed both to his development and his prospects. He was severed from dilettantism, drawn close to a mother who now put aside 'junketing' to give all her wisdom and her tenderness to her family, and invested with a sense of responsibility for his brother and sisters and for the family estates. As a peer he became a person of greater consequence ; and as the fatherless son of popular parents he could count upon increased interest and tutelage from men able to do more for him, in some respects at least, than ever his father could have done. Of these at least two were diplomatists, and one the possessor of administrative talent as well. Lord Minto, who had already served two years as minister plenipotentiary to Austria, and was soon to achieve some measure of fame as a prudent governor-general of India, regarded him with an affection that was quite fatherly : Lord Malmesbury, who was almost the personification of skilled eighteenth-century diplomacy, shared the boy's actual guardianship with Lord Chichester, a member of the great Pelham family. Both guardians, it may be noted, were Pittites. It was to Malmesbury in particular that he turned, choosing to spend much of his holidays with the deaf but still vigorous ambassador. He could scarcely have found in England a man better fitted to familiarize him with the great European courts from Madrid to St. Petersburg, or to offer him glimpses from behind the scenes of the tactics and strategy of eighteenth-century diplomacy. Nor could he easily have found a mentor who had observed from a greater number of angles the shifting scene of British politics. For Malmesbury had once stood with Fox ; had left Fox to take his place with the 'old' Whigs ; and now ranked as a trusted adviser to Pitt, leader of the 'new' Tories, and to George Canning, the new Tories' rising star. This may explain why the Whig Mintos, though closely connected by marriage with Malmesbury, looked upon the growing intimacy between Palmerston and his illustrious guardian with some regret.

In accordance with plans made in his father's lifetime, and adhered to scrupulously by his mother and guardians, Palmerston, having said good-bye to Edinburgh, was admitted to St. John's College, Cambridge, in 1803. In later years he was reported by credible witnesses as saying that one could learn boating at Cambridge if nothing else, and that he had spent his time there ' very much in forgetting what he had learned at Edinburgh.' But admissions in his autobiography that 'it became necessary to learn more accurately at Cambridge what one had learned generally at Edinburgh,' and that ' the habit of mind acquired by preparing for . . . examinations was highly useful,' tend to offset these obvious indulgences in hyperbole. And, if he found Cambridge an intellectual waste, it is hard to understand why he took his life there so seriously. As a nobleman he enjoyed the privileges, not only of sitting at high table and wearing a gold-laced gown, but of eschewing examinations and taking a degree without even a pretence at work. Yet, according to all available accounts, he proved himself as much a paragon at St. John's as at Dugald Stewart's house, rising punctually at seven, keeping ' in the first class ' (whatever that may have meant) and submitting regularly to examinations like any commoner. It would be sad to think that Cambridge was quite unworthy of such perfectibility, or that such virtue went without reward.

Whatever Palmerston may have learned or forgotten during the years when he was an undergraduate at St. John's, some of the events of this time must have impressed themselves indelibly on his memory. With the French threatening a descent on the south coast, the lay members of the University organized a cadet corps, and elected the young Irish viscount one of its officers. But he had in later years memories more vivid than that of drilling his ' division ' on Cambridge lawns. He was passing through Doncaster on one occasion when an alarm was raised :

A court-martial that was sitting immediately broke up, and the officers ran to the top of the steeple to see Rendlestone Beacon smoking. Nobody knew what the cause of alarm was, but all supposed the French to be landed, but whether at Liverpool, Scarboro', or Harrowgate, none could tell.[3]

French military preparations, and the very name of Bonaparte, were to make him uneasy for well-nigh sixty years.

Before he took his degree at Cambridge, in 1806, fresh

sorrow and fresh responsibilities had come to him. His mother had died, after exhibiting, through a long and very painful illness, a cheerful resignation that was sufficient in itself to establish her strength of character. Had she lived only a little longer she would have seen the opening of a great career to which she had greatly contributed. For her elder son was just preparing to step forth into the world of politics.

The English world of politics was a very confused one at this time—a world where parties lacked definition, cohesion and discipline, and yet where one great party held distinct ascendancy. Except when some specific party issue drove party leaders to sudden remembrance of party tradition and principles, it was often difficult to tell a Tory from a Whig. For the Whigs were, on the whole, quite satisfied with the constitution as it stood ; and had long ceased to question the necessity of England's fighting it out with Napoleonic France : while the Tories, finding but little incentive to assert themselves in defence of ' Church and King,' were commencing to be merely conservative. Secessions of individuals or groups—almost invariably from Whig to Tory ranks—were likely to occur, and coalition governments to be a necessity. For both parties were divided within themselves by differences of opinion and by rivalries as to leadership. Yet Tory ascendancy was becoming if anything more pronounced, thanks largely to the continuance of the war, and the part played by Tory leaders in waging it. The men who had brought England safely through the perils she had encountered since '93, and on whom England expected to rely for security during the perilous years to come, were either Pittites or men whose Toryism was older and more inveterate. The Whigs had, for the time being, no corresponding hold on popular confidence. Many of the old titled chiefs seemed merely selfish, haughty and party-bound ; while the leaders of the more liberal and active group—the ' Foxite ' Whigs who commenced to congregate at Holland House—appeared insufficiently ' patriotic,' and too sympathetic with radicalism, for a nation which feared France and the new subversive ideas above all things. It happened, too, that a good proportion of the Tory leaders were able to remain in the lower house of parliament; while the Whigs showed a tendency either to inherit peerages or to burn out their energies far too soon. Young Lord Palmerston, who was quite naturally planning to offer himself for election as a Tory candidate, was enlisting on the side of the big battalions.

The conditions just sketched were neatly illustrated at the very time of his début. In January 1806 Pitt died, broken-hearted over the news of Austerlitz; and the King admitted to office the coalition government of 'All the Talents'—in reality a combination of conservative and liberal Whigs with Sidmouth's anti-Pittite Tory group. Its titular head was Grenville and its great figure—for the eight months of life that remained to him—was Fox. The talented ministry had but a brief career. Realising its insecurity, it sought fresh support by bringing on a general election in the late autumn. Though its quest proved vain, it embarked hopefully on a programme of reform, pushing through a bill to forbid the slave trade to British possessions everywhere, and taking up the question of removing certain disabilities from Irish (and incidentally English) Catholics. But the question of Catholic relief was peculiarly dangerous, since it involved issues concerning both Church and State. The cabinet quarrelled, both within itself and with the King; and George III, in March 1807, used certain rather impossible demands made upon him by the more liberal of his ministers as an excuse for dismissing all of them. Since the bulk of his subjects were as bigoted with regard to Catholics as he was himself, his action was entirely safe. But it was of more than doubtful constitutionality.

To these circumstances Palmerston owed his start in public life; but the initiative was his own. During the year 1806 he made two attempts at entering parliament: in the spring by contesting the seat for Cambridge University vacated by Pitt's death, and in the general election of November by standing for Horsham, a borough in Sussex.

His attempt at Cambridge[4] revealed him as a young man endowed with a fair degree of self-confidence. For he was not only aspiring to Pitt's seat, but was contesting it with two exceptionally gifted and powerful young Whigs who held posts in Grenville's new ministry. One was Lord Henry Petty, son of the famous Shelburne, and soon to achieve fame for himself as the third Marquis of Lansdowne, who had just become chancellor of the Exchequer ; the other was Palmerston's old schoolfellow at Harrow, Lord Althorp, heir to Lord Spencer, and just entering upon office as a junior lord of the Treasury. Yet Palmerston's self-confidence in confronting them was not unjustified. The Whig vote would be split ; and, what was more, the terrible epithet of ' lurking dissenter ' had been applied by rumour to Petty, the stronger Whig candidate. The Irish viscount, on the other hand, was reputed firm in his desire that the Test Act should be retained, and relief to Catholics refused. He seems to have impressed people by his sincerity. ' I can assure you,' Isaac Milner wrote, ' a more ingenuous appearance I never saw. The young man's conscience seemed hard at work for fear . . . of saying more than he could justify to his mind.'[5] And the young man had still another ground for optimism. The other university seat had been held for more than twenty years by still another Whig heir-apparent, Lord Euston, the duke of Grafton's son. Surely, under all the circumstances, Cambridge would show enough regard for ' Church and King ' to give half its representation to so sound a young Pittite. At any rate the young Pittite, reckoning among his assets the pride of his fellow-Johnians and the personal influence of such friends as the Malmesburys, believed that he might defeat Petty and would certainly make a better showing than Althorp. Petty agreed with him ; and so, as readers of *Hours of Idleness* may remember, did Lord Byron :

> Then would I view each rival wight,
> PETTY and PALMERSTON survey ;
> Who canvass there, with all their might,
> Against the next elective day.
> One on his power and place depends,
> The other on—the Lord knows what !
> Each to some eloquence pretends,
> But neither will convince by that.[6]

But all three were wrong ; for Petty stood at the head of the poll, while Palmerston was third. Perhaps Byron was not altogether wrong in connecting Petty's success with Petty's power :

> They know the Chancellor has got
> Some pretty livings in disposal :
> Each hopes that *one* may be his *lot,*
> And, therefore, smiles on his proposal.

Palmerston frankly took the same view. But according to Adam Sedgwick, who knew as much about Cambridge as any man, and to William Wilberforce, who was the highest of authorities in any issue that pertained to slavery, the question mainly at issue was the real or supposed attitude of the candidates towards abolition. That Palmerston of all British statesmen should at any time have been identified with the perpetuation of slavery seems well-nigh incredible; but Brougham for one certainly opposed his return on the ground that his family were notoriously anti-abolitionists, and that the new viscount would presumably be the same. It is worth noting, too, that Petty had the determined support of the Prince of Wales. The Prince was, of course, acting on what with him took the place of convictions ; but Palmerston's first encounter with the monarchy in politics was not of happy augury.

No account of his experience in standing for Horsham could offer much improvement on his own :

> In November, 1806, Parliament having been dissolved, a general election took place. Lord FitzHarris [later the second earl of Malmesbury] and I stood for Horsham. The borough was burgage-tenure, and the return of voting disputed. There was a double return ; each party petitioned, and the committee seated our opponents. FitzHarris and I paid each about £1500 for the pleasure of sitting under the gallery for a week in our capacity of petitioners. We thought ourselves very unlucky ; but in a short time came the change of government and the dissolution, in May, 1807, and we then rejoiced in our good fortune at not having paid £5000 (which would have been its price) for a three months' seat.[7]

The unreformed House of Commons was an expensive club.

The dissolution of May 1807 found Palmerston, though not in parliament, at least in public life. On Grenville's dismissal the Tories had returned to power, under the leadership of the septuagenarian duke of Portland, a veteran Pittite. The premier was too old and infirm to take any real direction of affairs; but he had insured the strength of his ministry by enlisting the services of Canning and Castlereagh. Incidentally, and at the request of his friend Malmesbury, he had made Palmerston one of the six junior lords of the Admiralty.[8] As a junior lord was scarcely expected at that time to do much more than sign his name, the appointment was not an especially flattering one. But Palmerston took it seriously—so seriously as to win both commendation and the nickname of 'Sir Charles Grandison.'[9] And it may have been due in some measure to his rather superfluous diligence that in August of this year a great opportunity almost came to him. Canning, who held the Foreign Office and needed a new under-secretary, would apparently have offered him the post had it not previously been promised to Charles Bagot, the future diplomatist.[10] Fortune had proved fickle to her one-time favourite. But it was not the first nor even the second time.

For she had also deserted him in the general election of May 1807, when he had stood again for Cambridge, with what seemed greatly increased prospects of success.[11] Not only had the influence of his friends, and the claims he had established on the party by his two attempts to enter the House in 1806, made him an official nominee, but the Tory strength in the university had suddenly revived. The reason is amusingly obvious. Since the ministry of 'All the Talents' had gone out mainly on its refusal of a pledge not to suggest further measures of Catholic relief to George III, and since the bulk of the nation had as usual applauded one of the most lamentable exhibitions of the King's wrong-headedness, the Tories saw that an appeal for loyalty to 'Church and King' would once more constitute an effective battle-cry. Deliberately played up throughout the country, and issuing, be it noted, in this case from the new holders of 'place and power,' the appeal had a striking effect on the Cantabrigians. The academic voters drove out Petty ; yet they did not, for a curious reason, send Palmerston to parliament. What happened was that the government, hoping to defeat not only Petty but Euston, the other Whig candidate, sent down Sir Vicary Gibbs, the attorney-general, to ' help ' the favourite and, if possible, to secure second place in the poll. Palmerston, to the chagrin of some of his backers, agreed with Gibbs that each Tory voter should be asked to cast one vote for each Tory candidate ; and Gibbs beat him by a majority of three. The Whigs, throwing many double votes to Euston, placed him just ahead of Gibbs.

Defeated in three elections, and yet holding a minor office in the ministry, Palmerston was an obvious nominee for some close borough at the disposal of the government. How ' close ' the borough was may be judged from a passage in his autobiography :

> Soon after this I came into Parliament for Newtown, in the Isle of Wight, a borough of Sir Leonard Holmes'. One condition required was, that I should never, even for the election, set foot in the place ; so jealous was the patron lest any attempt should be made to get a new interest in the borough [12]

No one could ever say that Palmerston lacked intimate knowledge of the old system of representation.

After a year of obscurity, the twenty-three year old junior lord of the Admiralty who sat for Newton made his maiden speech.[13] It is interesting to remember that he first addressed the House not only in defence of Canning, but of the most high-handed act for which Canning ever shared responsibility. The opposition had moved for papers on the bombardment of Copenhagen and the seizure of the Danish fleet ; and Palmerston had the privilege of helping to explain why the motion was resisted by the government. He chose the occasion, so he informed his sister, because ' it was impossible to talk any very egregious nonsense upon so good a cause.' His half-hour oration, composed and memorised with care, and embellished with references to ' the blessings of a free constitution ' and ' the law of nature which . . . commanded self-preservation,' was well delivered so long as memory served him, and was

A Meeting of the Board of Admiralty

APPOINTMENT TO THE WAR OFFICE

favourably received. He stood within the range of possible preferment when Portland's retirement should bring about a reconstruction of the ministry.

And the circumstances surrounding the reconstruction when it came, in 1809, gave him better chances of promotion than he could have hoped. They also separated him from Canning for several years. A quarrel between Canning and Castlereagh, for which each was in some degree to blame, caused a duel between the two ministers, and the resignation of both from the cabinet. The amiable Spencer Perceval, who accepted the task of forming a new ministry, found it almost too much for him. The Whig leaders, Grenville and Grey, refused to form a coalition; Sidmouth's group of Tories could not be fitted in; and some of Canning's friends, including Huskisson, declined to take office without their chief. But Palmerston seems to have been one of those who found Canning very much at fault.[14] He had no reason, then, to be surprised when Perceval called him, in the third week of October, from the pleasures of a three days' sailing trip, to receive the offer of a ministerial appointment. What did surprise him was that he should be offered the chancellorship of the Exchequer with a seat in the cabinet. He had neither experience in speaking nor any knowledge of finance.

Caution and modesty, which could certainly not be reckoned among the salient characteristics of the Palmerston of later years, were strongly in evidence in the Palmerston of 1809. Doubtful whether in accepting Perceval's flattering offer he would be acting fairly either to the premier or to himself, he turned to his guide and mentor, Lord Malmesbury, to his chief at the Admiralty, Lord Mulgrave, and to his friend, Plumer Ward.[15] Decision was difficult; for the situation was distinctly complicated. Perceval, foreseeing possible rejection on Palmerston's part, had offered two alternatives: a seat in the Treasury, to be exchanged for the Exchequer after a short period of apprenticeship, and a reversion to the secretaryship at War, in case this last-named office should be refused by another rising young Tory, 'Orator' Milnes. But the acceptance or rejection of the Exchequer was the question of the moment. The advice tendered by Palmerston's friends constituted as great a compliment as the offer. Malmesbury would have counselled acceptance in less troublous times ; Ward considered Palmerston capable of mastering the administrative side at least ; and Mulgrave thought that he should take the post, unless he felt ' nervous about it.' But Palmerston was more than nervous. He believed that ' by fagging and assistance ' he ' might get on in the office ' ; but being a person ' not born with the talents of Pitt or Fox,' he would have to make many bad speeches at first if called upon to deal with many subjects.

> . . . a bad speech, though tolerated in any person not in a responsible situation, would make a Chancellor of the Exchequer exceedingly ridiculous, particularly if his friends could not set off against his bad oratory a great knowledge and capacity for business ; and I should be apprehensive that instead of materially assisting Perceval, I should only bring disgrace and ridicule upon him and myself.[16]

In the end he rejected the Exchequer and the accompanying cabinet rank, at a time when it was still uncertain whether he would receive the appointment of secretary at War.

On October 26, however, Perceval finally offered him the War Office, and, in defiance of precedent, a seat in the cabinet along with it.[17] The office he was glad enough to accept ; but, contrary to Malmesbury's advice, he declined to enter the cabinet. Although perfectly conscious of the honour and the increased chance of future preferment which he was giving up, he allowed himself to be ruled by a prudence so marked as to be extraordinary :

> The office is one which does not invariably, or, indeed, usually go with the Cabinet. A seat there was consequently not an object to me for appearance' sake ; and considering how young I am in office, people in general, so far from expecting to see me in the Cabinet by taking the War Office, would perhaps only wonder how I got there . . . and the business of the Department will, I take it, be quite sufficient to occupy one's time without attending Cabinet Councils.[18]

Yet, as a comment made by Lady Lyttelton suggests, he was not entirely wrong :

> That place [of secretary at War] is now made use of as a sort of

seminary for beginners in politics. I suppose we must be glad of it, as it may divert his Lordship from flirting, in the same way as people rejoiced at his predecessor's appointment because it was to cure him of gambling.[19]

It is time to consider how Palmerston appeared to the great world as a whole.

The gay and talented circle of his parents, still gay but becoming somewhat less talented as the celebrities of the Literary Club passed gradually out of view, must have seen him as a promising recruit.[20] Able, good-looking, athletic, dandified, genial and high-spirited, he possessed plenty of aptitude for society. He was not very tolerant of bores—of the sort of people who were constantly asking his opinion of *Marmion* and *The Lay*; but to be among the clever and the charming, especially when they were women, delighted him. And almost from the first he singled out for the object of his particular admiration the young Countess Cowper, sister of the rising politician, William Lamb, who would rise in time to the premiership as Lord Melbourne. She seems, indeed, to have been the one woman to whom he showed a really enduring attachment in all his life. While the dowagers shook their heads over the introduction of a foreign and almost improper dance, Lady Cowper, who could subdue even dowagers, taught Palmerston to waltz. He had no need of training in more masculine accomplishments favoured by society.

But the great world, even while it welcomed him, must have realized that here was no true successor to the second Viscount Palmerston. Here was no devotee of pleasure, but a young man who fitted pleasure into life. Here was no gentle wooer of the arts, but a vigorous and rather matter-of-fact person, intent on using his abilities for the promotion of his own and his family's interests. Where the second Viscount had charmed sentimental ladies with verses about 'trembling anguish' or 'enchanting nymphs,' the third discovered a certain facility for composing clever doggerel about the Whigs. The *New Whig Guide*, published in 1815, has embalmed some specimens attributed to his pen. Thus, the Whigs, pondering 'the Choice of a

Leader,' had 'met to prepare their annual bill of political fare':

> But while they prepared the defeat of their foes
> Within their own camp civil discord arose
> And famished and gaunt Paddy Ponsonby's pack
> Like the hounds of Actaeon their huntsman attack ;
> ' What boots our debate ? ' Thus the rebels began,
> ' What avail the discussion of topic or plan ?
> With a leader who neither can lead us or drive.
> . . . .
> Expect then to see half the party secede or
> Provide us with someone more fit to be leader.'
> . . . .
> At length 'tis proposed to allay all their grudges
> That Grenville and Grey shall conjointly be judges.
> Unable their rancour a moment to smother
> The followers of neither will trust in the other
> . . . .
> And lest the one worthy his brother should trick
> Like two Brentford kings they must both hold the stick.

Perhaps, among the dozens of stanzas, that satirising the conclusion of a speech delivered by Whitbread, whose fortune came from brewing, added most to the Tory joy of living :

> My rhet'ric alone will suffice to your aid
> And of *it* I may say as we did to the trade
> Of the prices of beer (to detain you no longer)
> ' You can't have it cheaper but shall have it stronger.' [21]

Even if the attribution happens to be false, the breeziness, the flippancy, the rather coarse humour and the sarcasm all ring true to the Palmerston of history.

Still others of these rollicking couplets ridiculed not only the Whigs but some of the articles of their faith. Whig speakers were, for example, represented as ' roaring of popery ' and drawling ' all the twaddle of all the Dissenters.' No one would, of course, class Palmerston as an orthodox Tory on such evidence ; but it seems clear that he found himself quite at home with his party during the years of his very early manhood. He recognised much of the greatness and all of the lovableness that had been in Fox; but regarded him as having been so 'infected with the disorder' of the French Revolution as justly to have forfeited public confidence.[22] When the ministers of 'All the Talents' were dismissed, he blamed them for pressing Catholic relief at all in face of the known sentiments of the country and the King, and found their conduct at the time of the final break irreconcilable 'with the respect which they owed to their Sovereign, or the constitutional principles by which it was their duty to have been guided.'[23] In 1811, Plumer Ward identified him again and again with a group of young Tories who 'hoped and expected to keep together,' were 'enthusiastic for such a leader as Perceval,' and entertained 'a general sentiment against Canning.'[24] Other evidence of his Toryism might be found in his conduct during the riots of 1815, when the London mobs, enraged by the passage of a 'corn law,' designed to benefit the landed proprietors by keeping up the price of food, threatened to attack the houses of the ministers. For he ordered his servants to 'meet the first discharge of stones with a volley of small shot from a bedroom window,' since this would 'pepper the faces of the mob without any danger of killing any of them,' and serve as 'an earnest of what a further perseverance in the attack might produce.'[25] Yet, be it noted, one may look in vain for convincing evidence that he ever sympathised with the stubborn and reactionary 'old' Tory group represented by such men as Lords Eldon and Bathurst. It is true that he blamed the ministers of 'All the Talents' for their break with George III; and that he was regarded as an enemy to Catholic emancipation during his first Cambridge canvass. But this was when he was very young and had not even crossed the threshold of his career. Moreover, in criticising Grenville and his ministers for breaking with the King (the criticism is found only in his diary) he was careful to point out that he was condemning, not the principle of Catholic relief in any of its projected forms, but merely the action of the ministry in pressing it at that especial time. One suspects that he was less 'ingenuous' than Milner thought. In throwing himself into the spirit of convivial Tory dinners he was perhaps testifying to his youth as much as to his principles ; and in protecting his house against the London mobs he was acting less as a Tory than as a rather callous property-owner of the period.

It was not long before he became clearly identified with the more liberal Tory group in one essential at least. By 1812 his advocacy of Catholic emancipation was drawing complaints from the duke of Richmond ;[26] in 1813, it was announced in one of the very few noteworthy speeches which he made during his early years in parliament.[27] Not only his attitude but his line of argument was significant. He would hear nothing of Catholic 'rights' ; for the sovereign parliament of Great Britain was entitled to secure the 'welfare and safety' of the nation by putting upon Catholics such disabilities as might be requisite to that end. But, according to his view, it was essential for the very welfare and safety of the nation that Catholic disabilities of all kinds should be removed :

> There is both inconvenience and danger in the continuance of the present anomalous state of things. . . . We have, in the bosom of the empire, a large mass, considerable by its numbers, by property, by rank, by talent, and activity, . . . circumscribed and cut off from the rest of the community. . . . Is this a desirable state of things ? can we be said to have, at our command, the full natural resources of the united empire ? . . . If it had unfortunately happened that by the circumstances of birth and education, a Nelson, a Wellington, a Burke, a Fox, or a Pitt, had belonged to this class of the community, of what honours and what glory might not the page of British history have been deprived. . . . The question is not whether we would have so large a part of the population Catholic or not. . . . It is in vain to think by any human pressure we can stop the spring which gushes from the earth. But it is for us to consider whether we will force it to spend its strength in secret and hidden courses, undermining our fences, and corrupting our soil, or whether we shall, at once, turn the current into the open and spacious channel of honourable and constitutional ambition, converting it into the means of national prosperity and public wealth.

It may perhaps be said that there was no 'liberalism' in such an argument, but merely a touch of nationalism combined with hard common sense. Yet it would have been hard to persuade Eldon and Bathurst that Palmerston's Toryism was orthodox.

Since the party could not dispense with its 'Catholic' wing, the secretary at War's views constituted no necessary bar to such advancement as he might earn. And that he had some claim to promotion there is no doubt. As will later appear, his work at the War Office was not only assiduous but highly efficient and even enterprising. Though he seldom spoke in parliament, and then usually to no great effect, the military estimates which he had yearly to lay before the House were prepared and presented with a skill and clarity which brought him commendation from all sides. As early as 1811, so prominent a member of the opposition as Whitbread had congratulated him both publicly and privately.[28] And on one occasion at least his own colleagues proved ready to mark their recognition of his services. In the summer of 1812, some months after Liverpool had taken Perceval's place as premier, Palmerston was offered the chief secretaryship for Ireland. It was, as he recognized, a post 'more important, more active, and more likely to lead to distinction' than the office of secretary at War; but, on account of 'particular circumstances and considerations' which he seems never to have specified, he refused it immediately.[29] Peel accepted it, and made it one of the great stepping-stones of his career.

One wonders whether the 'particular circumstances and conditions' had anything to do with the attention which Palmerston was giving to his family and his estates. No matter of detail seems to have escaped his grave consideration.[30] He decided that the drawing-room curtains at Broadlands should be 'applied to mend the chairs and sofas' which were in 'great decay,' and that other rooms should have 'new curtains of the *suppressed* green, with carpets less likely to show stains than the present' ones. He was careful to specify what horses from the Broadlands stables his brother (who was not much younger than himself) should ride. Perhaps his attitude was a little more paternal than was necessary; but his letters were bantering and affectionate. They showed, too, how deeply concerned he was in furthering William Temple's prospects in life, and how sympathetic to his sisters' purchases of smelling-bottles and other proper appurtenances of débutantes of that day.

As landlord of a ten-thousand-acre estate lying on the west coast of Ireland around Sligo, he lost no time in planning improvements on an impressive scale. If he was to be an absentee he intended to be a model one, visiting his property annually for some time at least, and developing it in every manner possible. He was quite awake to the financial advantages that might accrue from the reclamation of bogs and the improvement of ' the arable ' ; but what he seems to have been most intent upon was the well-being of his swarming tenantry. He described his plans to one of his sisters in 1808:

> The present objects which I must in the first instance set about, are to put the parish church in a state of repair . . . to establish schools, to make roads, and to get rid of the middlemen [tenants who made a profit by subdividing and subletting their holdings] . . . where it can be accomplished. After that, as opportunities occur, I mean to endeavour to introduce a Scotch farmer, to teach the people how to improve their land ; to establish a little manufacturing village in a centrical part of the estate, where there are great advantages of water and stone ; and to build a pier and make a little port near a village that stands on a point of land projecting into Donegal Bay, and called Mullaghmore.

He wrote of the smallholders with genuine commiseration and sympathy :

> They are too poor to improve their land, and yet it is impossible to turn them out, as they have no other means of subsistence.[31]

He was always to be known in Ireland as a kind landlord.

In 1813, Palmerston, completing the third decade of his life, could still regard fortune as a friend. The prudent game, which he had so far preferred to play, seemed bound to yield substantial returns before many years. Two years previously, one of his minor ambitions had been realised ; for his university had at last chosen him as one of its representatives in parliament.[32] What was more, it had elected him by a large majority. No doubt his success was partly due to the fact that he had nursed the seat carefully, giving up more promising diversions to play whist and drink punch with the Johnians ; but when the time for the election came, his party ' made the most of the ability displayed by Lord Palmerston in the administration of the country.' The phrase has a decidedly electioneering sound ; but even as early as 1811 it had become obvious that he was a highly efficient secretary at War.

CHAPTER II

THE WAR OFFICE, 1809–1828

ONE meets some formidable obstacles in attempting to follow Palmerston's activities at the Horse Guards. The vast accumulation of War Office papers covering the period of his incumbency are so forbidding in content as well as bulk, that it will take unusual enterprise and diligence to refine them down to a usable product. Until the task is done, one must be content to pick up what can be learned elsewhere, and supplement it with what an occasional dip into the main repository may reveal. Nor is lack of precise information the only obstacle. It is, and always has been, difficult to explain just what the secretary at War was supposed, and was not supposed, to do.[1]

His duties were primarily financial. It was a long-established principle that army finances should be controlled by the House of Commons through the secretary as a responsible minister; while, on the other hand, the 'discipline and management' of the forces—regarded as belonging to the royal prerogative—rested in the hands of the non-responsible commander-in-chief. Questions of military policy fell within the province of the secretary of state for War and Colonies. Even had the lines thus drawn been absolute, the position of the secretary at War would have been rather a difficult one; but, unfortunately, the division of functions between his office and that of the commander-in-chief was not clear either in theory or in fact. When the commissioners of Public Accounts attempted, in 1808, to define the position of the secretary, they were informed only that he was 'to govern himself in the charge of his duty by the existing rules of the Service, as ascertained by law, by His Majesty's warrant, or by established practice.'[2] As the warrant was ambiguously worded, and as some of the statutes had been carelessly drafted, the commissioners were forced to conclude that the authority of the secretary was 'grounded in most instances on usage.' It was largely because of their quite excusable failure to draw a more tangible line between the powers of the commander-in-chief and those of the secretary at War that the duties of the latter were at times performed in circumstances of great difficulty, and that Lord Palmerston had abundant opportunity to exhibit his official personality.

Since military finances touched military administration at many points ; and since parliament, perennially suspicious of the ' standing army,' desired to make the ministry responsible for certain kinds of military activities, the secretary's duties were almost as heterogeneous as they were laborious. To begin with, the superintendence of army finances comprised the preparation of estimates, the supervision of expenditure, and the audit of accounts. The estimates were prepared on the basis of the total establishment authorised by parliament, and the detailed tables of organisation prepared by the commander-in-chief with the consent of the Crown. Supervision of expenditure, extending down to that of regimental accounts, was provided for by a rule that the paymaster-general and the storekeeper-general should issue money and supplies only upon warrants signed by the secretary at War. Audit extended to the accounts of all officers charged with the payment of military personnel. But the duties of the secretary extended beyond matters purely financial. It was for him to frame the annual mutiny bill and the articles of war; and to wield a patronage by no means limited to the persons under his immediate control. Moreover, he had, in certain departments of military administration, some independent authority. This was true, not only where money matters were concerned, but where certain classes of orders and regulations were to be disseminated. He was even required, under certain contingencies, to exercise authority over military personnel. Thus, it was his duty to remove all troops from the vicinity of places where elections were in progress ; and to protect civilians against ' oppression and misconduct ' on the part of military persons. It seems that one of the qualifications especially needed in a secretary was tact—tact great enough to serve him even in dealing with persons so difficult as commanders-in-chief are wont to be.

Assiduity was also a qualification, and one in particular demand when Palmerston first appeared at the Horse Guards. For, needless to say, the secretary and his staff were obliged to work under tremendous and unprecedented pressure by England's great and growing part in the Napoleonic war. Palmerston's responsibilities at the War Office expanded with those of Wellington in the Peninsula. He had to keep his eye on at least a quarter of a million regular troops (reliable figures seem difficult to obtain), and a hundred thousand or so of militia.[3] The militia, tied up as they were with the interests and susceptibilities of country gentlemen whom the government had to treat tenderly, must often have been a pest.[4] And even the regular units must have been difficult to supervise from their infinite variation. There were, to take unusual examples, the forces operating under the East India Company ; the ' foreign corps ' (consisting mainly if not entirely of German troops) ; and a regiment of Greek light infantry, under mixed British and Greek command, and bearing arms and accoutrements ' in the Albanian fashion.'[5] At one time the War Office was even considering what sort of presents, adapted to savage tastes, would be most useful for recruiting in Africa![6] Lacking not only the methods and equipment which would be regarded as essential at the headquarters of a single regiment to-day, and working under a system of military administration almost incredibly disarticulated and confused, the secretary might well have found his burden almost unbearable. One wonders whether it was ignorance or incurable optimism and energy which caused him to declare, on his induction to office, that he found plenty to do, but ' not of a nature to alarm one.'[7]

He must soon have been conscious that his duties involved a mass of the most petty and tedious routine. A few volumes of the War Office papers, taken at random,

THE ADMIRALTY, THE WAR OFFICE AND THE TREASURY [1804]

will tell the tale.[8] At one moment he or his deputy was trying vainly to secure from the Army Medical Board information that would enable him to pass on the appointment of an army surgeon for service on the continent ; at the next he was informing the adjutant-general of mistakes made in the shipping of arms and accoutrements. Next, perhaps, came the duty of instructing the storekeeper-general to forward clothing (even to a single overcoat) according to careful specifications regarding size ; and this task was followed, in all likelihood, by that of writing the commissary-in-chief for accounts of food supplied, in order that the secretary might next instruct the paymaster-general to deposit funds in payment at the bank. Recruiting, transportation, billets, water supplies and a dozen other such matters had to be dealt with constantly. But it was the individual soldier who was responsible for much of this overwhelming correspondence. If he were an officer, his appointment, the regulation of his pay, his subsistence and other expense accounts, his leaves and his retirement might all find some record in the files of the secretary at War. And, were he officer or private, his financial claims against the government (including those for disability or prize money), his admission to a hospital, and the final disposal of his back pay and effects might be noted there as well. Even evidence as to his morals might be in the same manner preserved to posterity if, for example, he required bail for having enjoyed the privileges, without entering the bonds, of holy matrimony. Since Palmerston, as will presently appear, reorganised his department with striking efficiency, it is curious to find that he dealt personally with much of this detail. One finds him deciding upon the amount of pay due to a single veterinary surgeon, and even upon the disposal of one unserviceable horse.[9] He probably wasted a good deal of time ; but he displayed a penchant for detail which has its part in the make-up of a good administrator.

In parliament, too, the secretary's responsibilities were wide. He had naturally to introduce and defend, as well as frame, the estimates and mutiny bills ; and, since these provided the means by which the House controlled the 'standing army,' their passage sometimes gave rise to important debates. Moreover, he was, ' by ancient custom and usage . . . aided by the Judge Advocate-General . . . the mouthpiece of the Government to sustain any attacks that might be made upon the Commander-in-Chief or his office.'[10] This function was greatly stressed by Liverpool and Castlereagh in 1820, when the election to parliament of Sir Herbert Taylor, secretary to the commander-in-chief, the duke of York, aroused their fears that the Duke might use Taylor as an independent representative in the House. 'The command of the army being one of the King's most peculiar and important functions,' and the commander-in-chief being considered as the King's executive officer, 'any direct official communication' between him and the House might, they urged, lead to encroachments upon the prerogative.[11]

Under the most favourable conditions and with the best of will on both sides, such division of responsibility in military matters offered infinite possibilities of disagreement between the secretary at War and the commander-in-chief. The position of the secretary was of course the more difficult one. Subordinated to the commander-in-chief by his commission,[12] and yet invested with some independent authority by parliament ; responsible to the cabinet and to the House for administering the army economically against the frequent and not unnatural opposition of the army's non-political head ; called upon at times to enforce a discipline which it was not his to frame, and to justify measures in which he had not concurred, the secretary was between the upper and the nether millstones. Indeed, he was hard put to it to avoid being forced into the impossible position of a powerless yet responsible subordinate to an irresponsible military chief.

In such a situation personalities counted heavily ; and the personality which Palmerston encountered in the office of the commander-in-chief was not only rugged but, in a marked degree, antipathetic to his own—the personality of Sir David Dundas.[13] Dundas was a self-made Scotsman, now aged seventy-four, 'a tall spare man, crabbed and austere, dry in his looks and demeanour.' As a veteran of distinction in the field and in army administration ; as author of the leading British work on tactics, and of the rules and regulations under which the army fought ; as a favourite of the King and *locum tenens* for the temporarily discredited duke of York, he was not the man to give ground before a dandified whippersnapper secretary at War of twenty-five. And yet this iconoclastic youth dared to beard him from the outset, dared to defeat, by appeal to the secretary of state for Colonies and War, the appointment of Dundas's father-in-law to a comfortable sinecure. It was true that the father-in-law's demonstrated dishonesty gave grounds for Palmerston's conclusions that ' old Dundas has a strong national propensity to a job ' ;[14] but the commander-in-chief was not any the more content for that. Palmerston had found a second ' Goliath.'

The battle which ensued on his preliminary skirmish with Dundas was not long deferred ; but even before it opened he had begun on one of the most important and the most pressing of his tasks, the reform of his own department. The importance was obvious, since on the proper functioning of the department would depend the value of Palmerston's principal contribution to the prosecution of the war. The planning and conduct of campaigns could be none of his work ; but to do his share in the work of keeping the army paid, supplied, and reinforced was to play no insignificant part. And reform was pressing, too, not only in the needs of the immediate military situation, but because it had already begun.[15]

The War Office, housed in the old Horse Guards, was a large government establishment for those days, and was being constantly enlarged by the swelling demands of the war. Its graded ranks of clerks, split into divisions and subdivisions, now numbered one hundred and twenty or thereabouts. And salaries as well as numbers had shown steady increase.[16] Yet, despite this, the business of the office had slipped more and more into arrears ; and when parliament, in 1805, ordered the appointment of seven commissioners ' to enquire and examine into the Public Expenditure and the Conduct of Public Business in the Military Departments,' the War Office came under fire.[17]

The commissioners sat for six years, and those three of their nineteen reports which dealt with the office of the secretary at War had been laid before parliament by the end of January 1809. While the commission relied for its information almost entirely on the officials of the War Office staff; and while there is good reason to believe that part of this information was never put in print,[18] the evidence that was published, the recommendations of the commissioners, and the work commenced by Leveson-Gower and carried through by Palmerston, gave ample proof that reform had come none too soon.

The young secretary lost no time in studying defects and applying remedies. He had made up his mind to embark on a campaign of reform before he had occupied his new post for two weeks:

> . . . *if they leave us in long enough, I trust much may be accomplished in arranging the interior details of the office, so as to place it on a respectable footing.*
> *Its inadequacy to get through the current business that comes before it is really a disgrace to the country; and the arrear of Regimental Accounts unsettled is of a magnitude not to be conceived.*[19]

The magnitude soon became conceivable in the figure of forty thousand accounts in arrear, of which some extended back to 1783.[20] Reform through a board had been projected; but Palmerston soon decided that such a method of procedure was too dilatory, and that only the strictest personal supervision, combined with the fixing of responsibility upon individuals, could give real results.[21] Personal supervision soon showed him what was wrong.[22] A five-hour day, Saturday leaves during the recess of parliament, liberal allowances for extra work done out of hours and sometimes off the premises, and a general slackness that was revealed in many details, made the office thoroughly wasteful. Carelessness and disorganisation resulted in the constant loss of documents. Clerks were allowed to draw additional incomes from sinecures, army half-pay, or even from agencies. To the reform of these conditions Palmerston brought unrelaxing insistence upon regularity, and upon economy of time. The office instructions soon put

SYSTEM AND DISCIPLINE

into force [23] read like those of a well-run business establishment in our own time. A six-hour day was established, with daily reports on attendance and punctuality, and with rigid scrutiny of excuses when either punctuality or attendance failed. Restrictions were placed upon visitors; the doors between offices were closed during business hours; the holding of outside positions was forbidden; and promotion was no longer determined by seniority alone. As for the care of documents, the instructions for initialling, docketing, indexing, copying, and registering could scarcely have been more minute. The secretary himself was constantly to be informed concerning papers which appeared 'to have been unacted upon longer than they ought.' Legislation alone could not, as Palmerston soon found, ensure enforcement, but the tone in which breaches of regulations were condemned shows that enforcement was a stern reality.

Having occasion perpetually to observe the loss of papers in the office, which is disgraceful to the office and injurious to the business of the Public, I desire that it may be notified that if any paper is lost after the 29 Instant, I shall mark my displeasure in an effectual manner on the Clerk at the head of the subdivision to the business of which the paper belongs.[24]

And again:

Inform the subdivisions that I *insist* upon obedience to my repeated orders . . . and let them take care that I have no further occasion to take notice of any further neglect.[25]

And take care they did, by all appearances.

For results were soon apparent. In 1817 Castlereagh's Select Committee on Finance [26] noted that 'in the current accounts the arrear is inconsiderable, and by the more modern and judicious arrangement, a considerable proportion of the Establishment has been transferred (without any interruption of the current business) to the examination of the periods in arrear; by which means nearly the whole of the outstanding accounts from the year 1784 to the year 1797 have been settled.'[27] In point of fact, the office had learned to keep up with current business some years before; and the signing of peace in 1815 had been the signal for the transfer of an increasingly large proportion of the clerks to the work of cleaning up arrears.[28] By 1821, their work had resulted in the saving of more than £100,000, or the cost of the secretary's office for two years.[29] When, in 1834, the deputy secretary at War, testifying before a new set of commissioners, summed up the achievements of Palmerston's incumbency, he was able to show, not only that the War Office had been brought to a high state of efficiency, but that, coincidently with the rapid reduction in staff and expenses from 1815 on, the office had not only cleared up all arrears, but had absorbed a considerable amount of business from other departments.[30] When Palmerston left office, the number of clerks had been reduced from 170 to 75; £300,000 had been paid in as a result of the examination of accounts in arrear; and the business of four minor departments, which had employed scores of clerks, had in whole or in part been absorbed.[31]

Meanwhile there had been time for a series of encounters with Sir David Dundas and the duke of York. The details of this Battle of the Horse Guards seem sadly tedious and trivial nowadays; and, though Bulwer has reason for saying that Palmerston successfully defended the War Office against threatened subjugation by the army,[32] it cannot be claimed that he gained much ground. Ten years later the then secretary at War complained of 'the intolerable interference of the military authorities' sanctioned by arrangements to which Palmerston was forced to submit; and deplored the 'turmoil, intrigue, and perpetual discord' which arose between his office and that of the commander-in-chief.[33] Enough, then, to take one or two phases of these operations, with the object of discovering the nature of Palmerston's aims and the tactics which he employed. There is good reason for doing this. His tactics revealed a side of his official personality which must be taken very much into account in following his career.

One of his first objectives was to obtain for the War Office some control of the financial operations pertaining to the clothing of the enlisted personnel.[34] Now this clothing, according to the curious system of the day, was paid for from stoppages on the soldiers' pay, such stoppages being treated in effect as part of the personal income of the colonel, and assigned by the colonel in advance to an agent, who paid the clothiers. Since the stoppages were calculated according to the numbers of the authorised personnel of the regiment, and the clothing supplied only to men actually in the service, an annual surplus—ranging from £400 to £1000—accrued to the colonel as a recognised perquisite. To interfere with it was to touch the whole officers' corps at an especially sensitive point. But the faults of the system were obvious and had, long previously, come under fire. In June 1810, Palmerston found himself in a position to interfere. For in that month parliament, without, it appears, any prompting from Palmerston, and equally without the knowledge of Dundas, passed a bill providing that all assignments of stoppages for clothing should be transmitted to, and checked by, the office of the secretary at War; that they should be paid by warrant of the War Office; and that the secretary at War might make regulations concerning them. Palmerston, having thus obtained the power of withholding warrants, discovered that, according to the strict letter of the Mutiny Act, assignments were to be made, not to agents, but to the persons by whom clothing was actually supplied. Whether, as he claimed, he considered these acts mandatory upon him, or whether he merely seized a welcome opportunity, he lost no time. Little more than a month after the new act came into force, he wrote the commander-in-chief to inquire why the intention of parliament was frustrated, and to demand that the clothiers should have better security for payment than dependence on the agents. Had he stopped there, his action could hardly have been open to criticism; but, with the same impulsiveness and intractability which were to become so familiar in later years, he took action without waiting for a reply. Two days after sending his protest, he returned some assignments to the agents, with a statement that payment would be authorised only when they presented written evidence that the clothiers were contented that the agents should be the assignees. That Dundas should contest this action, which made his colonels dependent for the payment of a considerable portion of their incomes on the consent of tradesmen, and this by the action of an official whom he regarded as a subordinate, was natural. As natural was it that he should appeal to the prime minister. The contest was brief. Perceval, while deciding that Palmerston's interpretation of the law was justified, requested him to allow the old procedure to be followed until remedial legislation had legalised it again. Palmerston consented, with apparent willingness and undeniable good-nature.

But the battle had widened to cover far more important ground. Dundas, in his irritation, had repeatedly called upon the premier to declare that in no case could regulations or even interpretations be issued by the secretary at War without the concurrence of the commander-in-chief; or, where such concurrence was refused, without reference to the Crown. Palmerston resolutely held the ground that his office exercised 'a free and separate jurisdiction' in matters of finance, and could naturally promulgate orders under it. The contest was now over a highly important principle. Hence, when Perceval refused to pronounce judgment, Dundas confidently appealed the whole matter to the Prince Regent. The Regent's decision, delivered on February 28, 1811, was all that even Dundas could have desired. In the Regent's opinion, the function of the secretary at War was merely to supply 'a well arranged check upon expenditures of the army' and 'a vigilant control of the financial details.' No communication in the shape of orders or regulations could be made by him without the concurrence of the commander-in-chief. The appearance of this decision, followed almost at once by the return of the duke of York to the office of commander-in-chief, might have awed many a young minister into acquiescence. But Palmerston's courage was not to be daunted even by royalty. Appealing from the decision on the ground that he had had no opportunity of making a defence, he presented in the following August a memorial that is notable, not only for clarity of reasoning and statement, but for the research on which it is based.[35] Covering the precedents of a century and a quarter in copious extracts from some fifty volumes of manuscript, he asserted the independence of his office in words quite as forcible as any that he had used to Dundas:

he must beg leave humbly to submit to His Royal Highness . . . that if it should be his Royal Highness's pleasure to make the office of Secretary at War dependent upon that of Commander-in-Chief, it would in some important particulars require the authority of Parliament to alter those laws which have imposed special duties on the Secretary at War.[36]

His head was bloody, but it was still unbowed.

And so it remained as the dreary conflict progressed. The Duke and Palmerston managed to conduct hostilities in a manner entirely courteous and impersonal; nor did the secretary allow their differences to detract from his admiration for his royal adversary.[37] But neither would recede a step; and the struggle became more inveterate and involved. In December 1811, the Prince Regent, apparently wearied of appeals, insisted that the premier should investigate and report to him all issues on which agreement could not be reached. Perceval wisely referred the matter to Liverpool, as secretary of state for Colonies and War, Charles Yorke (the first lord of the Admiralty), as a former secretary at War, and the lord chancellor, as a legal and constitutional authority. The decision of these experts gave Palmerston a very barren triumph. Pointing out the conflict of precedents, they showed that, since the statutes 'implied an independence in the office of the Secretary at War,' it would be impossible for the Regent, without reference to parliament, ' to declare the complete dependency of the office of the Secretary at War on that of the Commander-in-Chief.' Moreover, any proposal to diminish, through act of parliament, the independence of the secretary ' would be worse received and with more jealousy than almost any proposal which could be made.' On the other hand, they advised that the Regent should order the secretary not to issue any new orders or regulations, however much connected with finance, without informing the commander-in-chief. In case of disagreement, the matter should be referred to the prime minister or the secretary of state for Colonies and War. This decision formed the groundwork of a settlement which was not finally concluded until June 1812. In the meantime Palmerston, still resistant, tried to secure a ruling that the duty of communication should be mutual. But in vain. His office, while retaining an independence of which it could never have been permanently deprived in the face of parliament, had secured no augmentation of power.

But, if defeated, he was not subdued. Another foretaste of his later career appears in his occasional, and possibly continual, violations of the settlement of 1812.[38] In 1822 and 1823 there occurred some amusing examples, one of which may be worth following in brief.[39] Late in 1822, the secretary at War was informed by the Treasury of the transfer of the Barrack Department from the jurisdiction of the Quartermaster's Department to that of the Ordnance. Wishing, properly enough, to take advantage of what economy could be effected by the exchange, Palmerston at once circularized the commanders on foreign stations, directing the dismissal of clerks whose services had been rendered superfluous. But, in palpable violation of the settlement of 1812, he sent out the circulars without taking the trouble to communicate with the commander-in-chief. The duke of York, in some natural indignation at this attempt 'to encroach upon his province and set aside his authority,' struck back by informing Palmerston of his intention of ordering the commanders in question to disobey the War Office circulars. The preliminary announcement of his intention, coupled with a subsequent statement that previous appeals to higher authority in such matters had failed to establish his position, create the impression that, in default of better means of maintaining his authority, he was attempting both to bluff the secretary at War and to compel action on the part of the government. If so, his manœuvre succeeded to perfection; for Palmerston himself proposed submission of the case to the premier. Liverpool having condemned both Palmerston's action and that proposed by the Duke, the matter ended in the most charming expressions of mutual regard, and in a concord which was probably not disturbed until the next occasion when Palmerston was tempted to forget the arrangement of 1812.

It should, perhaps, be noted again that Palmerston took his office very seriously. It was not merely that he showed exemplary devotion to his work, or that he amused Wellington by donning a uniform and taking salutes at the Horse Guards.[40] He seems to have imbibed some army spirit, to have cherished some ambition to effect reforms, and to have developed a determination (a lifelong determination it was to prove) that England should always be in a state of adequate defence. The army spirit became evident in his support of army discipline. Quite genuinely disliking autocratic government in civil life, he insisted that the unfettered power of the higher command to dismiss an officer without showing cause should be preserved.[41] As genuinely sympathetic with human suffering and intolerant of brutality, he persistently defended the flogging of enlisted men; and at one time even maintained that the infliction of corporal punishment was essential to the very existence of the army.[42] When it is remembered that men were literally flogged to within (and occasionally beyond) an inch of their lives, that six hundred lashes (delivered by instalments, if necessary, on the advice of an attendant surgeon) were sometimes inflicted for one offence, it is hard to escape the conclusion that the secretary at War was somewhat militarised. It is true that he censured an officer for bestowing twenty-five lashes on a man who carried two cartridges in his pocket instead of his cartridge box; but the sentence had been imposed by drumhead court-martial, and the officer who inflicted it was appealing to the House against his own forced retirement on half-pay.[43] It was only at the end of Palmerston's incumbency that he made any noticeable effort to keep flogging within ascertained bounds.[44]

Just how much Palmerston did in the way of army reform still awaits discovery. One important improvement, however, has been placed to his credit by the army's most distinguished historian.[45] It would be hard to better the description of this improvement which he himself offered to the House:

> Formerly, a regiment consisted of ten companies or eight; all of which went on service, leaving only the skeleton of one company to recruit. Each regiment now consisted of ten companies, six of which were sent on service, the remaining four companies being left at home to recruit. These companies disciplined the young soldiers,

and sent them from time to time to the battalions abroad. It was a literal fact, that when a comparison had been made between regiments consisting of the same number of men, those which had only six companies abroad . . . were found to be stronger and more efficient than the regiments with ten companies. . . .[46]

Not only was the system of recruiting more effective, but there were other substantial advantages. Invalids received full opportunity to recuperate in English air ; and officers worn and stale with foreign service were restored to vigour by a term at the depôt. Moreover—and this probably counted greatly with Palmerston—the ten companies, always maintained at numbers far below the authorized, offered a framework through which a rapid increase of personnel could be effected in time of need. Such increase he seems to have had very much in mind.[47] When reduction in the rank and file became unavoidable, he preferred to carry it out by suspending recruiting, and allowing a sufficient number of enlistments to lapse, rather than by disbanding any unit as a whole.[48] Thus the skeleton of a larger army was disposable at any time. The 'weeding' of companies would have produced a like result ; but this method,[49] which involved considerable outlay for pensions, he rejected in the interests of economy. The plan followed was not original,[50] nor is it, perhaps, certain that it was he who suggested its application at this time. But at least he promoted and defended this and several minor reforms [51] with all the enthusiasm which an author could have shown. He had ready replies when the opposition jeered at him for making 'fine gentlemen' out of artillerymen by allowing them to discard their leather breeches in favour of pantaloons ; and for replacing the 'little cocked hats' of the cavalrymen by helmets 'which could not be knocked off, and the metal of which would turn the edge of a sword.' His reforms must have found favour with contemporaries. For in 1832, when Hobhouse, one of his successors, suggested fresh improvements to the cabinet, it was decided that they should 'be finally determined on by Palmerston.' [52]

Some of his attitude on defence is discernible in his anxiety to maintain the framework of a large standing army at all times : more of it is seen in his *obiter dictum* that 'amongst nations weakness would never be a foundation for security.' [53] In so far as he could contrive it, Britain and her possessions would always be armed against attack. It was not his function to decide on the tactical distribution of British troops ; but he was interested in the question none the less, and quick to note how the improvement in the means of transportation affected it. In 1827 he wrote his deputy that the introduction of steam navigation entirely altered the situation in so far as Ireland was concerned : since, for military purposes, it made the British Isles one.[54] After all, however, his main exertions in the matter of defence were made in combating the demands of members of the opposition, such as the economical Joseph Hume, who were incessantly demanding reductions in appropriations and personnel.

Behind his exertions in behalf of discipline, reform and defence, the grinding routine went on year after year. The cessation of the war undoubtedly brought some relief ; but when the country found itself at peace again the work of the War Office was infinitely complicated by the demobilization, within three years,[55] of 220,000 men, and by domestic disturbances for which the sudden coming of peace and demobilisation were largely responsible. In 1817, some 40,000 to 50,000 letters from private persons were being dealt with by the War Office annually, and more than double that number of letters were sent out.[56] Then, in the twenties, as civil discontents died down, fresh augmentations and dispositions of the forces of the Crown were called for by disturbances on the continent, expeditions in the East, and the growth of Irish discontent. The chief of the War Office, presiding there for nineteen years, found that each one of them brought its own measure both of anxiety and monotony. How well he survived these years has been pointed out by the latest and most gifted of his biographers :

. . . this long imprisonment failed signally to impair him. The assiduous minister was always alert, and sometimes sprightly. Drugged with official detail, he retained his spirits with a bright observant eye for Paris and the *beau monde*. His style survived his drafting ; and for nineteen years Lord Palmerston sustained without ill effects the blameless *rôle* of the Industrious Apprentice.[57]

An apprentice in the craft of high politics, he was, of a certainty, industrious. But if the rôle were blameless, the player was far from being considered so by army officers, War Office clerks, and, unfortunately perhaps for him, certain persons very highly placed.

For the same faults of temperament, the aggressiveness, impulsiveness and hauteur, which had appeared in his relations with the commander-in-chief, had been displayed in others of his contacts. The action of the Prince Regent in expressing through his secretary his 'surprise' at what seemed to be a slight dereliction of duty on Palmerston's part, brought to the Prince's guiltless amanuensis the haughty announcement from Palmerston that : 'it is quite impossible for me in the official station which I have the honour to hold to receive through you any expression of the Regent's dissatisfaction '; and to Liverpool a protest against 'a degradation to which it would be impossible to submit.'[58] Affable, and ready for give-and-take on most occasions, his tone became insufferable when he feared that his dignity might be compromised. No one had more occasion to realise this than the prime minister. Liverpool, under whom he served for fifteen years, had not only to mediate between him and the duke of York, not only to reprimand him sharply on his own account,[59] but to review disputes in which Palmerston's intolerable pomposity constantly emerged. In 1817, for example, he received from a well-known firm of army agents a set of letters covering a quarrel which they had been carrying on with the War Office for at least four years.[60] Of the several letters addressed by the genial secretary to the head of the firm, two will bear sufficient testimony to his tone :

SIR,—I have to return an act of Parliament contained in your letter of the 4th Inst., to which letter I am unable to give any reply, from not having succeeded in understanding its meaning.

As gracious was the other :

. . . with respect to what passed in the personal interview referred to in . . . your letter I can only say that as it had intirely escaped my recollection that I had had the honor of conversing with you upon this subject, I cannot certainly pretend to charge my memory with what passed on that occasion, but can only observe that every day confirms me in an opinion . . . that the most satisfactory mode of discussing an official question is by letter . . .

The use of such cool and studied insolence, alternating with temperamental displays of a disturbing character, constituted the great flaw in a service that seems otherwise to have been entirely admirable. This flaw did not perhaps greatly detract from, and may even on some occasions have contributed to, the effectiveness of Palmerston's departmental work. But it must occasionally have given food for thought to some of the Tory chiefs who for so long a period held the question of his advancement in their hands.

CHAPTER III

THE BREACH WITH THE TORIES, 1826–1828

IF present-day terminology had been in use a century ago, people would certainly have spoken of Palmerston's official career as exhibiting a strange case of arrested development. There was always, indeed, some suggestion if not of arrested, at least of retarded, development about his whole life. One has only to remember that he commenced to enjoy, more or less simultaneously, high office, popular esteem and the sobriquet of 'Cupid' when he was already middle-aged; that he made his romantic marriage only when middle age itself had virtually gone by; and that he began a decade of service as a vigorous and successful premier at the age when, according to Scripture, his time for earthly services of any sort was past.

At any rate, he halted for an abnormally long time on the threshold of his real career. He, who had refused the chancellorship of the Exchequer and a seat in the cabinet at the age of twenty-five, and had accepted the post of secretary at War merely as a good 'leaving off' place, was still to be awaiting advancement at the end of nineteen years. Yet throughout that time he had deserved well of his party; and his party had been continuously in power. Was he the victim of oversight or injustice on the part of those in whose hands his fortune lay, or was it his own fault that promotion passed him by? No definite answer to the question can even yet be made; but the search for an answer brings to light the fact that, during his years of waiting for preferment, he became gradually and, as it was to prove, permanently alienated from the Tory party as a whole. The process of alienation was by no means steady or continuous; it seems, like most political schisms, to have

ENTERPRISE AND KINDLINESS

developed not only out of differences of opinion but out of the clash of personalities. As usual, too, it was rather involuntary on both sides.

Palmerston's personal development in the years that followed Waterloo [1] was such as to make him more than ever a typical representative of the early and mid-nineteenth century type of sporting politician and aristocrat. He was one of the most prominent habitués of Almack's, that famous rendezvous of the socially eminent; he was the most successful gun at Chatsworth on a day when 'they were all frantic with delight'; and he was commencing to figure prominently on the turf. Under the management of John Day, one of the most successful trainers of the time, his horses were seen on many a track, and gathered in many a cup and purse.[2] Their owner's letters to his brother abound in accounts of their pedigrees, their speeds, their health and their public performances. Apparently he raced them for pure love of sport; he was never greatly given to betting. Equally wanting is any suggestion that he thought of them as being useful politically. But his colours must have made his name familiar for the first time in many an English community.

On the other hand, it is impossible to treat of him merely as the representative of a type: he showed too much vitality, too eager an interest in achievement of all kinds, too much gaiety and kindliness, for that. Even a couple of his letters, taken almost at random, make this clear. In 1820 he was urging upon Liverpool the desirability of giving an official trial to a new type of steamboat, on the ground that both the postal service and the navy might profit if the invention should prove its worth.[3] And he had been interested enough to acquaint himself with the specifications of the boat in some detail. But his personality emerges far better in a letter, written in 1816 to Peel on behalf of the Irish poet and dramatist, Charles Mathurin. Mathurin, a curate and schoolmaster, was threatened with dire punishment by the (Anglican) Archbishop of Dublin for writing a tragedy in which Palmerston thought to discern the marks of genius:

> I really think that a proceeding such as he [the Archbishop] antici-
> pates would be a disgrace to the nineteenth century. . . . Had this

reverend divine [Mathurin] been guilty of the unbecoming levity of a farce, or even had he disported himself in the easy walks of genteel comedy it would have been difficult to have witnessed such episcopal wrath without exclaiming *tantaene animis celestibus irae* ! But when the sacred thunderbolt is levelled at a legitimate tragedy in five acts of the full standard length and weight, in which all the rogues & whores are brought to the most condign and exemplary punishment in a manner that must be admitted to be most edifying even by the most active and zealous members of the Vice Society, the archbishop's lightning seems to be like that of Jupiter which *saepe nocentes praeterit exanimatque indignos inque merentes.* Pray if you possibly can exert yourself in behalf of this poor gentleman.[4]

It is sometimes forgotten that there were perfectly valid reasons for much of Palmerston's popularity.

He also departed somewhat from type, perhaps, in the amount of attention he gave to his properties. His great estate at Sligo engaged his attention most of all ; and before he had left the War Office he had made great progress in realizing his early schemes.[5] A harbour of ' enough depth to admit vessels of 300 tons, and as much as any harbour on the west coast of Ireland ' had been built for the fishery and the coasting trade ; and plans for getting other persons to lay down a railway connecting it with forty miles of interior navigation had been made. The bogs had been surveyed, and some parts actually drained and brought under cultivation, by scientific methods which the owner was able to describe in great detail. He had commenced with his ' worst bog ' and was able to figure that he would make some twelve per cent. a year. Sandy areas were being reclaimed by the planting of bent ; an ' infant linen market ' and a limekiln had been established ; and the people were building a village according to plans laid down by Palmerston and his engineer. Two schools had been erected ; and a ' concordat ' made with the Catholic bishop concerning the schoolmasters. There had been a clash between the two great powers ; and Palmerston had meditated the rather Napoleonic stroke of obtaining from Cambridge the services of ' some zealous Simeonite who would curb the ardent enthusiasm which would impel him to the banks of the Ganges, and might content himself with winning his Jerusalem spurs by a campaign in the parish of Ahamlish.' But, in the end, he conceded all that the bishop asked. Henry Crabb Robinson, visiting Sligo in 1826, noted the improvements, and heard Palmerston praised ' as a generous landlord to the Catholic poor.'[6]

At Broadlands and on the Yorkshire estates the same story would probably have been told. Certainly both Romsey and Fairburn had to thank Palmerston wholly or in part for schools; while Fairburn, too, had its lime works. Nor did his business ventures stop there. In the twenties he and his brother were actively interested in the ' Cornwall and Devon Mining Company' and in the ' Welsh Slate Company.'[7] The former was to involve him in trouble and disappointment in more ways than one ; and the latter, while ultimately profitable, was for a time so unsuccessful that Palmerston, feeling responsible as a director, bought in the shares of many of his friends. It was probably due in large measure to his taste for such speculation that he was frequently, if not chronically, hard up. Day pictured him as dilatory in the payment of his debts ;[8] and other contemporaries held that money difficulties more than once affected his political career.

How diversified were his interests appears again from his own account of three visits which he paid to France in these years.[9] On two occasions, in 1815 and 1818, he seems to have gone in part at least for official reasons, since his time was largely spent in viewing the troops of the allied armies of occupation. But official duties by no means prevented him either from enjoying himself or from storing his mind. Whether he was dining with the Tsar, the king of Prussia, or Castlereagh ; whether he was climbing the arch on the Carrousel to examine the ' exquisite workmanship' of the great bronze horses that were being prepared for their journey home to Venice, or obtaining the exact measurements of the Scheldt-Oise canal ; whether he was ' doing ' Paris or drinking in landscapes, little failed of observation or of graphic description in his diary. Most interesting, perhaps, in view of later events, were the observations he recorded concerning the effects produced on a people by the extinction of liberty. While one sees no signs of sympathy with revolutionary violence, it is clear that Napoleonic despotism, the dragon against which St. George and England had fought during his most impressionable years, had made its mark upon his mind ; and, perhaps fostering a natural propensity, had imbued him with dislike for autocratic government. ' It is indeed quite striking,' he wrote of the people of Rouen in 1815, ' to observe how totally everything like manly feeling and independent spirit has been crushed by the successive tyrannies under which the people have suffered since the Revolution, and it is hardly possible to extract from any man a political opinion.' The ' devil's son,' who was later to disturb Metternich's dreams, was already beginning to appear in Palmerston—bred by an independent and sympathetic temperament, not out of romanticism or the ideas of the philosophers, but out of an exaggerated conception of the political superiority of his countrymen. Nothing, in fact, emerges more clearly from the journals of these trips than the evidences of his insular and rather blatant type of patriotism. With what joy did he note that the British forces manœuvred without the piles of straw which Prussian commanders used to mark objectives for their troops ; with what exultation chronicle Alexander's order that his men adopt the freer British stride ; with what emotion hear the ' hurrah ' which marked the British capture of a position in some sham warfare. His pride and confidence in the British army were unbounded. But they were not greater than his pride and confidence in the nation which the British army served.

He made considerable display of these feelings in parliament. For, although his infrequent speeches there related almost solely to military affairs, he was at no loss to flavour them with expressions of his patriotism. A suggestion that economy might be effected by discontinuance of the military college, elicited his famous remark that ' he wished to see the British soldier with a British character, with British habits, with a British education, and with as little as possible of anything foreign.'[10] His defence of the constitution, though less quoted, seems quite as notable. When the opposition complained of the danger involved in the existence of a ' standing army,' he scoffed at the idea that

THE BLESSINGS OF THE CONSTITUTION 49

such danger could be existent while the country was enjoying 'the practical blessings of freedom in a greater degree than had ever been done by any other country, and . . . in a greater degree than even this country had ever enjoyed at any former period.'[11] Answering criticisms of the use of troops to suppress civil disturbances, he became more emphatic still :

> No man who had the slightest opportunity of witnessing daily and hourly, in private life, the blessings derived from the constitution under which they lived, could entertain any other feeling but a determination, if necessary, to sacrifice his life in its defence.[12]

He even displayed traces of what has, in later times, been designated as 'imperialism.' Proposals that a reduction of the forces of the Crown might be effected by the withdrawal of colonial garrisons impelled him to ask the House whether they wished to give up recent conquests overseas which, in serving as naval stations, protected British trade 'in every part of the world.' And if so, were they prepared to see England abdicate her great position in Europe and resign herself to the position of a secondary Power ?[13]

Save, perhaps, for his privately noted and probably quite unknown expression of disgust over the effects produced by autocratic government on the people of Rouen, there was nothing in all of this to alienate him from any section of his colleagues. And, in practice as well as precept, his allegiance to the Tories apparently remained unabated through years when the faith of the more kindly and liberal-minded members of the party must repeatedly have been put to the test. High prices, unemployment, and other social disorders incidental to the ending of so vast and prolonged a war, stirred the populace to a series of threatening demonstrations, including an attempt upon the Prince Regent's life. The ministry, in which the more unbending Tories played a dominant part up to about the year 1822, had no answer to make to these demonstrations other than repression of the sternest sort. Their policy reached its culmination in 1819 through the passage of the notorious 'Six Acts,' which placed severe restrictions on the right of the people to hold public meetings or to publish their political views. Palmerston, with whom a dislike of popular insurrection seems to have been ingrained, apparently accepted this policy without protest. Bulwer, his friend and 'official' biographer, pointed out that he said no word in parliament in defence of the 'Six Acts.'[14] But, in view of Palmerston's parliamentary habits the fact is almost devoid of significance; while a letter which he wrote to his friend, Lord FitzHarris (Malmesbury's heir), in November 1819, suggests that in feeling at least he was distinctly with the government:

> This is no ordinary moment and everything depends not merely upon the cold support of the friends of social order, but upon their displaying a zeal and alacrity in some measure corresponding with the activity of those who are endeavoring to overthrow our institutions.[15]

One can find, too, evidence of his willingness to support the ministry generally. Witness a letter which he addressed to Peel in the summer of 1817 offering to 'make from 280 to 290 voters' in county Sligo, by giving leases to tenants-at-will on his great Irish estate.[16] He even spoke on one occasion in behalf of the established church, expressing his conviction that 'tithes . . . were as much the property of the church as any property was of the landlord.'[17]

Why, then, did he remain in a minor office and outside the cabinet? Though the question is not definitely answerable, it is, because of the light it throws on his position in the party, definitely worth considering. One very suggestive fact is that the leaders of the party were generous and flattering to him in their offers of outside posts. He refused, not only the chief secretaryship in Ireland, as has been seen, but, on two occasions, the splendours of the governor-generalship of India.[18] On the other hand, Liverpool, in 1821, made a determined effort to deprive him even of the War Office.[19] It is true that this effort was made in behalf of Huskisson who, dissatisfied with his lowly position as chief commissioner of Woods and Forests, wished to become secretary at War. But the premier's suggestion that the two men should exchange offices, and that Palmerston should receive a British peerage to balance the scales, showed how little he desired to have Palmerston either in the House or in the cabinet. But why? Croker has been credited with supplying the explanation by pointing out, in 1822, Palmerston's lack, as a speaker, of ' that *flow* of ideas and language which can run on for a couple of hours without, on the one hand, committing the Government, or, on the other, lowering by commonplaces or inanities the station of a Cabinet Minister.'[20] But Croker was merely explaining why he, in disagreement with ' many persons,' did not consider Palmerston ' fit to be a lieutenant-general, and command the right wing of the army.' And Croker agreed that Palmerston was ' the very ablest ' of departmental heads in repelling attacks upon his own branch of the government. Hence one is forced to seek for other explanations of Palmerston's failure to advance. Was it because his haughtiness as secretary at War, and his impulsive way of taking things into his own hands, had been forced so often upon the attention of the prime minister and other members of the cabinet? Or, were ministers suspicious of the orthodoxy of a man who frequented Whig society, formed no intimacies personal or political, and openly announced his ' Catholic ' proclivities? In all likelihood it was his ' Catholic ' proclivities which worked most to his detriment, They rendered him definitely unacceptable for certain posts, such as the Home Office ; and they made his inclusion in the cabinet through any post seem undesirable to men determined that the cabinet should contain a ' Protestant ' majority.[21]

After 1820, Liverpool's ageing cabinet (one can hardly think of it without remembering that old age brings hardening of the arteries) went through a process of rejuvenation. It was responding both to the spirit of the time and to changes in personnel. Not only was repression, now almost as unnecessary as it was unpopular, given up ; but a spirit of innovation was at work in the ministry. Peel, at the Home Office, opened his attack on the cruel and antiquated system of criminal law ; Canning, taking charge of foreign affairs in 1822, cast loose from treaties and congresses with the reactionary Powers ; and Huskisson, presiding at the Board of Trade, hewed away some of the regulations which had confined British industry and commerce—thus proclaiming himself a disciple of Adam Smith. Since most of the energy and talent in the ministry belonged to this group, and since to the support they received from the rank and file of the party was added that of the Grenville Whigs, who were now voting with the government, they were able to prevail over the old Tories at nearly every point. In fact, the government's policy was more acceptable to the opposition than to some of its own chiefs. And, incidentally, it was distinctly to the taste of Palmerston. His humanitarianism responded to Peel's activities, his dislike of autocratic government to Canning's, and his interest both in the new economic theories and in the Empire to Huskisson's.

He left the party no room for doubt that he stood upon the liberal side. At a time when Bathurst and even Canning were content merely to regulate colonial slavery, he warned the colonists that an institution so contrary to the spirit of Christianity and of the British Constitution (the two were perhaps never entirely separate in his mind) could not for long be permitted to exist.[22] And he seemed almost as clearly to threaten the Test Act when he disclaimed being ' one of those who wished to see political distinctions established between religious sects.'[23] On the one occasion when he defended Canning's foreign policy, his defence was far from that which might have been offered by a Tory advocate of ' legitimacy ' on the continent. In 1823 the opposition attacked the ministry for allowing France to crush the Spanish liberals without trying to restrain her by attacks on her commerce and colonies, or even by the use of threats. Palmerston's justification of ministerial inaction sounded rather perfunctory. Was England to convict herself of greed and hypocrisy by using the fleet to her own profit, while she left the Spanish liberals to meet the French armies without aid ? And as for the use of threats :

To have talked of war, and to have meant neutrality, to have threatened an army and to have retreated behind a state paper, to have brandished the sword of defiance in the hour of deliberation and to have ended with a penful of protests on the day of battle, would have been the conduct of a cowardly bully. . . .[24]

This part of the speech seems well worth quoting for future reference ; as it might well have issued from the lips of one of his own critics in later years. But at the time it merely helped to define the position occupied in the party by a minor member of the ministry.

His position was even more clearly marked on two other issues which, at the time, were of greater importance in marking off the liberal Tories from the more orthodox. The lessons that he had learned at Edinburgh made him an uncompromising supporter of Huskisson's policies :

. . . our adoption of the principles of free trade was not a course which would render the country poor, and unable to bear expense, but a course which had been resolved upon from a conviction of its superior profitableness and expediency.[25]

He had, in fact, not only kept in mind the teachings of Adam Smith, but had kept pace with Smith's successors. Witness a long memorandum which he sent to Peel in 1823, respecting a bill then under consideration for the ' composition ' of Irish tithes.[26] By maintaining, through laboured arguments, that tithes fell, not upon the landlord, but upon the consumer, he showed himself abreast of his time in being a Ricardian. With Canning and Huskisson he was, of course, also at one concerning *the* great issue of the middle twenties—the question of Catholic emancipation. His attitude was disturbing to some of his academic constituents. The Master of St. John's, whom he had helped, in 1820, to become Dean of Ely, wrote him, three years later, warning him that in view of prevalent sentiment at the university it would be better for him not to speak upon the question, however he might vote.[27] That the warning was not an idle one he discovered when he stood for re-election in 1826.

It has not infrequently happened that a particular election has served to mark a crisis in some statesman's life, by bringing to himself and to others a realisation of his position in politics, and so helping to define his path.

Anyone seeking an election which played such a part in Palmerston's career would unquestionably settle upon his campaign at Cambridge in June 1826.[28] His own reference to it as ' the first decided step towards a breach ' between himself and the Tories, seems a decided understatement of its significance.

There was nothing at first to indicate that it would be especially important. The general election of which it formed a part was in no way remarkable, save that some bitterness was shown concerning the Corn Law, and a good deal concerning Catholic Emancipation. Palmerston opened his canvass six months in advance, with little or no anxiety regarding his prospects. The university had returned him as a ' Catholic ' three times ; the other sitting member was a ' Protestant ' ; and the government was operating under a gentlemen's agreement that its members were free to hold such views on the Catholic question as they wished. Moreover, the Whigs, who as a party were fervent ' Catholics,' showed no inclination to put forward a candidate. There seemed no reason why an able minister, who had represented the university for fourteen years, and who could appeal, for different reasons, to both Tory and Whig voters, should fear for his seat. He was disagreeably surprised. Two new Tory candidates, Copley and Goulburn, appeared, both of them ' Protestants,' and both vigorously supported by the King, the duke of York, Eldon and Bathurst. Palmerston was forced to conduct a protracted and exhausting canvass ; and was brought in second to Copley only by the strenuous exertions of the Whigs. He had protested to Bathurst, to Canning and to Wellington against what he regarded as a gross breach of faith ; and he had informed Liverpool that if defeated he would withdraw from the government. He made no suggestion of having received less than his due from the party in previous years ; but his tone suggests that long-standing irritation had reached its climax.

Any further evidence that might be required as to the importance of this episode is supplied by his own words. Liverpool, he felt, had run true to form in acting ' shabbily, timidly and ill '[29] ; but Liverpool was only a ' spoony ' after all. It was the old-fashioned section of the party with which he had lost all patience :

> . . . the real opposition of the present day sit behind the Treasury Bench ; . . . the stupid old Tory party, who bawl out the memory and praises of Pitt . . . are opposing all the measures and principles which he held most important ; it is by these that the progress of the Government . . . is thwarted and impeded. On the Catholic question ; on the principles of commerce ; on the corn laws ; . . . on colonial slavery ; . . . on all these questions, and everything like them, the Government find support from the Whigs and resistance from their self-denominated friends.[30]

Again and again he referred to the Whigs, always in terms of gratitude, and sometimes in terms of something more. ' He says,' wrote Frederick Lamb to his sister, Lady Cowper, ' he feels like Caspar in the Fr[e]i[s]schutz Story, quite afraid L[or]d Grey should come with his long arm, & claim him as his own.'[31] He was not really much alarmed lest that prince of darkness—that advocate of thorough-going parliamentary reform—would carry him away ; for he had hopes of the young and ' more liberal ' Tories who would sit in the new House.[32] But he had discovered in himself a strong affinity with the bulk of Grey's followers.

His comments on the election show, too, how deeply he had Catholic emancipation at heart for its own sake :

> I think that the question has gained by the general election . . . the grand point is, that the No Popery cry has been tried in many places and has everywhere failed ; and we may now appeal to the experience of facts to show that there does *not* exist among the people of England that bigoted prejudice on this point which the anti-Catholics accused them of entertaining.[33]

He was always anxious to believe that his fellow-countrymen shared his ideals.

In April of the following year, 1827, it seemed that his allegiance to the more liberal section of his party and his affinity for the Whigs could be perfectly reconciled ; for Canning became prime minister of a coalition government composed of these two elements. Liverpool's health had broken down in February ; and George IV, after postponing so unpleasant a decision for two months, had been forced to entrust Canning with the task of forming a new ministry. A secession of all the 'Protestant' Tories, including Peel and Wellington, had immediately taken place ; and the new premier had been glad to enlist the support of most of the Whigs, under the leadership of the former Lord Henry Petty, since 1809 the marquis of Lansdowne. The Whigs, anxious above all things to keep the old Tories out of office, and quite conscious of the potential advantage of a Tory schism, had agreed to co-operate on generous terms—allowing Catholic emancipation to remain an open question in the cabinet, and postponing for the duration of the coalition any attempt to press a general measure of parliamentary reform. Grey, who considered these terms much too generous, and who was piqued that the bargain had been concluded without his acquiescence, stood, with some of his friends, scornfully aside.

Palmerston's time, it seemed, had come at last. Of the Tory 'sergeants and corporals,' as Lord Londonderry called them,[34] who had clung to Canning, he was certainly among the most able and most prominent. And Canning, after expressing a desire to have him at the Home Office, offered him what Portland had offered eighteen years before—the Exchequer, with a seat in the cabinet. But ill fortune, assisted by his taste for speculative enterprises and his carelessness in looking after them, once more dashed his hopes.[35] The cabinet seat he accepted immediately ; but his transfer to the Exchequer was deferred until the close of the session, in order that he might be spared the necessity of asking re-election from his Cambridge constituents at an unfavourable time. But the transfer was never to take place ; for Canning not only withdrew the offer of the chancellorship, not only left him at the War Office, but tried to remove him from the ministry by sending him abroad. Palmerston left two (and partially conflicting) accounts of the affair, in both of which he attributed Canning's change of front to his (Palmerston's) misfortune in having displeased the King, and to the King's desire for a compliant person at the Exchequer. But these accounts are sadly disingenuous. For there is accumulated evidence

THE COUNTESS COWPER

to show that his reputation in financial matters temporarily disqualified him for taking over a great financial post in the government. Perhaps it was only his directorship in the Cornwall and Devon Mining Company that counted against him ; but that seems to have been quite enough. Some of the company's shareholders claimed to have been swindled by the directors ; and the matter was, by petition, aired before the House.[36] The members, after two debates, in April and in May, passed on to other business without attempting to decide whether directors or shareholders had been at fault ; and apparently accepted Palmerston's emphatic disclaimer of having known that anything fraudulent was afoot. But he was certainly convicted of some negligence. Painful scenes ensued between the premier and the secretary at War. When Canning offered him the governorship of Jamaica he laughed Canning out of countenance—and sought consolation from Wellington ! At a renewed offer of India he could not laugh ; but he could and did announce his intention of remaining at the War Office. He had apparently learned a bitter lesson ; for one finds no record of fresh speculations on his part from that time on.

What else he may have learned, or what he did, during the three months that Canning survived after becoming premier, does not appear. The speeches he delivered were as few as they were insignificant ; and there are apparently no records of the part he played in Canning's short-lived cabinet. Indeed, his footing there must have been too precarious to allow him any scope. But at least he must have seen something at close range of Canning's diplomacy, and at a time when Canning was dealing with two questions which were to engage his own attention through many years : the question of the Near East and that of Portugal.

The situation in Portugal had lately offered attractive possibilities to a British statesman of Canning's liberal proclivities. The government was carried on in the name of an infant queen, Maria, and under a fairly liberal constitution presented to the people by Maria's father, Dom Pedro, the emperor of Brazil. Queen and constitution were naturally supported by the real or self-entitled constitutionalists among the Portuguese. As naturally, the large number of Maria's subjects who regarded infant queens and infant constitutions as undesirable, preferred to follow Pedro's younger brother, Dom Miguel, who was more than ready to take his niece's place. Many of the Miguelites, finding Portugal uncomfortable, crossed into Spain, and, with the scarcely concealed assistance of King Ferdinand, organised military expeditions against Maria's government. In December 1826, the ministers who ruled in Maria's name appealed to Liverpool's ministry for help. Since England was bound by treaty to protect Portugal against outside attack, Canning was in the happy position of being able to send British troops to the assistance of the constitutionalists without actual interference in Portugal's domestic politics. While he had allowed himself the satisfaction of calling down the blessings of heaven on the constitution, and, by implication, on its supporters, not even Metternich could find fault with what he had actually done. Palmerston, while quite appreciating this, was doubtless more impressed by Canning's sentiments, by his frank avowal of sympathy with the Portuguese liberals, and by his rapid and effective action, than by his regard for the letter of the law.

The issue of the moment in the Near East had, of course, to do with the revolution of the Greeks against the Turks ; and Canning's problem had been to see that Russia did not use it to ' swallow Turkey at one mouthful and Greece at another.'[37] Having long preserved an attitude of neutrality, and having tested the possibilities of mediation, either single-handed or along with the Russian government, he had been forced into a more active policy by the hideous excesses of Turkey's Egyptian auxiliaries in the Morea, by the realisation that the Greeks could not be subdued save by measures which civilised nations could not contemplate, and by a conviction that Russian intervention of some sort was inevitable. That Russia, which had a long list of real or supposed grievances of her own against the Sultan's government, should intervene alone ; that she should have free scope to crush the Turks and dictate terms of peace that would strengthen her grip on the Ottoman Empire and make her the great patron of the new Greek state— these were developments he was determined to forestall. And within a month before his death he had apparently forestalled them by one of his most famous pieces of diplomacy—a treaty concluded at London, which provided that Russia, France and England should take joint action, even by force, if necessary, to compel a cessation of Greco-Turkish hostilities. They were also to co-operate in arranging a final settlement. Again Canning was able, in promoting British interests, to promote also those of continental liberalism. This phase at least of his policy must have been explained to the cabinet in the presence of Palmerston.

In 1860 a London firm of publishers, desirous of obtaining biographical notices of important persons, had such notices drawn up, and sent for correction to those whom they concerned. By a stroke of good fortune the notice sent to Palmerston, corrected in his own hand, survives.[38] Among the deleted passages are two which touch upon his relations with Canning. One of these reads:

> It may be said with great truth that Canning the statesman made Palmerston a politician in reality and depth.

A statement that Palmerston, after May 1828, 'aimed at acquiring the reputation of being Mr. Canning's successor,' was also excised. Whether these elisions, comprehensible enough in any case, made the document a more or less truthful representation of the facts, it is difficult to say; but the deleted passages certainly contained some exaggeration. It is clear, for example, that Palmerston was so fitted to fall in with most of Canning's ideas, both by temperament and by his own views on foreign affairs, that he was able to take them for his own quite naturally and with his whole heart. In how far he justified his discipleship is not the question here. What must be noted is that in his preference for things English, his desire that England should stand upon her own feet, his appreciation of the great force of public sentiment, and his taste for constitutional government as the proper medium between autocracy and democracy, he was a natural-born Canningite. There were matters of technique which he may or may not have learned from Canning—in particular the value of appealing to public sentiment both in England and abroad through the power of oratory : and there were certain of Canning's perceptions, such as that of the power of nationalism on the continent, which he failed to appreciate. But this is not to say that the 'reality and depth' of his policy was acquired from his great forerunner, nor that ambition to take Canning's place alone accounted for the increasing devotion to questions of foreign policy which his friend Mme. de Lieven, the Russian ambassadress, noted in him from the time of Canning's death.[39]

The ministry headed by Canning's successor, Goderich, lasted only through the later months of 1827. Its history is merely that of the decline and break-up, for lack of a leader, of the coalition which Canning had so hopefully formed. In the rather apt phrase of a journalist, the coalition 'put Canning to death and Goderich at his wit's end.' The latter, who had been chancellor of the Exchequer from 1823, and secretary of state for War and Colonies during Canning's 'hundred days,' was an essentially weak man, placed in a position where an exceptionally strong one was required. Both George IV and the Whigs wished to alter the personnel of his ministry ; and both continued to harass him by their conflicting demands until the end of the year, when he gave up his task in absolute despair.

Goderich's difficulties and his pliability brought fresh disappointment to Palmerston ; but he bore it, as he had apparently borne his earlier political reverses, with exemplary cheerfulness. Once more the offer of the Exchequer was made to him and withdrawn.[40] The fault on this occasion was entirely with the King, who insisted that John Herries, a 'Protestant,' an 'anti-Liberal,' and a man whom George expected to find compliant with his own personal demands, should have the post. Palmerston gave way immediately, moved in some degree, perhaps, by considerations of self-interest, but also by dread of the consequences which would ensue from a break-up in the ministry :

> One of two things must follow : either a mixed Government would be made by Goderich of some of his present colleagues and the Tories, or the whole Cabinet would march, and the Tories come in bodily. The last, it is obvious, would be most unfortunate in every possible way, and would produce the worst consequences on our foreign relations and domestic policy, including commerce and Ireland. The first event would bring back a Government just like Liverpool's, consisting of men differing on all great questions, and perpetually on the verge of a quarrel ; the result of which is that nothing is done, each party giving up their own views on condition that a corresponding sacrifice is made by the others.[41]

Unhappily such very reasonable arguments were powerless to save the paralytic cabinet, to which a quarrel between Herries and Huskisson gave the *coup de grâce*. In December, Goderich secretly and fretfully begged to be released ; and in January 1828 the old King—attired in his greasy jacket and nightcap—ordered Wellington to form a ministry.[42] The coalition which had enabled Palmerston to reconcile so neatly his party alignment with his personal opinions was at an end.

It was now to be seen whether his dire predictions would be fulfilled—whether the country would have either an old-fashioned Tory government or one 'just like Liverpool's.' Wellington seemed to incline to the second alternative ; for, strongly urged by Peel, he at once invited Huskisson and the other Canningites to co-operate in the formation of a united Tory ministry. But he had not the least intention of playing the conciliatory rôle of a Liverpool. Instead, he expected to be a political chief of staff, surrounded by helpful and disciplined staff officers. On the other hand, the Canningites, failing or perhaps refusing to realise this fact, hoped to sell their assistance to the Duke at the price of his acceptance of their doctrines. And, according to William Lamb (who did not become Lord Melbourne until the following year), Wellington and Peel spread a little bait for the liberal Tory group. 'One thing . . . in his [Huskisson's] favour,' wrote Lady Cowper, shortly afterwards, 'is that Duke W. and Peele are become so liberal. William says to hear them *talk*, one only feels inclined to say to them, " Why in the name of wonder did you not stay in with C[anning] ? " '[43]

Yet Huskisson and ' the Triumvirate,' as he called Dudley, Palmerston and Charles Grant, kept political London in suspense for nearly a week.[44] They were too wary to accept mere talk for pledges ; and it was a question whether, even with pledges, they could honourably take office under Wellington. To do so was to re-enlist with Tories who had deserted Canning in his time of need, and to dissociate themselves from those Whigs who had given him support. There was another consideration. ' The part of the transaction which will appear extraordinary,' wrote Charles Greville, ' is, that the Government having been broken up by a quarrel between Huskisson and Herries, the opposite party come in and both of these Ministers remain with them. In private life the transaction would look very like a fraud, and be open to great suspicion.'[45] But the Canningites were under great temptation to make terms with the Duke. Considering the weakness and disunion of the Whigs, and the small number of votes which Huskisson could command in parliament, there were good grounds for believing that only through a liberalised Tory party could Canning's principles be made to prevail. If considerations of a less altruistic sort swayed the group, there was much to set their consciences at rest.

Whatever his motives for wishing to join Wellington, Palmerston, in common with his friends, felt the need for guarantees concerning the acceptance of their policies ; and more than his friends, perhaps, showed suspicion of the Duke's new-found ' liberalism.'[46] On the Catholic question, and the related question of the administration of Ireland, he demanded specific pledges on his own account. He stipulated that Catholic emancipation should be an open question in the cabinet, that patronage should be distributed between pro-Catholics and anti-Catholics with strict impartiality, and that neither the lord lieutenant nor the chief secretary should be of pronounced anti-Catholic views. The first point the Duke conceded without hesitation. For the second, he suggested that Palmerston should trust his honour as a gentleman, and for the third an equal confidence that he was not mad. Restive under the rebuke, Palmerston hesitated to the last over the relinquishment of his demands ; but he seems to have given in, comforted by the knowledge that the cabinet contained a majority of 'Catholics.' After all, his interest in Ireland and emancipation was being rapidly eclipsed by his taste for foreign affairs.

But, if he had not received all the personal assurance which he had sought, he believed that the general influence of the group was sufficiently secured. A letter written to his brother, on the day when agreement was reached, speaks of no such definite pledges on the part of Wellington as his autobiography was later to record,[47] but breathes genuine confidence :

> The Duke . . . wishes to form a strong Government, and a liberal one. . . . Canning's principles of policy will be preserved. . . . Dudley will carry them on in our foreign relations ; Huskisson and Grant in our colonial and commercial. Peel will probably return to his Home Office, where he will prosecute his system of reform. All this, instead of a pig-tail Tory Government, shows the great strides which public opinion has made in the last few years. Such a Government as Liverpool's even cannot now be established ; and such a one as Perceval's could not be for a moment thought of.[48]

His attention was fixed especially on foreign affairs :

> The Duke . . . declares that ' *The King's treaties must be observed.*' So that there will be no change of policy about Greece ; indeed, Dudley's continuance would be a security on this point.

Other passages in the letter showed that he was still a little uncertain as to the strength of his group, and that he felt the need of some self-justification with regard to the abandonment of the Whigs :

> The Whigs of course will be furious and violent, and lay about them to the right and left. *I very sincerely regret their loss, as I like them much better than the Tories, and agree with them much more ; but still we, the Canningites, if we may be so termed, did not join their Government, but they came and joined ours* ; and whatever regard we may feel for them, we have not enlisted with them, so as to be bound

to follow their fate and fortunes, or to make their retention a condition of our remaining ; and, indeed, if we had all gone out, I should certainly not have sat with them in the House of Commons, but should have taken an independent and separate position.

A Whig-Canningite combination was ideal, so long as the Canningites had the upper hand, and so long as the combination enjoyed some prospects of success. But Palmerston did not find the prospect of attaching himself to the weak and disorganised Whig opposition an enticing one. Better it seemed, to join the Duke, trusting in his honour and sanity, in general assurances, and in the fact that the most active cabinet posts would be in ' liberal ' hands.

The re-united Tory government had a hard road from the first. A chorus of resentment greeted its very emergence.[49] Wellington was sharply attacked by the ultra-Tories for concessions, both in principle and in appointments, to the Canningites ; but it was the latter who bore the brunt of the abuse. Lady Canning was ' much hurt ' and ' very violent ' ; and, while the majority of her husband's followers fell into support, there were many who criticised Huskisson, either for making the bargain at all, or for not making a better one. As for the Whigs, they were as ' furious and violent ' as Palmerston had foretold. Only a few, like Lady Granville, were convinced of the purity of Huskisson's motives, and saw in his acceptance of office under Wellington a painful sacrifice.[50] Far more serious than any outside criticism, was the fact that the new Government had all the weaknesses of a coalition, and of a coalition divided, not only on policy, but by distrust.[51] Before it had had time to compose its differences in private, public disagreements between its chief and Huskisson as to the ' guarantees ' which the Canningites had received, made its disunion public property.[52] ' Ministers blackguard one another like draymen,' wrote Mme. de Lieven.[53] Small wonder that, for all the efforts of Peel to keep the peace, the meetings of the cabinet frequently did little more than register acrimonious disputes. ' We should have no Cabinets after dinner. We all drink too much wine, and are not civil to each other,' wrote Lord Lyndhurst, the chancellor.[54] Actually, the most dangerous disagreements were over domestic issues ; but Palmerston's battles in the cabinet had to do mainly with foreign policy. In 1851, Lord Aberdeen, called upon to advise a distracted sovereign on means for disposing of the foreign secretary, 'well remembered that, when he had been in office with him under the Duke of Wellington, the constant disputes with him (who was then only Secretary at War) on the foreign policy were anything but pleasant.'[55] Aberdeen had reason to remember. Persuaded by the Duke to accept a cabinet seat without portfolio in order that he should have time to 'assist' Dudley (Dudley, who was one of Huskisson's 'guarantees') in the conduct of foreign affairs; and accepted by the compliant Dudley as his '*coadjutor jure secessionis*,'[56] he must have held many a tilt in memory. Palmerston was showing a certain inclination to be Dudley's coadjutor on his own responsibility.

It was with respect to British policy in the Near East that the maintenance of Canning's principles was most clearly at stake. No British government could, indeed, with any face denounce the treaty of the preceding July; but, since the means by which it was to be carried out had not been specified, the ministry could virtually nullify it by mere inaction. To do this was, of course, utterly to reverse Canning's policy ; but Canning's policy had been disliked, in so far as it had been understood, by Wellington and Aberdeen.[57] There was little exaggeration in Palmerston's summary of the situation :

The Duke has the strongest dislike to Russia. . . . Ellenborough is even more adverse than the Duke : Aberdeen is Austrian, and Bathurst anti-Russian and Austrian ; all these would give anything to get out of the Greek treaty, which they hate, and they set about it dextrously. The Duke I believe to be in correspondence with Metternich, and tries to play his game of delay and procrastination.[58]

As for the Greek cause, the Duke was his own witness :

. . . there never was such a humbug as this Greek affair altogether. However, thank God, it has never cost us a shilling and never shall.[59]

Moreover, events in the Levant had been moving rapidly to a crisis since Canning's death. In November, while

Goderich was still in office and the treaty was being vigorously executed, the naval forces of the three Powers had practically annihilated a Turco-Egyptian fleet in the Bay of Navarino, in order to stop further operations against the Greeks. But what made the continued execution of the treaty especially vital from the point of view of the Canningites was the fact that Russia was about to go to war, whether with or without England and France. There was also a closely related issue : that of the boundaries to be assigned to the new Greek state. Wellington and Aberdeen, ' pro-Turkish ' even as against the Greeks, were for confining the new state to the Morea and some neighbouring islands ; the Canningites for giving it better prospects of real independence and prosperity by adding territory to the north.

And even among the Canningites, Palmerston stood out in his vigorous advocacy of the dead leader's policy. Of the others, only Dudley seems to have shown an equally sustained interest ; and Dudley seldom ventured on his own initiative to oppose Wellington and Aberdeen.[60] The secretary at War was particularly assertive with respect to the policy to be followed in the Near East ; for the battle of Navarino and the imminence of Russian action had, if possible, hardened his resolution. He had joked about the battle as ' a slight act of remonstrance struck parenthetically into unbroken friendship '[61] ; but he had hailed it as clarifying the situation for the British government. ' The treaty of London,' he wrote, ' *must* be carried into effect, cost what it may, and oppose it who will.'[62] At that time Goderich was still prime minister.

With Wellington for his chief, Palmerston realized that some concessions would be necessary ; but he made them only under pressure and very grudgingly. When, on two occasions, he was forced to defend in parliament Wellington's reference to the battle of Navarino as an ' untoward event,' he allowed his own sentiments to be pretty accurately inferred by translating ' untoward ' into ' unexpected.'[63] But it was naturally in the cabinet that his real efforts to salvage Canning's policy were made. In working for the Greeks, he found allies in Peel and other non-Canningites ;

MUTINY IN THE MINISTRY

and had the satisfaction of seeing Wellington defeated several times.[64] The amount which the Duke would have had the new Greek state pay as tribute to Turkey was cut down; his proposal for maintaining a Turkish agent in Greece was rejected; all plans for requiring Greece to assist Turkey in war were tabled; and the participation of Turkey in the choice of a Greek ruler limited to the right of rejectng the first two candidates named. Even this last provision was too much for Palmerston. But his greatest concern was with regard to the frontiers of the new state. His aims and difficulties may be judged from an entry in his journal under date of April 2 :

> Cabinet this evening after dinner at Apsley House. . . . *As usual, much discussion and entire difference of opinion*; the Duke, Ellenborough, and Aberdeen being for cutting down the Greeks as much as possible; Huskisson, Dudley, and myself for executing the treaty in the fair spirit of those who made it. . . . The limits were proposed to be the Morea and islands. I again urged that Livadia, or at least Attica, should be added; but nobody else supported this opinion.[65]

With regard to Russia, too, he justified his discipleship. In March came the announcement of the Tsar's intended declaration of war on Turkey, and his threat that, failing allied co-operation, he would proceed solely with regard to Russian interests. Palmerston, for a time persuaded of the impracticability of co-operation, and suspicious of Russia's ulterior designs,[66] soon swung around. In opposition, as usual, to the Duke, he urged that an Anglo-French expeditionary force should be sent to Greece, that the British and Russian admirals should act together under identical instructions, and that the conference between the three Powers should be resumed.[67] But it was an uphill fight; and all that the Canningites could do was to temporise :

> Huskisson, Dudley, Grant, and I try to keep things together, and have done so; and if Russia and France are *civil* to us, we shall manage it still; but if they send us uncivil papers, we shall not be able to prevent a separation of the alliance.[68]

To preserve the alliance, he ventured upon a curious diplomatic indiscretion. ' You will probably hear it alleged,' he wrote on May 8 to his brother, then chargé at St. Petersburg, ' that our Government wishes to break with Russia and abandon the Greek cause ; you may with truth say that this is not the feeling of some of the most influential members of the Cabinet ; and that if Russia shows a disposition to abide by the treaty we shall not depart from it.' [69] This was acting the part of coadjutor to Dudley with a vengeance. And it was also an admission that Wellington and Aberdeen had, in the larger issues, won the game. Russia received no British co-operation or encouragement through the efforts of the Canningites.

They failed again in urging what they represented as a logical development of Canning's policy in Portugal ; but in this instance Wellington had a stronger case. For they were attempting to help the constitutionalists without having Canning's excuse. Soon after his death it had been arranged that Dom Miguel should accept the constitution and marry his niece, the Queen—thus putting an end to all danger of invasion from Spain, and all technical justification for the presence of British troops. But when Miguel's arrival produced a panic among the constitutionalists (with only too good reason, as events were soon to prove) Huskisson insisted that the British force despatched by Canning could not in fairness to the liberals be withdrawn. Palmerston, fuming with impatience, declared that the overthrow of the constitution would make the British ministers ' appear to have been so many *dupes*.' [70] But the cabinet stood with the premier. British influence in Portugal was to be exercised through the presence of a single line-of-battle ship, and the use of ' the strongest terms ' to Miguel.[71]

The Canningites never actually broke with Wellington on any defined issue ; but they came nearest to doing so over the corn law. The details of the affair scarcely call for record in a short sketch of Palmerston's career ; for the defence of the liberal point of view in economic matters fell naturally to Huskisson, and to Grant, the president of the Board of Trade. The issue was one peculiarly fitted to divide the two sections of the cabinet. For Canning had attempted, during the preceding session, to substitute a sliding scale for the high fixed duty on imported grain established by the law of 1815; and had been defeated in the House of Lords on an amendment proposed by Wellington. In March 1828 the details of a new corn bill were discussed at several stormy meetings of the cabinet; and a compromise arranged to which all the ministers with one exception were willing to agree. But the one exception was the president of the Board of Trade, on whom the task of moving the 'corn resolutions' would necessarily devolve. Unable to accept a rate as high as that proposed, Grant resigned on March 24. Palmerston, describing in his journal his efforts to induce Grant to change his mind, explained with great precision the very embarrassing situation in which he and the other Canningites were placed :

If he [Grant] went out, Huskisson must go too, although prepared to support the measure. . . . If Huskisson went out I must do so too, for similar reasons, and because if his influence were withdrawn from the Cabinet, the arbitrary party would soon predominate, and I could no longer co-operate with my colleagues. We should then all of us make ourselves highly ridiculous ; we had said when the Government was first formed, that before we joined it we had explanations and understandings with the Duke on all important points of policy ; and now it would appear that on one most important point, . . . we had had no understanding at all.[72]

Once again he argued that Canning's followers could best pay tribute to his memory by serving under Wellington :

. . . if we all went out there must be formed a purely Tory Government, that would speedily throw over all those measures on which Canning had founded his fame. We should break immediately with Russia, probably also with France, back out of the Greek treaty, and unite ourselves again with Metternich, and adopt the apostolical party in Spain and Portugal.

This was before the final contests on the Near Eastern question had occurred. In the end, Grant gave in ; but the abnormal dissensions in the cabinet continued, in spite of all that Peel could do. Even Palmerston, combative as he was, grew tired of them.[73]

The end came, late in May, through the unintentional

resignation of Huskisson.[74] On May 18, he and Palmerston voted against the government on the disposition to be made of a seat recently forfeited by a corrupt borough : Huskisson because he considered himself pledged to do so, and Palmerston as a matter of personal conviction. The vote involved no real principle ; and they had reasons for believing themselves entitled, by previous agreement, to take which side they chose. But when Peel, who did not consider the agreement operative in this case, showed some of his not infrequent irritability, Huskisson acted with his customary impulsiveness. Without consulting any of his friends he sent Wellington a letter which he apparently intended as a formal and courteous offer to resign, but which could be interpreted as a definite resignation. The Duke, long outraged by the concerted opposition of ' the four,' as he called Huskisson, Dudley, Grant and Palmerston, accepted it in the definite sense. What was more, he persisted in doing so after Huskisson had protested repeatedly that he had not intended to give up his post. For Wellington expected to profit in any case. If Huskisson, admitting that he had actually resigned, requested to be taken back, his influence would be diminished both in the cabinet and in the House. Or, if his resignation stood, the Duke would be rid of at least two members of the insubordinate liberal clique, under circumstances decidedly damaging to them. For it was known that Palmerston would follow Huskisson. But he was perhaps the greater nuisance of the two.

Indeed, according to Huskisson, it was the conduct of the secretary at War which finally provoked Wellington to risk the break ; and it was only Palmerston and Grant whom he wished actually to extrude.[75] Huskisson was laying a little too much unction to his soul ; but there is no doubt that Palmerston had particularly enraged the Duke and the more orthodox Tory ministers. In the debates over the repeal of the Test and Corporation Acts he had spoken vehemently for Catholic emancipation. He was entirely of the opinion, so he told the House, that the Test and Corporation Acts should disappear ; but he could not be a party to the removal of the ' theoretical, or at least extremely trivial ' disabilities of the dissenters until the

DISHONOURABLE DISCHARGE

'real' grievances of the Catholics had been redressed.[76] In the cabinet his incessant 'pecking' (the word was Ellenborough's) [77] seemed like insubordination to his chief; and in the House he came to what Wellington characterized as 'mutiny' when, on May 14, he was called upon to answer an inexcusable attack on Canning's memory:

> He could not allow that statement to remain uncontradicted, considering, as he did, that the government of this country would be entitled to parliamentary support, in proportion as it adhered to the principles of Mr. Canning, whose name would be venerated long after his detractors had been consigned to oblivion.[78]

This was not only to touch Wellington at a very tender point, but to make his position extremely difficult.[79]

Whatever his share in bringing on the crisis, Palmerston showed to great advantage in meeting it.[80] Huskisson abased himself too far. Dudley appeared to worse advantage still. From the first he was in 'the agony of doubt and hesitation,' pleading that he could not bear to hurt the King who had been pleased 'to take a great fancy' to him, and holding his place until even the Prussian ambassador had warned him that he would be '*perdu de réputation.*' Grant, presumably, and Lamb and Palmerston certainly, were firm in their attitude from the first. It is true that Palmerston was more involved than the others, and that he had to resist none of the blandishments offered by the Duke to Dudley and to Lamb. But his quiet resolution to go out with Huskisson, maintained along with determined efforts to heal the breach, was admirable. His steadfastness had its reward. Huskisson was severely blamed in many quarters, and even regarded as having 'acted like a knave throughout.'[81] Palmerston appears to have received abuse only from the ultra-Tory duke of Cumberland; and this he regarded as a high compliment.

Looking backward, one can see that his 'mutiny' against the Duke was the climax of a long repudiation of 'the stupid old Tory Party.' One can see, too, that it was doubtful whether his separation from the Tories would be permanent. Let 'liberalism' within the party once more gain the upper hand, and there would be nothing to prevent him from rejoining it *totis viribus*. For to him, as to others of his time, the vital distinction was not between Whig and Tory, but between the open-minded and the blindly reactionary. The spirit of the times had borne him along to belief in Catholic emancipation, a freer economic policy, and the wisdom of encouraging the movement for self-government on the continent. He was even commencing to appreciate that there were rotten spots in the otherwise perfect British system of parliamentary representation.[82] If the Tories would also move with the spirit of the times, so much the better. If not, well, there would always be the Whigs, with whom he had already co-operated so pleasantly. Some of them—the Mephistophelean Lord Grey in particular—were inclined to take grave liberties with the constitution. But the party was still lacking in any real cohesion or discipline ; and it might be held to prudent courses through alliance with sensible Canningites. Obviously, the immediate task for any aspiring Canningite was to advance himself to a position in parliament which would give him stronger bargaining power with either side.

CHAPTER IV

THE JUNCTION WITH THE WHIGS, 1828–1830

TIME was when men asked how Palmerston became a Whig ; but it has been realised in later years that he was never actually a Whig at any time. He was, in fact, so self-willed and so given to opportunism, so impatient of restraint imposed by traditions and principles, that his identification with any party was a matter of convenience, almost of accident. Whereas the ordinary minister had only to subordinate a few of his opinions and policies to those of his colleagues, Palmerston had sometimes to subordinate so many that he could, with a different but not appreciably greater sacrifice, have served equally well upon the other side. But he was able to remain long and continuously a cabinet minister because, on those occasions when he found it impossible to have his way, his sportsmanlike good nature and his love of office taught him to compromise. Not having achieved cabinet rank until 1827, he had had little opportunity to exhibit his characteristic independence during his service in the successive Tory ministries. But it was sufficiently well developed to leave him undecided as to his future party affiliations during the two and a half years which elapsed between his break with Wellington and his acceptance of the Foreign Office under Grey. In so far as opinions and policies were concerned he became no less a Tory and no more a Whig. He remained a Canningite, and an independent one at that.

The position of the Canningites on the morrow of their break with Wellington was far from a happy one. No one seemed to hold them in much regard. The two choruses of critics who had respectively denounced their apostacy to Canning in January, and the effrontery of their opposition to the Duke during the ensuing months, now joined to celebrate their expiation. The old Tories were pleased at their predicament; while so good a democrat as Hobhouse noted that 'the Canningites have fallen without a tear being shed for their loss, a good lesson for unsteady politicians.'[1] Some rehabilitation in the estimation of parliament might have come to them had they been able to carry on a vigorous opposition; but fate and Wellington denied them the opportunity. The very question of Catholic emancipation began to fail them as a fighting issue at the moment of their fall. For their resignation necessitated the reconstruction of the cabinet; and the reconstruction made necessary the famous election in county Clare, at which O'Connell and the Catholic Association convinced Wellington and a good many other 'Protestants' that emancipation could not long be deferred. Moreover, the Duke, anxious to reinforce his majority, and relieved of the fear that he would be accused of acting under compulsion from 'the four,' showed a distinct tendency to steal some of their ammunition by partially reversing his policy in the Near East.[2] His cabinet, reorganised into a very fair imitation of a general staff, seemed quite at his command. And the Canningites were deprived not only of ammunition but of followers. A few of their previous associates were seduced outright by the Duke's offers and promises; others gave a wavering allegiance at best. Small wonder, since the former Canningite ministers showed little either of cohesion or of leadership. Any or all of them might from time to time be found voting with the government. Goderich made a singularly artless bid for the captaincy, and was rejected with decision by Palmerston and the rest.[3] Huskisson retained what primacy there was, but seemed discouraged. Before the session was over, he had gone abroad.

Yet the future prospects of the 'Liberals,' as Palmerston termed the group, were not unfavourable by any means. If they numbered, even before the seductions, only twenty-seven in the Commons, and eleven in the Lords,[4] they included not only the five leading secessionists but other men of talent and standing such as Stratford Canning,

Goderich, Granville, Sturges Bourne and Littleton. Even in ordinary times no party could have neglected them or failed to covet their support ;[5] and their position was rendered doubly advantageous by the persisting division of the Whigs and the rapidly increasing signs that Wellington was to have a 'mutiny' in the rank and file of his right wing. By August his conversion to the 'Catholic' cause was rumoured everywhere ; by November it was being predicted that the die-hard Protestants of his following would leave him, and that he would be compelled to turn to Huskisson. With four other groups, two of them Tory and two Whig, on the look-out for allies, the talented Canningites, disorganised as they were, would not be hard put to it in finding friends.

Palmerston bided his time, holding himself free to make any political connection that might suit him, and showing entire independence in the expression of his opinions. He did not seem to be counting upon an early reconciliation with the Tories ; for Hobhouse reported, at the beginning of 1829, that ' he " talked " Liberal, just as well and as freely as if he had played the part all his life,' espousing the cause, not only of Catholic emancipation, but of O'Connell and the Association.[6] Yet he had chosen, a month after his resignation from Wellington's cabinet, to accentuate the great barrier that lay between him and the Whig leaders as a whole—their advocacy of, and his determined opposition to, any general reform of the system of parliamentary representation. In advocating the application in one specific instance of 'piecemeal' reform (*i.e.* the transference of the right of representation from individual boroughs which were notoriously corrupt to counties or to unrepresented towns), he put himself on record before parliament in the most emphatic terms :

Lord Palmerston expressed his wish, that the franchise should be extended to a great town, not because he was a friend to reform in principle, but because he was its decided enemy. To extend the franchise to large towns, on such occasions as the one in question, was the only mode by which the House could avoid the adoption, at some time or other, of a general plan of reform.[7]

The fact that his openly expressed convictions made him

ineligible for office either as a proper Tory or a proper Whig, strengthens the supposition that he hoped to see the coalition of 1827 revived. He was certainly suspected of doing so by some of Grey's friends. Lady Grey, in January 1829, wrote her eldest son of Lord Rosslyn's anxiety that Grey should absent himself from London at the opening of the session lest ' many things might occur to force him, even against his will, into an active opposition to the Duke, of which all the Canning party would be too happy to avail themselves. . . . He might assist Lord Lansdowne and the Huskissons to overthrow the Duke, but it would be to bring *them* into power, from which they would again exclude him. . . .'[8] But if such a plot were maturing in Palmerston's head, he seems to have kept it to himself. His one obvious desire was to make an impression on the House during the session of 1829.

It was very probably to fortify himself for the debates on foreign affairs which he intended to bring on, that Palmerston spent the three weeks immediately preceding the opening of the session in Paris. As usual, he gathered and recorded lively and clear-cut impressions of all he saw. What he saw in particular was that the French, or most at least of those who governed them, were looking for an opportunity to upset the generous territorial arrangements accorded their country at Vienna in 1815, in order to seize territory lying beyond their eastern frontier :

. . . there is growing up among public men a *French* feeling, and this is directed for its first object to the recovery of the provinces between the northern frontier and the Rhine—Belgium, in short, and part of the Prussian territory. The ultra-Liberals say they would support any minister who would recover this territory for France. . . .[9]

Sebastiani[10] even told him that so long as England was ' opposed to these resumptions ' she might expect to see France unite with other Powers.[11] Casimir Perier, Royer Collard and Pasquier seem to have made a better impression ; but Palmerston felt some uneasiness :

This country is, however, making rapid strides in improvements of all kinds ; and, as Miss Berry said last night, ' It is a joke to talk of danger to Europe from Prussia ' ; if any exists, it is from France it is

THE SHIFT TO FOREIGN POLICY

to be feared. However, this is a chapter far on in the volume, and we have a long way to go before we come to it.[12]

Little he knew that Charles X's government would be planning to justify his suspicions within the current year.[13]

Another notable feature of his visit was a long conversation with Pozzo di Borgo, the Russian ambassador to France, on the situation in the Near East, and its relation to European politics as a whole.[14] It was a friendly conversation, but not quite so friendly as Pozzo might have expected had he seen the report of the Princess Lieven to her brother at St. Petersburg in the preceding May. The Princess had quoted Palmerston as declaring himself one of those who ' trust, eyes open or eyes shut, in your Emperor.'[15] With all suitable allowances for exaggeration on both sides and for Palmerstonian gallantry, there is still room for the supposition that Palmerston, since making his fervid declaration, had undergone some change of heart. Labouring to persuade Pozzo that it was to Russia's interest to agree with her adversary quickly, he suggested that the Powers might put an end to the war by laying down for Turkey the terms on which she should, in their opinion, be prepared to make peace, and threatening to abandon or even to take sides against her if she refused compliance. ' I did not add to Pozzo what, however, would in that case be indispensable, namely, that we should say to Russia, we will leave Turkey to you, or even help you against her ; but then, mark you, you must make peace when you have beat her, without taking any of her territory in Europe.' This, while friendly, was not exactly ' trust, eyes open or eyes shut.' And another possible development, discussed with equal frankness, was that England and Austria might join the Turks ; and that England, sending a fleet to the Black Sea, might cut the Russian communications. Both men, however, ' hoped that no such rupture would take place.' A similar discussion with the Princess would not have ended so complacently.

Filled with information and animation, Palmerston returned for the opening of the session that was to bring him fame as a speaker, and some recognition of his aptitude for handling foreign affairs. Throughout its course he really exerted himself only twice, once in favour of Catholic emancipation, and once in criticism of the government's foreign policy. For it was only after careful preparation that he could rise to his own full powers in public speech. In 1829 he had not only every chance for preparation, but every incitement to do his best. The group to which he belonged was still intact, but still in the wilderness. It could come to no satisfactory agreement either with the Whigs or with Wellington.[16] Cumberland and the ultra-Tories, burning to revenge themselves on the Duke, for conceding Catholic emancipation after all, were reported ready for a junction; but the Canningites repudiated the idea of an alliance so unnatural.[17] Ambition, then, and love of the game spurred on Palmerston; but genuine conviction shaped his course. Catholic emancipation had long lain near his heart; and Aberdeen's (or rather Wellington's)[18] foreign policy he regarded as a national disgrace to which an apathetic country should be aroused. He was preparing to attack it, and coaching at least one of his friends to do the same, fully two months in advance.[19]

On March 18 he made his principal speech on Catholic emancipation.[20] No gloss can convey the flavour of any speech, and, since Palmerston's position on Catholic emancipation was already clear, the flavour was what made, and still makes, his oration notable. One can scarcely, indeed, find more typical examples of his parliamentary speaking at its best than those which he offered to the House in this session of 1829. After giving the 'Protestants,' who rested their case on the principles of 1688, the rather surprising information that William III came to England ' with peace and toleration on his lips, and civil and religious liberty in his heart,' he let loose a torrent of emotional eloquence :

> Can one believe one's ears when one hears respectable men talk so lightly, nay, almost so wishfully, of civil war; do they reflect what a countless multitude of ills those three short syllables contain? It is easy to denounce against a nation this awful doom; but when Heaven shall once have opened the windows of its wrath, when the foundations of social order shall once have been broken up, when the deluge of civil war shall once have burst upon the land, where is the

INTERIOR OF THE OLD HOUSE OF COMMONS

man who shall presume to set limits to its fury, or foretell the extent of devastation.—It is well, indeed, for the gentlemen of England, who live secure under the protecting shadow of the law, whose . . . harvests have never been trodden down by the conflict of hostile feet, it is well for them to talk of civil war, as if it were some holiday pastime or some sport of children :

> ' They jest at scars who never felt a wound.'

But, that gentlemen from unfortunate and ill-starred Ireland, who have seen with their own eyes, and heard with their own ears, the miseries which civil war produces, who have known by their own experience the barbarism, aye the barbarity, which it engenders—that such persons should look upon civil war as anything short of the last and greatest of national calamities, is to me a matter of the deepest and most unmixed astonishment.

If the nation is overflowing with so much suppressed pugnacity ; if like an overcharged thunder-cloud we are bursting with accumulated fire, which a fourteen years' peace has rendered unbearably irksome, let us vent it on any and every other nation of the earth, let us not exercise a suicidal fury on ourselves.

And there was much more than emotional oratory in the speech. Certain passages showed that their author possessed an understanding of the Irish situation rare enough among Englishmen of his time :

If I wished to convince an impartial Englishman of the policy of repealing these laws, I should bid him repair to the south of Ireland ; . . . to see what a fierce and unsocial spirit bad laws engender ; and how impossible it is to degrade a people, without at the same time demoralizing them too.

But if this should fail to convince him, and his judgment still hung in the balance of doubt, I should then tell him to go among the Protestants of the north. There he would see how noble and generous natures may be corrupted by the possession of undue and inordinate ascendancy ; there he would see how men, naturally kind and benevolent, can be brought up from their earliest infancy to hate the great majority of their countrymen with all the bitterness, which neighbourhood and consanguinity infuse into quarrels ; and not satisfied with the disputes of the days in which they live, raking up the ashes of the dead for food to their angry passions ; summoning the shades of departed centuries to give a keener venom to the contests of the present age . . . .

There was convincing logic, too :

> We are called upon to maintain these disabilities, in order to preserve the integrity of the British Constitution. . . . Does the British Constitution consist in . . . keeping down the people by the sword ? . . . for some time past, five-sixths of the regular infantry at home, have been employed in Ireland, in preserving a forced tranquillity. . . . Is this the principle of the Revolution of 1688 ? "

It would take further quotation, not only from this but from other speeches, to show the warmth and more especially the generous spirit of his advocacy. He protested against coupling the suppression of the Catholic Association with the removal of Irish disabilities ;[21] and he objected even more to the disfranchisement of Irish forty-shilling freeholders.[22]

The great speech of March 18 produced all the effect that its author could have wished.[23] Greville wrote that it ' astonished everybody ' : Tierney regarded it as ' an imitation of Canning, and not a bad one ' : Sturges Bourne declared that Canning's eloquence had risen from the dead : and Lord Howick (Grey's son and heir), whose circle was anything but Palmerstonian, heard that it was ' excellent & very well listened to.' If Palmerston had missed advancement for lack of oratorical power, he had now become far more eligible. But the House had still to learn what he could do in the way of slashing assault, withering scorn, and appeals to British pride. This was demonstrated on the night of June 1, when he made his long meditated assault on the government's foreign policy.[24]

His main attack was launched at Wellington's and Aberdeen's relations with Portugal, where Miguel had progressed from the status of regent to that of sovereign. An absolutist rising, and the calling of a notoriously packed Cortes, had given him despotic power, which he was using in utter disregard of his undertakings not only to Pedro but to the British government. The constitution was torn up ; and its more loyal supporters despoiled, and either executed or driven into exile. So flagrant were Miguel's cruelty and bad faith that even the despotic sovereigns, with the sole exception of Ferdinand of Spain, withdrew their diplomatic representatives. What, in the first place, infuriated Palmerston was that Wellington had done no more than the reactionary courts. Surely England, the friend and ally, the patron and protector of Portugal ; England, the fountain of constitutional government ; England, the country to which Pedro had given his confidence and Miguel his most specific assurances, had a special function to perform. And Wellington's sins were not merely those of omission by any means. Alone of the Portuguese dominions in Europe the island of Terceira had held out bravely for the Queen ; and the refugees from Miguel's cruelty who had found asylum in Britain had sailed for Terceira to give its defenders help. But, on the specific orders of Wellington's government, British ships had forcibly prevented them from carrying out their plan. Considering how more than doubtful was Miguel's claim to sovereignty, Wellington's ' neutrality ' seemed to a good many Englishmen a little overdone.

In his strictures on this affair, the militant Palmerston of history first appeared in full panoply. For the first time he indicted a continental despot for the edification of a British audience :

> The civilised world rings with execrations upon Miguel ; and yet this destroyer of constitutional freedom, this breaker of solemn oaths, this faithless usurper, this enslaver of his country, this trampler upon public law, this violator of private rights, this attempter of the lives of helpless and defenceless women, is in the opinion of Europe mainly indebted for the success which has hitherto attended him, to a belief industriously propagated by his partisans, and not sufficiently refuted by any acts of the British government, that the cabinet of England look upon his usurpations with no unfriendly eye.

The government had attempted to justify its attitude by appeal to the doctrine of non-interference in the internal affairs of other states. But Palmerston, in words of engaging frankness which were more pregnant than any of his hearers could have realised, proceeded to lay down the doctrine on which he was himself to act for many years :

> If by interference is meant interference by force of arms, such interference the government are right in saying, general principles

and our own practice forebade us to exert. But if by interference
is meant intermeddling, and intermeddling in every way, and to every
extent, short of actual military force ; then I must affirm, that there
is nothing in such interference, which the laws of nations may not in
certain cases permit. . . .

After declaring that Anglo-Portuguese relations had
been 'almost one unbroken chain of such interference,'
he proceeded to exhibit the chain, link by link. In particular, parliament was asked to consider a letter of Miguel's
on which the constitutionalists had relied ('written under
the eye, if not under the dictation, of the English ambassador at Vienna'), the hospitality and confidence shown
him when he stopped in England on his way to Portugal ;
his escort to the Tagus by a British squadron and a British
ambassador ; and the protection he had been able to derive
from the very British troops which Canning had sent in
1826. Then came a thoroughly Palmerstonian appeal to
British pride :

The conduct of Don Miguel has been no less affronting to the
king of England, than it has been disgraceful to Don Miguel himself.
Was it fitting that the king of England should be made the stalking-horse under whose cover this royal poacher should creep upon his
unsuspecting prey ? Was it becoming that the king of England
should be made use of, as the attesting witness, to engagements never
meant to be fulfilled, and to oaths forsworn by the heart ere yet they
had found utterance from the lips ? I say, that if the insulted honour
of a sovereign is a legitimate ground of national quarrel, we are
intitled to demand, and to extort, reparation from Don Miguel.

Wellington and Aberdeen had failed to secure redress
even for the ill-treatment of British subjects :

The British government have submitted to usage from Miguel,
which coming from any other quarter, would have roused them, like
a lion from his slumber. Well, Sir, then comes the case of Terceira,
and here indeed the lion has put forth his strength, when it were much
to be wished, he had still continued to repose : or here rather we performed the functions of a less noble animal, and hunted down the
prey, that another might step in and devour.

The *civis Romanus,* even at a comparatively early age, had
an effective way of putting things.

From Portugal he turned, in the same speech, to Greece, taking up again the struggle for more liberal frontiers that he had waged in the cabinet a year before :

> Shall I be told . . . that the Morea and the Cyclades are to be this liberated Greece, and that the Isthmus of Corinth is its northern boundary ? I say that will not be, that cannot be, it is impossible that it should be ; a larger and wider limit, extending at least to the line drawn from Volo to Arta, is indispensably necessary, for Greece, . . . and even those, who were the greatest sticklers for the Morea simply, must now abandon the notion of establishing a Greece, which should contain neither Athens, nor Thebes, nor Marathon, nor Salamis, nor Platae, nor Thermopylae, nor Missolunghi ; which should exclude from its boundaries, all the most inspiring records of national achievements, whether in ancient or in modern times.

It was this passage which made the deepest imprint upon the mind of his contemporaries. In curiously effective contrast stood another, which, in arraigning the Tory party for its ignorance of the true sources of political power, purported to present the speaker's own philosophy of political life. It was in the familiar rationalistic style, stressing the power of mind over matter, and instancing the harnessing by the human ' insect ' of the power of winds and waves. Not improbably was it a reminiscence of the Dugald Stewart days. Yet anyone who read that speech in the later months of 1848, and reflected on the positions of Palmerston and Metternich, might have found it something more than pedantry clothed in pompous rhetoric:

> Those statesmen who know how to avail themselves of the passions, and the interests, and the opinions of mankind, are able to gain an ascendancy, and to exercise a sway over human affairs, far out of all proportion greater than belong to the power and resources of the state over which they preside ; while those, on the other hand, who seek to check inprovement, to cherish abuses, to crush opinions, and to prohibit the human race from thinking, whatever may be the apparent power which they wield, will find their weapon snap short in their hand, when most they need its protection.

The speech remains one of peculiar significance, quite apart from the evidence it gives that Palmerston believed in ' intermeddling,' in making England the patron of liberal parties and small states, in berating foreign sovereigns and bemusing a British public, many months before he passed the Foreign Office doors. It was so deliberate an effort that one is tempted to see in it another bid for high preferment, another 'imitation of Canning,' and hence a demonstration to Canningites and Whigs that they had among them one fit to take up Canning's work in the field of foreign policy. It may have been all these things ; and, if so, Palmerston was able to congratulate himself once more on achieving remarkable success. For, although the speech was delivered at a late hour and in an almost empty House, it produced an even deeper effect than the speech on Catholic emancipation.[25] But, if the skilful preparation and delivery of the speech owed much to Palmerston's ambition, there is no doubt that its fervour owed much to his sincerity. Proof of this appears only in his private letters, and in the record he established at the Foreign Office in later years ; but some apparent confirmation can be found in a characteristic step which he took at this time. In writing his brother about the speech, he added :

> I had taken measures to insure these matters being touched upon also in the French Chambers, because that was the way to stir up the French Government to more active feelings about them ; and I trust that some good may be the result.[26]

It is just possible that he hoped to embarrass the ministry by 'stirring up' the French to take the lead in foreign affairs. But he was apparently far less anxious to upset Wellington than to drive out that well-meaning and rather ingenuous admirer of continental autocracy, Aberdeen. It is worth noting, too, that, whatever his ambitions and ideals, he was willing to consecrate to them some real work. For several weeks after parliament rose he remained in London as 'by far the best place to read in,' a place where one was not 'tempted to be out all day.'[27] The autumn was the time for visiting his estates and the country houses of his friends.

The autumn of 1829 brought him not only recreation but some rather curious evidence of the extent to which he had enhanced his standing in the political world.[28] During the foregoing session Wellington, failing to conciliate the ultra-Tories for his *volte face* on Catholic emancipation, and feeling his exposure to the increasing power of the Whig and Canningite assaults, had shown his desire for auxiliaries. But the part of auxiliaries was one which neither Whigs nor Canningites aspired to play, whether to Wellington or to one another; and the House remained roughly divided into five, or (if the radicals were counted) six groups. In this situation, some at least of the ultra-Tories, relying on the King's disappointment in Wellington, and his distaste for the Whigs, seem to have conceived the idea that they might revenge themselves and return to power if they bid high enough for outside help. In order to be able to assure King George in advance that they could form a really powerful cabinet, they sounded some of the desired auxiliaries, including Palmerston. The tempter was Sir Richard Vivian, member for Cornwall; the place, the Travellers' Club; the time, late October. Vivian, declaring that a new government must soon come in, suggested that Palmerston might have the Colonial Office and the leadership of the House in a government to be built around Mansfield, Eldon, Newcastle and Knatchbull. Would he allow his name to be mentioned to the King, and would he, if necessary, take office without Huskisson? The Tories regarded him as 'committed' only on foreign policy, and not on financial and economic questions. The only interest attaching to the episode is to be found in Palmerston's definition of his own position. He felt quite free, he told Vivian, to take office without Huskisson, but not to take office in a cabinet which would 'retrace the steps' which Huskisson had taken in matters of trade and currency. Nor would he undertake to join any government without definite knowledge as to its policies and personnel. In writing of the affair, he defined his position still more specifically:

> ... it seems to me that my interest as well as inclination leads me to adhere to the party with whom I am thrown. I consider myself as being free if I choose, because we never have met or consulted as a party, and have upon no occasion voted as a body. ... But as to going to the Tory party ... though I should not be quite in the same false position as Peel, because he has always concealed his

opinions more or less, and I have avowed mine, yet still to belong to people you do not think with cannot answer.[29]

In just a year he was to resign himself to the fact that, to belong with people he did not 'think with' in at least one very fundamental matter, was a hard necessity.

In December, he went once more to Paris, where he was becoming more and more at home. His position and reputation insured him reception at court and at the great political houses ; and his membership (by unanimous election) in the new Anglo-French Club gave him as he said, ' a *Pied à Terre* immediately for news, & society.'[30] His letters show him to have been at once a witty gossip, a student of broad interests, and a farsighted observer of men and events. A recognised entertainer of society, such as Joseph Jekyll, might have written a letter which Palmerston sent at the time to Lady Cowper :

You say Bingham Baring has lost his Teeth, but you do not mention how or where the Loss occurred. I could get him a Set in the Palais Royal if he would send me the Measure of his Mouth, and there is a Man who advertizes that he makes Chins & Noses to order, who might perhaps be useful to Ly Harriet, & give her a better Nose, in exchange for her Redundancy of Chin.[31]

Yet this debonair gossip, this middle-aged man of fashion, had stayed in London to read through hot midsummer days ; and now, with all the diversions of Paris at his command, was 'attending some lectures of Guizot, Villemain, & Dupin, upon the Early History of Civilization in Europe, upon the Progress & Origin of European Languages, & upon the State of the Mechanical Arts & Industry of the Civilized World.'[32] In political matters the French lust for expansion again impressed him unpleasantly, though he was naïve enough to regard the danger as remote so long as parliamentary government continued :

It is quite astonishing how every Frenchman you meet raves about ' *nos frontières,*' and declares he would cut off his two hands to get back the Rhine, Alps, and Pyrenees as boundaries ; all this, however, is mere froth and vanity ; and while they have Chambers who must levy taxes to carry on a war, nothing but egregious folly on our part can bring on a war between the two countries.[33]

As for French domestic politics, his foresight was remarkable. He did not, indeed, believe that Charles X and Polignac would be mad enough to persist in their reactionary course ; but he prefigured to a nicety the developments that persistence would bring :

> . . . the Duke of Orleans might be invited to step over the way from the Palais Royal ; . . . There are too many millions of proprietors of land and funds in France to let it be possible that anything should happen endangering the safety of either one property or the other.
> The army, however, would not support the Government in any violent proceedings. . . .[34]

Conservative liberalism, *i.e.* compliance with the desires of the nation, when these should be definitely ascertained, and expressed in terms of constitutional government, seemed to him the one safe policy for France. The year just opening was to show that he would make some sacrifice of personal conviction for the application of the same policy at home.

The obvious desire to make his mark in the House, and the equally obvious resolution to let events shape his course in domestic politics which Palmerston had shown in 1829, were at least equally evident in his conduct during the following and much more fateful year. In the face of approaches from both Tories and Whigs, he held his decision regarding any fresh party affiliation in reserve as long as possible. He had no intention of repeating his experiences of 1828 in the Wellington cabinet ; nor was he ready to become merely a member of some Whig cabinet. There would be need for too much concession in either case. What he apparently desired was a reconstruction of the Wellington ministry, by the introduction of a predominating group of Canningites and Whigs. So broad-bottomed an administration could make what small concession to public opinion was necessary in the matter of parliamentary reform, and could pick up again the policies of Canning's coalition. Only when all prospects of such an outcome vanished, did Palmerston make his choice between two parties he could not ' think with.'

But, while waiting, he was careful not to forfeit his

newly acquired standing in parliament. Together with the other Canningites, he continued his attacks on Aberdeen's foreign policy. His opportunities were now somewhat restricted ; since Russia and Turkey had made peace, and Miguel's ascendancy seemed assured. But he could still complain that the treaty of 1827 had not really been carried out ; that the government had allowed Russia to extend her boundaries at the expense of European Turkey, while refusing to support the Greeks in securing enough territory to allow of their enjoying an independent and prosperous future. And he could criticise Aberdeen's contemplated recognition of Miguel.[35] The House was again impressed by the effectiveness of his speaking ; [36] and Peel was driven to make a passionate response,—accusing Palmerston, even at this early date, of wishing to use ' the principle of interference ' to involve England constantly in war.[37] It was the beginning of a twenty years' duel between the two ; and it seems to have exhausted Palmerston. By the end of March Jekyll reported him ' pale and jaded, and five years older since last summer, from his parliamentary anxieties and displays.' [38]

His anxieties were no doubt enhanced by the increasing interest shown by parliament and country in the question of parliamentary reform. With respect to this, he and his group usually acted in concert, and in strict consistency with Palmerston's declaration of the year before. On various motions for disfranchising East Retford, for enfranchising Birmingham, Manchester, and Leeds, and for breaking the duke of Newcastle's influence in Newark, they were with the reforming Whigs ; but when general schemes of reform were advanced, they sided with the government.[39] Their attitude constituted no bar to eventual reconciliation with their former associates ; for even Tories as sound as Croker were coming to regard the adoption of ' piecemeal ' reform as the safest course.[40] But, taken all in all, the Canningites were still a centre party. Grey confidentially applied to Palmerston's friend, the Princess Lieven, as a first-hand authority on the prospects that the Huskissonians would develop into a real opposition. ' Are they sufficiently united,' she wrote, ' sufficiently determined ? It appears to me more than doubtful. I would wager that no one of the party yet knows on which side he will ultimately find himself.'[41]

But now fortune, which had been so kind to Palmerston at first, and then had seemed to desert him for so long, commenced to smile again. The death of George IV, on June 26, proved the first of a series of fortunate occurrences, by bringing on a general election at a time peculiarly unfavourable to the existing government. It had been realised for some weeks that the King could not live long; and Wellington had hoped that the election necessitated by his death would give the ministry increased strength. But at the critical moment liberalism flared up across the Channel ; and the French justified Palmerston's predictions to the letter. Refusing to allow Polignac to '*terrasser*' them, they disposed of him and his master at a stroke. The duke of Orleans stepped across from the Palais Royal ; signed a compact with his subjects ; and became, to outward appearances, a fair imitation of an English king. In France, ' Church and King ' and their supporters in the territorial nobility had received a fatal blow ; the middle class had acquired a dominant position in politics ; and the Paris mobs had shown again that force could accomplish much. The reflection of these events was seen in England as the voters went to the polls : in false reports that Wellington had been in secret league with Polignac, and in the sudden increase of agitation for reform.[42] The conservative *Annual Register* lamented that ' the general election took place in a period of greater public excitation, directed towards great changes in the frame of the government, than had occurred since the period of the French Revolution,' and without the ' restraints ' which French excesses ' had then imposed on the restless love of innovation.'[43] When the results were measured, there seemed little doubt that the Duke would have to overhaul both his ministry and his policies if he hoped to remain premier. And where would he turn first but to the Canningites ?

Meanwhile Palmerston had been displaying an enthusiasm over the events in France hardly exceeded by that of any Whig or even that of any radical. He may have seen that the 'glorious days' in Paris were producing a situation at home which favoured his prospects; but his private letters show beyond doubt that what he gloried in was the triumph of constitutional government. Thus, to Sulivan, his brother-in-law, on August 1 :

> We shall drink the cause of Liberalism all over the world. Let Spain & Austria look to themselves; this reaction cannot end where it began, & Spain & Italy & Portugal & parts of Germany will sooner or later be affected. This event is decisive of the ascendancy of Liberal Principles throughout Europe; the evil spirit has been put down and will be trodden under foot. The reign of Metternich is over & the days of the Duke's policy might be measured by algebra, if not by arithmetic.[44]

And again to Graham three days later :

> The contrast between the conduct of the French now and in the time of Louis is truly striking. Then the resistance which patriotism rendered legitimate against tyranny seemed only to be the pretence for arriving at the most horrible excesses. Now no violence seems to have been committed, beyond what was absolutely necessary for the security of the Constitution. Is not this the most triumphant demonstration of advantages arising from free discussion, from the liberty of the Press, from the diffusion of knowledge, and from familiarising even the lowest classes with the daily examination of political questions ? For to what else can be ascribed the honourable contrast which the proceedings of last week exhibit with those of the beginning of the last Revolution ?[45]

The end of July found him on good terms with the world. He had just enjoyed a quiet and successful election, and incidentally a convivial reunion, with his friends at Cambridge;[46] and his feeling of contentment must have been deepened by the knowledge that Wellington had already been appealing to Melbourne for Canningite support.

It is curious to observe the obscure negotiations which went on during the summer and early autumn months, and especially curious to see what convenient lapses of memory on the part of Wellington some of them entailed. At the beginning of July he did not think that he 'could or ought to sit in a Cabinet again as the First Lord of the Treasury with

Mr. Huskisson, Lord Palmerston, or Mr. Charles Grant.'[47] But before the month was out—and perhaps when the result of the elections could be in part foretold—he asked Melbourne to join the ministry and to bring with him Grant and Palmerston.[48] Melbourne closed the negotiation by asking that the reconstructed cabinet should be broad enough to include Grey and Huskisson. The latter apparently conducted some unsuccessful *pourparlers* of his own ; but these seem to have been especially obscure. The Whigs were not as yet prepared to make counter moves ; but they were looking in the same direction as Wellington for additional support. On the first day of September, Durham wrote Brougham that ' no efficient government ' could be formed without Palmerston, Grant and Huskisson. He feared, however, his party, by forming ' an open junction ' with them, might forfeit the aid of the ultra-Tories in upsetting Wellington.[49] Thus, approximately, did matters stand at the middle of September, when Huskisson, impulsive and clumsy to the last, was run over and killed by an engine at the opening of the Manchester Railway.

Before Huskisson was in his grave, the political world was busied with speculation as to the effect of his removal upon the futures of the other Canningites.[50] The consensus of opinion was that they would now find it easier to coalesce with either side ; since Huskisson had been *persona non grata* both to Wellington and to many of the Whigs. The Duke was expected to make the first move ; and his chancellor, Lord Lyndhurst, urged him to bid not only for the Canningites but for Grey as well.[51] On the other hand, the Whigs, now rapidly progressing towards reunion under Grey's leadership, were more and more inclined to claim Palmerston and his associates for their own. Palmerston's fear of Grey's long arm, if he still cherished it, was far more justifiable than in 1826.

In this agreeable and flattering situation the new Canningite leader—for as such he was generally recognised —maintained an attitude of scepticism, caution and reserve. To him it seemed that the Duke, delivered of so formidable an adversary as Huskisson, might continue in office without reconstructing his cabinet, provided that he showed himself a friend to 'piecemeal' reform. The Canningites might be well advised to offer 'co-operation' to the Whigs, but would do better to avoid 'incorporation.'[52]

At the end of September—a month before the date fixed for the opening of the new parliament—the Duke's memory again began to play him false. Not only was it impossible for him to remember that there had ever been any 'personal or political hostility' between himself and Palmerston, but he was unable even to recall 'any material difference of opinion.' He sent word that he would be glad to have Palmerston rejoin the ministry. Palmerston replied politely that he could remember no 'personal hostility' in the past ; but that he could not see his way to joining the Duke alone.[53] His reasoning was reserved for a more intimate correspondent :

> I did not say that it was like asking me whether I was disposed to jump off Westminster Bridge . . . it is not the accession of one or two, or even three individuals that would strengthen the Government. Such accessions would exterminate the men who became his [Wellington's] new instruments without adding materially to the force of the Government. He must either go on as he is, or make up his mind to a reconstruction of his Government upon an extended principle. This was poor Huskisson's decided opinion. . . . Every public motive which led us to go out in 1828 would equally have operated against going in now, and there are many new reasons. . . .[54]

According to his autobiography, he told Lord Clive, who conducted the negotiation for Wellington, that he could not join the cabinet unless places were provided for Melbourne, Grant, Lansdowne and Grey.[55] As Wellington was apparently hoping to get rid of Grey by sending him to Ireland,[56] and as Grey was hoping soon to head a cabinet of his own,[57] the suggestion was not a very fruitful one. Nor does Palmerston seem to have been anxious to press it ; for, on October 12, he placed himself beyond reach of further offers by setting out for Paris. It is not unlikely that he thus avoided approaches from both sides. For Brougham and Durham, now that Huskisson was dead, were urging an immediate 'union' of their party with Grant and Palmerston ;[58] while Prince Leopold (later of

Belgium) was offering to negotiate with the latter on Durham's behalf.[59]

When Palmerston arrived back from France, on the eve of the opening of parliament, negotiations proceeded with great rapidity. On October 30, the day after his return, he was telling Wellington, in an interview at Apsley House, that he and his friends could not accept an invitation that did not include some of the Whigs:[60] on the day after that, he was informing a Whig deputation that he was ready to support their party in so far as he could without sacrifice of his principles; but that he and his friends were not prepared for a formal coalition.[61] Still another day, and Littleton, a minor and most unreliable Canningite, was assuring one of Wellington's friends that the Canningites would join the ministry without stipulating for any Whigs if the Duke would take up 'piecemeal' reform.[62] But Littleton had no authority to speak for his associates, and was probably misrepresenting their leader's attitude. From first to last Palmerston seems to have played for time.

It was, of course, Wellington's announcement, on November 2, of his opposition to reform of any kind, that drove Palmerston to make terms with the Whigs. With his keen appreciation of the force of public sentiment, he recognised that reform of some sort was inevitable. Witness the account he gave of an interview with Croker, when Croker, on November 6, carried to him the Duke's last bid of all:

> After talking for some time, he [Croker] said: 'Well, I will bring the question to a point. Are you resolved or are you not to vote for Parliamentary Reform?' I said, 'I am.' 'Well, then,' said he, 'there is no use in talking to you any more on this subject. You and I, I am grieved to see, will never sit again on the same bench together.'[63]

But he and his friends did not conceal their reluctance to enlist on the reformers' side. In notifying the Whigs, on November 7, of their willingness to help in turning out Wellington, they agreed to support a general resolution on reform.[64] But if they did not specify, as Hobhouse claimed, that it should be 'vaguely worded,' there is little doubt that they wished it to be as vague as possible. Still, they had turned the corner, and could not go back. Lord Howick was justified in hoping that they would go much further in their acceptance of reform when the question of constructing a new ministry was raised. On November 15, they kept the first part of their promise by assisting the Whigs, the ultra-Tories and the radicals to turn out Wellington.

As the Whig motion on reform was immediately postponed, the Canningites had not to fulfil the rest of their undertaking until after Grey had chosen his ministry. It was not difficult for the new premier to assign them to high posts ; for they measured up satisfactorily to his demands not only for men of talent and experience, but for aristocrats. Palmerston received the post which he probably most coveted ; for which he had sedulously prepared himself ; and which, if the Princess Lieven is to be believed, he had pestered her to procure for him.[65] Grey had thought of him for home secretary ; but after Lord Lansdowne, and apparently Holland, had refused the Foreign Office, it was tendered to Palmerston on Lansdowne's advice. Probably Mme. de Lieven, who was allowed by Grey to believe that the appointment was her work, had some influence. At any rate she pronounced the new foreign secretary ' perfect in every way.' [66] As the Princess shared her court's general dislike of all statesmen who encouraged liberalism, this eulogy, pronounced in a private letter, seems a little curious. But, after all, Palmerston had stood for co-operation with Russia in the Near East, was not ' Austrian,' like Aberdeen, and seemed very much on the alert regarding the dangerous tendencies of France. She was convinced, too, that no one need be uneasy over the advent of a cabinet containing so many aristocrats of ' moderate ' views, and several of her own friends. At any rate she gave her benediction to the new foreign secretary just a week before the Poles broke into revolution at Warsaw.

No doubt the Canningites shared Mme. de Lieven's satisfaction in the ' moderate ' temper of the new cabinet. They themselves had fared extremely well, with Melbourne at the Home Office, Goderich in charge of War and Colonies, and Grant as president of the Board of Control (India). Of the other ten cabinet ministers, only two could be suspected of radical sentiments ; while one, the duke of Richmond, was an ultra-Tory. Even on the question of reform—the only question which was likely to produce marked divergence—there seemed no great reason for alarm. Conservatism was still strong both among the Whig leaders and the parliamentary rank and file. Certainly Palmerston, plunging with zest into the Foreign Office papers, seemed perfectly content. He had not only helped to drive out Aberdeen, but secured the glorious opportunity to rectify some of Aberdeen's mistakes. Seldom if ever could one have a party which one could entirely ' think with,' after all.

CHAPTER V

Parliamentary Reform and Settlement in Greece, 1830–1832

The Palmerston who took over the Foreign Office in November 1830 with such zest, was a person of too many sides to be described in any single phrase ; but one may gain a fair impression of his personality by noting once more that he represented a very well-marked type, and then giving a little consideration to a couple of his sobriquets. In type, he was, of course, the early nineteenth-century statesman-aristocrat of sporting proclivities. He felt it both his duty and his right to take a part in ruling England and her empire, fitted as he was by education, abilities, wealth and rank. Class stood to him as one of the great realities both in government and society. But he exhibited neither the aloofness of a Grey, nor the contempt for the rabble of a Wellington. He could stoop to conquer, exhibiting his wit, his joviality, and his very genuine kindliness to a crowd, or even to a lowly individual—provided that the lowly individual did not presume. No account of his life has been considered quite complete without reference to the radical butcher of Tiverton, with whom he exchanged handshakes and badinage in campaign after campaign, to the delight and edification of his constituents. But less known is a story related by the trainer of his horses, Day, concerning his treatment of another butcher, who forced his way into the statesman's presence to secure payment of an account long overdue. When this butcher, paid at last, had written a receipt, Palmerston, after ostentatiously drawing on a glove, threw out of the window the polluted pen.[1]

His most famous nickname, that of ' Cupid,' recalls the

fact that he was an engaging member of society, a gay spark in spite of his forty-six years, handsome in face and figure, dressed in the height of fashion, and still notable among the beaux.[2] He was, in fact, like his mother, but for very different reasons, inclined to take a protective attitude towards ' demi-reps.' He was even inclined to display his conquests rather ostentatiously. Regarded throughout Europe—and apparently with every reason—as Lady Cowper's lover,[3] he allowed his name to be linked with those of various ladies of varying degrees of fair fame. Mme. de Lieven, in one of her especially vicious moods, remarked that a certain spinster of high position, who reputedly hoped to marry Palmerston, was like the housemaid who advertised : ' A housemaid wants a situation in a family where a footman is kept.'[4] Footmen were regarded as sad dogs in those days. Hence Palmerston gained a nickname which long outlasted the graces of his person, though not his gallantries. The name was a little contemptuous ; but *The Times*, which was credited with originating it, had not learned to take Palmerston seriously.

' Lord Pumicestone '[5] was a sobriquet little used but infinitely more significant ; for it pointed to a characteristic which always to some extent marred his character and clouded his official prospects. His roughness, expressing itself more especially in an intolerable arrogance, and sometimes in an apparent desire to wound, was rather oddly distributed.[6] The presumptuous butcher saw it, and so did the Foreign Office staff ; but in the cabinet it was scarcely, if at all, perceptible. Yet it was not merely the roughness of a bully or a snob to those less highly placed. For he despised those who toadied to him ;[7] and kept his worst manners for the statesmen of other countries and their envoys at the British court. Let one of them go too far in opposing the British government or its policies, and he might at any moment have occasion to intone with Metternich :

> Hat der Teufel einen Sohn
> So ist er sicher Palmerston.

Thus the trait is a little difficult to analyse. In general, it probably represented the impatience of a man nervously organised, engrossed in a vitally important task, convinced of his infallibility, and determined that no obstacle should block his course. When displayed to foreign ministers and their envoys, it certainly derived to some extent from his insularity and his belief in England's might—perhaps even from his sporting instincts. What England, under proper direction, wished or did, was for the benefit of mankind. To those who were stupid or criminal enough to reject this truth, admonition must be given. And, if gentle admonition failed, there was nothing for it but to use harsh words. He had been just three months in office—as a pupil of the circumspect Lord Grey—when he undertook to put the French foreign minister, Sebastiani, in his place. In a letter addressed to the British ambassador at Paris, but sent through the French Foreign Office so that it would be opened and read there, he delivered a tirade :

> Sebastiani really should be made to understand that he must have the goodness to learn to keep his temper, or, when it fails him, let him go to vent his ill-humour upon some other quarter, and not bestow it upon England.[8]

He concluded by accusing Sebastiani of pursuing 'a course of miserable intrigue.' The device he used for administering this unofficial reproof was by no means new ; but such roughness was, to say the least, unusual. He was making the great game of diplomacy a game not only of the chessboard but of the professional football field. It was a pity if the other great courts could not appreciate rough-and-tumble play—combined, of course, with plenty of strategy—but why concern himself greatly over that ? England was not afraid of any or all of them. In fact, the more numerous her opponents, the more did her superiority become evident. And she was always right.

The foreigners would not have minded Palmerston's game so much if he had not been guilty of so many incivilities. He seems never to have accepted the maxim that tact is the essence of diplomacy. Unfortunately, he often saw in the sending of a despatch which transcended the bounds of diplomatic courtesy, or in the exhibition of intolerable hauteur to a distinguished and dignified envoy, a method

HIS INCIVILITIES

of scoring neatly on behalf of his country and himself. And personal rudeness which was no doubt often quite unintentional—the result of his devotion to work and his incurable unpunctuality—was frequently regarded as of a piece with the deliberate unmannerliness to which he sometimes resorted officially. It was not only that so aged and distinguished a person as Talleyrand would be kept waiting in an anteroom for an hour or two : even the ladies were not spared. When Palmerston, giving a great dinner to the diplomatic corps in honour of the King's birthday, invited for the first time the wives of the envoys, he did not reach the drawing-room until after his guests. Nor, according to Talleyrand's niece by marriage, the duchess of Dino, did he trouble himself even to apologise.[9] It is impossible to regard this rudeness as deliberate ; for Palmerston, during the short period when he enjoyed the happiest relations with Queen Victoria, was on several occasions to be late for dinner and for drives when his sovereign was his guest or he hers.[10] But Mme. de Dino by no means forgot the occurrence in making up against the offender her own and her uncle's account. Nor was her personal ill-will a negligible factor in the circumstances which combined to give Palmerston a bad name. For she possessed excellent brains, a decidedly vengeful temperament, and a circle of influential relatives and friends which extended from Paris to St. Petersburg.[11] Her influence and that of her ally, the Princess Lieven, may have made material contribution to the growth of a feeling, both in England and abroad, that Grey had made a sad mistake in choosing his foreign secretary.

It was, however, only by degrees that ministers and envoys of the continental courts became conscious that an *enfant terrible* was presiding at the Foreign Office. For then, as always, the premier and foreign secretary divided the direction of diplomatic relations pretty much according to the ability, experience and strength (personal and political) which each possessed. And Grey had by far the greater advantages. As the undisputed leader of the Whigs ; as head of a ministry which contained a surprising number of his relatives and friends ; and, most of all, perhaps, as a statesman whose great character and talents were universally recognised, his decisions were not lightly to be challenged by any member of his cabinet. Moreover, foreign policy happened to be his speciality. His only ministerial service had been as foreign secretary in the Ministry of All the Talents ; and he had given close attention to foreign relations ever since. He would gladly have returned to his old post in 1830 had this been practicable. But he would have laboured under marked handicaps. He was an old man at sixty-eight, disliking office and longing to retire to the beauty and quiet of Howick House.[12] Pessimism descended upon him from time to time : disputes took heavy toll of his patience and his nerves. He was impressionable, too, and sometimes irresolute—longing to achieve great things but hesitating at the price, especially where the price involved sacrifice of principle. Palmerston's advantages lay in youth and vigour ; in sureness of aim, and remarkable ability to estimate the chances of success ; in audacity, and lack of scruple where national interests were concerned.

With Grey as mentor and Palmerston as pupil, excellent results were possible, so long as the two men stood in satisfactory relations : and their relations were apparently all that could have been desired.[13] Grey seems to have found no fault in Palmerston save his official obnoxiousness ;[14] and Palmerston wrote his brother that ' no two men . . . ever went on better together in office, and very few half as well.'[15] It was no perfunctory tribute which he paid in a private letter on Grey's retirement in 1834 :

> The country has sustained a loss of the heaviest sort, and I individually have been deprived of a guide whose direction was invaluable, and whose kindness was unlimited . . . daily and confidential intercourse of three years and a half . . . has made me intimately acquainted with one of the most statesmanlike minds and with one of the noblest natures that has ever yet appeared. . . .[16]

Perhaps even better evidence of his feelings lies in the fact that, self-willed and self-sufficient as he was, he readily accepted the gentle and expert tutelage of his chief. According to all accounts, he submitted not only to a constant revision of outgoing despatches,[17] but to certain actions of Grey's under which he might well have chafed. The premier, adopting the prevalent method of conducting delicate negotiations through private correspondence (which could never be called for by parliament), sometimes took communications with the French government into his own hands, by writing personally to the British ambassador.[18] That he could or would have done this without Palmerston's consent seems inconceivable. Moreover, Grey at times took the appointment of diplomatic envoys into his own hands, 'settling' with Palmerston afterwards. One case in point is that of the appointment of Stratford Canning as a special envoy to Spain in 1832.[19] And there is another case of much greater interest.[20] When the cabinet was being reconstructed in May 1834, the prime minister, wishing to rid himself of the presence of his too temperamental son-in-law, Durham, decided upon his appointment to the Paris embassy. Palmerston, convinced that Durham would wreck his policy, and ignorant that Durham had no intention of obliging Grey, protested vigorously, but apparently gave in. Rarely did he stand out against his chief: and never, in so far as one may judge, did he attempt to proceed beyond the decisions of the cabinet. But a useful check was provided at this time: every cabinet decision was recorded in a cabinet minute. The Whigs were to sigh over the relinquishment of this procedure at a later period.

It would be easy to assume from all of this that Grey should receive much the greater share of credit for the diplomatic successes of his ministry—easy, but after all quite unjustifiable. So closely did the policies of the two men in most instances coincide, and so much mutual loyalty did they show, that to divide the credit with even approximate exactitude would be impossible. Clearly, however, Palmerston's part was no minor one. His most private letters bear witness to his intense enthusiasm for the policies he carried out, and at times to a sense of personal achievement which he was not a man to feign, or even greatly to exaggerate. His speeches on foreign affairs, relatively few and ineffective as they were, rang with sincerity. The actual management of affairs was almost invariably in his hands ; and the rapid, sure and daring decisions ; the sharp, jaunty and even in these times frequently provocative despatches, were obviously far more his than Grey's. Contemporaries frequently showed their realisation of this in assigning praise or blame ; and, occasionally, in begging the prime minister to use his moderating influence. 'Lord Pumicestone' appeared even during the early months of the ministry ; and, as time went on, and Grey became more and more distracted by domestic questions, and more and more anxious to retire, the influence of that formidable personage was more and more evident. Metternich, Talleyrand, Mme. de Lieven and their like passed from surprise, through dislike, to resentment and disgust. But there were other and less splendid figures in England and on the continent, Belgians or Greeks, exiled Spaniards or Poles or Portuguese, who, turning their eyes gratefully to the two masters of British diplomacy, turned them first to Palmerston. Mme. de Dino, in describing Lady Grey's last reception, noted this with the utmost scorn :

. . . la nouvelle Espagne, le nouveau Portugal, la Belgique, à peine ébauchée, tout ce qui a besoin du désordre et de la faiblesse des grandes puissances pour se sauver des mauvaises conditions de son origine, regardaient lord Palmerston avec des regards d'angoisse qui, bientôt, et lorsqu'on a supposé qu'il restait aux affaires, se sont changés en regards d'amour et de triomphe.[21]

Behind his harshness, of which some even of them had quite sufficient experience, they saw a champion of constitutional government, putting his beliefs into practice with as much consistency as his power in the ministry, and his obligation to think first of British interests, would allow.

It was, however, with a certain reluctance that he gave his patronage to revolutionists and advanced democrats. He preferred to see liberalism advance by timely compromise, so that the nations of the continent could keep to the middle road. And for him there existed only one middle road for nations and peoples of all sorts—the road which had led England to such order, prosperity and happiness. If only each continental sovereign would grant to his people a constitution of the English type, a constitution providing government by a king and a parliament representative of the intelligent and propertied classes, all would be well. As he explained to the House, in 1832, he regarded the spread of constitutional government, not only as desirable in itself, but as conducive to British interests :

. . . the independence of constitutional States, whether they are powerful, like France or the United States, or of less relative political importance, such as the minor States of Germany, never can be a matter of indifference to the British Parliament, or, I should hope, to the British public. Constitutional States I consider to be the natural Allies of this country ; and . . . no English Ministry will perform its duty if it be inattentive to the interests of such States.[22]

And he was frank in confessing that he had never abandoned his belief that diplomatic 'intermeddling' was perfectly justifiable :

. . . the pledges given by his Majesty's Ministers, on their accession to office, were Reform, Retrenchment, and Peace . . . there was nothing about non-interference . . . the principle for this Government to proceed upon, was that of non-interference by force of arms in the affairs of any other country ; but he did not think that we should be precluded, where it was expedient for us to do so, from interfering by friendly counsel and advice.[23]

Interference by 'friendly counsel and advice' was to be directed especially to the peaceful establishment of liberal constitutions in as many countries as possible. It might, indeed, involve the patronage of revolution where kings were obdurate ; but kings who refused sound British advice would have occasionally to take the consequences. Even in his own country Palmerston was, as he felt, witnessing a demonstration of the danger of resisting too long a popular demand for constitutional change. It was in this light that he viewed the struggles incidental to the passing of the Great Reform Bill of 1832.[24]

Difficult as Palmerston had often found it in his Tory days to square his position with that of his colleagues, it is doubtful whether he had ever been in a less comfortable position than that in which he found himself on the evening of March 1, 1831. Young Lord John Russell had just explained to a House of Commons in which mirth, horror, and incredulity were exhibited on every side, that the government would ask it to pass a bill taking the right of representation from boroughs having less than two thousand inhabitants, reducing to single member constituencies all others of less than twice that size, enfranchising £10 householders in the towns, and effecting other changes which seemed nothing short of revolutionary. Palmerston, though bound as a minister to advocate and share responsibility for the measure, did not believe in it. It was not to be expected that he should. In striking the Whig-Canningite bargain of November 7, he had agreed to abandon the position which he had stated so uncompromisingly in 1828, and to vote for *a* general measure of reform. But he had never promised to endorse a bill such as this. For it represented, not general Whig sentiment, but the distinctive views of the Whig left wing, and of their auxiliaries, the radicals. Lansdowne, great Whig leader as he was, disliked and opposed it almost as much as Palmerston.[25] The foreign secretary could see no real justification for its terms. In his view they went beyond the public demand, and would certainly be unacceptable to the House.[26] Hence, insistence upon them would mean a general election at a time when political ferment, in Ireland especially, rendered an election particularly undesirable.[27] Yet his agreement with the Whigs, and his recognition of the strength of public sentiment for reform, prevented him from suggesting the withdrawal of the bill. The country, he wrote Granville, now ambassador at Paris, was 'decidedly for it, and enthusiastically.' Consequently, it would 'not be Revolution, but the reverse.'[28] What he demanded was a modification of the 'arbitrary' figures on which its provisions had been based.[29] He was quite ready to agree to three basic 'principles': that nomination boroughs should be wiped out; that representation should be given to large towns; and that a large middle class element of the population should be enfranchised. But that did not involve an acceptance of anyone's arithmetic.

Hence, Palmerston attempted from the beginning to act as a brake upon the more liberal section of the cabinet. Long before the bill was introduced, he warned the premier that he could not bind himself to the support of its 'details';[30] and, after March 1, he urged on Grey that modifications should be made, and negotiations with some of the doubtful Tories set on foot. In parliament he proved a very poor advocate.[31] He defended his change of front since 1828 by sneering at 'the puerile vanity of consistency'; but he showed himself fairly consistent after all. For, while declaring his acceptance of the three principles, he justified his support of the measure as it stood, only as a concession to public sentiment. Quoting Canning with excellent effect, he taunted the Tories with lack of foresight in so long resisting 'piecemeal' reform as to make that sentiment irresistible :

> Those who resist improvements because they consider them to be innovations, may be at last compelled to accept innovations when they have ceased to be improvements.

He was showing himself a reformer of a very lukewarm sort ; but at least he was frank enough.

As the spring wore on, and the government, defeated in committee, appealed to the country in spite of all that he could do, his attitude hardened if anything. He was running counter now to a growing public sentiment for 'the bill, the whole bill and nothing but the bill.' On the other hand, the question had in a way become more personal. For in the election (which he had tried to prevent) his share of responsibility for the reform bill (which he did not like) had cost him his hardly won seat at Cambridge, held without interruption for twenty years.[32] He was at pains to point out to the premier that his own objections to the bill were shared by 'staunch and tried Whigs & reformers of long standing,' and by most of his constituents at Cambridge who had remained loyal to him. When, in July, the new House of Commons proceeded to give a great majority to a second bill open to all the objections he had urged against the first, he still remained obdurate.

In fact, his essential conservatism, where the constitution

was concerned, now, and quite naturally, asserted itself with double force. For the ministry was in clear sight of its conflict with the peers. It was bad enough that the basis of representation for the House of Commons should be changed so radically ; but it was worse that such a change should be effected by the subjugation of that pillar of the constitution, the House of Lords. Feeling thus, there was only one thing, short of resignation, that he could do : to work harder than ever for compromise.[33] Nor was he without legitimate ground for hope. The premier viewed with great repugnance the idea of swamping the anti-reform majority in the Lords by a creation of new peerages which would both weaken the constitutional position of the upper House, and diminish the distinction and value of an individual peerage. 'Damn Reform ! I wish I had never touched it,' may not have been Grey's words ;[34] but they represented what was apparently at one time his attitude. Surely, then, he might accept a reasonable alternative. On the other hand, there were Tory lords who, in their anxiety to avert a crushing blow to their order and their House, were earning the name of 'Waverers' by their known willingness to compromise. Hence Palmerston reached out with one hand to the 'Waverers,'[35] and with the other attempted to extract concessions from his chief.

Long and complicated were the negotiations with the 'Waverers,' and the struggles in the cabinet. Palmerston, enjoying the general co-operation of Lansdowne, Melbourne, Richmond, and, to a lesser extent, Stanley,[36] worked hard through the autumn and winter months to persuade the cabinet to alter its arithmetic and explore all possibilities of compromise, before exerting increased pressure on King William and the House of Lords. For the Lords, decisively rejecting the second bill, had taken up an attitude of defiance to the Commons and the cabinet ; and William had refused consent to a wholesale creation of peerages. Fortunately for those who write books about Palmerston, few phases either of the negotiations or the struggles throw much light upon his political views or his character. Indeed, there is little evidence that he had developed any very reasoned views on constitutional questions at this time. As for his character, the two things most apparent were his dogged resistance in the face of discouragement, and his cheerful acceptance of defeat, when further resistance became dangerous to the existence of the cabinet and the preservation of order in the country.

Capacity for resistance he had exhibited plentifully to Wellington : hence his acceptance of defeat seems more notable. His first great concession was made early in March 1832, when he promised Durham in future to support a provision of the bill to which he had been especially opposed—that enfranchising the £10 householders.[37] But he had not yet given up his negotiations with the 'Waverers'; [38] and his great and most graceful surrender waited on the exciting developments of the later spring. When, in early May, the Lords again threw out the bill ; when the public, now exasperated to a dangerous pitch, signed covenants, refused to pay taxes, and threatened to 'go for gold' to the banks, Palmerston, like a good sportsman, himself proposed in the cabinet that the King should again be asked to promise a wholesale creation of new peerages.[39] He was far from convinced that either the bill or the one possible means of securing its immediate passage was desirable. But he found 'the excitement of spirit . . . universal & alarming' ;[40] and he believed that a government which would not go far to avert revolution was inexcusable. He was soon to be preaching this to many a ruling sovereign on the continent. It was something that he could show consistency on his own part in May 1832.

The continental sovereigns, however, gave no thought to that. Since the time of Palmerston's advent at the Foreign Office they had been to an extraordinary degree engrossed in taking practical measures for keeping intact their sovereignty. When his example of submission to popular pressure was displayed to them, they were interested only in the practical side of his foreign policy. But their interest in that was intense. Not for some time had the gaze of Europe been so centred on Downing Street.

In fact, conditions on the continent at the time of Palmerston's advent at the Foreign Office gave him an extraordinary opportunity. He had arrived in power at one of the critical junctures in nineteenth-century history : at a moment when liberalism was resurgent from Lisbon to Warsaw, when movements for self-government and national independence were in progress, or soon would be, in all the Latin countries, in Belgium, in Germany and in Poland. And as these movements gathered force, assuming in most cases the form of armed revolts, the reactionary rulers of Russia, Prussia and Austria drew together to preserve the constituted order in government, society and international boundaries. It was obvious that the scattered, ill-armed and ill-led liberal bands would have no chance unless they could obtain the active assistance of some great Power ; but their doing so was by no means beyond the limits of possibility. If the more revolutionary element among the French were to have its way, then France would almost certainly revert to the rôle she had recently played with such success, making herself the militant champion of self-government and nationality, and at the same time forcibly establishing her rule over non-French territory. In such case, nothing could save Europe from a general war, and from one of the bitterest of wars. For it would be a war of opinion, a war, that is, of propaganda and of hate.

In this crisis Palmerston faced responsibility as great even as his opportunity. London was, for the time, the diplomatic capital of Europe. Its position was not derived merely from the strength of England, nor from the prestige that Castlereagh and Canning had bequeathed. It did not depend primarily upon the presence there of the most eminent diplomatic corps in Europe, nor the holding of conferences in which the attitude of the Quadruple Alliance to the new French government had been settled and the problems of Greece and the Netherlands were being solved. Each of these factors had its part ; but some were in the nature of effects as well as causes ; and, taken all together, they do not quite supply the key. The vital facts of the situation were that the fire of liberalism, which burned strongly but as yet steadily in France, was fanning by its draught the embers that smouldered throughout most of Europe ; and that the developments of the immediate

BLOWING UP THE FIRE

[1830]

future seemed to depend upon England more than upon any other single Power. Grave danger, for her as well as for Europe, lay to right and left. Let her but give assent, and Metternich might send his bands of '*pompiers*' (in Russian and Prussian as well as Austrian helmets) to smother the fires and drive them underground— even perhaps in France itself. What then of England's reputation and influence ; and what would happen when the fires, driven underground, burst out again ? Another danger and a worse : let the flames in France leap up too high, let them advance to meet surrounding fires, and England, in the very instinct of self-preservation, might be forced to join the *pompiers*. Was she to be drawn into a new war of opinion, another devouring conflict, and on the anti-liberal side ?

But the opportunity was well worth the responsibility— the opportunity of reversing the rather shabby part that England had played since Canning's death, and re-establishing her prestige. Continental liberals, who had taken heart at Canning's voice, were hopefully watching Grey and Palmerston. Louis Philippe (of whose position and policy more anon) leaned on the British ministry for support. For once a French government seemed ready to accept English direction, so long as this might decently be hidden from French eyes. And with France in leading strings, how fine the opportunity to beard the Powers of Eastern Europe which Canning had defied ; to support liberalism and the principles of 1688 by speeches which would flatter English pride and the English public's liberal proclivities ; to lecture haughty and despotic courts, and show them how low they fell beneath the new standards which England was proclaiming to the world. And, in several areas where liberalism stood in need of help, in Belgium, in Italy, in Spain and Portugal, there might be a chance to use England's only real fighting arm, sea power. How soon or how completely Palmerston saw his opportunity it is impossible to tell ; but the realisation was certainly not long delayed.

Fortunately for Grey and Palmerston, opportunity and responsibility could best be met by the moderate course which they preferred on general principles—by supporting yet restraining France. For they had no choice. It was not only that such perils lay on either side : they were committed in more ways than one. They had come together and won their way to power on programmes differing in detail, but not on the general principle of conservative liberalism. Their platform called, not only for retrenchment and reform, but peace ; and peace was to be maintained only by advancing with Louis Philippe along the middle road. The Foxite tradition of so many of the Whigs—the predilection for co-operation with a liberal France—dictated the same course. Hence Palmerston could announce it frankly to the house :

> . . . the interest of England was the maintenance of general peace throughout Europe, and this object was, in the mind of his Majesty's Government, most easily, most safely, and most securely to be attained, by the maintenance of a firm and strict alliance between France and this country.[41]

Two years later, in March 1834, the *Standard* complained :

> Lord Palmerston has but one answer for everything that could be said against the foreign policy of the Government—The French Alliance.[42]

There was indeed no 'alliance' in the ordinary sense. What existed was the first *entente cordiale*.

Yet the establishment and maintenance of an entente was difficult. The old hostility between the two peoples was still strong enough to enable the opposition in either parliament to embarrass ministers by claiming that the other partner in the entente had assumed the lead. Again, the interests of the two countries conflicted at several vital points—in Belgium, in the Iberian peninsula, and in the western and central Mediterranean. And for Palmerston it was, in some respects, particularly difficult to conduct the English side of this delicate partnership. Not only were his traditions Pittite and consequently somewhat anti-French, but he was inclined to ignore French difficulties and susceptibilities ; to harbour suspicion, and to make hard terms. His suspicions, grounded on observations of many years, and deepened by his recent visits to the French

THE FIRST *ENTENTE CORDIALE*

capital, were nourished by the duplicity which he detected almost from the first in the French conduct of foreign policy. In part, this duplicity was the outcome of the peculiarly difficult position in which Louis Philippe found himself; but, unfortunately, he and his ministers not infrequently went beyond the strict necessities of finesse, and attempted to play a double game. Palmerston, whose own diplomatic sins were never of this sort, found such cheating unsportsmanlike and very hard to bear. He drove hard bargains, partly because he was so sure his own diplomacy was right, and partly because there was inherent in his policy the selfishness of what is now known as an 'integral nationalist.' There were times when his little finger seemed thicker than Canning's loins. All the more remarkable and the more creditable does it seem, that he and Grey, by patience and by firmness, did their part and more in preserving the entente through long stress and strain.

They were, of course, immensely aided by the necessities of Louis Philippe and the diplomatic skill of Talleyrand. The king of the French, like Grey and Palmerston, had no choice but to take the path of moderate liberalism. He knew that alignment with the forces of reaction in France and eastern Europe would make him an exile overnight; while endorsement of European revolution would bring the coalition of 1814 back to life, and just as surely expel him from his throne. Only 'non-intervention' and Talleyrand remained. The adoption of the non-intervention formula would bind him to England, its professed inventor and champion—England, the only Power with which his subjects would permit him to combine, the Power which might save, and could assuredly ruin him. And Talleyrand, the adjuster and adjustable, the aristocrat and revolutionary, a man acceptable both to Europe's older statesmen and the leaders of her nascent democracy; Talleyrand would be able both to understand and to execute. Hence, the best possible plan was to send Talleyrand to England as ambassador, at the same time making him the confidant, and even to some extent foreign minister *de facto* of his King. The plan had worked well. Louis Philippe's ambassador and policy had won some favour from Wellington's ministry, and were sure to win more from Grey's. But the real tests were still ahead. The liberals were stirring to action all through Europe. Each manifestation increased the twofold peril of the French government and made English friendship more necessary. Here was the British foreign secretary's *point d'appui*. And in using it he had the special incentive of knowing that he was engaged in a duel with the forces of reaction in the east. For Metternich, old and discouraged as he was, soon set his heart on making Vienna the real centre of diplomacy, and defeating from this vantage-ground the dangerous policies of the British foreign minister.[43]

The issues raised by the revolutionary movements of 1830 claimed his attention immediately; but he had also to take an important part in liquidating an earlier revolution —that of Greece. At the end of 1830 the new state lay very much at the disposal of England, France and Russia, the three Powers which had assisted at its birth. Hence there was still time to reverse the pro-Turkish policy of Wellington and Aberdeen, to apply once more the generous principles of Canning, and to see that the Greeks were provided with a constitutional monarchy. The question of the northern boundary, although not taken up seriously until September 1831, was of first consequence.[44] Palmerston, who at this time believed the dissolution of the Turkish empire imminent,[45] was anxious that Greece should be strong enough to take advantage of it when it came. Hence he urged the fixing of the boundary at the Volo-Arta line,[46] —the line for which he had vainly pleaded in 1828.[47] Grey, who had for some time held the same view,[48] cooperated heartily; while the French and Russian governments were quite ready to acquiesce. By November 1831, only one obstacle remained. The Turks, who very much disliked bartering away their lands, were especially reluctant to relinquish territory to the Greeks. As a means of surmounting this difficulty, the appointment of Stratford Canning as British negotiator, in face both of the objections of Sir Robert Gordon, the ambassador to the Porte, and of Canning's consequent reluctance,[49] was probably as effective a move as the British Foreign Office could have made.

THE LAUNCHING OF GREECE

When Palmerston warmed the heart of the returning and successful envoy with a pat on the shoulder, and the simple words : 'Canning, you are the man,'[50] he was paying an unconscious tribute to himself.

But nations do not live by boundaries alone : what the Greeks needed most of all was a properly organised government. With the assassination of their president, Capodistrias, in October 1831, the anarchy and disorder already existing became intolerable.[51] Rival governments succeeded in nothing but in opposing one another : and the hapless peasants fled for refuge to strongholds or to the Ionian Islands. The three 'protecting' Powers had still to set Greece on her feet.

It is easy, from the vantage ground of later years, to criticise the arrangements that were made ; but it is not so easy to show what Palmerston could have done to better them. He was ready enough to admit in later years that he made a grave mistake in helping to place the seventeen-year-old Prince Otto of Bavaria on the throne ;[52] and Stratford Canning claimed that the mistake would never have been made had Palmerston taken the trouble to seek the information and advice which Canning had to give.[53] But princes at once suitable and willing were not easily found ; nor could the British government make its own choice. Palmerston would greatly have preferred Prince Frederick of Orange, both because he was old enough to administer the government himself, and because his choice might 'soften' his father, the king of the Netherlands, with respect to Belgium.[54] The only danger was that 'the mania of the Palais Royal for marrying off French princesses' might be vented on Frederick. But the foreign secretary's fear proved too groundless, if anything ; for the Palais Royal objected to Frederick's choice. Thus, it was partly by elimination that the three Powers finally agreed upon Otto. According to gossip of the more authentic sort, the Bavarians, who had been haggling for some time, were brought to terms by Palmerston in May 1832, by warnings of impending changes in the British and French cabinets.[55]

Nor did Otto seem at the time so bad a choice. His

family associations were constitutionalist and Philhellene;[56] and his functions were at first to be exercised by an able and experienced group of regents, headed by Bavaria's reputedly liberal minister, Count Armansperg.[57] The protecting Powers were sufficiently confident of his success to guarantee a Greek loan of 60,000,000 francs, of which a third went to Turkey in payment for the territory she was relinquishing. Perhaps it was a little hard upon the Greeks that a foreign youth, supported by foreign advisers, foreign money and even a foreign bodyguard, should be placed over them;[58] but for the time being they seemed quite content. Before the year was up 'the reviving country of a Solon, a Plato, a Pericles,' was rejoicing 'in the conviction that a worthy guide of its destinies was about to reach its shores.[59] Palmerston had his reasons for contentment, too. Here was another young and healthy state, with the proper kind of government, and possessed of every reason to look to England for guidance.

Unfortunately, there soon proved to be too many guides in Greece; and Palmerston, who recorded happily in March 1833, that 'the Greek affair . . . is well settled, just as I wished it,'[60] was disillusioned before many weeks had passed. From the very outset the agents of the three guiding Powers, acting more or less under directions from London, Paris and St. Petersburg, manœuvred for influence at the Greek and Bavarian courts. And in doing so, they accentuated, if they did not cause, irreconcilable divisions between the members of the regency. France and Russia both threw the weight of their influence against Armansperg, who was considered much too English in his sympathies; but it was between Russia and England that the sharpest rivalry arose.[61] Palmerston's case is best summarised in a memorandum, written on March 30, 1834, and containing instructions to be observed by the permanent under-secretary for foreign affairs, John Backhouse, in an interview with the Greek envoy (and later foreign minister) Tricoupis:

. . . I wish you to explain to him that what the King [William IV] said to him had reference . . . to the general desire which we know to exist in the Russian Government to establish a predominant influence in Greece, for the purpose of directing the external relations of Greece in such a manner as to make the policy of that country subservient to Russian objects, and for the purpose of prescribing such a system of management in the internal administration of Greece as might prevent any free or liberal institutions in that country, and might assimilate its organisation as nearly as possible to that of a despotic Monarchy.[62]

Palmerston, with his habitual plea for the preservation of 'liberal institutions,' showed, by this very memorandum, his readiness to meet the Russians at their own game. But it was for the capture of the Bavarian rather than the Greek government that he played his best cards. Thus, when Russia delayed in fulfilling her agreement to guarantee (along with France and England) the first instalment of the loan, he informed the Bavarian government that Nesselrode was trying to win special concessions from the Greeks by taking advantage of their necessities.[63] Whether the charge was just or not, he won the first rubber of the game.[64] In February 1834, the Greek government asked that Dawkins, the over-zealous British envoy, should be recalled. Palmerston, refusing the recall and accepting Dawkins' denial of any guilt, complained to the Bavarian court that his agent was the victim of a plot in which one or more members of the council of regency had borne a part. Two months later Maurer, the most pro-Russian of the regents, was withdrawn, leaving Armansperg stronger than before. But 'the Greek affair' was no more 'settled' than it had been sixteen months previously ; and one of the most sordid of diplomatic games was to trail its wearisome length into mid-century politics. Fortunately, Palmerston was able to demonstrate in Belgium that, given a fair opportunity, he could do much better in helping to launch a new state on its career.

CHAPTER VI

THE BIRTH OF BELGIUM, 1830–1832

IN an access of gratitude and enthusiasm a Belgian historian once dubbed Palmerston the *père de la Belgique*.[1] Though not inclined to under-estimate his own achievements, it is not recorded that he himself laid claim to such paternity. On the other hand, writing thirty years after the event, he did, by certain implication, maintain that Belgium owed more to Great Britain than to any other Power :

> . . . they owe their independence to us more than to the French —and without our interference and assistance Belgium would . . . either have been forcibly re-united to Holland or have been reduced to be a province of France. . . .[2]

And, since he was foreign secretary throughout the time when Belgium's debt to England was incurred, he was certainly placing no mean estimate on his own services.

This in itself would be reason enough, perhaps, for following his handling of the Belgian question during the early 'thirties with especial care. And there are other reasons at least equally cogent. At the very moment when his longing to take charge of England's foreign relations had been satisfied, he found himself handling an issue of the most vital and far-reaching kind : during the months when he was acquiring the technique of diplomacy he was forced to bring his every faculty as a statesman repeatedly into play. And the personages with whom he had immediately to match wits were the shrewdest and most experienced diplomatists of the age. Metternich, the Princess Lieven and Talleyrand, to mention only three of the most formidable, would be ready to note and seize upon each mistake. But Palmerston advanced to meet them with a surging confidence and an obvious pleasure in the fray. Perhaps he may even have experienced satisfaction in realising that, of the peoples menaced by the political counter-reformation, those who first cried to him for aid inhabited the Netherlands. He was to show a marked proclivity for harking back to Elizabethan precedents.

To appreciate the skill which he displayed, one must follow his activities through months of the most involved diplomacy. Indeed, so tangled is the skein that it is impossible even to indicate his aims and achievements within reasonable space except by following some special line. And the best line to follow seems to be that of his duel with the French.[3] For it was this aspect of the question which involved the greatest threat to the success of his foreign policy in general, and which at the same time demanded his greatest dexterity. The situation proved to be curious and even ironical. It was mainly through their co-operation in the Belgian question that the British and French governments developed the first *entente cordiale* : yet in dealing with that question they were seldom really at one, and several times bitterly, even dangerously, at odds. If ever the familiar analogy of a juggler walking on a tightrope applied to Palmerston's diplomatic activities, it was in this case. Feeling his way step by step for means of keeping on peaceful terms with France without sacrifice of British and Belgian interests, he had at the same time to keep three other great Powers and two small but exceedingly refractory states moving within a given orbit. Grey was no doubt in considerable measure responsible for the performance of the feat ; while Durham and others lent aid from time to time. But such definite appraisal as might be possible of the contributions which they made would involve the introduction of far too much detail.

Palmerston's performance was, of course, no solo act in so far either as the British cabinet or as diplomatic Europe was concerned ; but he occupied the centre of the stage from the outset. When, in October 1830, the king of the United Netherlands, unable to subdue the revolt of his Belgian subjects, appealed to the Powers for assistance in retaining the Belgian provinces handed over to him in 1815,

Wellington's government assumed the leadership by suggesting an international conference.[4] Louis Philippe and Talleyrand, anxious to reassure the other Powers as to their pacific intentions, were only too happy to concur ; while the Russian, Austrian and Prussian courts acquiesced almost as readily. Since haste was essential, and since both Talleyrand and his master preferred that the old diplomat should do his work at a safe distance from the French foreign minister and the too ' patriotic ' Parisians,[5] France soon agreed that the negotiations should take place in London, where the Russian and French ambassadors were already discussing with the British foreign secretary the affairs of Greece. The conference had just gotten fairly under way and arranged an armistice between the Belgians and the Dutch, when Palmerston supplanted Aberdeen. In doing so he became host to the other members of the conference. And the policy of Grey's cabinet rendered his position more important still ; for it made him an intermediary between revolutionary France and the three reactionary eastern Powers. Nor was this the only difficult and important rôle which he was called upon to play. He had not only to reconcile the policies of the five great Powers, but to resist the efforts of the king of the Netherlands and the Belgian national congress to convert one or more of them to views concerning which no reconciliation would have been possible. Finally, Palmerston's relations with France were the most delicate of all, and as paradoxical as delicate. Working with the French government to shield the Belgians against hostile moves on the part of the reactionary courts, he had an even more difficult task in protecting the interests of Belgium—and England—against the cupidity of France herself. Nor was even this the worst. Co-operating with Talleyrand to prevent the propagandist and expansionist policies of the French ' party of movement ' from becoming the official policies of France, he had constantly to block Talleyrand's own moves. Talleyrand would have no talk of annexation and propaganda ; for annexation and propaganda smelt of revolution and gunpowder.[6] But he well knew that partition, compensation and equilibrium—principles of diplomatic action consecrated by the high priests of the old regime—could be employed with quite equal benefit to France. When French policy appeared to follow one line at London, another at Paris, and still another, possibly, at Brussels ; when pronouncements from the Tuileries were designed, now for French ears, now for Belgian, and now for ears far to the east and north, the mediator of the London conference had need to tread warily.[7]

During the first month, however, no great complexities appeared. Palmerston's obvious task was to prevent the armed intervention of the three reactionary great Powers, and to secure a general acknowledgment of the Belgian provinces' self-declared independence. His special aim for the moment was not so much the establishment of Belgian independence as the preservation of peace. Indeed he frankly admitted that, in his view, the continuance of the union of the Dutch and Belgian provinces ' would have been most advantageous to the general interests of Europe.'[8] And ' Europe,' in Palmerston's scheme of policy as much as in Canning's, was usually interchangeable with ' England.' Accepting, however, the breakdown of the union as ' an irreversible fact,'[9] he set himself to prevent armed intervention in order to prevent an armed conflict. He did not find the task especially difficult. Talleyrand, who dreaded war not only for itself but lest it should deprive the French king of his throne, gave him valuable aid. And still greater assistance came from the Russian Poles, whose pitiful revolt, breaking out at just this time, engrossed much of the attention of the three eastern courts. On December 20, when the establishment of Belgium as a separate state was agreed to by all five Powers, peace seemed assured.

But, as Poland and the London conference delivered the Belgians from some of the dangers which had threatened from the east, new dangers from the west emerged, and Palmerston's most exacting work began. Independent Belgium had to be supplied with proper boundaries and a proper king : with boundaries which should not satisfy the cravings of French expansionists, and a king who would not take orders from the Tuileries. But none of the French were inclined to recognise any such necessity. At Paris, the boulevards were chanting ' *Le Rhin lui seul peut retremper nos armes* ;[10] and the 'party of movement,' with its demands for an aggressive and acquisitive foreign policy, was threatening to prove too strong for the prudence of the sovereign. Sebastiani, the French foreign minister, talked of 'disinterestedness' and 'loyalty,' but still hoped the Powers would see that 'some arrangement other than her [Belgium's] independence would more certainly secure the peace of Europe.'[11] Partition between Belgium's neighbours is almost certainly what he had in mind. Talleyrand, on the other hand, was ready to assent to 'the creation of a kingdom of Belgium'; but added the proviso that it should be 'placed under the sovereignty of some prince who should be too weak to give us any anxiety, and who should not even possess the means of keeping up the garrisons in the belt of fortresses.'[12] Moreover, he hoped to secure territorial acquisitions at Belgium's expense. Palmerston was soon to find that the disagreeable impressions of French policy which he had formed during his visits to Paris in the two preceding years had been only too well justified.

Determined to resist both French covetousness and the untenable claims of the Belgians to all the territories (including Luxembourg) which had taken any part in their revolt, he took for his own a plan of settlement which probably reconciled as well as any plan could have done the demands of abstract justice, of British interests, and of the general sentiment of the London conference.[13] Holland should return to her boundaries of 1790 ; Luxembourg should remain a state of the German Confederation under the king of Holland's rule ; and Belgium, which, as he pointed out, had never been independent, and could plead no right of *postliminium*, should have the rest of the territories which had constituted the United Netherlands. Not one acre of those territories was to go to any other state. His efforts to secure the complete adoption of this plan met with violent opposition from the Belgians and the Dutch, and with various objections from the other four great Powers. But of the latter, France was the only one which showed actual cupidity. Moreover, she was the only Power which tried to secure the Belgian crown for a puppet of her own. Palmerston did what he could to further the election of the

Prince of Orange, son to the king of the Netherlands, nephew to the king of Prussia and brother-in-law to the Tsar.[14] But in all the negotiations on this point he showed himself determined only on one thing—that the French should not succeed in installing a prince subservient to their orders and their interests.[15] Like his great collateral ancestor, Sir William Temple, he was embarked upon a diplomatic defence of the Low Countries against France.

His campaign can be followed with less difficulty if certain dates are kept in view. As the most prominent of these one would be inclined to take off-hand January 20, 1831, the day on which the delegates of the Powers to the conference signed a protocol fixing boundaries for the new Belgian state, and recording their assent to the proposal that it should be neutralised. On the other hand, when one remembers that some of Palmerston's greatest exertions were required to make Belgium's independence actual as well as theoretical, February 4 seems at least an equally important date. For it was on this date that the French government finally promised that Louis Philippe's second son, the duke of Nemours, would not accept the Belgian throne. With these two dates in mind it is not difficult to obtain a general view of Palmerston's successive (though naturally overlapping) activities. Up to January 20, he was mainly occupied in circumventing Talleyrand's efforts to secure, by bargain, some territorial advantages for France. In the fortnight which followed, he was contending against some very tortuous and apparently aggressive moves on the part of the government at Paris to establish a predominant influence in the new state. A third period, extending from February 4 to the establishment, on March 13, of a more conservative and pacific French cabinet, presented on a reduced scale similar dangers and difficulties. After March 13, Palmerston's path was for some time relatively clear.

For convenience, then, one may think of Palmerston as devoting his principal energies from December 20, 1830, to January 20, 1831, in repelling Talleyrand's attempts to secure some enlargement of French possessions to the east, and in discussing with the members of the conference generally the advantages of neutralising the new Belgian state. But, unfortunately, one cannot separate these two sets of activities, or even consider the two of them alone. For Talleyrand, with subtle effrontery, attempted to make French consent to the neutralisation scheme conditional upon the satisfaction of French wishes regarding the frontier ; and, not satisfied with this, brought into his attempts at bartering for territory the question of the selection of a Belgian king.

Talleyrand's demands and his efforts at bargaining were disposed of quite summarily ; but they are too illuminating to be passed by. At the very beginning of 1831, the Prussian envoy warned Palmerston that the French ambassador was hinting that the Prussian Rhineland might go to France, Saxony to Prussia, and the king of Saxony to Belgium.[16] Unsubstantial as this ghost of the Vienna congress may have been, the apparition was a disturbing one. And even Talleyrand's more modest suggestions to Palmerston [17] were utterly inadmissible from the standpoint of British policy. One of his first proposals was that Luxembourg might be assigned to France. When Palmerston replied that 'any territorial acquisitions of France such as this' would make it impossible for the British and French governments 'to continue on good terms,' the old ambassador held out for a *pourboire*. He asked for the border fortresses of Philippeville and Marienbourg, which France acquired from Spain in 1659 and lost to the United Netherlands in 1815. In exchange he offered French support to the candidature for the Belgian throne of Leopold of Saxe-Coburg, who would, of course, be expected to espouse a French princess. Since Leopold had lived much in England, and would have become Prince Consort had his wife, the daughter of George IV, survived, some English diplomatists might have regarded this offer as worth considering. But Palmerston, resolved to abide by his principles, would have none of it. Louis Philippe would have to satisfy the Paris *boulevardiers* as best he could.

Not even the proposal of neutralisation—a proposal which seems first to have been made in concrete form by Palmerston himself[18]—put an end to Talleyrand's attempts at bargaining.[19] He fought 'like a dragon' to have Luxembourg included in the scheme, so that the German Confederation's military command of the Metz-Coblenz line would be removed. Failing to secure this, he offered to take Philippeville and Marienbourg as a substitute. To Palmerston this seemed merely bluff. His own warm approval of the neutralisation scheme arose, not only from the conviction that it would make for general peace, but also from a real desire to offer to the French something which would seem contributory both to their self-respect and to their security. It hardly appeared necessary to buy Talleyrand's consent to an arrangement which took from the fortress-studded Belgian territory the aspect of a memorial to Waterloo and a bridgehead ready to serve the foes of France ; and made it, ostensibly at least, a screen protecting the French as much as it did any of their probable adversaries. Moreover, as he pointed out, Talleyrand and the more conservative element in France would be able to use the neutralization of Belgium in resisting the demands of the expansionists :

The possession of Belgium, somehow or other, and at some time or other, seems to be the object to which tend the unremitting efforts of a party in France, whose strength and activity appear to embarrass, and almost to controul the Government. The engagements entered into by the French Plenipotentiary . . . to respect the perpetual neutrality of Belgium, and the integrity and inviolability of its territory, must furnish the French Government with an argument not to be refuted, against those who may seek to drive them into war for the acquisition of Belgium.[20]

Talleyrand's claim that France should be paid for consenting to the neutralisation was not only unjustifiable, but one which the British government could not with any propriety satisfy :

First, we had no power to give what belongs to Belgium and not to us, and we could not, under the pretence of settling the quarrel between Holland and Belgium, proceed to plunder one of the parties, and that too for the benefit of one of the mediators. Besides, if France began, the rest might have a right to follow the example.[21]

His account of Talleyrand's surrender, much quoted as it is, will bear repetition :

At last we brought him to terms by the same means by which juries become unanimous—by starving. Between nine and ten at night he agreed to what we proposed, being, I have no doubt, secretly delighted to have got the neutrality of Belgium established.

The terms which Talleyrand had accepted, now safely embodied in the protocol of January 20, seemed to dispose of French aggressiveness. For they bound France, as they did her co-signatories, to renounce 'any augmentation of territory, exclusive influence, or isolated advantage' in the new state.[22]

The protocol was, perhaps, signed just in time. For the French double policy was in operation ; and Sebastiani, the French foreign minister, was exerting himself for the adoption of a plan which might well have given France 'augmentation of territory' at no very distant date. Personally an ardent expansionist, he was incited to action by the fact that a Francophil minority at Brussels was petitioning for the annexation of the Belgian provinces to France, and by a fear of the effect which the rejection of the petition would have upon the more nationalistic Parisians. Hence he caught at a suggestion, thrown out just previously by Talleyrand, that Belgium should be constituted as a federal state,—in other words, as an eventual French artichoke. On January 19, he placed this scheme before the British ambassador, Lord Granville, as his own.[23] Moreover, he urged it in terms that were half pleas, half threats, suggesting 'the impossibility of Peace if France were still to continue under the humiliation imposed upon her in 1815.' At the same time he sent to London a special envoy, whose real mission was to discuss the plan with Talleyrand.[24] When Talleyrand pointed out that the moment for suggesting a federal Belgium had already passed, Sebastiani gave in with rather surprising suddenness, and announced his decision to ratify the protocol of January 20. There is no particular reason to assume that, in executing this sudden change of front, he was actuated by anything save common sense ; but Palmerston may have been right in suggesting to Granville that the French Foreign Office was not unmindful of a certain unwonted activity in British dockyards :

Talleyrand read me to-day part of a letter he had received from Sebastiani, which was very satisfactory. . . . It sanctioned the signature of the . . . protocol [of January 20] . . . it renewed the former declarations that the French Government would neither consent to a union of Belgium with France, *nor accept the crown if offered to Nemours. . . . It is no harm, however, that the French should think that we are a little upon the alert with respect to our navy, because I believe it is the fear of a naval war which has greatly tended to induce the French Government to make the efforts necessary for the preservation of peace.*[25]

Certainly, a new situation which was evolving even at this time, was to justify his belief in the necessity for inculcating prudence at the Tuileries.

Throughout the crisis which developed at the beginning of February 1831, Sebastiani was again at fault; while the French government's capacity for indulging not only in double policies but in double dealing was strikingly displayed.[26] The question at issue was that of the election of a Belgian king. The French foreign minister, still fearful of displeasing the expansionists, discovered that the election, fixed for February 3, was sure to result in favour either of the duke of Nemours or the duke of Leuchtenberg. Since the French government had twice promised that neither Nemours nor any other son of Louis Philippe would be allowed to accept the Belgian crown; and since Leuchtenberg (a grandson of the former Empress Josephine) was entirely unacceptable to the Orleans monarchy, an appeal to the London conference would apparently have been the wisest course. But Sebastiani preferred, unfortunately, to handle the situation by himself, and to secure the defeat of Leuchtenberg in a particularly secret and underhanded way. First, Count Bresson, who, with Lord Ponsonby, represented the London conference at Brussels, but who also took orders from his own government, was confidentially instructed to give 'unofficial' support to Nemours. Considering that Bresson himself regarded this as an indication that Nemours might be allowed by his father to accept the throne in spite of all previous promises, it is not strange that the Belgians considered the acceptance as virtually assured, or that the other Powers were seriously alarmed. Nor was this all. On February 1, another letter from Sebastiani to Bresson announced that the French Foreign Office was unprepared to adopt a fresh protocol signed by Talleyrand five days before, and even doubtful whether the famous protocol of January 20 could be ratified after all. Since this was done without previous notification to the conference, Sebastiani was violating accepted canons of international usage and good faith. And, since both protocols had aroused resentment at the Belgian capital, it seemed obvious that Sebastiani's second letter was designed as a fresh attempt to assure the election of Nemours. Moreover, as though this were not enough, Talleyrand refused (also on February 1) to subscribe, otherwise than *ad referendum*, to Palmerston's proposal of a joint undertaking by the plenipotentiaries of the five great Powers that no prince of their reigning houses should accept the Belgian throne. He even ' sounded ' Palmerston as to the possibility that England would change her mind about Nemours.[27]

It seems probable that the French government had as yet failed to realise into what hands the conduct of British foreign policy had come. If so, enlightenment was not long delayed. Palmerston, writing to Granville on the situation, first pointed out that France seemed quite incorrigible :

... I must say that if the choice falls on Nemours, and the King of the French accepts, it will be proof that the policy of France is like an infection clinging to the walls of a dwelling, and breaking out in every successive occupant who comes within their influence.[28]

And he went on, in the firmest and most dignified manner possible, to promise that the necessary method of correction should be applied :

The Cabinet have considered the question of the Duc de Nemours, and have determined, as I tell you in my official despatch, that we must require from France the fulfilment of the engagement by a refusal to accept for him the crown if offered.

We are reluctant even to think of war, but if ever we are to make another effort this is a legitimate occasion, and we find that we could not submit to the placing of the Duc de Nemours on the throne of Belgium without danger to the safety and a sacrifice of the honour of the country.[29]

The outcome is well known : Nemours, elected with Sebastiani's help, refused the Belgian crown.

The French game had been, in all likelihood, one of bluff ; but the chronology of some of the developments is worth noticing.[30] On February 3, Sebastiani's attitude on the protocols was made known in the Belgian capital, and Nemours elected by a comfortable majority. On the day following, Sebastiani's special envoy, Count Flahaut, returning from London, reached France in time to have informed his chief before evening of the British cabinet's threat of war. Whether he did so is not clear ; but we know that Sebastiani, who seemed to Granville ' warm, warlike, and mounted on his highest horse ' at one o'clock, was all friendliness and conciliation before the afternoon had closed. ' Tell Lord Palmerston,' he said graciously, ' that we will not have a thought concealed from him.'[31]

Palmerston, having given France her lesson, returned to the quiet pursuit of his general policy. As Sebastiani's gracious message came to him at a time when French ' thoughts ' on the protocols—as conveyed to Brussels— were being revealed at Downing Street, he was so unappreciative as merely to threaten serious consequences if double dealing should be renewed.[32] But, as one of his letters shows, he was keeping the larger aspects of the question steadily in mind :

. . . our position at present ought, I conceive, to be that of impartial mediators between France on the one hand, and the three other Powers on the other ; . . . as long as both parties remain quiet we shall be friends with both ; *but . . . whichever side breaks the peace, that side will find us against them.*[33]

Unfortunately, the way of the mediator continued to prove hard. Nor did the British Foreign Office find the display of French thoughts sensibly increased.

If one should make a chart representing the developments in the Belgian question during the third decade of the nineteenth century, the result would suggest that a political fever had been prevalent in the Low Countries. The political temperature, always somewhat above the normal, rose and fell from time to time, leaping occasionally to a point which was distinctly dangerous. Needless to say the tensity of diplomatic relations varied with this temperature. So did the diplomatic preoccupations of Viscount Palmerston.

During the five or six weeks which followed the critical days of early February, the situation, while greatly improved, remained disquieting. In Paris, the 'party of movement' was still influential and aggressive: in London, Talleyrand still intent on bargaining. There were reports of military preparations among the French; there were attempts to use the newly bought French influence at Brussels to secure the Belgian throne for a Neapolitan Bourbon, who, as both nephew and son-in-law to Louis Philippe, would be a fair substitute for Nemours;[34] and there were fresh hagglings for rectification of the Franco-Belgian frontier. To make matters worse, the Belgians, greatly dissatisfied with the terms accorded them, encouraged by the French attitude, and apparently heedless of the danger of a general war, assumed a position of almost open defiance to the Powers.

Palmerston's letters show that his temper and his gorge both rose.[35] He was not greatly concerned to explore the underlying aims and motives of the French government. Remarkably forthright in his own diplomacy, he was genuinely disgusted by what seemed to him the 'underhand proceedings,' the 'endless intrigues and plots,' and the 'unceasing disposition to pick a quarrel' displayed by the French ministers. Why could they not 'make up their minds to be honest with stoutness, or to play the rogue with boldness'? Why must they be 'scrambling and intriguing for such pitiful objects as the ruined castle of Bouillon'? The only proper way of dealing with them was to refuse concessions of any sort:

> The moment we give France a cabbage garden or a vineyard, we lose all our vantage-ground of principle; and it becomes then a mere question of degree or the relative value of the different things which, one after the other, she will demand.

As for Sebastiani's blustering, he instructed Granville how to deal with that:

Pray take care in all your conversation with Sebastiani, to make him understand that our desire for peace will never lead us to submit to affront either in language or in act.

It will be remembered that he had already taken personally in hand the education of Sebastiani in the amenities of diplomatic intercourse.[36]

From March 13, Sebastiani's deportment did improve, though hardly as a result of Palmerston's tutelage. It was, of course, the accession to the French premiership of Casimir Perier, a representative of conservative French liberalism, which wrought the change. For Perier effected a re-orientation of French relations with England along those lines of action for which Talleyrand had always stood.[37] ' Scrambling ' and intriguing, not only for ruined castles and cabbage gardens but for greater stakes still, came to the attention of Palmerston from time to time ; but his steady policy of refusing, by ' the buying off of the Danish ravages,' to offer a ' temptation to a speedy repetition of such profitable attempts '[38] bore fruit. After France announced, on April 17, her full acceptance of the two great January protocols, she was able to avoid any vital disagreements with the British government until the close of the following July.

In the intervening months Palmerston was once more the mediator, compromising with his convictions as to the proper division of the territory of the Netherlands, in order to find an arrangement to which the Belgians would voluntarily accede ; and taking a leading part in the difficult negotiations which placed Leopold of Coburg on the throne.[39] It seemed at last that only two things were wanting for final settlement. The first of these was the submission of the Dutch to concessions made to Belgium in June, and embodied in the famous Eighteen Articles ; the second was the conclusion of arrangements for the destruction of certain fortresses on the Franco-Belgian frontier. But, in August 1831, the two matters became intertwined ; and intertwined in such fashion as again to involve Palmerston in the duel with France.

It may be worth while to recall the circumstances surrounding the question of the Belgian fortresses.[40] When the Allies of 1814 decided, as part of their scheme for holding France in bounds, that the Belgian part of the United Netherlands should be plentifully supplied with forts, England at once became especially responsible for the project. It was the British treasury which subscribed most liberally ; and it was the duke of Wellington who assumed direction of the work. By 1830, some twenty-five fortresses had been constructed or rebuilt at a cost of more than £7,000,000. Of these, some on the Scheldt and the North Sea were designed to give ingress, in case of need, to British troops ; while others, situated on the Meuse, were to serve as gateways for the Prussians. Thus the garrisons of still other forts, placed mainly along the Franco-Belgian frontier, and designed both to check a French advance and to serve as a bridgehead for a possible allied offensive against north-eastern France, were supposedly assured of English and German reinforcements. On paper the plan looked well enough ; but by 1831 there were good arguments for revising it. Reports drawn up in the autumn of 1830 concerning the danger that France would go to the assistance of the Belgians had revealed the fact that most of the border fortresses were in no condition to withstand serious attack.[41] If the king of all the Netherlands had found the maintenance of the whole system too much for him, what could be expected from the sovereign of the merely Belgian provinces ? Moreover, the French, who had bitterly resented the whole project from the first, showed that they would regard it as still more intolerable if maintained in connection with an independent and neutralised Belgium.[42]

Until August 1831, the question, while arousing considerable feeling at Paris, and receiving careful attention from the Powers, provoked no disputes. In April, England, Austria, Russia and Prussia signed a protocol which provided for the demolition of some of the border fortresses,[43] and to which the Belgian king—not as yet elected at this time—was expected to subscribe at the first opportunity. But, although France was no party to the protocol, and was to be denied all voice in deciding which of the fortresses were to be destroyed and which retained, no objections came from her representatives or her government. Indeed, Talleyrand had urged that the agreement should be made, and had been delighted to send confidential news of it to Louis Philippe and Casimir Perier.[44] He even boasted of its conclusion to the King as a diplomatic victory; while the King, in July, announced it in the same manner to the French chambers.[45] Nor were Talleyrand and his master without some apparent justification in thus referring to the protocol. The four Powers undoubtedly signed it mainly from the feeling that they would do better to destroy some of the fortresses than to leave them as a certain prey to France at the first outbreak of hostilities;[46] but they were probably actuated in some degree also by a desire to placate French public sentiment. Thus matters went along smoothly for some months. Yet the seeds of trouble lay underneath. Even in April Talleyrand had shown that France wished to be consulted regarding the selection of the fortresses to be destroyed.[47]

Then, at the beginning of August, a new crisis in the Belgian question united the two outstanding matters and gave the French their chance. The Dutch king, enraged by the concessions made to Belgium in the Eighteen Articles, sent his troops into Belgium; the Belgians, after a brief resistance, fled; and Leopold sent urgent appeals for help to Paris and London. Within two hours (so Palmerston claimed)[48] of the time when the appeal reached Downing Street, orders had been sent to Admiral Codrington, cruising off the Scilly Islands, to bring back his ships for service in the Scheldt. But the winds were contrary; and so long a delay ensued that British action in the Scheldt became superfluous. For a great French expeditionary force had sent the Dutch hurrying home. Palmerston wondered whether it would even be quite safe to have British ships far up the river, with a French army on the banks.[49] For all his mistrust was now aroused again. He even suspected that the French had instigated the Dutch attack, in order to secure an excuse for sending in their troops and forcibly settling the question of the fortresses.[50] Perhaps for a short time he was reassured. So specific were the undertakings given by Casimir Perier's ministry to withdraw their troops as soon as Holland did the same, that the London conference adopted French military (as well as British naval) action for its own; and Grey assured parliament that it need have no fears regarding French good faith.[51] But, when the French forces showed no intention of going home, and the familiar evasiveness commenced to replace specific assurances at the French court, both the foreign secretary and parliament took alarm.

Within a fortnight or so, the new crisis had produced a crop of actual and potential dangers which seemed more threatening even than those of the past winter and spring. Talleyrand once more threw out suggestions to the Prussian minister at London that their governments might divide up the Belgian territories with the king of the Netherlands.[52] French expansionists and Belgian annexationists seemed to take new heart; while Belgian patriots were encouraged by the sight of French troops to resist certain changes in the Eighteen Articles which the conference now judged necessary. Leopold, contrasting French promptness with British delay in sending aid, and noting the pro-Dutch tone of the British press, British society and the British opposition, listened to French suggestions for a separate Franco-Belgian accord on the question of the fortresses.[53] The central fact of all was that Belgium lay in the French grasp; and that France, despite her assurances, intended to exploit the fact to her own benefit. Even had the British cabinet been inclined to submit to this, it would have been prevented from doing so by parliament. Palmerston summed up this situation in writing to Sir Robert Adair, who had been rushed to Belgium as a special envoy:

> We should be compelled either to go out, or go to war, and from the jealous feeling of the cabinet upon the subject, I have little doubt that we should take the latter alternative.[54]

He was ready to accept it himself if necessary, but in the meantime he would use every possible means of keeping the peace.

Through all the rumours and alarms, the question of the

THE BELGIAN FORTRESSES

destruction of the Belgian fortresses emerged as an international issue of the first consequence. Talleyrand, who at first thought that the French expeditionary force might demolish the fortresses before returning home at the cost of nothing more than ' irritation ' on the part of the Powers, soon changed his mind.[55] But Louis Philippe's ministers, anxious as usual to appease the ' party of movement,' and noting that Belgium had not yet endorsed the April protocol, decided to explore two possibilities.[56] One was to refuse the recall of the expeditionary force until French wishes on the fortress question had been acceded to by the Powers ; the other to come to a separate understanding on the question with the Belgians. Success in either project would show Paris and all Europe that the Allies of 1814 were no longer able to take action without regard for France. But Palmerston had no intention of allowing Louis Philippe's ministers to decide the selection of the fortresses by either means. ' You might as well consult the housebreaker which of the bars & bolts of your doors & windows you might most safely dispense with,' he wrote disgustedly.[57] Nor was the housebreaker to have his way through any show of arms :

> If they want a coup de theatre & to impose humiliation on the rest of Europe they will fail in their object, for we will not allow them to dictate to us at the point of the bayonet.[58]

His annoyance was deepened by the fact that the French ministry, disagreeing with Talleyrand's view that good relations with England were more important than success concerning the fortresses, kept even their own delegate to the conference ignorant of their moves.[59] But, on this occasion, no complaints of the double policy could have been more bitter than Talleyrand's own.[60]

The lines of action to be followed by Palmerston were so obvious that he had to consider only the question of tactics. Diplomatic pressure had, of course, to be exerted at Brussels and Paris to secure the French evacuation of Belgium, to block the conclusion of any separate Franco-Belgian accord, and to convince Louis Philippe and his ministers that in the selection of the fortresses they could never have more than a consenting voice. Leopold was deluged with arguments from the foreign secretary's busy pen.⁶¹ Was it not clear to him that he should take the British policy for his own? Did he wish to encourage Belgian annexationists, or to see his country become a theatre of war? Could he not see through French cupidity and French intrigue? Was it not obviously to his own and his country's interests that he should ask for the retirement of the French expeditionary force, that he should ratify the April protocol, and that he should give full powers to his agent in London to accept necessary alterations in the Eighteen Articles? Let him remember that before long the Polish resistance to Russia would collapse, and the pro-Dutch sympathies of the eastern Powers have freer play. But the effect of all this dialectic on the astute Belgian king was not as immediate or conclusive as it might have been. For Leopold, who knew full well what danger to his throne and his adopted country could come from offence given to the French, and who expected to meet it by becoming Louis Philippe's son-in-law, tried to avoid committing himself too much to either side.

At Paris, Palmerston's tone was naturally a different one. Addressing the French government through Granville, he used not arguments so much as threats:

One thing is certain—the French must go out of Belgium, or we have a general war, and war in a given number of days. . . . With regard to the fortresses, make them understand that their pretensions are utterly inadmissible . . . to dismantle these fortresses while the French have them in possession would be a disgrace to all the five Powers; and as to making France a party to the treaty for their demolition, that is impossible . . . they will find that a war with all the rest of the world, brought upon them by a violation of their word, will not turn to their advantage, nor redound to their honour . . . the ministry will be turned out, and the King may go with them.⁶²

It is to be presumed that the last warning was not conveyed to the Tuileries.

If the English government was not to be dictated to at the point of the bayonet, the French government could scarcely do anything but submit when a pistol was levelled at its head by its only possible ally. The greater portion of its troops were recalled without delay, and the remainder

THE WITHDRAWAL OF THE FRENCH

drawn back close to the frontier. Talleyrand begged that, as 'a little help and a small act of friendship,' the Powers would decide about the fortresses before the withdrawal was complete. The plea was not quite in vain. The British government was willing that the four Powers should at once commence to discuss the question of the fortresses with Leopold, so long as France took no part, and the principle of separation between the questions of evacuation and the selection of the fortresses was preserved.[63] At Leopold's request a small French force was allowed to remain for his security; but, on September 15, the French government, 'of its own free will,' announced that even this contingent would be at once withdrawn.

For the time being at least the air seemed cleared; and the London conference was able to concentrate again on its long and involved task of working out boundaries, financial obligations, riparian rights, commercial routes and all the other matters incidental to a just division of the Netherlands. On October 14, its members, after working as Palmerston said 'like dray horses,' embodied the results of their labours in a long protocol,—the protocol of the 'Twenty-four Articles.'[64] In order to obtain the adhesion of the Belgian government to the terms laid down, the conference proceeded to promise that it would take upon itself the obligation of securing the consent of Holland to these terms, 'and would guarantee their execution.' An identical inducement was offered to the Dutch.[65] Rather unexpectedly, the Belgian government accepted while the Dutch refused. But Palmerston was glad enough to make the protocol into the famous treaty of November 15, 1831, between Belgium and the five great Powers.[66] On the first anniversary of his entrance to the Foreign Office he was writing happily:

> At last you may wish me joy. This morning, between two and three, we signed, sealed, and delivered six copies of the treaty of friendship and acknowledgment between the five Powers and Leopold . . . the Dutch King may sulk if he will; but he can no longer endanger the peace of Europe, since all the five would be equally bound to resist him. . . . We signed also between the four powers and Van de Weyer an agreement to serve as the basis of a Convention about the fortresses. . . .[67]

In his happiness he could not resist an amusing little jibe at Talleyrand :

> There was a doubt at one time last night whether all the things could be got ready in time to sign, and I said to Wessemberg that perhaps we should have to put it off till today. 'No,' said he, 'old Talleyrand won't quit this roof without signing ; his orders to his stockbroker are all given, and he must have the treaty signed before tomorrow morning.' . . .

Apparently Palmerston did not realise how much trouble about the fortresses there was still in store.

The trouble was serious ; for France threatened to withhold her ratification of the treaty if the fortress question were not settled to her taste ; whereas such a settlement would give excuse for non-ratification to any or all of the three eastern Powers.[68] Only Palmerston seems to have felt any enthusiasm for the Twenty-four Articles. Compelled to take sides on the fortress question, he still maintained that the 'housebreaker' should have nothing to say about the 'bars & bolts.' And he repeatedly instructed Adair [69] to explain to Leopold the principles on which the selection of the four Powers had been based :

> Their interest in this matter is . . . to dismantle those fortresses which are too near the French frontier to be secure against a sudden attack, and which from their very proximity are a temptation to France ; and to keep up those which being more remote from the frontier are safer from a surprize, and which being nearer to Prussia & England might receive succour from those two quarters.[70]

Hence there could be no talk of the destruction of the forts on the seacoast or the Meuse, nor acceptance of the French demand that the list of fortresses to be demolished should include Tournai and Charleroi and exclude Philippeville and Marienbourg. Tournai and Charleroi could be defended even by Belgium, and would be of the greatest service in holding up a French advance on Brussels. Moreover, Charleroi was a source of strength to Namur. As for Philippeville and Marienbourg, they were certain to be captured, and perhaps to be retained, by France when hostilities should break out. It seems never to have occurred to him that France or any other Power would be restrained from violating Belgian neutrality by anything save the risk of meeting a coalition on the other side.

In the end he prevailed over the French government as he had so often done before. A Belgian agent, General Goblet, sent to London to win general acceptance for the terms of a Franco-Belgian understanding reached at Brussels on September 8, ended by signing, on December 14, a convention with the four Powers for the destruction of the fortresses on their list.[71] There was an outburst of rage in Paris, and the utterance of various threats, levelled in particular at Belgium and the unhappy Leopold.[72] Louis Philippe addressed a haughty letter to his would-be son-in-law, commanding that Goblet's action should be disavowed.[73] But Palmerston, scornfully discounting the French threats, adjured the Belgians to stand firm. Thus, on December 27, to Adair:

> I see clearly that the French will give in . . . Leopold need not fear that the fortresses will deprive him of his bride ; and unless Belgium be finally settled that bride would not be tempted from the Tuileries by the demolition of all the fortresses from the Meuse to the sea. . . .[74]

And (this letter seems curiously indiscreet), on December 22, to Goblet:

> I have too much respect for the king your master and the king I have the honour to serve to make it possible I could ever consent to yield to the insolent tone the French government has judged it proper to assume on the subject of these fortresses. Prince Talleyrand and General Sebastiani must learn that they are no longer the instruments of the imperious wishes of a Napoleon ; and it is necessary also that Louis Philip should know that the laurels of Valmy and Jemmapes [*sic*] cannot serve as a bugbear to all Europe. . . .[75]

He saw no inconsistency in using language of this sort to denounce as 'unseemly and unworthy' the 'flourishes' of Sebastiani and Talleyrand. But he consented, at the end of January 1832, to the drafting of a note which mollified the French by declaring that the destruction of the fortresses was to be regarded as an act of Belgian sovereignty, and that the relations of France to Belgium were to be the same as those of all the other Powers.[76]

So much for Palmerston's Belgian paternity. How he shielded and succoured the infant during the following year by helping to drive the Dutch troops from Antwerp is a story in itself, a story too long and too involved for relation in this place.[77] Suffice it, then, that the London conference broke down; and that sharp despatches and British naval power produced the desired results. An episode less familiar than the bombardment of the Antwerp citadel was soon (as will be shown) [78] to shed a more revealing light on Palmerston's attitude toward Belgium and her fortresses.

CHAPTER VII

Palmerston's first 'Intermeddling' in Spain, Portugal, Germany and Italy, 1830–1834

The report of Palmerston's appointment as foreign secretary must have come as news of peculiar interest to all persons, in England and on the continent, who were interested in the Spanish peninsula. Not only was a disciple of Canning's to deal with a question in which the master had achieved some of his most spectacular successes, but it was less than eighteen months since the disciple had delivered a great philippic against Miguel. Some of the periods of that speech must have lingered in men's minds :

> . . . Miguel . . . this destroyer of constitutional freedom, this breaker of solemn oaths, this faithless usurper, this enslaver of his country, this trampler upon public law, this violator of private rights, this attempter of the lives of helpless and defenceless women. . . .
> I say that if the insulted honour of a sovereign is a legitimate ground for national quarrel, we are entitled to demand, and to extort, reparation from Miguel. . . .[1]

Not only had these passages suggested that Palmerston was consumed with eagerness to avenge the honour of his country and the woes of any number of Portuguese from Queen Maria down, but they had contained the faint suggestion of an almost Elizabethan touch,—of a tendency to singe royal beards worn by champions of a discarded faith. True, the faith now in question was political ; the treasures to be seized on bore the drab guise of mere bills of exchange ; and the suggested method of warfare was no more heroic than that of ' intermeddling in every way, and to every extent, short of actual military force.' But it was not Palmerston's fault if the brighter times of Elizabeth were past; and liberalism was the best possible nineteenth-century substitute for protestantism, in providing a cause for St. George and England. The political counter-reformation threatened to roll back the spread of constitutional government on the continent, leaving England, in Palmerston's view at least, sadly wanting in ' natural allies ' and in influence. In Belgium, the dark forces of reaction were being held at bay; but more than this might be achieved by an adventurous British secretary, acting in concert with a very liberal premier, and not too much weighed down by regard for the proprieties. And the best field of action lay south of the Pyrenees.

The situation in the Peninsula seemed almost to have been made for Palmerston. Even he rarely found an opportunity to be at once so good a patriot and so stout a liberal. Here was a part of Europe where liberalism, trembling in the balance, might triumph with a little aid; and where British influence, recently in decline, might thereby be restored. And a broader vista opened. The triumph of the reactionary governments in Poland, Germany, and Italy, where their armies would always make outside patronage of liberalism futile, might be counter-balanced by the success of the liberal governments of England and France in this region, where naval power could easily be the determining element. Indeed, considering the importance of sea power and the dependent position of the French government, it did not seem impossible that British influence might become predominant throughout the whole Peninsula.

At home, too, there were sweet fruits to be garnered: justification of that flaming speech of June 1829; satisfaction that would lie in the rescue of Canning's policy; and the pleasure of wielding the weapon of Canning's discovery, the power of popular sentiment. For popular sentiment on this question was growing strong, as people noticed in the streets of London more and more exiled constitutionalists from Portugal and Spain—interesting strangers who attracted the same sympathetic and romantic interest that Italians and Hungarians were to enjoy in later times.

Indeed, the actual situation in the Peninsula was in

some respects less important to the foreign secretary than the emotionalised conception which most of the English public held. In Portugal they saw the wicked usurper Miguel, dressed in the black garb of absolutism, flaunting the favour of the reactionary northern Powers, and depriving of the throne a gentle—though, withal, somewhat stout—young niece, who yearned to endow her doubly deprived subjects with a good, sound British type of government. That the gentle young Queen Maria had a father, Pedro, who was uncommonly like his brother Miguel, was not as yet quite realised. In Spain events were shaping to produce a situation well-nigh identical. Old Ferdinand VII was sinking miserably to his grave. The crown would go either to his infant daughter, Isabella, or to his brother Carlos, according as Ferdinand's young wife, Christina, on the one hand, or the clerical and reactionary band of Carlos on the other, held sway over the decrepit monarch in the last months of his life. Let him die still upholding the Salic law, and Carlos and reaction would not only rule in Spain, but throw support to Miguel in Portugal. Let Isabella receive the crown, and the Dowager Queen Regent (for reasons which the public would not be too anxious to analyse) would give constitutional government. Thus Spain, like Portugal, would have its innocent girl queen fighting for the political faith of which England was the great expositor, against a benighted (and incidentally very anti-English) uncle.

It was, naturally, the Portuguese uncle to whom Palmerston's attention was first turned. Certain orders which he issued at the outset testify, by their unobtrusiveness, to the sincerity of his interest in the Portuguese constitutionalists. He had not been in the Foreign Office for three weeks when he directed the packet agent at Lisbon to discontinue ' the habit of publishing a list of all letters arriving . . . by the English mail and of thus pointing out to the persecution of the Portuguese government all those persons in Lisbon who hold correspondence with the Portuguese emigrants in England.'[2] Shortly afterwards he forwarded to Maria's servants at Terceira copies of a note on Portuguese affairs which he was sending to the Spanish government, and of a despatch which he had written to Sir Frederick Lamb, England's envoy to Miguel.[3] But he made no effort to veil his sympathies. A British consul, Hoppner by name, whom he sent to Lisbon, and with whom he corresponded confidentially and frequently,[4] was regarded by Lord William Russell as a '*sanguinaire sans-culotte.*'[5] What the British government did for Pedro and Maria in a naval and military way constituted a frank avowal of its partisanship to all the world.

In his unabashed advocacy of giving naval and military assistance to Maria and Pedro, Palmerston again displayed the Elizabethan—one is tempted to say the freebooting—touch. For, abetted by other ministers, he conducted hostilities against Miguel under the pretence of peace. The pretence was, of course, quite necessary. Isolated intervention might entail dangerous international complications ; joint intervention with the French would strengthen French influence ; while intervention of either sort would invite political assaults at home, and create precedents most useful to the northern Powers in their dealings with constitutional governments. Hence, none more insistent than the British foreign secretary on the neutrality of his government.[6] But neutrality is at all times an elastic state, and Palmerston knew how to draw it taut. Long afterward, he enjoyed boasting that 'the liberties of Portugal . . . the question between constitutional and arbitrary power' had been 'decided' by the active assistance which British subjects, acting with the scarcely veiled approval of their government, gave to Pedro's and Maria's cause.[7] In how far Portugal's 'liberties' were actually enhanced was questionable ; nor was it proper to forget that the French were also to a large extent responsible for what changes may have taken place. But there was none to gainsay his claim of having contributed to Miguel's defeat.

The manner in which active assistance was given to Pedro and Maria would doubtless have made Canning rub his eyes. Peel pointed out to the House,[8] just sixteen months after the inauguration of Grey's government, that thousands of British subjects were being enlisted in England for the cause ; that British naval officers, acting under assumed names, were in command of Portuguese constitutionalist ships; that British-built vessels, pierced for guns, and manned by British crews, were setting out from British ports for destinations ultimately Portuguese; and that materials for full armament accompanied them in other ships. And apparently Peel himself was not aware that the foreign secretary was helping Maria's agents to recruit even in Belgium.[9] But Palmerston was imperturbable under Peel's assaults. Resting on the civil law for the justification of the sale of ships and arms, he simply denied any knowledge of the other facts, with an apostrophe on interference with 'the property and pursuits of individuals.'[10] Why should he know or care if certain British naval officers were dropped temporarily from the navy list? Why indeed? When, in June 1833, Wellington carried what amounted to a vote of censure in the Lords, Palmerston, reminding the Commons that 'the principle of embarking in the contests of other countries had prevailed, and had been acted upon, in the brightest periods of our history,' triumphed in the lower House by an overwhelming vote.[11] He was able to point out that Miguel also had been allowed to buy supplies and raise recruits; but it did not appear that English poor-houses had been emptied for his support as for Maria's![12]

The highly irregular proceedings of the British and French governments soon commenced to obtain what justification success could give. In July 1832, the taking of Oporto by the constitutionalists dealt Miguel a serious blow. Just one year later, Admiral Carlos Ponza (known previously and subsequently as Captain Napier, R.N.), executing a stroke foreseen, if not recommended, by Palmerston three months previously,[13] seized upon Lisbon, and placed Miguel on the defence. Though the end was still far off, Maria's prospects had become promising. Meantime, however, the issue was becoming more and more complicated from the diplomatic point of view by the increasing necessity of taking into account the policies of the French and Spanish governments.

'I little thought a year ago,' wrote that great diplomatist Stratford Canning, in December 1832, 'that there was anything in negotiation more impossible than the Greek question, but the enigma of the two Doms [Miguel and Pedro] beats it hollow.'[14] As Canning's dictum is unlikely to be disputed even now, it is perhaps fortunate that the diplomatic exchanges which went on between England, France, Spain and Portugal through these years need not be traversed here. But it seems essential to note the difficulties which confronted Palmerston, and the way in which his path at last was cleared for the conclusion of his famous Quadruple Alliance of 1834. What made his way so hard was that France had so great an interest in Spain, and Spain in Portugal. Nor did the views of either the French or the Spanish government fit in with those of Grey's ministry. The ministers of the sick and ageing King Ferdinand were for the most part as reactionary as Miguel. Even Zea Bermudez, the minister with whom the English government had most to do, and who was by no means the most extreme, regarded Miguel with what Palmerston called 'the passion of a mother for her deformed child.'[15] Hence an Anglo-Spanish intervention in the affairs of Portugal, which would have suited Palmerston perfectly, and which would not have been objected to by the French, proved impossible to arrange. Instead of co-operating, the British and Spanish governments watched each other jealously for evidence of any clear breaches of neutrality.[16] Palmerston hoped to convert Zea to better courses, or, failing that, to compass his downfall. But, in pursuing this laudable enterprise, he found it impossible to secure any backing from the French. Louis Philippe's ministers acted to his complete satisfaction where Portugal only was concerned.[17] They assisted Maria in much the same manner as the British government, and heeded British warnings not to bombard Lisbon or to land troops when exacting redress for outrages perpetrated by Miguel. But not even their appreciation of the *entente cordiale*, not even their strong desire that a general defensive alliance should take its place, could bring them to acquiesce in British policy respecting the government of Spain. For their interests bade them to foster strong, not to say repressive, rule at Madrid. Disorder might necessitate French intervention ; and the fate of Napoleon, the danger of tying France's hands in the southwest while danger threatened her from the three eastern Powers, was very much before their eyes. Moreover, an autocrat would be much more susceptible to the diplomatic *ménagement* of the Spanish government on which France was bent than would be any group of impulsive and unpractised Spanish constitutionalists.[18] Even while the British and French governments were still engaged mainly with the affairs of Portugal, the latter refused to make any show of force against Ferdinand and his chief minister, or to approve the exclusion of Don Carlos from the Spanish throne through the abrogation of the Salic law[19].

As a result of these complications, and of the British government's reluctance to sanction French interference in Portugal, Palmerston was unable for some time to achieve anything by diplomacy. Yet he made several attempts. Stratford Canning's disgusted comment marks the fact that, in December 1832, when Ferdinand was very ill, Canning was hurried to Madrid. His mission was to persuade the King and Queen that, as their daughter Isabella was likely soon to find herself in a position only too similar to that in which Maria stood, the Spanish government would do well to assist the British in disposing of Miguel.[20] Queen Christina saw the point. But Zea also hung over the sick bed ; and, as Ferdinand's health improved, so did he harden his heart against Canning and the Queen. Canning went home : Miguel and Pedro, who now headed his daughter's cause, fought on: and the unfortunate Portuguese paid for the disagreements of the great. Palmerston, never really daunted, was planning a new mission to be carried out by George Villiers, the future great earl of Clarendon, when circumstances commenced to play into his hands.

In September 1833 (the September of the 'Holy Alliance' meeting at Münchengrätz) Ferdinand was gathered to his fathers, leaving behind him neither son nor Salic law. On the proclamation of Isabella as queen under Christina's regency, the late king's brother, Carlos, broke into revolt ; and, most unwisely, soon allowed his cause to be identified with that of Miguel in Portugal. Thus even Zea Bermudez could no longer, without disloyalty to his government, support his Portuguese favourite. Though not even yet prepared to champion Maria's cause, he would no longer stand in England's way. No more would France. An Anglo-French-Spanish intervention was still the policy which she preferred; but she had no intention of urging it too far. Louis Philippe was ready to make any reasonable sacrifice to the hope of securing a general defensive alliance with the British government. At the beginning of 1834 isolated British intervention in Portugal would apparently have been unopposed.[21]

And Grey, at least, regarded the situation as having become so acutely dangerous to European peace that intervention could no longer be delayed.[22] His argument was that Miguel's support of Carlos might force the French to send troops into Spain for the support of Isabella's government; that this ' w'd be considered by ye despotic powers as affording a favourable opportunity for ye execution of ye hostile designs agst ye liberties of ye smaller German States, which they are known to entertain '; that France would in return feel justified in rousing ' ye discontented spirit which is so ready to break out in Germany and Italy '; and that Europe would then be in danger of a general war. England, he decided (this was in January 1834) should immediately send 6000 troops to Portugal, thus averting the whole danger at its source. Whether or not Grey's elder son was right in believing that the premier had been led to these conclusions by Palmerston (and the evidence points rather the other way) the foreign secretary, with about half the cabinet, supported the premier. But three other cabinet ministers, including Althorp, not only opposed the expedition but threatened to resign; and anxious days ensued.[23] Grey seemed determined to have his way, or to break up the government by leaving it; but Palmerston gave in to Althorp and the other dissentients. In the end the premier, exasperated and mortified, yielded to the entreaties of the cabinet that he should sacrifice his convictions to the survival of the ministry. The governments of the two queens were informed, to their consternation,

COUNTERPOISE TO 'HOLY ALLIANCE' 147

that nothing could be done for them; and the wretched civil wars dragged on.

But not for long in Portugal; since Palmerston's famous Quadruple Alliance between the four 'liberal' western governments was soon to compass the ruin of Miguel. A characteristic account of the genesis of the alliance was given by its proud author in a letter to his brother written in April 1834 :[24]

> I have, ever since Ferdinand's death, felt that morally this alliance must exist; but it was not till a fortnight ago that I saw the opportunity of giving it a substantive and practical form. The communications of Miraflores [the Spanish minister], and his renewal of the Spanish wish that we should send troops to Portugal, suggested the idea to me. . . .

As originally drafted, the treaty was to be concluded only between England, Spain and Portugal. The privilege of being 'acceding parties' was offered to the French :

> I carried it through the Cabinet by a *coup de main*, taking them by surprise, and not leaving them time to make objections. I was not equally successful with old Talley and the French Government, for they made objections in plenty. . . .

In fact 'old Talley' brought Palmerston to time.[25] The honour of being 'acceding parties' was so little appreciated by the French that they refused to accept it unless a general alliance with the British government was offered them as well. After a lively diplomatic skirmish both ideas were dropped; Palmerston's treaty was redrafted; and the alliance for disposing of Miguel and Carlos became in the fullest sense a quadruple one.

Like many other quadruple structures, it was hollow behind its imposing face. At first glance the terms appeared satisfactory enough : Spain to send troops against Miguel; England to give naval aid; and France, in case of need, to offer co-operation of a kind unspecified. But the two great signatories did not err on the side of generosity. Talleyrand assured his government that France was 'not pledged to anything '—that she could, in fact, ' play politically an equal part with England, without employing an additional soldier or spending a sou.' [26] Palmerston could boast of equally admirable economy :

> Our naval co-operation is merely put in to save appearances, and to prove our goodwill, for there is nothing for us to do in that way, unless Miguel and Carlos were to attempt to sail away to Madeira, and even in that case Napier would be too many for them.[27]

In other respects the two statesmen were not so well agreed. The French ambassador's claim that the English ministry had ' submitted its policy in the Peninsula to our control ' seems a little out of key with Palmerston's condescending report : ' I have . . . satisfied their vanity by giving them a proper place among us.' But it is with respect to the general significance of the alliance that the contrast between the two views is most marked. Talleyrand seemed primarily concerned that the jealousy of ' the great Northern Powers ' and their desire to break up the entente would make them ' more friendly ' to the French government.[28] Palmerston struck a very different note :

> I reckon this to be a great stroke. In the first place it will settle Portugal, and go some way to settle Spain also. But, what is of more permanent and extensive importance, it establishes a quadruple alliance among the constitutional states of the west, which will serve as a powerful counterpoise to the Holy Alliance of the east. . . . I should like to see Metternich's face when he reads our treaty.

He must have felt deep satisfaction as he wrote these words. For he doubtless remembered that the Russian and Austrian envoys at Madrid had urged Ferdinand and Zea to assist Miguel and maintain the Salic law.[29] Nor can he have been sorry to answer in so direct a fashion the understanding concluded by ' the great Northern Powers ' at Münchengrätz.

For some time he was able to glory in the treaty as ' *a capital hit, and all my own doing* ' ; [30] but some of his jubilation died away as the year 1834 wore on. On May 16, a Portuguese constitutional army, assisted by Spanish troops, defeated Miguel ; a week later the two reactionary uncles capitulated and agreed to leave the Peninsula. Palmerston was in high feather :

> *Nothing ever did so well as the Quadruple Treaty : it has ended a*

DOWNING STREET [1827]

war which might otherwise have lasted months . . . the normal effect of the treaty cowed them all. . . . The case of Carlos is now desperate. . . .[31]

His self-congratulations were destined to be short-lived. At the beginning of July, Carlos, who had taken refuge in England, escaped without notice by the Dumas-like device of employing an impersonator to converse with visitors from his bed. A few days more and he was back in Spain, opening the wearisome series of 'Carlist' civil wars. The Quadruple Alliance, having proved inadequate, Palmerston and Talleyrand negotiated some additional articles, providing, among other things, that France should refuse the passage of Carlist arms through her territory, and that England should sell arms and ammunition to Isabella's government.[32] But in essence the agreement was no more substantial than before. Talleyrand, in pointing out to his government the gratifying fact that France would again escape the necessity for outlay of any sort, while England would send supplies for which she never would be paid,[33] showed once again how little the understandings between the two great liberal Powers rested upon any veritable *épanchement de cœur*.

In 1836, Palmerston, a little disillusioned of his treaty, wrote of it to Russell in a somewhat apologetic tone.[34] The government, he pointed out, had measured the assistance it gave the queen of Spain, not by the extent of its good will towards her, but by its 'opinion of the disposition of parliament to vote . . . supplies.' But he had no apologies to make for his policy as a whole:

. . . what would have been the more just and wellfounded attacks of our friends if when the struggle for liberty began in Spain . . . the Whig government of England . . . had tamely and passively allowed despotism and the Inquisition and Holy Alliance ascendancy to be again reestablished in Spain ; and if in Spain eventually in Portugal also ?

The government had been blamed enough for not offering more resistance to Russia in the Near East and Poland, though in those regions 'ready means of action' were not at its command.

But it must have been obvious to everyone that when the battle between the two great parties which divide Europe was transferred to the Peninsula all the advantages of nearness and easy contact were on our side.

Glad as he was to have given succour to the constitutionalists of Portugal and Spain, it was always to the broader aspect of the whole question that he ultimately turned.[35] The 'Holy Alliance' was the great enemy, and he had called a new league into existence to redress the balance of the old.

He had made western Europe as safe for moderate and constitutional liberalism as it could be made; but what of the centre and the east? The question is very pertinent. For diplomatic intervention in the Low Countries and the Spanish peninsula was a very different thing in more than one respect from interference in the affairs of Germany, Italy and the kingdom of Poland. In Belgium and Portugal, England's interests were traditional and beyond dispute, her intervention was almost unavoidable, and her prospects of success were excellent. But none of these things could be said where the other three regions were concerned. Hence one might hope at least to find in any efforts made by Palmerston in behalf of Italian, German or Polish liberals a somewhat better test of the extent to which genuine interest in liberal movements for their own sake entered into his foreign policy. The more remote were British interests, the more gratuitous was British interference, and the more unpromising were Palmerston's chances of securing even the intangible benefits of a diplomatic victory, the more discernible was the altruistic element in his policy.

And it seems worth while inquiring, from the very outset, to what extent Bright, Cobden and the heirs to their views have been justified in sneering at Palmerston's claims to be regarded as 'liberal' in his foreign policy. The answer must, of course, depend in large degree on one's own conception of 'liberalism.' If the only true faith was that of the advocates of the Spanish constitution of 1812, of the Poles who proclaimed the deposition of the Tsar, or even of the leaders of Young Italy, the jibes of the Manchesterites and their heirs will stand. But if one thinks of liberalism in constitutional and evolutionary terms, of that liberalism, in fact, which achieved the most substantial and most lasting gains during the sixteen years when Palmerston was foreign secretary, the question becomes a very different one. If he was unfaithful to liberalism of this type, his ceaseless defence and praise of constitutions and constitutionalists, in speeches, despatches and, above all, in letters of the most private sort, constituted one enduring piece of mere hypocrisy. Under the same proviso his efforts to give the Belgians and the Greeks a freer and healthier development, to moderate the vengeance of the Tsar against the Poles, to encourage the Italian rulers in reform with smiles, and restrain the German Diet with protests,—these were mere cloaks to officiousness, pomposity and a desire to further British interests.

Of the sincerity of his enthusiasm for liberalism one must, of course, judge for oneself. But of his influence there can be no doubt. Many years later Turgeniev told of a peasant who crawled out of the reeds of a marsh in one of the most remote Russian provinces to ask: 'Who is this Palmestron?' And Turgeniev added: 'I have often asked what glory is. I know now.' A contemporary French historian, in reviving this well-known story,[36] concludes that Palmerston's liberalism was only the means to an end; that having no interest in territorial acquisitions in Europe, and every incentive to maintain the balance of power by curbing the stronger states, pure national interest led him to patronise the peoples whose struggles for self-government would weaken the great Powers as regards both fighting strength and commerce. Thus, his impelling motive was a patriotism '*violent, égoïste, avide, impitoyable, dédaigneux des hommes, des théories, des principes.*' But it is possible that this historian has not read his most private communications or noted certain quite unobtrusive acts which he performed. One must not forget, for example, that this man, driven to exhaustion by unremitting work, turned from his major operations on European politics to protect German and Polish refugees in Switzerland,[37] and to request the release of revolutionary subjects of the Pope captured in their flight across the Adriatic by the Austrians.[38] But only a review of all of his diplomatic activities gives a basis for conclusions on either side. Something may be gleaned from his dealings with the German section of middle Europe.

What strikes one more than anything else, perhaps, in Palmerston's first dealings with the German states, is the evidence he gave of his jaunty and incorrigible optimism. Optimism was needed by a British minister who attempted, during the early thirties, both to preserve some of England's former ability to flood the German market with her goods, and to shield the half-stifled flame of constitutionalism at some of the lesser German courts. In the one case, he was opposing the firm and relentless advance of the Prussian Zollverein; in the other, the inveterate determination of a German Diet, directed by Metternich and supported by all three of the great reactionary Powers. And among the reactionary German princes of secondary rank stood the king of Hanover, who reigned also in England as William IV.

While Palmerston showed a certain persistence in meeting both the Diet and the Zollverein, there is no evidence that in his encounters with the latter he was animated by any particular enthusiasm.[39] Commercial diplomacy he seems always to have taken as a task to be performed conscientiously, not to be seized and driven through with the absorbed interest that he could give where boundaries, where constitutions, and, above all, where questions of Britain's prestige and Britain's fighting strength entered in. So it was here. As a free trader he deprecated 'the Prussian tariff' (even while admitting that retaliation might become unavoidable):[40] as a good politician and Englishman he resisted the development of the Zollverein as a threat to British trade. Hence, some of his agents at the smaller German courts were directed to encourage resistance to the Prussian league by smaller leagues from which England might hope for better terms, or offer commercial treaties with the British government to individual states which might serve as centres for the distribution of British goods.[41] Among these, Frankfort, a free city for five centuries, an emporium for several more, and still a trade centre with few rivals on the continent, was the focus of England's most definite attempt to keep open a commercial path through Prussia's enveloping lines. Nor was Frankfort difficult to woo. For one thing, her senate argued that the small share of the duties collected by the Zoliverein to which the principle of distribution by population would entitle her, must fall far short of what she collected as an independent entrepôt. Some of her merchants felt, too, that since she was almost surrounded by territory included within the Zollverein, she could make all the greater profit from traffic in British goods. Hence, in May 1832, she signed a treaty with the British government, providing for 'most favoured nation' treatment on both sides, and thus disqualifying herself for membership in the Zollverein.[42] The treaty was to run without renewal for ten years. It seems that Palmerston was fortunate in getting the treaty signed when he did. For the ink was hardly dry when the Foreign Office found itself confronted with a question involving the fortunes of constitutional government in Germany. Whether it also involved a threat to peace; and whether, on this or on any other account, Great Britain was entitled to intervene in any way, it was largely for Britain's foreign secretary to decide.

In the late spring and the summer of 1832, the revolutionary wing of the German liberals, whose activities centred in the Bavarian Palatinate, staged a series of demonstrations at Hambach and neighbouring points which alarmed moderate as well as reactionary circles all through Europe. Visions of a German revolution, sustained by the French, and leading to that nightmare of the time, a general 'war of opinion,' troubled statesmen everywhere. The reactionary German courts, seeing no cure save intensified repression, and encouraged by the Tsar's promise to send help should France intervene, passed through the Diet six articles which abridged the sovereignty of the German states and erected obstacles against constitutional development. The moderates, in England and elsewhere, had now to deplore provocative excesses on both sides.

Palmerston, as one of these, felt called upon to define his policy with unusual clarity. He believed that revolution and the resulting danger of war were as much prompted by the Six Articles as by the Hambach festival; and that every successful blow at constitutional government in Europe was an indirect impairment of British influence. Besides, his hand was forced. On August 2, Henry Lytton Bulwer moved an address, requesting the King 'to exercise his influence with the Germanic Diet in opposition to the course pursued by them, contrary to the liberty and independence of the German people.'[43] Bulwer's oratory was of a type to appeal to Palmerston himself:

> It was in the free forests of Germany that the infant genius of our liberty was nursed. It was from the free altars of Germany that the light of our purer religion first arose. It was from one of the minor states of Germany that our Constitutional Monarchs came.

But, in point of fact, it was, as Bulwer doubtless knew, precisely from the opinions of England's constitutional monarch that one of the British cabinet's difficulties in dealing with German affairs arose. William, as king of England, had not only lived up to the constitution but shown some Whiggish proclivities: as king of Hanover he apparently concurred in thought and action with the more illiberal German sovereigns.

The situation created something of a dilemma for Palmerston; but he also found in it an opportunity to declare his policy. It was incumbent on him to resist Bulwer's address, if only as constituting an encroachment upon the executive by the legislature. His general principle of discountenancing revolution required, too, that he should condemn the disturbance of 'internal tranquillity' occasioned by such 'public meetings' as that at Hambach, and disclaim the right of interference upon 'uncertain facts and doubtful surmises.'[44] But he was careful that the Diet should glean no atom of approval or encouragement from that. The German sovereigns, he pointed out, might imperil peace if they undertook such infringements of individual liberties as would be permitted them by the resolutions which the Diet had just passed. Then, choosing this occasion for his declaration of England's interest in the welfare of all constitutional states, he warned the reactionaries of central Europe that if their measures should bring on a war, Great Britain ' would not only be entitled, but called on, to take such steps as circumstances might require to preserve Europe against the consequences of such an injurious and extensive principle of warfare.'

This was in perfect accordance with a line of policy which he had previously marked out : a careful dissociation of the British from the Hanoverian attitude, through the despatch of warnings and admonitions to the German courts. In addition to this, the Foreign Office decided to make at least an ostensible attempt to deprive those courts of the Russian government's support. Now the dissociation of British from Hanoverian policy involved notification to the King that in German affairs William of England must be a person professing and acting upon principles almost diametrically opposed to those which guided William of Hanover. To this delicate task Palmerston addressed himself three days after Bulwer's speech.[45] The instructions which the Foreign Office proposed sending to the British agents at the Austrian and all the German courts stood, he admitted, in opposition to opinions of the King, opinions which were ' deeply rooted, founded upon principle, and therefore not readily to be abandoned.' But his Majesty was reminded that these instructions were based upon principles identical with those which underlay the British constitution itself, and that his ministers, while ready to discountenance popular violence at any time, would ' look with alarm at any endeavour, by the exertion of overruling power, forcibly to deprive nations of rights and privileges which have been solemnly conferred upon them.' For, the sermon proceeded, ' violent changes so brought about are revolutions also ' ; and, by exciting resistance, ' lead to the same consequences which spring from popular violence.' Then followed the application of these rather shop-worn truths :

> . . . Viscount Palmerston is alarmed at the possible consequences which may ensue from the recent proceedings of the Frankfort Diet. He fears that those proceedings may be followed up by violent infringements of the existing constitutions of Germany. He believes the German nations who live under those constitutions to be . . .

not likely to surrender them without a struggle ; and in the present agitated state of Europe, and in the temper of men's minds, from Italy to Belgium, and from the western provinces of France to the Lithuanian Governments of Russia, he thinks that nothing could be more dangerous to established institutions than a war of political opinions commenced upon the Rhine, by the aggression of power against legal rights.

William, with his sailor's appetite, seems to have swallowed both instructions and sermon without visible ill effects.

For the more pampered and sophisticated palate of the Tsar the dose had to be seasoned with some spice of self-interest. The responsibility for dealing with Nicholas was confided to Grey's son-in-law, Lambton, who is more conveniently referred to under the title of earl of Durham, which he was soon to bear. Durham, arch-aristocrat and, as most Englishmen saw it, arch-radical, was sent on a special mission to Nicholas (of which more anon) in the summer of 1832. His instructions laid particular emphasis on the necessity for securing better behaviour from Nicholas regarding the affairs of the Low Countries ; but he was ordered to do all he could in persuading Nicholas to refrain from promising support to the reactionary forces in Germany. Some of the arguments he employed with Nicholas sounded strangely from his lips ; but his instructions had been pitched to the old refrain.[46] Let Nicholas beware of offering military support to Austria and Prussia in any measures they might take to put down German liberalism, lest he help to involve Europe in a general war.

The effectiveness of Durham's mission may be considered more conveniently in another place : here it is sufficient to notice that Metternich's policy of crushing German constitutional development sustained no check either from the British or the Russian government. Palmerston's insistence that England was exercising her treaty rights and performing her duty in protesting against the repressive measures adopted with respect to the German states merely offered Metternich the welcome opportunity of using a little sarcasm on the officious British minister.[47] Austria, he pointed out, was acting with strict legality ; and the Diet was quite competent to look after its own affairs. 'Pray inform Lord Palmerston in a friendly manner of these facts,' he wrote. 'I should not wish him to waste his precious time, which is required for other matters of greater urgency.' The British secretary, quite unabashed by this insolence, became more admonitory still. At last, in October 1832, Metternich, with something of the air of a tutor forced to take measures against an errant child, circularised the other German governments.[48] Regretfully he called on them to take note of the 'complete ignorance of the federal constitution of Germany' and of 'the mass of contradictions in fact and in logic' which Palmerston's presentation of the British case revealed. But he used another tone when he called upon them to defend the independence of the Bund by '*repulsing resolutely and energetically all arbitrary interference in the internal affairs of Germany.*'

For most British foreign secretaries one experience of this sort would probably have been enough. But it was not so with Palmerston. Two years later he had a very similar rencontre. A foolish outbreak by a handful of irresponsible liberal extremists at Frankfort itself, in April 1833, had led to the occupation of the city by troops acting under federal authority. At the beginning of 1834 new measures for curbing liberal activities in Germany were put through by Metternich. Apart from the fact that England had a commercial treaty with the Frankfort senate (from which the latter was already trying to escape) no concrete reason for British interference seems discoverable. Certainly the city requested nothing of the sort.[49] Yet Palmerston, supported by the knowledge that the French government was taking similar action, pushed in. On May 15, 1834, he condescendingly pointed out the great forbearance of Great Britain in not interfering earlier, 'although fully entitled so to do as a contracting party to the Treaty of Vienna, and although authorised, even had no such treaty been signed, to regard as a British interest the maintenance of the political independence of the smallest State in Europe.' Persistence by the Diet in its evil course 'must be regarded by the British Government as a violent infringement of the rights of an independent State, and as involving considerations of a much more serious and extensive nature than belong to a merely federal question between the Diet and a member of the Confederation.'[50] Similar communications, embellished with elaborate arguments founded on the text of the treaties of 1815 and final act of 1820, were forwarded in rapid succession both to the Diet and to some at least of the German courts.[51] Such diplomatic gesturing could have no tangible result save to provoke a fresh diplomatic snub. On this occasion the Diet spoke up bravely for itself. In a set of resolutions, and in notes to the British government which were prepared in part at least under Metternich's eye, and were nothing if not forcible, it followed out to the letter the Austrian chancellor's injunctions of October 1832.[52] But the Diet had no weapons to inflict deep wounds on England ; and each of the active participants gained something after all : Palmerston, the pleasure of bringing his ingenuity, his love of preaching, of arguing, and of blustering into play ; the Frankfort senate, the satisfaction of being justified and encouraged in protesting against the treatment it had received; and the Diet the gratification of reproving an officious British minister.

It seems curious that episodes so barren should reveal so much. They show that Palmerston, even in the time of Grey, had adopted his distinctive course in diplomacy. It was a course which was making his name anathema to most European courts and a troublesome factor in the calculations of the Whigs ; but which was also making that name an elixir for hard-pressed liberals from Warsaw to Madrid, and the boast of the masses of his countrymen. Meddlesomeness, obstinacy, touches of bombast and hauteur, the tendency to create enmities and invite slights, all were there. But with these went evidences of sincerity, of clear and moderate aims, of firmness of purpose, and of the generous if narrow patriotism of him who longs that other countries may enjoy the same constitutional blessings as his own. Practised statesmen could claim that Palmerston was showing himself deficient in the more dignified and far-sighted type of statesmanship ; but for those of his day who feared and hated the polished wiliness of Metternich, or wearied of the cautious correctness of Aberdeen, a combination of sound knowledge, directness, ingenuity and courage had great charms. The simplest could understand ; the most unfortunate could hope.

Meanwhile, Palmerston was being forced to realise the hopelessness of attempting to keep Frankfort outside the Zollverein. The reasons for his failure were summarised by the British envoy to the German Diet, Thomas Cartwright, in December 1834 :

> . . . hemmed in by a line of Custom Houses all round the Gates of the Town, its [Frankfort's] commercial intercourse with the Interior of Germany was greatly harassed and restricted . . . its Commerce and Trade had already fallen off considerably, and . . . great apprehensions were entertained that its Fairs would be irretrievably injured unless the Union with Prussia was speedily effected ; . . . the British Houses . . . finding their old customers deterred from frequenting the Fairs and their buyers diminish, had themselves become the Advocates of the Union with Prussia. . . .[53]

Palmerston showed himself very reluctant to admit that his calculations had been wrong.[54] In February of that year he had been working at Berlin to reduce the pressure on Frankfort : in March he had ordered his minister to Nassau to suggest a commercial treaty which ' might have a beneficial effect in indisposing the Nassau Government to the anticommercial league.' Even when, in May, it became apparent that Frankfort would shortly ask permission to put an end to the treaty of 1832 as a preliminary to her submission to the Prussian league, Cartwright was instructed to avoid discussion of the affair. He might as well have been ordered to avoid discussion of the weather as a method of averting rain. England agreed to release Frankfort from the treaty before the year 1834 had closed.[55]

Remembering how impetuous and aggressive Palmerston showed himself with respect to the affairs of Germany—a country of which he knew and for which he cared comparatively little at any time—one is at first surprised to find that he was correctness and cautiousness itself where Italy was concerned. In February 1831, liberals in Parma, Modena, and the Papal States rose against their autocratic and reactionary governments; and Austria lost little time in sending assistance to the Pope. Yet no denunciations of reactionary rule, no invocations of international arrangements, no declarations even of British interest in fostering the development of constitutional governments, seem to have issued from the fulminator of Downing Street. Indeed, when one remembers the passionate hopes and fears, the romantic longings and deep depression which filled so many Italians at this time, Palmerston's tone seems almost glacial. It may very likely be that Grey and the cabinet exerted themselves for the maintenance of this tone in all pronouncements of an official kind; but Palmerston seems to have adhered to it even in what he wrote privately. His restraint probably testified not only to his dislike of revolution in the abstract, but to the fact that he could master his own proclivities where danger plainly threatened European peace and England's interests. In the Spanish peninsula and at Frankfort the danger of starting a general conflagration was comparatively remote. In Italy, as in Belgium, it was perilous to play with fire. And Palmerston, realising this, struck from the outset what was always to be the keynote of his Italian policy. The great concern of his Majesty's government in giving its attention to the affairs of Italy, he informed the British ambassador at Vienna, on March 22, 1831, was 'the maintenance of peace and the preservation of the balance of power in Europe.'[56] In other words, his main care was to restrain the French and Austrians from once more making a battlefield of northern Italy, lest they should upset the balance which Castlereagh had done so much to produce, and, in doing so, bring on the dreaded general war.

It was not his first pronouncement on the subject. Until March 13, when the French government was taken over by the more moderate French element under Perier, he had gone through very anxious days. When Austrian troops advanced to the assistance of the Pope, France, while receding from an original threat to intervene, insisted that the Austrian occupation should not be prolonged. Faced with the possibility of war, Palmerston summarized England's position neatly to Granville:

It will be impossible for England to take part with Austria in a war entered into for the purpose of putting down freedom and maintaining despotism ; neither can we side with France in a contest the result of which may be to extend her territories ; we shall therefore keep out of the contest as long as we can.[57]

Another letter emphasised still more the fact that in this case his concern for continental liberalism was a secondary matter—almost an afterthought :

If we could by negotiation obtain for them a little share of constitutional liberty, so much the better ; but we are all interested in maintaining peace. . . .[58]

For all that, he was able to work in accordance with his general principles. As the immediate danger of war diminished, he could recollect that the chances for future tranquillity and peace in the Italian peninsula would be greatly furthered by the progress of constitutional reform. Even Metternich, though far from admitting this, acknowledged that the excellent Pope's most execrable government should be improved without delay. Palmerston had apparently failed as yet to realise what small appeal ' a little share of constitutional liberty ' would have for any considerable section of the subjects of his Holiness.[59]

Since the British foreign secretary was all discretion, and since there was nothing like the usual divergence between his policy and that of Metternich, the story of what ensued belongs rather to diplomatic history than to any attempted delineation of the official personality of Palmerston. His belief in the development of constitutional government as the best safeguard against revolution and a possibly resultant war was steadily put forth ; but put forth in a manner studiously unobjectionable. Through the despatch of March 22, in which Palmerston had outlined British aims, Vienna was assured that the Foreign Office had no desire to discuss ' the abstract and not easily defineable principle upon which interference or non-interference should depend,' or to argue whether the notorious grievances of the Pope's subjects had furnished ' a justifiable cause of revolt.' But it would discuss the restoration of tranquillity ' upon such terms as might hold out the prospect of permanent stability,' and was convinced that no permanent stability could be secured through 'the temporary application of external force.' Only such reforms in the Pope's government as might 'render it more consistent with the spirit of the age and the feelings and interests of his people' would be conducive to real settlement. And England agreed with France that the reforms should precede, not follow, the submission of the Pope's subjects to their legitimate government. There was stress, much stress, on this English agreement with the French (Casimir Perier, be it noted, had been in office for nine days), and almost as much on the risk Austria ran of involving herself in a probably unsuccessful war, either with Casimir Perier's or with some more radical and bellicose French government. One feels that Grey, the temperate, may have revised this communication line by line.

England, through Grey and Palmerston, was really proving herself the steadiest friend to Italian liberalism among the Powers. Russia and Prussia consistently supported Metternich. The French government, eager to exploit the situation in its own interest, and driven this way or that by gusts of popular sentiment, now lulled the Pope, now encouraged the liberals. But Palmerston held to his course. He warned France, on the one hand, against encouraging Italian revolutionaries,[60] and Austria, on the other, against fostering the influence of 'the violent party' among the French by allowing her troops to tarry in the Papal States.[61] And he gladly accepted the invitation of both Powers to send a representative, Sir Brook Taylor, to a projected conference on reform between the papal government and the Powers.[62] He realised that his action was certainly irregular, probably unpopular, and quite opposed to 'the Praemunire Law'; [63] but he did not hesitate even to send a second envoy, Sir George Seymour, when the conference reconvened in 1832. Nor did he allow discouragement to halt him in his course. When Austria's influence during and after the conference prevailed, and the other Powers, including France, declined to impose effectual constitutional reforms upon the Pope, he dissociated himself from their common policy. But he strove steadily, by

ENCOURAGING THE ITALIAN LIBERALS

warnings and protests, to bring them to his own unaltered point of view.[64] Moreover, he gave the whole question a publicity which was highly disturbing to the friends of 'order,' by allowing the publication of letters exchanged by the British and Austrian representatives at the conference.[65] Metternich was excessively annoyed:

> The exposure of the British cabinet's views unquestionably constitutes an incitement to revolt for the people of the Roman states, and consequently for those of the entire peninsula . . . . It is impossible to foresee the effects of such a piece of radical folly upon the repose of Italy and that of all Europe.[66]

Even William IV, who approved of Palmerston much more than he did of most of the members of the cabinet,[67] complained that in connection with Italian affairs the Foreign Office was making too much concession to 'the spirit of the times.'[68]

A severe test of Palmerston's ability to cling to his pacific and moderate policy came in 1832. The incompleteness of the Pope's concessions, and his failure to make even those effectual, brought on fresh revolt and a fresh occupation of papal territory by the Austrians. Louis Philippe, 'a grocer put up to be shot at,' in Montalembert's vitriolic phrase, decided that some patriotic gesture was essential for the preservation of what little prestige adhered to his very bourgeois government. Hence a French landing was made at Ancona, where the upholders of French influence flew their tricolour, danced during mass before a church, and disarmed some papal troops. The incident was highly disquieting for Palmerston.[69] Full well he knew that, of the various explanations offered for the French move, that which represented it as 'a countercheck to Austria' and the assertion of 'an equal right of interference' was the most genuine. Yet, feeling that his policy was best served by a show of complete understanding with Louis Philippe's government respecting the affairs of Italy, he adopted the official French contention when explaining the incidents at Ancona to the House. The occupation was designed, he said, only ' to restore the papal states to such a degree of tranquillity as would enable the sovereign to perform those engagements into which he had entered.'[70] The wisdom of his course seemed demonstrated, as the crisis passed rapidly.

In so far as tangible improvements in the Italian situation were concerned, he had to admit ruefully, in 1833, that nothing had been achieved :

> The affairs of Italy seem to be in a miserable state. . . . I speak more particularly of the Papal States and Modena : as to the latter, the Grand Duke is mad. . . . The cardinals are supposed to be in their sound senses, and it is lamentable to see what the sound sense of a cardinal amounts to.[71]

Yet he had achieved some measure of success. He had not only contributed something to the preservation of peace, but had done something to nourish in Italy ' the spirit of the age.' In these and in the following years, informed Italians knew that the government of England would give them at least sympathy in the prosecution of moderate demands. Some of them may even have been aware that the British foreign secretary was, unofficially at least, urging Italian princes to draw together against Austria, and to treat their subjects with some liberality.[72] Whatever his motives, Palmerston's policy in Italy was conducive to something more than ' the maintenance of peace and the preservation of the balance of power.'

CHAPTER VIII

Palmerston and Eastern Europe, 1830–1834

Palmerston was always inclined to be apologetic for his failure to afford any succour or protection to the Poles during and after their first great revolt against the Russian government. When, in 1836, he deplored England's lack of any 'ready means of action' in eastern Europe, he was voicing afresh regrets that he had more than once expressed during the preceding four years. And those regrets pursued him even to his latest days. In 1863, when the Poles were making their second pitiful attempt, he wrote Lord John Russell, his foreign secretary :

> In past times personal influence did much to embarrass the action of the British govt. Mad. Lieven had great influence over Lord Grey and put much water into my wine ; while at Petersburg Durham's inordinate vanity and desire to be well with the Russian court intirely gagged him as our mouth piece about Polish affairs : and accordingly we do not I think stand quite satisfactorily as to our language and course in those times.[1]

His memory, like that of most aged statesmen, was far from trustworthy ; but there is significance in the fact that dissatisfaction had rankled with him for more than thirty years.

And, quite apart from this evidence that his interest in the Polish question was an enduring one, there are special reasons why his reaction to the first Polish revolt should be carefully scrutinised. For there was not in Europe any band of revolutionaries whose cause had less discoverable connection with British interests, or was less fitted to yield even a barren triumph to British diplomacy. The Foreign

Office might excusably, and perhaps wisely, have abandoned the Polish insurgents to their fate in so far as British obligations, interests, or chances of scoring diplomatically were concerned. Whether it could safely have done so in view of the great sympathy with the insurgents displayed by the public and by members of parliament is questionable ; but in any case a gesture or two in favour of the Poles would probably have sufficed. Whigs and Tories were both, though for very different reasons, reluctant to press on the government an active pro-Polish policy.

It is hard to say whether Palmerston's dissatisfaction in later years arose from a feeling that he had done too little for the Poles, or too little in bringing to time the haughty Russian government. His humanitarian sympathy for the insurgents was genuine ; and, in so far as private expression went, quite unconcealed. But his desire to see them succeed in their revolt apparently arose only when the first stage of his duel with France concerning Belgium came to an end, and there was less probability of his needing Russian support to hold a chauvinistic France in check. The Russian tone concerning Belgium, he wrote Granville, four days before Casimir Perier took over the French government, would change when the Russians had subdued the Poles, ' which,' he added ' (were it not for the ill-concealed spirit of aggrandisement of France) I should say I am *afraid* they will.'[2] It was probably no accident that when, two months later, the danger of French aggression in the Netherlands seemed past, and Russia appeared a greater obstacle than France to a final settlement there, his expressions of sympathy for the Poles (still private, of course) were unreserved. For example :

> One cannot help wishing the Poles heartily success ; and one should be glad to help them in any way consistent with our good faith towards Russia.[3]

But what did this solicitude for ' good faith towards Russia ' signify ?

Apparently it signified two things : that good relations with Russia were still highly desirable, whether victory or defeat should perch on Russia's arms ; and that England's stand in treating diplomatically of the Polish revolt was to be taken on the treaty settlements of 1815. For it was on these principles that he based his policy from the outset.[4] And, for all his subsequent dissatisfaction, for all the reproaches he had to sustain from the radicals, it is hard to see that any other policy was possible. Though he urged Austria to observe strict neutrality, and to seize any opportunity for mediation that might present itself ;[5] though he warned Prussia that England would make no move should a Prussian march into Poland cause a French march to the Rhine,[6] both the great German Powers placed themselves firmly on the Russian side. British or French intervention must then have been abortive save through war ; and how could a war which brought the Holy Alliance armies into united action have profited the Poles ? There was little exaggeration in Palmerston's later statement to the House :

> A general war it must certainly have been . . . Austria and Prussia . . . were ready to maintain their opinions at all risks. . . . If, therefore, the Government wished to render the fate of the Poles certain . . . they had but to declare their determination of enforcing the Treaty of Vienna by arms.[7]

He might have added—what must have been equally present in his mind—that such a war would have been fraught with peril for the Belgians and the liberals of central Europe generally. Sound sense, the pledges of his party, the interests of his country, even regard for continental liberalism in its broader aspects, all forbade any action in favour of the Poles save a cautious use of diplomacy.

Even mediation was impracticable. The French government, forced to take heed of a traditionally pro-Polish public sentiment, suggested joint action of this sort in July 1831. But Palmerston declined in no uncertain terms. He was not satisfied merely to point out that Russia's inevitable rejection would present ' an embarrassing alternative' to the mediating Powers. Russia, he informed the French ministers, had lately ' performed . . . all the offices of a good and faithful ally,' and had acted with ' perfect fairness ' with respect to Belgium.[8] He would perhaps have added, had perfect candour been compatible with diplomacy, that he was glad to excuse himself from an acquiescence that would have destroyed his early policy of balancing Russian friendship against French. Nor is it improbable that the Polish envoys were correct in believing the British cabinet definitely concerned 'to prevent Poland, whom it regarded as the natural ally of France, from becoming " a French province upon the Vistula."'[9] At any rate, Palmerston not only refused to consider mediation, but went out of his way to pay public compliments to the Tsar. As late as November 1831, when such cordiality as had at first existed between the Whigs and the Tsar's government was already cooling rapidly, he informed the House that Russia had not been 'in the slightest degree the aggressor' in her recent wars with Turkey and Persia, and that Nicholas, ' a man of high and generous feelings,' was not responsible for cruelties inflicted on the defeated Poles.[10] Two accompanying circumstances lend significance to these praises of the Tsar. For one thing, Palmerston, in delivering them, was risking some unpopularity. For another, he was sending lively protests to St. Petersburg, quite privately of course, at this very time. Public flattery (at some personal cost), combined with private expostulation, constituted his method of working for the Poles.

To be not only *fortiter in re* but *suaviter in modo* was far from his bent; but he seems to have followed the Roman adage in this case at least. No doubt Grey steadily encouraged, if he did not direct, this policy. For the two men seem to have agreed perfectly.[11] Both felt that the Poles in declaring their independence (an independence denied them not only by Russia but by the signatories of 1815) had put themselves in the wrong. Both admitted that Russia could scarcely have acted otherwise than as she did in suppressing the revolt. On the other hand, both were resolved to neglect no means of persuading Nicholas to treat the conquered insurgents mercifully, and of holding him to the grant of Polish autonomy incorporated in the treaty settlements of 1815. Neither premier nor foreign secretary was prepared to sanction breaches of those settlements on either side.

Even within the circumscribed field of action thus marked out, the two directors of British foreign policy had some latitude. There were ways and ways of treating the succession of Polish envoys who came to England to appeal for help ; and there were ways and ways of appealing and protesting to the Tsar. The Polish envoys were frequently received by Palmerston as well as Grey ; but, in their passionate desire for commendation and encouragement, they found him very cold.[12] Their proclamation deposing Nicholas had, he told them, deprived England of the only ground on which she could have interfered. And to what purpose could she interfere ?

We cannot send an army to Poland, and the burning of the Russian fleet would be about as effectual as the burning of Moscow.[13]

All he could do was to tell them unofficially of his regret that their struggle ' had such an unfortunate result,' and to promise that every diplomatic effort should be made on their behalf. Grey gave them little more satisfaction.[14] In one breath he admitted that his government had been ' too timid,' and in the next asked what England could do against Russia, Prussia and Austria. Mme. de Lieven, who protested violently but ineffectually at his inviting Czartoryski to dine with him, admitted his ' very loyal conduct towards Russia during the struggle in Poland.'[15]

There was nothing really distinctive either in Palmerston's policy or in his dealings with Polish envoys ; but there was something decidedly characteristic in the exhortatory tone of his communications concerning the treatment of the conquered insurgents. When the Austrian government imprisoned some Poles who fled across the border for security, handing over their arms and horses to the Russian government, Metternich was informed that such unneutral proceedings produced ' consequences . . . repugnant to the common feelings of mankind.'[16] As for Nicholas and Nesselrode, they were importuned in the name of ' humanity and policy ' to grant complete amnesty to all save assassins, and in the name of the Polish constitution to forbear all proscription and confiscation. The question of ' policy ' was strongly emphasised :

Is it in the very outworks of defence that a prudent administration would incur the risk of having a population disaffected to its government, and ready to join any invader, who might promise them a milder rule, and a better fate ?[17]

Nesselrode accepted with perfect equanimity such of these rather gratuitous admonitions as the prudent British ambassador passed on to him ; and it is possible that they had some effect. It is possible, too, that the 'merciful ukase' which Durham prided himself on having obtained from the Tsar[18] alleviated the miseries of the prostrate rebels. But, if this be so, one shudders to think of the punishment which would otherwise have been inflicted on them.

It need hardly be said that the British government failed utterly to persuade Nicholas that he should leave to his subjects in 'congress' Poland the autonomy conferred on them by the Vienna settlement. But this was not because Palmerston omitted the use of any possible argument.[19] In a series of long and laboriously reasoned despatches he insisted that, since the terms of the treaty of Vienna attached the kingdom of Poland to Russia only through the Polish constitution, the disappearance of the constitution would automatically extinguish Russia's right of sovereignty. Moreover, good faith to the great Powers and consideration for their security were involved. It had been felt in 1815 that Poland garrisoned by native troops would be a very different thing from Poland as a Russian military outpost ; and these considerations had 'acquired additional weight since that time in consequence of the increased security which Russia has acquired on her southern and her Asiatick frontiers.' In other words, Russia would be moving her military frontier westward by some two hundred miles. Nesselrode, while of course denying the validity of those arguments, apparently received them more patiently than Metternich would have done. But, for all that, England's interference, and the dispute which it brought on, must have impaired the friendly relations which had prevailed between the two governments when Grey and Palmerston first came to power.

As a matter of fact, Palmerston's dialectical duel with Nesselrode over the treatment of the Poles constituted a mere side issue in a half-obscured but almost unremitting diplomatic struggle which went on during the early 'thirties between the two greatest empires in the world. It was, of course, largely because England and Russia possessed such strength that the latent hostility between them was never really submerged. Even their disagreements regarding the treatment of continental liberalism were the more pronounced because England's naval supremacy seemed so great a potential asset to the liberals of the west, and Russia's huge armies constituted the final resource of the autocracies of the centre and the east. It was true that Russia operated under great disadvantages in making her policy effective in Greece, in the Low Countries and in the Spanish Peninsula ; and that England could offer little but sympathy to Germans, Poles, or even Italians when the weight of the 'Holy Alliance' pressed down on them. But the two governments did not love one another the better for the fact that neither could prevail where the other's allies and principal fighting arm gave distinct superiority. As for geographical points of possible contact or actual rivalry between the two empires, these points seemed almost to stretch 'from Greenland's icy mountains to India's coral strand.' Or at least the English saw them so. The Russian octopus was using one tentacle to fortify the Aaland Islands and another to penetrate Khiva, thus challenging the British empire's defensive power at points two thousand miles apart. And most of the tentacles, so it seemed from the windows of Downing Street, were closing in around the decadent but very useful Turkish empire, threatening to cut off England's influence at the Sublime Porte, to strangle her Black Sea trade, and from a second direction to threaten India. The growing Russian pressure on Persia was but another move in the same nefarious game. Even had the Foreign Office realised that Russia had, for the time being, relinquished the idea of taking any more of Turkey's European territory, its general attitude towards the Tsar's government would probably have been much the same. Russia was too powerful and too bent on becoming more powerful still.

Yet Mme. de Lieven had been quite delighted at the

advent of the Whigs, and especially of Grey and Palmerston. The reason was, of course, that the war of Greek independence had momentarily abated the anti-Russian feeling of the new ministers. The Whigs for a brief interval saw Russia as a protector of the abused and struggling Greeks : the Canningites shared some of the same sentiment, and remembered, too, that to restrain the Russians by embracing them had been their dead master's policy. But, Greece once free, Russia appeared again as the dark champion of autocracy at every European court, and especially as the brutal oppressor of the Poles. Rapidly she became once more antipathetic to both Whigs and Canningites ; and as rapidly all her offences against England, actual and putative, again became evident. While the ministry was in its infancy, the Princess Lieven found the Whigs desirous of 'a good understanding with all—but especially with Russia'; nor did she know anyone of 'better judgment, juster views, and greater propriety' than Palmerston.[20] Nesselrode regarded the future as full of hope.[21] Even as late as May 1832, Count Orloff, on special mission to the British government, reported that both Grey and Palmerston were anxious to continue on good terms with the Russian government.[22] This was doubtless true ; but it was also true that both had become suspicious and irritated. The sending of Durham to St. Petersburg at this time, itself a friendly act, was witness to the dissatisfaction which Palmerston and Grey shared.

For Palmerston instructed Durham to turn the Tsar from evil courses by gentle remonstrances, by assurances regarding England's policies, and by a warning, delicate but quite discernible.[23] Since, in the Belgian question, England's 'main difficulties for the last year and a quarter' had 'come directly or indirectly from the Emperor Nicholas,' Durham's first task was 'to work a change in the feelings of Russia' regarding this issue. But he was also to exert himself 'in favour of the wretched Poles' ; to 'get Russia to lean a little to the view of England' where the papal dominions were concerned ; to argue against the Tsar's promising military support to Metternich in 'the conflicts about to take place in the south-west of Germany' ; and to discuss 'the designs supposed to be entertained by Russia upon the district of Khiva . . . the possession of which would place her in immediate contact with rivers, navigable down to the northern frontiers of our Indian possessions.' He was to give Nicholas the comfortable assurance that the Whigs, 'though friends of free institutions,' were neither 'promoters of revolution' nor bound in any 'connection offensive in its tendencies' with the French. But he was also to see that the Tsar realised the existence of a close Anglo-French 'defensive connection.' The instructions were issued just eighteen months after Mme. de Lieven had found Palmerston 'perfect in every way.' Grey, who was, of course, jointly responsible for them, had given emphatic expression to his irritation over Russia's activities in the Belgian and Polish questions during the preceding January.

The effects of the Durham mission are hard to gauge.[24] The Tsar, anxious at all times to weaken the Anglo-French entente, and well coached by his indefatigable ambassadress at the British court, overwhelmed the envoy with flatteries from the outset.[25] He bestowed on Durham the signal honour of meeting his vessel at Cronstadt. Indeed, according to report, nothing would do but that he should go aboard the ship, taste the sailors' soup, and drink the health of William IV (knowing well that William detested him) in sailors' grog. At St. Petersburg Durham was again cajoled in a manner that might have been offensive to a man less consumed with vanity. And, while he did not receive very definite assurances of any sort, the Tsar and Nesselrode poured out soothing words. They took especial care, it seems, to contrast British honour with Louis Philippe's unreliability;[26] and even attempted to trap Durham into a step which might have damaged the Anglo-French entente.[27] At any rate, Durham regarded his mission as a great success. He wrote that he had even induced Nicholas to send Pozzo di Borgo on a special journey to Vienna and Berlin, where he would presumably second British efforts to combat Austrian and Prussian pressure on the minor German states. Palmerston no doubt shared some of Durham's satisfaction that the mission had gone well, but hardly Durham's confidence as to its probable results.[28] That he spoke of it as having been 'perfectly successful' in the House [29] can be taken both as a defence of his own policy and as evidence of his desire to keep Nicholas in play. He even seconded Durham's efforts, by deprecating the violent attacks being made on the Tsar in parliament.[30]

He might have kept the Russian court in play longer still if Durham and the Princess Lieven, counting on the influence each possessed with Grey, had not forced themselves too much into the game. Each was haughty and officious; and each was a trial to Palmerston. No doubt he made allowances for Durham's ill-health and terrible domestic griefs; but Durham's known desire to have the Foreign Office seals, his conviction of his own infallibility, and his tendency to bully Grey, his father-in-law, would have made him a trial to a foreign secretary far less self-willed than Palmerston. As for the fascinating and redoubtable princess, one must regretfully conclude that she was not only an arch intriguer but a spy as well. As gifted as she was unscrupulous, as enticing as she was false and passionate, she had achieved a commanding position in the coterie which dominated English society and politics.[31] She used this position not only for the advantage of her own government, but for the support of reactionary principles everywhere. She had wormed her way into the affection and confidence of Grey, only to send reports of his every utterance to St. Petersburg, and to deride and abuse him when he especially displeased her by his policies.[32] She had established an affectionate intimacy with Lady Cowper, and was said to make capital out of being on such terms with the foreign secretary's reputed mistress. And Palmerston, knowing these things, knew also what her friendship had cost some of his former Tory associates. Outwardly, he and she remained on the best of terms; but, in the autumn of 1832, there was developing between them a contest which deeply involved the relations between their respective governments.

This contest had to do with the appointment of a new British ambassador at St. Petersburg.[33] When Lord

Rischgitz

THE PRINCESS LIEVEN

(*From Lawrence, in the National Gallery*)

Heytesbury, an appointee of Wellington's, and a man *persona gratissima* to the Russian court, resigned in 1832, Mme. de Lieven sent home the information that Stratford Canning was likely to be appointed in his place. Since Canning was due for appointment to some high diplomatic post, since his career had given him an almost unrivalled personal knowledge of affairs in the Near East, and since he had served at St. Petersburg in 1824, the appointment was obviously a proper one. But Nicholas and Nesselrode had been fearing and attempting to forestall it ever since the advent of Grey's ministry. Although unable or unwilling to support their action by any excuse save Canning's undoubted faults of temperament, and the fact that it was especially important to have a British ambassador with whom they could work easily at a time when a new crisis was developing in the Near East, they used every device to gain their point. They asked both Durham and the Princess Lieven to block the appointment ; they 'implored' Palmerston to send someone else ; and they ended by instructing the Russian ambassador that Canning would not be acceptable. It is possible that, had the matter rested there, Palmerston might have given in. But the Princess Lieven and Durham, who had imprudently given separate assurances to the Russian court that the appointment would never actually be made, bestirred themselves with Grey.[34] Hence Palmerston was doubly challenged, and doubly determined to persist. Believing that Russia's real objection either arose from a fear that Canning would serve his country all too well, or else was ' a mere remnant of the apostolical and holy-alliance abomination of the name of Canning,'[35] he considered that British prestige was involved. Irritated that the Princess Lieven and Durham should try to override him in a matter that lay peculiarly within his own province, he felt the issue to be personal as well. Yet it is unsafe to assume, as did Talleyrand, that the issue was primarily personal. Grey and the cabinet would hardly have given the foreign secretary firm support merely to gratify his *amour propre*. And support him they did to such effect that Canning's appointment was gazetted at the end of October 1832. A dispute between the two governments, trivial in origin but none the less damaging to good relations, had begun.

The diplomatic exchanges by which it was carried on show once again that Palmerston's provocative and haughty manner was in evidence long before he was freed from the tutelage of Grey. As the quarrel progressed through the autumn of 1832 and the winter and spring following, Nesselrode passed from protests to entreaties, from entreaties to a bribe in the shape of the highest Russian order for Canning, and at last to a flat refusal to receive the man whom Nicholas had just offered to decorate. Palmerston, who, on account of Russia's unpopularity with the British parliament and public, and of the ministry's desire to avoid open hostility between the two countries, lived 'in daily dread of having the whole matter forced into discussion in the House of Commons,'[36] apparently conducted all real negotiations by private correspondence with Bligh, the attaché at St. Petersburg. No despatches could have been firmer in tone. Thus, on October 27 :

> With respect to Nesselrode's own objections, *if he should continue to press them*, make him understand very civilly that the King of England is the best judge of whom it may be for the good of his service to employ . . . and that we cannot allow any foreign authority to dictate to us on such matters or to *taboo* our best men *merely because they are so* . . .[37]

And on May 14, 1833, when Nesselrode protested that England was departing from established international usage :

> . . . even if it were the universal rule of the Continent, that is nothing to us ; it is a rule we cannot subscribe to on account of our peculiar constitution.[38]

Yet he seemed at this very time genuinely desirous of securing a friendly settlement of the dispute. He asked Canning's reception not only as a right but as a 'kindness' ; and promised that Canning, once received, should immediately be withdrawn. But Nicholas, refusing to give way, and unwilling any longer to be represented at London by an ambassador while England had only a chargé at his court, had apparently decided to recall the Lievens before Palmerston's letter of May 14 had reached St. Petersburg.

It is rather a nice question whether Talleyrand was right in asserting that Palmerston manipulated the affair with a deliberate intention of removing the Princess Lieven from his path.[39] If so, he left little trace of his design. He certainly foresaw, as early as December 14, 1832, that the Lievens might be recalled.[40] But, in so far as actual evidence goes, it seems impossible to go beyond the ambiguous explanation which the well-informed Lady Cowper gave, in February 1833, to Charles Greville:

> Palmerston was provoked with her [the Princess Lieven's] interference ... and ... he had thought both *she* and her *Court* wanted to be taken down a peg ... and, what had done more harm than anything, she had appealed to Grey against Palmerston, and employed Durham to make a great clamour about it. All this made Palmerston angry, and determined him to punish her. ...[41]

Whatever his intentions, he had brought upon the Princess a punishment which almost broke her heart. And, incidentally, he had done much to sweep away the veneer of cordiality which had been maintained between the British and the Russian governments.

In any case, appearances of cordiality could not long have been maintained; for Grey and Palmerston were learning (if they had need to learn) how utterly Durham had failed to convert Nicholas and Nesselrode. By October 1832, both were complaining bitterly that Russia still stood in the way of a final settlement in the Low Countries;[42] the Princess Lieven had discovered that Palmerston was 'a poor small-minded creature'; and Bligh was explaining to Nesselrode that England, no longer able to work with the despotic Powers, was being forced into closer union with France. In early December Grey pointed out to the Princess that Pozzo's promised German tour had not worked out at all as Durham had foretold:[43]

> There is not a Court in Germany through which he has passed, from which we have not had accounts of his holding the most hostile language, and describing this Administration as Jacobinical, and so reprobated by the most powerful classes in the country that it could not stand.

Pozzo, Grey added, could hardly have used such language 'if he had thought it would not be approved of' at St. Petersburg. And how could the Princess justify Pozzo's incitement of the Spanish government to give aid to Miguel? Palmerston, who was at least equally incensed, reserved a good deal of his own particular ammunition to be fired at Pozzo direct. When the Russian envoy reached England in January 1833, the foreign secretary fell on him with all of Grey's charges and a surprising catalogue of new ones.[44] Pozzo was accused of inciting the Spanish government to attack the French in case France and the Holy Alliance came to blows; and of offering Russia's 'Polish' army to the Prussian king. Again, Palmerston charged the Russian government with trying 'to drive Prussia and Austria into a war,' and the Russian embassy at London with conspiring with the Tories against Grey's government. While the last-mentioned accusation was unquestionably true,[45] some of the others were so far-fetched as to raise the suspicion that Palmerston was 'drawing' Pozzo. Even at that, his recriminations show how far the two governments had drifted from their former cordiality. The point is worth stressing when one remembers that, while Palmerston was berating Pozzo, and while the diplomatic world was still wondering what was to be the outcome of the dispute over Stratford Canning's appointment at St. Petersburg, a new crisis of first-rate importance was developing in the affairs of the Near East.

The new crisis arose from the first war of Mehemet Ali, the able, ambitious and warlike pasha of Egypt, against his suzerain, the Sultan. Encouraged by the apparent imminence of the break-up of the Turkish empire, and considering himself ill requited for his services against the Greeks, Mehemet set out to secure by force the government of Syria and, if possible, a more independent status for Egypt. Month after month his armies pushed on through Jaffa, Acre, Damascus and Antioch, until in the autumn of 1832, the Sultan, fearing that the Egyptians might even cross the Straits, appealed to the British and French governments for aid. Russia, all eagerness to use so heaven-sent an opportunity, offered, on her own initiative, all the help that the

Sultan could want. Here, indeed, was a call to action for any Canningite.

But Palmerston's problem was a far more complicated one than that which Canning had faced five years before. It was no longer merely a question of keeping Russia from feeding on the Turkish empire. The spectacular rise of Egypt as an oriental Power which might rival or even displace Turkey was a new element of vast significance. And of vast significance for England in particular. Steam transportation was making the Mediterranean once more a great highway to India, and the favoured route lay through Egypt. Just at this time, too, the possibilities of developing the alternative route by Asia Minor and the Euphrates were being probed.[6] Considering this, would it be to England's profit or to England's loss if Egypt became independent or quite autonomous ? Would it be wise or unwise to permit her expansion to the east, when this expansion would give her command of both overland routes to India ? Would Mehemet, if allowed to increase his power, facilitate or obstruct Russia's advance, especially where Persia was concerned ? Or would he deliver himself to France ; and would France, as Metternich suggested, secretly abet Mehemet in his schemes, even while pretending to co-operate with the British government ? French ambitions in the Mediterranean were becoming more apparent year by year. Such were some of the eventualities which Egypt's new position opened up ; and Palmerston, considering them, had also to keep in mind the old dangers which sprang from Russia's desire to dominate Constantinople and the Straits. Russian naval superiority in the eastern Mediterranean would always threaten the overland routes to India ; and Russia, so long as she controlled the Black Sea, would be well-nigh invulnerable in so far as England was concerned.

Since most if not all of these questions must have presented themselves to Palmerston at a moment when his attention was being claimed by developments throughout western and central Europe, it is hardly to be wondered at that he hesitated as to the line of policy that he should pursue. For hesitate he did. When, in December 1832,

Stratford Canning sent a despatch urging him to assist the Turks without delay, he annotated it copiously with shrewd queries and comments which show how open was his mind.[47] Was not 'the unwieldy extent of the Turkish Empire one great check to the improvement of its industry and commerce, and possibly one great cause of its external weakness?' He could not see that 'progress in civilization and reform' had been advanced by England's previous restoration of Egypt to Ottoman suzerainty ; nor that Mehemet's 'forcible suppression of minor nationalities' was essentially less 'legitimate' than the Turk's. As to one matter, however, he was quite decided. For practical reasons, he dismissed the suggestion that England should intervene single-handed and blockade the coasts of Egypt and Syria.

With respect to the negotiations which progressed from October 1832 to the following July, it is more interesting to know what Palmerston thought than what he did. For the negotiations were quite ineffectual in so far as he was concerned. In spite of him, Russia was able to make herself the saviour of the Turks by the use of ships and troops, and to exact a heavy price. In spite of him, Mehemet took possession of Syria. But Palmerston at least gained experience and a definite point of view on Near Eastern affairs—commodities which were to come in very useful before many years had passed.

There is some evidence that, during the first months, he showed himself not only undecided in his views, but less quick to take up his dead leader's line of policy than were some of his colleagues. On December 21, the Turkish armies, making a last stand at Konieh, were completely crushed. The French government, as concerned as the British to rob Russia of her opportunity, and working as usual to stimulate British fears of Russian encroachment,[48] proposed to Palmerston a joint armed mediation in which Austria should be asked to join.[49] Palmerston agreed ; but the cabinet, more Canningite than he, decided that Russia should also be invited to take a hand. In the end the project came to nothing. Metternich might have co-operated with England ; but he suspected the French of giving Mehemet secret support.[50] And there were those in France who felt that Talleyrand, in urging joint action, was playing England's game.[51]

By mid-February of 1833 Palmerston had come to a definite position, and even to the line of policy which he was to follow for many years. He had reached it in part at least during his discussion of joint intervention with Talleyrand; and he elaborated it, on February 17, in a letter to Lord Ponsonby, his ambassador at the Porte.[52] England would object both to any increase of Egypt's autonomy and to Mehemet's acquisition of all Syria:

> The danger likely to result from the occupation of Syria by Mehemet is that he might thereby acquire the command of Mesopotamia down to the Persian Gulph. This would certainly follow if he had the Pashalik of Aleppo; Acre alone, or even with Damascus added to it would not give him the command of the Euphrates.

It was to become almost a maxim of the British Foreign Office that Egypt should not control both routes.[53] Palmerston went on to confess his inability to decide whether Russia wished Mehemet to weaken Turkey's power, or whether the Tsar's respect for 'legitimacy' would induce him 'as a point of honour and precedent' to compel Mehemet's 'unconditional submission to his Sovereign.' But England could always proceed on one safe principle:

> In the absence of grounds for judgment one must go by the general rules and believe that where Russian agents are employed there must be intrigue on foot.

It is hardly too much to say that this, too, became or perhaps better remained, a maxim of British foreign policy. Finally, Palmerston suggested a line of action on which England and other would-be preservers of Turkey were long to act. The Sultan should modernise his country by employing European experts, and, in particular, British officers to train his navy and his troops. Moreover:

> He should place his fiscal system upon a better footing: prevent his pashas from plundering his subjects . . . pay . . . fixed salaries . . . to his pashas . . . his wealth and resources would rapidly increase. . . .

So, and in considerable detail, Palmerston's charmingly

optimistic plans for the regeneration of the Turkish empire flowed on. It all seemed so very obvious to a minister who had presided in the Foreign Office for little more than two years. Strange to say, he did not suggest for Turkey a constitution of the British type, admitting handsomely instead that the Koran was 'a very good code of human laws.' But he urged that the Sultan should give his sons an European education ' above all.'

Whatever the virtues of these policies, they could not yield immediate fruits ; and suggestions for saving Turkey by a five-Power conference were denied even a trial by the fact that Palmerston and Metternich were each resolved that discussion should take place at his own capital.[54] Hence Syria and the ports of Adana soon passed into Mehemet's hands. In April and May, the British Foreign Office even assisted in reconciling the Sultan to their sacrifice. And, what was far more serious, the British and French governments entirely failed to balk the Russians of their desires. The Tsar took advantage of the misunderstandings and dilatoriness of England, France and Austria to make himself the saviour of the Sultan by sending ships and troops against the Egyptians. Palmerston fumed to the Austrian envoy in London about the necessity of ' breaking up Russia's influence ' and ' forcing back to its proper limits this half-barbarian nation,' which had ' nothing in common with modern civilization ' ;[55] but fuming did no good. It seemed more to the point that when terms of peace between Turkey and Egypt were agreed upon, and the Tsar invited to call his soldiers and sailors home, British and French squadrons lay off Smyrna to assist the Sultan, if need arose, in speeding his now useless guests.

But even this warning gesture proved of no avail ; for, as Palmerston was so ready to assume, Russian ' intrigue ' was very much at work. The Russians departed with good grace. But, as London and Paris discovered at the beginning of August, they shackled the Turks in return for their aid. The treaty of Unkiar Skelessi, which they signed with the Sultan's ministers on July 8, was bad enough in establishing a Russo-Turkish alliance, with provision for mutual assistance in time of hostilities. But when it transpired (Lord Ponsonby at Constantinople discovered the fact within four days) [56] that the Russians had in addition secured a secret Article, which bound Turkey in wartime to open the Straits to Russian ships alone, the worst fears of the British and French ministers appeared to have been realised. Russia had, as regards naval warfare, become almost invulnerable ; England's power in the Levant, naval and commercial, had apparently received a staggering blow ; and Turkey, which Palmerston had tried at least to rescue from Egypt, seemed delivered over to the Russian octopus. To see the situation in this light was, of course, to see it at its worst, and under the fullest developments which could be drawn from it by Russian policy. There was still the question whether those developments need be permitted to transpire. It was one of the greatest challenges which Palmerston had so far faced.

No doubt he found the situation especially humiliating from the fact that, during the three days which followed the signature of the treaty, he had twice assured parliament of his trust in the Russian government's good faith.[57] He seemed at the time almost to have divined the fact that Russia had temporarily given up the idea of expanding at Turkey's expense. For he informed the House that 'he had great doubts that any intention to partition that empire at all entered into the policy of the Russian government.' After news of the treaty of Unkiar Skelessi had arrived, he could do no more than excuse the government's failure to help Turkey in the autumn of 1832. He pointed out that the naval operations in progress at that time on the coasts of Holland and Portugal made it impossible to spare ships for the Levant from the establishment which parliament (not then in session) had authorised.[58] His excuse was an honest one enough ; but it did not in the least alter the fact that he had been deceived by Russian 'intrigue,' and that his policy had received a serious check. In diplomatic intercourse his rage quite got the better of him. So intemperate were his expressions regarding Prussia's 'cowardice and weakness' that he found it necessary to apologise.[59]

For the time being there was not much that could be

done. 'They are half dead with fright,' wrote the delighted Princess Lieven, ' and all we need do is to jeer at them.'[60] Palmerston warned the Turks that, in fulfilling their treaty obligations, they might at some future time compel England to treat them as enemies : but the ratification of the treaty was rushed through before his threats and protests reached the hands of the Sultan. In September, the 'Holy Alliance' meeting at Münchengrätz strengthened Russia's position by re-affirming the solidarity of the relations between the great eastern Powers. The British could do nothing but sputter threats.[61] The King delivered one of them in closing parliament ; and Palmerston was gratified that he brought out the words with emphasis and watched the impression they made on the Russian ambassador.[62] More offensive by far, however, to the Tsar and his government was a note of protest indited jointly by the French and British governments.[63] It was, according to Pozzo, the fact that the note was a joint one which especially grated on Russian sensibilities ;[64] and Palmerston, in forwarding it to Bligh, took pains to rub this feature in :

> The Russian government must not be surprized if other combinations should be contemplated for the purpose of counteracting the dangerous consequences which might result to other States.[65]

He obtained the reward of learning that he had produced irritation not only at St. Petersburg but at Berlin.[66]

These sputterings would have been quite inexcusable if real and deep anxiety had not lain behind. Reports were reaching London that insurrection at Constantinople was probable.[67] Hence, the Russians seemed likely to return under the terms of the treaty of July, and England to be faced with the alternative of abandoning Turkey to her fate or embarking in what was likely to prove a general war. For months the danger lingered on, with the fleet prepared at need to force the Dardanelles and meet the Russians in the Bosphorus.[68] At Christmas-time it was, as the Princess Lieven said, *chance égale* that peace would be maintained.[69] Grey showed little more optimism.[70] Only in the middle of February 1834, could Charles Greville conclude that 'the storm that impended over Europe' had 'blown off.'[71]

The war clouds passed because no occasion for testing the treaty of Unkiar Skelessi had happened to arise, and because both England and Russia wished to avoid a clash. Palmerston made a conciliatory overture by suggesting that frank explanations should be exchanged ; and Nesselrode responded eagerly.[72] The treaty of July should, he declared, be regarded merely as a moral guarantee that Turkey should not be invaded or conquered by an Arab Power. Nor did Russia expect to draw from it any exclusive advantages for her flag. Palmerston was glad to transmit these assurances to parliament ;[73] but in his dealings with the Tsar's government his tone remained distinctly tart. He was happy to note Russia's friendliness and disavowal of all hostility ; but he found several of the recent actions of the Tsar's government insufficiently accounted for. He could not understand why the Russian Black Sea fleet had just been re-equipped, why the Crimean army was still concentrated, why new fortresses were being built in Poland, and, above all, why the Aaland Islands were being fortified. The frank explanations had not done much to abate his hostility ; and he was able to give his hostility free rein. 'Lord Palmerston laughs at his colleagues' game and at all the world,' wrote the Princess Lieven, bitterly.[74]

He was, in fact, as far as possible from being at ease concerning the Near East, or from feeling any confidence in Russian protestations of friendship. For he had reverted to an entire misunderstanding of Russian policy. Thus, he had written Ponsonby on December 6 :[75]

> No reasonable doubt can be entertained that the Russian Govt. is intently engaged in the prosecution of those schemes of aggrandizement towards the South, which ever since the reign of Catherine have formed a prominent feature of Russian policy.

He had gone on to point out that, while he could for the present only 'wait to see the course of events,' he hoped, with the co-operation of the French government, to prevent the Russians from being able to put their treaty into force :

> ... Russia would not risk the consequences which would follow a reoccupation of the Bosphorus, without an invitation from the Sultan ; & the Sultan would not give her an invitation unless to

relieve himself from some great and pressing danger. That danger could arise only from a renewed rupture with Mehemet Ali, or from some serious insurrection in some part of the Turkish Empire.

The influence of Great Britain & France has been, & will be, exerted to prevent Mehemet Ali from commencing any aggression against the Sultan ; and while those two Powers have a strong naval force in the Mediterranean, there can be little chance that the Pasha of Egypt will, in neglect of their remonstrances, again take up arms against his Sovreign [sic].

Your Excellency is instructed, on the other hand, to take every proper occasion strongly to deprecate any proceedings on the part of the Sultan, calculated to excite Mehemet Ali. . . .

And he had closed with a warning to the Sultan :

. . . if the British Govt. should ever be reduced to the necessity of choosing between the Establishment at Constantinople of the Power of Mehemet Ali, or the subjection of that Capital to the Power of Russia, it would be impossible that we should not prefer the former of these alternatives.

This threat, repeated to Prince Lieven, and apparently conveyed to St. Petersburg in garbled form, had drawn complaints from Nesselrode.[76]

'Wait to see' had become, and was for some time to continue, the motto of Palmerston in his Near Eastern policy. While waiting he would do his best to prevent a fresh Turko-Egyptian war, and to assist the Sultan in strengthening his country in view of a possible contest.[77] And he would keep a particularly watchful eye on proceedings at St. Petersburg. Though written in April, 1834, a letter to his brother gives a fair idea of the state of Anglo-Russian relations when, seven months later, he gave up the Foreign Office seals : [78]

With Russia we are just as we were, snarling at each other, hating each other, but neither wishing for war.

Although suspicions concerning French designs in North Africa and the Levant were already thoroughly aroused,[79] so thoroughly that Peel had referred to them in the House,[80] Palmerston still preferred to reserve all or nearly all of his misgivings regarding the Near Eastern question for the Tsar.

CHAPTER IX

PALMERSTON, THE WHIGS AND THE ENTENTE CORDIALE,
1834–1835

ON the night of November 14, 1834, Palmerston, on his way back from a dinner at Holland House, called in to see Melbourne, and received the startling news that he and all his colleagues were to have an involuntary holiday. Melbourne, who had replaced Grey as prime minister in July, had just been dismissed by the King. The foreign secretary, though very much surprised, took the news calmly; for he was rightly convinced that parliament and country would make short work of the Tory government under Peel and Wellington which King William was preparing to install.[1] In fact, he was cheerful enough to indulge in an unheard-of piece of *gaminerie*. He directed his envoy at Vienna to hand Metternich a letter in which he expressed his conviction that the news of his fall from power would give the Austrian chancellor such pleasure as he had never before experienced.[2] Cuttingly, Metternich replied that he was sorry to note this new instance of Palmerston's frequent errors concerning facts and persons. Being as yet unable to determine what effects the change at the Foreign Office might produce, he felt not pleasure but merely ' hope.'

William's irregular action in dismissing his prime minister was bitterly resented and criticised : but it was taken with some collusion on Melbourne's part ; and it gave the Whigs a useful breathing space. For the ministry, although still commanding a safe majority, was encountering difficulties on every side. The King, offended and alarmed by the Reform Bill, by the measures taken to pass it into law, and by other aspects of the cabinet's domestic and foreign policies, had been hostile for some time. The House of Lords was now Tory by a large majority ; most of the press was unfriendly; and there were sections of the party's supporters among the electorate which showed dissatisfaction with the cabinet, either for listening too frequently to the advanced wing of the party, or for not listening frequently enough. Worse still, divisions of opinion had appeared among the ministers and among their supporters in the lower House. The touchstone, as with so many nineteenth-century ministries, was the question of Ireland. In 1834 two phases were involved : the repression of disorder through coercion acts, and the reform of the Irish church. Differences of opinion regarding both phases produced, or helped to produce, successive crises in the cabinet, —crises which had the general effect of liberalising the conservative Whig-Canningite ministry which Grey had formed.

Palmerston's privately expressed comments on these crises afford much of what little light is to be had on his relation to domestic policies at this time. In May 1834, Graham, Stanley, Goderich and the duke of Richmond resigned in protest against their more liberal colleagues' view that the government had the right to dispose of the surplus revenues of the Irish church. Palmerston blamed Durham, quite unjustly as it seems, for producing the crisis in the hope of replacing Grey ; and regretted the loss of Graham, Stanley and Goderich as ' most intimate friends.'[3] But he showed neither inclination to follow them, nor even dissatisfaction over the removal of their conservative influence from the cabinet. And in public he decisively took the other side, declaring in the House his conviction that 'the property of the [Irish] Church was not to be looked at in the same light as the property of individuals, and that it was for the Legislature to determine in what manner that property . . . should be distributed.'[4] The Tories later accused him of pandering to radicals and O'Connellites through love of ' place ' ; but he had always shown liberality where religion was concerned. His attitude towards the Irish question in general was defined in a letter to his brother concerning the Coercion Bill of 1833 :
. . . this reformed House of Commons is passing the most violent bill ever carried into a law . . . but . . . there is the difference

THE 'DISMISSAL' OF THE MINISTRY

between us and Metternich or the Pope ; we coerce as they do, but then we redress grievances as they do not.[5]

He was in a ' middle ' position as usual.

The succeeding cabinet crisis in July, which resulted in fresh liberal gains, left him equally unperturbed.[6] He was sorry to see the substitution of Melbourne for Grey, even though the new prime minister was Lady Cowper's brother, and a man of conspicuously easy-going temperament. But it was enough for him that government by ' extreme parties ' should be avoided, and the administration left in the hands of Whig moderates. As usual, he had his eye partly on the continent :

> The result which has now happened must surely undeceive those foreign governments which have been speculating on the return of the Tories to power. It must prove to them that the Tories cannot come back to office, let what will happen to be the government of the day. . . . That consequently . . . the political system of England is settled and unchangeable. They ought, therefore . . . not to be perpetually thwarting us. . . . This has been the mistake of Metternich in all his dealings with England since 1830.

There was a good deal of political insight in his perception, so early as the summer of 1834, that the old Tory party had passed away.

And now, in November, there had come the dismissal of the ministry.[7] Althorp had been forced by the death of his father to go up to the House of Lords ; and Melbourne, in consulting the King with respect to the choice of a new leader in the lower House, had inquired in his casual way whether his Majesty would prefer ' seeking other advice.' William, disturbed over the question of the Irish church, had pondered the matter and decided in the affirmative. It has been noted that Palmerston had no fear that Peel and Wellington would be able to carry on for any length of time; but he was very much concerned lest ' the collateral effect of the storm ' by which they would be ' driven away ' would work out to the benefit of the group soon to be known as Chartists. What would the Tories do ?

> Either they will dissolve, or they will not. If they do not, they will be outvoted in the Commons, and every man there expecting a

dissolution, every man who has liberal constituents will be making violent speeches and declarations, in order to curry favour with his electors. If they dissolve, then matters will be worse, because, though they may gain sixty or seventy votes, yet that will not give them a majority ; and the greater part of the rest of the House will have been tempted on the hustings to pledge themselves chin-deep to most extravagant measures. Triennial Parliaments, ballot, and universal household suffrage will be the cry on almost every hustings, and no man who does not bid as high as that will have any chance in the great towns. The Tories will be turned out ; and then it will be difficult to make a Government which shall be acceptable to the Commons, and shall not at the same time consist of men pledged to all sorts of extreme measures.[8]

His dislike of ' extreme parties ' was always in evidence.

He was, in fact, quite generally in sympathy with his late colleagues' policies. By 1833 he had lost all fear of the consequences of the Reform Bill :

. . . I must say that this reformed House of Commons is growing to be wonderfully like all its predecessors : impatient of fools, intolerant of blackguards, tired with debate, and disposed generally to place confidence in Government upon all matters which the members do not understand, or in which their particular constituents have not a direct interest. Property and land are strong in this House, and it is highly Conservative.[9]

Of the principle of free trade he was as much as ever the advocate, promising the House that England, by repealing protective duties, could compel other nations to follow her, and arraigning English protectionists as ' the true encouragers, both of smuggling and prohibition in other countries.'[10] It is true that he opposed any immediate alteration in the corn laws ;[11] but here he was acting with the ministry ; and he was careful to point out that he considered action inadvisable only for the time. If he had little or no part in the great humanitarian reforms to which the Grey-Melbourne ministry so largely owes its fame, it is probably because he really lacked the time.

For he had given almost all his thought and energies to the Foreign Office, performing there what he believed to be ' more intense and uninterrupted labour than almost any man ever went through before.'[12] It had unquestionably been far more exacting than that of his War Office days. At the beginning he had felt himself 'like a man who has plumped into a mill-race, scarcely able by all his kicking and plunging to keep his head above water.'[13] That feeling passed; but there were times when he regarded with consternation the piles of Foreign Office boxes which pursued him everywhere. He found it consoling, when the influenza laid him low, to shut out the diplomatic world, so that he would not be 'tied to the stake, to be baited as long as they chose to bestow their tediousness' upon him.[14] Otherwise, he seems never to have relaxed. It was a matter of pride that the business of his office should never be more than one day in arrear, and seldom as much as that.[15] Brougham regarded the Foreign Office as one of the two 'best administered' departments in the government;[16] and the House had the satisfaction of seeing diplomatic and consular salaries greatly reduced.[17] But it was not merely his fidelity in performing the ordinary functions of a foreign secretary which made his labour so intense. To an extent which cannot accurately be determined but was certainly unusual, he conducted some of the more delicate diplomatic negotiations by private letters written with his own hand. According to Wellington, he employed this method in commencing the mediation between France and the United States;[18] and he certainly used it in connection with the later phases of the Belgian question[19] and in the dispute with Russia concerning Stratford Canning's appointment as ambassador.[20] He paid the price of his diligence in confinement to the house in London and even in the country at times when his soul longed for horse and gun. But he retained his 'usual and habitual state of uninterrupted good health'; and snatched such exercise and relaxation as he could.[21] He would sometimes ride before breakfast out to Wormwood Scrubs; he would even slip away with his papers to the Star and Garter at Richmond, work and sleep there, and ride back into London for another busy day. Now and then he would escape to Broadlands or Woburn, or join one of Lady Cowper's parties at Panshanger. His social life in London was much curtailed.[22] For a time at least ' the Romsey Dandy ' (there seems to have been no end to his nicknames) attended no parties save the 'diplomatic' Sunday evenings of Lord Grey. Indeed, as Bulwer his friend and first biographer took note, he did not always shed his official cares even at gatherings held under gayer auspices :

> I then for the first time made Lord Palmerston's acquaintance at a party at Lady Cowper's, and still remember his appearance as that of a man in the full vigour of middle age, very well dressed, very good looking, with the large thick whiskers worn at that time. His air was more that of a man of the drawing-room than of the senate; but he had a clear, short, decisive way of speaking on business which struck me at once. All the questions he put to me went straight to the point; and one could see that he was gathering information for the purpose of fortifying opinions.[23]

One wonders how intentional was the sting conveyed in the last phrase. Now, however, Palmerston was entering upon five months of rest. Relieved of his cares, he could review the labours and achievements of his busiest four years.

He must, for example, have found it especially interesting to look back on the vicissitudes of what he called the 'cordial union' with France.[24] Accuracy would have been better served had his conception of patriotism allowed him to use the word ' entente ' ; and even cordiality between the two governments had frequently given way to suspicion or clear hostility. Still, the understanding had been kept alive by its indispensability to British and French policies, and by outward demonstrations of mutual esteem between the governments. Moreover, each government had realised that the fall of the other might bring worse things. Louis Philippe had had every reason for praying that Grey's government would keep the Tories out of power.[25] Peel had publicly compared the French king's constitutional position with that of Miguel. Wellington had privately attacked the entente as existing only for the benefit of France, and sympathised with Talleyrand's complaints that the Whigs had pushed France ' forward in a course of Jacobin foreign policy ' ! Aberdeen, of whose ' factious malignity ' in the upper House Grey more than once complained,[26] had arrived at his apparently lifelong conviction that the July revolution ' was undoubtedly at the time a great mis-

fortune for France and for all Europe.' In November
1833, he wrote that the meeting of the Holy Alliance rulers
at Münchengrätz had given him more satisfaction than any
other recent event, since 'the cordial and intimate union of
the Northern Powers' was essential for 'preserving the tranquillity and happiness of Europe against the disorganizing
and revolutionary policy of the present governments of
England and France.' Palmerston was, on the contrary,
quite solicitous for the welfare of the French government.
Not only was his general viewpoint opposed to that of his
old associates, but he reasoned that the French middle
classes, from whom the Orleanist dynasty drew its principal
support, would be so eager to foster commercial prosperity
as to adhere to the principle of 'non-intervention,' and thus
to the way of peace.[27] Of course, his faith had wavered
from time to time; but there had been reason for that.
For one thing, Talleyrand, who had been regarded with
grave suspicion by Grey and other Whigs at the outset,[28]
proved enigmatic enough to puzzle any man. Having
emerged on the winning side through every major change
in French government since 1789, he still posed for his
public, and still gave contradictory indications concerning
his real proclivities.[29] On his arrival, he had amused
London with his tri-coloured cockades and entourage of
young *sans-culottes*: and he was later quoted as declaring
that the terms 'intervention' and 'non-intervention' were
practically synonymous, and that 'a trifle of conquest'
was necessary for the stability of any French government.
But to Mme. de Lieven he spoke constantly of the '*repos
et bonheur pour les individus*' which were attainable only
under the '*vieux gouvernements.*'[30] As the same conflicting tendencies were equally observable at Paris, it says
something for the persistence of Grey and Palmerston that
they continued for four years to make the 'cordial union'
the keynote of their foreign policy.

Since the entente in large measure owed its existence
to the British government's desire to check the interventionist tendencies of the three autocratic eastern Powers, it
had, generally speaking, gained strength as the British and
Russian ministers passed gradually from exchanging smiles

to exchanging snarls. Very weak in the early months of 1831, it had grown firmer as the crises of that year concerning Belgium were safely passed. Palmerston had formally announced it at the opening of parliament in 1832;[31] and in the same month Talleyrand was toasted with great heartiness at the Mansion House.[32] In June, de Rémusat, writing from London, referred to the French ambassador's position there as '*une des forteresses de la France.*'[33] When, a fortnight later, Talleyrand went on leave, Palmerston sent him a surprisingly cordial farewell note :

. . . take care of your health, get over the fatigues of our long conferences as quickly as you can, and come back here soon ; but above all—come back.[34]

Evidences of friendliness continued up to the fall of Melbourne's ministry. In September 1832, the ministry drove Charles X and his *émigré* court from Holyrood to Austria, on Charles' refusal to give up all correspondence with the French Carlists.[35] In 1833, the British gave an impressive reception to the duke of Orleans,[36] and exerted themselves to reconcile France with Sardinia.[37] In January 1834, Talleyrand noted with deep satisfaction that the *Globe*, regarded as a ministerial organ, was giving the understanding warm support :[38] and in the month following, almost on the second anniversary of the day when the 'cordial union' had been first announced by Palmerston, the speech from the throne referred to ' the good understanding which has been so happily established between my Government and that of France.'[39] Neither the irritation produced by Palmerston's proposal to make the French mere ' acceding parties' to his alliance for settling the affairs of Spain and Portugal, nor the resignation of de Broglie, Louis Philippe's very pro-entente foreign minister, destroyed the desire for co-operation between the two countries. During this very spring, Palmerston began his efforts (of which more anon) to heal the diplomatic breach which had occurred between the governments of France and the United States over the repayment of the French loans.[40] And Talleyrand continued to urge the idea of a general defensive alliance on the British government. When Grey and Palmerston declined on the ground of parliamentary difficulties, and of the probability that such an alliance would drive Metternich to further coercion of the German states, Talleyrand admitted the force of their arguments.[41] But he was prepared to resume his efforts at the first favourable opportunity.

There was also an economic side to the entente, which further investigation may show to have been a decidedly important one.[42] A French scholar has already pointed out that English complacence regarding French policy in such matters as the expedition to Ancona and the siege of Antwerp show a suggestive correspondence in point of time with minor concessions made by France respecting her tariff and port dues. For in economic matters all the initiative was on the British side. France, so far from responding to Huskisson's establishment of less onerous customs dues, and his attempts, through reciprocity agreements respecting shipping, to foster a freer system of international trade, had become increasingly protectionist. Hence the British Foreign Office and Board of Trade made repeated efforts, at Paris and through Talleyrand, to secure laws or ordinances that would open a better French market for British manufacturers. In these efforts Palmerston, of course, bore a proper part; but his general correspondence affords at least negative evidence that the issue did not seem a very great one in his eyes. With much British capital and many skilled British workers operating within France, the prospects of increasing the British market there were not promising. Germany and the countries reached through Germany offered a better field; and Britain's most important markets were overseas. Hence, though Granville, Bowring, Villiers and Durham, to say nothing of the president of the Board of Trade himself, made what efforts they could to secure the adoption by the French of lower customs and port dues; and though Talleyrand urged upon his government the advisability of doing something which would at once conciliate the British cabinet and strengthen its hold on parliament, the commercial negotiations between the two countries seem to have been quite subsidiary to the diplomatic ones. Although the French concessions were extremely small, it has yet to be shown that the strength of the entente was sensibly affected by any resultant disappointment or resentment on Great Britain's part.

On the whole, however, the entente, while fairly stable as ententes go, never attained to any marked degree of solidity ; and Duvergier de Hauranne, whose opinion as a contemporary man of affairs and historian deserves some weight, was probably correct in saying that its lack of substantiality was due in part to the personal relations between Talleyrand and Palmerston.[43] It is especially worthy of remark that, writing in 1841, at a time when Palmerston's name was anathema in France, he placed much of the blame for the lack of good understanding between the two diplomatists upon the shoulders of the French ambassador. Palmerston, he pointed out, became the target for the ill will of the reactionary courts against what they regarded as Grey's revolutionary government, either because it was with him that they had most of their contacts, or because they regarded him as a renegade from Tory ranks. In this situation he naturally expected evidences of personal good will and support from Talleyrand. Instead, he met with indifference and disdain, arising largely from Talleyrand's preference for Tory ideas and society, and his contempt for the Whigs as ' a bastard party without principles, without consistency, and without future.'[44] Whatever the correctness of Duvergier's view, there is evidence that Palmerston was latterly much to blame. Perhaps it was merely because he had come to look upon Talleyrand as an incorrigible trickster ; perhaps he was sensitive, as men said, to the criticism represented by cartoons in which he found himself represented as a fly in the French net, or a blind man seated on a lame man's back.[45] At any rate, some of his discourtesies towards Talleyrand had the appearance of being deliberate. That he kept the old ambassador waiting so long in his anteroom may indicate no more than adherence to his rule that all his visitors should take their turns ;[46] but it seems hardly possible that he forgot to inform Talleyrand either of Don Carlos' arrival in England or of his escape.[47] And, as though the relations between the two men were not unsatisfactory enough, Mme.

de Dino did her best to widen the breach. Her diary reveals the final scene.[48] When Talleyrand prepared, in August 1834, to leave England for good, Palmerston, as in duty bound, gave a farewell dinner for the ambassador. But what was the lady's rage at finding among the other guests only a few diplomatists 'of the second order' and not a single person 'of eminence in English Society.' Hence she enjoyed herself by telling her host 'a few home truths,' and 'introducing many hints and double meanings and sly digs' into the conversation which they carried on. So Talleyrand and his niece went back to France to amplify the reports of Palmerston's offensiveness. It was not difficult for them to show that his record for quarrelsomeness was a surprising one.[49] And, needless to say, they made no allowance, as Grey did,[50] for the provocations he sometimes received from foreign emissaries.

Curiously enough, it was Talleyrand who bore the most striking testimony to Palmerston's ability as a foreign minister. Writing from London to a friend in Paris, he referred to Palmerston as the 'one statesman' among the British ministers. And his memoirs show that he did not change his mind:

> Lord Palmerston is certainly one of, if not quite the ablest of statesmen I have ever met with in all my official career. He possesses ... extensive and varied information, indefatigable activity, an iron constitution, inexhaustible mental resources and great facility of speech in Parliament ... furthermore, he has great social qualities and highly finished manners.[51]

It is true that the old diplomatist went on to say that all these gifts were outweighed by Palmerston's tendency to sacrifice 'the greatest interests' to his 'personal feelings,' and it is true also that other foreigners, marking the passion displayed in his letters and his speeches, subscribed to the same charge. But it is noteworthy that judges so competent as Brougham and Lady Granville laid some emphasis on his indifference to personalities and abuse ; and that others of his countrymen who were able to compare at close range his policies with his performance, failed to show agreement with Talleyrand. Neither, it seems, did Molé, twice Louis

Philippe's foreign minister, when he classed Palmerston with Russell and Holland as '*constituants, des hommes de 1791, travaillant pour le genre humain, comme Voltaire et les encyclopédistes écrivaient pour lui.*' [52] Sometimes even the envoys of the reactionary eastern Powers gave the foreign secretary praise. Metternich's haughty ambassador, Esterhazy, while deploring Palmerston's *insouciance*, and agreeing with Talleyrand that he was swayed by personal feeling, considered him the one member of his party who was ' practical and well-informed about foreign affairs.' [53]

By several of the most competent judges among his countrymen Palmerston's success was equally recognised. Charles Grey, the second and the more judicial of the premier's sons, paid tribute in a sentence : ' I think few people have a better right to look back with satisfaction on a four year's [*sic*] administration than he has.' [54] Brougham was even more appreciative, when giving his considered estimate later on :

. . . he was firm, and even bold ; quite steady to his friends ; indifferent to abuse ; full of resources ; using his pen better and more quickly than almost any body ; and not punctilious or vain, or standing upon trifles and personalities . . . I highly disapprove his foreign meddling ; but I speak of his general talents.[55]

Charles Greville, who had begun by accepting the estimates of Palmerston's enemies and crying him down, was surprised to get good reports of him from the Foreign Office staff :

They said that he wrote admirably . . . that his diligence and attention were unwearied—he read everything and wrote an immense quantity ; that the foreign Ministers (who detest him) did him justice as an excellent man of business.[56]

By 1836, Greville learned that ' the excellent man of business ' was rated more highly still at the British embassy in Paris :

It is surprising to hear how Palmerston is spoken of by those who know him well officially—the Granvilles, for example. Lady Granville, a woman expert in judging, thinks his capacity first-rate ; that it approaches to greatness from his enlarged views, disdain of trivialities, resolution, decision, confidence, and above all his contempt of clamour and abuse.[57]

His abilities as a foreign minister were, in fact, established for all time.

But recognition by the circle of the well informed does not necessarily bring advancement in politics; and Palmerston, as he quite realised, had done little to establish himself with parliament or with the electorate.[58] Engrossed by the affairs of his department, he had persistently neglected his parliamentary duties as a cabinet minister. The Whigs, who had enlisted the Canningites largely for the purpose of remedying their party's lack of debating talent in the lower House, had found their allies a disappointment, and Palmerston the greatest disappointment of them all. He, who in opposition had startled and delighted the House by his oratory, who had been proposed for the leadership by Stanley,[59] and had been counted upon to 'speechify in the House for Althorp,'[60] had remained, month after month, and session after session, almost dumb. He had seldom risen save when foreign affairs or such related matters as colonial questions or military estimates were before the House, and even then had rarely given much evidence of power.[61] Apparently he had not learned to talk extemporaneously, and grudged the time necessary for the preparation of a speech. Brougham, who arraigned the other Canningite ministers bitterly for their failure to do their duty in the House, excused him as 'worked and worn to death': [62] but the general impression was unfortunate. James Grant, recording his *Random Recollections*, attributed Palmerston's frequent absences from the House to indolence, and criticised his harsh voice, his gestures, and his stuttering address.[63] A changing House of Commons began to forget that he had ever possessed any claim to being an orator; while House and country both had reason to doubt his interest in the great reforms which the Whigs were placing upon the statute book. What is available of his correspondence suggests that in as far as these reforms left the constitution undisturbed, he entirely approved of them.[64] But his letters were not available to the public or to parliament.

This may in some part account for the fact that the middle classes who, in later years, were to lavish on him their admiration and support, barely commenced to turn to him at this time. His haughtiness and impatience made a sad impression on enthusiastic reformers who aspired to guide his hand in the patronage of continental liberalism. In 1831, the 'Westminster Union' presented to him a petition asking intervention on behalf of the Poles :

> ... they complained that the noble Lord had treated their memorial with the utmost contempt, not having condescended to make any reply to it. They contrasted the noble Lord's uncourteous conduct with the urbanity manifested by Earl Grey, who returned an answer to the memorial presented to him by the Birmingham Political Union and concluded by praying the House to address his Majesty to dismiss Lord Palmerston from his Councils. . . .[65]

Before Melbourne's dismissal there were some signs of change. The appearance in London of Spanish and Portuguese exiles commenced to stir the pride of the populace in seeing England serve as an asylum for the victims of autocracy, and hence to create appreciation of a foreign secretary who had obviously done much to make such pride possible. But 'Lord Pumicestone' was far from being as yet the beloved 'Pam.' He had not as yet much hold even on the press. It was rumoured that the *Globe* followed him ;[66] and it is certain that he made some effort to woo *The Times*.[67] But the Thunderer usually joined the majority of the papers in attacking him. According to Brougham, the Whigs saw in the attitude of the London editors in general one of two important reasons why he should not again receive the Foreign Office seals.[68]

The other reason was, of course, his excessive unpopularity with many persons with whom he had to deal officially. Brougham found this very hard to understand.[69] Personally, he had never known 'a man whom it was more agreeable to act with '; for 'his temper was excellent,' and he gave ' universal satisfaction ' to all of the cabinet save Durham. Melbourne reported that 'Palmerston exhibited no signs of temper or arrogance with his colleagues, but quite the reverse.'[70] But in the Foreign Office and the diplomatic service a very different account was to be heard.

It is an old story, and probably a true one, that the Foreign Office staff longed to illuminate the windows when the door closed on their chief in November 1834. But to accept it is not necessarily to say that the chief deserved all his unpopularity.[71] Palmerston, working tirelessly himself, imbued with a not unnatural suspicion that civil servants seldom exerted themselves to their capacity, and under pressure to play his part in the policy of retrenchment to which the ministry was vowed, demanded that his staff should do an increased amount of work. If all the business of the office grew in proportion to the number of despatches which were to be copied under the personal supervision of the permanent under secretary before being sent abroad—210 in 1829 and 1566 in 1832 [72]—the increase of pressure on the staff must have been severe indeed. Moreover, Palmerston insisted that all work should be done in such manner as to spare his own time and energies. Hence his insistence that all incoming papers written badly or in too small a hand, should be copied out for him; and hence his scribbled comment on some circulars prepared for signature, that they were 'most ingeniously folded up, each separately, so as to take the maximum of time in signing.'[73] Some of his instructions suggest that even in the Foreign Office his orders were not always scrupulously obeyed:

> The best manner of acting upon what I understand and suppose to be a general regulation of this office, seems to be *to act upon it*.[74]

Fortunately, his sense of humour sometimes tempered his official manner. The conclusion of a serious memorandum for the permanent under secretary with the words, 'I . . . have been suffering under a severe attack of Zea all morning,' is quite typical.[75]

But strong circumstantial evidence that Palmerston's nervous impatience made the life of a Foreign Office clerk in the early 'thirties very hard, is to be found in the numerous instances of his harshness to British diplomatic envoys of all grades. Hertslet's story of the incoming despatch which he filed with the endorsement 'Goose, Goose, Goose,'[76] reflects the temper in which many an outgoing reprimand was composed. Nothing irritated the overworked secretary so much as infractions of the little directions on routine which he had chosen to send out. Offenders were treated like delinquent schoolboys. Witness the reproofs administered to three envoys who served at Washington.[77] Sir Charles Vaughan received back a despatch and set of enclosures 'to be rewritten in blacker ink'; Sir Richard Pakenham, who seems to have used the same writing fluid, was informed of the secretary's hope that he should 'not again have to observe upon such a neglect of the standing instructions'; while Sir William Ouseley, guilty of the use of 'Gallicisms,' was forbidden to employ the term '*corps diplomatique*,' and reminded that '" to resume " does not mean " to sum up " or " to recapitulate," but " to take back again."' Perhaps Mr. Dawkins, minister plenipotentiary to Greece, had the crowning experience in receiving 'a specimen of the large round office hand for his sedulous imitation,' together with a hint that 'ink ought to be black.'[78] No doubt all of these gentlemen realised that such pettiness and irritability were not to be taken too seriously; but there were some of Palmerston's agents who felt deeply aggrieved at his methods of treating them, and who poured their woes into the receptive ears of the Princess Lieven and the duchess of Dino. The duchess reported, for example, that Lord William Russell (Lord John's brother) accused Palmerston of wishing to be served only by such men as 'would distort the truth to suit his prejudices,' and of having at one time vented his displeasure by attacking the reputation of Lord William's wife.[79] Charges of this sort, preserved through the offices of two angry gossips, cannot, of course, be relied upon; but Palmerston's general unpopularity with the members of the diplomatic service seems beyond dispute. There were British diplomats, such as Sir Henry Bulwer, who felt admiration and even liking for their chief; but they seem to have been few. Perhaps the majority had still to realise that against Palmerston's harshness could be set the generous commendation and loyal support which he gave to those who carried out his orders with courage and diligence.[80] With his subordinates, as with parliament, the public and the press, he began badly, but grew in favour as time went on.

He was not only a toil-worn and formidable, but a rather lonely figure in those years. His ' intimate friends ' seem to have been mere political associates, and he lacked even substantial party ties.[81] He had cared so little about identifying himself with the Whigs that he neglected even to join Brooks's for some time. Nor had the Whigs altogether accepted him. He had played their game well enough so far, both in domestic matters and abroad ; but they were beginning to take alarm.[82] The roughness of his methods and the resultant alienation of England from the great eastern courts seemed to most of the cabinet deplorable and unnecessary. Even the entente with France, the object of their special solicitude, had obviously been strained by his relations with Talleyrand. Melbourne, it was already seen, would not be capable of restraining him ;[83] and Melbourne was virtually certain to head the next Whig ministry. There is every indication that the party leaders, like Metternich, looked upon Palmerston's departure from the Foreign Office in November, 1834, with hope that a successor of different type could be put in his place when the next Whig ministry was formed.

They made no secret of this hope in April 1835, when Peel resigned, and Melbourne set about forming his second ministry.[84] It is true that Grey and Lansdowne snubbed the envoys of the three eastern Powers when those gentlemen protested in advance against Palmerston's return to Downing Street. But in private Lansdowne called attention to Palmerston's seeming inability to get along with foreign diplomats ; Grey, declining the Foreign Office seals himself, expressed the hope that they would be given to some one other than Palmerston ; Holland stated the same wish without reserve ; and Russell showed himself eager to supply in his own person the some one else whom Grey and Holland hoped to see in Palmerston's old place. Most active of all, seemingly, was Grey's brother-in-law, Edward Ellice, who later boasted of his efforts to exclude Palmerston from the ministry, or at least to force him to accept some other portfolio. Melbourne, whether by conviction or persuasion, fell in with the Whig desires. Interviews and letters on the subject multiplied. But the premier's hands were tied. He could not adopt suggestions for excluding Palmerston altogether from the ministry and trying to persuade him to go to France or Ireland or India ; for this might be interpreted as condemnation not only of the man but of the foreign policy in which the rest of the cabinet had concurred. And it might also carry the man, not abroad, but into the opposition camp. The obvious solution, then, was that Palmerston should take some other portfolio. But on this point he was adamant. He would, and did, join in asking Grey to take the Foreign Office ; but he would give way to no one else.[85] And in the end the Whigs could only bow to what Ellice called a ' cruel necessity.' Palmerston had, for the first but by no means the last time, forced himself by sheer strength on a party that wished but did not dare to be rid of him. How far he realised the situation it is impossible to say ; but he was to have ample demonstration of the feelings of the Whigs before he had filled out his coming six years' term.

But he was at least identified with his party in the public eye. This appears in his relations with his new parliamentary constituents. Since 1832 a member for South Hants, he was the only minister to lose his seat in the general election which had followed upon the dismissal of Melbourne.[86] When he re-entered Parliament in May 1835, a month after his re-appointment as foreign secretary, he did so as member for a borough which he was to represent for the remainder of his life.[87] This was Tiverton, a town of some 10,000 inhabitants on the coast of Devonshire. This ancient place, which could boast of modern manufactures and a small race meet, had retained double representation in parliament under the bill of 1832. One of its seats was held impregnably by a Mr. Heathcot, the leading manufacturer, and the other by a Mr. Kennedy. In May 1835, Mr. Kennedy most conveniently decided that he could not afford the luxury of a seat in parliament ; and the caucus obligingly adopted Viscount Palmerston in his place. The fact that the departing member soon secured appointment on a commission to investigate the slave trade, and not long thereafter became a judge, did not escape comment. But the interesting possibilities of this borough,

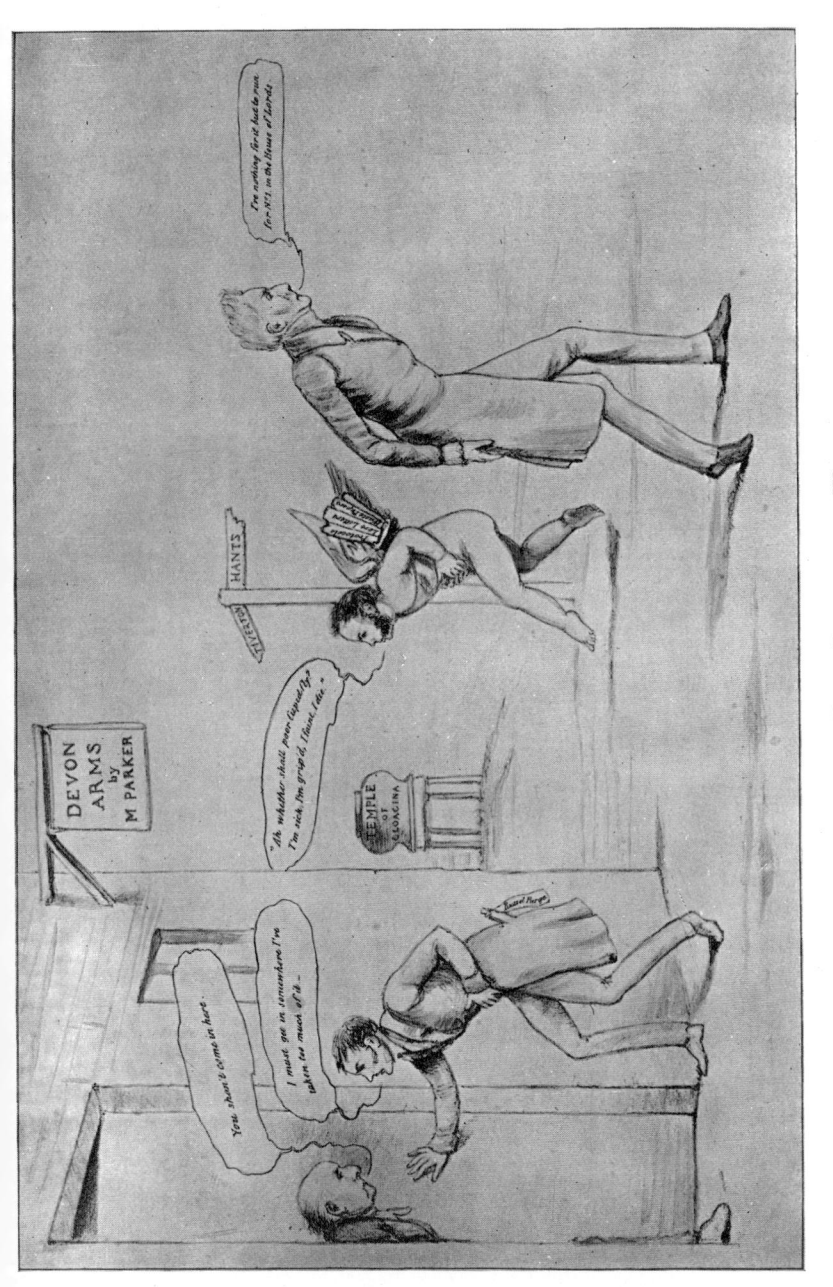

The Russell Purge Beginning to Work
or
Three Secretaries in Search of a Close Seat

half manufacturing centre and half market town, a place where conservatism, liberalism and even radicalism could be found side by side, did not become apparent until 1837, when Palmerston for the first time solicited the votes of his constituents.

The electoral contest of 1837 in Tiverton was nothing if not a lively one. Palmerston's Tory opponent placed an open Bible on his standard; but forgot some of the biblical injunctions regarding openhanded generosity. 'The old gentleman would rather open his Bible than his pocket,' some of the intelligent and high-minded electors jeered. The local Tory leaders, neglecting nothing, turned their hands to campaign literature. Remembering how Palmerston had first secured his seat, and perhaps resentful of the aspersions cast on their own candidate, they put into the foreign secretary's mouth a parody of the most famous of soliloquies :

> To stand or not to stand—that is the question—
> . . . to stand—to canvass—
> Perchance the election lose ; aye there's the rub.
> For since I first became that Borough's member
> By means of which remembrance makes me blush
> The slaves have soon rebelled—this bids me pause
> Ere at the same vile rate I buy their votes—

They suggested, too, that as a reformer he was somewhat lacking in sincerity :

> Who'd puff ' the poor laws ' and cry out ' Reform '
> But that the hope, the burning hope of place
> And eke of pension spurs on my ambition.

And ' Junius,' re-incarnated for the occasion, pictured Palmerston as the servant of the radicals :

> Who has been the obsequious humble servant of the Tories, Whigs, Whig-Radicals, O'Connellites etc. in order to *continue* a *Placeman—PALMERSTON !*

Who, asked Junius, had assisted in the passage of the ' cruel and un-Christian Poor Law ' ; who was the ' encourager of the Free Trade Mania ' ; who had ' on many occasions voted with and encouraged that English Radical humbug "black-and-white" Joseph Hume'; and who was one of the chief promoters of the 'infamous new Marriage Act' —which had ' taken away the religious obligation from and destroyed the sanctity of the Nuptial Vow '—who but ' sly CUPID'? 'Sly Cupid' contented himself with much more commonplace tactics. Neglecting the resources of literature, he depended on a mere election speech, in which he assured the presumably gratified burgesses of his realisation that their votes could not be bought for less than the price of ' a Principality anywhere,' or ' even some Kingdoms in Germany.' He gloried in the abolition of an electoral system that had allowed his constituents to know no more about the election of their representatives than ' the sheep of Old Sarum or the stocks and stones of Gatton.' Nor did he deny, as, for any evidence to the contrary, he might very well have done, his promotion of ' the infamous new Marriage Act.' It would scarcely have been wise to do so; since the Dissenters of the constituency held the balance. On election day the town beheld four nonconformist parsons leading thirty or forty burgesses in procession to vote for the liberal foreign secretary. They gave him a comfortable majority over the economical champion of Holy Writ, and an enduring realisation that liberalism in religious matters may bring political rewards.

Palmerston's rather detached position with respect to Melbourne's second cabinet, and the Tory charge that he pandered to the radicals and O'Connellites, arouse some curiosity as to his relations with the ministry's supporters in the House. To the duke of Bedford, hereditary leader of the Whigs, the government benches were occupied, in the spring of 1835, by a ' noisy and turbulent pack of hounds.'[88] For the party, relieved of its more conservative leaders including Grey himself, and furiously resentful over the King's dismissal of Melbourne, had made common cause in the ensuing elections with radical and even O'Connellite candidates. The result was curious and unfortunate. The radicals, drawn to some extent from the aristocracy but more from the middle class, bitterly resented Whig condescension and what they regarded as Whig timidity. Feeling their power, they

THE VALUE OF THE RADICALS

were even more determined to force the pace with Melbourne's ministry than they had been with Grey's. But the Whigs would not, and perhaps could not, respond. 'Sir William Harcourt said that Whiggism trying to translate itself into Liberalism was like an old mail-coachman trying to turn stoker.'[89] No wonder the 'hounds' were 'noisy and turbulent.' At first sight it would seem that Palmerston in particular must have found the situation embarrassing. It is true that in his actual views of most leading issues he does not seem to have stood far from Russell or the other leaders of the younger Whigs. But by tradition, service and general inclination he was distinctly more conservative. Yet the situation also held for him one interesting possibility. If the Whigs objected to his foreign policy, might not the more advanced members of the party's rank and file give him useful support? He could pose as a good liberal, and could do so with some conviction where economic and religious issues were concerned. And when, as foreign secretary, he undertook the patronage of continental liberalism and, still more perhaps, the flouting of autocratic foreign rulers, he and the radicals might join in combating Whig 'timidity.' Radical members of parliament and the public which supported them would be free from the restraint imposed on his colleagues by responsibility and by full knowledge of the dangers to be run. Whether he saw it or not, the possibility was there.

CHAPTER X

THE FADING-OUT OF THE ENTENTE AND THE DECLINE OF BRITISH INFLUENCE IN SPAIN, PORTUGAL AND GREECE, 1835-1841

THE enticing prospects which had greeted Palmerston when he made his début as Grey's foreign secretary—the opportunity and responsibility, the call to high adventure in the service of England and of the political principles which he had adopted as his own—were sadly diminished by the spring of 1835. Through middle and eastern Europe liberalism seemed quiescent, not to say prostrate; and in those countries where it could still be served by outside aid, its most conspicuous British patron had only the relatively uneventful work of carrying through unfinished tasks. He had still to see that Holland accepted the settlement of November 1831; that Greece received her promised constitution; that Portugal was reduced to order; and that Carlos was expelled from Spain. But if a less adventurous course now lay before him, he was not less resolute or less confident in following out his aims. No matter what Burke had taught, no matter what his agents on the ground might write, he still believed that every European country should, in Britain's interests and its own, have a constitution of the British type. As Raikes once remarked, he possessed a peculiar ability to believe what he wished.

It may very well have seemed to him that the five months of Tory rule had been a mere punctuation point in so far as the conduct of foreign relations was concerned. When he took over the reins again at Downing Street he was delighted to find that Wellington had acted 'in the most fair & honourable manner,' and proved himself 'a great practical statesman,' by living up to all engagements contracted by England during the four preceding years.[1] Indeed, the only very noticeable effect of the Duke's incumbency was that London had regained some of that diplomatic eminence which it had enjoyed in 1831. The Austrian and Prussian envoys, Esterhazy and Bülow, who had found it more pleasant to go on leave than to have intercourse with 'Lord Pumicestone,'[2] were once more at their posts ; while Lieven's place had been given to one of the most astute and experienced Russian diplomatists, the old Corsican, Pozzo di Borgo. True, Sebastiani was rather an inadequate substitute for Talleyrand, but Anglo-French relations were handled by Granville at Paris to the satisfaction of both governments.[3] Moreover, from Palmerston's point of view, the general alignment of the Powers remained unchanged. Thus, he wrote Melbourne as late as March 1836 :

> The division of Europe into two camps . . . to which you so much object, is the result of events beyond our control, and is the consequence of the French Revolution of July. The three powers fancy their interests lie in a direction opposite to that in which we and France conceive ours to be placed. The separation is not one of words, but of things ; not the effect of caprice or of will, but produced by the force of occurrences. The three and the two think differently, and therefore they act differently, whether it be as to Belgium or Portugal or Spain.
>
> This separation cannot really cease till all the questions to which it applies are decided—just as it is impossible to make a coalition ministry while there are questions pending in which public men disagree.[4]

In one particular at least he was perfectly correct ; the solidarity of interests between the three eastern courts was as strong as it had ever been. Affirmed at Münchengrätz in September 1833, it was reaffirmed at Teplitz in September 1835. And Palmerston still thought to counter it effectively with the *entente cordiale*, and with the Quadruple Alliance of April 1834. Here again his wishes seem to have been somewhat the parents of his beliefs.

For the relations of the Powers, and the diplomatic position of England in particular, were being modified to a pronounced degree in 1835. The modification arose mainly from certain changes in the disposition of the government of France, or rather in those of its head, King Louis Philippe.[5] In brief, the Orleanist king was persistently feeling his way to the realisation of suppressed desires. He had always wished to rule as well as reign, and to make his peace with the three great eastern courts. Not only did their ideas of government correspond fundamentally with his, but they had it in their power to bestow certain advantages which he craved. Their friendship would at once lend to his government a desirable appearance of legitimacy, and free it from a humiliating dependence on England. Fear that an attempt to realise these desires would cost him his throne, by driving moderate French constitutionalists into the ranks of the republicans, had restrained him to this time. But in 1835 he was able to take heart. France was settling down more and more to bourgeois rule; and the republicans had gone so far in irritating the champions of order and property that the King could venture to crush them utterly. Not only were the leaders deported, imprisoned, or placed under surveillance in the summer of 1835; but the 'September' laws reduced their chances of acquittal at all future trials, and virtually wiped out their press. 'I wish that Louis-Philippe would come over and govern this country for six months, it would be better for all of us," wrote Wellington.[6] Moreover, by making any question as to the authority of the government a crime, the French king practically declared his rule legitimate. One step he had still to take: to make himself independent of parties and of party leaders who, like Casimir Perier, would allow him to reign but not to rule. He did not as yet dare to take it completely and openly. French public opinion was not prepared for such a change; and if Casimir Perier were dead, three ministers, Broglie, Guizot and Thiers, seemed to stand very much in his place. He was forced once more to 'swallow' Broglie in March 1835. But he was gaining steadily; and, as he gained, he turned his face more and more to the east and his back to the Quadruple Alliance of 1834 and the entente.

He had been feeling his way for some time toward better relations with the eastern courts;[7] and, as the year 1834 closed, he had found his sentiments strongly reinforced. Talleyrand, encouraged and applauded by a circle of followers among whom Mesdames de Dino and Lieven were conspicuous, preached that the entente had already been exploited by France for all that it was worth.[8] Still, Louis Philippe was forced to proceed cautiously. Repudiation of entente and alliance would arouse British animosity, and place France too much at the mercy of the eastern Powers. Nor could he as yet count on securing and sustaining ministers who would endorse a diplomatic *volte face* so complete. Hence he continued for years to speak, with apparent sincerity, of the solidarity of the entente, the while he secretly reassured the envoys of the eastern Powers,[9] and sought an Austrian bride for his heir, the duke of Orleans. As for the supposed directors of French foreign relations, their policies fluctuated incessantly. Broglie, in power to February 1836, favoured the entente, but made concessions to his master's desire for an Austrian duchess of Orleans. His successor, Thiers, appointed as a pliable minister and a disciple of Talleyrand, was quite pro-Austrian until Metternich decided that the Paris climate was not good for the Austrian archduchesses. Swinging vengefully to the opposite extreme, and showing an unlooked-for determination to have his own way, he went out of office, in September 1836, on his insistence that French troops should intervene in Spain. Molé, who with the assistance of Guizot then took the reins, was a man much after the King's own heart. 'We might nearly as well have had Nesselrode at Paris,' was Palmerston's comment on Molé's fall in January 1839.[10] Optimistic as ever, he cherished some hopes that the entente, to which he had been trying to hold the French for well-nigh four years, might 'revive' with the removal of Molé's 'benumbing touch.'[11] But the history of his relations with succeeding French foreign ministers belongs in another place.

The fact was that he tried to give new life to the entente, only to find the effort vain. In 1835, he mediated with great tact, ingenuity and success in a dispute over the settlement of certain French indebtedness to the United States.[12] His *démarche* was not, indeed, disinterested; for, as he pointed out to Grey, 'a war between those Powers would have been in many ways embarrassing and inconvenient for us.'[13] None the less, he was entitled to the thanks of both disputants. That warm public acknowledgments came to him only from Washington was possibly the result of mere inadvertence at the Tuileries;[14] but, be that as it may, the entente was doomed. The growing alienation of the two governments—seen in re-orientation of policy in Paris, resentment in London, and the breakdown of diplomatic co-operation everywhere—was accompanied by a growing alienation between the peoples whom they served. 'They are beginning here to hate us,' wrote Lyndhurst from Paris in 1836.[15] The traditional antagonism, temporarily obscured, was laid bare again by the press, and deepened by the conflict of economic interests.[16] The cry was going up in France that England, not content with seizing her rival's colonial empire, was aiming at economic domination even on French soil. Hence the French bourgeoisie set out to 'emancipate' itself from the British middle class. Government loans were floated without British co-operation for the first time in twenty years. Strong pressure was put upon the government to maintain a high tariff wall against British manufactures and British coal, and to bar the employment of British capital, material, and engineering skill in the construction of railroads. Palmerston found the language and the actions of the French government 'anything but friendly' with respect to commercial interests, and was surprised at the 'irritation and resentment' on the subject shown in parliament.[17] How far these misunderstandings on economic matters affected the diplomatic relations of the two countries it is difficult to say. But their very existence must have given Louis Philippe encouragement in following his new policy —the policy of departing from the entente and from the Quadruple Alliance of 1834.

In January 1835, Metternich, recklessly mixing his metaphors, had declared the Quadruple Alliance a 'phantom,' a useless weight which the British and French governments had bound themselves to drag after them, and a bowstring which constricted their policies.[18] Prejudiced as the Austrian chancellor was, it seems impossible to deny that his views had some validity. And he might have gone on to show that the alliance, in binding the two Powers to interfere, under certain contingencies, in the affairs of Spain, bound each to take action which was calculated to arouse the other's jealousy. It remained for the Spanish 'constitutionalists' to make such jealousy certain. Too Latin to remain united even in face of the danger from Carlos, they split into a so-called 'moderate' section which leaned for support on the increasingly conservative Louis Philippe, and a 'progressive' which looked to Palmerston. To make matters even worse, the progressives were more or less closely linked with a revolutionary element abhorrent to Christina, the Queen Regent, and determined to establish what Palmerston called the 'absurd and stupid' constitution of 1812. Unfortunately, too, it soon appeared that the British government had hopes of securing payment for its services to the Spanish queens in the form of reductions in Spanish tariffs on British goods.[19] '*Mais quelle alliance, grand Dieu!*' wrote Metternich later on, '*que cette alliance pour le Roi des Français! Lui qui, avant tout, aurait besoin de repos et d'appui. . . .*'[20]

And truly repose was the last thing that could be thought of in the later 'thirties by any government which concerned itself with the affairs of Spain.[21] The Carlist war was being carried on with such exhibitions of bestial ferocity as the mutual murder of hostages, and with a growing threat to the government of Christina and Isabella, the mother and daughter Queens. At the end of May 1835, the government of the Queens appealed to England, France and Portugal for aid. It seemed apparent that such aid as had been promised under the Quadruple Alliance and the additional articles would not suffice. Reinforcements to the Queens' army were needed urgently; and the Portuguese government, which alone had promised troops, had few to spare. Would, then, England and France, or either of them, send out an expeditionary force? The question was answered without delay in a manner which went far to justify Metternich's strictures. The Melbourne ministry, whatever its members may have desired, could not even hope that a parliament still devoted to retrenchment and to peace would vote money for an adventure of this kind. It was graciously disposed to allow the French to intervene in Spain ; but Palmerston, probably acting under instructions, was careful to point out that they would have to do so solely on their own responsibility.[22] Hence, Louis Philippe, who was very attentive to Austrian persuasions and to Prussian threats, was provided with an additional excuse for resisting Broglie and refusing French troops to the Spanish queens. A little later he fell back on the device of sending 'indirect' aid.[23] So did the Melbourne government.

For Palmerston decided that what he had done for a Portuguese queen he could now do for a Spanish one— with slight improvements suggested by experience. His colleagues seem to have been cold to his suggestion that they should help Queen Christina to negotiate a loan for the payment of British auxiliaries (secured, perhaps, by a mortgage on some Spanish colonies), and make themselves 'masters in chancery' for the protection of the lenders.[24] But at least Christina was given facilities for the purchase of arms and ammunition in any desired quantities ; and it was somehow contrived that British vessels going to the Spanish coast—solely, of course, to preserve order and to protect British interests—carried quite remarkable numbers of marines. However, the real improvement in procedure consisted in the issue of an order in Council suspending the Foreign Enlistment Act. Thanks to this, Christina's representative, General Alava, was able to enlist some 10,000 British subjects (many of them Irishmen assembled by O'Connell, it was said) for service in the Peninsula.[25] Colonel Delacy Evans, a radical firebrand who had served Maria of Portugal, took command. Although, in deference to the Mutiny Act, all organisation, training, and equipment of the British volunteers were done outside the British realm, this means of sending aid was hardly 'indirect' enough for some members of parliament. Aberdeen was not the only member who found it ' a disgraceful and a barbarous thing, that an independent nation should be

THE ELIZABETHAN TOUCH FOR SPAIN 215

delivered up to the ravages of foreign mercenaries.'[26] But Palmerston was unperturbed. In serving ' the cause of constitutional liberty' in Spain, was he not serving also the balance of power, and perhaps even the balance of trade ? If the suspension of the Foreign Enlistment Act was a bit irregular, was not the action taken under it fully covered by precedent ? Once more he recalled to parliament the stirring days of Elizabeth.[27] And once more parliament acquiesced. The more readily, perhaps, that one Tory member who had taken the occasion to condemn the furnishing of supplies and money to the Spanish queens, found to his horror that he had been indicting not only Palmerston but Wellington ![28]

Once again, too, Palmerston was active in helping to recruit Belgians for service in the Peninsula. No summary could do justice to the letter he wrote upon the subject to Adair :

> My view of the question about the Belgian recruiting for Spain has been a little modified by reading the 6th & 7th Chap. of the 3d Book of Vattel. I believe that other writers on the Law of Nations hold different opinions on these matters, but where doubt is, prudence counsels forbearance. I talked this matter over yesterday with Bulow & afterwards with Vandeweyer & read Vattel with them. Bulow seemed to think that his Govt would be satisfied if the Belgian Govt abstained from making any formal convention for allowing Spain to raise troops in Belgium, and that nothing would be said if the Belgians merely winked at the inlistment of individuals in the same way as in the case of Don Pedro ; . . . I pointed out to Bulow that Prussia would have some difficulty in making a remonstrance because to do so she must declare herself a party interested, that is to say an ally of Carlos, which she has not hitherto avowed herself as being. That at present Carlos is the only party who could have a right of war against Belgium on account of supplies furnished to Isabella, and that the five Powers as guarantees of Belgium could only say, if Carlos makes war upon you for having aided his enemy remember that we shall not be bound to protect you.[29]

Alas, that one has no recorded comment of Metternich's on this interview !

What the British legion, and the employment on at least one occasion of British marines,[30] contributed to the success of Christina's and Isabella's cause, it is of course impossible to estimate. Not a great deal in all probability; for the story of the ten thousand seems to be one of ineffectiveness on their part, of neglect, ill-treatment, and bad faith on the Spanish side, and, naturally, of constant quarrels.[31] Nor was Carlos a redoubtable foe at best. But it is certain that in 1839, through mediation by the British government which Alava regarded as ' beyond all praise,'[32] the pretender was persuaded to say good-bye to Spain. After this, *Sir Delacy Evans, K.C.B.*, and Palmerston exchanged congratulations; while the respective parties at Madrid which professed allegiance to the Queens proceeded to quarrel at ease and involve their two great patrons at every step.

But not even Palmerston could really have congratulated himself on the effects of that policy in Spain of which he had formerly been so proud. He had seen the Queen Regent, a prisoner in the hands of the extremists, compelled to proclaim the constitution of 1812 : he had seen the constitutionalist forces, to which he steadily gave aid, compete in savagery with the Carlists, even where the assassination of women was concerned. At times he had frankly confessed his discouragement and disgust :

> The Queen's party want nothing to ensure them success *but* money, honesty, ability, and courage, *slight* requisites, and found in Spain on every roadside.[33]

And, in spite of Carlos' agreement to leave Spain, the final outcome gave him cause for anxiety. For Queen Christina betook herself to Paris, to become, as he believed, 'a mere instrument in the hands of the King of the French.'[34]

Moreover, it seemed not only to him, but to many other Englishmen, that the French had played a very shabby part.[35] Villiers sent home warnings that they were covertly assisting the Carlists.[36] Grey wrote sadly that bad faith seemed ' a strong feature in the character of Louis Philippe . . . brought into action by personal motives of different kinds,' such as his jealousy of British influence in Spain, ' his foolish desire to conciliate the Northern Powers,' and ' Talleyrand's hatred of Palmerston.'[37] The British ministerial press was filled at times with recrimination and re-

THE SPANISH MARRIAGES—FIRST PHASE 217

proach against England's partner in the entente.[38] As for the foreign secretary, he took his accustomed way. Granville was instructed to warn Molé that his policy was fraught with the danger which isolation would involve for the security of France, and popular discontent for the stability of the July Monarchy;[39] Villiers was ordered to enlighten the Spanish government;[40] while the world was informed of England's displeasure by the deliberate and much remarked omission of any reference to France or the entente in the speech which opened William IV's last parliament.[41] These measures were all, of course, quite in vain. In vain, too, Victoria, less than a fortnight on the throne, pleaded with her uncle Leopold of Belgium to persuade her ' kind and dear friend Louis Philippe . . . to do something for poor Spain.'[42] The French king, well coached by Metternich, snatched what ' repose ' he could, intoning that most useful motto : ' *La France garde le sang de ses enfants pour sa propre cause.*'[43] And Molé spoke to Granville ' *with the greatest openness and confidence about the weather, and the French elections . . . and so forth.*'[44] Not the least striking feature of the situation was that Palmerston, only too ready to condemn the French for their infidelity to the alliance from the first, persisted in his efforts to hold them to it until the very end.

And finally, to insure that his distrust of Louis Philippe and his anxiety concerning Spain should continue in full force, there had arisen, as early as 1836, the question of finding a suitable husband for the young Spanish queen.[45] Palmerston, while quite reasonably insisting that all discussion on the point was premature (Isabella, it will be remembered, was the same age as the July Monarchy) found it necessary to raise objections to several suggested husbands before leaving office in 1841. An Austrian archduke he rejected as an Austrian ; the eldest son of Don Carlos as certain to prove an autocrat ; and another first cousin of the Queen's, the young duke of Cadiz (who was later the Queen's husband, and was almost certainly impotent) for ' natural defects.' But most emphatic of all was he in repelling suggestions, put forward as early as 1836 and never really disposed of for ten years, that Isabella should marry a son of the French king. All in all, he had been sorely disappointed in his hopes concerning Spain. He had gone out of office in 1834 confident that his Quadruple Alliance had prepared the way for the evolution of a new Spanish monarchy, constitutionalist and friendly to England. He was to leave office again in 1841 with the alliance in ruins and Spain a country which he could regard only with disappointment and anxiety, not to say disgust.

If he was disappointed by the developments in Spain, how much more bitter must have been his disillusionment concerning Portugal? He had not even the comfort of feeling that in this case any fault could be imputed to the French. All that he asked of France was that she should not interfere. And Louis Philippe, exemplary *père de famille* as he was, declined in 1836 to allow his son, Nemours, to become the second husband of the already widowed Queen.[46] As usual, there was a young Coburg, a nephew of Leopold's, available for the place. But, lacking his shrewd uncle's tact, he became, as the Queen's consort, a new source of disturbance in what was perhaps the most disturbed country on the continent.[47] There seemed little save disturbance in Portugal.[48] Instead of the ordered constitutional government which, in Palmerston's dream, was to have strengthened the bonds between England and her oldest ally, Portugal presented as sad a spectacle of incompetent administration, of banditry, of riots and mutinies, of revolution and counter-revolution, as could be conceived. There was all too much truth in Raikes' remark that the error of Grey's ministers had been in thinking that they could ' obtain all the popularity of advocating revolutionary principles, and yet establish *a medium point.*'[49] In the very year of the Queen's remarriage mutinous soldiers and revolutionary civilians demanded the proclamation of a constitution of the most democratic type. Applied to a populace ignorant and undisciplined, it produced something akin to sheer anarchy. In vain the Queen retired from her capital ; in vain British warships were stationed and marines landed for her support.[50] Rather than lose her crown she returned to Lisbon virtually a prisoner, bound to gratify the wishes of the populace. And the populace turned with fury against the British government,[51] which, they felt, had been attempting to dominate their government and to exploit their country economically. New tariffs were loaded upon British goods, and the British minister was forced, from motives of mere prudence, to forbid British subjects in Portugal to seek interviews with the royal pair. As for England's attempts to secure payment for services rendered in men and material during the Peninsular war and the struggles of Pedro and Maria against Miguel, the Portuguese passed from evasion to flat repudiation. Even the duke of Wellington's pension was unpaid. The surviving British volunteers of the early 'thirties were requited only with danger and hardship.

Palmerston, mortified by the whole affair, abused by the British press,[52] and blaming Queen Maria for bringing on the counter-revolution too precipitately,[53] tried to carry off the situation with his usual jauntiness. 'Peninsular affairs,' he wrote, in December 1836, 'are so bad that they cannot become worse, and must therefore become better.'[54] When the Queen's government regained some control of the situation, in 1838, he was quick to revert to his old claim that Spain and Portugal, if they could be made 'independent, free and prosperous,' would 'become a most valuable addition to the balance of power in Europe.' But he added an unlooked-for comment :

. . . the time may come when Austria and Prussia will heartily thank us for having done that which they have so stoutly resisted. France and Russia may, naturally enough, take a different view of the matter.[55]

What had become of the league of the four constitutional Powers, of that counterpoise to the Holy Alliance on which he had congratulated himself just four years previously ? Had Metternich been right in calling it a ' phantom ' ?

Others of his hopes had gone glimmering—in particular those which he had cherished with respect to Greece. In the manœuvring for position which went on incessantly at Athens between the envoys of the Powers, England— represented by the energetic Sir Edmund Lyons from the summer of 1835—on the whole maintained first place.[56]

That the Greek government still found the services of General Church, the 'liberator,' indispensable to its army; and that England showed herself more ready than France or Russia to guarantee further instalments of the Greek loan, were facts which in themselves gave Lyons some predominance. Yet Palmerston, rightly or wrongly, believed the Foreign Office to be putting up a losing struggle against the Austrian and Russian moves.[57] He saw Russian gains in the growing influence of the patriarch of Constantinople, and in the attempts of King Otto to crush the Athens press. He perceived, correctly enough, that Otto's marriage, in November 1836, with a princess of Oldenburg, established a closer connection between the Russian and Greek courts. As for the Austrian influence, his feelings emerged in a letter which he wrote the young Queen Victoria in 1838.[58] The Archduke John of Austria, after visiting in Greece, had declared the country to be handicapped by the 'German pedants,' the intriguing and too intelligent Phanariots, the 'swarm of half educated young men from Capo d'Istria's Colleges' and the foreign diplomats resident at Athens. Palmerston's scornful comment on the assumption of such an attitude towards all the inhabitants of the country who had 'any considerable share of education and knowledge' is notable in more ways than one:

> Your Majesty will not fail, however, to observe . . . traces of the strong prejudices which are entertained in Austria against everything that savours of education and improvement . . . the reasoning of the Archduke John is . . . much the same as the argument which is often employed against education, by those who dislike improvement. Ignorance, they say, may be bad, and perfect knowledge may be a very excellent possession, but a *little* knowledge is a dangerous thing, and as masses of men cannot at once become fully informed, but must begin by having a little knowledge, it is better to leave them in absolute darkness than expose them to the danger of a partial sight. But it is unnecessary to expose the fallacy of an argument which if admitted would be a bar to all improvement in the condition of nations, and which is not more founded in truth than would be the assertion that a little wealth is a bad and dangerous thing. . . .

As so often, he felt that he was fighting the powers of darkness, and that in his fight he stood alone. Certainly he failed to secure the co-operation which he incessantly demanded of the French.[59] For the French gained in prestige by refusing to take sides, thus giving to Otto the impression of some disinterestedness.[60]

But deeper disappointment came to Palmerston from the fact that the constitutional government, which he had taken such pains to promote, did not appear.[61] Though the granting of a constitution was called for by the agreement which had placed Otto on the throne, the King and his Bavarian advisers steadily evaded it. Palmerston, who had at first hoped great things from the Bavarian premier, Armansperg, and his colleagues, reluctantly came to the French view that the Greek administration should be 'nationalised' and the Bavarians sent home.[62] But not even this could be achieved. Year by year the administration proved itself more unpopular and more incompetent, especially where finances were concerned. And, year by year, Palmerston's tone became more bitter and more menacing. What makes this dreary story worth the telling is the evidence it gives, not merely of his failure and disillusionment in a cherished policy, but of his readiness to abuse a powerful government, and to bully a weak one, which arrayed themselves against the powers of righteousness. That he had no hesitation in extending to Metternich's policies strictures even more severe than those he had applied to the views of the Archduke John, is seen from a despatch to the British ambassador, Sir Frederick Lamb :

It would afford H. M. Govt. great pleasure if they could see that Austria had become reconciled to the independence of Greece which she so strenuously endeavoured by every means in her power to prevent. . . .

But H. M. Govt. lament to see that the same spirit of enmity to the development of any germ of liberty in any part of Europe, which set Austria in opposition to . . . the emancipation of Greece, still continues to direct the policy of Austria towards the Greek nation, and that instead of encouraging and aiding the Greeks in their efforts to become independent and prosperous, she seems to aim only at reducing them to the nearest approximation to torpidity and political stagnation consistent with the arrangements of the treaty of 1827, and having failed to perpetuate in Greece one foreign yoke is endeavouring to substitute for it another.[63]

Disappointment seems to have been envenoming his pen.

In hectoring the Greek government he appears to have been well served by his envoy ;[64] but he took no risk that Lyons would not perform the task with sufficient energy. In 1839 the Greek minister to England reported that Palmerston had treated him to a torrent of abuse, ordering him to tell his master that until he granted a constitution he ' never should have a moment's peace,' and that the Foreign Office would not hesitate about communicating to the Greeks the opinion that, so long as the constitution was withheld, they would have good justification for revolt.[65] Since Palmerston detested revolution at all times, he was, if correctly reported, indulging both his temper and his tendency to bluff. And, on one occasion at least, his irritation got the better even of his common sense. For he gave the French government the fullest opportunity to increase its influence with Otto at the expense of England's own. To demand the dismissal of a Greek minister accused of using torture was certainly an act most commendable. But surely it was not the part of wisdom to inform Guizot—at a moment when Guizot's bitter resentment towards Melbourne's ministry in general and Palmerston in particular were unconcealed—that Otto ' pertinaciously ' clung to a ' disgusting system of torture ' and that the minister of whom complaint was made was merely the Greek king's ' chief instrument.'[66] The stage was being set for the entrance, nine years later on, of Don Pacifico.

Of what may be termed Palmerston's constructive diplomacy during his first four years as foreign minister, there remained only the work he had done for Belgium. This gave promise of enduring, both because it was fortified with so many treaties and protocols, and because Louis Philippe, as the father-in-law of King Leopold, could now be counted upon to make Leopold's interests to a large extent his own. Yet the king of Holland's acceptance of the settlement had still to be secured ; and it seemed to Palmerston that the matter was one of some urgency. He had scarcely been a month in office when he wrote Adair that all the 'ill-humour' which England encountered in Germany, and all the obstacles to a 'cordial union of the Powers of the west, against the encroachments & ambitious schemes of Russia' could be traced to 'the unsettled state of the dispute between Holland & Belgium.'[67] Consequently, he decided to send Adair on mission to Berlin. For he believed that it was principally from Prussia's foreign minister, Ancillon, that the Dutch government received encouragement in refusing to accept the treaty of November 1831. Ancillon, he complained, seemed 'to consider himself tutor to Belgium' and to act on the maxim, 'Spare the rod & spoil the child.' Adair's mission would be to convince him that Prussia, in persuading Holland to accept the Twenty-four Articles, would put an end to Belgium's dependence on the French government, and perform a service as valuable to herself as to all the other Powers.[68]

But Adair, on his arrival in Berlin, found himself obliged to deal with an issue of a more specific sort—with a new development in the question of the Belgian fortresses. For some time the Belgians, apprehensive that Holland might attack them with the acquiescence, if not the covert approval, of the three eastern Powers, had been maturing plans for the fortification of their northern frontier. Ancillon, seeing in the execution of these plans a possible strategic advantage for the French; and claiming, at least, to see a departure from Belgium's obligations in the matter of neutrality, objected vigorously. Palmerston was as ready as ever to spring to action where the Belgians were concerned. In his official communications he argued temperately enough that a neutral state, like any other state, was the only judge of the measures necessary for its security, that Belgium and Holland were still in 'a state of war,' and that history proved the inadequacy of treaties as a substitute for forts.[69] But his private letters to Adair show that his suspicions of the three eastern Powers were scarcely if at all less lively than those which he had previously entertained concerning France:

It is all very well to say that the independence of Belgium is guaranteed by the five Powers . . . we have all seen how bitterly three out of those five Govts repent having taken that engagement and how gladly they would escape from it, if they could.[70]

Was not a Dutch army ready to march on Brussels at any time ? And, in such case, what could be expected from the eastern courts ?

If King William were to order the Prince of Orange to march what good would the Belgians derive from the guarantees of Prussia Russia & Austria ? The armies of those three Powers are too far to afford any assistance, and if they were close I do not believe that a man of them would stir ; at least not until the Dutch had been defeated : They would wait to see whether the Dutch succeeded. If Leopold was driven out the three Powers would loudly condemn the attack of the Dutch, but say that after all the King of Holland had never acknowledged Leopold, nor made any compact with him, and had a right to recover his own ; and they would say that the ' Fait accompli ' annulled the Treaty of 1831.

Haunted by such fears, he supported Belgium steadily, as the dispute dragged on into 1837, to be handled by Werther in place of Ancillon and Lord William Russell instead of Adair.

In the late summer of 1837, Palmerston, whose patience seems to have been wearing thin, and who apparently transferred to Werther much of the feeling he had entertained regarding Ancillon, decided to administer a little chastisement at Berlin. Sir George Hamilton, who was temporarily in charge of the legation there, was ordered to show to Werther the copy of a despatch on the fortification question which the Foreign Office had sent recently to Brussels.[71] In this Palmerston advised the Belgian government to return a courteous answer to Werther's remonstrances, but ' to go on with the works just as if that remonstrance had never been made.' For, so the foreign secretary judged, Werther was employing no arguments which were not ' unreasonable ' and ' destitute of any just foundation,' no arguments in fact, of which the ' fallacy ' had not been ' amply demonstrated.' The effect on Werther must be described in Hamilton's own words :

Baron Werther had not read above twenty four lines, when he gave way to a paroxysm of violence such as I have seldom witnessed in any Individual. The expressions used by His Excellency with respect to Your Lordship were so strong that I more than once begged him to recollect that my conference with him was an official one and that I should think it my duty to report to my Government what took place at it, and I desired that he would tell me word for word what part of his conversation I should report to Your Lordship. . . . I found him too much excited, to believe he meant me to communicate every thing that had escaped him. After a long interval I persuaded Baron Werther to continue to read the Despatch which he had thrown aside, and at its termination, he desired me to state to Your Lordship as follows,—

'That he would not enter with me into the subject of that Despatch, and that he would never more receive any communication from Your Lordship connected with the Belgian Fortress Question,—that he considered Your Lordship's language with regard to himself personally, as *highly unbecoming* ' (these words were made use of in English) ' and that he had too much respect for his own character as a Gentleman, and man of Honour to reply to Your Lordship in your own terms, and that whilst Your Lordship thought that you were striking a blow immediately at him, you were insulting the Prussian Monarch who had deigned to approve of, and to sanction the Instructions he had sent to Baron Arnim [Prussian minister to Belgium] and which Your Lordship had been pleased to qualify as unreasonable and fallacious,—and that he should take care to communicate to His Sovereign the terms employed by Your Lordship in that Despatch.' [72]

In order that there should be no mistake Werther's statement was repeated, both in German and in English, more than once. True, he later apologised for his loss of self-control; but he renewed his complaint of 'the tone and manner' in which Palmerston's arguments were conveyed, and failed to withdraw his carefully phrased reply. There was a certain rather charming naïveté in the comment which Palmerston pencilled on the margin of the despatch:

There was nothing in that despatch about Baron Werther *personally*. The despatch dealt with Baron Werther's arguments. . . .[73]

Perhaps he never really understood why other diplomatists objected to his rough-and-tumble game.

This imperturbability of his, which, in so far as they knew of it, must have irritated the statesmen of other courts as much as his deliberate insolence, was displayed equally to Metternich. The old chancellor had not only lined up squarely with Werther, but had declared that the fortification question was for Prussia a question of peace or war.[74] The British government, Palmerston placidly replied, felt no apprehension on this score, counting the Prussian minister 'much too enlightened not to . . . be aware of the inconvenient consequences to Prussia herself which a war so commenced would inevitably produce.'[75] And he really felt himself compelled to say that the conduct of the eastern Powers respecting Belgium had not 'formed any striking exception to the warning to be derived . . . from the experience of preceding times' concerning the value of 'paper securities.' Had Metternich forgotten that, in the autumn of 1831, the Powers had secured the adhesion of Belgium to an arrangement which Belgium did not like, by promising that the consent of Holland should also be secured, and the terms of the arrangement actually put in force? Had he forgotten that, in spite of this, the eastern courts had abstained from any effort to bring the Dutch to terms, and refused to co-operate with the English and the French in expelling them from the Antwerp citadel? Surely it was not surprising if Leopold found it wiser to provide means for his defence than 'to trust for his safety to the already broken guarantee of the 3 Powers.' In the end, Belgium's dispute with the two great German Powers was compromised, and most of the projected fortifications given up; but Palmerston could feel that he had not failed his former protégés. In one respect his connection with them had become more than ever close. For William IV's death had recently given him, for a new sovereign, Leopold's niece, Victoria.

And it seemed at first that Palmerston would enjoy the happiest relations with his Queen. Perhaps, apart from Melbourne himself, he stood as close to her as any of her first ministers.[76] It was not merely that her foreign secretary was bound to command her interest, not merely that he was intimate with Melbourne, of whom she could not see enough, not merely that she liked sprightly and good looking men. Palmerston's closest friends stood near the throne: for Lady Cowper soon became one of Victoria's '*only real*

SCENE IN THE NEW POLITICAL PANTOMIME [1838]

friends,' her son, William, a groom-in-waiting, and one of her daughters a trainbearer at the coronation. He himself was singled out for favour, too. In London he appeared at the first state dinner of the reign—late as usual. At Windsor he cantered beside the royal carriage when the Queen went to Virginia Water; though when it came to embarking, he preferred, quite typically, to row himself in a small boat, rather than to miss his exercise by joining others of the noble company on a barge. He even shared with Melbourne alone the honour of being a guest at a 'little party' which the Queen found 'very social and agreeable.'

What was more, he shared with the premier the task of instructing Victoria in chess, in politics, and in foreign policy. He taught her the meaning of the word bureaucratic—'a name fabricated in imitation of the words "aristocratic" and "democratic," each being compounded of the word "cratic," which is a corruption from the Greek word "kratos," which means power.' He ordered special atlases to be made up in the Foreign Office so that she might find the foreign despatches more comprehensible. And apparently she found not only Palmerston but his policy quite to her taste. Witness the diplomatic dinner that she gave, just after her coronation, at which the guests were limited to the representatives of France, Belgium, Spain and Portugal. And Palmerston, on his side, was charmed not only by her graciousness and dignity but by her intellect. He pointed out to Creevey in the first months of the reign that 'she was no ordinary person,' having 'an understanding of her own that could have been made by no one.' There were several symptoms which might have disturbed him: the Queen's confidence in Leopold and Leopold's *fidus Achates*, Baron Stockmar; the 'obstinacy' and 'very high opinion of herself,' which Lady Cowper saw; her diligence in reading despatches from the first; and her rather alarming decision that public business would not allow her to take more than two or three days for her honeymoon. But he had no immediate occasion to feel alarm. Victoria's willingness to accept the advice of her ministers seemed exemplary. There was the best possible demonstration of this in connection with the final settlement of the Belgian question during the years 1838 and 1839.

The finale of the Belgian question, or rather the finale of its initial stage, was a dramatic one. In March 1838, the king of Holland announced his acceptance of the settlement of 1831. The Belgians, who had been holding in pledge parts of Limburg and Luxembourg assigned by treaty to the Dutch, and who felt that they were now called upon to abandon people bound to them by religion, by revolution, and by political union for eight years, demanded that the Twenty-four Articles should be revised. Violent demonstrations in Brussels brought on a dangerous economic crisis. There were military mobilisations in Belgium, in Holland, in Prussia and in other German states. Louis Philippe found it necessary to effect some cautious re-disposal of his troops. A Belgian revolution and a general war seemed quite within the range of possibilities. The conference of the Powers on Belgian affairs re-convened in London ; but it could not guarantee the maintenance of peace. The eastern Powers presented a united front against any alteration of the articles ; Leopold pleaded that alteration was essential to the tranquillity of his country and the safety of his throne : while the French government, placed in a serious dilemma, dissembled and temporised. Once again the British attitude was of vital consequence. But there was no longer a Talleyrand nor a real entente. Instead, there was a Queen Victoria, of whose support Leopold—with great justification, be it said—wrote hopefully and even boastfully.[77] Louis Philippe also had reason to build hopes on the accession of the Queen. On the other hand, her youthful Majesty was seeing a great deal of Melbourne and of Palmerston. The first of a long series of little dramas—comedies for the most part—in which she and Palmerston would play leading parts, with Europe for a stage, was about to be played out.

It was a very simple little drama after all, in which Palmerston successfully insisted upon the preservation of the Twenty-four Articles ; while Victoria trustfully followed her ministers. The king of Holland's change of heart was announced on March 14 ; and Palmerston, after some

THE DISAPPOINTMENT OF KING LEOPOLD 229

temporary hesitation, took his stand definitely with the eastern Powers.[78] Lord William Russell wrote delightedly from Berlin that the foreign secretary had ' got the right sow by the ear ' at last ;[79] while Leopold plaintively expressed fears to his royal niece that he ' had been put aside as one does with a piece of furniture which is not longer wanted.' Then begging forgiveness for such lack of confidence, and delicately reminding her that he wished always to be ' in the position of having rendered services without wanting any return for it,' he enjoined her to suggest to ' good Lord Melbourne' that England should not ' take the *lead* ' in bringing ' *destruction* ' upon Belgium.[80] From April on, Palmerston apparently ceased to be regarded as his ' clever and well-informed friend.' But good Lord Melbourne could see no justification for Leopold's complaints, nor reason for disagreeing with Palmerston. And all the comfort that went to Brussels from Buckingham Palace was Victoria's cool assurance that her ministers would ' do *everything* in their power to promote the prosperity and welfare ' of Belgium.[81]

What Leopold most resented was that the British government pressed France to join in urging Belgium's acceptance of the Twenty-four Articles. French historians are wont to suggest that Palmerston, in applying this pressure, was actuated by a desire to punish Louis Philippe, or to demonstrate the fact that Victoria was dominated by her ministers. But a more matter-of-fact explanation seems preferable. Only through agreement between the Powers could peaceful settlement be reached ; and there was every reason to suppose that the eastern Powers, having conceded to Belgium more than they had wished to do, would treat her harshly if she held out for better terms. Both the British and French envoys at Berlin emphasised the real and growing danger that Prussia and the other German states would attack her if her submission was too long delayed : while the Austrian and Prussian delegates to the London conference flatly refused to consider territorial readjustment of any sort, and suggested that German troops and Dutch ships should co-operate in bringing Leopold to terms. When Palmerston demurred to this, they insisted that the other four Powers should 'press France to take a straight line about the territory and to stand by the treaty.'[82] And press France they did, until Molé and Louis Philippe wrote Leopold that he would look in vain for help.[83] There ensued a widening of the breach between the Belgian king and Palmerston. Though the latter, co-operating with the French ambassador, secured for Belgium a reduction in the share of the debt of the United Netherlands for which she was to be held responsible,[84] Leopold was too resentful and disillusioned to show appreciation of the fact. And Palmerston, nettled, perhaps, at Leopold's long resistance and his attempts to influence Victoria, inflamed the wound. It was 'preposterous and most unjust,' he told the House, that the Belgians, after appealing for eight years to a treaty, ' as the charter for their existence and the record of their rights,' should attempt to upset it for their convenience.[85] He was not the man to dissemble, even when the object of his wrath had peculiar means of access to a British sovereign. Indeed, it did not seem at the moment that he had much to fear. Victoria, not long afterwards, wrote Prince Albert, her cousin and fiancé, that ' dear Uncle ' was ' given to believe that he must rule the roast [sic] everywhere.'[86] She omitted to remark that he was also a man of much patience and of tenacious memory. Palmerston, if he did not know this, was to discover it in due time.

There were those who found him deserving of the highest praise. Thus, Lord William Russell, perhaps the bitterest of all his critics in the British diplomatic group, praised the 'great ability and extraordinary patience' he had shown, and even declared him deserving of being made an earl.[87] He himself was apparently much of Lord William's mind, pronouncing the settlement 'a capital job . . . which ought to be satisfactory to both parties.'[88] There must have been satisfaction in knowing that, in one case at least, he had been able to continue with success a policy initiated under Grey.

CHAPTER XI

PALMERSTON'S WAR AGAINST THE SLAVE-TRADE AND FIRST RELATIONS WITH THE UNITED STATES, 1830–1841

IF the patronage of continental liberalism had, with the defection of the French government, become a discouraging and rather lonely task, Palmerston was commencing to taste success in the great humanitarian enterprise of his life—his attempt to exterminate the African slave-trade.[1] To attack this disgrace to nineteenth-century civilisation was, of course, an obligation which he had inherited. From the year 1807, when the Ministry of All the Talents had forbidden the trade to British colonies, a circle of English humanitarians had encouraged and applauded the efforts of successive cabinets to bring various foreign governments into line. But, from November 1830, the crusade was carried on—by the Foreign Office in particular—with unexampled energy and thoroughness. Palmerston gave to it all his vigour, his stubbornness and his sometimes ruthless audacity. In this case at least, personal feeling certainly found expression in his policy. As tales of hideous atrocities in Africa or on the 'Middle Passage' came to him, he expressed his loathing in terms of indubitable sincerity:

> I will venture to say, that if all the other crimes which the human race has committed, from the creation down to the present day, were added together in one vast aggregate, they would scarcely equal, I am sure they could not exceed, the amount of guilt which has been incurred by mankind, in connexion with this diabolical Slave Trade.[2]

Still deeper evidence of his feeling lies, perhaps, in the fact that his letters on this subject, unlike those on almost any other subject of which one can think, seem never to have been touched with flippancy. And with Palmerston to feel deeply was to act. No matter how engrossed in domestic or international affairs, he was always ready, with the help of a specially designated Foreign Office clerk,[3] to attack the slave-trade hydra at any vulnerable point. In fact, he seemed at times to put the prosecution of this great crusade before the promotion of Britain's material interests. His most ruthless steps were taken against Portugal, his special protégé, and England's oldest and still highly prized ally : while the greatest pressure possible was brought to bear on the United States, a country which he was particularly at pains to please. The reason seems to be that, as he told the House in 1841, he felt his country's moral leadership to be involved :

> As long as England shall ride pre-eminent on the ocean of human affairs, there can be none whose fortunes shall be so shipwrecked, there can be none whose condition shall be so desperate and forlorn, that they may not cast a look of hope towards the light that beams from hence ; and though they may be beyond the reach of our power, our moral support and our sympathy shall cheer them in their adversity. . . . But if ever by the assault of overpowering enemies, or by the errors of her misguided sons, England should fall . . . for a long period of time, would the hopes of the African . . . be buried in the darkness of despair. I know well that in such case, Providence would, in due course of time, raise up some other nation to inherit our principles, and to imitate our practice. But . . . I do not know any nation that is now ready in this respect to supply our place.[4]

This blend of patriotism and humanitarianism sustained him in the struggle for more than thirty years.

The difficulties which confronted him at the outset were enough to have daunted any ordinary man. Almost every government was ready enough to proscribe the trade in so far as the mere enactment of penal legislation and subscription to promises of a general description were concerned. But, when it came to the actual enforcement of the penal laws, and to the acceptance of treaty provisions of a specific and effective sort, few states were at first prepared to accede to the wishes of the British government. And certain very specific provisions were indispensable.

THE TACTICS OF THE WAR

It was, for example, necessary that a slave-ship could be condemned on the evidence of her merely possessing equipment for the trade, without proof that she intended to engage, or had engaged, in it. Otherwise, she could proceed to the coast of Africa with absolute impunity; and there was always the sinister possibility that a trader, threatened with capture on the voyage back, would seek safety in the wholesale drowning of his incriminating passengers. Again, unless each condemned ship were broken up, she was apt to reappear on the Slave Coast almost immediately. And—most important of all—unless nations conceded to one another's navies a mutual right of visit and search, a sufficient number of slave vessels would always escape to make the traffic pay. Any trader might hope to elude capture by flying the colours of some state of which the government was too indifferent, or too poor in ships, to send out adequate patrols. And, if he did meet a cruiser under the colours he was wont to use, he was customarily prepared to exhibit another flag, other papers and another crew. Only an international police could deal with the situation on all the coasts and islands of Africa and America where slaves were loaded and disembarked. Hence, to secure agreements with all countries for a mutual right of search was Palmerston's most important task. And also the most difficult. It was not merely that rich traders found methods of influencing governments. England had humiliated other nations by forced search in times of war; and her great naval superiority would give her dominance in any international policing of the seas. But there were ways of getting at least partially around the difficulty. The seizure of a slaver carrying the flag of some other Power could be made by a British vessel acting under warrant from that other Power's own Admiralty. The proudest states, with one exception, were willing to concede, by 1841, that the slight derogation to their dignity which an arrangement of this kind involved was more than atoned for by the service to humanity. The exception was the United States.

With other countries Palmerston made steady progress from the first—driving the slavers from refuge to refuge.

On coming into office under Grey he had found them flourishing under the French flag. But his relations with Louis Philippe's government had enabled him to secure, in 1831 and 1833, treaties which provided not only for the mutual right of search, but for 'equipment' and 'breaking up' articles.[5] When the slave-merchants laid aside their French captains, French papers and French flags, to acquire Spanish ones instead, they found him on their heels. For in 1835 he used his influence with the Spanish government to secure a treaty which gave him all that he had obtained from France.[6] In the five years which ensued, British cruisers seized over one hundred slavers of alleged Spanish nationality, of which only eighteen were actually carrying slaves.[7] But the next step in the pursuit of the malefactors was more difficult. Diplomatic measures were not enough to drive them from the next sanctuary they claimed—the disavowed but quite effective protection of the Portuguese.

Palmerston's indignation with Portugal was profound.[8] From 1810 she had signed several treaties and given endless promises regarding the extinction of the trade. She had accepted from England nearly £500,000 (quite apart from £300,000 paid to Portuguese ship-owners in compensation for their ships) as a virtual bribe for making good her word. And now, as the foreign secretary pointed out indignantly to the House, she refused, not only to fall in line with France and Spain, but to live up to her earlier promises :

> She has violated them in a greater degree, I will venture to say, than any country in the history of the civilized world could be found ever to have violated the solemn obligations of treaties. . . . For, instead of suppressing the Slave-trade and abolishing it, she encourages it. . . .[9]

He was not unmindful of his own especially close relations with the new Portuguese government, but

> . . . he could assure the hon. Baronet [Peel] that no predilection of his in favour of the system of government now fortunately established in that country, or any degree in which he might have identified himself with the support of that system . . . would he allow to interfere by mitigating, in the slightest degree, the indignation which he felt . . . on this subject.[10]

Neither did it mitigate the action which he judged necessary. For in 1839, having exhausted all the possibilities of persuasion and argument,[11] he obtained from parliament an act which permitted British cruisers to search and seize suspected or actual slavers flying the colours of Portugal, almost precisely as though they had been sailing beneath the Union Jack.[12] There was little exaggeration in Tory complaints that the bill authorised proceedings tantamount to acts of war ; but, when the Tory peers at first rejected it, Palmerston discussed the possibility of directing British cruisers to take action without authority from parliament.[13] It was remarked that neither he nor Brougham ' was quite accountable for his actions where the Black Man was concerned.'

The foreign secretary's ruthless determination to exterminate the trade was equally well shown in the year following.[14] When Captain Denman, R.N., destroyed a barracoon on the west coast of Africa in which some negroes of British citizenship had been confined, and conveyed all the slaves he could gather, irrespective of ownership or nationality, to the free colony at Sierra Leone, he dangerously exceeded his authority. But Palmerston and Russell both hastened to write the Admiralty, commending Denman's action, assuming responsibility, and recommending that officers on the Slave Coast should be authorised to imitate Denman's step wherever British negroes were confined, or where approval could be secured from native chiefs. As a result, Denman was promoted and rewarded, as well as secured against all suits for damages ; while orders were issued by the Admiralty according to Palmerston's desire. In 1842 the cautious Aberdeen withdrew official approval, and surrounded with safeguards any future action of this kind. But enough had been done to strike terror on the African coast, and so retard the trade.

The events of the year 1840 also produced an interesting demonstration of the manner in which Palmerston's anti-slave-trading crusade might interfere with his other policies. In this case British relations with Texas were concerned.[15] The Texans had been asking British recognition of their republic for three years. They had offered the enticing prospect of a great new agricultural state, which would throw wide its markets to the manufacturers of Yorkshire, and emancipate Lancashire from dependence on the cotton of the United States. Various factors in the situation enjoined caution upon Palmerston and his colleagues ; but he was obviously attracted from the first. On the other hand, his convictions, and the merest deference to consistency, forbade him to accord the favour of recognition to a new slave-trading state. He had even to consider how he would meet the criticisms of Tories and abolitionists in parliament for extending the hand of fellowship to a new nation in which slave-holding was the rule. It is obvious that he found the situation an embarrassing one. In 1837, when the subject of recognition was first broached, he had not only inquired carefully about the possible cotton crop, but ' observed rather archly ' that he believed Texas had abolished slavery.[16] As the negotiations progressed, he came to realise, if he had not done so from the first, that to demand abolition in Texas would be quite futile. But he warned the Texans more than once concerning the slave-trade ; and ended by making its abolition a ' preliminary and indispensable condition ' of the recognition which they craved.[17] Thus, because of his humanitarian crusade he was forced to imperil good relations with a state from which England might have much to gain, which France and the United States had already recognised, and which he was evidently anxious to conciliate. Witness the ' noble frankness and cordial confidence,' the ' friendly & considerate regard,' of which Hamilton, the Texan agent, could not say enough.[18] And Hamilton noted that the foreign secretary lived in mortal dread lest their negotiations be rendered abortive after all by premature disclosure to the British abolitionists. Yet Palmerston imposed a ' preliminary and indispensable condition ' which might easily have been rejected by the Texan government. Hamilton dared not write his chief that he had agreed to it, until he could send the news by an influential and persuasive friend.[19]

The anti-slave-trade treaty with Texas, although not ratified until 1842, was, of course, a portion of the vast net which Palmerston was constructing for the capture of all sea-going slave-traders of the world. In 1830 there had merely been treaties—and very inadequate ones at that—with Spain, Portugal, Brazil, Sweden and the Netherlands. But by 1841 his agents had concluded, or had every prospect of being able to conclude, effective treaties with every European court that showed its flag upon the sea, and with nearly every state of Central and South America.[20] In assuring parliament, in May of that year, that the last of his negotiations held every promise of success, he was able to conclude :

> Well, then, if we succeed . . . we shall have enlisted in this league against slave-trade every state in Christendom which has a flag that sails on the ocean, with the single exception of the United States of North America.[21]

And that the exception existed ; that Portuguese, Brazilian and Spanish bootleggers of human souls found it a shelter from his wrath, was not his fault. Apologists for America are apparently correct in pointing out that there were British merchants who did not scruple to assist in fitting out vessels for the trade ;[22] but any proof of connivance by the government will be a discovery indeed.

It is not a pleasant task for an American to write of his country's attitude towards the slave-trade in the third to fifth decades of the nineteenth century. As the slave states consolidated their power and brought it to bear at Washington, the national government and a great proportion of the populace displayed what now seems an almost incredible indifference to the infringement of the law, and to the bestial cruelties which this entailed.[23] Partial enforcement there was, of course, even at the worst of times ; protests that there was not more, reached Washington even from men who owed their positions to the government.[24] But successive cabinets and congresses lacked will or power to abate the national disgrace. The honour of the flag was supposedly upheld by repeated and increasingly uncompromising rejections of British proposals for a mutual right of search. There were obvious reasons why the idea conveyed by the phrase was especially repellent to Americans. But, except in origin, there was no real identity between the right of search which had done so much to cause the war of 1812, and that for which Palmerston pleaded in the interests of the blacks. Even James Hamilton, the Texan agent to England in 1840, himself a South Carolinian, a slave holder and a veteran of the war of 1812, saw this :

> . . . the right of search in the Treaty [between Texas and England] . . . is no more like the right of search which Great Britain exercised for more than fifteen years on board of American vessels than a naked act of violence is analagous [*sic*] to the execution of the Judgment of a Court of Justice. I have not been alarmed by the potency of mere names against the evidence of what things really are.[25]

But Hamilton had the incentive and the will to see : the politicians at Washington had not. As for most of the populace, it was much as in 1920, when Americans, alone among the great peoples of the occident, yielded to persuasion that they would sacrifice national sovereignty by entering the League. Palmerston was persuasive too ; but his arguments probably reached the ears of few possible converts.

In fact, Palmerston was all persuasiveness for several years. With Martin Van Buren, who was American minister to England from 1831 to 1832, he began in the gentlest manner possible, professing his anxiety ' to promote the views of the two governments,' and apparently showing no resentment when Van Buren explained that popular sentiment in America would prevent the federal government from conceding even a modified right of search.[26] Through the four years when Aaron Vail represented the United States at the British court, and even for two or three years after the arrival, in 1836, of Andrew Stevenson as American minister, there seems to have been no serious difficulty. The nearest approach came in the interchange of some rather heated notes concerning the American demand that compensation should be paid for slaves brought by bad weather to British colonies, and liberated there.[27] Palmerston, stoutly invoking ' the Law of Nations ' to prove that any state might refuse to admit the existence of slavery on its soil, and 'the Law of Nature' to establish a distinction between 'laws bearing upon the personal liberty of man, and laws bearing upon the property which man may claim in irrational animals, or in inanimate things,' refused indemnification in cases where the liberation of American slaves had occurred after the abolition of slavery in all British territories. But he arranged for the payment of what Stevenson considered 'highly liberal and satisfactory' compensation in the case of slaves emancipated on British soil in earlier years. Hence the disagreement between the two governments did not even approach a climax until 1840, when slavers of every known and unknown breed, finding even the Portuguese flag unsafe, crowded for protection under that of the United States.[28] The issue was squarely joined.

The American position, summarised by Stevenson as a determination that the flag should '*cover all that sails under it*,'[29] was, in the eyes not only of Palmerston but of Aberdeen, quite preposterous. Strictly applied—and neither Stevenson nor his government seems to have been willing to consider anything but application of the strictest sort—it meant that any rabble who chose to hoist the Stars and Stripes would be immune from capture or control of any sort, save in the circumstances of their being brought to by some American cruiser on patrol. Since American patrol ships were reputedly slow and few;[30] since condemnation for the possession of equipment was not provided for by law; and since double sets of colours, papers and mariners were not difficult to procure, the risk of slave-trading under the American flag, though quite appreciable, was far from sufficient to offset the gain.[31] Small wonder then if Palmerston protested that to concede the American position would be to make the extermination of the hideous traffic impossible. Aberdeen later pointed out that it would prevent England from punishing miscreants among her own subjects, and might even afford a screen to piracy.[32]

Deeply engrossed as he was, during 1840, in the Near Eastern crisis and the European complications which it entailed, Palmerston found time to bring continuous and increasing pressure on the American government.[33] He begged that American laws should be enforced in America's own ports, and that an adequate number of cruisers be sent to Africa. He forwarded reports of British commanders on patrol, admiralty letters, and despatches from the slave-trade commissioners at Sierra Leone to show that his entreaties and protests were based on solid evidence. He appealed repeatedly to Stevenson, and furnished him with a memorandum, written in his own hand, which pointed out the 'perfect immunity' enjoyed by fully equipped slavers under American colours on the eastern trip, and 'suggested' that the United States should pass a law making the possession of equipment sufficient ground for punishment. For all the good it did, he might have spared his pen and breath.

But, during this year and 1841, the issue was growing more and more serious. For the British ministers, determined to suppress the trade, and finding all persuasion vain, encouraged their cruisers to overhaul allegedly American ships. Stevenson's protests were ignored as long as possible ; and Palmerston, when he found himself compelled to deal with them, usually declined to give redress.[34] Lieutenant Payne, U.S.N., who commanded what seems to have been, in March 1840, the only American cruiser patrolling the Slave Coast, gave him an excuse of which he made full use.[35] For Payne, wholeheartedly anxious to use his ship as effectively as possible, agreed with the officer commanding the British patrol to institute what amounted, for the locality, to a mutual right of search. But Payne's action was speedily disavowed, and Palmerston forced to base his refusals of redress on broader grounds. What he did was to develop the theory that the right of visit was quite distinguishable from the right of search :

> But there is an essential and fundamental difference between searching a vessel and examining her papers to see whether she is legally provided with documents entitling her to the protection of . . . the country whose flag she may have hoisted at the time. For though by common parlance the word 'Flag' is used to express the test of nationality ; and though according to that acceptation of the word Her Majesty's Government admit that British cruizers are not

entitled in time of peace to search merchant vessels sailing under the American flag, yet Her Majesty's Government do not mean thereby to say that a merchantman can exempt herself from search by merely hoisting a piece of bunting with the United States' emblems and colours upon it ; that which Her Majesty's Government mean is that the rights of the United States flag exempt a vessel from search when that vessel is provided with papers entitling her to wear that flag, and proving her to be United States property and navigated according to law.

But this fact cannot be ascertained unless an officer of a cruizer . . . shall board the vessel, or unless the master of the merchantman shall bring his papers on board the cruizer, and this examination . . . is a proceeding which it is absolutely necessary that British cruizers employed in the suppression of the slave trade should continue to practise.[36]

These words were written to Stevenson at the end of August 1841, when Palmerston was preparing to hand over the Foreign Office to Aberdeen ; and it is not unlikely that the arrogant phrasing reflected his realisation that his responsibility was at an end. Nevertheless, he was perfectly sincere. The position which he assumed had been almost as clearly stated in earlier communications with Stevenson ;[37] and had been set forth as a basis for naval action in a letter despatched by his under secretary, Lord Leveson, to the Admiralty three months before.[38] Nor was it really abandoned on Palmerston's fall. Although Stevenson protested hotly to Aberdeen, he received little satisfaction at the outset. The new foreign secretary's first answer, though draped in phrases of charming amiability, appealed to Stevenson's ' candour '—he ' had almost said to the dictates of plain sense '—and declared the right claimed by Palmerston to be ' indispensable.'[39] Three months later Aberdeen charmed Everett by disavowing Palmerston's pronouncements, and doubling his own civilities. Yet the ' marked change ' of which Everett wrote was not in position but in ' tone.'[40]

Palmerston's attempts to bring pressure on the United States had also had quite another side. When he boasted to parliament, in May 1841, that he expected to enlist against the slave-trade ' every state in Christendom which has a flag that sails on the ocean, with the single exception of the United States of North America,' he was announcing the approaching realisation of a plan for throwing a spotlight on America's delinquencies. What he worked for above all, and was on the point of obtaining in the summer of 1841, was a treaty between the five great European Powers, concluded on terms similar to those of his treaties with the French government. Thanks to the circumstances of his break with France, which must be related in due course, it remained for Aberdeen to reap where Palmerston had sowed. Nor, as events soon proved, did the great republic find itself in the position of being 'the single exception' after all. But most of its citizens would not have minded much. They were far more sensitive to the efforts of a pugnacious British statesman to reform them in spite of themselves.

The peculiar sensitiveness of Americans regarding these disputes over the slave trade—a sensitiveness to which the possession of guilty consciences no doubt contributed—must have helped to foster the belief that Palmerston was inimical to the United States. His bluntness, determination and occasional high-handedness in all diplomatic intercourse must have operated in the same way. Hence it is a striking fact that Van Buren, writing his autobiography in 1854, went out of his way to combat this belief:

> During . . . a period of about eleven years, [1830–1841] there did not arise a single important question between our respective Governments with the superintendence of which he [Palmerston] was not charged or in which I did not take a direct part, or over the disposition of which I did not exert a material influence either as Secretary of State, Minister to England, as the confidential counsellor of President Jackson, always consulted on such occasions, or as President. . . . Among those questions were that of the North Eastern Boundary between us and Great Britain, in the worst and most menacing aspects which that subject ever assumed, and that presented by the mutually disturbing and irritating occurrences growing out of the Canadian Rebellion and the unauthorized participation of our citizens in its prosecution, including the affair of the *Caroline* and the case of McLeod.
>
> I have seen, with regret, that an impression has, to some extent at least, secured a lodgment in the public mind here that Lord Palmerston

has imbibed prejudices against this Country which have made him less disposed than other British statesmen to do us justice. I feel bound to say that with the opportunities I have had, perhaps as full as those of any other person, I have seen nothing to justify this notion but much to disprove its correctness. . . . I never had occasion to suspect him of professing opinions he did not sincerely believe to be well founded . . . to this day I retain a gratifying and abiding recollection of the constant occasion I found to admire the candour and integrity of his conduct and of the facilities for the performance of official duties which were afforded by his genial and conciliatory dispositions.[41]

Since the 'impression' which Van Buren deplored eighty years ago has shown rather a tenacious hold on life, and since it may be guessed that age or personal prepossessions brought the former president to show undue tolerance toward his principal diplomatic adversary, some examination, however casual, of Palmerston's attitude on the questions referred to seems desirable.

It may be well to go back for a moment to Palmerston's relations with the Jackson administration from 1830 to 1834. There can be no doubt that he showed himself quite friendly and accommodating at this time. He accepted immediately the award of the king of the Netherlands concerning 'the North-Eastern Boundary'—*i.e.* the boundary between northern New England and eastern Canada—although its terms were less favourable to England than those of the Webster-Ashburton treaty which he was to denounce so violently in 1843. Van Buren found him 'disposed to enter liberally' on the American attitude towards impressment, and very appreciative of America's willingness to defer settlement until the Whigs had had time to dispose of the question of reform.[42] Indeed, he did not fail in actual blandishments—in the avowal, for example, that England had 'experienced better treatment' at Jackson's hands than at those of any of his predecessors.[43] Altogether, Van Buren found the British foreign secretary's conduct 'of the most fair, liberal and friendly character'; and Aaron Vail, who took over the American legation in 1832, wrote to the same effect.[44]

Nor did these halcyon days of Anglo-American relations

end with Palmerston's first term at Downing Street. Returning to his post in the spring of 1835, he preserved the old tone of friendliness, in spite of the existence of various minor difficulties.[45] American fishermen might encroach in the St. Lawrence; American citizens in Massachusetts, Connecticut and Maine might raise protests against the activities of British abolitionists; the southern states might imprison, or even enslave, free coloured subjects of his Majesty, and refuse all intervention by the federal government; but the relations between Downing Street and the White House remained undisturbed. When citizens of New Hampshire attacked, wounded and abducted a Quebec justice of the peace, Palmerston privately stigmatised the act as 'a most violent and inexcusable outrage';[46] yet, officially, he kept his temper and his head.

'I believe,' wrote Henry Fox, the British minister at Washington, in June 1836, 'that there is no other Country on the globe, amongst whose inhabitants it would at the present moment be more difficult, than amongst the Americans, to provoke feelings of hostility against Great Britain.'[47] Fox's discernment seems to have been decidedly at fault. Yet, thanks largely, no doubt, to the British mediation between the United States and France, the old cordiality between Van Buren and Palmerston, and the fact that disputes over the slave trade had not yet become at all inflamed, the period from 1835 to 1837 seemed one of 'hands across the sea.' Certainly compliments flowed back and forth in a manner highly unusual if not unprecedented. In December 1835, the redoubtable 'Lord Pumicestone,' 'taking the liberty' of recalling himself to Van Buren 'as a private friend,' overflowed with assurances concerning the confidence reposed in Jackson's trusted counsellor by the Foreign Office and the King.[48] Van Buren, answering, was happy to report that Jackson quite shared his own conviction of the resolution of the British government to maintain 'the most just & friendly relations with the U. States.'[49] And why should not the president have felt so, when Palmerston pointed out to parliament that the conduct of America regarding Texas had been 'consistent with the most scrupulous feelings of honour and delicacy towards other powers,'[50] and when the American chargé pictured the British cabinet as ' every day becoming more . . . anxious to draw closer bonds of friendship ' ?[51] In 1836, when Stevenson was preparing to take up his post in London as American minister, Vail prophesied that he would ' have an easy berth of it,' provided, at least, that he was not instructed to reopen the question of the north-eastern boundary.[52]

Nor, in an atmosphere of such friendliness, did the boundary question seem at all dangerous. True, it had reached something like a deadlock by the time Palmerston was re-established at Downing Street in the spring of 1835, —a situation which was in no wise altered by his withdrawal, six months later, of the British offer to accept the king of the Netherlands' award.[53] But amicable negotiations could and did proceed.[54] Palmerston, who seems never to have had much respect for the peace commissioners of 1783 and their ' erroneous ' maps, persistently urged the judgment of Solomon—bisection of the territory in dispute. But Maine refused to hear of such dismemberment ; and the federal government demanded a new international commission of exploration and survey. Palmerston, still genuinely sceptical, it seems, as to the possibility of arriving at a settlement by such means, gave in. But he did so with a proviso which, as he expected, proved unacceptable to the United States ; and which would, in any case, have made final settlement by the proposed commission impossible. What had to be decided, above all, was the location of a certain height of land which formed a watershed for rivers flowing to the sea. The ' key to the whole question,' as Palmerston saw it, was what the sea comprised. If it included the Bay of Fundy, as the Americans maintained, the height of land lay well to the east ; and most of the disputed territory went to the United States. But he would concede nothing of the sort. Nor —and here was his proviso—would he allow the proposed commission to decide the point. His attitude, at first so accommodating, and still friendly enough, seemed to be hardening. Perhaps the opposition from Washington, and the news of clashes between the patriots and soldiers of New

Brunswick and of Maine, were responsible for this. And, since the potential dangers of the European situation had become relatively slight, he had more time and energy to spare. Even at that, he showed no incivility or unfriendliness. Hence the negotiations pursued a leisurely and not unfriendly course to 1837, when rebellion broke out in Upper and Lower Canada, and American citizens in the border states insisted upon helping the Canadians to be 'free.'

Of the burning of the *Caroline* and the other 'border incidents' which supervened, it seems needless to speak. Of the ripples which they produced on the smooth tide of at least outward friendliness between the representatives of the two countries, one rather enlightening example may suffice.[55] In November 1838, a 'Hunters'' lodge in Michigan attempted an attack on the little Canadian town of Windsor. But government officials interfered; and Van Buren issued a proclamation calling on every citizen of the United States to protect the national 'honor and good faith' by doing his best to check such ' nefarious ' activities. News of the raid reached London before that of Van Buren's proclamation; and it seems probable that for once Palmerston's attitude of studied equanimity gave way. At any rate, Stevenson wrote to him sharply concerning an editorial in the *Chronicle*—an editorial which particularly sinned in referring to the New York *Inquirer* (a strongly anti-Van Buren sheet) as 'a paper of very high character.' But when the American minister followed this up by sending a copy of the proclamation, the reconciliation was immediate and apparently complete. Palmerston wrote to Stevenson of the ' high tone of national honour ' on which the proclamation of the president was ' conceived,' and Stevenson to Van Buren of his own intense gratification at receiving the ' highly flattering answer' of the British foreign minister. 'Flattering' was just the word to describe the foreign secretary's attitude towards the federal government and its representatives at this time. In February 1838, he had testified to parliament in glowing terms of the ' friendly spirit ' and ' high sense of honour' displayed at Washington in communications concerning the destruction of the *Caroline*.[56] In the spring of 1839, being called upon to advise his sovereign concerning the acknowledgement of certain gifts from the United States, he suggested that 'the sensitive pride of the American character' made advisable the despatch of a print of her august Majesty's portrait.[57] He even begged that court etiquette be relaxed in favour of certain friends of Daniel Webster, he being 'a person upon whom an act of civility would be usefully bestowed.'[58] And—most flattering of all—he actually used the words 'deep regret' when writing, in 1840, of a new border incident in which the Canadians were obviously to blame.[59] European Powers were hardly accustomed to such courtesies at his hands.

Then, suddenly, in 1841, the two countries came to the very verge of war concerning that bibulous and boastful Scotch-Canadian, that self-proclaimed participant in the wretched *Caroline* affair, McLeod. The only interest here attaching to this oft-told tale lies in observing just how Palmerston bore himself. And one might begin by noting a rather striking demonstration of his brand of psychology. He had heard that Francis Granger, the friend and future postmaster-general of Harrison, the president-elect, had made a jingoistic speech in Congress, promising that McLeod, if found guilty, should be hanged, and daring England in such case to do her worst.[60] Palmerston's comment in a *private* letter ran :

> When a man connected with a government that is or is to be holds such language in Parliament, it seems clear to me that it is for the purpose of holding high a principle which he thinks will not be carried into practice.[61]

But he was perfectly prepared to go to war if by any chance Granger's threats were to be made good. It seems that he really would have had no choice.[62] Not only did the Tory opposition promise full support, but, as Stevenson pointed out, the nation as a whole was determined that McLeod should either be rescued or avenged. This being the case, it is notable that war-mongers, if there were such in England at the time, received no shadow of encouragement from the chauvinistic foreign minister. While he showed ' much more caution and reserve ' to Stevenson, he went out of his way to prevent dangerous discussions in parliament.[63] He pointed out to the American minister that McLeod's life would have to be paid for in the blood and treasure of both countries; but he was careful to do so in a private and informal interview.[64] And when he conveyed the same warning to the American government through the British envoy at Washington, his tone was dispassionate as well as firm.[65] A final demonstration of his desire to keep the peace was given when the Supreme Court of New York decided that McLeod's case would have to take its course. For he assured Webster of his ' entire confidence in the just intentions of the Federal Government,' and readily acceded to Stevenson's request that no further steps should be taken until after McLeod's trial.[66] There were, of course, times when sharp letters passed between the American legation and Downing Street. In this same year Stevenson protested angrily against Palmerston's assertion that Great Britain had from the first assumed official responsibility for the attack upon the *Caroline*, and that the American government had allowed the matter of settlement to lie quiescent for three years, rather than invite a certain rebuff.[67] This, perhaps, makes it the more notable that, during the real crisis, Stevenson had apparently no fault to find.

But after all, if one is interested in checking the correctness of Van Buren's statement, and that of the ' impression ' which he was at pains to counteract, it is necessary to concentrate on Palmerston's attitude toward the question of the north-eastern boundary. For the most common charge against him is that he allowed the negotiations on this issue to reach a dangerous *impasse* by the late summer of 1841. The *impasse* and the danger are, of course, undeniable; but the final apportionment of responsibility—if such apportionment is really possible—seems to wait upon final research. And one wonders whether the prevailing idea may not owe something to the accused's virulent attacks on the Webster-Ashburton treaty in 1843. If this be true, it is well to bear in mind that party government in England has often had the effect of impairing memories; since the opposition must manage, somehow or other, to find fault with most of the proceedings of the government. It seems, for example, a matter of some interest that Stevenson, writing to Forsyth on the boundary question in March 1839, showed considerable misgiving lest the Tories should come into power.[68] While he believed the Whig government and the mass of the populace entirely bent on peace, the speeches of Peel and Wellington seemed to him ' anything but pacific, or conciliatory towards America.' He found the same division in the press. The *Chronicle* was quite subdued ; but *The Times* and *Standard*, opposition organs both, were 'insolent and belligerent.' To point this out is not, of course, in any way to exculpate Palmerston, but merely to suggest a broader view, which may in some degree explain Van Buren's general attitude. There is a good deal of explaining to be done. For Palmerston became more and more haughty and exacting between the spring of 1839 and the summer of 1841. If one asks why, at least four possible explanations present themselves. There was the irritation caused by incessant bickerings over the slave-trade ; there were what he regarded as constant ' encroachments ' by American frontiersmen in the disputed area ; there was the long-sustained refusal of the American government to accept, first an arbitral award, and then a conventional settlement ; and there was his obviously sincere belief that he had, by 1840, come into possession of new evidence supporting the most extreme of his claims. The last point requires some emphasis. Van Buren, it will be remembered, laid much stress on two things : that Palmerston had no 'prejudices' against the United States, and that he was always convinced of the justice of his demands.

But to stress this latter point brings up, alas ! the ' battle of the maps.' If one could but be certain even now of the part he played in that still lingering contest ! The accepted story is that Palmerston, finding that the British Museum contained the 'Oswald' map of 1783, and that its display would be fatal to the British claims, removed it to the Foreign Office files—just as Webster concealed *his* knowledge of a map which would have been treasure-trove at Downing Street. The reader is sometimes told that Palmerston withheld knowledge of the map even from Aberdeen, and is permitted to infer that Aberdeen would not have connived at proceedings of this sort. The story may be true enough. But one wishes that it were based on evidence more direct than that furnished by a speech from the passionate and sometimes very unreliable Lord Brougham.[69] And, of course, Palmerston could be defended on almost the same grounds as those used to justify Webster.[70] As for Aberdeen, there is reason to regard his connivance as entirely probable. For, if Charles Greville was not grossly misinformed by a member of the State Paper Office personnel, Peel's whole cabinet was concerned in sequestering still another apparently inconvenient map, unearthed about June 1842.[71] Elucidation of the whole matter will provide the chance for the telling of a very pretty story by some historian—a story which may light up Palmerston's exact motives for objecting, in 1841, to any search of public records by the international commission urged by Webster at the time, and his seemingly artless remark that each government could voluntarily share with the other such information as it might possess![72] But one thing can be established with certainty: his contempt for the famous Mitchell map. He expressed it most clearly in August 1841, when writing Fox of his objections to certain proposals just received from Washington:

> But of all the propositions made by the American counter draft none can be more inadmissible than that contained in article 10. For that article again proposes that Mitchell's map shall be acknowledged as evidence . . . whereas everybody who has paid any attention to these matters now knows that Mitchell's map is full of the grossest inaccuracies as to the longitude and latitude of places, and that it can be admitted as evidence of nothing but of the deep ignorance of the person who framed it.[73]

Beneath this hyperbole there lay some truth;[74] but the essential point is that Palmerston's lack of confidence in the Mitchell map helps to explain his attitude throughout.

Forced by the American government to consider what settlement might be arrived at by a new international commission of survey, he still boggled over the terms under which the commission was to be sent out.[75] And, even in face of the danger which clashes in the disputed area entailed, he persisted in believing that an equitable settlement must take time. As he explained to Russell in October 1839, when Lord John was in a nervous mood, surrender could be effected immediately, but the acceptance of just terms must wait on the pleasure of America.

> . . . do not suppose that I wish to *decide* to defer a settlement of the boundary question for two years—on the contrary I should be delighted to settle it in two days ; but . . . if we mean to keep that which rightfully belongs to us, and which I believe will turn out to be, very nearly all we have ever claimed, there are but two ways of doing so, the one by going to war . . . the other by negotiating, and proving to the Americans that we are justly intitled to what we ask. The first mode is out of the question, and the latter requires time. [76]

It would take time, he pointed out, for the surveyors ' to cut their way at the rate of four miles a day ' ; and the season when even this was practicable was so brief that the summer of 1840 might not be enough. Hence 'it would be forming a very sanguine expectation to hope that any satisfactory and final agreement could be come to . . . till the year 1841 was pretty far advanced.' Even then arbitration or agreement on a conventional line might have to be adopted after all.

That war over the boundary dispute was ' out of the question,' he apparently believed from the beginning to the end. Certainly he expressed such belief frequently enough, often introducing a variation which reflected the circumstances of the moment and his own resultant mood. There were occasions when he blustered, expressing (quite privately, of course) his scepticism as to the willingness of the federal government to ' involve itself in a war to please a few speculators in Maine.' [77] There were others when he counted upon the fact that the Americans were ' in a condition of general bankruptcy,' and that this would not ' give a fancy for maritime war to a nation who live by commerce and who have made no naval preparations whatever for a fight by sea.' [78] And there were times when he took broader and firmer ground. 'Commercial interests on both sides are so strong,' he wrote Granville, in March 1839, 'that it would require a very extraordinary state of things to bring an actual war.'[79]

His attitude hardened from the spring of 1840 on, because he was convinced as never previously that he could make good England's claim to the lion's share of the disputed land. In 1839, he had sent out two surveyors, Mudge and Featherstonhaugh, to gather data on England's own account. When, in this same year, the cabinet seemed inclined to close with one of the projects for settlement of the whole dispute then offered by the American government, Palmerston successfully importuned them to wait for Mudge and Featherstonhaugh's report.[80] This report, which, to judge by Palmerston's own calculations, was prepared in an amazingly brief space of time, was presented in the April following. Pronounced in recent years by the best Canadian authority to be 'as strongly partisan a document as could possibly be produced,' and as showing highlands which 'had no real existence,'[81] it was seized upon by Palmerston with every appearance of complete credulity as well as delight.[82] Thus, on April 22, he wrote exuberantly to Melbourne:

> It quite knocks over the American claim, and I think it sets up ours; and surely if the unanimity of the Americans in favour of their own claim is founded . . . upon a universal belief that their claim is just, one way of breaking up that unanimity must necessarily be to show them that their claim is erroneous.[83]

He still, of course, continued to negotiate for a bi-partisan survey. In fact, within six weeks he had accepted the 'fundamental principles' of a new proposal by Van Buren that a joint commission should be sent out, and that, with the help of arbitration where agreement proved impossible, the commissioners should come to a final settlement.[84] But drafts and counter drafts for the regulation of details were soon passing backwards and forwards between London and Washington, and were to do so until the Foreign Office had changed hands. Where reason lay it is not always easy to decide, but it is obvious that Palmerston was most anxious to avert a break. When, in his last despatch to Fox, he declared the latest American counter draft quite inadmissible, he suggested that it be treated as *non avenue* rather than as rejected by the British government. Moreover, Fox was carefully enjoined to give to Webster only the *substance* of the criticisms which the despatch contained.[85]

It must be said, however, that a letter which he sent to Russell in January 1841,[86] suggests an irritability on his part which was not conducive to sweet reasonableness. In how far his strictures were applied merely to the inhabitants of Maine, and in how far to the American nation as a whole, it is impossible to say ; but the immediate occasion for his rage seems to have been the arrival of news that Maine had claimed ' exclusive occupation & possession ' of nearly all the disputed territory lying south of the St. John's. After demanding that the lieutenant-governor of New Brunswick should immediately be recalled for ' his folly & weakness ' and his habit of exceeding his authority, that further American ' encroachments ' should be ' stoutly resisted,' and that ' Sydenham's plan for making settlements ' should be carried through, he indulged in an outburst such as those which he was apt to apply to sinners on the European continent :

> With such cunning fellows as these Yankees it never answers to give way, because they always keep pushing on their encroachments as far as they are permitted to do so ; and what we dignify by the names of moderation and conciliation, they naturally enough call fear ; on the other hand as their system of encroachment is founded very much upon bully, they will give way when in the wrong, if they are firmly and perseveringly pressed.
>
> I quite agree with Sydenham that their scheme is to consent to no settlement of the boundary question by negotiation, which shall not give them all they ask ; and while they are spinning out the negotiation by refusing one after the other all our just and reasonable proposals, and by starting successfully the most unfair propositions of their own, they mean practically to determine the matter their own way, if we are supine enough to allow them to do so, by forcibly occupying and seizing hold of the territory in dispute.
>
> I am convinced that we can establish a just claim under the treaty of 1783 to a large extent of country south of the St. Johns ; in fact to nearly all we have ever claimed ; and it would be a thousand pities

to lose de facto by want of energy, that which we might be able to prove ourselves intitled to de jure.

One might easily take it that the writer of such a letter, however shrewd, and however convinced of the justice of his cause, was a menace to peace, and even to international comity. But it seems that these fulminations did no harm. Certainly the American minister failed to hear of, or had learned to discount, them.

For it is a fact—and one of much significance—that Stevenson, returning to the United States in the autumn of 1841, carried with him an impression of Palmerston and Palmerston's conduct which was by no means unfavourable. Thus Broughton, after sitting next to him at dinner in May of that year, reported that ' he praised Lord Palmerston much ' ;[87] while Lady Palmerston, three months later, wrote happily to Mrs. Huskisson that Palmerston, in ' explaining the American affair ' to the House, ' did himself credit and satisfied everybody, even Mr. Stevenson.'[88] And it seems evident that the American envoy, while he had apparently recovered from some of his apprehension concerning the bellicose attitude of the Tories, felt no particular pleasure in the change of government. In late August, and again in mid-September, he wrote Webster that he was unable to foretell what effect upon Anglo-American relations the change at Downing Street would entail.[89] Further, on the very eve of his departure for America, he summed up the situation in much the same fashion to an old friend in Virginia :

> Now between ourselves matters are a little ticklish here ! I cant say wht [sic] the Tories will do— They appear to be pacific, but are to be tested. So far I like Lord Aberdeen. . . . Now I must let you and Mr R—— into a secret.— On the eve of Lord P—— going out, he let off some heavy artillery which I returned—all however in good feeling personally. . . . He also shot off an arrow on the subject of the African seizures.[90]

It really does not seem that Stevenson—a sturdy protagonist of the American position on every point—was seriously alarmed, or in fundamental disagreement with Van Buren's view of Palmerston. His disagreement seems rather with those Tories who, replying in 1843 to Palmerston's intemperate attacks on Ashburton, accused him of having, to an unprecedented degree, endangered peace with the United States.[91] But, with the customary lapse of party memories, these Tories overlooked the fact that some of their number had once alarmed Stevenson more than Palmerston had done; that on the single occasion when war was really near (*i.e.* when the execution of McLeod seemed possible) they had promised the cabinet full support; and that until the very end the American minister had been uncertain as to whether they might not prove more bellicose than their predecessors. And if Palmerston endangered peace, it was certainly not for lack of wish and effort to avoid hostilities. Until he shot off his 'heavy artillery' on the eve of resignation, he was very circumspect. But he had decided that war was almost, if not quite, impossible. And he had decided, too, that undue concessions to what he regarded as a grasping adversary would involve improper sacrifice of his country's interests, without really fostering peace. 'His principle and his practice too,' wrote Melbourne to Victoria, in October, 1841, 'is that nothing fails, except weakness and timidity, and this doctrine is generally right.'[92] But Melbourne, still shaken, no doubt, by his alarm of the preceding year over the danger of war with France, added a qualification as necessary as it was trite : 'at the same time it is possible to be too bold.'

CHAPTER XII

PALMERSTON AS A SEASONED DIPLOMAT AND CABINET
MINISTER, 1835–1841

DURING the six years of his second term of service at the Foreign Office, Palmerston became a personage. His name, which in 1835 had meant little to those who stood outside the confines of government and society, was by 1841 a household word in England and in certain regions of the continent. The emotions which it called up were of infinite variety even among his own countrymen ; but the masses were certainly beginning to take him to their hearts. What minister had ever in times of peace given them sensations more pleasurable ? What a glow of satisfaction came in feeling that, through him, England flouted and preached to the haughtiest and most powerful monarchs of the continent, dispensed her patronage to oppressed masses who longed for the blessings of the British form of government, and showed herself not only enlightened but humane by fighting the slave-trade. And Palmerston took measures to make sure that they appreciated him. Following the common, though by no means universal, custom of the time, he supplied news and even leading articles to certain favoured newspapers. But if the public warmed to him increasingly, the same could not be said of his official associates. For all his breeziness and bonhomie, for all his cheerfulness in sickness and adversity and his readiness to sympathise with others in failure or success, he was regarded as a tyrant by his subordinates, a *mauvais coucheur* by his fellow ministers. The latter became increasingly uncomfortable as the six years wore on. More and more self-willed and self-satisfied, unrivalled as to his knowledge of and technique in foreign policy, Palmerston was both unmanageable and indispensable. The Lamb family were partly responsible. Melbourne, the easy-going and cynical, did not attempt to manage him. And Melbourne's sister, Lady Cowper, helped to make him indispensable. She did so by the simple process of marrying him.

His famous or, as some would have it, notorious, connection with the press was just developing : but even at this early stage it was significant in its suggestion of Palmerston's indifference to party claims, and deference to an element in the electorate which the party was reluctant to conciliate. Witness the complaint made in 1839 by Sir Denis Le Marchant, the secretary of the Board of Trade, who, with Thomas Drummond, the under secretary for Ireland, was ' managing the press on the part of the Government.'[1] Palmerston ' would see any newspaper editor who called on him, and often communicate to such persons matters of great delicacy ' ; but with Sir Denis, of all persons, he was reticent. Or note his relations with the *Morning Chronicle*. Since this paper was ' renovated . . . and set on its legs ' in 1835 by the more liberal Whigs,[2] it was natural enough, and quite in keeping with the practice of the time, that Palmerston should supply its editor with confidential news or even with anonymous articles.[3] But when, four years later, the *Chronicle* deserted the ministry to seek the favour of the radicals,[4] the connection was apparently maintained.[5] True, the Whig *Globe* was also in receipt of favours at the foreign secretary's hands,[6] and joined the *Chronicle* in defending the Foreign Office against *The Times* and *Morning Post*; but it could not seem proper to good Whigs that the *Chronicle* should remain Palmerston's journalistic *maîtresse en titre*. It was an odd liaison certainly, but very useful to a minister who was not quite accepted by his colleagues.

Such readers of the *Chronicle* as had the opportunity of seeing Palmerston could not fail to note that the vigour and the optimism which found expression in his policy were true reflections of the man.[7] Well past fifty now, he was still the sportsman and athlete. At every opportunity he made for the country, to enjoy the ' springy and elastic ' action of a horse, instead of ' taking physic in London ' like such persons as his old friend, Lord Glenelg. At Windsor he would appear for his usual hearty breakfast ' as fresh as . . . an old river-god ' after rowing and swimming for two hours or more. His sobriquet of ' Cupid ' still followed him : his racing colours still adorned a winner now and then. But some of his letters and speeches indicate that confinement, incessant work, and nervous excitement were beginning to take their toll. Whatever he did, he did with all his might. Dedel, the Dutch envoy, who was anything but his friend, paid tribute to his ' peculiar talent ' in coming to a diplomatic conference ' fully and completely master of the subject of it in all its minutest details.' No wonder, if he was justified in boasting to the House that he read ' every report, every letter, and every despatch received . . . down to the least important letter of the lowest vice-consul.' And his readiness to do work that others would have left to subordinates was remarked upon even by his critics. ' Palmerston,' wrote Ellice in 1839, ' as I have heard . . . would save the labour of any horse in the stall by dragging any dray himself.' But he paid the price. In June 1838, came ' a slight threatening of gout,' which incapacitated him for at least ten days. In November of that year he lost his only surviving sister, Mrs. Bowles. On New Year's Day of 1839 the Queen wrote that ill-health had driven him to Broadlands : ' He had gone through so much grief and labour, that it was absolutely necessary for him to recruit his strength.' But the cure did not take long. Two weeks later the patient reported that a ' course ' of hunting and shooting had quite set him up again. And his spirits, if they had ever flagged, recovered almost as rapidly. In early March he wrote the Queen to suggest that the duke of Lucca, as a sovereign prince, should be invited to dine with her by note and not by card : ' Your Majesty may think this a small matter, but the Duke is a small Sovereign.' Two months later, when the cabinet resigned (only to be brought back to power immediately by the ' Bedchamber ' episode), Palmerston was preparing to give a dinner in honour of the Tsarevitch. Hobhouse inquired whether this would be given up. ' What ! ' was the answer, ' lose my place, and my dinner too?' Resilience such as this was a political asset.

But he had the best of reasons for exhibiting cheerfulness as the year 1839 went on ; for Lady Cowper, now a woman of fifty-two and a widow for two years, was making up her mind to marry him.[8] Whether because her children, or some of them at least, raised opposition to the match ; or whether she herself shrank from the new responsibilities it would entail, she hesitated for some time. But Palmerston's perseverance, ' so very unlike what one ever meets with,' as Lord Beauvale remarked, was at last to win the day. It is no wonder that he persevered ; for the union was, in almost all respects, an ideal one. The two were curiously similar in some ways.[9] Each, for example, combined a taste for gaiety with a deep love for country life ; and each stood ready to put personal gratification of either sort aside, under pressure of affairs. In each a cheerful paganism went hand in hand with Christian kindliness and sympathy. They were alike in independence of merely conventional loyalties and ties, alike in bravery, alike even in their utter inability to be punctual. Lady Lyttelton described a visit which the Queen paid to Panshanger (Lord Cowper's principal seat) in the summer of 1841 :

> The visit is very agreeable, surprising from absence of formality, contrived by Lady Palmerston and her daughter-in-law. The only fault is that they are immensely unpunctual, and make the poor Queen wait for dinner and drives till anybody but herself would be furious.

It was soon to be a jest in London that Lord and Lady Palmerston had never seen soup served. Fortunately, their characteristics were also complementary. If Palmerston brought the greater sum of knowledge and pure intellect to the partnership, his lady was richly dowered in other qualities : sound sense and delicate sensibilities, warmed by beauty and good-heartedness into charm ; shrewdness, so linked with impulsiveness that one wonders still how far her ' indiscretions ' were planned for effect ; earnestness and enthusiasm that admit of no such doubt. There was no more fortunate day in Palmerston's long life than that of his marriage on December 16, 1839.

Nor is it likely that the events of any other single day contributed as much to make his political advance irresistible. His marriage did not, indeed, so much betoken his 'settling down' as certain writers, especially Gallic ones, have been ready to suppose. Gallant, dandy, lover of Lady Cowper, adventurer at times in politics and policies, all these things he had been and would remain. Yet his life was radically changed. For the first time since his boyhood he could always count on intimate, sympathetic companionship and unremitting care. The tone of Lady Palmerston's letters to him is unmistakable. Thus, from the country in January 1841 :

> I do so long to get back to you ! Not but what it is all very well here, every body very kind and courteous—but still there is *something* wanting, and I am so glad to think this is the last day. . . .
> It is idle of the housemaids to leave your Windows open & fire out, and you should send and scold them, for it might give you a very bad cold after coming from your warm writing-room.[10]

And, for the first time in his career, he could make a political and social centre of his London house. This was a fact of real political significance. The number of great Whig houses in the capital had dwindled rapidly ; and, in 1840, the death of Lord Holland practically closed the greatest of them all. Earlier in this same year Palmerston's town house, now provided with a great hostess, threw wide its doors. Not that it resembled Holland House, that charming rendezvous of Whigs and litterateurs, where eccentricities flourished, where hospitality and conversation were alike lavish, unrestrained and rather casual. In Lord and Lady Palmerston's hospitality there was from the outset something purposeful, a note of political values which not even the graciousness and geniality of host and hostess ever quite concealed.[11] But theirs was soon *the* political house. There all accepted members of the great world, irrespective of party affiliations, sooner or later found themselves : and there, too, the aspiring—who could be of great service to a rising minister—hoped to find themselves. What is more, those who came were usually charmed. In so far as people in London were concerned, Lady Granville proved herself justified in a prophecy she made when the coming marriage was announced. 'Foreign Affairs,' she wrote, ' will be more come-at-able, I suspect, than they have been for a long time. Lord Palmerston's incivilities will obtain a varnish.'[12]

Lady Granville had reason to know whereof she spoke when she suggested that Palmerston's official manners required 'varnishing.' Not only was her husband still British ambassador at the Tuileries, but her son, Lord Leveson (the ' Puss ' Granville of a later time) was serving at the Foreign Office, and was soon to become Palmerston's parliamentary under secretary. Even this fortunate and suave young man found his chief approachable only through Lady Palmerston, and conformed at first to the practice of communicating with him on official business only by writing.[13] Later, at the suggestion of Backhouse, the permanent under secretary, he reverted to the ' custom of under Secretaries when Canning was Minister,' and bearded the ogre in his den.[14] He wrote of being graciously received ; but he gave a sad account of Palmerston's general relations with others of the staff :

> I think I may be of use, from having more opportunities of seeing Ld. Palmerston and not being so dreadfully afraid of him. It is impossible to have a glimpse of him in the Office—he comes down very late, having kept quantities of people waiting for him and before he has seen them all goes down to the House—the clerks detest him and have an absurd sort of fancy that he takes pleasure in bullying them.[15]

Palmerston was up to his old tricks. Unless Leveson re-wrote drafts 'drawn out by some of the oldest and best clerks in the office,' they would come back ' slashed about with very cutting remarks.'[16] One of these remarks, anent the sentences in a certain draft, has been preserved elsewhere : ' Life is not long enough to correct them and put them into plain English, planting Sugar Canes would not be more laborious.'[17] Harder still it must have been for the unhappy clerk to be informed that ' sentences should be constructed to begin with the nominative, to go on with the verb, and to end with the accusative.' And if Palmerston could not understand why his staff should fail to emulate the simplicity and precision of his style, neither could he see why they should not display some of his own industry. When he found empty places in the office on a Sunday morning, Lady Palmerston had to remind him that people did go to church sometimes.[18] He was so prone to convict his staff of idleness. Note his comment on Russell's suggestion, in October 1839, that promotion by merit should be established at the Foreign Office by order in Council :

> The clerks will of course object to any principle that breaks down the prescriptive right of idleness and dulness to succeed hackney coachlike from bottom to top of an office by dint of mere living ... I should think that practically it would not often happen that a man would be found to possess such superior merit & qualifications, as ... to be transferred from A to C without passing through B, at least I fear there [are] no such bright geniuses in the Foreign Office ; but I am quite ready to adopt your principle.[19]

The clerks seem to have repaid their chief's contemptuousness with something more than mere dislike. The chief of them told Greville that 'Palmerston's tone on every occasion, and to every Power ... disgusted them all.'[20]

He does not seem to have been on a much happier footing with the most important of his envoys.[21] His inveterate tendency to play the schoolmaster to all persons from imperial chancellors to class C clerks was still in evidence. And so was a lack of understanding with respect to policy between Palmerston and his Whig ambassadors. Sir Frederick Lamb, ambassador at Vienna (created Lord Beauvale in 1839) could not conceal his dislike for Palmerston from his sister, Lady Cowper, even when her second marriage was afoot. Nor did he hesitate on one occasion at least to suppress a despatch of which he disapproved. Lord William Russell at Berlin wrote frankly to his brother, Lord John, of the foreign secretary's 'mismanagement.' At St. Petersburg, Durham was reported as admitting to the Austrian ambassador that Metternich had justification for slighting England through her foreign minister. And as for Ponsonby, England's veteran representative at the Porte, his attitude of defiance reached the scandalous. Applying for leave of absence, he found that Sir Charles

Vaughan had been sent on a ' special mission ' temporarily to fill his place. Suspecting with reason that the home government wished the substitution to be permanent, he forbade Vaughan even to place his foot on shore. And Palmerston, of all men in the world, 'knocked under,' as Greville reported wonderingly. Perhaps the foreign secretary was complacent because Beauvale was Lady Cowper's brother, because Russell was a Russell, and because Durham and Ponsonby were practically Greys. But it is fitting to remember, too, that he gave his firm support to every envoy who did satisfactory work. Durham was obviously touched at being assisted by his chief in reporting his diplomatic activities in the most favourable light, and at receiving undiscriminating praise from the foreign secretary in the House.

However justified the critics of Palmerston's official manners may have been, it must in fairness be remembered that he was tried by manifold anxieties. It has been seen that western Europe, the United States and the slave trade furnished a plentiful supply of these : eastern Europe, southern Asia and northern Africa offered even more. In August 1840, Lord John Russell, rising one morning earlier than was his wont, performed a still more unwonted act by listing some of them in doggerel :

> The Chinese at Canton
> Prodigiously rant on
>
> . . . . .
>
> Our prospects in Turkey
> Are lowering and murky
> The Frenchmen will task us
> With thoughts of Damascus
>
> . . . . .
>
> But though we have stayed in
> The snug post of Aden
>
> . . . . .
>
> And we're not such a fool
> As to give up Cabul
>
> . . . . .
>
> By such plagues are we curst
> Those of Egypt the worst.[22]

It will be noted that Russell suggested problems at point after point along a great arc stretching from Canton to Constantinople and Cairo. Nor did even this sweep of territory cover the field of Palmerston's diplomatic activities. A second if less important arc passed up through the Balkans to the Baltic Sea : a third stretched westward along the south shore of the Mediterranean.

His attitude toward developments in these three arcs is not easy to define. While he lacked the expansionist visions of a Disraeli, he was not content with the merely watchful attitude of a Pitt. It was not enough for him merely to remain on guard against the many threats to British commerce, security and prestige which he saw or thought he saw in the East and in the Mediterranean. He was determined that aggression or arrogance, whether from Peking, St. Petersburg or Paris, should be dealt with firmly and decisively from the outset; and that Britain's position should not only be defended but consolidated at every convenient opportunity. Note his reaction to the statement that Russia was unprepared for war :

... knowledge of that fact ought ... to encourage us to make a stout stand against her systematic encroachments on Peace ; as we ought to be convinced that she is always pushing on as far and as fast as she can go without war ; but that whenever she finds that perseverance in encroachment will lead to forcible resistance, she will pull up and wait for some more favourable opportunity of carrying on her schemes.[23]

And, again, his dictum regarding British ' influence ' :

Our influence is like the tide, which, though it advances and then recedes, yet steadily gains ground.[24]

In so far as territorial possessions were concerned, his doctrine was merely that of ' What we have we hold.' But, since he was abnormally sensitive to any moves made by England's two great rivals in Asia and Africa ; and since it sometimes seems that a government can hold what it has only by acquiring more, Palmerston became at times an involuntary expansionist.

Of England's two great rivals in Asia and Africa, Russia continued, in these years, to arouse most of his anxiety. It was comparatively easy to keep an eye on France, and to persuade her cautious king that any steps toward making the Mediterranean a Gallic lake had better be deferred. But it seemed to Palmerston that the Russians were engaged in no end of nefarious and half-veiled activities at points distributed along two arcs. They fortified the Aaland Islands, thus threatening Sweden and creating a new base of operations for any future naval war. Together with their Austrian and Prussian friends they occupied the tiny Polish republic of Cracow, challenging not only the territorial settlements of 1815, but the British foreign secretary's well-known championship of ' liberal ' governments. They were apparently bearing down on the Serbian as well as on the Greek government ; and, as usual, they were menacing the sultan of Turkey, his capital and his Straits. In face of this Palmerston could only ' snarl ' at Russia, assure parliament that the treaty of Unkiar Skelessi had no real force, work for the rejuvenation of Turkey, and attempt to hold the Sultan and the pasha of Egypt apart, as one would hold two quarrelsome dogs. Such measures could not allay his anxieties. Let Sultan and Pasha come again to grips, and how could he keep the Russians from mastery of the Straits ? And that day would be a very evil one for the interests which he had in trust.[25] Russia would become invulnerable in the Black Sea—invulnerable at what, in so far as England was concerned, was Russia's most vulnerable point. What chance would then survive of harassing any movements Russian troops might at some future time make through the Caucasus on Mesopotamia, Persia and the Persian Gulf ? And what would become of that promising artery of British commerce which passed through Germany down the Danube, with an entrepôt at Galatz, and so across the Black Sea to Trebizond ? What, for that matter, would become of England's more convenient routes to India, the old ' overland ' route by Alexandria, Cairo and Suez, and the new ' alternative ' route—this latter a premature and British *Baghdadbahn*, in which the Tigris and Euphrates served in lieu of rails ? If Russia's Black Sea fleet could emerge from the Dardanelles at will, and if her Baltic fleet could arrive in the Levant, as it had done in 1827 to aid the

Greeks, England would be hard put to it. There were
'ifs' in plenty to all of this; but fears and suspicions of
the Tsar and his empire had attained fantastic dimensions
in British minds. In March 1839, the cabinet authorised
Palmerston to use secret service funds in probing a report
that Nicholas had approved the project of sending a fleet
and army to India. The modest aim of the expedition,
according to the informant, was 'to seize . . . the three
[Indian] Presidencies' ![26]

Dangers on dangers ! It seemed to Palmerston that
an even more immediate threat loomed in the Middle East
from Russian activities in Persia and Afghanistan. The
Tsar's agents were ingratiating themselves at the Persian
capital, inciting the Persians to take the Afghan border
town, Herat, and 'intriguing' at Cabul, the capital of the
strongest of the Afghan principalities. Some of the Tsar's
troops were undertaking a supposedly punitive expedition
against the khanate of Khiva. There was ground for suspicion, then, that Nicholas had some great plan afoot; and
what could this be save to use his own forces and those of
his Asiatic allies or satellites in an advance against the
north-western borderlands of India ? To Palmerston,
rendered all the more nervous by delay and difficulty in obtaining news, confirmed in his fears by most of his agents
on the ground, the Russian danger seemed at first more
pressing in the Middle than in the Near East. As for the
Far East, 'the Chinese at Canton' were causing trouble
purely on their own account. But he must have known
that there had been a Russian church and school at Peking
for some time.[27]

It may be long before all the steps he took to preserve
British commerce, security and prestige against real or
imagined dangers in these regions become fully known.
How he and his consul encouraged King Milosch of Serbia
to resist pressure from St. Petersburg :[28] how he warned the
Russian government not to interfere with Khiva's independence, and asked the honour of knighthood for a British
officer who had helped to compose the Khan's differences
with the Tsar ;[29]—there are episodes such as these which
one can merely mention in passing. But, leaving aside

matters which are obscure or of minor interest, one is still embarrassed by the number of his activities. To take the most characteristic and the most important seems the only way. And, for the sake of clarity, it may be well at first to clear the sheet of issues which lay outside his resistance to Russia in the Middle and Near East.

Very characteristic of his methods in diplomacy was his reaction, in 1836, to the occupation of Cracow.[30] This tiny Polish republic, the independence of which Metternich ascribed to the 'spirit of false generosity, which so often misled the Emperor Alexander,'[31] existed under the Vienna treaty of 1815.[32] Declared neutral, and placed under the 'protection' of Russia, Austria and Prussia, whose Polish territories encircled it, the little state occupied a peculiarly ambiguous position under the provisions of Article IX. For this article, after declaring that no armed forces should enter the republic on any pretext, 'expressly stipulated' that Cracow should afford no asylum to 'fugitives, deserters and persons under prosecution' who were subjects of the protecting Powers. To say that just such persons thronged into it, especially after the Polish rebellion of 1830–1831, is almost superfluous. Nor does one need much imagination to conceive the feelings entertained on the subject by Metternich, Nesselrode, and Ancillon. Each saw on his country's frontier a breeding-place for plots which might cause trouble at any time, and which were bound to keep alive the spirit of resistance in Russian Poland and in Hungary. In the latter part of February, 1836, the three 'protecting' governments seized the pretext offered by a murder and by some disorders of a minor sort to effect a military occupation of their protégé. They were perfectly aware of the resentment this would rouse in Downing Street.

What is more, Metternich went out of his way to be offensive to the British government. He gave formal notification of the occupation to France, as one of the five great signatory Powers of 1815; but purposely omitted offering the same courtesy to England.[33] The reasons are not especially far to seek. At Paris, Thiers, who had just displaced Broglie, was seeking an Austrian bride for the Dauphin, and in other ways arousing hopes that the *entente cordiale* was at an end. And the Austrian chancellor was glad to seize so safe an opportunity of flouting Palmerston. When Barante, the French ambassador at St. Petersburg, asked Ficquelmont, the Austrian ambassador, why discrimination had been made between the partners of the entente, he was told not only of the ' *bienveillance* ' of Louis Philippe and the French ministry, but of the ' *malveillance, méfiance, hauteur* ' of Palmerston.[34] Barante was not impressed. ' This proceeding of M. de Metternich,' he wrote, ' seems to me petty and puerile.' What Palmerston thought of it need scarcely be a matter of record.

Of course, some move on his part would have been inevitable in any case. He admitted privately that there was ' something to be said for the three courts ' ;[35] but he neither would nor could allow them to take such highhanded action without protest. Even had he been willing to conceal his sympathy with the Poles, and forego the pleasure of making himself the champion of oppressed liberals, British public sentiment would have forced his hand. At the outset he showed unwonted circumspection by consulting the king's advocate in advance of making any move ;[36] but the identical despatches which he sent to St. Petersburg, Vienna and Berlin on April 15 showed his customary joy in giving free play to his pen.[37] He complained of the lack of any intimation or explanation to the British government ; and he denied—on the basis of some very close and legalistic reasoning—that the action of the three Powers in coercing Cracow had conformed at any stage to the terms of the treaty of 1815. Instead, he found it ' sweeping . . . precipitate and . . . violent.' Apparently warming to his work, he went on to remind the three offending governments that ' many of the Powers of Europe ' possessed no better claims to certain of their territories than Cracow did to immunity from attack. And he coupled his protests almost immediately with a threat—the threat of accrediting a consul to Cracow.

Thanks, however, to the hardihood of the Prussian foreign minister, Ancillon, this was merely a prelude to the

METTERNICH

real cannonade.[38] Ancillon, pleading his desire 'to avoid entering into a polemic discussion' with Palmerston, at first refused to receive a copy of the protest, or even allow it to be read to him. Only when the British envoy (after pleasantly assuring him that Palmerston did not mind polemic in the least!) threatened a diplomatic break, did he give in. And his 'polemic' proved almost worthy of his British adversary. Regretting that friendly relations with England were rendered impossible by the 'erroneous views . . . taken by His Majesty's Government of the state of Continental Affairs,' he announced that the protecting Powers would not permit the appointment of a consul at Cracow. For this would not only constitute 'a direct insult,' but would supply a rendezvous for 'the discontented and intriguing.' Then were the thunders of the Foreign Office really unloosed. Ancillon's assertions and his 'unjust and offensive imputations' were cast in his teeth. And Palmerston, as if anxious to enlarge the battle-ground, proceeded to condemn the eighteenth-century partitions of Poland, to point out that they had 'borne at various times . . . appropriate fruit,' and to claim that England would 'long and justly' reap honour for her sympathy with the Poles. The Prussian Foreign Office was probably still smarting from its wounds when it again came into collision with Palmerston over the question of Belgian fortifications in the year following.

Palmerston, on the other hand, probably enjoyed it all. Note the sprightly tone in which he wrote his brother, on July 9:

Metternich has taken a fling, as if bit by a horse-fly, and Ancillon has mimicked him as a donkey would do.[39]

There was a separate bout of 'polemic' with the Austrian chancellor, arising from Metternich's profession of belief that Cracow was the centre of a great international conspiracy, and that the appointment of a British consul there would constitute a deliberate blow at Austria's internal tranquillity. But the Austrian 'fling' was much more discreet and less productive of recriminations than Ancillon's.[40]

Most notable, however, was the great moderation displayed by Nicholas and Nesselrode. Lord Durham, the British ambassador, was showered with attentions which were interpreted in the diplomatic world as expressing more than Nicholas' personal regard for him.[41] The French ambassador reported to his government that there was ' no complaint about the language of Lord Palmerston ' and that ' all irritation was sedulously repressed and concealed.'[42] And the Russian answer to the note, restrained all through, went no further than the expression of a ' strong wish ' that the appointment of a British consul at Cracow should not be made.[43] Palmerston was ready to make full acknowledgment :

> The communications of the Russian Government on these matters have been courteous in manner, and have been marked by a degree of moderation which forms a contrast with the tone assumed by the Governments of Austria and Prussia.[44]

The cessation of ' snarling ' between London and St. Petersburg was attributable not only to the efforts of Durham, but to a sincere desire on the part of Nicholas for better relations with the British government.[45] Anxious to remove a possible obstacle from his path by separating the partners of the entente, he found it less distasteful to make advances to William IV's ministers than to the usurper at the Tuileries. As one looks back, his policy attracts attention mainly as an earnest of his success in pursuing it some four years afterwards ; but it smoothed the way for Palmerston's inevitable retreat in the matter of Cracow.

But to speak of ' retreat ' is not entirely suitable ; for Palmerston continued to protest the presence at Cracow of an Austrian force[46] until 1840, when he admitted his powerlessness to the House :

> . . . it was one thing to express an opinion, and another thing to take hostile steps . . . and especially in a case where, from local and geographical circumstances, there were no means of enforcing the opinions of England.[47]

Even the sending of a consul had been given up at the discreet request of the Senate of Cracow. What then, if anything, had he obtained to counterbalance the increased enmity of the German courts ? At first sight only the joy of lecturing the three eastern Powers in the rôle of a defender of treaties and mouthpiece of British liberalism. But he could add the approval of a large section of his countrymen and the gratitude of the Poles. With such gains he was more apt than most men to be content.

CHAPTER XIII
FURTHER PROBLEMS IN THE EAST, 1835–1841

THE question of 'the Chinese at Canton' was as far removed from the Cracow affair in nature as it was in space. If only one might pass it by ! For the issue, instead of being one ' of the simplest,'[1] as Lord Morley incautiously allowed himself to write, is too complex even for cursory treatment in restricted space. But omission seems impossible. For one thing, the results which British diplomacy and arms achieved were as epoch-making from the standpoint of world history as any developments of the time. And there is another reason, too. Morley and other leaders in English letters, thought and politics, moved consciously by moral fervour and unconsciously by prepossessions that were, perhaps, somewhat political, have drawn a sad portrait of Palmerston. One sees him bullying a helpless Chinese emperor—an emperor consumed with zeal to cure his subjects of their greatest vice—into opening his ports to British opium. Though specialists have long declared the picture false,[2] the eminence of its authors has caused it to linger in the public mind. It seems impossible to pass over so great a difference in portraiture.

Palmerston's diplomatic contact with the Chinese dated back only to 1833, when the government of Great Britain took the monopoly of Chinese trade from the East India Company, and threw it open to all Englishmen. And, even subsequent to that date, there was no diplomatic contact in the ordinary meaning of the term. For the Son of Heaven, regarding all occidentals as barbarian rebels too contumacious to prostrate themselves with tribute before his throne, and fearful that any apparent diminution of his sanctity would enhance the disorders by which his empire was already torn, declined to acknowledge such equality with the white races as the establishment of diplomatic relations would imply. He permitted them to trade at and around Macao and Canton, but only under conditions the most conducive to his financial profit and the maintenance of his divine superiority. Trade was to be conducted only with a hong, or guild of Chinese merchants, whose members could be milked of their profits and held responsible for any misdeeds of their barbarian customers. And only through the guild could the barbarians approach the sacred throne—transmitting ' petitions ' and receiving ' orders ' in return. The East India Company, a commercial corporation whose status did not involve directly the dignity of the British government, and whose monopoly of Britain's Chinese trade enabled British traders to present a united front against the hong, was able to accept such terms. But the superintendents of trade who went out after 1833 had to be sent as representatives of his Majesty's government. Otherwise the rather motley group of British merchants would have lacked both protection and control. Were these official representatives of the British crown to exchange ' petitions ' for ' orders,' and that through the lowly medium of a Canton merchant guild ? Assuredly, said the Chinese. Not by any means, said Palmerston. Hence, since the Son of Heaven would not condescend even to negotiate, a trial of strength was unavoidable, unless the protection supposedly enjoyed by Englishmen abroad was to be surrendered on the China coast. Nor were the issues involved merely those of prestige and dignity. The Chinese had, for foreigners as well as nationals, a theory of joint responsibility. It was customary to hold all occidentals of one nationality responsible for the misdeeds of an individual ; and there were cases in which men entirely innocent had been executed according to the peculiarly unpleasant methods prescribed by the Chinese penal code. Horrified by tales of oriental tortures and other brutalities, the British people were unwilling that even a detected British wrongdoer should be placed in Chinese hands. Their foreign secretary quite agreed with them.

For six years Palmerston, engrossed by other problems,

seemed, if anything, too indifferent to the situation at Canton.³ Instead of sending out accredited envoys, he conformed to Chinese wishes and to the custom followed before 1833 by appointing only superintendents of trade. Moreover, the instructions issued to the successive chief superintendents were inadequate and contradictory. According to general instructions, they were to conform to established practice and avoid all friction with the Chinese government. But more particular instructions forbade them to communicate with the Chinese emperor through the Canton guild, or to frame their communications as petitions,—forbade them to do, in other words, those very things which observance of tradition and avoidance of friction especially required. They might conceivably have been able to follow their particular instructions had their advice and that of the merchants been accepted by their government, and a display of force been made. But it was not until 1838 that this was done. In natural consequence, the earlier superintendents, having found that obedience to the particular instructions merely exposed them to humiliation and to risk, learned rapidly to ignore them. When Charles Elliot, who took up his post in December 1836, made an effort to carry out the stronger policy which Palmerston preferred, he found the Chinese quite convinced that coercion was the proper treatment for barbarians of the occident. He found out, too, that he lacked sufficiently defined authority over the British subjects on the Chinese coast. But the effects of Palmerston's indecisive policy were not fully seen until, in March 1839, the Chinese made their spectacular seizure of opium at Canton.

Their action in this affair was nothing if not violent. A high commissioner, Lin by name, sent by the Emperor to stop the importation of opium at Canton, decided to settle the matter at one stroke. Acting on the Chinese doctrine of responsibility, and confident that coercion would produce results, he ordered the first superintendent to compel the surrender, not only of such opium as was actually in port, but what was in the holds of ships which lay outside. He was, as Palmerston later pointed out, compelling the representative of another Power to enforce Chinese law, and to do so by issuing orders to persons over whom he had no authority.[4] Pending full acquiescence, the British residents of Canton were cut off from communication with the outside world, surrounded by Chinese troops, deprived of servants, drinking-water, and food supplies, and placed, if not in actual danger, certainly in apprehension of the most distressing kind.[5] Such refinements as the strangling of a Chinese criminal in the square outside the British factory were a little hard on British nerves.[6] And there were other factors to obscure the moral issue on which Palmerston's critics have been wont to concentrate. The wishes of the Son of Heaven both to put the occidentals in their place and to prevent them from depleting China's silver currency, were obviously involved. And although his wish to stop the trade in ' bootleg ' opium was undoubtedly sincere, there were circumstances which at the moment raised some doubt. Domestic production of opium was permitted to go on ; and bootlegging by traders of all nationalities had thriven and was sure to thrive through the notorious venality of the mandarins who acted as ' prohibition ' officers. Indeed, the sacred one himself furnished a pattern for those twentieth-century defenders of American abstinence who ' drank wet ' and ' voted dry.' Palmerston had justification when he complained that the penalties of enforcement fell on foreigners alone, and that ' a Law . . . for a great length of time . . . allowed to sleep as a dead letter ' was ' suddenly . . . put in force with the utmost rigour and severity.'[7]

But the moral question seems somewhat beside the point in so far as the foreign secretary's indictment is concerned ; for he did not deny that, in excluding foreign opium, the Chinese empire was within its rights. The first superintendent had been warned, if somewhat tardily, that his government could not ' interfere for the purpose of enabling British subjects to violate the laws of the country to which they trade.'[8] And Palmerston made the same declaration both to the Chinese emperor and to the House.

Her Majesty's Government . . . had no intention to dispute the right of every Government to prohibit the importation of any foreign commodities which their Government might choose or think it right to prohibit, or of enforcing that prohibition by means and authority of its own.[9]

He even admitted that the Chinese commissioner would have been justified in seizing all opium found in Chinese territory. What he complained of was that a representative of the Crown had been treated with violence and contempt, and that British subjects, innocent of any wrong, had been abused. It is a reasonable supposition that Macaulay, speaking in the foreign secretary's defence, voiced what was in his heart:

. . . they belonged to a country which had made the farthest ends of the earth ring with the fame of her exploits in redressing the wrongs of her children ; that made the Dey of Algiers humble himself to her insulted consul ; that revenged the horrors of the Black Hole on the fields of Plassey ; that had not degenerated since her great Protector vowed that he would make the name of Englishman as respected as ever had been the name of Roman citizen.[10]

And it is equally reasonable to suppose that Palmerston stored away Cromwell's[11] and Macaulay's reference to the *civis Romanus* for his own use at some later day.

Macaulay's speech was made in April 1840, in the course of a prolonged debate.[12] The critical eyes of the Conservatives had been on the government's dealings with China for some time ; and their leaders hoped that the radicals would join in giving the Melbourne government a fatal blow.[13] Graham, who took the lead, had called for papers until, as Palmerston complained, the Foreign Office clerks had been ' almost killed ' with work, and the weight of accumulated type had broken through one of the Foreign Office floors. Then, having got his papers, he had introduced a motion of censure on the cabinet for failing to give proper orders and instructions to the superintendent at Canton. He had shrewdly opened the debate by claiming that cessation of the Anglo-Chinese trade would cost the United Kingdom and India something like one-sixth of all their revenue ; and he had closed his speech by throwing all the blame on Palmerston. The discussion, proceeding in an Anglo-Saxon atmosphere, quite naturally took on a highly moral tone. Young Mr. Gladstone, Conservative member for Newark, waxed so fervid in defending the Chinese as to let drop the words : ' of course they poisoned the wells.' His party hung their heads ; but the battle was soon taken up by Peel, who spoke with all his great ability and with his personal animus against Palmerston. The foreign secretary was virtually the last to rise. His speech is remembered chiefly for his success in twitting Gladstone on maligning the Chinese, and appearing to defend ' doctrines so monstrous ' as the propriety of poisoning wells ; but the real reasons for his success were pointed out by Hobhouse in his diary :

> Palmerston concluded the debate and made a very effective party speech, defending himself valiantly and attacking his accusers vigorously. He did not argue much . . . but . . . He was so gallant and confident, and claimed the support of all on our side with so much gay assurance, that he completely succeeded in his appeal, and sat down amidst thunders of applause, which lasted some time. We divided 271 to 261. The Conservatives cheered a good deal. . . .[14]

The victory was all the more impressive in view of the previous nervousness of the whips, and of the surprising number of ministerialist absentees.[15] Nor was it due to any access of ' patriotism ' in parliament ; since the ' Opium War ' had not as yet begun.

For, be it remembered, the war was by no means a direct result of Lin's seizure of opium and mistreatment of the British at Canton. Though British chambers of commerce indignantly demanded energetic measures from the Melbourne government, no more was done than the sending of naval reinforcements to Elliot.[16] Even Palmerston seems to have been hesitant about compelling the Chinese government to offer reparation, apologies and future security for British trade.[17] It was mainly the triumphant and exacting Lin who brought matters to extremities. As his quarrel with the foreign devils developed through the year 1839, the opium issue became more and more obscured, and the gulf which lay between oriental and occidental ideas of procedure more and more evident. When fresh disputes occurred, the Son of Heaven's officials forced the English to take refuge on shipboard, attempted to deprive them of supplies, incited the populace to attack any of them who went on shore, and threatened even to burn the ships. Elliot, whose patience seems to have been exceptional, fired on the Emperor's war junks only when they threatened his vessel. And this because he refused to surrender some undesignated Englishman in place of the undetected slayer of a Chinaman. Perhaps the story if told from the Chinese side might have sounded differently ; but the main facts seemed incontestable. Considering that Palmerston and his colleagues would never have submitted to a tithe of such provocation from an occidental Power, they can scarcely be called bullies for deciding that the Son of Heaven would have to be chastised. It is doubtful whether the foreign secretary had any passion or even deep interest to spare to the Chinese issue from the far more vital matters which were on his hands from 1839 to 1841. It occupied surprisingly little space in his private correspondence for those years.

But, when the British punitive expedition had done its work, and the dangers nearer home were virtually past, he displayed all that alertness which one would expect from him. Having secured ample and expert advice, he ordered his plenipotentiaries to demand the cession of Hong Kong, the opening of five ' treaty ports,' a virtual abolition of the Chinese guild monopoly, and the establishment of the principle of extra-territoriality—in short, all measures necessary for the opening up of China to the merchants of the west.[18] And he was utterly resolved to have them, too.[19] When Captain Elliot, the chief plenipotentiary, disobeyed orders, and signed articles of peace which not only spared the Chinese treasury but passed over the ' capital point ' of opening the Chinese coast northward from Canton to British trade, Melbourne was inclined to ratify. But Palmerston carried the cabinet with him in disavowing the articles and ordering the recommencement of hostilities. Thanks, largely, to Elliot's disobedience, Peel's government made the final settlement by the treaties of Nanking and the Bogue, of 1842 and 1843. But Aberdeen adhered to Palmerston's demands, even to the exaction of an indemnity and of compensation for the surrendered opium.[20] The question of future smuggling was treated in the most delicate manner possible. So much for the moral fervour which parties in opposition show.

For all the display of characteristic Palmerstonian diplomacy afforded by the Cracow affair, for all the permanent gains secured from the Chinese, these matters were but sideshows in Palmerston's eastern policy. What really held his attention were the moves and counter moves in the vast game he was playing with the Russian government, over an area which stretched from the Indus to the Straits. In a sense it was not one game but two : there was a clear distinction between the problems of the Middle and Near East. But these problems were Siamese twins of diplomacy, individual but inseparable. And the connecting-link, from the Foreign Office point of view, was furnished by the government at St. Petersburg. Hence Palmerston had really to keep in view three things : general relations with the Russian government, the curbing of Russian activities in the Middle East, and the guardianship of Turkey and her Straits.

His feeling about relations with Russia was summed up rather cynically in a letter which he wrote to his brother in the summer of 1836 :

> Russia is coquetting with Durham ; and in order to cajole him is obliged to be civil to us ; so his appointment has answered.[21]

Perhaps, a little later, he would have written in a somewhat different tone. For Durham was able to back his conviction that Russia had neither the will nor the means to commence a European war, by announcing that her troops would evacuate the Turkish fortress of Silistria, occupied since 1829.[22] But Palmerston's suspicions, almost inveterate in any case, were kept alive by disturbing reports from British agents in the Middle and Near East. His attitude seems to have been that of letting Russia call the game.[23] A mild flirtation with St. Petersburg would come in rather handily. France had deserted him even in the Cracow imbroglio, even when he was befriending her favourites, the Poles.[24] Why not, then, make what use he could of Nicholas' desire to lay the ghost of the entente, and of that desire for Anglo-Russian commerce which was felt so strongly at St. Petersburg ? Flirtations do not obviate watchfulness.

But the flirtation had to be exceedingly discreet ; for many Englishmen, and some very influential ones, were bound to be censorious. The King, for example, and Lord Ponsonby, the British ambassador at the Porte, were violent Russophobes. The Tory opposition were inclined to treat any apparent complaisance to the Tsar as compromising England's dignity : the merchants to regard it as betokening forgetfulness of their interests in the East. And, more to be considered still, there were the radicals, both in and out of parliament, with whom tsar-baiting was a favourite sport. Small and poorly led as was their representation in the House, its support was almost indispensable to the Melbourne government. And Palmerston, for reasons of his own, was courting radical support. Too liberal for the Tories, yet never on terms of full understanding with the Whigs, he had evidently commenced to realise how useful it would be to have the backing of public sentiment. If the heads of old Whig houses were affronted by his rough-and-tumble methods in diplomacy, his insolence to the greater governments and his rather indiscriminate championship of continental states or parties which passed for being liberal, the British public was beginning to be distinctly pleased. And it was the radicals who might be counted on to open the applause whenever the English champion of liberalism took the stage. It was difficult to flirt simultaneously with them and with the Tsar ; but Palmerston seems to have attempted it. In 1835, the year when Nicholas was gratified by the appointment of Durham as British ambassador, David Urquhart received the post of secretary at the Porte.

The young secretary's appointment was made in September ; and it struck people at the time as curious. No one could deny that Urquhart was able, well versed in the affairs of the Near East, and utterly sincere. He had impressed both Stratford Canning and Ponsonby. But, for all that, he seemed anything but fitted for his post. It was not merely that his romantic and adventurous career had given him little training in diplomacy : what mattered more was his temperamental unfitness to be a diplomat. He was not only a fanatic, but a dangerous one. Suspicious and credulous at all times, he needed only the conviction that he was fighting a good cause to become vituperative and utterly indiscreet. He had, in fact, a pronounced and highly developed talent for publication and publicity. Add to this that he was a pronounced radical and Russophobe, and it does not seem surprising that Wellington wrote to warn Palmerston that the Foreign Office was taking a great risk.[25] But there were arguments for the appointment, too. Ponsonby had no influence at the Porte ; and Urquhart, who had changed from an ardent Philhellene into an equally ardent Turcophil, was certainly well liked. Moreover, he had completed an important investigation of commercial conditions in the Turkish empire during the preceding year, and was full of schemes for a commercial treaty with the Sultan's government and the development of a new route for British commerce in the Black Sea area. Finally—and there were those who said that this was a deciding factor in the case—his appointment was very pleasing to his friend and fellow-Russophobe, the King.[26] Although Urquhart seems to have ignored his instructions even during his commercial investigations of 1834,[27] it is possible that Palmerston knew little of his faults in September 1835. But he could not plead ignorance of some of them when Urquhart, early in the following year, departed for Stamboul. For the secretary of embassy had meantime committed a blazing indiscretion and ' put all diplomatic Europe in a flutter ' by helping to bring out the first numbers of the *Portfolio*.

What made this curious serial the sensation of the hour was the fact that it contained a group of highly compromising Russian documents.[28] These had been seized in 1830 by the Polish insurgents at Warsaw and conveyed to England by Polish exiles. As they showed Pozzo, then Russian ambassador to England, at his most intriguing and his worst, as they contained the most offensive references to the duke of Wellington, and as they were calculated above all to annoy and disgust Metternich, the *Portfolio's* editor was obviously intent on raising up enemies to the Russian government. Whether, as Urquhart later claimed, the publication was undertaken with the active co-operation of the Foreign Office and its head, or whether, as Palmerston asserted on his solemn word of honour to the House, the charge was false,[29] one vital fact remains. Although Urquhart's connection with the *Portfolio* was known immediately,[30] he did not lose his diplomatic post. Indeed, the inconsistency of sending Urquhart to Constantinople and Durham to St. Petersburg does not seem to have troubled Palmerston until a small British vessel called the *Vixen* made a rather famous voyage to Circassia late in 1836.[31]

Circassia, which Russia claimed to have obtained from Turkey by cession in 1829, was of considerable interest to Palmerston just then.[32] He had doubts as to the legality of Russia's claim ; and, both because he disliked Russian expansion, and because there were possibilities for British commerce there, he was anxious that the claim should be disproved. Again, the sympathy aroused in England by the Circassians' valiant and hopeless struggle against Russian troops made him apprehensive lest the matter should come up in parliament. But when a merchant by the name of Bell informed him of his (Bell's) intention to ' test ' the Tsar's suzerainty by sending a trading vessel to the Circassian coast, the foreign secretary, according to his own account at least, declined to commit himself.[33] Urquhart, on the other hand, as usual threw discretion to the winds. If he did not originate the scheme of sending the *Vixen* to Circassia, he persuaded Bell to go ahead with it when Bell, warned by Ponsonby, had decided to withdraw.[34] Hence the *Vixen* carried a cargo of salt from Constantinople to the Circassian coast, and was promptly seized for the violation of customs regulations established by the Russian government. It then became quite obvious that those responsible for the voyage were in hopes that it would do more than test Russian suzerainty. When news of the *Vixen's* seizure was received, British enemies of Russia, both in and out of parliament, demanded that Nicholas should be forced to give redress, or that the foreign secretary be called fully to account. Palmerston's ' own Radical supporters . . . in the House' contributed to the outcry.[35] The double flirtation had become impossible.

It was not long before Palmerston became the *bête noire* of the radical Russophobes.[36] They were indignant that he showed himself content when Nicholas upheld the *Vixen*'s seizure, and made it clear that he gave money compensation for her cargo only *ex gratia*.[37] The fact that Palmerston had taken the opinion of the king's advocate did not mollify them in the least. They were again annoyed to find that the Foreign Office took a moderate tone regarding the Russian title to Circassia. True, Palmerston persuaded Metternich to join in urging that operations against the Circassians be given up, and things left as they were : but not even these gentle measures were persisted in when Nicholas proved stubborn.[38] And the foreign secretary's greatest crime of all was his treatment of Urquhart.[39] After being excluded by Ponsonby from the embassy for living *en Turc* and consorting with persons considered undesirable, Urquhart was quietly recalled within a few months of the *Vixen* episode. His insistence that Palmerston had selected Russian documents for the *Portfolio* was met with flat denials. Even his beloved commercial treaty[40] was put aside, to be revised and concluded by Bulwer in 1838. Hence Urquhart devoted his very facile pen to the ceaseless revilement of Lord Palmerston. And he did much more. Apparently under his inspiration, a section of the radicals had formed 'foreign affairs committees,' with headquarters at Birmingham, to supply expert advice on foreign policy to the government.[41] The indignation of some of these earnest citizens concerning Palmerston's policy toward Russia knew no bounds. They soon discovered the appalling fact that England's foreign minister was determined to hand over Turkey to the Tsar, and so to betray his country's most vital interests ! It is related that the more fervid demanded that the traitor be impeached, and even hoped to see him beheaded at the Tower.[42] Certainly they could and did interfere with his comfort. Urquhart's flood of books and pamphlets supplied excellent ammunition to his enemies ; and it was not many years before these radicals were joining hands with another midlands group which had Bright and Cobden at its head.[43] This did not mean, of course, that Palmerston was cast out by all the 'radicals.' The men who earned this name by deep-seated discontent with the existing state of things, political, economic, and religious, were too divided and diversified to unite on anything. But there were groups, by no means insignificant, who had nothing but bitter words for him. That Russophobes should have abused him at this time is by no means incomprehensible. He could hardly inform them and the world at large of the precautions he was taking in the Middle and Near East.

It is really more convenient to speak of Palmerston's precautions than of his policy in the Middle East.[44] With respect to regions where, as he complained, his instructions could not be received until the developments which prompted them were five or six months old, it was necessary to act on general principles and leave wide discretion to agents on the ground. His ability to handle the situation effectively was still more limited by the fact that the central issue was the security of India. Responsibility in this matter lay primarily not with him but with Hobhouse, president of the Board of Control, and with Auckland, the governor-general. It was for them to decide upon and execute such measures as those which precipitated the Afghan war of 1839. But this is not to say that Palmerston was not in part responsible. It was principally from Russia and Persia that danger, real or imaginary, came; it was on the reports of diplomatic and consular agents that Hobhouse and Auckland had chiefly to rely; and the cabinet must have deferred considerably to Palmerston where the external relations of India were concerned. His personal activities centred at St. Petersburg and Teheran; but his influence was felt at Calcutta and at the capitals of the Afghan principalities, Herat, Kabul and Kandahar.

His interest in the whole matter was intense; for he saw British interests vitally affected in several ways by Russian pressure on Persia, and Persian efforts to conquer Herat. Although he once assured the House that 'the course . . . pursued was entirely with a view to the security of our Indian empire,'[45] his tone in private correspondence could be a very different one. Thus, to Melbourne on October 31, 1838 :

> ... If we succeed in taking the Afghans under our protection and in garrisoning (if necessary) Herat, we shall regain our ascendancy in Persia, and get our commercial treaty with that power.[46]

He had still more in view than India's security and British commercial interests :

> ... British ascendancy in Persia gives security on the eastward to Turkey, and tends to make the Sultan more independent, and to place the Dardanelles more securely out of the grasp of Nicholas. Again our baffling on so great a scale of intrigues and attempts of Russia cannot fail to add greatly to the moral weight and political influence of England, and to help us in many other European questions; while it must also tend to give us strength and authority at home.

Given to reflections such as these, it is no wonder that he believed in an active, not to say aggressive, policy.

The restoration of British 'ascendancy' in Persia and the conclusion of an Anglo-Persian commercial treaty were placed in the forefront of his aims. He was, as he wrote Victoria,[47] merely claiming what England had possessed or been promised long before his time. By a treaty of 1814, the Shah was to prevent any Russian advance on India through his domain, and to conclude a commercial arrangement of some sort.[48] While the latter stipulation had remained unfulfilled, Anglo-Persian relations had been satisfactory up to 1834. But a new Shah, who in that year had mounted the peacock throne with the aid of Palmerston,[49] had turned out to be sadly Russophil. Not only was the signing of a commercial treaty still put off, but Russian 'ascendancy' was soon in clear evidence at the Persian capital. By 1837, the British minister, McNeill, was being treated with contempt. In June 1838, the situation became so serious that McNeill severed relations with the Persian government. What had brought matters to this extremity was that the Shah, acting with Russian encouragement, and despite McNeill's protests, had set out to conquer the neighbouring Afghan principality of Herat.

On October 1, 1838, Palmerston explained to Russell how he viewed this Persian move :

... the Success of the Shah [of Persia] in Affghanistan would be full of danger and embarrassment to us in India. ... He is in this matter acting avowedly as the Tool of Russia; and the Proceedings of Russia in Affghanistan are certainly as direct an approach to British India as it is *at present* in her Power to make.[50]

What should be done? McNeill suggested the landing of an expeditionary force at Persia's principal port, Bushire, and its advance to Ispahan or Teheran. But such an operation would be costly; it would weaken or possibly dethrone the Shah; and it would even be somewhat dangerous in view of the possibility that Russia might 'throw away the Scabbard . . . and attack us.' If any land operations were required it would be better to undertake them on Afghan, rather than on Persian, soil:

... any forward movement into Affghanistan would, if successful, be clear gain, as we should permanently retain any advantage we might gain, and should thus make a permanent Barrier for India.

It is probable that Palmerston was contemplating the possibility of a 'forward movement' to Kabul. Someone had certainly suggested that Ranjit Singh, the Maharajah of Lahore, should be assisted by the government of India in taking the offensive in Afghanistan; and the Maharajah had no apparent reason for moving against either of the other Afghan principalities, Herat and Kandahar. But Palmerston, at this time, hoped to avoid land operations anywhere, and to bring the Shah to terms by the occupation of Karrak, an island which commanded the harbour of Bushire:

... the occupation of Carrack and the landing at Busheer, if it should take Place, may as a diversion in the Rear of the Shah, compel him to give up his attack, and may thus effect our object at less Expence and with less Trouble than if we pushed on Runjeet Sing aided by a Body of the Company's Troops through Affghanistan. ...

My own belief is that our Demonstration, [at Karrak] together with the Gallant Resistance of the People of Herat, will have induced the Shah to abandon the Siege and retire, and if that should be the Result we shall have had a good Escape, and shall then be able to enter into alliance with the Affghans and make with them the proper arrangements for their future Security and our own.[51]

RESPONSIBILITY FOR THE AFGHAN WAR

Neither he nor any member of the cabinet knew, at the beginning of October 1838, what measures Auckland might decide upon :

> Hobhouse was to say to Auckland that the Government is sure he will have adopted the Course which he and his Counsellors will have thought on the whole best, and that he will be supported.

In point of fact, Auckland had decided, nearly five months before, to effect a change of rulers at Kabul, and to do so with the help of Ranjit Singh.

There seems to be entire agreement that the adoption and execution of this project was a blunder of the first magnitude. The Indian government attempted to establish its control over a warlike and freedom-loving people inhabiting a country remote and inaccessible. What was worse, it tried to do so by dethroning Dost Mohamed, a prince both capable and popular, in favour of Shah Shuja, a British puppet as weak as Dost was strong. And the use of Ranjit Singh, who had taken Peshawur from the Afghans a short time before, was bound to heighten Afghan susceptibilities. It has seemed, then, that the rebellion and massacre at Kabul and the annihilation of the retreating British troops—those terrible events which brought the short reign of Shah Shuja to a close—could easily have been foreseen. At any rate, there has been almost universal condemnation of the three men held primarily responsible, Auckland, Hobhouse and Palmerston. Both of the former accepted full responsibility ; and in one respect Auckland was especially culpable. In spite of news that the Persians had given up the conquest of Herat—largely as a result of the occupation of Karrak—he persisted in sending the expedition to Kabul.

But Palmerston has borne a goodly share of blame. For it seems that he and Hobhouse, by October 24, 1838, and before the first news of Auckland's decision had reached them, resolved that Shah Shuja should be enthroned.[52] Apparently, in just three weeks, he had experienced a change of heart. Were fresh reports responsible for this, or did he allow himself to be won over by Hobhouse ? Nothing is clear, save that Hobhouse regarded himself as the patron of the expedition among the members of the cabinet. Note this entry in his diary, made when the expedition had seemingly achieved success :

> Of all our colleagues, the one that was most pleased with these successes was Lord Palmerston ; and I always found in him a cordial sympathiser in every variety of fortune, more particularly in success—a very rare quality. . . .[53]

The question of prior responsibility is, however, somewhat beside the point ; for Palmerston's approval of the expedition was unmistakable.[54]

His critics have laid great stress on his ' fantastic ' fears, and on his failure to perceive that the expedition to Kabul was sure to prove futile. As for his fears, a wide divergence of opinion still exists as to whether the danger to India's disturbed and unprotected borderlands was or was not actual.[55] And Kaye, the first authoritative historian of the war, and one of the most unsparing critics of those whom he regarded as responsible, has pointed out that there were other considerations which could not be overlooked :

> . . . the result of all these disturbing rumours was an aftergrowth of new perils springing up almost at our very doors. The Native States on our own borders were beginning to evince signs of feverish unrest. . . . Even in our own provinces, these rumours of mighty movements in the countries of the north-west disquieted the native mind. . . . Among our Mussulman subjects. . . . it was believed that countless thousands of true believers were about to pour themselves over the plains of the Punjab and Hindostan, and to wrest all the country between the Indus and the sea from the hands of the infidel usurpers. The Mahomedan journals, at this time, teemed with the utterances of undisguised sedition. There was a decline in the value of public securities ; and it went openly from mouth to mouth, in the streets and the bazaars, that the Company's Raj was nearly at an end.[56]

Be it remembered, too, that Palmerston's ' fantastic ' fears of Russia's proceedings in the Middle East were shared by those who were supposedly the best informed,[57]—by Hobhouse, the member of the cabinet primarily responsible for the direction of affairs in India, by Auckland, by the two ministers to Persia, Ellis and McNeill, by Auckland's agent on the northwest frontier, Captain Wade, and even by Dost

Mohamed's friend and advocate, Sir Alexander Burnes. Whether or not his apprehension may now be looked upon as fanciful, it is difficult to see on what grounds he could have dissented from the judgment of this group. There seems to be a better case for criticising his judgment as to the practicability of the enterprise. But when Hobhouse and Auckland were so confident, a very optimistic foreign secretary, if anything less informed than they, and deeply engrossed in matters nearer home, was not likely to dissent. One wonders whether the persisting impression of Palmerston's great culpability may not owe something to the oratory of John Bright.

Bright's charges were most vigorously pressed in connection with a side issue of the Afghan war, the falsification of the despatches of Sir Alexander Burnes in the papers laid before the House in 1839.[58] Burnes, an able, experienced and devoted officer, who had done his best to persuade Auckland to strike a bargain with Dost Mohamed—at the almost certain price of a struggle with British India's powerful neighbour, Ranjit Singh—was assassinated at Kabul in 1841. Before his death he had complained of the garbling of his despatches to Auckland in the blue book of 1839. Hence a number of persons, including his brother and the 'foreign affairs committees' which owed so much inspiration to Urquhart, carried on a long agitation for the publication of full texts. They secured the publication in 1859; and two years later proceeded to the indictment of Palmerston.[59] The latter, then of course prime minister, had to meet the demonstrated fact that those parts of Burnes' letters in which he pointed out the evidences of Dost Mohamed's desire to ally himself with the British government —on condition that it would help him to recover Peshawur —had been carefully excised from the papers given to parliament. So, too, had been Burnes' professions of faith in Dost Mohamed's honesty, and his pleas that Auckland should meet Dost's terms. The excisions changed the purport of some letters fundamentally, even to conveying the impression that Burnes agreed with Auckland's policy. Palmerston pleaded that the rules of the game had been observed. It was not the custom, nor for the public interest, that unabridged sets of papers should be given to the world ; and the regular procedure was that the government should offer parliament an exposition of those facts and arguments on which its actions had been based. What had been omitted were parts of Burnes' despatches in which ' his personal opinions, evidently arising from confusion of ideas, misconceptions, and overcredulity, were stated, at variance with the views justly entertained by the [Indian] Government under which he was acting.' It had been recognised that Burnes was ' acting according to the best of his judgment ' ; and, if parts of his despatches had been omitted, so had the severe reprimands administered for his failure to abide by his instructions, and for unauthorised communications concerning the progress of his negotiations to the newspapers of Bombay. Who had been responsible for the excisions the premier did not say. Nor did the efforts of Bright to ' drag the delinquent before the public ' avail. Russell fully endorsed Palmerston's defence ; and Disraeli, leader of the opposition at the time, supported him as being technically in the right.

But Bright had used his extraordinary gifts of invective and of emotional oratory to indict his enemy. The mutilation of the despatches, he declared, was nothing short of forgery, of the sort of thing certain persons did to coins and notes and deeds. Palmerston, ' throughout the whole of his speech ' had ' stooped so low as . . . to heap insult upon the memory of a man who died in the execution of . . . a duty which was thrust upon him by the mad and obstinate policy of the noble Lord.' Such carelessness regarding facts was hardly becoming in a critic of the blue book ; but speeches of this kind leave their mark. Those who sympathised with Bright, they and the generations following who have looked with distaste on the mutilations of the Burnes papers, have not always been over careful to inquire just how much ' the mad and obstinate policy of the noble Lord ' had to do with the genesis of the first Afghan war.

CHAPTER XIV

THE NEAR EASTERN CRISIS, 1839–1841

THE diplomatic triumph which Palmerston achieved through his handling of the Near Eastern question in the years 1839–1841 was a happy offering to his devoted and ambitious bride. It was one which any wife in Europe might have worn with pride, being secured, as Lady Palmerston wrote gratefully, by 'extraordinary courage under circumstances that would have made many a stout heart flinch.' Yet, ironically enough, it was anything but the kind of triumph her knight had at first striven for. His general line of action concerning the Turkish empire did not, indeed, undergo any change. Never did he swerve from that policy of at once defending and reinvigorating Turkey, of which he had made himself the first great British exponent : [1]

As to the Turkish empire, if we can procure for it ten years of peace under the joint protection of the five Powers, and if those years are profitably employed in reorganizing the internal system of the empire, there is no reason whatever why it should not become again a respectable Power. Half the wrong conclusions at which mankind arrive are reached by the abuse of metaphors. . . . Thus people compare an ancient monarchy with an old building, an old tree, or an old man, and because the building, tree, or man must from the nature of things crumble, or decay, or die, they imagine that the same thing holds good with a community. . . . Than which there cannot be a greater or more utterly unphilosophical mistake . . . the component parts of a community are undergoing daily the process of physical renovation and of moral improvement. Therefore all that we hear every day of the week about the decay of the Turkish empire, and its being a dead body or a sapless trunk, and so forth, is pure and unadulterated nonsense.[2]

But in defending Turkey from the dangers which threatened her, in 1839, both from the north and from the south, he was forced into unexpected relations with two other Powers. He found himself co-operating with the Tsar to confound Louis Philippe ; whereas he had been contriving for years how he and the French king might circumvent Nicholas.

During those years of worry over the Russian threat to Constantinople and the Straits which had followed the conclusion of the treaty of Unkiar Skelessi, he had stood defiant and alone, warning Turks and Egyptians impartially against flying at one another's throats,[3] and promoting Turkey's rejuvenation against the eventuality that his warnings should prove ineffectual. A statesman less given to independent action might well have sought to eliminate all risk through an understanding between the Powers ; since the French were at first more than ready to co-operate, and Metternich was willing to lend some aid.[4] Break with Nicholas the Austrian chancellor would not, so long as 'order' in Europe was menaced. But the two had agreed at Münchengrätz, in 1833, to abstain from all immediate aggression in so far as European Turkey was concerned ; and Metternich would have liked an understanding on the subject with the British and French governments. Had the Austrian chancellor realised this wish, Europe might have avoided the crisis of 1839–1841. But in that case Palmerston would have missed an opportunity to score heavily off Louis Philippe, to show his independence of the Whigs, and to reach the peak of fame as a foreign minister.

Some of his reasons for running counter to Metternich's desire appeared in the winter of 1835–1836, when he urged the conclusion of a treaty binding the British, French and Turkish governments to resist the transfer of Turkish territory to any Power.[5] He proposed that after the conclusion of the treaty Austria should be invited to concur, and even, if she wished, to suggest concurrence to her two great friends. But when half the cabinet, including Melbourne, insisted that she be given the opportunity of becoming an original partner, Palmerston would not hear of it. He was 'fully convinced,' he wrote, that she would not separate herself from the Russian and Prussian governments.[6] That being the case, England, having once invited Austria to be an original partner, would have three possible courses of action : to show herself ' baffled ' by giving up the suggested treaty with the French ; to assume an ' air of defiance ' to Austria by signing it without her ; or to accept ' a congress of the Five Powers at Vienna upon the affairs of the East, or rather upon the affairs of Europe.' He went on :

> As to a congress or conference at Vienna, how could a Whig government enter upon such a career ? For my part what I have seen of such negotiations during the continuance of the Belgian Conferences, would lead me to decline signing the instructions of a British ambassador to take part in such a conclave.

For one thing it was impossible to tell what decision on the Eastern question the five Powers might reach :

> . . . there is a wide difference between proposing to Powers to accede to a treaty, the four corners of which we have already traced out & bounded, or proposing to such Powers to enter into negotiation for the purpose of coming to some treaty or other. The first course is definite & known, the second is boundless & uncertain.

And the ' conclave ' might embarrass the British in another way :

> . . . if we ask the Three Powers to talk with us about Turkey, on what ground are we to refuse to let them talk to us about Spain ?

It accorded far better with his general policy to reach understandings with a complaisant French government, and let the other Powers accept or reject these as they chose. Hence, when it proved that neither he nor the cabinet would give way, all chance of a preliminary settlement of the Near Eastern question disappeared. In vain Metternich tried to draw him into some congress or conference, or at least into an exchange of views between the Powers. For two years and more he preferred to watch events and trust that he would be able to deal with any developments which might arise.

Only in the summer of 1838 did he change his mind.[7] By that time the Egyptian Pasha's announced intention of declaring himself independent made a Turco-Egyptian conflict so probable that it was necessary to lay plans. The British cabinet decided that it would be better to give naval assistance to the Turks than to let Russia ' save ' them under the terms of Unkiar Skelessi. But the foreign secretary had no desire to act alone. Believing that an understanding existed between the Pasha and the Tsar, and feeling that *the one great danger to Europe* lay in *the possibility of a combination between France and Russia*,' he longed more than ever for a convention with France and Turkey such as he had urged in the winter of 1835–1836. But, whether he considered it useless again to press this policy upon the cabinet, or whether he gave it up in face of Turkey's fear of offending Nicholas and the obvious partiality of Molé for the Pasha, he decided at last to work for an understanding to be concluded in London between the five great Powers. He seemed to make no real progress. Russia and Austria, supported as usual by the Prussian court, refused to take part in a conference in London ; while the tardy acquiescence of the French government did not conceal its ' cold reserve.' But in one respect the British Foreign Office had distinctly scored : a declaration made to Russia that England would not allow her to work her will on Turkey a second time, and was resolved on concerted action by the Powers, produced a useful and lasting impression at St. Petersburg. Meanwhile, the crisis was approaching fast. In the early months of 1839 the Sultan, confident that he was strong enough to punish the Pasha at last, concentrated his army on the Euphrates for a campaign in Syria. The worst could happen at any time. Some reassurance came, however, to the British government. In January 1839, Molé resigned, to make room at the French Foreign Office for the more friendly Marshal Soult. It seemed to Palmerston that, if general co-operation of the Powers should prove impossible, the partners of the entente might prevent the Russians from exploiting the situation after all.

He attacked the problem with real zest. The Tsar had worsted him six years before ; and now opportunity for a reckoning had come. Not only should Russia be prevented from profiting by the new developments, but, if the Foreign Office could compass it, she should be forced to relinquish whatever advantages she had acquired at Unkiar Skelessi. He poured out his hopes and plans in a series of letters to Granville. 'The first step would be to establish a perfect understanding between England and France,' thus eliminating the dire possibility of a separate agreement between Louis Philippe and Nicholas : the second, the despatch of an Anglo-French squadron to enforce an armistice.[8] But the armistice would not really be enforced against the Turks :

If the Sultan's troops were successful in the outset his general would refuse the armistice, and Ibrahim [Mehemet Ali's heir, who commanded the Egyptian army] would agree to it. In that case it seems to me that our admirals could do nothing but wait.

For, being determined that the Egyptians should be expelled from Syria,[9] he would not admit that the treaty by which Mehemet Ali had become master of the Syrian pashalics had any real validity :

The Sultan is the sovereign & though he may have been the aggressor . . . still he has right on his side. There was no treaty at Kutayah. There could be none ; The parties there were a sovereign & a rebel.—No *treaty* can be made between such parties. There was indeed an agreement, and the Sultan conferred certain governments upon Mehemet & Ibrahim. But those governments were given during pleasure, and the Sultan has a right to resume them . . . and to say the truth it would be very much for the advantage of every Power in Europe except Russia, that the Sultan should be able to resume what he then conferred.[10]

But, should the Turks accept an armistice and the Egyptians refuse, the fleets should intervene by cutting Ibrahim's water communications with Egypt and bottling or destroying Mehemet's fleet at Alexandria. Such one-sided intervention might seem unjust, but :

The maintenance of the Turkish Empire ought to be the basis of our policy ; for its maintenance is essential for . . . the upholding of the independence of Eastern Europe—a partition of Turkey would be fatal to the independence of Austria & Prussia . . . and it could not be accomplished without a general war—No ideas therefore of fairness towards Mehemet ought to stand in the way of such great & paramount interests : But in fact there is no question about fairness towards Mehemet . . . a robber is always liable to be made to disgorge. . . .

Palmerston sometimes displayed a genius for *ad hoc* reasoning.

Along with these proposals for immediate action went some rather prophetic suggestions for 'a final settlement . . . and not a mere patching up.'[11] The treaty of Unkiar Skelessi might, he thought, be replaced by a guarantee of Turkish independence and integrity on the part of the five Powers, and Mehemet might be forced to relinquish Syria, receiving in return some more permanent hold upon Egypt for his family. But how was Mehemet to be got out of Syria?

Not by his own good will certainly : But if the five Powers, or if the three Powers England, France and Austria, or the two Powers England and France were to tell him that he *must* go, go he would, for go he *must*.

And the situation in the early summer of 1839 offered an opportunity not to be lost :

This is a most favourable moment . . . Russia has been foiled and exposed by England in the East, and has found by the personal experience of the Emperor that she has lost her influence in the West—She is embarrassed by her Circassian war and by the discontent in many of her provinces—Her treasury is poor and she could not find easily the means in men ships or money to make war except in self defence. A year or two hence she will have rallied. . . . You should always deal with a bully when he has just had his nose pulled. Again you may never have France in better trim for acting fairly on this question. Soult is a plain straightforward soldier and very sincerely desirous of acting cordially with England, partly from his own conviction, partly to do the reverse of what Molé did.

He was more doubtful of Austria : for he saw Metternich,

Timid of course, as usual . . . trying to hide from himself the truth, fearing to face difficulties or opposition—truckling to self-styled friends whom he knows to be enemies at heart, and endeavouring to get into smooth water by always sacrificing the great interest of the future, for a little ease and comfort in the present.

But it might be possible ' to work him up to concert pitch,' and thus persuade him to ' do more to consolidate the peace of Europe than any man has done since the 15th of June 1815.' In fact, everything seemed possible so long as Soult remained 'straightforward . . . and very sincerely desirous of acting cordially with England.' Deceived, perhaps, by the fact that France sent a naval expedition to the Syrian coast, Palmerston was hopeful that Louis Philippe's ministers would help him confine the Pasha to Egypt. He was not without his suspicions regarding their sincerity[12]; but he seems to have been honest when he assured the House, on July 9, that ' the English and French governments perfectly understood each other and were acting in concert.'[13] ' Soult is a jewel,' he wrote Russell on that day.[14] Events had meantime travelled with disconcerting rapidity. The Sultan's army had been almost annihilated by the Egyptians at Nezib, late in June ; the Sultan had taken this most inconvenient moment to die and leave his kingdom to an incompetent youth ; and the Turkish fleet, with the reported connivance of French naval officers, had voluntarily given itself up to Mehemet Ali at Alexandria.

What must, however, have been far more disconcerting to Palmerston was to find that he had been wrong—most egregiously wrong—in his calculations concerning the attitudes which would be adopted by the French and Russian governments. The discovery did not come at once. Even after news reached Paris and London, on July 22 and 23, of the battle of Nezib, he and Soult both believed that it would be possible for them to co-operate.[15] Palmerston saw in the battle ' the triumph of Russian intrigue ' directed toward the weakening of Turkey ; and believed that Soult would prefer the maintenance of ' the balance of power ' to the replacement of the Sultan by the former ' waiter at a coffee shop,' Mehemet Ali.[16] But, before the summer was out, he found the radiance of the ' jewel ' among French ministers dimmed by the breath of French public sentiment. In fact, he soon came to suspect that it was a base stone after all. The French press celebrated the battle of Nezib as a French victory over England and her Turkish protégé,[17] and demanded that the gains of the victory should be enlarged. Louis Philippe and Soult, fearful of stirring up dissatisfaction, and utterly miscalculating Mehemet's fighting strength, decided to take the nationalistic side. Slowly Palmerston discovered that, so far from helping him expel the Pasha from Syria, they were inclining to make its possession hereditary in his house, and even to support him in his claims to temporary possession of Candia. They flatly rejected his conciliatory suggestion that Mehemet should be allowed to keep the pashalic of Acre, minus its fortress—presumably for the period of his life.[18] In pleasing contrast, the Tsar, deciding that the advantages to be drawn from the treaty of Unkiar Skelessi would be too dearly purchased by a struggle with England, and seeing a godsent opportunity of depriving the 'revolutionary' Orleans monarchy of the British support which alone made it really dangerous, surprised Palmerston almost from the outset by an apparently ready acceptance of his views.[19] In fact, as early as February 1839, Nicholas had remarked to Barante, the French ambassador at St. Petersburg, that England, now establishing herself in the Persian Gulf and the Red Sea, would want the control of Egypt for her lines of communication with India. And Barante had been quick to draw the inference : 'I saw his wish and his hope that we should become embroiled with England.'[20] And two months later : 'One can no longer doubt that the cabinet of St. Petersburg . . . will promise England certain advantages to persuade her to separate her interests from ours.'[21] In spite of these warnings the French government disappointed Palmerston by refusing, as he wrote disgustedly, 'to run counter to that little cabal at Paris' which had from the first taken Mehemet 'under the wings of its protection.'[22]

A 'little cabal' was all that Palmerston could see—or chose to see—in the French chauvinists. But Louis Philippe's ministers saw more. They saw that France was growing bored. Montalembert's gibe that the establishment of that Orleans monarchy was like 'putting up a grocer and his family to be shot at'[23] was highly appreciated : and the Napoleonic legend grew apace. Not the mere transfer of Napoleon's ashes would abate the murmurs for the resumption of French leadership on the continent, for 'natural' frontiers or at least some revision of the hated treaties of 1815, and for a curb on the growth of England's commerce and prestige. In regard to Egypt and Syria,

LOUIS PHILIPPE

linked to France by her oldest and newest traditions of overseas enterprise, and lying within her natural field of expansion, Frenchmen were bound to be especially sensitive. Such considerations weighed deeply with the French government and with many Englishmen. On both sides of the Channel, then, it was pointed out that a serious rebuff to the Orleans monarchy in the Near East might mean the appearance of a republican or Napoleonic France, ready to bring on Europe the perils of a general and revolutionary war. But the British foreign secretary was not to be diverted from his policy by mere possibilities. The French government had agreed to protect the integrity of the Turkish empire ; and it was to be forced, if need be, to live up to the agreement in the sense in which the agreement was interpreted by Palmerston.

The breach between the partners of the entente widened rapidly.[24] By September the hopeless divergence between their views was clear ; in November, Palmerston was incorporating in his despatches to Granville facts and arguments which, as he quite realised, would ' touch Louis Philippe in the raw ' ; in December he was complaining of French journals and French armaments, and threatening to strengthen the Mediterranean squadron. He had given up hope of voluntary co-operation from the French, but not his determination as to the final settlement. The ' miserable . . . shifts and changes in the opinions and schemes of the French Government,' its ' wishes and objects at bottom ' which they were ' ashamed of confessing,' merely made it necessary that the matter should be settled by a concert of the Powers. In changing his tactics he was perfectly honest. As early as September, he solemnly warned Louis Philippe's ministers that if co-operation was not to be had from them he would seek support from other Powers ; and the warning, frequently repeated in the following months, was taken seriously by the French ambassador. He had not far to seek for aid. Scarcely had he issued his first warning to the French when Russia's suave envoy, Brunnow, arrived in England with the most satisfactory assurances.[25] Russia was willing to co-operate against Ibrahim, to permit the lapse of the treaty of Unkiar

Skelessi, and to arrange peace terms in a concert of the Powers. Austria and Prussia were at her back. So well did matters go that Nesselrode was, in October, full of hope that the 'baneful' entente would be '*ipso facto* dissolved.'[26] He had not long to wait. In January 1840, Soult was complaining of a new 'Grand Alliance' against France;[27] and in March Palmerston was telling the House that 'it was impossible for any government to have acted with more honour and good faith in any matter' than Russia had been doing with respect to the Near East.[28] It was almost the same language he had used eight months before respecting France.

This month of March brought a short-lived hope that England and France might come to some understanding after all. For a new French ambassador came to London in the person of Guizot, well known to be a friend of peace and the entente, and respected as a 'sensible and enlightened' man by Palmerston. But almost immediately arrived the news that Soult had made way for Thiers, for Thiers the ardent nationalist who had just declared his disapproval of any measures of coercion against Mehemet Ali.[29] The breach became complete when Palmerston learned that, while Guizot was talking of joint action in London, his government was secretly trying to arrange a separate agreement between the Sultan and the Pasha which would assure the triumph of her pro-Egyptian policy.[30] Not that any open unfriendliness between the two governments ensued. France helped England to arrange a dispute over a sulphur monopoly with the Neapolitans;[31] and Palmerston, in writing to facilitate the transfer of Napoleon's remains from St. Helena to the Invalides, expressed the hope that 'if any animosity still existed between the two nations, it might be buried in the tomb which France would raise to the Emperor.'[32]

It cannot be said, however, that he did much towards the accomplishment of this pious wish. For, having discovered that France was quietly endeavouring to present the other Powers with a *fait accompli* in the Levant, he arranged that the presentation should be from the other side.[33] He proposed that the four Powers should proceed at once to fix by convention the terms of settlement between Egypt and Turkey, and the means to be adopted for imposing them. Melbourne and Russell heartily approved the step. But others of his colleagues did not. Since January, as Louis Philippe and Nesselrode well knew,[34] the cabinet had been divided over the irritation felt by some, and the ' blind partiality ' (as Melbourne put it) exhibited by others, with respect to France.[35] Hence it was not surprising that, when Palmerston asked sanction from his colleagues for the conclusion of an agreement with the three eastern Powers, two of them, Holland and Clarendon, refused. Holland's stand is perhaps best explained by Guizot's remark that this charming nephew of Charles James Fox would have been as much at home in his (Guizot's) eighteenth-century Paris salon as at Holland House.[36] Clarendon merely felt himself a better judge of foreign policy than the foreign secretary.[37] There was a short deadlock.[38] Palmerston, maintaining that the question was whether England was ' to remain a Substantive Power, or . . . to declare herself a dependency of France,' offered to resign. So did Clarendon ; and Melbourne begged that ' for God's sake ' no one should resign at all. No one did ; for Holland and Clarendon contented themselves with solemnly recording their objections in a memorandum to the Queen.[39] Palmerston thus being free to act, the British, Russian, Austrian and Prussian governments proceeded, without final warning to the French ambassador, to sign the convention on July 15.[40] It gave Mehemet Ali ten days to settle with his suzerain by accepting Egypt as an hereditary pashalic and southern Syria (Acre) for life, or twenty days to accept Egypt alone : and it did away with the treaty of Unkiar Skelessi by placing the Straits under international guardianship according to ' the ancient rule.' One of Palmerston's great diplomatic aims had been achieved. Yet the real crisis, in so far at least as he was personally concerned, had just begun.

For the signature of the treaty was a challenge, not only to France and her Egyptian satellite, but to Whig Francophils, to Manchester pacifists and to the many other Englishmen who feared that France would revert to revolution and to war. The immediate reaction at Paris was, as the Austrian envoy wrote, '*foudroyant.*'[41] The renewal of the 'coalition' against France, the breaking of the entente, and, most of all, perhaps, the fact that no final warning had been given to Guizot, roused a storm of indignation at Paris. The boulevards resounded with the Marseillaise and with angry boasts that France would meet the coalition as she had done in '93 : the carriage of Lord Granville, the popular British ambassador, was attacked. And the resentment of Louis Philippe was no whit less bitter than that of his subjects. It mattered not that France would not have signed the convention in any case ;[42] that Guizot had warned his government as late as June 15 ;[43] that the four Powers had plausible arguments for preserving secrecy ;[44] and that they communicated the convention in the gentlest manner possible.[45] The French king complained that he had been placed upon a *poudrière*, and that the ardour of the populace might force him to hostilities if concessions were refused.[46] Reserves were called up, Paris fortified, and negotiations opened with Naples and Piedmont. And, while the Gallic rage was concentrated on Palmerston,[47] it seemed that France would relieve her feelings in the traditional way by marching on the Rhine.

Needless to say, the attitude of the French destroyed such inclination to make conciliatory overtures as had existed in Britons of Palmerston's type. Its effect on the foreign secretary was very clear. 'Of all mistakes, in public affairs as well as in private,' he wrote Bulwer, 'the greatest is to truckle to swagger and bully, or even to unjustifiable violence.'[48] Hence, after asking Clarendon to write a soothing letter to Thiers, he decided that French threats made its despatch impossible.[49] Instead, he demanded an explanation of French armaments, and talked of asking parliament to vote the credits which might be required for war.[50] As he told Bloomfield, his ambassador at St. Petersburg, the attitude of the French people and their press convinced him that they needed the lesson they had just received.[51] True, Melbourne later found him 'not averse' to a suggestion that the July convention should be merged into a larger arrangement in which France could have a share ;[52] but he seems to have been quite content that the suggestion should prove abortive, and the ' lesson ' be prolonged. Of war with the French he had at this time little or no fear. He had diagnosed the attitude of their government.[53]

Pre-eminent among his countrymen in ability to recognise a bluff, he was not fearful of immediate hostilities ; but he realised that if delay were to ensue the danger might become actual. The British, in whose hands the principal share in the naval and military execution of the July treaty was to rest, were preparing to enforce it against Mehemet Ali by blockades, bombardments, and the landing of troops to further a rebellion of the Syrians. Mehemet was threatening to reciprocate by a thrust at the Turks of which the ultimate objective would be their capital. Now such a thrust might bring Russian forces on the scene ; and there was reason for taking seriously the warning of Guizot that if the four Powers came to some further arrangement without France, or if Russian troops appeared at Constantinople, the French government would scarcely be able to refuse a national demand for war.[54] Certainly there were limits to the ' grocer's ' influence over an inflamed Paris. Lord William Russell wrote of ' the total discredit into which the King and all public men ' had fallen ;[55] and Croker bemoaned that there was ' no man in France ' who had ' legitimate authority or commanding influence over the public mind.'[56] Hence, for the allies to delay, was to give time for the massing of French chauvinists as well as armaments. There had either to be rapid and successful action or else retreat from the agreement of July 15. Needless to say, the latter alternative never received a moment's consideration from Palmerston. Protests and menaces broke over him as waves over a well-worn rock. Thus to Melbourne :

> If the French attempt to bully and intimidate us as they have done, the only way of meeting their menaces is by quietly telling them we are not afraid, and by showing them, first, that we are stronger than they are, and, secondly, that they have more vulnerable points than we have.[57]

To his ambassador at Paris :

> . . . if Thiers should again hold to you the language of menace

... convey to him in the most friendly and unoffensive manner possible, that if France ... begins a war, she will to a certainty lose her ships, colonies and commerce before she sees the end of it; that her army of Algiers will cease to give her anxiety, and that Mehemet Ali will just be chucked into the Nile.[58]

and to Guizot :

Oh ! Mehemet Ali will give in ; he cannot be expected to give in at the first summons ; but let him have a fortnight and he will end up by capitulating.[59]

His confidence in the success of Britain's fighting forces and of his own policy was absolute. What gave him real concern was a combination of persons in England and abroad who were determined that his policy should not prevail.

To observe as well as possible the make-up of this combination and the methods it employed is but common fairness to Palmerston.[60] Otherwise it would be impossible to appreciate his difficulties and his dauntlessness. And it would also be impossible to make allowances for the unaccustomed resentment which he showed towards English adversaries and, most unfortunately, towards France. In the cabinet the first leaders had been Clarendon, who seems to have had a habit of carrying the tricks of diplomacy into domestic politics, and Holland, who openly lavished civilities on Guizot and expressions of his dissent from Palmerston's policies on every visitor to Holland House. Then, with French threats of war, there appeared a more dangerous adversary still in Lord John Russell, the leader of the House. That he, who had warmly supported the conclusion of the treaty of July 15, now opposed Palmerston's efforts to give it effect, merely bears witness to the impressionability and consequent instability that so often marred his great career. Apparently some of the Whig leaders outside the government, with the duke of Bedford and Lord Spencer at their head, decided to use Lord John in making effective their predilection for the French, and their resentment at the unwhiggish character of the Palmerstonian policies. Russell, drawn by their persuasion from one of his characteristic fits of boldness into an equally characteristic fit of nervousness, and stimulated into resenting Palmerston's domination in matters of foreign affairs, went no further in publicly disowning Palmerston's policy than to repudiate the opinions of Palmerston's organ, the *Chronicle*. But he caused infinite trouble by threatening constantly to resign—being prepared, however, to let Palmerston resign instead, and himself to accept the Foreign Office seals. Lansdowne, the president of the Council, took the anti-Palmerstonian point of view, but was correct in his conduct at all times. The other members of the cabinet, at first rather neutral but inclined more and more to go with the dissidents as the danger of war seemed more threatening, found themselves borne along in a policy they did not really approve by Palmerston's weight of knowledge, determination and resourcefulness. And Melbourne, cynical and incapable of making a determined stand, was borne along with them. Reported at times to be 'at his wit's end,' and even too worried to eat, drink or sleep, he proved equally unable to check his foreign secretary or to see that the cabinet left him in peace.

Palmerston also had a group of adversaries outside the cabinet, a varied and much scattered group, but all of them connected in some way. Prominent among them was Charles Greville, clerk of the Privy Council, gossip and diarist *par excellence* and intriguer intermittently. His milder methods of attack consisted in helping to foment trouble in the cabinet, and writing articles for *The Times*. But he also pumped Melbourne, Lord and Lady Palmerston, the three leading cabinet dissidents and the duke of Bedford quite impartially, and, on the strength of the information thus and otherwise acquired, helped the French ambassador to combat the foreign secretary. He suggested to Guizot what offers on his part would most impress the cabinet as a whole ; pointed out which of its members would be most influential in checking Palmerston ; and, at Guizot's request, attempted to swing *The Times*, through Barnes its editor, into a pro-French policy. But there was an even more interesting side to Greville's activities. Long before the crisis was over, his young friend Henry Reeve went to Paris and established intimate relations with Thiers and other French ministers. Greville apparently helped him to secure the insertion in *The Times* of anonymous articles which might almost as well have emanated from the French government itself. Moreover, Greville kept Reeve, and presumably, therefore, the French ministry, informed of all, or nearly all, he knew! Nor was Louis Philippe's government obliged to rely only on Reeve for unofficial information and advice. For Edward Ellice—the 'Bear Ellice' of the diarists—was frequently in Paris, too. Member of the inner circle of the Whigs, brother-in-law to Grey and friend to Holland and Clarendon, he was believed by most persons, and not least by himself, to have exceptionally accurate knowledge of what went on behind the scenes at Westminster. Intensely critical of the foreign secretary and his policies, he had been and was to be a thorn in Palmerston's side for several years. At this time he was, on the one hand, writing letters to Bedford which were used to influence Russell, and on the other conveying to the French court glad tidings of the dissatisfaction with Palmerston, and the pure and undefiled love for France which animated all true Whigs. Madame de Lieven, now at odds with her husband and her Emperor, and utterly attached to the interests of Guizot, welcomed Reeve and Ellice at her Paris residence with open arms. There was still one more line between Paris and London, a line which went via Brussels. King Leopold, naturally appalled at the prospect of a general war, and above all one in which his niece and father-in-law would be on opposite sides, was using all his craft and all his influence to sway Melbourne and Victoria against Palmerston. The Queen and Prince Albert, who were married in February 1840, at first resisted their uncle's arguments; but they urged conciliation more and more strongly as the crisis progressed. No wonder Louis Philippe proved so obstinate, knowing all these things. He may even have heard that Urquhart, convinced that Palmerston's 'treachery' was laid bare at last, was stirring up resentment in the cities in the Midlands; and that Cobden, as a pacifist, was assisting him. For Urquhart, too, was welcomed in at least one French ministerial salon. If France, as one of her historians has said, went from mistake to mistake and from disillusionment to disillusionment,[61] she might in fairness have laid much of the blame on the well-wishers who deluded her.

The demands which these persons made of Palmerston in the summer of 1840 and in the autumn months, do not seem inherently unreasonable. They asked concessions to France which would bring her back to the concert of Powers and save her dignity; and they felt that everything could be arranged if Palmerston would only give way with respect to Syria. When the French, in September, 'persuaded' Mehemet to agree to peace on terms somewhat more to his advantage than those which the four Powers had, on July 15, given him ten days to accept, the opponents of the foreign secretary would have had their government seize the occasion for a *rapprochement* with the Tuileries.[62] But there was much that they overlooked. Palmerston was executing a convention between four Powers, and a convention from which England had already obtained great advantages. Moreover, there was reason to fear that if he did not hold to its terms Russia would resume an independence of action which would be fatal to his hopes. Nor could he be expected to overlook the question of British prestige and British influence. France had chosen to resort to open threats of war; and if in face of these the Melbourne government seemed to retreat, the effect upon the eastern Powers, the Turkish and Egyptian governments, the Paris chauvinists and the British populace could easily be foretold. And was the question of Syria so immaterial after all? Melbourne pointed out that to renew Mehemet's tenure was to make that tenure permanent;[63] and there was little doubt that Mehemet would use Syria as a base of operations for the conquest of Mesopotamia and Arabia. Were both routes to India to be in the hands of the grateful friend of France? Palmerston, rightly or wrongly, would not take the risk. He was ready enough to readmit France to the concert, but only if she would join in securing the submission of her protégé.

'The greatest difficulties I had to encounter in the whole transaction,' he wrote long afterwards, ' arose from the unprincipled intrigues in our own camp.'[64] Even language so strong as this does not seem to have been unjustified. Since the French would not come to any terms which he regarded as admissible, the essential thing was to restrain them from aggressive action of any sort until British vessels, Austrian and British troops and native insurgents had expelled Mehemet's forces from Syria. And to exercise restraint it was, of course, important that the British government should give the appearance of a united front. What, then, were Palmerston's feelings on discovering that plans for opposing him at a certain meeting of the cabinet had been concealed from him but known beforehand at Paris ![65] There was, indeed, no end to his troubles with his colleagues.[66] At every important juncture Russell would threaten to resign and Clarendon to go with him. Of all the contemporary comments on the situation there is none, perhaps, more striking than Shaftesbury's :

> Did ever country present such a spectacle in its administration ? Their differences and cabals are become notorious as the secrets of the town-crier ; one-third is with Palmerston, one-third, it seems, against him, and one-third do not know which way to go. The ' Bear ' Ellice, they say (and it must have been a pure love of intrigue and mischief), urged Thiers to resist the policy of Palmerston, assuring him that the Cabinet would never meet any *real* French resistance.
> . . . Lord Holland writes to Guizot, and tells him everything. Clarendon talks to everybody, follows in the tail of Charles Greville, and throws confusion into the Cabinet. . . . The Duc de Broglie writes to Lord Lansdowne, and Lord Lansdowne writes to Broglie ; can this be done without communication . . . of his misgivings, waverings, &c., &c., and all the mischievous puerilities of the English Cabinet ? . . . The fact is there has been foul intrigue to displace Palmerston and get his office ; the plotters designated Clarendon to the situation (did they think him more docile to themselves personally ?) ; he, forsooth, saw the thing, and asked no questions. Meanwhile, Melbourne, the Prime Minister, suffers all this, having neither authority nor principle ![67]

Shaftesbury made no mention of the leader of the House ; though Palmerston might justly have parodied the doggerel written at the time by that most troublesome of his colleagues : ' By such plagues are we curst, those of Russell the worst.' But he pressed on resolutely in a way that won admiration even from those who would have blocked his path. Witness Lady Clarendon's journal :

> . . . George says, disapproving as he does of Lord Palmerston's policy, there is something grand in the way he braves everything in spite of all opposition from his colleagues—in spite of the Queen's fears—in spite of events at home and abroad—he goes steadily on, undertaking the awful responsibility which must fall upon him from the course he pursues, with a courage and calmness which would be admirable indeed if they did not proceed from a crotchet. . . .[68]

That he had taken on his own shoulders full responsibility for England's policy and the risks that it entailed was well understood abroad. Even Mehemet Ali is reported to have said that he was not at war with the British nation, but only with Lord Palmerston.[69]

At times he gave vent to his irritation by outbursts in conversation and correspondence ; but he usually tried to keep up appearances. When the duke of Bedford and Lord Spencer were working on Russell, he and Lady Palmerston were reported by Lady Clarendon as remarking that it was ' a great shame that the policy of England should be disturbed because the two greatest fools had influence over the weakest man in it.'[70] And he wrote bitterly of the ' Whig friends and grandees ' who, ' by giving way to unfounded alarms and holding what is called conciliatory language,' had ' very much encouraged the French in their attempts to bully.'[71] Nor is there reasonable doubt that he used the *Chronicle* to veil his most intemperate attacks—attacks aimed even at his colleagues.[72] But in general he played the game. When feeling was at its highest Lord and Lady Palmerston went frequently to Holland House, dined Guizot, and, in so far at least as Lady Palmerston was concerned, seemed ready for a chat with Greville at any time. When things were at their worst in the cabinet, it was Palmerston who sought Russell, and not Russell Palmerston. No doubt agreeing with his wife that cabinets were superfluous, to say the least, where foreign policy was concerned, he could on occasion lay his case before his colleagues ' very temperately.'[73] That was not to say, however, that he did not get his way. Charles Greville has left an account of one crucial meeting of the cabinet which, for all its probable exaggeration, is too precious for transcription or even for much abridgement :

September 29, Wednesday, [1840] : 'The Cabinet met on Monday evening and sat till seven o'clock. . . . It must have been *à payer les places* to see. They met, and as if all were conscious of something unpleasant in prospect, and all shy, there was for some time a dead silence. At length Melbourne, trying to shuffle off the discussion, but aware that he must say something, began : " We must consider about the time to which Parliament should be prorogued." Upon this Lord John took it up and said, " I presume we must consider whether Parliament should be called together or not, because, as matters are now going on, it seems to me that we may at any moment find ourselves at war, and it is high time to consider the very serious state of affairs. I should like," he added, turning to Melbourne, " to know what is your opinion upon the subject." Nothing, however, could be got from Melbourne, and there was another long pause, which was not broken till somebody asked Palmerston, " What are your last accounts ? " On this Palmerston pulled out of his pocket a whole parcel of letters and reports from Ponsonby, Hodges, and others, and began reading them through, in the middle of which operation someone happened to look up, and perceived Melbourne fast asleep in his armchair. At length Palmerston got through his papers, when there was another pause ; and at last Lord John, finding that Melbourne would not take the lead or say a word, went at once into the whole subject . . . in an admirable, though very artful speech. . . . He . . . then threw himself back in his chair, waiting for what anybody else would say. After some little talk, Palmerston delivered his sentiments the other way, made a violent philippic against France. . . . There then ensued a good deal of talk (in which, however, the Prime Minister took no part). . . . The result was an agreement, that it would be disrespectful to Lord Lansdowne . . . to come to any resolution in his absence ; and . . . that the discussion should be adjourned. . . .'[74]

When the cabinet reconvened, Palmerston consented to consult the envoys of the eastern Powers concerning a move for reconciliation with the French, correctly foreseeing, almost certainly, that he could thus delay matters until Mehemet had been subdued.

His shrewdness in sizing up England's opponents abroad was as impressive as his doggedness and resourcefulness. Never for a moment did he, like the French and so many of his own countrymen, accept Thiers' portrayal of Mehemet as a nineteenth-century Alexander the Great. Instead, he saw only 'an ignorant barbarian,' whose 'boasted civilization of Egypt' was the 'arrantest humbug.'[75] And one of the secrets of his cool and steady resistance to the French was his realisation that the peace-loving bourgeoisie of France was still the dominant element in society and government. Note some passages from his letters, written at a time when most of the British ruling class were convinced that war was imminent:

> France now is a very different thing from the France of the empire. Then war was the only way which anybody had of getting money; now war would put an end to most people's chance of getting money. A quarter of a century of peace does not pass over a nation in vain.[76]

And again:

> I conclude by the great anxiety that some [French] parties have to settle the matter soon, though at our expense, that they look forward to a speedy settlement of differences at the Bourse at the expense of other people; and that, having made a large sum by the fall, they want to double their profits by the rise. Pray let me know when the next settling day happens at the French Bourse. I should like to know what day it will be, as I foresee that it will be a critical period.[77]

Of course, he had other reasons for confidence:[78] Bulwer's assurances, his appreciation of the German 'spirit of nationality,' the fact that it would have been madness for France to go to war with the other four great Powers, and his conviction that Louis Philippe was 'not a man to run amuck.' The striking fact is that, in being so confident, he stood so much alone. Clarendon, for example, was all fears, though he could not share the foreign secretary's vivid recollections of France under Napoleon. Palmerston, as the autumn advanced, came to realise that war was possible;[79] but he was ready to gamble for great stakes at what, by careful calculation, he knew to be immensely favourable odds. He was delighted but not much surprised when news arrived that Mehemet's Syrian strongholds had fallen like the walls of Jericho, before British assaults.

Between the early days of October and the Christmas season, he reaped from his foresight, energy, courage and good luck a triumph as complete as the most patriotic and ambitious of statesmen could have desired. His enemies seemed to consume away before his eyes, and his colleagues to be confounded in their pessimism. His conviction that British operations on the Syrian coast would be not only successful in themselves, but would force Mehemet to recall his forces to Egypt, was justified with a speed and completeness which amazed Europe. And he had the satisfaction of knowing that the supreme operation—the reduction of St. Jean d'Acre, which had defied Napoleon—was due to his insistence that Napier, the second in command of the British squadron, should have his way.[80] What counted for still more, of course, was that the enforced submission of Mehemet involved that of France, and that the French collapse left him triumphant over all those of his countrymen who had tried to block his policy.

Yet he was forced to fight for that policy even in the time of his success. Indeed, his hardest struggle occurred after news came, on October 4, of the first great military success, the storming of Beirut.[81] The *furia francese* again rose to dangerous heights. Even Greville complained that the French acted as though British vessels had bombarded Boulogne or Toulouse, and that the newspapers loudest in outcry were those connected with Theirs and with the government.[82] None the less, his opponents once more attempted to force him into the adoption of a conciliatory attitude. They demanded overtures to France, some part of Syria for Mehemet Ali, and the recall of Ponsonby, who had encouraged the Sultan to declare Mehemet deposed as viceroy of Egypt. And they were formidable as never before. Victoria, seriously alarmed for the French dynasty, was clearly on their side. And so was Melbourne, who was pessimistic concerning further successes, and believed —on what grounds it seems impossible to say—that Palmerston wished to drive Mehemet even from Egypt. There was a new ultimatum from Russell ; there were new scenes in the cabinet ; and the foreign secretary, for the first of many times, was called to a serious interview with

THE APPRAISAL JUSTIFIED

his sovereign. Once again it became a question whether he could hold out until the complete triumph of British arms over Mehemet was secured. Fortunately for him, the French again went too far. Their ' insolence and unreasonableness ' disgusted Greville[83] ; the appearance at Thiers' house of Urquhart—a ' mad political dervish ' even to Reeve—shocked other persons of conservative bent ;[84] and Thiers' menacing demands for still more troops were too much for Melbourne.[85] The British premier, working tactfully through King Leopold, warned Louis Philippe that England would not endure such threats. Hence, when Thiers insisted that the King himself should echo them in a speech from the throne, Louis Philippe preferred to let his minister resign. There were rumours that the whole matter had been pre-arranged ; but in any case Palmerston was excusable in feeling that his contentions had been justified :

... the French armaments have been ... a mere trick. ... The King gave Thiers permission to bully and swagger and threaten, and to gain all he could by so doing, provided he did not go to the extent of war ; and the King himself ... did all he decently could to back up Thiers and help his stratagem. ...

Well, we have stood firm, and have not allowed ourselves to be made dupes ; and therefore Thiers goes out. The question then was, how he was to get off the stage. He could not go off kneeling ... and so, according to the most approved method of getting the hero away, he went off in *heroics*.

If you remember, Seymour [the British minister to Belgium] told us a fortnight ago that he knew the Queen of the Belgians had heard from her family that Thiers was to propose things which he knew beforehand the King would not agree to. . . .[86]

And some of the French ministers, when they made their explanations to the French chamber, justified Palmerston in the eyes of most of his British critics.[87] Years later, Theodore Martin, writing his *Life of the Prince Consort*, with the enthusiastic approval of Victoria, quoted the words of de Rémusat, minister of the Interior, to explain that the purpose of France had been ' to establish a second-rate maritime power [Egypt] in the Mediterranean, whose fleet might unite with that of France, for the purpose of serving as a counterpoise to that of England.'[88] Thiers, though less indiscreet, seriously damaged his own cause. And he repelled many an English sympathiser by an exhibition of bad taste. For he used in his defence the name of Lord Holland, whose death had just caused the deepest grief to men of all parties.[89] All in all, he probably did his great British adversary more good than harm when he declaimed : 'France has been grossly duped . . . I do not accuse the English people, I do not accuse the English cabinet, but I do accuse one man, and that man is Lord Palmerston.'[90]

But many of those who were ready to confess that the foreign secretary had had justification for holding out against Thiers, found it impossible to excuse his conduct to Guizot,[91] who, on Thiers' retirement, became foreign minister and real, though not titular, head of a new French ministry. Guizot, regarded as so pacific that Parisian students invited him ' *à la lanterne*,' and anxious to smooth the way for his new ministry and for his sovereign, begged, *ad misericordiam*, for a concession of some sort that could be used to mollify his disillusioned and embittered countrymen. Perhaps Palmerston would have listened had he not been so deeply resentful of the 'unprincipled intrigues' against himself and his policy in which Louis Philippe and Guizot had borne a part. He did, in fact, promise to treat any 'friendly communication' from the French 'in the spirit in which it was made.' But he proved deaf to appeals that Mehemet's retention of Egypt might publicly be ascribed to French efforts. He would not, even by implication, allow any kind of French ' protectorate ' on the Nile. And this was not his worst offence. At the time when Thiers fell, France was awaiting the answer to a note which merely demanded that the Sultan's deposition of Mehemet as viceroy of Egypt should be overruled. As the British cabinet had never intended that the deposition should take effect, the French demand had been met without delay, and Ponsonby instructed accordingly. But Palmerston, in sending a formal answer to Guizot, declared haughtily that the Sultan would decide the question for himself. Worse still, the answer was immediately published in Palmerston's organ, the *Chronicle*. True, a translation of the French note which he was answering had appeared in the British press (thanks, by the way, to Reeve) simultaneously with its arrival at Downing Street. But, whether or not this fact was taken into due account, Charles Greville was apparently recording a general impression when he wrote :

. . . where he [Palmerston] is and always has been wrong is in his neglect of forms . . . he has never said what he might have done to conciliate, to soften, and to destroy those impressions of intended affronts and secret designs which have produced such violent effects on the French public. On the contrary, he has . . . said what is calculated to irritate and provoke them to the greatest degree. . . .[92]

The same criticism was implicit in Granville's complaint that he alone of the ambassadors of the four Powers at Paris could administer no soothing unction at the Tuileries.[93] To Metternich it seemed poor diplomacy : ' Lord Palmerston . . . for the first time in his career as a Whig has taken the right side ; but . . . in his desire to secure a triumph he is acting like those gamblers who try to break the bank.'[94]

For the moment, however, such criticisms went almost unheard in the chorus of praise elicited by Palmerston's triumph.[95] He had not only saved Turkey from partition, not only done away with the treaty of Unkiar Skelessi, but made England's influence supreme at the Porte and greater among the Powers than it had been since Waterloo. It was natural that Melbourne should be ' in roaring spirits ' and that Wellington should jeer : ' The French can only sing the " Marseillaise," and talk of *la perfidie Anglaise.*' But Palmerston must have been gratified in noting how many of his opponents and critics were willing to let bygones be bygones, or even to own that they had been in the wrong. Russell was mollified in being reminded that he had been primarily responsible for the cabinet's acceptance of the treaty of July 15. Grey, that great Foxite Whig, wrote from his retirement that he had come to almost complete approval of Palmerston's policy up to the time of Thiers' fall. Reeve, impatient at last of the ' wretched mistakes, doubts and pretensions of the French Government,' wondered whether he had not taken the wrong view from first to last. Greville decided that ' Mr. Pitt (Chatham) could not have manifested more decision and resource.' Tributes came from more unexpected sources still. Mme. de Lieven confessed that ' the success and the glory ' belonged ' entirely to Lord Palmerston,' though she feared that England might pay too high for them if concessions were withheld from her friend Guizot. And at least one French statesman, Molé, cleared Palmerston of blame : ' We shall emerge from this Turco-Egyptian affair red with shame ; and the humiliation which we shall endure will be the result of our own actions. No one dreamed of inflicting it on us.'[96] There were, of course, some persons even in England who refused to alter their views or abate their criticisms. Of these, Greville singled out Lord Ashburton.[97]

The fact that there were even Frenchmen—Frenchmen in opposition to the government, of course—who could privately exonerate Palmerston, makes it especially unfortunate that he went out of his way to insult the French nation publicly in the summer of 1841. The occasion was a speech delivered at the end of June to his constituents at Tiverton.[98] He had not even what excuse for indiscretion a doubtful canvass would have supplied. For the Tory candidate, finding his chances unpromising, had retired, and the foreign secretary's only opponent was the Chartist butcher, Rowcliffe. He was not carried away by momentary enthusiasm ; for the speech had been carefully prepared. But, whether it was a desire to smother debates over Chartism under something more sensational, whether he could not resist the temptation to ' score off ' France, or whether, as he himself claimed, his indignation had been genuinely aroused, his speech passed beyond any possible bounds of propriety :

> There is a contrast of which we may have reason to be proud, between the progress of our arms in the East, and the operations which a neighbouring power, France, is now carrying on in Africa. The progress of the British army in Asia has been marked by a scrupulous reference to justice, an inviolable respect for property, an abstinence from anything which could tend to wound the feelings and prejudices of the people. . . . The different system pursued in Africa by the French has been productive of very different results ; there the French army, I am sorry to say, is tarnished by the character of their

THE GRATUITOUS INSULT TO FRANCE 317

operations. They sally forth unawares on the villagers of the country ; they put to death every man who cannot escape by flight, and they carry off into captivity the women and children (*shame, shame !*) They carry away every head of cattle, every sheep, and every horse, and they burn what they cannot carry off. The crop on the ground and the corn in the granaries are consumed by the fire (*shame !*) What is the consequence ? While in India our officers ride about unarmed and alone amidst the wildest tribes of the wilderness, there is not a French man in Africa who shows his face above a given spot, from the sentry at his post, who does not fall a victim to the wild and justifiable retaliation of the Arabs (*hear, hear !*). . . .

Leaving aside any question of truth or falsehood, the speech and its publication in the *Chronicle* would have been unpardonable at any time. Coming when they did, they give weight to Peel's later charge that Palmerston's habit was ' to fester every wound.' And no Frenchman could have been more wounded than Guizot, now settling into his long term of office as Louis Philippe's principal minister. In a letter written three weeks later he gave an estimate of Palmerston which must be read exactly as he set it down :

Je fais grand cas de son esprit. J'ai confiance dans sa parole. Sa manière de traiter, quoique un peu étroite et taquine, me convient ; elle est nette, prompte, ferme. Je ne crois ni à sa haine pour la France et le roi, ni à ses perfidies ; et quant aux difficultés, je pourrais dire aux désagréments que jettent dans les affaires son goût passionné pour l'argumentation, sa disposition à s'enfermer dans ses arguments et à les pousser jusqu'au bout sans rien voir au-dessus, ni au delà, ni à côté, je ne m'en choque point, je ne m'en plains point ; c'est la nature même de son esprit. . . .[99]

The phrases are so studied that one wonders whether he was able to maintain so detached an attitude after all ; and one feels a settled conviction on his part that Palmerston's faults were utterly incurable. Nor did Guizot show any philosophical detachment by his acts. The five-Power treaty which was to have dealt a mortal blow at the slave trade—the treaty over which Palmerston had worked so long and which he had so utterly at heart—was ready for signature at this time. And Guizot, foreseeing the early advent of a Tory government, took his revenge by refusing to affix his signature while Palmerston was in power.[100] As events proved, his action was destined virtually to wreck Palmerston's whole scheme. And the bitter estrangement between the two foreign ministers was in another respect significant. It was sure to render difficult if not impossible any real co-operation between their governments at any time when they might simultaneously be in power. This circumstance did not improve Palmerston's prospects of continuing to serve the Whig-Liberals as foreign secretary.

And the Near Eastern crisis had laid bare another situation which must have been disquieting to his friends: the equivocal position in which he stood with respect to the two great parties. His spirited resistance to the French had been in the Conservative tradition; and not a little of the support which had carried him through his difficulties had come from Conservatives and Conservative journals.[101] It is true that Wellington and Aberdeen, who believed that a maintenance of the entente constituted the best possible restraint on France, felt that he had gone too far in risking war. But they had otherwise approved what he had done; and there were doubtless other Conservatives who shared some of the enthusiasm which Disraeli was to voice in his *Tancred*:

> When we consider the position of the Minister at home, not only deserted by Parliament, but abandoned by his colleagues; the military occupation of Syria by the Egyptians; the rabid demonstrations of France; that an accident of time or space, the delay of a month or the gathering of a storm, might alone have baffled all his combinations; it is difficult to fix upon a page in the history of this country which records a superior instance of moral intrepidity. The bold conception and the brilliant performance were worthy of Chatham; but the domestic difficulties with which Lord Palmerston had to struggle place the exploit far beyond the happiest achievement of the elder Pitt.[102]

As for the Conservative press (the *Standard* in particular), Palmerston acknowledged that it 'had smoothed ten thousand difficulties.'[103] All this being the case, there had naturally been rumours that he would cross the House. The rumours grew when Melbourne, his premier, brother-in-law, and friend, made no answer to them save to rub his

MISUNDERSTANDINGS WITH THE WHIGS 319

hands, chuckle and ejaculate, ' I don't know.' Certainly, Palmerston had not strengthened his connection with the Whigs.[104] Instead, he had more than realised the dire apprehensions expressed by many of the party at the formation of the Melbourne ministry in 1835. He had run away with the premier and the cabinet, dragging them into a most unwhiggish policy : he had defeated the Whig Nestors, from the duke of Bedford down. Resentment was added to their fears : and resentment burned also on his side. Russell was too honest and too impressionable to be an object of dislike. Holland had died late in October ; and Holland's congenital lack of discretion had been forgivable even in his life. But Palmerston could not easily pardon Ellice and Clarendon. All Clarendon's protestations of admiration for, and gratitude to, his erstwhile diplomatic chief could not conquer the suspicions of Lord and Lady Palmerston that, in his ' depth of cunning,' he had plotted with Ellice to obtain the Foreign Office for himself. And there were other Whig sins which could not be forgotten easily. One can almost imagine Palmerston echoing Melbourne's ' I don't know.'

Disquieting again, at least as a portent, was the alteration in Victoria's attitude toward her first mentor in foreign policy.[105] By the summer of 1841 she had become critical if nothing more. There was, indeed, no sign of lessened friendliness. At the beginning of August she paid visits to Lady Palmerston at Brocket and Panshanger, the principal Melbourne and Cowper seats, and, amid bands and flowers and cheers, was very gracious to her foreign minister. But charming amenities and confidence are different things. She had been amazed at Palmerston's ' coolness and indifference,' frightened by his audacity. And doubtless she knew that the master of Brocket, still her trusted adviser and dear friend, had been worried to distraction by his brother-in-law's policy. Her doubts and fears had been fostered in the shrewdest manner by King Leopold. Quotations from one letter to Prince Albert, written in November 1840, will suffice :

. . . Palmerston, *rex* and autocrat, is . . . far *too irritable and violent*. One does not understand the use of showing so much hatred and anger. What he says about the *appeal to the personal feeling of the Queen, on the part of the King of the French,* is childlike and malicious, for it has *never* existed.

The King was for many years the great friend of the Duke of Kent, after whose death he remained a friend of Victoria . . . she was for a long time an object of hatred in the [British royal] family. . . . Many of these things are quite unknown to Victoria, or forgotten by her. Still it is only fair not to forget the people who were her friends before 1837 ; after that date there was a violent outbreak of affection among people who in the year 1836 would still not go near Victoria. October 1836, when he sat next her at dinner, was the first time that Palmerston himself had ever seen Victoria except at a distance. . . .

As to danger, it was very great in September. . . . Towards the end of October, when Thiers withdrew, there was a possibility of a [French] revolution, . . . at once democratic and bellicose . . . and only a fairly fortunate combination of circumstances saved matters. . . . If the poor King had been murdered, or even if he were now to be murdered, what danger, what confusion would follow ! All these things were met by Palmerston with the excessively *nonchalante* declaration, *it was not so, and it is not so* ! Those are absolutely baseless assertions. . . . I should think the Revolution of 1790 *et ce qui s'en est suivi* had done a brisk enough business in Europe, and to risk a new one of the same kind would really be somewhat scandalous. . . .[106]

What better tactics could have been employed than the play on Victoria's almost overdeveloped sense of family ties, the appeal to loyalty and gratitude, the threat of revolution, *and* the expression ' Palmerston, *rex* and autocrat ' ? One wonders whether the stinging phrase was lingering in Victoria's mind when she wrote a certain letter, five months later, to the prime minister.[107] She feared, it said, that some despatches were submitted for her approval after being sent, and others which were ' rough in language ' were never submitted to her softening influence at all. Would Melbourne please find out ? It was the first sign of a contest between the Queen and Palmerston of which all Europe would take cognizance in time, and which would end only with Palmerston's death.

As against these disturbing facts he could place a reassuring one. He had discovered what, at critical moments in the future, was to prove his great resource : the liking and admiration of his countrymen. It was a great resource ; and yet it could not assure one's inclusion in any cabinet. It was necessary to think first of party leaders and of the Court. All in all, it behoved him to make careful use of the period of opposition which, in the summer of 1841, lay before him and all Whig-Liberals.

CHAPTER XV

Palmerston's Longest 'Holiday,' 1841–1846

Palmerston's triumph over France, as the Whigs must reluctantly have recognised, alone shed lustre on the last days of Melbourne's government. Never too robust at any time, it had long been moribund. Since the Bedchamber episode of 1839 it had 'tottered on,' largely by grace of Victoria's support and the opposition's tolerance. In some respects it had merely been unfortunate. It had incurred unpopularity through poor law legislation which was unavoidable, and through the occurrence of economic depression which it could not remedy. It had been divided within itself, and put under new pressure from the radicals, by the growth of the movement for free trade. On the other hand, it had justly incurred blame where its handling of financial and economic matters was concerned. Year after year it had failed to make ends meet or cover previous deficits ; and its timidity regarding the free trade issue was almost ludicrous. The most important innovations which the ministers ventured to decide upon in the spring of 1841 were that the import duties on foreign sugar and Canadian timber should be cut down, and that a low fixed rate be substituted for the sliding scale on corn. This was referred to as an advance toward 'free competition,' not free trade. Such regard for the susceptibilities of Whig landed proprietors was really touching ; but it was calculated to hasten rather than postpone the cabinet's demise. Some of the ministers realised as much. Early in March Russell was asking whether it was worth while going on, and Lord Alvanley complaining that the smell of burning papers filled the air in Downing Street.[1]

If it had not been for Palmerston the end would very

THE END OF MELBOURNE'S GOVERNMENT

probably have come in May, when the ministry was defeated on the budget. Peel of course led the attack, declaring for protection and the sliding scale on corn, taking a high moral tone on the evils of encouraging slavery by fostering the production of sugar by foreign slaves, and making the House laugh with his picture of 'a Chancellor of the Exchequer seated on an empty chest—by the side of bottomless deficiency—fishing for a Budget.'[2] Palmerston, who had been almost silent on domestic issues for six years, made an effective and much noticed speech, in which he undertook to expose Peel's 'hypocrisy' on the question of slavery.[3] What, he asked, of slave cotton and slave coffee ? And what of Britain's attempts to persuade other nations that they would gain by the abolition of the slave trade and of slavery :

> The great argument, then, of these Gentlemen is, that the free-labour sugar of the West Indies cannot compete with the slave-labour sugar of the Brazils ; now what is this but declaring to the Brazilians and the Spaniards, that we have been telling them untruths all this while, as to the comparative cheapness of free labour ? Will they not think that we have added to the odiousness of our commercial hostility the meanness of duplicity and falsehood ; that we have been endeavouring to trepan them into an abolition of their slave-trade upon false pretences ; . . . Let us convince them that we do believe free labour to be, as it unquestionably is, cheaper than slave labour. Let us do so by admitting their slave-labour sugar into competition with free-labour sugar in our market, . . . I cannot but think that the respect which foreign nations have hitherto felt for the sincerity, the plain dealing, the straightforwardness of the British character, will be lowered, when they see the House of Commons adopting a resolution by which the principles of humanity and justice are (I am sorry to say so), prostituted to serve the party purpose of a day. . . .

But he could not avert the rout of his party. Peel drew votes from humanitarian supporters of the Melbourne ministry who took him seriously on the slavery issue, and from Whig landowners who, with good reason, suspected party leaders such as Palmerston of preparing to desert the agricultural interest. Of course Peel's success meant more than that. The country was turning to him, as the personification of 'enlightened Prudence,' as a leader whose proved capacity promised an era of steady and well-administered government. It seemed incumbent on the Whig-Liberal ministry to resign for the sake of its very dignity.

So thought Melbourne; but so did not Palmerston. On the alternative of resignation or dissolution, he appears to have been the most insistent of all the ministers that the cabinet should take the latter course.[4] Charles Greville put this down to mere pugnaciousness. 'Palmerston . . .' he wrote, ' has never any doubts or fears, and is for fighting everybody.' If Greville's estimate of the situation was correct, one must conclude that Palmerston was less gifted in estimating the strength of Tories and radicals than of Egyptians. But he may have had another reason for his stand. The outcome of British operations in China and Afghanistan was still in doubt; and two great international conventions, the Straits convention, which temporarily closed the question of the Near East, and the five-Power treaty concerning the slave trade, were still unsigned. Palmerston was no doubt anxious to gain even a little time. And he did win some respite. Slowly the majority of the cabinet came over to his view; and, in June, after a fresh defeat, Melbourne dissolved. When, in August, the new House convened, the Conservatives soon made any further postponement of resignation impossible. But the Straits convention had been signed.

From the summer of 1841 Palmerston was to be in opposition for five years, by far the longest period which he spent out of office during his whole career. After more than a decade of incessant labour he could refer to it as a holiday; and in some sense so it was. No longer did boxes of despatches dog his footsteps every day throughout the year; no longer were his mornings and his early afternoons filled with endless interviews, and with the drafting of communications to representatives at scores of courts and consulates. No longer need he, day and night, write those innumerable letters—extraordinary in vigour, clarity, and caligraphy, extraordinary again in the sureness which made erasure or correction superfluous—by which he conducted so much of his diplomacy, and maintained relations with his Sovereign and his colleagues. Yet there was little genuine relaxation associated with this holiday. He was constantly battering at the Conservative government, and laying plans against the day when the labour and the cares of office would come to him again. From the first he was especially distressed that the direction of foreign policy had been entrusted to Aberdeen.[5]

Still, he found it pleasant to be once more the landed proprietor and man of affairs.[6] In about eighteen months, he thought, he would probably wish to be in harness again : in the meantime it was pleasant to find himself ' much the better . . . in health, and much the freer and more amused in mind.' Once more he could look after his properties, and ' make exercise a religion, and be punctual in the observance of it.' Galloping was ' capital exercise,' and gallop he did at every opportunity. There was obvious relish in his accounts, not only of visiting, shooting and hunting with his friends, but of ' marking young trees for thinning the plantations ' at Broadlands, and establishing a new flower-garden there. He and Lady Palmerston undertook with zest the task of teaching a new gardener ' the management of fruit and flowers, and how to plant trees.' Not even these activities were pursued in a haphazard way ; for he was ' busy reading books on agriculture and horticulture, and trying to acquire some knowledge on those matters,' which had ' now become sciences.' Reading before breakfast seems to have been one of his fixed habits, even at Broadlands. In 1841 and 1845 he visited Ireland, and was delighted to find that his good works at Sligo, commenced so long before, were beginning to bear fruit. The harbour, built at ' enormous ' expense, was nearly finished now, and regarded by his neighbours as ' a great advantage to all that part of the Country.' The reclamation of land through the sowing of bent had proved a great success ; and his nine hundred tenants seemed ' better clad, and living in better houses ' than when he had last seen them, twelve years before. Lady Palmerston, inquiring as to the effects of the education offered by his schools, learned ' that it has had a great effect upon some of the turbulent Spirits of the South to be taught Geography, and to be shewn on the map the small space that Ireland holds in the world.' And Palmerston's financial prospects seemed more encouraging. He was gratified to discover that the slate quarries in northern Wales, which had always cost more than they brought in, promised to be a drain no more, and might pay dividends. Though he had been receiving a salary of £5000, he could hope to find himself 'none the poorer for being out of office' after all. Even his racing, and the moderate betting done for him by his trainer, were proving remunerative. Life smiled on him, and in nothing so much as in his wedded life. 'The Anniversary of my marriage,' he wrote, on December 16, 1841, 'two years that each deserve a flitch of bacon.'

As his habits and breadth of interests had survived the long Foreign Office grind, so too had his eagerness for exact information and his sometimes informal methods of obtaining it. The most famous instance was recorded by Philip Grant, the author of a history of factory legislation and at one time a labour delegate.[7] Grant and a fellow delegate were desperately anxious to convince Palmerston of the hardships endured by children in the textile mills before a certain division on Ashley's Ten Hour Bill should take place in the House. Arriving at Carlton Gardens just as Palmerston and his wife were starting for a drive, they would have been turned away had he not heard their protests and taken them into his dining-room. To make their case convincing they imitated the actions of the young unfortunates in the textile mills, using the heavy dining-room chairs to represent machines. To their surprise and delight their host and a footman were soon acting with them, so that the demonstration might be complete. By this means, and by exhibiting the scars of work, they secured Palmerston's promise of support. It was a promise, wrote Grant gratefully,

. . . which that great man ever afterwards kept, and on all occasions when the subject was before Parliament, he diligently performed by speaking and voting in favour of the 'poor factory child.'[8]

Even before Grant's visit he had been won over to the support of Ashley's famous bill in so far at least as the provisions relating to young children were concerned. ' They are not free agents,' he wrote Russell, ' and seem entitled to protection against the combined cupidity of parents and masters.' [9] In opposition to some of the leaders of his own party, and of course to the Bright-Cobden group, he stood with Ashley for the establishment of the ten-hour day, in 1844.[10] After all, the radicals had reasons for liking him, quite apart from his foreign policy.

Once more he showed his zest for travel, and for making himself familiar with all the aspects of continental life and continental politics.[11] It was a valuable trait in a British foreign minister. Scarcely was he out of office before he planned a trip that was to centre in Germany but extend to Austria, Italy and France. During the two years that followed, Melbourne, broken in health and spirits, needed Lord and Lady Palmerston, and 'of course all other considerations gave way to this.' Only at the beginning of August 1844, did they set out. Travelling by Dover, Brussels and Cologne, they made a short cure at Wiesbaden before going on to Frankfort, Dresden and Berlin. Although the tour was much punctuated by contacts with royal and official personages, Palmerston found time to set down in his diary a mass of information of the most varied sort: on the size and cost of the French army, and especially such of it as was in Algeria; on the condition of the French clergy and the efforts of the Jesuits to control the upbringing of the young; on the views of Cornelius, the German fresco painter, concerning English painting, and on those of the Prussian minister of instruction regarding the education of the Prussian youth. Nothing seems to have impressed him more than the 'mental endowments' and 'intellectual activity' of the subjects of Frederick William IV, and the leadership in German civilization which they had attained. He carefully recorded the amazing fact that every Prussian might learn to read and write. How much more he would have learned, had he been able to carry out his plans of visiting Metternich in Vienna, and proceeding from Vienna to Paris, it is almost alarming to contemplate. But the travellers stopped at Prague. The waters of Wiesbaden, Palmerston thought, had been too much for both of them ; and by November they were home again. The visit to Paris was not paid until 1846.

In London his unofficial life went on much as before. Lady Palmerston was still the great Whig-Liberal hostess, her Wednesday and Saturday receptions thronged by all the notables.   There were political dinners, too, dinners which reached a picturesque climax when Admiral Sir Charles Napier was invited to meet his late victim, Ibrahim Pasha. Lord Minto departed wondering which had drunk the more and was 'the greater blackguard' of the two.   Such were Palmerston's diversions during the five years of his 'holiday.' They were happy years, but shadowed, too.   For Melbourne, despite periods of apparent convalescence, was sinking to his grave ; and to his comfort his sister and her husband sacrificed themselves unsparingly.   Tact and discretion, as well as sacrifice, were requisite.   For it was thought politically advisable to conceal Melbourne's decline as long as possible ; and he himself refused to face the truth until almost the end.

Politically, Palmerston was energy itself.   Politics, he explained, were 'an amusement, and not a labour, for those who are out of office.'[12]   And no doubt he did find it amusing to sit in parliament among the besiegers instead of the besieged, and to be free of the trammels of cabinet responsibility.   Unable to enjoy the sport of lecturing and perhaps confounding the ministers of other states, it was a pleasant diversion to practise on those of his own.   Hence he spoke, and sometimes with much eloquence, on most of the important issues dealt with by parliament in these years.   But his assiduity and his aggressiveness showed that he was in deadly earnest, too.   It was not pure love of the game that made him, in August 1842, 'the last rose of summer, all blooming alone' on the bench which faced the ministry,[13] or that lent such bitterness to his attacks on the new foreign secretary, Aberdeen.   His motives demand analysis.

Ambition and pique were among them without doubt. His position in Melbourne's cabinet had latterly been such that Prince Albert regarded him as second only to the premier.[14]   As the permanence of Melbourne's disablement appeared more probable, it was only natural for him to hope that he might soon be premier himself.[15] True, Russell had become leader of the opposition in the lower House ; but it was Palmerston who had given most of what prestige it had to the moribund Melbourne ministry. As naturally must he have been piqued by the curious revival of the entente with France which ensued upon his fall. Since 1830 the predilections of the Tories as a whole, and of Aberdeen in particular, had been decidedly anti-French.[16] Yet no sooner was Aberdeen in power than he made every effort to conciliate those two great enemies of Palmerston, the French king and Guizot. No doubt the 'noble thane's' pacific temperament, his appreciation of Guizot's growing conservatism, and the belief of some Tories that England could best restrain the French by linking arms with them, were in large degree responsible ; but no one could be blind to the growing mutual esteem which bound the British and French foreign ministers. There were even circumstances, such as the renewed friendship between Guizot's dear friend, the Princess Lieven, and the noble thane, which suggested that common dislike of Palmerston and his policies was another, if perhaps unconscious, bond.[17] Even more disturbing to the self-appointed guardian of British leadership must have been the growth of intimacy between the French and the British courts. King Leopold, who had naturally long wished for it, found valuable allies in Aberdeen and Peel. For Peel seems to have admired Louis Philippe almost as Aberdeen did Guizot. Palmerston could hardly look forward without trepidation to a time when, as foreign minister or premier, he would find the Court as Francophil as any of the Whigs. Already he could see too well what the effects might be.

For what spurred him most to action was not ambition nor yet pique, but the belief that Aberdeen was squandering British prestige. He had built it up so proudly and so carefully that it had become the object of his intense solicitude ; and solicitude now impelled him to play the part of a national watchdog. Irritation and the liking for a rough-and-tumble fight made his performance a very noisy one. Real evidence as to the genuineness of his anxiety is not, of course, derivable from his philippics to the House, his constant cry that 'resistance at home and concession abroad' were the principles of the Conservative government's policy. But it can be found in various private letters to associates, such as one he wrote to Lansdowne in November 1842 :

> Our foreign affairs seem to have got upon a sliding scale, as well as the corn duties, and we are in that respect sliding downwards, by a very decently rapid descent. . . .[18]

The reason for the descent he found in ' a general disposition on the part of the Government to sacrifice in every direction abroad the future and permanent interests of the country in order to procure relief from momentary embarrassments.'[19] In the end the nation, browbeaten once too often, would be forced to go to war. His sincerity was the more apparent from the fact that he continued his outcry in spite of the protests and warnings of his late colleagues. Such applause as he drew from certain elements of the public was dearly bought at the price of a new breach with his party.

And a serious breach occurred before the end of 1842.[20] Those great Whig magnates, the duke of Bedford and Earl Spencer, took the lead by protesting to Russell against ' the tone that had been taken on foreign questions, especially the American ' by Palmerston and the *Chronicle*. Lord John, after consulting Clarendon and Lansdowne, sent the offender what was apparently a tactless note. For he not only warned Palmerston that he might be disavowed in parliament, but brought in the hated name of ' Bear ' Ellice. No characterisation of Palmerston's reply could convey a full impression of his bitterness, his attitude of defiance and studied insolence :

> What you say of Ellice confirms what I had heard of his underminings for some time past. But indeed it is no exception from his usual course. Cabal & intrigue are . . . natural to him. . . . I suppose that all parties in this country and everywhere else, have been beset by these intrigues, just as most animals have their adherent vermin ; and therefore one ought not to regard as a peculiar grievance that which is a general dispensation. Ellice however has invariably bestowed upon me perhaps more than my proper share of his sapping

Rischgitz

THE FOURTH EARL OF ABERDEEN

NEW CONTESTS WITH THE WHIGS 331

& mining faculties. . . . He set out in the days of Durhams ambition, to endeavour to turn me out of the Foreign Office, in order to get Durham in ; & well punished he was for his treachery ; by the bitter disappointment which he felt at its failure. He . . . has never forgiven me ; & . . . even now from time to time exhales his wrath, by swearing by his honour, that I shall never return to that office, in the event of our party regaining power.[21]

He was not to be dictated to by Ellice, nor yet by Ellice's converts :

It seems however according to what you say that some of our party, Radicals and old Whigs are disposed to take their views of our foreign relations from Ellice. God help them, say I ; . . . as I have no respect whatever for Ellices opinions when coming straight from himself, I am not prepared to defer to them a bit the more, because they come echoed back from others. But if those others chuse to follow Ellice in these matters let them do it ; I pretend to guide nobody, except so far as reasons which I may give in Parliament and arguments which I may there employ may influence the minds of fair & impartial men.

And (like Chatham) he could if necesary look beyond parliament itself :

If I am right I am quite sure that my arguments & reasoning will have weight with the country, even if not in the House of Commons. . . .

This epistle, apparently dashed off in a passion, is almost unique among his letters for its abusiveness. Yet, read in its entirety, and with due discount made for his loss of self-control, it seems to offer a fair summary of his views on politics, domestic and foreign, in 1842. ' Bears or Radicals or old Whigs,' would have to accept his views or dispense with his services. Russia in her burrowing for expansion, and Austria in her contest against the ' principles of political liberty ' would find him in their way. ' Occasional raps on the knuckles ' would be administered to France and the United States when they forgot themselves. He might have added that he was using, and intended to use, a bludgeon on Aberdeen.

Condemn as one may the violence of his attacks on Aberdeen's foreign policy, it is only fair to remember that he saw positive evil in his successor's course. Nothing, for example, incensed him more than his conviction that Aberdeen was throwing away the gains that he had made in the suppression of the international slave trade.[22] Although there can be no doubt that Aberdeen's intentions in the matter were of the best and that he achieved a good deal in some ways, this conviction was not unjustified. Reports that the new foreign secretary disapproved Captain Denman's action in burning the barracoons were received with joy on the slave coast ; and the importation of slaves into Cuba seems to have risen accordingly.[23] And infinitely more damaging to the anti-slave-trade cause was Aberdeen's passivity towards the defection of the French.[24] Thanks to Guizot's rather petty desire to punish Palmerston for the speech at Tiverton, and to strengthen the Tories by letting them reap where the Whigs had sowed, France, though an original partner with England in projecting the five-Power treaty that was to have made a 'single exception' of the United States, did not sign the treaty until December, 1841. And then the French king and Guizot, indifferent to international usage and good faith, refused to ratify. There was absolutely no excuse, save that the French (even to their naval officers) had always been lukewarm or worse regarding the suppression of the trade ; and that they were now so envenomed against all Englishmen that ratification would have proved unpopular. True, the American minister at Paris, General Cass, worked might and main to encourage Guizot in this breach of faith ;[25] but his exertions were apparently superfluous. And the French government was not content merely to wreck Palmerston's great scheme. Soon the British Foreign Office was informed that even the Anglo-French agreements of 1831 and 1833, with their provision for a mutual right of search, would have to be given up. Instead, an agreement providing for a restricted right of visit and for co-operation between patrols, which France only partially observed, was patched up in 1845. And Aberdeen ? He protested, yes—and protested in strong terms. But the cordial understanding was so perfectly complete that Guizot, for all his idealised dependence on the British government,

ABERDEEN AND THE SLAVE-TRADE

could receive and turn aside the protests without fear that unpleasant consequences would accrue.

Nor were these all the concessions made by Peel's business-like and pacific government at the expense, or so it seemed to Palmerston, of a myriad of tortured blacks. Lord Ashburton, with the somewhat reluctant approval of Lord Aberdeen, made his contribution, too, in negotiating and signing the treaty which settled the Maine boundary. Avoiding all discussion of that right of visit which Aberdeen had been at first so determined to uphold, he accepted an undertaking that an eighty-gun American patrol should be maintained on the Slave Coast.[26] It seemed more important, he wrote Aberdeen, to show a disposition 'to be satisfied with reasonable terms' than to look for 'any advantages to be gained in the details of a bargain.'[27] In Palmerston's view it was a little hard that African slaves should pay the price for such amiability and loftiness. Ashburton did not hesitate to assert that the new arrangement would have 'advantages . . . over any founded on a reciprocal right of search'[28]: but, considering that he was innocent of any practical knowledge or experience, the statement was a shade presumptuous. At any rate, the right of visit had been given up. Official circles in America were divided between those who (like Palmerston)[29] held that England had now implicitly acknowledged its illegality, and those who regarded her as having merely accepted an arrangement which made its exercise inexcusable. But, since Aberdeen soon admitted that it was legally indistinguishable from the right of search,[30] the controversy did not last long. Neither did the American eighty-gun patrol. And the amiability of Ashburton and Aberdeen was in another respect unfortunate for the Africans. As Palmerston foresaw, it gave France the needed encouragement to repudiate the agreements of 1831 and 1833.[31] These things, and the state of mind which they induced, are not to be entirely overlooked in considering Palmerston's attacks on the Webster-Ashburton treaty.

'Never was there imbecility like that of Ashburton, if it was nothing worse,' Palmerston wrote Russell, when news of the treaty came to him in September, 1842.[32]

Obviously, passion had caused him to throw discretion and even good taste to the winds. Conviction and righteous indignation partly accounted for his fury; but it is hard to avoid suspicion that personal feeling entered in. Not even his distress at the undoing of his work or his taste for polemic of the most violent sort need have carried him so far. He made no secret of his chagrin that great credit for 'gloriously' repairing the 'mischief' he had done in the Far and Middle East was going to Aberdeen;[33] and it is not unreasonable to suppose that he was piqued at seeing congratulations offered to the 'noble thane' for his retreat from the Palmerstonian contentions on the slave trade and the Maine boundary. And he may have remembered that Ashburton, before all things a banker and financier, had been one of his most unrelenting critics in the Near Eastern crisis of 1840–1841. Whatever the reasons, Palmerston degraded himself by his intemperance. Though both Conservative and Whig leaders agreed with him that the government had made large concessions to the United States, it was absurd to write of the treaty as 'one of the worst and most disgraceful treaties that England ever concluded,'[34] and inexcusable to refer to Ashburton, however privately, as 'a half Yankee' who 'would sacrifice anything and everything but his own private and personal interest.'[35] His public utterances[36] were almost equally unseemly and, of course, far more unwise. To speak in parliament of Ashburton as 'the most unfit person that could have been selected for so important a mission,' and to state flatly that the Americans had insisted upon territory to the north of the St. John's in order to have 'additional means of threatening us in case of new differences, or of attacking us in the event of war' was to damage both his case against the treaty and his reputation as a responsible statesman. To encourage or allow the *Chronicle* to exhaust itself in similar abuse, and to pretend that he was innocent of complicity, was perhaps to hurt his reputation even more.[37] No one could regard his disclaimers as containing more than a modicum of truth. It was not merely that the editor was unquestionably amenable to his influence. Some of the *Chronicle's* most vituperative articles were so definitely ascribed to Palmerston's own pen as to be collected and reprinted as his work.[38]

Yet, for all his attacks on the Webster-Ashburton settlement (and quite irrespective of what Van Buren said) it cannot be assumed that he was actuated by any unfriendliness towards the United States. If he denounced the settlement as 'a most disgraceful surrender to American bully,'[39] he does not seem to have blamed the bullies for getting what they could. Instead, he spoke of them quite graciously. No doubt it was true, he told the House, that 'nations have no cousins'; but the relations of Great Britain and America came nearest to disproving the maxim.[40] And he referred to Americans as men ' whose fathers gained the double victory of right and of might over our own.'[41] Writing to Russell, he insisted that the *Chronicle's* criticisms of the treaty would give no real offence to Webster's countrymen :

> The fact indeed is that these articles will be looked upon in the United States as complimentary because they tended to show that Webster proved himself what according to Dickens the Americans call a *smarter* man by far than Ashburton ; and no nation is much offended by its being shewn that they have concluded a negotiation with another and with a stronger power by a treaty in all respects greatly to their advantage.

When he talked of the 'Ashburton capitulation,' it was the 'capitulators' against whom he directed his real animus.

His tirades against the treaty brought him reprobation from many quarters, and desertion by his own party.[42] Peel countered his long and able speech of March 21, 1843, by quoting the similar expressions used in Congress by Benton, 'the Palmerston of America.' And, admitting that England had made great sacrifices, he delivered the unkindest cut of all :

> I approve of this treaty . . . I recognize the eminent services of the distinguished individual who has negociated and brought it to a satisfactory conclusion. . . . But I must condemn the conduct of the noble Lord opposite, [Palmerston] in having weakly conceded so much, as to have rendered such a compromise necessary.[43]

Brougham and Hume, those great spokesmen for the radicals,

moved votes of thanks to Ashburton in the two Houses. And Palmerston's former colleagues, having admonished him in vain, left him to take his punishment. Lansdowne and Clarendon promised to refrain from criticism of Ashburton unless forced into it by some move of the government. Grey wrote that 'such attacks [as Palmerston's] coming from such a quarter' created 'only feelings of disapprobation and disgust.' Russell, after twice changing sides, seems to have returned to his first view that 'Baring and Co. [the banking house controlled by Ashburton and his relatives], and the land sharks of Maine' would be 'the only gainers':[44] but even he pointed out that Palmerston had blundered in his tactics and failed to gain the public ear. There are other indications that Palmerston's chief fault in the eyes of his party was not his attitude toward the treaty but his impolitic vehemence. Lord Howick, Grey's heir, and a man as far removed as possible from the fire-eating sort, found 'something quite intolerable in the tone of insolent superiority the Americans were allowed to assume,' and felt that Ashburton's 'cringing' had invited fresh encroachment on their part.[45] But he kept such reflections for his intimates; whereas Palmerston, in making a violent and inevitably unsuccessful attack upon the government, had damaged the prospects of the party. Raikes wrote that 'the ill-success of Palmerston in his attacks on Peel's Government' had 'thrown a damp on the Whig-radical spirits,' and that nothing was to be heard in England 'except a snarl from the ultra-Tories about corn and tariff.'[46] And Palmerston for once owned himself dispirited. He admitted that he and his friends could 'do nothing, except make motions for their amusement,' until they could 'gain some *elections* and lose some of their associates.'[47]

Meanwhile he had to stand aside while Aberdeen, frankly conceding the predominance of French interests in Spain, gave up all attempts to foster British 'influence' there. He found it a very mournful spectacle.[48] At the time when he left office, Britain's position at Madrid had seemed excellent. Espartero, most capable of the generals who had defeated the Carlists, and a member of the 'progressive' party which looked to England for support, had made himself dictator and titular regent. But the country was not tranquillised. Revolts broke out, stimulated in some part at least by reports of commercial concessions which Espartero was prepared to make to the British government. And from Paris there operated a combination which included Moderates (members of the Francophil party), discontented Progressives, the former Regent and Queen-mother, Christina, and even—it was said—Carlists. In 1843 Espartero was overthrown. Whatever the true facts may have been, it was believed by the British envoys at Paris and Madrid and by most Englishmen who watched affairs that Louis Philippe had been secretly and deeply concerned in Espartero's fall. Certainly he had bullied the Regent on a question of mere etiquette, and had rewarded the French consul at Barcelona, who was known to have encouraged a revolt. Even Victoria, as late as December, 1842, expressed her disgust at '*French intrigues*' against 'by far the *most honest* Spaniard in existence,' and her fear that the French king was involved.[49] Aberdeen was quite passive through it all—except, indeed, when he reprimanded the British minister to Spain for undue zeal, and forwarded a copy of the reprimand to his friend Guizot. There were soothing influences at work, such, for example, as Guizot's charming Russian friend. They did not, however, soothe Palmerston. Nothing, wrote Greville, could be 'more virulent, bitter, and contemptuous' than Palmerston's attacks on Aberdeen in the *Chronicle*:

> However, the war that is waged by him, and against him, is very entertaining; he is an adversary well worth battling with, a *magnus Apollo* of newspaper writers.[50]

The *magnus Apollo* did not care to accept such compliments. Instead, he deprecated any attempt 'to exercise too minute a control over a paper whose general tendencies are right,' on the principle that 'a horse sometimes goes the safer for having his head given to him.'[51] He was in the habit, he pointed out, of reading the *Chronicle* with great attention, and had never noticed that it contained anything really objectionable.

Probably the worst blow of all to Palmerston in this year of 1843 was the establishment of intimate relations between the British and French courts.[52] The prime mover in this development was apparently King Leopold ; for the Belgian queen (Louis Philippe's daughter) seems to have persuaded Victoria and Albert to visit the French king. To many it seemed an event of happy augury, constituting, as it did, the first full recognition of the Orleans dynasty by one of the great courts, and incidentally the first visit of a reigning British sovereign to France since the time of Henry VIII. But Palmerston, who realised that it placed the seal of royal approval on the Guizot-Aberdeen version of the entente, was very much disturbed. Indeed, if the Princess Lieven is to be believed, it was because of the criticisms he was sure to make that plans for the visit were kept a secret from everyone in England save the prime minister and foreign secretary. Not even Wellington was informed.[53] Palmerston, on hearing the visit rumoured, declared it utterly impossible.[54] But, at the beginning of September, Victoria and Albert, accompanied by Aberdeen, were landing at Tréport on their way to the Château d'Eu.

The success of the visit was best described by Mme. de Lieven on the strength of letters from Guizot :

> The weather charming, and everyone in good spirits. The King and the Princes making the Queen of England laugh, the people cheering. *God save the Queen* very popular and very much applauded. (Who could have said that a year ago ?) M. Guizot passes his time (and does not waste it) with Lord Aberdeen. He is perfectly satisfied. Lord Aberdeen saying : 'We really must see each other from time to time, what good that will do.' . . . Lord Aberdeen impressed by the King, by his conversation, by his firmness ; impressed by the royal family ; impressed by everything ! Really this trip ought to be very useful.[55]

In the resultant atmosphere of happiness and confidence Guizot and Aberdeen proceeded to discuss the Spanish question on its most delicate and vital side, the marriages of the thirteen-year-old Queen Isabella and her sister, the Infanta Louisa. As certain differences of opinion were evident, even in the atmosphere of the Château d'Eu, decision was postponed ; but Guizot was 'perfectly satisfied.'

And well he might be. Victoria, always impressionable, had felt perfectly at home with the 'admirable and truly amiable' French royal family : Prince Albert had been delighted with 'the good kind King.' Given proper cultivation, the new friendship between Windsor Castle and the Tuileries might yield rich returns to the Orleans monarchy and its favourite servant. Palmerston looked on gloomily. Here was fresh evidence that his government was succumbing to French wiles. It would be hard to re-establish British leadership among the 'constitutional' states should he again receive the post of foreign minister. Any hopes of higher preferment must have perished by this time, shrivelled in the cold atmosphere of Whig discontent, and blighted again by Victoria's increasing preference for persons and policies that were anti-Palmerstonian.[56] Moreover, Russell was strengthening his hold on the Whig-Liberal leadership by putting himself forward on the two most debated issues of the time, the tariff and the treatment to be accorded to Ireland.

The question of the tariff stood, of course, in the forefront. Peel, though opposed to free trade in corn until his term of office had come almost to a close, busied himself with the schedule of import duties from the outset. Realising that the day when the landed interest could rule England had passed with the enactment of the Reform Bill of 1832, and that the interest of both nation and party demanded greater consideration than formerly for the industrial element, he decided to deal 'a hard right-hander' at the peers and country gentlemen by a reduction of the sliding scale on corn, and a 'left-hander' by the imposition of an income tax. Even the timber on the great estates was to lose much of the value which high protection had given it. Peel's policy was bound to create doubts and heart-burnings. For it involved the further depression of a class of Englishmen which for centuries had led Europe in the art of government, and was regarded by its members as taking 'a larger view of the national interest . . . than the manufacturer or tradesman.' And it would, of course, make England more dependent on other nations for her food supply.[57] It was a bitter draught for Peel's Conservative followers ;

and it placed the Whig-Liberals in something of a quandary. Among their leaders great landed proprietors were still predominant ; yet the party, as being more ' liberal,' might be expected to show less tenderness to the landholding class than would the Conservatives. Especially was this true in view of the fact that the contemplated detraction from the economic importance of the landed element would be complementary to the detraction from their political strength which had been involved in the passage of the Reform Bill of 1832. What the Whig-Liberals did in their dilemma was to cling to their programme of 1841, especially to the low fixed import duty upon corn.

Palmerston went with his party ; but he regarded himself, and was regarded by others, as an advocate of free trade. In 1839 he had voted with Russell and Villiers that the House should go into committee of the whole on the Corn Laws.[58] In 1841, he had denounced all protective duties before parliament,[59] and urged the electors of Tiverton to ' extend to the principle of commercial monopoly the same condemnation which had been pronounced . . . upon the principle of political monopoly.'[60] During the session of 1842, when Peel advocated the reduction of corn duties, but the retention of moderate protection and the sliding scale, Palmerston placed himself definitely on record.[61] He ridiculed extreme protectionists' fears of freer trade by reminding their leaders of the ' visionary ' and ' groundless ' apprehensions which they had entertained as to the results of parliamentary reform. He argued that a fixed duty on grain would put an end to gambling, and give England a more secure commerical footing in those new countries where her commercial future lay, especially the United States. And, maintaining that the duty should be imposed only for revenue, he presented some plain but frequently neglected free trade arguments :

> You cannot send your commodities to a foreign consumer unless you take in payment what he has to give. If you do not take his corn, except perhaps once in four or five years, you can have no means of paying with your goods for that corn when you want it. You must, therefore, send out bullion for that corn. You must take it from the Bank, and then comes the derangement of your currency.

Your currency must be restricted, and panic, distress, and bankruptcy follow.

He had an answer, too, for those who claimed that England should be independent of other nations with respect to food :

> Why, what a childish doctrine is this ? Independent of foreign nations for its supply of food !—a nation in which several millions of men live by foreign commerce calling itself independent of foreign nations for the means of subsistence for its people. Why, Sir, those who depend on foreign commerce for the means by which they buy their bread, are, to all practical purposes, as dependent on foreign nations for food, as if the food which they bought was grown on a foreign soil.

His self-proclaimed devotion to free trade seems to have been accepted by others as quite genuine. In 1844, when he was travelling on the continent, the British ambassador at Paris wrote that he was gathering information ' to prove the advantages which would result from the abrogation of the Corn Laws and the establishment of a free trade in corn.' [62] It will be remembered that no established leader of either great party ventured to advocate the importation of corn without duties of some sort until Russell startled the Whig-Liberals by taking this step in November 1845.

One feels that Palmerston was a believer in free trade, but one who kept his faith in firm control. At times he seemed to compromise with it, at others to make it more or less subserve his aims. He was impatient of Howick's ' ultra Free Trade Doctrines ' ; [63] and he was annoyed when Russell, without party sanction, subscribed to them in November 1845. [64] In the session of 1846, when Peel tried to induce the Conservatives to follow suit, Palmerston still advocated a fixed duty :

> I hold that there is no . . . reason why freedom of trade in corn should not be as advantageous to the country as freedom of trade in every other commodity. But by free trade . . . I mean trade free from duties laid on for the purpose of prevention or obstruction, but not trade free from duties laid on for the purpose of revenue . . . so moderate as not to cripple or impede commercial transactions . . . I am for a moderate fixed duty . . . this opinion was . . . taken . . . as far back as 1839 . . . I think that a duty of 4*s*. or 5*s*. would

not sensibly raise the price of corn in this country . . . it would produce a revenue not undeserving of consideration ; and, what is of more importance, it would enable us to accomplish a great transition with less violence to the feelings and prejudices of a large class of men.[65]

It is impossible to read the last phrase without suspecting that political considerations were present in his mind ; but it is impossible to review the whole without giving him credit for a large measure of sincerity.

The same mixture of conviction and expediency appears in a memorandum which he prepared in 1846.[66] For some time the German prophet of economic nationalism, Friedrich List, had been attracting attention in England, as elsewhere, by the arguments advanced in his *National System of Political Economy*.[67] Palmerston, attentive as ever to new theories, and confident as ever that he could cope with any specialist, composed a long reply. Perhaps List would have dismissed it as amateurish and naïve ; but it was written with obvious sincerity and decided forcefulness. List, according to Palmerston's interpretation at any rate, held that the Prussian Zollverein had performed its greatest benefit in giving protection to the Germans against the commodities of other lands. With this his British critic utterly disagreed :

> Commercially that institution has been most advantageous to Germany . . . for a reason precisely opposite to that on account of which Dr. List approves it. . . . The Zollverein has been eminently beneficial to Germany as a great machine for carrying into practice the principle of free trade. . . . The principle of protection has been only one of its incidental and accidental attributes.

He then modestly proceeded to show that List was ' utterly and entirely wrong ' in holding that protection could be the means of strengthening the German or any other state. For, he argued, national strength was inseparable from wealth ; and wealth came from production and from the accumulation of capital by saving. But the amount of production was lessened when a nation expended part of its energies in lines of production for which nature had not especially fitted it ; and saving was hindered when the domestic price of commodities was raised by a tariff. At the end of the memorandum the political motive came clearly into view : ' If the foregoing reasoning is well founded the British Government is doing no injury to Germany by endeavouring to persuade the Zollverein to diminish its protecting duties.'

Whatever may be thought of the purity of his motives, he could declaim free trade principles as effectively as their most devoted advocates. Having decided, in March 1846, that the Conservative protectionists and the free trade radicals had between them made the adoption of a fixed duty quite impossible, he took his stand with Russell and with Peel. And he denounced the protectionists in language such as Bright and Cobden might have used :

> Will the proud aristocracy of England contend for the continuance of a law, under which they are liable to have it cast in their teeth, that they derive a portion of their income from a poor rate—and a rate too, not levied on the wealthy for the support of the indigent poor ; but raised for the benefit of the rich, and wrung from the necessities of the poorest of the poor ? [68]

If Russell led the Whig-Liberals in their advance, Palmerston supplied some of the heaviest artillery.

Somewhat similar were the functions performed by the two men when the Whig-Liberals assailed the government on the conditions prevailing in Ireland. They were conditions to wring the heart of any understanding man ; for the Irish populace was in one of the worst throes of its long misery. With the established Church of Ireland still so richly and wastefully endowed as to seem a mockery to the starving Church that was really national ; with a vicious system of land tenure contributing to the chronic undernourishment of a great proportion of her populace, and keeping alive a burning sense of the wholesale confiscations practised by the British in earlier centuries ; with evictions threatening death by starvation to tens of thousands of her peasantry, mainly for the benefit of absentee landlords ; with the extremely small circle of her enfranchised population becoming smaller still ; and with administration placed in the hands of officials conspicuously lacking in understanding and in sympathy, the Irish were in a ferment of discontent. And, not unnaturally, if not quite logically, they concentrated their energies on the repeal of the Act of Union of 1801, which had extinguished their own parliament. Under O'Connell's leadership the 'repealers' stirred national feeling through the press, and held great meetings in the hope that the British government would be forced by pressure to surrender, as it had done in 1829. But the circumstances in the early 'forties were entirely different ones from those of fifteen years before. Though many Englishmen were ready to admit that the Irish had some grievances, there were few who had any patience with the agitation for repeal. As for the government, its first impulse was to use a heavier hand. A bill was passed to disarm Irishmen more completely than before; and troops were hurriedly despatched across the Irish Sea. Considering the insecurity of life and property in Ireland, and the violence frequently displayed, police and military measures were, perhaps, indispensable. But their execution made it the more essential that the principles of justice should be rigidly observed, and the harshness of coercion softened by determined efforts to afford relief. Unfortunately, Peel's government and, still more, the British people whom it served, paid scant regard to considerations of this sort. It was impossible to talk of justice when the Irish chancellor dismissed magistrates merely for showing sympathy with the advocates of repeal; and when O'Connell, after sacrificing much of his influence in efforts to avert bloodshed, was sentenced to heavy punishment through a trial that was little better than a travesty. As for relief, British indifference and bigotry were so pronounced that the utmost Peel could do was to make possible the endowment of Catholic charities, and increase the government's meagre subsidy to the Catholic religious seminary at Maynooth. In the end, order was restored by force; O'Connell's sentence was reversed by the law lords; and famine came to rob the Irish of capacity to accomplish much save ward off death.

It is interesting to recall that Palmerston attacked the abuses prevalent in Ireland long before Gladstone. He took up the Irish cause, not merely at the bidding of his strong humanitarian instinct and intuitive sympathy with the under dog, but because his very practical views on government persuaded him that redress of some sort was desirable. He understood perfectly that much of the agitation of the Irish for repeal was ' a conventional expression for their grievances ' ;[69] and he saw those grievances as clearly as any parliamentarian of the time. To say this is not to say that he was as ready as some others to support far-reaching measures of relief. He was not prepared to go as far as Lord Howick where the church question was concerned : nor did he agree with Conservatives of Stanley's type that more equitable conditions of land tenure should be set up by parliament. Instead of sharing Russell's shamed disgust at the scandals of O'Connell's trial, he speculated rather hopefully as to its effect, and privately vilified the great Irishman on his own account.[70] But he must be reckoned, for all that, with the minority who would gladly have righted some of Ireland's wrongs. It is true that he avoided speaking in the great debate of 1844, the debate in which Russell vehemently assailed the government, and Howick declared himself. But he must not be too much condemned for that ; since he had placed himself fully on record before parliament and people in the preceding year. And, in 1845, he gave Peel full support on the question of Maynooth, regardless of the unpopularity which he incurred. Considering that the Whig-Liberals were the ' popish ' party at the time, and that most of the Irish members were their allies, his attitude was to some extent conventional. But his vehemence, both in public and in private, was something more.

It was in June and July 1843, that Palmerston made his principal attacks.[71] Few features of the Irish situation escaped condemnation at his hands. He pointed out the inconsistency of the Irish system of registration and parliamentary franchise with the principles of reform adopted eleven years before, and now accepted even by the Conservatives ; he drew attention to shortcomings in the government of Irish municipalities ; and he emphasised the fact that Irish administration was in the hands of ' men . . . in the Castle in Dublin . . . who . . . had been known for years to be hostile . . . to the rights of the great majority of the people of Ireland.' Then, going deeper, he attacked two of the three great fundamental issues : the questions of the Protestant establishment and of land tenure. It was natural that he made no mention of the third. There was, as Russell said, entire agreement in parliament that the union of 1801 should be preserved. Incidentally, there was no one more resolved on its preservation than was Palmerston.

In dealing with the question of the church establishment, he talked of the national 'disgrace' attaching to the fact that the Catholic priesthood were ' so little cared for.' And in a later speech he portrayed the situation in vivid terms :

> Is it possible that you regard as permanent the arrangement that 6,500,000 or 7,000,000 of the poorest portion of the people of Ireland are to receive their religious instruction from a priesthood dependent upon the eleemosynary contributions of their flock, going from door to door, from farm to farm, and from cabin to cabin, to collect the wretched and precarious sums of which their income is composed ? . . . a provision by the State for the Catholic priesthood is a measure to which the Government and this House will at no distant period be compelled by their sense of justice to proceed. The great mistake made by Governments, not only in this country but everywhere, is to be too late in the measures which they adopt.[72]

To make provision seemed to him quite possible.[73] Even were the Church of Ireland to remain established, as he hoped, its surplus revenues could be drawn on for assistance to the Catholic priesthood. Should Catholics object that subsidisation would bring their priesthood into dependence upon a Protestant executive, there was at least one thing which parliament could do : it could see that Catholic priests were provided with glebes and glebe houses. Perhaps the expense of a general provision of this sort would prove to be too great ; but he thought that many Irish landed proprietors would welcome an enabling act, permitting them to establish Catholic glebes. He was speaking from the heart. ' To raise and improve the condition of the Catholic clergy,' he had written Russell on the day before he first discussed the matter in the House, ' is an object which all rational men must concur in thinking desirable.'[74] And, though he made no mention of the fact in parliament, he had assigned some land for the benefit of the priest or priests who ministered to his Irish tenantry.[75] With the Roman Catholic religion he had not the slightest sympathy. In another letter to Russell he stigmatised it as ' a bad political institution, unfavourable to morals, to industry, and to liberty.' [76] But he had as little sympathy with those who allowed religious prejudice to blind them to realities, and to the dictates of common sense and kindliness.

All the more striking is it then to find that his views on Irish land tenure apparently reflected his personal position as landlord. His heart was moved by the misery of the swarming peasantry : his indignation was aroused by the cruelty of landowners who evicted them. Thus to parliament in his speech of June 1843 :

> The people when turned out of their homes,—without the chance of obtaining a living—were driven to perish by the road side, or to eke out a miserable and lingering existence as squatters on the fringe of a bog, or in the outskirts of some neighbouring town.[77]

He had a special word of condemnation for landlords who ' had deliberately ejected good and sufficient and substantial Catholic tenants, in order to give their land to Protestants.' But he was opposed to any legislation for the correction of these ills ; and personal interest seems to have entered in. ' I, for one have no particular fancy,' he wrote Lansdowne, ' for being compelled to buy back my estate from time to time from my tenants.' [78] And the defence of his position which he made to parliament was nothing but an *ad hoc* application of a principle laid down by earlier generations for better purposes :

> He held that it would be unjust for Parliament to interfere in the arrangements between the landlord and tenant. To do so, would be to establish a principle of confiscation—to interfere with the rights of property, the foundation of all human society—property which the poorest man by his own industry and exertions, might acquire, as well as the wealthy and powerful.[79]

But let it be remembered that in taking this position he did not lack good company. The suggestions of a commission on Irish land tenure set to work by Peel could not secure even a hearing in either House. And Russell, reviewing Irish grievances in 1844, went beyond Palmerston only in suggesting definite reforms in municipal government and the parliamentary franchise. True, he talked of religious equality in Ireland at some future day; but he saw nothing in immediate prospect save glebes, glebe houses and a larger appropriation for Maynooth.

It was on this question of an increased grant to Maynooth that bigotry broke loose. 'No popery' petitions rained on parliament; and the Catholic Church was once more stigmatised as a 'harlot' and a 'beast.' Palmerston, whose stand on the matter had been unequivocal from the first, was called sharply to account by some of his Tiverton constituents. And surely no circle of bigots in all Britain was reproved in more stinging words than those of his reply.[80] This for the contention that the government should not subsidise the propagation of the 'errors' of the Catholic faith:

I fear that resistance to the bill upon this spiritual ground seems to have too much affinity to that most objectionable doctrine of the Catholic Church, held by the more ignorant, but disavowed by the more enlightened Catholics, that none can look with hope to an hereafter but those whose religious opinions shall in this world conform to a particular and prescribed creed . . . But I presume that no Protestant holds such an exclusive and uncharitable doctrine.

And this for objections that aid to Maynooth was inadvisable on 'temporal' grounds:

I can hardly conceive how any person who has attentively considered the state of public affairs can, in this respect, entertain a doubt of the propriety of the measure . . . we cannot prevent the Catholic priesthood from exercising an immense influence over six millions of the Irish people; but we may, by showing a kindly feeling and a liberal spirit, enlist that influence as an active auxiliary in the cause of good order and of submission to law; or we may, by harshness, by repulsion, and by a display of hostile feeling, render that influence at least motionless for good, if not occasionally active for evil.

Since he could and did point out that previous commitments would alone have forced him to support the Maynooth grant, his reproofs to the broad-minded burgesses of Tiverton may be taken as expressing what he felt. His courage, his haughtiness and his penchant for delivering homilies were not confined to his conduct of foreign policy by any means.

CHAPTER XVI

PALMERSTON'S SECOND RETURN TO THE FOREIGN OFFICE,
1845–1846

DURING the latter part of the five-year period which he spent in opposition, Palmerston, the exuberant and undisciplined, seemed restrained in most of his utterances on foreign policy. Various explanations of this phenomenon suggest themselves. No doubt he smarted a little from the chastisement he had received for his outbreaks concerning the Webster-Ashburton settlement; and it is certain that some Whig-Liberals, solicitous for the party's welfare, admonished him to guard his lips and pen.[1] He may have found it unusually easy to do this; since greater capacity for self-control goes with relaxed energies and rested nerves. And there were circumstances which could hardly fail of some effect on a man of such ambition and political insight. He must have been conscious that the Queen, without whose consent he could scarcely regain the post of foreign minister, was becoming more critical of his attitude as she became more intimate with the French royal family, and more convinced that the resignation of Peel's ministry ' would not only be for us . . . but for the whole country, and for the peace of Europe—a *great calamity*.'[2] He may even have seen that reaction was setting in against Aberdeen's over-gentle policies; and have decided that to bring their effects coldly and clearly before the public view would be his most effective course.

The Queen's growing taste for the Aberdeen-Guizot entente was evidenced by the frequency of royal visits in these years.[3] In the spring of 1844, Victoria's mother made a short stay in Paris, and was of course overwhelmed with attentions at the Tuileries. In the following October,

Louis Philippe took a squadron across to Portsmouth, and paid a visit to Windsor. Once again he and Guizot could congratulate themselves on marked success. In future the French king could wear the blue ribbon of the Garter, with all the greater of recognised monarchs. And, although the visit took place at a time when relations between the two countries were uncomfortably strained, he turned it to such good account that he left behind him feelings of affection and even gratitude. Victoria scarcely realised how aptly she used the adjective 'sagacious' to describe her guest. For he had addressed Albert, who still lacked the standing even of Prince Consort, as '*Mon Frère*'; and declared, '*Le Prince Albert, c'est pour moi le Roi.*' Nor did he forget, after getting back to France, to send a toy gun to the infant Prince of Wales, and a little work-box—exquisite emblem of Victorian domesticity—to the not yet four-year-old Princess Royal.

But it was the last of these cross Channel visits which promised to yield the French government the most tangible results. In September 1845, Victoria and Albert were once more at the Château d'Eu with their attendant ministers. Everything went as auspiciously as before. And on this occasion the ministers were able to come to an understanding about the marriage of the queen of Spain. Melbourne's warning to Victoria of two years before not to 'let them make any treaty or agreement there,'[4] was forgotten or put aside. That any understanding could be reached testified to the strength of the entente. Louis Philippe was resolved that no prince not like himself, of Bourbon blood, should share the Spanish throne. Realising, however, that the other Powers would not allow a son of his to become Isabella's king consort, he demanded that the happy man should be a Spanish or Neapolitan Bourbon, and thus a descendant of Philip V of Spain. More important still, he had set his heart on securing the Queen's sister, the richly dowered Infanta Louisa, for his son, the duke of Montpensier. On the other hand, Victoria had made no secret of her hope that one of her numerous Coburg cousins would secure Isabella's hand, or of her dislike for Louis Philippe's plan concerning

Montpensier.[5] Yet she and her minister, yielding to the insistence of their hosts, made concessions on both points. No active support would be given by the British government to the candidature of the Coburg prince. As for the Montpensier project, Aberdeen felt that it would not become a real issue for some time, and could probably be disposed of in the interim. He decided, then, that it ' might safely be left,' on the basis of Guizot's promise that the nuptials should not take place until ' *children, that were necessary to secure the succession* ' had been born to the Spanish queen and her future consort.[6] Any written agreement on the matter was apparently regarded as superfluous.

But Aberdeen's confidence in the French and in the good results of his conciliatory policy was finding less and less support among his countrymen. There were temperate men, such as Russell, who had been disturbed from the outset at the ' want of energy and boldness in the foreign department ' ;[7] and, by July 1844, a much larger number must have reacted sympathetically to a charge which Palmerston made in parliament :

> They [the Conservative ministers] cannot take a leading part in the settlement of any great European question, . . . because, dissatisfied apparently with the front rank position in which they found the country when they took the helm, they thought it more consistent with the modesty of our national character that Great Britain, under their command, should drop quietly astern, and take up her berth in the wake of all the great Foreign Powers.[8]

Justly or unjustly, it was felt by many that the French were taking undue advantage of the entente. Among the Whigs one may take Ellice, a man as pacifistic as Aberdeen, and for that reason an inveterate opponent of Palmerston's methods in diplomacy. Ellice complained to Russell in August 1844, that the French government as conducted by Guizot seemed almost as inclined as it had been in Thiers' day to intrigue against the British everywhere, and to make useless and vain-glorious abuses of its power. England, he added, would do well to keep on good terms with the other great continental courts, and to be ready with her fleet.[9] At the same time, Wellington was pointing out to

Charles Greville that the French insulted England ' whenever and wherever they thought they could do so with impunity, and that the only way to keep at peace with them was to be stronger in every quarter of the globe than they were.'[10] The fact that one of Louis Philippe's sons, the Prince de Joinville, had just published an indiscreet brochure calling for the building up of the French fleet confirmed the suspicions of many Englishmen.[11] As for Aberdeen's policy towards the United States, it will be remembered that Howick (who like Ellice was one of the most anti-Palmerstonian of Whigs) complained of Ashburton's 'cringing,' and of the unfortunate results it had produced in the American senate. Palmerston could well afford to moderate his expressions concerning other nations and their governments, and confine himself to cold but trenchant criticism of Aberdeen.

This was certainly his method of procedure when France, in 1844, aroused deep resentment among his countrymen by her proceedings in Tahiti and on the Moroccan coast.[12] The dispute regarding Tahiti, which came to a head during the spring and summer, was much the more serious. The island had been under the influence of British missionaries, of whom one, named Pritchard, was accredited as British consul. Its queen had twice requested a British protectorate ; and, although her requests were made in vain, it seems to have been generally understood that England would give her support in time of need. In spite of this a French admiral, acting without instructions, had forcibly established a protectorate and expelled Pritchard. Though the expulsion was by no means without cause, and did not take place until after Pritchard had resigned his consulship, British public opinion was dangerously aroused. Even Victoria and King Leopold agreed that the admiral had committed an ' outrage.' That war did not ensue was due mainly to the conciliatory attitude of the French government. Guizot, while not daring to give up the protectorate, apologised for the treatment of Pritchard ; and Louis Philippe personally indemnified the missionary-consul for the loss he had sustained. The trouble in Morocco occurred at the same time.[13] The bombardment of Tangier by French ships, with the object

THE SLAVE-TRADE AND FOREIGN POLICY

of persuading the Sultan that he must prevent his territory from being used for raids into Algiers, stirred up much feeling in commercial circles and created considerable uneasiness on the part even of Aberdeen.

Considering the strength of public sentiment and of Palmerston's own privately expressed disgust, the correctness of his references to these matters in parliament seems remarkable. In speaking of Tahiti he pointed out that the friendship between the British and French sovereigns seemed disappointing in its fruits, and reminded the House that Peel had referred to the treatment of Pritchard as a ' gross outrage.' But he carefully divided the blame between the two governments ; emphasised the sincerity of the French desire for cordial relations with the British ministry ; and declared himself ' not prepared altogether to say ' that England had any great ground to complain of the result. It could hardly be said that he went beyond the ministers of the Crown in criticising France. His principal complaint was that Aberdeen had not exacted such reparation as the French were willing to accord.[14] As for the bombardment of Tangier, he forbore even to catechise the ministers on the subject at the risk of impeding negotiations between London and Paris.[15]

But there was one subject concerning which he never showed restraint, the ministry's attitude with respect to the slave-trade.[16] He returned to the assault incessantly, making the most passionate and effective speech of his career on the brutalities which it involved, and exposing with all the fervour which he could command the results of the concessions made to France and the United States. Perhaps the most telling of all his attacks was delivered in March 1845. By quoting from French documents, he showed that Guizot had at first declared the abrogation of the treaties of 1831 and 1833 impossible, and had declined to invite rebuff by asking it from Aberdeen. And he showed, too, that after the terms of the Webster-Ashburton treaty became known in France, and after Aberdeen had proved so pliant with respect to Spain, Guizot had decided that abrogation could safely be demanded after all. Perhaps there was too much *post hoc, ergo propter hoc* in this assault; but the sequence of dates was a very striking one. Outside the House, and quite privately, he tried to hold the French to the undertakings they had made with him. While he was taking his cure at Wiesbaden, in September 1844, he sent Guizot a long and passionate appeal. He was sure that the abolition of the Franco-British agreement for a mutual right of search would mean the 'immolation' of perhaps a hundred thousand blacks a year; and surely nothing could so 'dishonour a civilised and Christian Power' as 'voluntarily and knowingly to have given encouragement and facilities' to the slave trade.[17]

He was equally his old self when it came to arraignments of Aberdeen's general policy.[18] Quite bluntly (and not without reason)[19] he accused the Foreign Office of sacrificing British interests to keep Guizot in power, and called upon the House to consider the results of the similar favour accorded to Prince Polignac by Wellington's government in 1829. Then came a piece of constructive criticism which contained the essence of what men were wont to think of as Palmerstonian doctrine:

> Influence abroad is to be maintained only by the operation of one or other of two principles—hope and fear. We ought to teach the weaker Powers to hope that they will receive the support of this country in their time of danger. Powerful countries should be taught to fear that they will be resisted by England in any unjust acts either towards ourselves or towards those who are bound in ties of amity with us. But after the abandonment of Spain by Her Majesty's Government, what weak power can retain any hopes of moral support or of effective aid from this country? And after we have ceded and given up the disputed territory in North America, what powerful country can entertain any apprehension of our resistance to encroachment?

It must have been clear to all the world that if Palmerston should return to the Foreign Office at the next change of ministry there would be a sharp re-orientation of British foreign policy. It was a matter to provoke speculation of the keenest sort. Would the Whig leaders and the Court attempt to relegate him to some other place in the new cabinet? Would he accept such relegation? And what would happen if he should refuse?

In the first week of December 1845, Peel's conversion to the principle of free trade in corn (following closely upon Russell's famous free trade letter of November 25) made all these questions of immediate interest. Peel, finding his party hopelessly divided from the cabinet down, resigned ; and Russell, on the eleventh of the month, received the Queen's command to form a Whig-Liberal ministry. On the two days following, the party leaders gathered at his London home and made provisional plans.[20] Their gatherings were rather gloomy on the whole. Peel, as Disraeli later said, was offering a ' poisoned chalice ' to the incoming cabinet. It would be no light task to repeal the Corn Laws, to decide about Ireland, to give a firmer but still pacific tone to foreign policy, and to secure increased appropriation for defence. Without assurances of support from Peel and from such of the Conservatives as clung to him, the task would obviously be impossible ; and no final steps could be taken in forming the new ministry until such assurances had been received. In the meantime, however, some of the party leaders proceeded to discuss informally certain matters of detail—in particular the question as to who should have the Foreign Office seals.[21] The Queen expressed to Russell her wish that it should not be Palmerston ; and the Whig leaders, almost to a man, it seems, agreed with her. Dissatisfied as they might be with the yielding propensity of Aberdeen, they did not care to reinstate a man whose name was anathema to almost every foreign government. But Russell and certain of the others realised that the wish would be difficult of accomplishment. They knew that the ' devil's son ' had no mind to accept exclusion from an office which he had thoroughly enjoyed, an office which had enabled him to satisfy his patriotic impulses and to overshadow Melbourne's ministry. His resentment of Whig criticism and his disgust with Aberdeen had each, in its own manner, hardened his resolve. Confronted with the probability that he would prove impervious to argument, the party leaders seem to have felt it would be less dangerous to yield to him than to risk his secession to the Conservatives. Perhaps he might be safely reinstated after all, provided Victoria told him personally of her strong wish that the entente should be preserved, and that his colleagues insisted on making foreign policy a matter of joint ministerial responsibility. They were confident that he would never run away with Russell, as he had done with the cynical Melbourne. In effect, the Whigs who first answered Russell's call wished, rather than expected, that Palmerston would accept some other office.

But the gathering of the clans had been so far incomplete ; and the situation became more difficult when the heads of the Grey section at last appeared.[22] Earl Grey, who, as Lord Howick, had been secretary at War in the last Whig cabinet, and who had succeeded to his great father's title in this same year, was slow in arriving from Northumberland. He had lingered a little to discuss matters with his uncle by marriage (and Palmerston's *bête noire*) ' Bear ' Ellice ; and had travelled to London with Ellice and with his cousin, Sir George Grey. What happened between Lord Grey and Ellice will never be known with any certainty. For Grey, though sincere and conscientious to a fault, was impressionable, proud and difficult : while Ellice was too much of an intriguer to be relied upon for literal truth. But they certainly agreed in considering Palmerston's reappointment to the Foreign Office highly undesirable. Grey had no feeling of personal animosity, being frank to confess that when he had been guilty of ' undue vehemence and pertinacity ' in opposing Palmerston, the latter had met him with ' perfect good temper and forbearance.' He was moved chiefly by the conviction that Palmerston's roughness of tone and reputation with foreign governments would cause them to resent proceedings on his part which would be regarded as unexceptionable if coming from some other minister.[23] The proceedings of the two men on their arrival in London were quite typical. Ellice hurried to Russell to assist him in the formation of his cabinet ; while Grey, besides seeing the prime minister elect, wrote him, on December 16, a letter in which he put forward the impractical demand that ' personal ' considerations should have no weight in determining the personnel of the cabinet.[24] Two days later, after the chiefs in full meeting had decided that a letter from Peel, promising qualified support, 'gave a sufficient foundation to form a ministry,' Grey had a private talk with some of them about the disposition of the Foreign Office.[25] He hoped that Palmerston might be bribed with a British peerage to employ his talents in some other post ; and proved his own intense sincerity by offering to give up to him the Colonial Office and the leadership in the House of Lords. The other Whigs whom he consulted were very much in favour of his plan, and talked of Clarendon as the man who should be made foreign secretary. They were, perhaps, ignorant that Palmerston had even by this time refused to consider any office except his former one. To do so, he considered, would be a tacit admission that his critics had been justified. Once again it was a question whether Whig opposition was to block his path.

On December 19 matters came to a head ; and Palmerston apparently sustained a serious reverse.[26] Russell, after vainly suggesting that he should give up the foreign secretaryship in view of an 'impression' which was admittedly unjust, offered him the post. The Queen had already given her consent. But Grey, on hearing this, declared that 'personal' considerations had entered in ; and refused to join the new cabinet in any capacity. Thereupon Russell hastened to notify Victoria that he could not proceed with the construction of a ministry. His motives remain even yet a matter of surmise. The injury to the party which Grey's defection might be expected to produce ; the reluctance of many of the leaders to accept the 'poisoned chalice' from Peel's hands ; and even his own and his sick wife's conviction that his assumption of the heavy burdens of the premiership would involve the 'desolation' of their 'domestic prospects' all seem to have weighed with him. But many persons, on both sides of the Channel, assumed that Grey's refusal to serve if Palmerston went to the Foreign Office had been the sole cause of the *débâcle* ; and drew inferences in accordance with their hopes or fears. Macaulay was afraid that Palmerston would be used as a scapegoat, and that he would 'sink' under the 'great storm of public indignation' which would burst on him.[27] Reeve wrote from Paris that if anything could increase the satisfaction of the French it was their knowledge 'of the actual cause of Lord John's failure.'[28] Greville told of the 'transports of joy' and increase in the price of all securities observable on the continent, and rashly predicted that Palmerston would never again be foreign minister.[29]

In point of fact, he was one of the few actual gainers by the episode. Russell, much criticised for giving up so easily, threw the blame on Grey.[30] And Grey found himself 'in the deepest disgrace with the whole party.'[31] Even Ellice, who, as Grey insisted then and later on, had encouraged him in resisting Palmerston's reappointment and in believing that he could be induced to take some other post, deserted him.[32] In a revulsion of feeling, the Whigs and the Court displayed an unlooked-for appreciation of Grey's 'victim.'[33] Lord John declared Palmerston 'the person in the United Kingdom best fitted' to direct its foreign policy. Minto found that the complaints against him were based 'specially upon the views and measures in which we were nearly unanimous,' and that it was the 'rabble' who had subscribed to Grey's 'nonsense.' But the most striking tribute came from Clarendon, who was greatly upset lest the talk of his own qualifications for the foreign secretaryship should have aroused fresh suspicions in the minds of the victim and his wife :

> My firm belief is that energy such as Palmerston's is at this moment greatly needed at the Foreign Office, and that it would tend, far more than the present system, to an *entente* really cordial between us and France. I have over and over again told Lord Aberdeen that his predilection for Guizot, and consequent partisanship in France was endangering the peaceful relations between the two countries ; because, on the one hand, it rendered hostility to England a natural and necessary weapon of attack against Guizot, and, on the other, this imposed on him the obligation to '*faire des niches à l'Angleterre,*' in order to prove his independence and keep his *portefeuille*.[34]

And Victoria, incensed at Grey's 'arrogant pretensions' in refusing to accept an appointment in which she had acquiesced, 'spoke most handsomely of Palmerston,' and announced her conviction that he would have performed the duties of a foreign secretary ably and faithfully.[35] Any momentary disappointment on his part must have been well recompensed by realisation that in the change of government which must soon occur the Court and party would be very much committed to giving him the Foreign Office seals. His family, and perhaps he himself, seem to have believed that even the premiership might not be beyond his reach.

Satisfaction of a minor character, yet not to be despised, he drew from the contemplation of his enemies' discomfiture. Witness the description of his meeting with 'Bear' Ellice at Lord Lansdowne's house during the Christmas week:

> He came uninvited, having proposed himself; and very unwelcome, as no one there wished for his company; Ly Lansdowne hardly spoke to him, though he sat himself next to her at dinner . . . certainly . . . he looked like a foxhound who has been chopping a hare in cover, and who sneaks up to the whipper-in with a down look that betrays consciousness of misbehaviour. . . . [36]

The two men had an amusing interview. Ellice threw all the blame of Russell's failure upon Grey, accusing him, who 'hardly knew how to speak French,' of having wanted the Foreign Office for himself, and blaming him for not stating his objections personally to Palmerston. The viscount's answer must have been a disconcerting one:

> 'Well, but Ellice,' said I, 'that was not the course which you yourself pursued when you made the same attempt in 1835.' 'Oh, but,' said he, 'you know I was not then going to take Office myself and that made a difference . . . it was very unfair of Melbourne to shew me up as he did on that occasion; besides, when I was then told that you positively refused to take any other Office, and Melbourne asked me what was to be done, I said there was no help for it, and nothing to be done but make the best of it.'

He could afford to treat Ellice lightly; and he may have realised that the days of Whig 'Bears' were virtually at an end. What disturbed him, and quite properly, were the operations of 'a certain clique' at the French capital.[37]

The activities of this clique furnished one of the most diverting as well as important aspects of the whole episode.[38] The central figure was still young Henry Reeve, now more than ever engaged in purveying to the French king, to

Guizot, and to Guizot's Russian Egeria the juicy morsels of political information which Charles Greville, as clerk of the Privy Council, was able so bountifully to supply. The ministerial crisis of December 1845, gave both men an exceptional opportunity; and Greville made full use of it by forwarding information concerning even the most confidential letters which passed between the principal actors. Nowhere can one obtain a better idea of what was going on than from one of Reeve's letters to his busy informant :

> Horace Walpole would have given his best piece of Sèvres to have written your two letters of Saturday, and his antique for two such auditors as Guizot and Madame de Lieven. Your description was so inimitably vivid and the events described so extremely agreeable that, I believe, they owe you one of the pleasantest moments of their lives.
>
> I was constrained after much entreaty to allow Guizot to communicate them to the King, under his royal promise of absolute discretion. . . . However, I demanded in writing a formal promise that the King should make no allusions to the contents of these letters, ' *dans ses rapports avec l'Angleterre* ' ; at least until he learned them from some other source. The fact is that with such intelligence and as your representative, ' *je joue le rôle d'un grand personnage.*' [39]

It was delightful for Greville to learn that the French king regarded his letters as ' *du Saint Simon tout pur*,' and very gratifying for Reeve, still rather an obscure young man, to feel that he could ' punish the presumption ' of Palmerston !

> I must say I respect Grey. . . . For my own part nothing would have induced me to sit in a Cabinet with that evil genius presiding over its foreign relations, and I am glad the Whigs are punished for their weak and culpable acquiesence in a foreign policy which has made Palmerston the bane of Europe. There is nothing in my own life which I can reflect upon with so much satisfaction as the having employed the last five years in an endeavour to punish the presumption of that man by an appeal to the public opinion of Europe. . . .

That he and other enemies of Palmerston had once betrayed the French government into over-confidence and might do so again, does not appear to have occurred to him.

In the effects which news of the crisis produced at the French court there was a decided element of comedy. For

Guizot and his master the essential fact was the virtual certainty, indeed the imminence, of Palmerston's return to power. The prospect was most discouraging. True, they must have learned from Reeve, if in no other way, that the Queen and the leaders of the Whigs intended to keep a tight rein on diplomacy. True, Disraeli, who was in Paris at the time, assumed the part of mediator ; promised that the entente would be preserved in any case ; and transmitted assurances to the same effect from Palmerston.[40] But Louis Philippe and his minister could not be cheered. Providing even that they gave Palmerston credit for sincerity, they knew too well the kind of entente he had in mind. Guizot, pointing out that he would not recognise France's ' superior influence ' in Greece and Spain, deplored his ' narrowness of views and *entraînement de caractère* '[41] :

> Lord Palmerston . . . concentrates all his energy on a point, and especially on a point where we happen to be at variance. *Il aime la lutte*, and the place where he is least master is that at which he is most anxious to become so . . . once engaged in this career his vivacity of temper prevents his stopping in it. That is the danger. *On tombe du côté où l'on penche.*

Granting the analysis to have been a true one—and few, perhaps, would disagree—the prospect that Palmerston would ever stand in cordial relations with the timid, ambitious and scheming Orleans government was slim indeed. To Louis Philippe, Palmerston, for all his new-found discretion, remained the ' *ennemi de ma maison* ' that he had been for several years.[42] But, *bon gré, mal gré*, he had to be treated with apparent cordiality. For Victoria, momentarily at least, chose to approve of him ; and Victoria had become the *grande amie de ma maison*. It would never do even for a royal personage to make Grey's mistake, to show such ' arrogant pretensions ' as to disagree with her Majesty that Palmerston would make a very proper foreign minister. Moreover, Palmerston was almost certainly coming back to power. Hence, while Guizot, to whom acting did not come easily, expressed a cold conviction that Palmerston sincerely favoured the entente,[43] Louis Philippe, ' radiant with smiles, was assuring the whole diplomatic circle that he was never less uneasy as to the prospects of Europe.' So Disraeli reported at any rate.[44] And, some time after the crisis was well past, de Tocqueville wrote of ' the cajoleries and graces ' shown by the French sovereign to the ' enemy of his house.'[45]

What made the situation more piquant was the growing connection between Palmerston and his ' acrobatic ' one time enemy, Thiers.[46] The connection apparently reached its peak in London, in October 1845, when they discussed the failings of Louis Philippe, reviewed ' with much good humour ' their struggle over the Near East, and parted, according to Palmerston's account, ' sworn friends.' Since Thiers was in rabid opposition to Guizot's government, the friendship, though declared on both sides to be of the most platonic and disinterested character, aroused suspicion in London and even stronger feelings at the Tuileries. The fact that the reconciliation of the two men had been in part brought about by the editor of the *Chronicle*, Sir John Easthope, seemed another suspicious circumstance. Easthope appears to have been a good deal courted at this time. Hobhouse, always something of a snob, was diverted when the editor gave a sumptuous dinner for Lord and Lady Palmerston ; and found it worthy of record that Lady Palmerston ' was as civil as if the hostess had been her fashionable friend of thirty years.' And great attentions had been paid to Sir John when he visited Paris in December 1844.[47] Perhaps the French government had heard that he was susceptible to flattery ; perhaps its reward for flattering young Reeve suggested that blandishments to other Englishmen connected with the press would pay. At any rate Easthope, ' a vulgar man enough,' according to Tocqueville, was treated as a great personage. Apparently, his pleasure was too manifest : for he was compared to the ass in the fable, which accepted for herself the adoration of the crowds when she bore sacred relics through the streets. Was the precious burden in this case the goodwill of the readers of the *Chronicle*, or the detachment of Easthope from Palmerston, or that of both men from the malign influence of Thiers ? At any rate, the French were playing a pretty comedy, almost as amusing as the little farce performed in England in January 1846, by certain personages at the Court, and, if not by Palmerston, by some of his closest relatives.

Peel's long continuance in office as a Conservative premier having become impossible, various moves for arranging the succession were immediately set on foot ; and it was in contributing some of these that Palmerston's relatives and their friends at Court played such intriguing rôles. The evidence now accessible is very incomplete ; but it is far too suggestive to be passed by. Briefly, it indicates that ' Palmerston House ' (as Greville called the group), lacking appreciation of the real feelings of the Queen, and under-estimating the courage and decision of which Russell was capable, conceived the idea that Palmerston might become heir to the premiership. This seems at any rate the natural interpretation to be placed on a correspondence carried on by Lady Palmerston with her younger brother, Lord Beauvale, and his wife at the beginning of 1846. Moreover, there are indications that Palmerston, then and for some time afterwards, contemplated the possibility of joining, if not leading, a combination of those Whigs and Conservatives who preferred a fixed duty on corn to the free importation advocated by Peel, Russell and Cobden.[48] Inconsistent as this may seem with his free trade principles, and his denunciation, later in the spring, of the protectionists, he had both incitement to take the step, and some ground for thinking that he could do it without entirely losing face. Grey's objection to his reappointment as foreign minister was an unpleasant reminder that he had never really been accepted by the Whigs. Russell's demonstration of weakness in the crisis which ensued—stamped upon the public consciousness by the famous *Punch* cartoon, ' You're not strong enough for the place, John '—had made the future one of great uncertainty. If, as seemed quite possible, Russell and his followers should coalesce with Peel and the free trade Conservatives including Aberdeen,[49] both Palmerston and much of what he stood for in foreign policy and the war on the slave trade would be put aside. It is probable that he sought, then, a possible haven for his ambitions and his policies. And a Whig-Conservative combination on the policy of a fixed duty on the import of corn was the only one in sight. The duty could be, or at least it could be called, one for revenue alone. With regard to foreign policy the protectionist Conservatives, with Stanley (later Lord Derby) and Disraeli at their head, would support him better than the Whigs.

To say that he reasoned in this way is in large degree to speculate : but 'Palmerston House' certainly entertained some ideas of this sort when Lord and Lady Beauvale visited at Windsor Castle, in January 1846, and wrote of their activities to Lady Palmerston.[50] Beauvale reported that Russell was so much out of favour for his hesitation and timidity that there seemed to be 'every disposition, if the case [of Peel's resignation] shld occur, to send to some other Person than Johnny' : and that it was 'impossible to stand better than P.[almerston]' did. The line of action was then to suggest most delicately to the Queen that she might dispel the false rumours concerning her own and the French king's objections to Palmerston's reappointment as foreign secretary by inviting him to Windsor before the opening of parliament. She would then, presumably, be impressed by his qualifications for a still more lofty post. The hopes of Palmerston House ran high. At one time it was believed that Lady Beauvale, the diplomatic daughter of a Prussian diplomatist, had 'managed it beautifully' with George Anson, who had once been Melbourne's secretary and was now serving Prince Albert in the same capacity. And Anson had done good work upon his own account, by calling the attention of the Queen to articles which treated the recent crisis from the point of view most favourable to Palmerston House. Thanks to him Victoria had 'split her sides' at Russell's expense over the *Punch* cartoon. Hence Beauvale gave a highly encouraging report :

In talking about Palmerston the Queen said to me that it was all in consequence of Syria and that the French had hardly yet got over it ; no, I said, nor never will, any more than they have got over Waterloo, but that is no reason for us to regret either one or the other, at which I had the satisfaction to see her chuckle with hearty glee, and this gave me an opportunity to repeat to her what Thiers

"I'M AFRAID YOU'RE NOT STRONG ENOUGH FOR THE PLACE, JOHN"

Punch, January 3, 1846

had said ' that He had no reason to be a friend to P. by whom he had been worsted, but that that did not prevent him from regarding him as the first Statesman of this age and perhaps of any other.' . . . All this and much more was corresponded to with full harmony by the Queen. She spoke about Ellice and asked if He was the cause of it all ? I told her that in my opinion He had been blowing it up for years but that the explosion had taken place against his will.[51]

The rest of Beauvale's report is somewhat cryptic ; but it seems conclusive as to the desires of Lady Palmerston and her brother :

I shld have much more to say to you if we were together but the above are the main points. Wild about free trade and the whole Household talking nonsense in the same direction. With this there is a great wish to undervalue the Aristocracy and (I doubt not) a great willingness to see them lowered. If the Protectionists had but common sense and wld yield what ought to be yielded, I firmly believe we should beat Johnny, Peel and the [anti-Corn Law] League united. . . .

I must add this whole affair [the crisis of December] seems to me to have turned out a triumph for P. instead of a check. . . .

What one yearns to know is in how far the Queen was acting too, and—still more of course—what Palmerston knew or thought of Anson's and Beauvale's activities. All that seems certain is that the hoped-for invitation never reached Broadlands.

At any rate, he could and did prepare for his almost certain return to the Foreign Office by crossing to Paris with Lady Palmerston at Eastertide. The visit had, of course, been planned for years, and would almost certainly have been paid in the autumn of 1845 had not Thiers advised its postponement until the opening of the Chambers had brought the ' people whom one should like to make acquaintance with ' to the French capital.[52] And the ministerial crisis of December had made it seem even more advisable. Disraeli, in acting as mediator, had suggested that Palmerston should make himself known to the ' impressionable ' French ; and Lady Palmerston privately avowed her hope that it would ' set to rest for ever all such absurd reports as L'd Grey put about.'[53] But if its purpose was serious, some of its incidents were amusing in the extreme. For both the visitor and his hosts were acting constantly ; and Palmerston, whose histrionic talents never ran much to light rôles, distinctly overplayed his part.[54] People were merely amused when he went about proclaiming on all sides his devotion to the entente, and lavishing cordiality even on some of those who made no secret of their hostility. But when he wrote a note of congratulation to Louis Philippe on having escaped unhurt from a new attempt upon his life—a step which even Aberdeen had not presumed to take—he was regarded as guilty of officiousness and impertinence. There were comments, too, on his action in rushing to call on Ibrahim, Mehemet Ali's heir and late general in Syria, before Ibrahim had been presented at the Tuileries. Reports had it that Ibrahim 'was so diverted at finding himself thus face to face with the great enemy of his house, that he burst into an uncontrollable fit of laughter,' before proceeding to welcome his unexpected guest. Such little departures from established etiquette perhaps gave Madame de Lieven the welcome opportunity of painting one of the most spiteful word-portraits of Palmerston which has survived.[55] His bearing was that of 'an old dandy of second-rate society,' quite lacking in dignity. And (this for Palmerston !) : 'Everyone says, "he has not the air of an Englishman."' Aberdeen, for whose special benefit the portrait was set down, acknowledged 'the likeness and excellence of the artist.'[56]

The acting of the French comedians was far superior. Palmerston's first real biographer, Bulwer, who supposedly had knowledge of the event, declares that ' Paris rang with praises of his good-breeding ' ; that ' " *ce terrible Lord Palmerston* " became " *ce cher Lord Palmerston* " ' ; and that ' before he returned to England all idea of there being anything to apprehend from his reappointment as Foreign Secretary had disappeared on both sides of the Channel.'[57] And Charles Greville, who had quite unnecessarily warned Reeve that the French government should keep in mind the extreme probability of Palmerston's return to power, at first believed the visit to have been ' triumphantly successful.'[58] He learned that Palmerston had been dined by the King and by 'political leaders of all shades,' and treated by some of them, as the Tory British ambassador wrote resentfully, 'more like a person who had rendered signal services to France than one who had by his conduct afforded her any grounds of complaint.'[59] No doubt Greville heard, too, that the French people, already somewhat appeased by the apparent rebuff which their great 'enemy' had sustained through Grey, were flattered to consider his visit an 'act of reparation and of deference towards France.'[60] Palmerston himself seems to have been well satisfied with the results of his visit.

But, in view of what lay ahead, it was the real feeling of the Court and of Guizot which mattered most; and in this there was no change.[61] The secret correspondence which went on between Aberdeen, Guizot, Madame de Lieven and the British and French ambassadors is full witness to that. Yes, the King had dined Palmerston as a statesman of a friendly Power. But, having promised in advance to converse with him only in so loud a tone that everything could be overheard, he had kept his word in a manner which was almost too much for his consort's gravity. True, Guizot had dined the visitor, too. But he sent at least one agent to pump him under cover of what was supposed to be a friendly call.[62] And he, the Princess Lieven and the British ambassador, explaining that 'necessity and seemliness' had forced the Court and ministers to show some cordiality to Palmerston, left Aberdeen in no doubt as to the sentiments prevailing at the Tuileries. Guizot wrote that the French could not forget so easily, and that, if Palmerston's position in England were altered by his visit to Paris, it would be because the English accepted appearances for realities. The Princess was more explicit still:

M. Guizot has not altered his opinion concerning him. He believes that Lord Palmerston will be circumspect, that he will restrain himself a little, and that he will perhaps even pretend to sentiments different from those which he had professed so far; but he is convinced that the former man will reappear . . . on the first occasion . . . and more than ever prays to God to be spared from him.[63]

The subsequent history of these letters from Paris has its

interest. Aberdeen was at this time telling Guizot of his desire to smooth the way for Palmerston, and pointing out that his disinterestedness in doing this, incomprehensible to ' mere politicians ' and probably to Palmerston himself, would be fully appreciated by a man of Guizot's type.[64] Yet he considered it quite consistent with his consciously high-minded attitude to send on the letters from his Paris correspondents to Victoria.[65] Naturally enough, the Queen enjoyed them to the full, and hoped that he would ' never hesitate to send her private letters of this sort.' Guizot and the Princess had no reason to complain. Whether they had intended it or not, they had given Victoria their own and the King's opinion of Palmerston without offending her. Indeed, she declared her complete agreement with the Princess's conviction that Aberdeen had ' the good wishes of all honest men ' and that Peel ' was the only man to govern his country.'[66]

If Palmerston had really shared with Beauvale the idea of ' beating Johnny, Peel and the League united,' as may almost be assumed, he had probably discarded it before his visit to Paris. During the session of 1846 Russell supported Peel in doing away with all duties on the import of corn; but no junction of the two men or their followers occurred. Russell's party, instead of splitting, stayed with him; and neither they nor the ' Peelites,' as the free trade Conservatives were from this time called, seemed content to make the adjustments which fusion would entail. Palmerston, thus lacking any strong incentive to part from his old associates, reluctantly gave up his idea of a compromise between the extremes of protection and free trade. On March 27, he admitted in the House that his conviction was unchanged; but his confession, he wrote Disraeli, was to be regarded as ' one " pitying tear to grace the obsequies " of fixed duty.'[67] There is, indeed, some indication that he reverted to his old policy in May. The Repeal Bill was then before the Upper House; and Lord Bessborough tried to unite anti-free trade peers of both parties on an amendment calling for a fixed duty. But Russell's energy and courage held his party firm. Calling a meeting of Whig peers at Lansdowne House, he announced his invincible determination to resist the mutilation of Peel's bill. Palmerston tersely announced the decision to Hobhouse : ' All unanimous against the Bill and all unanimous not to oppose it.'[68] The pithy sentence suggests that he was much dissatisfied ; and Charles Greville believed that he had supported Bessborough's move in the hope that Russell and the party could be brought to their earlier programme. But if Palmerston was really a participant in the Bessborough ' plot,'[69] he was remarkably successful in covering his tracks.

His return to the Foreign Office followed hard upon the conclusion of the Corn Law debates. The Conservative protectionists, led by Lord Stanley, Lord George Bentinck and the ambitious young Disraeli, were resolved to punish their former leader at all costs. Irish affairs gave the opportunity ; and, on the night of June 29, Peel, ' colder, dryer, more introverted than ever, yet to a close gaze showing the fullest working of a smothered volcano of emotions,'[70] made his farewell speech. It was a speech of peculiar interest to Palmerston ; for it announced that the controversy with the United States concerning the boundary of Oregon had been settled on what were virtually the United States' own terms. There seems little doubt that the imminence of his return to power determined the fashion of his reply. To him, as to Russell and Howick, and perhaps to most of the parliamentary leaders on both sides, the settlement represented another of Aberdeen's weak efforts to avoid trouble at almost any cost.[71] In February, when Russell had listened to a plea from the American minister that he should not attempt to block the settlement, Palmerston had tried to hold him firm. He had begged him not to encourage American ' violence and bluster ' as Aberdeen proposed to do ;[72] and had suggested that American diplomacy had much in common with the methods of ' gentlemen of the road.'[73] But now, in late June, the situation was a very different one. The question was settled for all time ; the Conservative ministry which had made the treaty was giving up the ghost ; Russell was committed to acceptance of its terms ; and Palmerston was almost certainly about to resume charge of England's relations with the

United States. No doubt he would best have served his later reputation had he held his tongue : instead, he chose to pretend that he was pleased. The settlement, he told the House, seemed ' equally favourable to both parties.' [74] Such a statement was extremely politic, whether from the domestic or the diplomatic aspect ; but those who called to mind his attacks on Ashburton must have smiled.

It was obvious that Russell was to be prime minister ; but there were disturbing rumours concerning his cabinet-making and his policies. The bishop of Oxford trembled at the thought that a tradesman and Dissenter (Cobden, of course) might be included in the cabinet, and heard ' whispers of Palmerston and War ; the Whig budget and deficiency.' [75] He must soon have been greatly reassured. The cabinet proved to be Whig and aristocratic to the core, the offices, as Sir William Harcourt later said, being ' parcelled out . . . among Greys, Russells, Eliots—and again, Eliots, Russells, Greys.' [76] Prince Albert pointed out that there was a ' Grey ' section, which included Clarendon, and a ' Russell ' section (stigmatised as ' old women ' by some of their colleagues) which counted Lansdowne, Minto, Auckland and Hobhouse.[77] Reckoned ironically enough as inclining to the ' Greys,' was Palmerston. This time no one seems to have thought of denying him his favourite post. Ellice, according to Lady Palmerston, had been ' sent to Coventry ' ; [78] and Grey (after facing exclusion on Palmerston's account) accepted the Colonial Office on an understanding that the premier would supervise foreign policy.[79] This understanding seems to have satisfied the other ministers ; but it was not quite sufficient for the Court. Clarendon, who, for all his private criticisms, had made Aberdeen's position ' a bed of roses ' in the House of Lords, was informed that the Queen and Prince Albert ' mainly counted on his judgement and influence to make matters go on smoothly abroad.' [80] Perhaps they shared the apprehensions expressed soon after the formation of the ministry by one of Greville's friends :

X—— said Lord John was well disposed to interfere in foreign affairs . . . but what he feared was that he would not find time, and that he would be overwhelmed with the multifarious functions

ALARM IN EASTERN EUROPE

that were heaped upon him . . . and the attendance in the House of Commons, where, for example, he was kept yesterday from twelve in the morning to twelve at night. All this he thinks will be too much for his health and strength, and above all will baffle his good intention of overlooking and controlling the other departments. [81]

But Prince Albert was quite prepared to do a little interfering on his own account :

The Ministers, however, find the Prince in a very different situation from that in which they left him, more prominent, more important, with increased authority. This was the result of Peel's and Aberdeen's administration, and their continual care and attention to all his wishes and the Queen's. [82]

It was not a very pleasant prospect for Palmerston, especially in view of the nervous and suspicious attitude of some of Albert's best friends on the continent.

It is almost a commonplace that the effect of Palmerston's return was to lower the price of foreign securities ; [83] and this has been laid solely to his chauvinism. But there is another explanation to be kept in mind. Already in this year there were premonitory signs of some of the movements which were to convulse Europe in 1848, and give Palmerston his second great opportunity to guide his country through a period of stress and storm. Nesselrode, alarmed at reports that the king of Prussia was planning to grant a constitution to his subjects, voiced his fears of Palmerston to the Russian envoy at Berlin.[84] Aberdeen, he pointed out, had discouraged Frederick William from making so dangerous an experiment, and, for all his ' cajoleries ' of Louis Philippe, had favoured the alliance of the three despotic eastern courts as a support for conservatism in government, of which England might wish to avail herself :

With Palmerston it will be the other way : he wants to see constitutions everywhere. He will be very careful not to discourage the ideas of the [Prussian] king ; *für ihn ist es ein gefundenes Fressen* ; he will encourage and strengthen these ideas . . . By this means he will hope to create a breach in our eastern alliance, which is a thorn in his flesh . . . he will thus attack the vulnerable point in our position, which is Prussia. Our task will be to thwart his desires and work.

A good many people were anxiously regarding the reinstated 'Lord Pumicestone,' and wondering how long it would take him to quarrel with the government of some other Power. The question was answered all too soon in the imbroglio known as the question of the Spanish Marriages.

CHAPTER XVII

THE SPANISH MARRIAGES, THE DEATH OF THE ENTENTE AND THE EFFECT ON CONTINENTAL POLITICS, 1846–1847

LOOKING at the dispute over the ' Spanish Marriages ' is somewhat like seeing Rome : one must do it very superficially if it is not to take an unconscionable amount of time. On the other hand, while the spectacle offered by the dispute had aspects which were extremely picturesque, it was far from edifying. The Spanish queens and their advisers outdid themselves in intrigue and untruthfulness ; the French government, to English eyes at least, offered a shocking exhibition of cynicism and trickery ; while Palmerston, though much less blameworthy in this respect, gave a poor account of himself as a diplomatist. He, so far the daring and the prompt, appeared cautious and dilatory : the expert calculator of chances calculated very ill indeed : the master of diplomatic secrets seemed insufficiently informed : the statesman who was so adept at the game of diplomatic chess suffered checkmate by delivering the Queen (quite literally) into his opponent's hands. Temporarily, then, he was forced to confess defeat : but he found plentiful compensation, too. For the time being he enjoyed the unaccustomed support of his colleagues, his political opponents and his sovereign ; later came opportunities of showing the French government that it must pay a heavy price for the sacrifice of the entente; and later still realisation that the victors would never obtain possession of the spoils. For the Orleans monarchy, in tricking Palmerston, helped to bring about its own downfall.

In the early summer of 1846 the situation with respect to the marriages was extremely delicate. The list of eligible husbands for the young Queen Isabella had to all intents and purposes narrowed down to three ; and to each of these there were objections of the strongest kind. Of Bourbon candidates there remained only two cousins of the Queen, sons of her father's younger brother, Francisco. The elder of these, Francisco, duke of Cadiz, was generally believed by the highly placed and well informed to be unfit for marriage and incapable of parenthood :[1] the younger, Henry, duke of Seville, described as 'a hideous little monster' by one Englishman at least,[2] was detested by the Queen-mother, Christina, for his intimate associations with the Progressive (and Anglophil) party.[3] The situation with respect to the third possible candidate, Prince Leopold of Coburg, cousin to Victoria and Albert, and brother to Louis Philippe's daughter-in-law, the duchess of Nemours, showed how unfortunate it was that no written agreement had been drawn up at Eu.[4] The French, determined as ever to keep their hold on Spain by preventing any prince not of the line of Philip V from sharing Isabella's throne, insisted upon excluding Leopold and treating him as a British candidate. They claimed, too, that in this matter Aberdeen had bound the British government to give the French policy full support, in return for Louis Philippe's refusal to let Isabella marry one of his sons. There were even greater complications regarding the marriage of the Infanta Louisa, or Fernanda as the French called her. Guizot admitted the undertaking given at Eu that she should not marry Montpensier until Isabella had borne children ; but he insisted that this undertaking was merely provisional. It was given, he claimed, only on condition that the British government refused even to admit that Leopold was an eligible suitor, and co-operated with the French in seeing to it that Isabella married a descendant of Philip V. England's failure to do this would release the French king from all promises. Incidentally, the French minister declared that Aberdeen had first suggested the Montpensier marriage. Finally, he insisted (although apparently without notification to the British government until February 1846) that France would be relieved from all undertakings if the marriage of *either* princess to a non-Bourbon prince should become 'probable and imminent.' Aberdeen's recollection of the conversations at the Château d'Eu was very different.[5] He was quite certain that he had never proposed the Montpensier marriage ; and could not remember that he had agreed to co-operate, even in so far as Isabella's marriage was concerned, in excluding the Coburg prince or other non-Bourbons. What was more, the French king's assurance regarding the Infanta's marriage had, to his mind, been absolute, constituting the indispensable condition upon which the British government was willing to allow the Montpensier marriage to take place at all. Prince Albert (and presumably Victoria) admitted that they had promised to support any Bourbon marriage for Isabella which was practicable ; but believed that the Bourbons had ' made themselves *impossible*,' and that ' for Spain, Leopold would be the best person.'[6]

The situation had, in fact, become greatly complicated by French activities, activities which were more or less connected with the virtual certainty of Palmerston's return to power. In December 1845, Guizot had instructed Bresson, his envoy at Madrid (chosen as a man who could be counted on to act with daring in case of emergency) that, should there be serious danger of Leopold's marriage with the Queen, he might at once arrange for her betrothal to a prince of Philip's line, and for Louisa's to Montpensier.[7] This step had been kept quite secret from Peel's government. But, in February 1846, the French ambassador had read to Aberdeen a formal notification that, should the marriage of either Isabella or Louisa to anyone save a descendant of Philip V seem imminent, France would regard herself as released from all promises concerning Montpensier. Aberdeen, characteristically enough, seems to have allowed this notification to pass without protest.[8] In the late spring there had occurred the last developments. At Easter, Palmerston had warned Guizot that the marriage of Montpensier to the Infanta would seem to him (Palmerston) ' nearly as objectionable as his marriage to the Queen.'[9] In May, Queen Christina had offered Isabella's hand to Leopold through his brother, the king consort of Portugal ; and, with the knowledge of Bulwer, the British minister, had conveyed the offer through a British agent.[10] Aberdeen, on learning this, had immediately informed Guizot, and reprimanded Bulwer in sharp terms. Whether, as was strongly suspected later on, this offer constituted a trap set for the British government by Christina and Louis Philippe,[11] it seems impossible to say ; but at the time it was regarded as *bona fide* by the British government and its envoy at Madrid.[12] When Palmerston came into office in the following month no answer from the Coburg family had been received.

Palmerston returned to Downing Street, ill-informed as to what had been taking place,[13] but with the firm resolve to reverse Aberdeen's policy with respect to Spain. His main idea, as Guizot at once suspected, was not so much to decide the question of the marriages as to rebuild British influence at Madrid through British patronage of the ' Progressive ' party there.[14] Having little interest in, or hope for, Leopold,[15] he seems to have been rather indifferent as to the marriages, save on one point. He was resolved, if it should in any way be possible, to prevent the Infanta Louisa from marrying a French prince.[16] It seemed that in order to do this he need only let well enough alone. Bulwer was sure that Christina was eager to have Leopold for a son-in-law, and quite ready to renounce an Orleans marriage for her younger child.[17] Still, Palmerston was not content, as Aberdeen had been, merely to wait and hope. It had been bad enough, he pointed out, for England to face a Family Compact in the eighteenth century ; and such a compact would be even more dangerous now that France had established herself in northern Africa.[18] As for Isabella's marriage, he declared that she and her mother should take their choice of the three candidates.[19] But he believed there were in reality only two, Henry and Leopold. The Queens, he was convinced, would never follow French advice to accept so poor a creature as Cadiz ; nor could England, in the name of common decency, recommend them to do so. And, as between Henry and Leopold, he felt, like Aberdeen, that he must give preference to the Spaniard. A Coburg marriage would provoke a break with France and might prove unacceptable in Spain. Hence Bulwer, who urged that England should bring off the

Coburg marriage and defy the French,[20] was told to follow Aberdeen's policy in so far as the marriage of Isabella was concerned. It must be emphasised that Henry was Palmerston's favourite, in so far as he had any, from the beginning to the end.[21] Once, indeed, he wrote Russell that, in view of Christina's determination, Leopold should consent to share Isabella's throne : [22] once he admitted that he found it difficult to decide that 'any given course' was best. But even the Princess Lieven admitted in the end that he had never supported Leopold ; while his insistence in urging Henry upon the Spanish queens was so constant as to bring many reproaches from Victoria and Bulwer then and later on.[23] What he wished was that Isabella should have Henry for her husband and Leopold for her brother-in-law : only if this arrangement should prove impossible would he be willing to see the positions of the two princes reversed. Either arrangement would, in excluding Montpensier, violate the spirit of the understanding reached at Eu. But Aberdeen, it seemed, had done no more than refrain from objecting to the Infanta's marriage with the Orleans prince (on condition that Isabella had children first); and Palmerston did not consider himself bound. That the Spanish court would yield to persuasion, and the French to reason and 'firmness,' he seems to have been quite sure. Victoria was apparently much of his mind, except in so far as his preference for the Progressives was concerned. Certainly she agreed to his views concerning the qualifications of the candidates, and especially to the virtual elimination of Cadiz.[24] Prince Albert was soon writing of the 'unjust requirements' and 'unreasonable obstinacy' of his French friends.[25]

Palmerston, while still in the early stages of following out his policy, made one of the most flagrant errors of his career as a diplomatist. He erred by writing a most impolitic despatch, and still more by dealing too frankly with the French government. For he furnished Guizot not only with information as to his own views and hopes, but with a weapon which the French minister could use in bringing all those very hopes to nought. What he did was to allow Jarnac, secretary of the French embassy, to take a copy of the first despatch on the Spanish question which he sent to Bulwer at Madrid.[26] In this he specifically ordered Bulwer to abide by instructions received from Aberdeen. After that, he named the three remaining aspirants for Isabella's hand, and announced that England would neither promote nor obstruct the candidature of any one of them. Leopold's name stood first among the three, but there was no indication, either in the despatch or in a letter sent to Bulwer on the same date [27] (July 19), that the order was intended to suggest preference. The despatch wound up with a stinging condemnation of the existing Spanish ministry,—a ministry made up of 'Moderates,' and supported by a notoriously packed Cortes. The despatch was intended for Bulwer's guidance, and only for his eye. According to Palmerston, Jarnac himself immediately pointed out that the latter part would be deeply resented by the Spanish government if any communication of it should be made.[28] Why Palmerston proved so trusting as to place it at the disposal of the French government one can only guess. His declaration that he and Guizot were 'personally upon the most friendly terms, and . . . equally anxious in the main to preserve the *entente cordiale*,' was coupled with a statement that they were playing at cross purposes.[29] Perhaps, as he later said, he was choosing 'the civilest way' of allowing the French to know the line he proposed to take ;[30] but another explanation is quite possible. In all probability he was desirous of marking his return to Downing Street by an act that would be pleasing to Victoria and the Whigs. Bresson had urged Lord Minto, Russell's father-in-law and lord privy seal, to persuade the foreign secretary to deal frankly with Guizot's government ;[31] and Palmerston assented good-naturedly.

Whatever his motive may have been, his action in letting Jarnac have a copy of the despatch to Bulwer came as a godsend to the French government. Despite all their assertions to the contrary,[32] Guizot and his master were not convinced, either before or after reading the despatch, that Palmerston had any intention of urging Leopold's marriage with the Spanish queen.[33] But they had been worried lest their old antagonist should restore British influence at

Madrid by renewed patronage of the Progressive element, and prevent Montpensier from securing the Infanta for his bride.[34] The despatch to Bulwer was precious in two ways. The mention of Leopold as a candidate for Isabella's hand, and the fact that his name happened to precede those of the Spanish dukes, made it just possible to claim that Palmerston had broken the bargain made at Eu in 1845, and thus released France from her undertaking regarding the Montpensier marriage.[35] And Palmerston's condemnation of the existing Spanish government was exactly what the French envoy at Madrid required for persuading the Queen-mother and her ministers to act in conformity with the French plans.[36] Palmerston, misjudging the situation at Madrid,[37] and trusting to Guizot's sense of decency in dealing with a confidential and highly compromising document, had given the French minister an opportunity to score a resounding triumph for himself and for the Orleans dynasty. Guizot had no compunction and no fears. The position of the Whig cabinet seemed to him 'feeble and precarious.'[38] Palmerston, he had already pointed out to Louis Philippe, was practically in chains :

> Jarnac's letter indicates that Palmerston's attitude towards us, while rather undecided, is well disposed and timid. It is the timidity which pleases me. Every one around him is co-operating in exercising surveillance and in restraining him, Lord John, the duke of Bedford, Lord Lansdowne, even his wife. . . .[39]

Of this situation one might make ' *bon ménage.*' Louis Philippe seemed equally confident. They had reason to place confidence in Victoria, and they could make use of King Leopold :

> He is excellently disposed towards us and very anxious for the fall of Ld. Palm., fearing that he might once more make us his dupes. No fear of that ! I shall show him how things stand, and, considering how well disposed Victoria is, I believe he will be able to do a good job. . . .[40]

With a light heart, then, Guizot decided that he could proceed apace with the realisation of his plans, and sent a copy of Palmerston's despatch to Bresson for communication to the Spanish government.[41] Bresson, instructed more than a fortnight earlier to arrange for Isabella's marriage to Cadiz and for the Infanta's to Montpensier, might now do everything [42] but give a ' formal ' promise that the marriages would be simultaneous.[43] That they were departing utterly from the bargain made at Eu; that they were committing a shocking breach of confidence ;[44] that their action was likely to condemn Isabella to a life of degradation or of misery ; that her sudden death might make Montpensier king consort ; not all these things were enough to give the French king and his minister much pause. In less than a month, *i.e.* as soon as consent could be wrung from the unfortunate young Spanish queen,[45] the marriages were arranged, blessed by the packed Cortes, and announced for early celebration to all Europe. If Bulwer is to be believed, the whole affair was of the most repellent nature possible.[46] Queen Isabella, who loathed the idea of marriage with Cadiz, consented to it under pressure and in floods of tears. Her submission was recorded by witnesses stationed for the purpose in adjoining rooms. And there was another aspect which savoured of indecency. The princesses were aged sixteen and fourteen years ; yet in the face of every British protest and appeal,[47] neither marriage could be delayed for a longer period than six weeks.

Louis Philippe bore joint responsibility with his leading minister for most of this ; but there is some ground for the King's suggestion that Guizot was the more to blame.[48] When, before the copy of Palmerston's despatch reached Paris, Bresson had reported discussion between himself and Christina, the Queen-mother, concerning the possibility of simultaneous marriages of the two princesses with a Neapolitan Bourbon and Montpensier, Louis Philippe had insisted that the idea should be formally disavowed.[49] His chief minister apparently urged him to relent, and was transported with delight when he learned from Bresson that simultaneous marriages with Cadiz and Montpensier had been arranged.[50] This is not the place for any assessment of Guizot's political morality ;[51] yet the British reaction, which was of deep significance to Palmerston, cannot be understood unless one understands how the episode appeared in British eyes. When Guizot said in one breath that he was forced into action by Palmerston's unmistakable efforts to promote the Coburg candidacy, and had done no more than give the Queens a free choice of candidates ; and when he added in the next that the Coburg marriage would have taken place but for Palmerston's indiscreet attack on Christina's government,[52] his friends in England hung their heads. When it was known that Jarnac had kept Palmerston in play by talk of joint action in favour of either of the Spanish dukes up to the very last, and that Guizot, on August 28, (the date on which the simultaneous marriages were arranged) had used similar language to the British ambassador, Normanby, his duplicity seemed beyond any limits permissible even in diplomacy.[53] When Normanby reported that Guizot had absolved himself from his promise that the marriages would not be simultaneous by pointing out that the marriage services were to be separate, Lansdowne let the paper fall from his hand in sheer disgust.[54] Guizot's unauthorised and misleading publication of extracts from the despatch of July 19 was not better received. People were not blind to the faults of Palmerston.[55] It seemed that he had been guilty of negligence and tardiness ; that he had been too insistent in urging the acceptance of Seville, that he had shown too great a preference for isolated action as usual, and had tried to undermine French influence at Madrid. There were, perhaps, others than Jarnac who blamed him for failing to reiterate to Guizot his objection to the Infanta's marriage with Montpensier. But, given all this, one thing seemed clear : his course, in comparison with Guizot's, seemed one of transparent honesty.

When Bresson's triumphant message of August 28 arrived at the Tuileries, Guizot and his master believed that they had pocketed the stakes ; but they were soon to find that they had committed a blunder of the gravest kind. They had expected to secure their triumph at the expense only of Palmerston. In the preceding April Guizot had warned him that if any break in the entente should follow his return to Downing Street the whole world would consider him at fault.[56] And Louis Philippe, before the marriages took place, informed Stockmar that the issue, instead of being national, was merely between himself and the British foreign minister.[57] But in aiming at Palmerston the two great promoters of the Spanish marriages had struck England as a whole, the Whigs in particular, and, above all, the Queen. It seems to have been true that in the whole country, as Russell wrote Victoria, there was 'hardly a dissentient voice.'[58] Greville and Aberdeen, between them, managed to moderate *The Times* and even to give it a somewhat pro-French tone.[59] But that was all. Normanby, the British ambassador at Paris, was shocked by such an 'extraordinary piece of trickery.'[60] The Conservatives, for all their wish to smite the government, found no defence for France. Peel, devoted friend to the French king and Guizot, an untiring critic of Palmerston and his policies, declared that he and his friends Graham and Aberdeen were as disgusted as any of the Whig ministers.[61] Aberdeen himself, while making every possible, not to say impossible, apology for Guizot, admitted that the 'breach of engagement' had given him much pain, and endorsed a scathing letter of condemnation written by Victoria.[62] Charles Greville, who had worked so hard to support the Guizot-Aberdeen entente, wrote with loathing of French trickery and of the extinction of 'the small remains of Spanish independence.' 'Certainly,' he added, 'never anything equalled the duplicity and bad faith of the French King and his Minister, and the manner in which we have been treated never can be forgiven or forgotten. . . .'[63] In vain Jarnac persuaded him to spend hours in reading papers at the French embassy and listening to the chargé's arguments; in vain Madame de Lieven and Guizot induced him to go over to Paris and consider all they could tell him of the case. He became much more critical of Palmerston's technique, but little less condemnatory of what the French had done.[64] As for Clarendon, on whom the Queen relied to keep things smooth abroad, he flatly accused of falsehood anyone who charged Palmerston with promoting Coburg's cause, and contemptuously told James Rothschild, sent from Paris to London to make the peace, that Palmerston 'would not walk across the room' to see Guizot removed from power.[65] Russell, not content with a bitter arraignment of the French government's procedure to Jarnac, added a fine tribute to his foreign secretary :

> I cannot but notice, though I will do so very shortly, M. Guizot's accusations against Lord Palmerston. In my opinion he has conducted himself with the greatest moderation and calm reflection throughout this painful transaction. I have the greatest reliance on his sagacious perception of the true interests of his country, and I have the truest satisfaction in constant co-operation with him upon all our foreign relations.[66]

But there was no one who took Palmerston's side more emphatically than Victoria.

What made the Queen so bitter was her utter disillusionment. Only a few days before Guizot had ordered Bresson to proceed with all speed at Madrid, she had written that Palmerston's return to Downing Street made it all the more necessary that Louis Philippe should visit her, and that she hoped to see him frequently. That he and the minister to whom she had been so gracious, and to whom she had reluctantly made concessions in the matter of Prince Leopold's prospects, should proceed to trick her and to force an impossible husband on the young queen of Spain fairly sickened her. It was '*infamous*' ; it was ' beyond *all* belief shameful, and so *shabbily* dishonest.'[67] Not all the arts of the Orleans family served to make her change her mind. When the queen of the French wrote a private letter enlisting Victoria's affection for her ' new child,' the reply was full of reproaches and stiff in every line.[68] When Louis Philippe, not venturing on a direct approach, sat up until four in the morning on three successive nights to write his daughter at Brussels a letter of explanation which would be sent on to Windsor, Victoria wrote what Palmerston joyously called a ' tickler ' in return.[69] And she did it quite on her own account, with no assistance from anyone save the equally enraged Prince Albert. Her tone was made none the sweeter by the fact that the French king, writing in the early morning hours, had made the extraordinary slip of suggesting that she saw things through the '*lunette*' of Palmerston. Indignantly denying this, she set forth her chagrin at having to ' acknowledge before the whole world ' that the behaviour of France was 'altogether contrary to the spirit of our *entente cordiale* and to our former stipulations.' Lord Aberdeen, she added, entirely agreed with her. That England had ever pressed the candidature of Leopold was something which she could ' *absolutely deny.*' She was in a position to '*affirm*' that the British policy had been ' unassailably straightforward and honest.' The letter concluded with a demand :

> I have . . . well considered everything . . . and it is impossible to acknowledge that the King could be released from his word . . . my only consolation is that this project, not being realisable without producing grave complications . . . may yet fall back before it is carried out. . . .

The Queen can scarcely have been mollified by learning from King Leopold (who privately expressed indignation quite comparable to her own) that his queen had been enjoined to let her ' French and Bourbon heart take pride in the noble victory ' by which her sire had ' added the brightest jewel to his crown.' [70]

It was partly, perhaps, the knowledge that he was receiving so much sympathy which enabled the foreign secretary to bear himself with a dignity and restraint which surprised and pleased everyone.[71] Quite typical seems to have been the language which he held to Jarnac, as reported by Guizot :

> This is the most patent act of ambition and political aggrandisement which Europe has seen since the [Napoleonic] Empire. I hope that at Paris they will reflect before going on with it. It is impossible that the relations of the two Courts and the two governments should not be completely altered.[72]

Victoria was especially gratified. It seemed that Palmerston was atoning for his error in backing the duke of Seville by behaving 'most openly and fairly towards France,' and, more still, by his readiness to be ' guided ' by her views.[73] But this is not to say that she appreciated the full range of his activities.

The pheasants at Broadlands had a peaceful time of it during the early autumn weeks ; for their owner had little

THE JOHN-BULL FIGHT OF LOUIS-PHILIPPE

Punch, November 7, 1846

time to think of anything save the Montpensier marriage. Short of helping to stir up a revolution at Madrid, there was nothing he did not do to postpone it, prevent it, or rob it of all political effect. To his envoys at the courts of Spain and all the four great continental Powers a stream of documents went forth.[74] The despatches, highly approved for the most part by Victoria, presented a long series of warnings, protests and appeals. From treaties—that of Utrecht in particular—and from old ordinances of Spanish kings, the foreign secretary drew elaborate arguments to prove the impropriety, the illegality, the danger of the threatened family compact. Over-elaborated and vain as these appeared even to many Englishmen, they were quite in accordance with correct diplomacy. But some of the private letters, to Bulwer in particular, were not so innocent. Bulwer was ordered to renew the British influence at Madrid to the greatest possible extent by patronage of the Progressives. And, if he was to have no traffic with rebels, he was not to discourage such of the Spanish queen's subjects as might plan a revolution on their own initiative. Apparently no harm was done ; but there seems to have been some under cover work. For Russell wrote the Queen that it would be well to leave to the discretion of the foreign minister whatever expenditure of money might seem requisite in Spain. It could be taken for granted that he would not stir up revolt.[75]

Palmerston's exertions were all in vain. His protests at the Tuileries were received by Louis Philippe and Guizot with fervent expressions of injured innocence. How the Spanish government reacted may be judged from a letter written to Bulwer by Queen Isabella's principal minister :

> Allow me to say that the sacred deposit of Spanish independence is not entrusted to the vigilance of any foreign nation. . . .
> The loss of her extensive Dominions abroad and of Gibraltar in her own territory ; the recent destruction of her Fleets in War, and the loss of the greatest part of her Colonies, when at peace, have left remembrances to Spain, which are neither forgotten nor unprofitable.[76]

Hence, on October 10, the two marriages—not ' simultaneous ' of course—were celebrated with great pomp ; and

Bresson wrote that the Queens, the Infanta and the populace were all alike radiant with joy.[77] Confronted with the accomplished fact, the British foreign secretary, actively assisted by Prince Albert,[78] set himself to the task of securing declarations from the other three great Powers that treaty obligations (the Orleans renunciation at Utrecht in particular) automatically disqualified Montpensier's descendants from succession to the Spanish throne.[79] But everywhere he failed.[80] Guizot was apparently holding out tempting inducements to the East, such as that of protecting Prussian commerce south of the Pyrenees. And, what doubtless counted for far more, the eastern courts had no mind to smooth the way for a renewed entente, or to help England's dangerous foreign minister secure a success which would strengthen him at home. Moreover, they were, at this time, just disposing of Cracow, an operation which called for an united eastern front, and for the utmost possible dissonance between the Poles' two former champions. It was easy for them to maintain that, never having recognised Isabella, their hands were tied. Hence Palmerston was left quite alone. He had only the encouragement of the warning sent by Metternich to Guizot : ' One does not with impunity play little tricks with great countries.'[81]

Yet, before the year 1846 was out, and more and more as the year following rolled by, it could be seen that misinformation and miscalculation had by no means been entirely on the side of Palmerston. If Bresson had really seen so many radiant smiles, he did not continue to bask in them long. Public opinion in Spain turned rapidly against the French ; while Isabella, released from the Queen-mother's guardianship, inclined to Bulwer and the more liberal element in the Cortes. And, though she did not seek the annulment of her marriage as Palmerston had hoped, she managed, according to popular report, to annul it in her own way. Palmerston joked about her lovers, and about the ' true spirit of inductive philosophy ' which led her ' to found her conclusions upon a great variety of experiments ' ;[82] but it was the pious Prince Albert who, six months after the marriage, made the most startling comment:

THE OUTCOME OF THE MARRIAGES

The couple have separated, . . . the Queen has her lovers. . . . Her mother, Christine, wanted to press a lover on her, one according to her wish. But the King's father, Old Don Francisco, succeeded in getting one of his party accepted. What will Louis Philippe have to answer for in heaven ![83]

All in all, it was extremely doubtful whether the Spanish marriages had been of any real service to France or to her government. And there was no question that the French sovereign and his favourite minister had done themselves great injury. Thiers and other opposition leaders, in striving to overthrow Guizot, denounced his trickery and his sacrifice of the entente. And part at least of the opposition press, wishing to clear the nation from any stain, inclined to throw blame on the King. In so far as regard for their own safety and for propriety would permit, the journalists exposed Louis Philippe's avarice, his dynastic ambition and his untrustworthiness. The general effect was obviously serious ; and, according to the Princess Lieven, Palmerston went so far as to say that ' Louis Philippe had better look to it that the Spanish marriage did not cost him his throne.'[84] At the moment such speculation must have seemed wild enough ; but it was not to be so very long before Paris mobs were singing their version of the consequences of the break :

> Si le militaire peureux
>   Prend les armes à la canaille,
> Si Louis Philippe heureux
>   Se sauve sous la mitraille ;
> S'il agit en polisson
>   C'est la faute à Palmerston,
> Et bientôt si l'on l'enterre
>   C'est la faute à l'Angleterre. [85]

But no one was really looking ahead to such developments in the autumn of 1846.

Instead of looking forward, men were watching curiously to see what re-adjustments the foreign secretary would make in his, or rather in his country's policy. Even before the marriage had taken place Molé had sounded a note of warning : ' *Mais manet alta mente. Gare aux revanches* !'[86]

Greville expected an alliance with the three eastern courts ; [87] and Metternich was sure that Palmerston would turn violently against the French. 'Lord Palmerston,' he wrote, 'makes arrows from every kind of wood, and he is a passionate and audacious archer.' [88] But those who counted upon any sudden and sensational change were very much at fault ; for Palmerston, officially at any rate, kept his head. His attitude was well portrayed in a letter which he sent in January 1847 to Bloomfield, his ambassador at St. Petersburg :

> Of course it is our object and interest to be upon good terms with France. England and France have many interests, commercial and political, all over the world, which are perpetually coming into contact; and a good understanding between Paris and London is necessary, in order to prevent that contact from degenerating into collision. But as to trusting the French Government . . . I think everybody in England have now had their eyes sufficiently opened to prevent them from falling into that mistake.[89]

And his actions well bore out his words. When fresh trouble developed in Tahiti—trouble which might easily have put the British public in a rage—Guizot was twice warned privately and unofficially against the danger of allowing the former irritation to revive.[90] When Normanby, whom Palmerston had sent as ambassador to France, took offence at what he regarded as reflections cast by Guizot on his veracity, the foreign secretary, to his envoy's great disgust, refused to make a serious issue out of the affair :

> The only thing for you to do is to stand your ground, . . . Guizot would never do anything which could be deemed an apology ; . . . we have published to all Europe that we believe you, and not him ; . . . It is always desirable to avoid making anything depend upon a foreign Government or a foreign Minister doing or saying any particular thing as a concession, unless one is prepared to go to all extremities. . . . There is no reason why you and he . . . should not do business again together as before ; . . .[91]

All appearances of ill feeling were to be avoided studiously. Later there were even cases—such as in the affairs of Portugal and the Argentine—where Palmerston felt it necessary to co-operate with Guizot. On the other

THE ANNEXATION OF CRACOW

hand, he no longer cared to preserve even the outward semblance of the entente. This was made quite evident in November 1846, at the time when danger of fresh trouble over Tahiti arose, and well before the quarrel between Normanby and Guizot. Austria furnished an opportunity through her annexation of Cracow.

Palmerston's official attitude in this affair showed not only cool detachment where the French government was concerned, but a much more tolerant bearing toward the three eastern Powers. In 1836, when Cracow had merely been occupied, he had outdone himself in recrimination and reproach. In 1846, when Russia, irritated by Polish plots, encouraged Austria to swallow the little republic whole, in clear defiance of the Vienna treaty, his tone was comparatively mild. Privately, indeed, he denounced the action of Cracow's three ' protectors ' as ' an abominable shame . . . executed by the most hollow pretences and the most groundless assertions,' and as an attempt to ' outdo Louis Philippe ' in their contempt for treaties.[92] A speech which he made later at the Mansion House was recognized by the Polish refugees through the presentation of a medal of Czartoryski, eulogistically and gratefully inscribed.[93] But, in his official communications, Britain's great guardian of oppressed peoples and the obligations of treaties surprised and delighted the Russian court. Nesselrode, happy in what he regarded as the first real success achieved by the three eastern governments since the advent of the Orleans dynasty in France,[94] had expected to receive ' a sheet of paper labelled protestation ' from London and Paris.[95] And, in view of the threatening language which the British Foreign Office had used to Austria and Prussia before the event,[96] he had looked for a communication that would be typically and detestably Palmerstonian. But the protestation which arrived from London emanated from the British government alone, and was, as its author himself pointed out, ' as civil & moderate ' as it could be made.[97] Nesselrode was charmed :

> Palmerston's protest is as moderate as it can be, and Cracow has not re-established the entente cordiale. . . . I confess that this result surpasses my expectations.[98]

The Russian chancellor went on to promise that Palmerston should not be left in ignorance of the appreciation felt at St. Petersburg of his '*bons procédés*.' Had Nesselrode but known it, there were other '*bons procédés*' for which he might have thanked the British foreign minister.[99] When the Russian and Austrian envoys called at Downing Street to request that the speech from the throne at the opening of parliament in January 1847 should contain no specific condemnation of their courts, and to explain that such condemnation would make it impossible for them to attend, he was all for giving way to them. 'Their absence,' he wrote Russell, 'might be turned to account by those who may wish to represent us as on bad terms with the three Powers.' It was Russell and the cabinet who decided that public reproof must be administered.

This change in Palmerston's attitude doubtless arose in the main from his desire to secure the support of the three eastern courts in depriving the Montpensier marriage of all international significance ; but he must have been gratified in observing that it embarrassed and even weakened the French king and his favourite minister. Guizot, who apparently hoped to eat his entente cake and yet keep some of it, had suggested a joint protestation from the French and British governments. Palmerston's answer, that the British government had already acted on its own account, was not only chilling but ominous.[100] Not even French jubilation over the Spanish marriages could conceal the fact that the Orleans monarchy, deprived of its only friend among the Powers, was for the moment impotent in international affairs. Since it dared not remain so, it had no choice but to seek reconciliation with the eastern Powers, and pay the price of abandoning any liberalism in its foreign policy. It was a dangerous proceeding at a time when liberalism was resurgent at Paris. It became more dangerous when, with the passing of the months, Palmerston re-emerged as the champion of liberalism in Switzerland and Portugal.

Palmerston found Portugal a sore trial in these years. Braganzas would be Braganzas ; Coburgs would be

THE 'LIBERAL' QUEEN OF PORTUGAL

Coburgs ; and Maria of Portugal had been married since 1836 to Ferdinand of Coburg, cousin of Victoria and Prince Albert. Maria, once represented as the hope of her more liberal subjects, had been behaving in a manner to win the full approval of her despotic uncle, Miguel.[101] By the autumn of 1846, all but the barest pretence of constitutional government had come to an end ; and once more a revolutionary junta at Oporto, supported by liberals and viewed sympathetically by the Miguellites, was making armed resistance to the throne. The Queen's government repelled Palmerston as much by its cruelty and bad faith as by its corruption and its tyranny. Forty revolutionary officers who laid down their arms on promise of being accorded the honours of war were sentenced to living death in Angola. And to persuade Maria to change her policy seemed impossible.[102] Ferdinand seems to have felt at times that his wife went too far ; but the German ' tutor,' Dietz, who had accompanied him to Lisbon, was said to give her the worst possible advice and to enjoy her fullest confidence. Rumour had it, too, that she was very susceptible to French influence.

Thanks to England's old ties with Portugal, and to the new ties between the Braganzas and the Coburgs (Portuguese and British), Palmerston had to do violence to his feelings by protecting the person, and consequently the sovereignty, of the erring Queen. As foreign minister in the Grey and Melbourne ministries, he had made England more than ever responsible for upholding the Portuguese government ; and neither a republic nor another aspirant to the crown could be thought of. He really could not help to place Miguel—now living in London in retirement and poverty—upon the throne ; and any other change of sovereigns would arouse the opposition of the other four great Powers and Spain. He could not even allow another state to intervene unasked ; since England would thereby resign her position as Portugal's protector, and default on her treaty obligation to defend the *de facto* Portuguese government against outside attack. And his task of dealing with Maria was greatly complicated by the attitude of his own sovereign.[103] His aims and hers were very much the same ; but, when it came to methods, a sharp divergence was at once in evidence. Victoria, though feeling that a constitution was 'an unfortunate thing in those Southern countries,' was quite ready to admit that, once granted, it must be observed. She regarded Maria's course as 'unconstitutional and unsafe'; and was willing that her ministers should urge a compromise with the 'Opposition,' a return to constitutional methods, and the inauguration of administrative reforms. But to her mind persuasion, and tactful persuasion, was the only method which could with any propriety be employed. Loath to believe any harm of 'her near and dear relations,' and always imbued with a sense of the sacredness of royalty even at its worst, Victoria could scarcely tolerate the fact that sharp admonitions were delivered by Southern, the British chargé at Lisbon, and that some sympathy with the rebel cause was displayed by Palmerston. She especially disliked the tone of some of his communications with Colonel Wylde, who was sent on special mission to Oporto and Lisbon.

Since Palmerston believed from long experience of Portugal that persuasion was wasted there unless backed up by the 'perspective' of force,[104] and since he felt that persons who rebelled against tyranny and cruelty should receive some marks of British sympathy, he was at odds with Victoria concerning British diplomatic activities at Oporto and Lisbon even while he was supposedly accepting her 'guidance' regarding the Spanish marriages. When he warned Maria and Ferdinand that they were courting destruction by retaining cruel, reactionary and corrupt ministers, and by dissolving and packing the Cortes, Victoria complained that he was persisting in that policy of supporting particular parties in other countries which had always been so fatal to British 'influence.' 'These peremptory and dictatory notes,' she wrote, 'these constant complaints, produce the worst and most unfortunate effect.'[105] The first weeks of 1847 saw the issue between British sovereign and minister clearly defined. Victoria's idea of correct procedure had been carried out in the original instructions given to Wylde.[106] On reaching Oporto he was merely to declare that Maria had promised to dismiss the reactionary ministers who were held responsible for her worst acts, and to return to constitutional government as soon as the rebels had submitted to her authority. He was then to warn the insurgents that they would incur the indignation of the British government if they refused to lay down arms in view of their queen's promises. But Palmerston, in writing Wylde, on January 26, took a very different tone.[107] Wylde was to 'negotiate' between the two sets of authorities at Oporto and Lisbon, and to do so only on condition that 'formal and positive' assurances concerning the treatment of the rebels were given by Maria and Ferdinand. These, thought Palmerston, should include promises of half pay for rebel officers temporarily retiring from the country, and abstention from the seizure of property belonging to civilians who also submitted to temporary banishment. Wylde was to explain to the insurgents that this offer of 'mediation' was all his government could do on their behalf, and that, should they continue to resist, Britain would deplore, but would not be able to avert, the evils they would bring upon themselves. Palmerston added for Wylde's benefit:

> We certainly think that it is the fault of the Court which has brought on the insurrection, but we take no part . . . except as mediators to put an end to it.

Windsor was scandalised; and Prince Albert, now well established as Victoria's *alter ego*, at once administered sharp reproof:

> The Queen of Portugal had addressed herself to her old ally and represented, that it was a prevalent opinion in Portugal that the resistance of the Rebels and consequent immense loss of lives and money . . . was to a great degree owing to the current impression that England wished well to the cause of the Rebels. . . . The language of the Morning Chronicle and the bearing of Mr. Southern amply justify such an impression. The Queen begged that before she was forced to attack Oporto . . . her old Ally should . . . declare to the Rebels, that she *does not* approve of their proceedings. . . .
> We thought you would be entirely justified as Minister of England to comply with that request and you would be anxious to seize this opportunity to prove that you do not sympathise with the insurgents as is believed, particularly if you could gain at the same time those

objects which alone *ought* to be of interest to England and to you, namely the Queen's immediate return to Constitutional Govt. the security that the Cabrals will not be restored to power and the safety of the Commercial town of Oporto.[108]

Instead there was talk of '*negotiation*,' of a royal ' pledge,' of amnesties, immunities and pensions, of the manner in which England would '*deplore*' further resistance and '*pity*' vanquished insurgents. Russell took Prince Albert's side; and Palmerston, having gained some slight concessions, gave way in so far as immediate instructions were concerned.[109]

The displeasure of his queen, and the fact that her willingness to see the insurgents severely punished must have been known at Lisbon, made Palmerston's task more difficult; but he stuck to his guns. He directed Sir George Seymour, appointed minister to Portugal just at this time, to explain to Maria and her advisers that ' a throne whose stability rests on the point of the bayonet ' had ' a very ticklish and uncertain basis '; and that they could expect no support from England ' to help them to continue a system of misgovernment.'[110] To Russell he pointed out that to pronounce judgment on the insurgents would be ' a very unusual measure for the British government . . . and . . . much more after the fashion of Austria and Russia.'[111] He was willing to urge them to submit, but only if and when Maria made specific promises to correct her errors and forbear revenge. Maria hardened her heart; and comminatory notes continued to pass from London to Lisbon. The foreign secretary had the satisfaction of knowing that the bulk of cabinet, parliament, and public supported him. Russell, while inclined to caution in so far as diplomatic action was concerned, wrote in terms as shocking to Victoria as those employed by Palmerston :

> The Queen [Maria] by suspending all the safeguards of Freedom . . . has outraged public opinion. . . . Recent events have exhibited a spirit of tyranny and cruelty in the decrees and acts of the Portuguese Ministers without a parallel in any part of Europe. . . . It would be impossible to support such atrocities by British arms without bringing disgrace on the British name. Either some security for Good Government must be given by a change of Ministers, or England must declare that she cannot attempt mediation with any hope of success.[112]

Fortified by such endorsement, Palmerston dashed off another letter to Seymour which was sadly at variance with their sovereign's ideas of propriety :

> If the Queen fears Don Miguel, she must make haste to make up matters with the Junta, . . . If Portugal is to be governed despotically and by sword and bayonet, a man is as good as a woman for such purpose, and it matters little whether the despot is called by one Christian name or another. Pray make this very civilly to be understood by the King and Queen.[113]

And still the Portuguese queen hardened her heart against making terms with the insurgents ; while British merchants complained of the damage to their trade.

And Maria in some degree prevailed. Slowly and reluctantly, in the spring of 1847, her tormentor found himself forced into a most uncongenial line of policy. In the first place, he had to adopt the idea of joint action with France and Spain.[114] He and Russell had more than once rejected it when suggested by the Portuguese ministers and by Guizot, maintaining that the Quadruple Alliance of 1834 had been fully executed, and that circumstances had so changed in the course of thirteen years that not even the 'spirit' of the alliance could be invoked. But now he altered his stand, for reasons which he explained later to the House.[115] The Spanish government was determined to intervene at Maria's invitation ; and, so long as the invitation was extended, England could not object. But Spanish intervention, if not controlled, would either establish Maria in her despotism, or produce such anarchy and chaos as would be fatal to British trade. The only policy, then, was to combine with Isabella's government, and to mollify the French by admitting them to a sort of sleeping partnership. The idea was distasteful, since England might have to aid Maria against some of those very persons ' by whose exertions, devotion, and sacrifices she was placed upon the throne.'[116]

But its adoption solved the main problem, the problem of securing 'formal and positive' guarantees that Maria would grant amnesty and the restoration of constitutional government. Russell fully agreed that the demand for such guarantees should be the basis of the agreement with Spain and France;[117] Victoria, obviously reluctant, gave her consent. And fortune favoured Palmerston. At Madrid there came to power a new ministry of liberal tendencies, indisposed to help Maria save in agreement with England: at Lisbon morale was low, food short, and money so scarce that Maria was advised to pawn her jewels. As Prince Albert said, she felt 'the knife at her throat.'[118] Thus the agreement was made, with England in pronounced control, able to dictate to Maria or to the junta at Oporto as occasion might require. It was the junta which had to be coerced.[119] Maria accepted the terms of the three governments; the insurgents held out; and British forces played a prominent part in defeating them.

Successful and true to his convictions as he really was, Palmerston had to show some of his fellow-countrymen that he was still a liberal. Prince Albert saw good omen in the fact that this was the first time a foreign Power had 'intervened in *internal* affairs in Portugal, in favour of the crown';[120] the radicals in parliament threatened the ministry by joining a protectionist assault on the foreign secretary's anti-liberal policy.[121] But they could hardly have done so with any conscience had they been able to read his letters to Seymour:

> Now then comes the time for keeping a tight hand on the Portuguese Government, as to the faithful and immediate execution of the four conditions, which they must not, under any pretence whatever, evade. . . . What we have intended to do, and what the Portuguese Government is pledged to us to do, is to transfer from the field of battle to the floor of Parliament the conflict of political parties in Portugal.[122]

When Maria showed herself restive under the 'tight hand,' he persuaded Victoria and Prince Albert to admonish her.[123] No less than in the days of the Grey and Melbourne ministries did he feel that he was making his country the proud champion of constitutional government on the continent. Thus, to the House on July 5, 1847:

> Our duty—our vocation—is not to enslave, but to set free; and I may say, without any vain-glorious boast, or without great offence to any one, that we stand at the head of moral, social, and political

civilization. Our task is to lead the way and direct the march of other nations. I do not think we ought to goad on the unwilling, or force forward the reluctant; but when we see a people battling against difficulties and struggling against obstacles in the pursuit of their rights, we may be permitted to encourage them with our sympathy and to cheer them with our approbation; and even, if occasion require, to lend them a helping hand, and bear them up against the difficulties that have beset them.[124]

Maria and her friends might still, as they did, evade their promises, demand Seymour's recall, and satisfy their resentment by discrimination against British trade.[125] Victoria might still complain of ' the taking up of party politics in foreign countries.'[126] But Palmerston stood strong in the faith, in the support of the majority of the cabinet and in the growing admiration of John Bull. It was seen that in Portugal he had achieved some measure of success; he was about to secure far more renown by intervention in the affairs of Switzerland.

CHAPTER XVIII

THE PRELUDE TO THE REVOLUTIONS OF 1848

ALL things considered, Palmerston did not come off so badly in his dealings with the affairs of Spain and Portugal ; but in 1847 it pleased certain of his adversaries to depict his own and his country's positions in very gloomy terms. Metternich, with unconcealed satisfaction, wrote a memorandum on the subject :

> Abandoned by France and defeated on every diplomatic field, England now finds herself alone and paralysed in face of the continental Powers. All her resources are inadequate for the purposes of her government, since she cannot make war for any of the ends which she pursues. She did not dare to do it when she had France at her side and could count upon allies in every European country. To-day, if she threw down the gauntlet to anyone, she would force France to take sides ; and there is no doubt as to which side France would take.[1]

Whether Palmerston attempted to conceal or to exploit the break-up of the entente he would still be powerless. Nesselrode, while showing less animus, was happily convinced that the three eastern Powers need take no account of Britain's adventurous foreign minister.[2] In England there was at least uneasiness. Charles Greville ' took the opportunity of pouring a broadside ' into Lord Lansdowne ' about the management of foreign affairs.' He had been assured by Aberdeen that ' nothing could exceed the abhorrence in which Palmerston was held all over Europe.'[3] But despite the pessimists and critics the foreign secretary seemed quite unconcerned by his country's or his own predicament. As he had written Melbourne some months earlier, the unfriendliness of any foreign Power was to him only a 'temporary inconvenience,' which the pursuit of British interests sometimes rendered unavoidable.[4] He could not, for example, copy Aberdeen by making ' English agents everywhere . . . subservient to the French.'[5] But that did not mean that he was indifferent to French hostility. He proceeded to meet this ' temporary inconvenience ' by urging extensive preparations for a possible conflict. And he was soon to show Prince Metternich that in England's case isolation did not necessarily involve impotence.

To be prepared against invasion, Palmerston had written Russell, in October 1845, is ' like an umbrella on a fine day. If you take it you are sure not to want it & if you leave it at home you are certain to be drenched before you get home again.'[6] He was merely paraphrasing language which he had used in the House of Commons four months earlier : ' There was no complete security for friendly relations between different countries, except in a state of mutual defence.[7] The contention was, of course, no more his special property than the very commonplace analogy ; but he became, from this time on, its most prominent and untiring advocate among Englishmen. He had, in fact, for years been interested in providing for England's security, though not necessarily by increase of armaments. Seven years before, he had suggested an agreement with another Power [8] which would have involved some limitation of naval armaments. In that case it was Russia which he had in mind ; but the clouds he watched most anxiously were nearly always over France.

Many a public man in England shared his anxiety during the middle 'forties.[9] When the dispute over Tahiti, in 1844, threatened an outbreak of hostilities, it seemed to many that England would be an easy prey. It was asserted, even publicly, that the defences of the south coast were utterly inadequate ; that dockyards and arsenals would fall at the first raid ; and that invading columns might reach the capital itself. And, since winds and tide had largely been conquered by steam power, men believed that raids or an invasion might come at any time. French hostility seemed as inveterate under Orleans as under Bonapartist rule ; and Napoleon had lacked, not only steam, but the system of strongly fortified harbours which Louis Philippe was building up. England's oracle on such matters, Wellington, demanded insistently that precautions should be taken without loss of time. It was owing mainly to his influence that Peel's ministry undertook the construction of new defensive works.[10] But parliament and public were as much affected by the words of Palmerston :

> France . . . has now a standing army of 340,000 men . . . and, in addition to that, 1,000,000 of the National Guard . . . competent . . . to take the internal duty, . . . and to set free . . . the regular force . . . if France were a country separated from our own by an impassable barrier . . . I should say this was a matter with which we had no concern. But . . . the Channel is no longer a barrier. Steam navigation has rendered that which was before impassable by a military force nothing more than a river passable by a steam bridge. . . . I venture to state that no country in Europe is in such a state of defencelessness as England. . . .[11]

So much was public opinion gradually aroused that Russell and his ministers arrived in power, in the summer of 1846, to find the matter of security a pressing one. Wellington, still gravely alarmed, turned to them of necessity, and was perhaps agreeably surprised. The traditional friends of France and friends of peace showed more energy than had the heirs of Pitt and Castlereagh in strengthening the coast defences and the Channel fleet.[12] This development doubtless owed something to the boasts of Louis Philippe that he had been ready to attempt invasion in 1844.[13] But it also had some connection with the fact that Palmerston's influence in the cabinet was second only to the premier's.

One vision occupied his mind—the vision of a French expeditionary force capturing England's dockyards and harbours from the rear, and advancing to London.[14] For what could the few thousand disposable British regulars do to bring it to a halt ? No doubt he sometimes exaggerated his alarm in order to secure the more effect ; but to some degree it was unquestionably genuine. It appeared with monotonous frequency in letters and memoranda of the most private sort. Quite typical is this passage from a memorandum of more than three thousand words, forwarded

THE APOSTLE OF 'PREPAREDNESS'

to Russell in December 1846, when the feeling roused by the Spanish marriages was particularly strong :

> It may confidently be affirmed that neither England nor any other first-rate power ever stood in such a condition of comparative military weakness as that in which the United Kingdom (to say nothing of our foreign possessions) is now placed . . . the French nation remembers the Nile, Trafalgar, the Peninsula, Waterloo, and St. Helena, and would gladly find an opportunity of taking revenge. . . . In regard to naval force, France may be said to be for present purposes on a par with us . . . in regard to her land forces, she has a war establishment in time of peace. . . .[15]

In case of war, he went on, the French fleet in the Channel might temporarily be superior. In a single night a crossing might be made, and debarkation points established for the hundred thousand troops which Louis Philippe and Guizot could so easily spare. Twenty to forty thousand could be pushed across for the initial blow.

Suggestions for meeting the French peril reached the prime minister from various members of the cabinet ; but there seems to have been no one so prolific of them as Palmerston.[16] Even in Peel's time he had pressed military reforms upon the government, and demanded that the Admiralty should call in ' the most scientific men ' to aid those of practical experience in designing ships.[17] Now he urged the rapid execution of the defence projects which had been approved, and offered suggestions of his own. He pointed out that the store of ' percussion muskets ' had fallen much too low ; begged that the central arsenal for the nation's munitions should be located well inland ; and concerned himself with the adaptation of merchant ships to warlike purposes. But there was one measure to which he always gave first place, and which he pressed insistently from first to last—the creation of a great militia force. He could not agree with those who wished to concentrate on the augmentation of the fleet ; for he felt that naval engagements, even in home waters, would never be decisive :

> The real danger is at home, quite at home, at the heart of the Empire, in our dockyards, and in London, by the landing of a French army on our southern coast. . . . The landing of a hundred thousand

would be the conquest of the country, or at least the submission of England to conditions of peace which would reduce her thenceforward to the condition of a Secondary Power. . . .[18]

It was 'nearly sure' that naval forces would be unable to prevent this ; and any real augmentation of the regular army was impossible. The addition even of 10,000 men to England's handful of home troops would put too great a strain on the government's income, besides arousing resentment and distrust. At half the cost there could be organised a militia of at least 100,000 men, recruited by ballot and enlistment, trained yearly, and liable for service anywhere within the island at any time. Nearly all the leaders of both great parties were agreed that the militia should be made into an effective force ; but they hesitated before obstacles which he brushed aside. If a measure embodying his scheme should alienate some of the Whigs' customary friends, he would take the risk of carrying it by agreement with the protectionists. And if objections should be made upon financial grounds (the government was facing a large deficit at this time), surely 'almost any expedient' was to be preferred to public confession that Englishmen 'were too poor and too distressed to defend the country.' Untiringly he drove his project home, freely criticising the more cautious proposals of the premier and secretary at War, and urging the cabinet to make haste at any cost.

Fortunately for English pockets, his fellow ministers refused in the end to be convinced.[19] The prospect of having to raise the income tax from sevenpence to a shilling had a sedative effect upon the members of the cabinet ; and Cobden's virulent abuse of the duke of Wellington[20] and other apostles of preparedness made them increasingly fearful of the effects of a militia bill upon the radicals. As Sir Charles Wood, the chancellor of the Exchequer, pointed out, the 'very best friends' of the ministry in the larger towns included the Quakers and peace societies.[21] And even Palmerston was temporarily reassured by improvements made in forts and ships.[22] Hence the militia bill hung fire, and talk of the French peril subsided by degrees until the revolutions of 1848 concentrated the attention of all the Powers on continental constitutions and

THE SONDERBUND

boundaries. But fresh alarms occurred from time to time ; and Palmerston eagerly made use of them to press his darling scheme. He met nothing save fresh disillusionment, disillusionment which he confessed to Russell in February 1851 :

> I am well aware that it is almost as difficult to persuade the people of this country to provide themselves with the means of defence as it would be for them to defend themselves without those means, and that although our internal conditions may still be 'the envy of surrounding nations' yet we have neither 'hearts resolved, nor hands prepared, the blessings we enjoy to guard.' [23]

But for him disillusionment was not defeat. He stood ready at any minute to place England's 'umbrella' in her reluctant hand. The safeguarding of his country and the suppression of the slave trade, he was wont to say in later years, had become the most abiding of all his aims. But he was never satisfied that England should merely be safe. Before the year 1847 had reached its end, he pained Metternich, Nesselrode and especially Guizot by executing a diplomatic coup in connection with the affairs of Switzerland.

In 1846 and 1847, 'Swizzerland,' as Palmerston always spelled it, enjoyed quite unaccustomed prominence in Europe's *haute politique*. Put very roughly, the principal issue was as to whether the majority of the cantons, Protestant in religion and liberal in politics, should be allowed to use force against the Sonderbund, a league of seven cantons formed in defiance of the constitution, and for the protection of conservatism and Catholicism.[24] What gave the affair particular significance was the fact that it involved a clash between liberal and conservative forces ; and that similar forces were approaching a conflict in the great states which bordered Switzerland on every side. The hospitality shown by the Swiss to political refugees aroused fears on the part of neighbouring governments that revolutionary movements in the lands under their rule would be encouraged and aided from across the Swiss border. And Palmerston's activities were also of special interest. It was not only that he scored a diplomatic victory against all four great continental Powers ; not only that his diplomatic skill, seemingly impaired in 1846, was fully in evidence again. The striking feature was that he achieved his customary aims by reversing his customary methods. What Europe had come to expect of him was set forth by Count Ficquelmont, that astute diplomatist who sat with Metternich in the inner council of the Austrian government:

No country has, for a long time, been so jealous of its influence as England. No minister has, for a long time, exercised that influence so actively as Lord Palmerston. . . . The Tory party took as the basis of its political action the principle of non-intervention. . . .

Lord Palmerston frankly gave up this policy, which he found too timid for England's pride. . . . He has not ceased to intervene . . . declaring this intervention as a right appertaining to England.

To supply a motive for exercising this right Lord Palmerston added to a policy based on interests one founded upon doctrines and principles. . . .[25]

Ficquelmont overlooked the fact that Palmerston could sometimes best follow out his ' doctrines and principles ' in the rôle of a non-interventionist.

Trouble between conservative and liberal elements had been brewing for some years in the majority of the twenty-two Swiss cantons. The liberals first took the offensive, demanding constitutional changes that would make the government at once more democratic and more centralised, and a wholesale expulsion of the Jesuits. Politico-religious clashes occurred ; and, in 1842, the seven most conservative and Catholic cantons formed a league, or Sonderbund, for the protection of their rights. Since this league was both unconstitutional and a threat to Switzerland's rather feeble national unity, twelve liberal cantons, led by the Bernese ' radical,' Ochsenbein, decided that it must be dissolved. In July 1847, the federal Diet voted the dissolution ; in August it decided that the constitution should be revised ; in September it took up a measure for the expulsion of the Jesuits. At the end of October, the deputies of the Sonderbund cantons, having vainly demanded the disarmament and disbanding of the federal troops, left the Diet. The country was obviously on the verge of civil war, a war in which the twelve cantons, which regarded themselves as constituting the old Diet, would almost certainly be victorious.

This prospect gave rise to a surprising amount of excitement at the great European capitals. It was natural, of course, that Metternich, fearing repercussions in the Austrian dominions and Italy, and strongly on the Catholic side, should resolve to save the Sonderbund. But the panic which the king of Prussia showed in a letter to Victoria seems curious, even when one remembers that the king was Frederick William IV :

> . . . there, in Switzerland, a party is becoming victorious ! ! ! which, notwithstanding the exercise of Christian charity, can only be called '*Gottlos und Rechtlos.*' . . . For Germany, the saving of Switzerland from the hands of the Radicals is *simply* a *vital question.* If they are victorious there, in Germany likewise torrents of blood will flow; I will answer for that. . . . Thousands of emigrated malefactors wait only for a sign (which their comrades and allies in Germany will not be backward in giving) to pour forth beyond the German frontier. . . .[26]

That all three eastern courts were prepared to support the Sonderbund there was no doubt : the uncertain factor was the government of France. For Guizot's dilemma was painful. Both because isolation was dangerous, and because the more liberal elements in France were the ministry's bitter enemies, he and his master would readily have joined the eastern courts in a diplomatic, and if necessary armed, intervention on behalf of the seven cantons of the Sonderbund. But to leave England and Palmerston alone, alone to champion the liberal cause in Europe by supporting the liberal Swiss Diet, was to court trouble both at Paris and in the Alps. The obvious thing was to obtain concerted action by all five Powers. This was the plan which Guizot urged for months upon the British government.

The curious thing about Palmerston's part in the whole Sonderbund affair is that he received credit at the time, and has received it ever since, for a shrewd manipulation of the circumstances which he virtually denied in parliament.[27] What he did, if contemporaries and historians are right, was to prevent the intervention of the Powers until the twelve cantons had subdued the seven by force of arms ; and then to insist that Europe should recognise the accomplished fact. Thus the Sonderbund was dissolved, the Jesuits expelled, and the constitution revised, in defiance of the other four great Powers, and because Palmerston so willed. If this interpretation is correct, he was brilliantly successful in three things : in persuading Guizot that his professed readiness to co-operate with the other Powers was perfectly sincere ; in encouraging the Diet to attack the Sonderbund ; and in calculating the time it would take the Diet's army to do its work.

There is much reason for believing that he deserved all the credit he received. He certainly delayed all concerted action among the Powers until the Sonderbund had been subdued ;[28] though he later explained most plausibly to parliament that he had merely been holding out for terms more equitable to the twelve cantons.[29] It is even probable that he encouraged Ochsenbein to attack. True, his official despatches[30] contained an emphatic warning that the Diet should avoid hostilities,[31] and offered no trace of his alleged advice to ' go ahead, provided that it showed itself prudent.'[32] But there was a suggestive postcript in a private letter which he sent to the secretary of legation, Peel, on November 17 :

> If the Diet take Friburg and make themselves afterwards masters, bad weather and want of money will probably suspend further operations, and both parties may be in a better mood for amicable arrangement of their differences.[33]

Peel was supposedly the person who advised the Diet's chief general to '*finir vite*' ;[34] and Ochsenbein may have obtained secret encouragement both from him and from England's special and very liberal envoy, Lord Minto. As for Palmerston's timing, he wrote Lansdowne, on November 10, that he doubted whether the contest would be ' very hard or very long ' ;[35] while Guizot, by his own confession, expected that the resistance of the Sonderbund would be ' strong and long.'[36]

Whatever the British secretary's deserts, his success resounded through Europe. Nesselrode held him responsible for the danger to Switzerland's neighbours which the existence of such 'a permanent centre of revolution and communism' would entail.[37] Metternich, calling attention to the fact that Europe's arch interventionist had had the impertinence to invoke the principle of non-intervention in order to prevent Switzerland's great neighbours from providing for their own security, declared it doubtful whether 'history would record a second example of a political game comparable to that of Lord Palmerston.'[38] Barante, summing up French sentiment, admitted that Guizot's foe had triumphed by 'making game of everyone.'[39] In quiet contentment, Palmerston allowed himself the luxury of drafting a sarcastic despatch to the Austrian chancellor :

> I have to observe that His Highness has misunderstood the opinion which is prevalent in England when he supposes that opinion to be that *Austria* is making common cause with *France* in regard to the affairs of Italy and Switzerland. On the contrary the opinion is that *France* has been making common cause in those affairs with Austria, as far as public opinion in France will allow the French Government to go, and that on the other hand Austria has sided with France against England in the question respecting the application of the Treaty of Utrecht to the right of succession of the descendants of the Duke of Montpensier to the throne of Spain.[40]

His success seemed to him a neat piece of revenge. He could hardly foresee that Beust would write years afterwards: 'The bankruptcy of the Metternich system took place neither in Vienna in the days of March [1848], nor in Paris, but in Switzerland in the previous year.'[41]

The 'devil's son' was at work again, and very much the same person that he had been ten or fifteen years before. For a man of sixty-three, who had lived at the centre of politics and society for forty years, his vitality was remarkable. Baron Bunsen, the Prussian minister, could never forget how Palmerston once took him from Osborne to London, steering a boat through an uncomfortably rough sea, and dashing to town in a special train, furnished by a reluctant company at his own risk.[42] In January 1849, in the midst of what to most men would have been an intolerable load of labour and anxiety, he shrugged away an inquiry about his health with the casual reply : 'I . . . had been a little overworked ; but what official man is not ? '[43] All who knew him realised that he took virtually no rest. He was able now to visit Broadlands at more frequent intervals, since the railway had reached Romsey. But even there he slaved incessantly. Work all the morning, an orange instead of lunch, a ride to keep him fit, and then more work—such was his customary day.[44] To Broadlands not only diplomatists but place hunters followed him ; and there are delightful stories concerning his methods of handling them. One was to invite the would-be office-holder to ride with him, and then to gallop so rapidly all the way that any solicitation was impossible.[45] But the people whom he treated in this way were probably grasping or importunate ; for his kindliness was no more abated than his energy. Witness the arrangements which he made when some of the starving peasants from his Sligo estate took advantage of the contract prices offered for emigration to America.[46] He was willing, it seems, to pay an extra rate in order that his tenants should have every possible comfort. And he is said to have presented the captain of every ship in which his tenants sailed with ten pounds for looking after them, and a supply of port and brandy to be shared with such of them as needed it. Only the protests of the Irish priests caused him to give up the practice of comforting his former peasantry faring overseas with a weekly treat of rum. Coffee and biscuits were substituted in the interests of temperance. Such bounty and thoughtfulness, extended where even appreciation was doubtful, went beyond the traditions of his class. Moreover, Palmerston ' had a way with him.' When Admiral Sir Charles Napier asked permission to use a Portuguese title, he was told that the ministers could not ' be parties to denationalising one of the brightest ornaments of the British navy.'[47]

That his good-heartedness, always pronounced, had if anything developed with the years was due, perhaps, to Lady Palmerston. It was almost impossible to think of him without her any more ; and she herself had developed into a real personage. Versed in the study of blue books, she would tilt with anyone, even with an editor of *The Times*, when her hero—for he seems to have been nothing less—was roughly used. At times she was violent and perilously indiscreet ; but her most effective ways of helping him were gentle ones. It was not merely that her famous dinners and receptions helped to win over such foes as the ubiquitous young Henry Reeve.[48] She had other ways of showing her political instinct, letting it be known that her splendid costumes were made solely from British goods, and not from the cheaper fabrics with which the French deluged the London shops.[49] She was as careful for his welfare as she had been in the first years :

> I grieved that you was not with me to feel the benefit of these healthy breezes, and the life you are obliged to lead, and the trial it is to your Constitution, makes me very unhappy.[50]

It was a delightful partnership, built on mutual affection, admiration and solicitude. The pathetic Chartist demonstration of April 1848, showed it in an especially charming light.

For all the demonstration was a tragedy to so many idealistic Englishmen, there was an element of comic opera in the reactions of the governing class. The windows of the Foreign Office were blocked with books, and its utterly unwarlike staff equipped with cutlasses and Brown Bess muskets that would have been more suitable as stage properties. The foreign secretary commanded the garrison.[51] Great town houses were barricaded and left to be defended by servants. Lady Palmerston, after walking out to see the sights, took refuge with her daughter, Lady Shaftesbury, and left it to her husband to decide whether she would have to ' *découcher* ': [52]

> If all remains quiet I am very anxious to return home in the Even[in]g . . . *Pray* therefore give me leave to do so, . . . as we have now a good exit to our House above & below, there can be no danger. I await your orders. . . .

The ' orders ' apparently not suiting her, she calmly disregarded them, and informed the commander of the Foreign Office fort that he would find her at home awaiting him. In a few hours the whole affair was at an end ; but, years afterwards, there was an interesting little piece of aftermath. Being appealed to on behalf of the poverty-stricken sister of Feargus O'Connor, the Chartist leader, Palmerston apologised for not being able to place her on the pension list, and saw to it that she was temporarily relieved. George Jacob Holyoake, the 'Agitator,' who recorded this, wrote of Palmerston's 'generous personal qualities which adversaries might trust.'[53]

It is rather startling to turn from this tribute to a letter sent by the generous adversary to Clarendon, the lord-lieutenant of Ireland, in November 1847. It dealt with murders committed by the Irish peasantry:

> I am glad you are taking vigorous measures. . . . The true remedy cannot in these days be applied, but if you *could* hang the priest of the parish whenever a murder such as these last was committed, I have a notion that lay Protestant life would be much more secure.[54]

Beneath the jocularity there lay real animus. Palmerston had shown bitterness against the Irish priests in a complaint to Russell, made three months earlier, when the results of the general election had become known.[55] He held them responsible for the ingratitude of the Irish electorate in forgetting England's bounty during the famine, and sending to parliament an almost solid body of members who stood for repeal of the Union. What was more, he accused the priests of acting from purely mercenary motives. But he was given to contradictions such as this. His tolerance and generosity often succumbed to temper when the established order was menaced. And menaced it really seemed to be. In spite of O'Connell's disappearance from the scene, in spite of the exhaustion which came from starvation and pestilence, the Irish agitation for repeal had grown more violent. And this fact was associated, how justly it is difficult to say, with a marked increase of assassinations and other crimes of violence. That members of the clergy encouraged or condoned these crimes there is, naturally, no conclusive evidence; but it is certain that at least some of the hierarchy supported the agitation for repeal. They would have none of England or her works. Thanks to their efforts, a papal rescript had condemned England's establishment of non-sectarian 'Queen's' colleges at Cork, Dublin and Belfast.[56]

IRISH AGITATION AND THE VATICAN

But, as Palmerston had for some time realised, two could play at the game of appealing to the Vatican.

Angry though he was with the repealers and the clergy who encouraged them, the foreign secretary was not so destitute of sympathy for the Irish people as has sometimes been supposed. Though he believed that ' a long continued and systematic ejectment of Small Holders and Squatting Cottiers ' was necessary to the future of the country,[57] he agreed that the law covering the Irish system of land tenure should be modified on behalf of the tenants-at-will :

> The grievance we apprehend is that when a tenant at will improves [his holding] the landlord sometimes takes advantage of the improvement either to exact a higher rent from the tenant before he has had time to repay himself by increased produce or else he turns the improving tenant out and gives the holding at an advanced rate to somebody else. I cannot believe that such cases are numerous, but they are possible . . . we ought to apply a remedy. . . . We propose to . . . say that when a tenant at will whose rent does not exceed a given sum . . . shall have his tenure put an end to by his landlord he shall be intitled to put in a claim to be decided by the assistant barrister. . . .[58]

What is more, he seems to have understood and trusted Irishmen more than some at least of his colleagues. When the cabinet was discussing plans for defence against the French, he argued against those who felt that an Irish militia would be too dangerous :

> The Irishman has a superstitious reverence for an oath and a great respect for the tie imposed upon him by any kind of enrolment.[59]

England would be all the more safe, he held, for putting the Irish on their honour, and showing that she trusted them. But the repealers had to be suppressed ; and in suppressing them he hoped to find an ally in the Vatican. As early as the autumn of 1846, he had made advances to the new pope, Pius IX, congratulating him on the introduction of administrative reforms and the building of railroads in the Papal States.[60] In doing this he had been thinking of probable developments in Italy ; but, by the summer of 1847, he saw the possibility of killing two birds with one stone.

The proposal for actual negotiations seems to have come, however, from the Pope. Pius IX, uneasy over Austrian hostility to the moderate reforms he was introducing in his civil government, desired the moral support of Palmerston.[61] At the beginning of August 1847, his desire was intensified by an Austrian move. Austrian troops, established by treaty in the citadel of Ferrara, took possession of the town.[62] Pius turned, in his anxiety, to Bishop (later Cardinal) Wiseman, who had arrived at the Vatican to urge that England should have a regular Catholic hierarchy, in place of the government by vicars apostolic established a century before.[63] The bishop communicated with Palmerston through one of England's great Catholic peers, Lord Shrewsbury ;[64] and Palmerston was soon urging on Russell that a special envoy should be sent to Rome.[65]

That he caught eagerly at the Pope's suggestion was due to his increasing anxiety about Italy. Though the great revolutionary storm of 1848 was still unforeseen, premonitory squalls, especially in the Italian states, had troubled him for at least a year. He could not forget how often the Italian peninsula had been a battleground for Austria and France, and how easily the conditions prevailing there might make it one again. He had communicated his fears to Russell on July 30, 1846 :[66]

Italy is the weak part of Europe, and the next war that breaks out in Europe will probably arise out of Italian affairs. . . . Outbreaks and insurrections and conspiracies have followed each other in rapid succession, . . . Leave things as they are, and you leave France the power of disturbing the peace of Europe whenever she chooses . . . the ascendancy of the Liberal party at Paris, whenever it may happen, . . . will soon be followed by an outbreak in Italy. That is the point to which the French Liberals look ; they know that if they tried to get back to the Rhine they would have against them all Germany united, Russia, and more or less England ; but in supporting an insurrection in Italy against Papal misgovernment, they would stand in a very different position.

But they would still bring on a war. Neither England, Russia nor Prussia would be likely to ' stir a foot ' :

But Austria *would* interfere, and could scarcely help doing so, . . . France and Austria would then fight each other in Italy, and

France would have all the Italians on her side. But the war, begun in Italy, would probably spread to Germany, and at all events, we can have no wish to see Austria broken down and France aggrandised, and the military vanity and love of conquest of the French revived and strengthened by success.

The letter is worth quoting at some length, since it prefigures the policy he was to adopt in 1848. It supplies, too, some of his most cogent reasons for wishing, in 1847, to open relations with the Pope. Believing that the principal danger spot was still in the Papal States, he was ready to apply his old and favourite remedy : to 'take advantage of the liberal inclinations of the new Pope to encourage and induce him to make reforms.'[67] But he also had his eye upon Piedmont. Her king, Charles Albert, had more will and power to resist the inroads of either France or Austria than any other Italian sovereign. And Italian nationalism was nowhere more ardent than at Turin.

He had no trouble in finding a suitable envoy.[68] Lord Minto, lord privy seal, and father-in-law both to Russell and to Abercromby, the British minister at Turin, was going to south Germany. Why not, suggested Palmerston, send him to Berne, Turin, Florence and Rome? In Switzerland he could warn the Diet against 'violent acts . . . which could afford either to Austria or to France any pretext for interference by force of arms' : at the Italian capitals he could urge the governments to stave off revolutions by making moderate concessions to the liberals. He could open the way for closer commercial relations between England and Italy, and request the Pope to make the Irish priesthood keep out of politics. He could also warn Charles Albert against 'any unnecessary rupture either with Austria or with France.' In these proposals one finds no indication that Palmerston was interested in Italian nationalism ; and it has been asserted, on the basis of a despatch which he sent in the summer of 1847 to the British ambassador at Vienna, Lord Ponsonby, that he showed as yet no grasp of the great issue which occupied the minds of the Italian liberals. But the phraseology of one of the instructions given to Minto, and of a draft prepared in late October for the British minister at Turin raises some doubt. Minto was to promote the formation of a commercial league which could serve as a basis for a 'national and united sentiment' ;[69] and to Abercromby it was pointed out that the league might further ' the formation of an alliance which would lay a solid and secure foundation for the political independence of Italy.' [70]

In arranging for the Minto mission, Palmerston encountered a force which was from this time on to hamper most of his efforts in behalf of the Italians—the opposition of Victoria. Under the combined influence of her beloved husband and uncle—the two influences were virtually one—she was leaving behind some of the teachings of Melbourne. Since 1832, Leopold informed her, the constitution had become ' bad ' ; and *the very spirit of the old Monarchy* ' had been '*abolished.*' [71] She must strive, above all, against her arrogant foreign secretary, to restore monarchy to its proper plane. Victoria was developing, too, her own conception of international affairs. Her idea of a properly constituted world rested on the conception of a group of monarchs, who should be high-principled, well-conducted and benevolent, but were virtually irremovable no matter what faults they might display. They should be devoted to their countries' interests ; but manage at all times to give their subjects the example of living in dignified amity. And with Victoria as with Palmerston, to believe was to act, and to act with all the power and influence that one could command. She did not forget the constitution ; but she realised that, although the last word lay with the cabinet, her ministers would accept some dictation on her part rather than confront the unpleasantness, not to say the scandal, of continual struggles. The preachings of Leopold and Albert, the deference and acquiescence of Aberdeen, and the consciousness of her own and her husband's very real ability, filled her with determination and self-confidence. She showed this above all in her attempts to influence foreign policy ; since foreign policy was almost a passion with her, with Prince Albert, and with King Leopold. Though she had taken her first lessons in diplomacy from Palmerston a scant ten years before, she had no doubt that she and her consort were better fitted to handle international affairs than he. She scarcely attempted to understand his aims ; and his methods outraged her sense of dignity and propriety. Contrasting her foreign secretary's policies with those of Aberdeen and Peel, she decided that he was usually wrong. With respect to the Italian situation, her views and his were to diverge more and more.

Some indication of this divergence could be seen even when the Minto mission was proposed.[72] Prince Albert objected that to encourage Pius in liberal reform by the sending of a special mission would be '*a most hostile step* towards our old and natural ally,' Austria. He suggested that the Foreign Office might, instead, issue a warning to the Austrian and all other European governments that armed interference by any of them in the affairs of another state for the purpose of checking constitutional reform would be ' an act of aggression ' which ' Europe and the Powers who signed the Treaty of Vienna ' could not ' look upon with indifference.' Thus would England make herself the loved champion of European liberals, ' particularly in Germany ' ; thus would she avoid encouraging reform which was not spontaneous ; and thus would she show regard for diplomatic propriety. Nothing could better have shown how essentially the Prince belonged among the idealistic German liberals of 1848. As the disagreement between the Court and the Foreign Office had only just begun, the difference concerning the Minto mission was soon composed. Palmerston and Russell tactfully stated that they quite approved Prince Albert's views ; and Victoria allowed Minto to be instructed as Palmerston desired, provided that his mission was previously explained to the governments of France and Austria. The Court even agreed that a naval squadron might go to the west coast of Italy, to encourage Italian sovereigns in spontaneous reform, and to discourage both absolutist intervention and popular outbreaks. The Queen was suspicious that England's ' old and natural ally ' might be fostering such outbreaks for her own purposes.

In so far as its minor purpose was concerned, the Minto mission was attended with some success. The Pope, through the Congregation of the Faith, reproved the Irish clergy for their political activities.[73] The Congregation, after expressing disbelief in reports that the Irish priesthood had desecrated churches 'for the purpose of aiding and promoting secular concerns,' and had even provoked or extenuated murder itself, sent an exhortation to some of the Irish bishops which lacked nothing in solemnity :

The Church of God should be the House of Prayer—not of secular concerns or the meeting place of politicians. . . . Ecclesiastics . . . are Ministers of Peace . . . who should abhor blood and vengeance . . . this Sacred Congregation deems it its duty to require satisfactory and speedy information concerning all these matters that it may know what importance it should attach to the above-mentioned damnatory reports.

The exhortation apparently had some effect ; but the outbreak of the Young Ireland rebellion in the spring of 1848 suggests that it did nothing to quiet the Irish agitation as a whole. It took the failure of the rebellion and the punishment of its leaders to compass that.

In fact, the whole project of establishing closer relations with the Vatican soon came to nought ; and this thanks largely to an attempt to place such relations on a permanent and conventional basis.[74] The cabinet decided on the passage of an enabling act, more impelled, it seems, by the political desirability of obtaining parliamentary endorsement than by any doubt that it possessed the necessary power under existing law. To gild the pill, Palmerston pleaded with the House to consider the possible benefits to British commerce, and the important part which projected Italian railroads might soon play in British communications with the East. Despite the opposition of alarmed Protestants, and of English and Irish Catholics who accused the government of wishing to use papal legates in controlling her Majesty's Catholic subjects, the measure became law. But the manner of its passing and its final form were so offensive to the Vatican that the act defeated its own ends. Russell declared, in the course of a debate, that he had no intention of allowing the creation of Catholic bishoprics in England ; and he pleaded for the passage of the bill by asserting that the non-existence of diplomatic relations left the Pope un-

NO RELATIONS WITH THE VATICAN

fettered in his spiritual influence. In point of fact, however, the upper House had already doomed the whole project to futility. It had inserted a stipulation that the Vatican should never accredit an ecclesiastic as its envoy to London. Members who were no friends to Catholicism pointed out that this was both to place an unwarrantable restriction on the Pope, and to deny the diplomatic equality of the British and Roman courts. Palmerston not only supported the stipulation, but stated his reasons almost as forcibly in parliament as he did in a private letter to Clarendon :

> I am convinced by my diplomatic experience that there would be no end to the embarrassments and inconveniences which we should suffer from having a Roman priest invested with diplomatic privilege holding his court in London surrounded by English and Irish Catholics . . . & capable of becoming an engine of political intrigue to serve all kinds of foreign interests.[75]

For once at least he agreed with Aberdeen.[76]

The effects of the Minto mission on the Italian movement are impossible to estimate. Minto doubtless attempted to execute his instructions faithfully ; and Palmerston later claimed that he had been instrumental in the establishment of constitutions in Piedmont, Tuscany and the Papal States. But Victoria and Metternich had reason for their belief that he greatly stimulated the revolutionary tendencies of Italian liberals. His sympathy with them was unconcealed, his popularity immense, the encouragement afforded by his presence undeniable. Another thing which seems incontestable is that he had been sent too late. There were riots in Milan, a conspiracy in the Papal States, a rising in Lucca, and, in the first days of 1848, a real insurrection in Sicily. If the bankruptcy of the Metternich system was evident by the end of 1847 in Switzerland, payment was already being called for in Italy. In fact, the day of reckoning for the whole of Europe seemed at hand. From Lisbon to Buda-Pesth the liberal groups, weary of the stagnation and repression of the 'Metternich' era, profoundly optimistic that new ideals of society and government would soon be realised, and drawing new resources in the more advanced countries from the economic transformation that had been

I. 2 E

going on, were ready for action. The nightmare that had haunted conservatives, and even 'moderate' men like Palmerston, the nightmare of disintegration, anarchy and wars of 'opinion,' bade fair to become a reality.

The Sicilians set the ball rolling; but their insurrection was not immediately recognised as an event of particular significance. Europe at large did not awake to the situation which confronted it until, at the end of February 1848, the Parisians rose, overthrew the Orleans monarchy, and established the second French republic in its place. This French revolution was like the breaking of a dam, the crumbling of one end of that structure of conservative or despotic monarchies and obedient armies which had been holding back the accumulating forces of liberalism. Throughout western, central and east central Europe, men who had been struggling to obtain some measure of self-government, to bring together each nationality into one independent state, or to do both, believed their hour had come. The movement was so widespread that the preservation of 'order' by bands of 'pompiers' was impossible. At Buda-Pesth, Vienna, Berlin, Turin and a score or more of minor capitals there were sudden uprisings. Riots became revolutions: princes and ministers bowed to popular demands and sometimes took to flight: constitutions, usually ratified by those who had refused them for so long, were hastily proclaimed: national groups repudiated alien rule and prepared to alter the frontiers of Europe according to the principle of nationality. When it was known that a liberal constitution had been accepted by the emperor of Austria; that the Hungarians had received complete autonomy; and that Metternich—the very keystone of the reactionary structure—had sought refuge in the country of Lord Palmerston, it seemed that the ultimate had arrived.

In England there was great alarm. The cooler spirits realised that the country's institutions were safe enough, for all the agitation of the Chartists and the revolutionary movement in Ireland. But there was no one who could say that a 'war of opinion' might not engulf Europe. It was not at all fanciful to fear that the second French republic would emulate the first, throwing its armies and its propaganda (now socialist as well as republican) far beyond its boundaries. Military glory, leadership among the Powers, and the acquisition of territories to the east had appealed far more to the advanced than to the conservative elements in France. No one knew, in fact, how much of Europe's existing order, national or international, political or economic, would survive. It was impossible even to predict how the new governments, evolving everywhere overnight, would finally align themselves. German liberals were flocking to Frankfort to found, by a voluntary union of constitutional governments, a united Germany which should fulfil the dreams of many years : contingents of soldiers from all the Italian states were hurrying to Turin ; and the Hungarians stood ready to defend by arms their newly won autonomy. What would France and Austria, even in liberal hands, have to say about a new Germany, a new Italy and a new Hungary, brought into being without regard for the permission or interests of the older Powers, and almost bound to repudiate their influence ? And would the Tsar, his authority and his great armies quite intact, desert his fellow sovereigns, and allow liberal ideas and institutions to sprout on his very frontiers ? Thus to paint the dangers of the situation in 1848 is, of course, to paint them imaginatively and at their worst, without regard for co-existing factors of stability. But those factors of stability were temporarily obscured ; and the most dangerous possibilities had always to be kept in mind by a person burdened with such responsibilities as a British foreign minister.

When Palmerston is praised as a diplomatist, the greatest testimony to his skill is usually found in his work in making Belgium an independent state, in handling the Near Eastern crisis of 1839–1841, and in assisting, twenty years later on, at the birth of the present kingdom of Italy. But one wonders whether at least equal emphasis should not be placed on his diplomacy in 1848–1849. Though his arrogance and intemperance in word and action were never more in evidence than at this time ; though he needlessly embroiled himself and his country with several courts ; the fact remains that he was never in any major issue drawn away from the cool and detached line of policy which he believed most conducive to his country's interests. And his influence, if impossible to estimate, would be difficult to exaggerate. It is true that the constitution makers of 1848 had no need of his patronage, and that he had little either of power or will to further the aspirations of the nationalists. But he had the task of guarding against a general war that would almost certainly have nullified the careful arrangements of 1815, and have upset the balance of power to England's probable detriment. The task of acting as an international gyroscope, of using just the right amount of pressure or persuasion to keep certain continental governments in check, required such calculation, such patience and such self-control as British foreign secretaries have seldom been called upon to exercise. In those years responsibility and opportunity once more called to Palmerston, and called on him to assume a leading rôle. No great government in Europe save those of England and Russia stood secure ; and, since Russia's attitude as the defender of reaction was known in advance, since her armies were so far away, England's position had almost incalculable weight. So had the personal attitude of Palmerston.

One must be careful, however, to understand just why this was. The impression frequently conveyed is that Palmerston ran away with Russell's ministry as he had with Melbourne's in 1839–1841. And to some degree this is quite true. If Melbourne had been too easy-going and cynical to keep his foreign secretary in control, Russell lacked the strength. Nor could party discipline be effectively applied. The Whigs, lacking a secure majority, ruled by virtue of the Peelite dread of a new corn law, by Irish recollections of Tory coercion acts, and by the favour of a large section of the radicals. And Palmerston, generally regarded as the 'strongest' member of the ministry, usually in favour with the Irish, and growing to be the idol of most of the 'political' radicals, was far too valuable an asset, far too dangerous a potential foe, to be allowed to cross the House. But the fact is that the cabinet was usually quite ready to accept his lead. In 1848 and the two years following, when panic, innovation, and impractical idealism were so prevalent, his experience, coolness, sound sense, and keen perception of British interests made it hard to gainsay his policies at any given point. True, his roughness and his ruthlessness were as distasteful to his correct and rather gentle associates as they had ever been. True, he frequently took action without consulting them, and sometimes in a way to which they would never have given their assent. But Russell more than once declared that his policies seldom diverged from those of Palmerston; and there were times when Russell was less inclined to support his foreign minister than were the other members of the cabinet. The devil's son seemed a *Deus ex machina* to his countrymen in those perilous days.

CHAPTER XIX

THE REVOLUTIONS OF 1848, AND PALMERSTON'S CONFLICT WITH THE QUEEN—I

REALISATION of what was happening on the continent during the spring of 1848 was strikingly brought home to Englishmen through the arrival in their midst of a flock of quondam rulers and celebrities.[1] In the first days of March, Louis Philippe, disguised in a rough pea-jacket, ' enormous goggles ' and a week-old beard, and escorting a heavily cloaked and veiled consort, was landed at Newhaven. In the course of the following few days most of the French royal family were installed in King Leopold's now dreary and unsanitary British residence, Claremont. Guizot, who had just preceded them, took up his residence in a small house at Brompton ; and commenced, appropriately, to write of the civilisation of his countrymen and England's revolution of 1688. The Princess Lieven, owing to an '*affreuse terreur*' of Paris, and a dislike for the smoke and activity of the London she had once so dearly loved, took refuge at Richmond, and there re-opened her salon. Soon she had as neighbours a Herr and Frau von Meyer, better known in better times as Prince and Princess Metternich. Herr von Meyer at first found Richmond rather dull. Not many people seemed in haste to pay homage to a fallen statesman who was old and deaf. Slowly, however, his circle of acquaintances increased ; and he found himself at dinners and soirées. One of these dinners was given for a Prussian prince who had found it wise to leave Berlin, and was visiting the duchess of Kent. At the Prussian legation he pushed aside the chair of honour offered him, with the remark, ' We must practise humility now.' He did not know that he was to be William the First of the nineteenth century German Empire.

The arrival of these humbled great ones in England justified many an admonition and prediction of Lord Palmerston's; but it was far from conducive to his peace of mind. And this, not merely because he disliked revolutions and dreaded the developments which might ensue upon the continent. The presence of his old foes was an annoyance and even something more. The French group went about declaring that he and Normanby were much to blame for the downfall of the Orleans dynasty, and secured a very sympathetic hearing in society and at Court.[2] Victoria, in her pity for the Orleans family, and her disgust that royalty should be treated so, forgot the Spanish marriages and showed all her old affection for her connections at Claremont. Albert himself, so it was said, had to remind her that reasons of state forbade the exhibition of too much sympathy. No such reasons, of course, prevented her from blaming Palmerston for having helped to bring her friends to such a plight. Other admirers of the exiles adopted the same attitude. 'Aberdeen,' wrote the Princess Metternich, 'shows an animosity towards Palmerston which surprises me; I did not believe that he could so far depart from his customary bearing, he who always knows so well how to remain calm and to restrain himself.'[3] In fact, the Princess took heart from the attitude of British society. It seemed quite possible that Metternich would be able to do some good by acting as a nucleus for the 'honest' men in London.[4] He made at least a beginning by assisting Disraeli to prepare a parliamentary attack on Palmerston.[5]

Palmerston seems to have treated the exiles very well. There were, indeed, reports, emanating from Claremont, that he acted in an unfriendly manner to Louis Philippe. But even Charles Greville was in doubt as to their truth.[6] And Greville was not one of the three or four people who knew that Palmerston had offered to relieve the French king's poverty from secret service funds which he controlled.[7] What is more, he was very courteous to Guizot,[8] greeting him with a message not only friendly but flattering, and inviting a group of notables to meet him at dinner.

'I thought Palmerston and Guizot would have shaken each other's arms off,' wrote Charles Greville, who was present, 'and nothing could exceed the cordiality or apparent ease with which they conversed.' He was equally civil, though naturally less cordial, to Metternich.[9] And he received but little credit for his pains. For the Metternich circle showed no compunction in abusing him as a 'red republican' for the delectation of the Hanoverian minister and of Victoria's relative, the duchess of Cambridge.[10] Palmerston's civilities are the more worth noting in view of the fact that one cannot weigh them wholly in the scale of amenity and kindliness. He had always to consider what effects his courtesies might produce abroad. In showing cordiality to Guizot he created some dissatisfaction at Paris;[11] and his diplomacy was focused there as much as it had ever been.

His attitude toward the French republican government exemplified the coolness and detachment, the ability to discern realities under appearances, which he showed so frequently in those confused and stormy years. Although he had regarded revolution at Paris as impossible up to within a few days of the time when it broke out,[12] he received the news coolly enough. He owned to some gratification in noting that all the authors of the Spanish marriages had destroyed themselves[13] (Bresson had blown out his brains some time before); but he was not too sanguine of any great political advantage from Guizot's fall. 'Any sucessor,' he had written, some months earlier, 'would in his heart be just as hostile to England.'[14] There had even been advantages, he felt, in having France governed by a man who had 'lost his means of imposing on the credulity of the British public.'[15] As for the new regime, he was revolted at the sight of 'a nation of 33 millions . . . despotically governed by eight or nine men who are the mere subordinates of 40, or 50,000 of the scum of the faubourgs of Paris.'[16] But he was not immediately disturbed. The Orleanists, he was sure, would soon be back in power;[17] and in the meantime there was little to be feared. If the new government proved sensible it might get on very nicely with England. The great thing to be sought was peace. Hardly was the revolution at Paris an accomplished fact, before he was assuring the three eastern courts of his confidence that the republic was pacifically inclined.[18] When Lamartine issued a manifesto, proclaiming that his government did not consider itself bound by the arrangements of 1815, Palmerston was quick to realise that it had been written for the consumption of the boulevards :

> . . . if you were to put the whole of it into a crucible, and to evaporate the gaseous parts and scum off the dross you would find the regulus to be peace and good fellowship with other governments.[19]

His optimism grew. Within a month he had decided that Lamartine was a great improvement on the Orleanist ministers, ' who were more bent on reducing and crippling the power of England ' than any men who had governed France since Napoleon's time.[20] England's relations with the republic must be of the friendliest.[21] No doubt he hoped that the French government, daring neither to follow a revolutionary foreign policy for fear of the three eastern Powers, nor a reactionary one for fear of its own citizens, might lean on England and Palmerston as much as the Orleans monarchy had done. But there was a far more pressing reason why he was willing to extend his patronage to the favourites of the faubourgs, a reason which had much to do with Italy.

If Paris was the focus of his diplomacy, northern Italy seemed to him the focus of danger, danger of international complications, and even of a general war. His fears were very much as they had been in 1846, save that they no longer centred in the Papal States, but in Piedmont. From the day when the French republicans expelled their king the danger of serious complications in northern Italy was quite visible : from March 13, when Metternich fled from Vienna, it was serious : during the fortnight following, when Milan and Venice expelled their Austrian garrisons, it became acute. What little can be said of Palmerston's attempt to meet it during the following eighteen months can best be understood if one submits to the tedium of analysis at the outset.

The *summum desideratum* was, of course, the maintenance of general peace. As Bunsen, the Prussian minister, pointed out to Frederick William IV, almost everyone in England was agreed on that :

> . . . Y. M. knows the manner in which Ld. P[almerston] views the relations, actual and eventual, with France. Whatever happens, no offensive war against France, still less a war of principles ; no compromise or alliance . . . to such an end, but an agreement with the other powers for the defence of the Status quo against unprovoked attacks on the part of France, of course on the basis of non-intervention in Italy and Switzerland. That is Ld. Palm's programme. It is that of the Cabinet ; at bottom, it is also that of Sir R. Peel and Ld. Aberdeen and their friends, it is that of the Leader of the Protectionists, Ld. Stanley. . . .
> The man who has reflected most deeply on the state of Europe in view of the catastrophe in France, is Ld. Palmerston. He is calmer and more serious than usual and even anxious.[22]

But whence did the greatest threat to general peace arise ? Apparently from the most advanced French liberals. The revolutionary, warlike and expansionist tendencies of '93 were in evidence in Paris. And the radical patriots yearned above all to liberate their oppressed brothers in Italy, and confound their common arch enemy, Austria. With these aspirations Palmerston could have a certain sympathy. But he realised that the heirs of '93 might do two other things with which he could have no sympathy at all, in setting up new republics, and asking territorial returns for their services to liberty. What was more, their intervention in Italy would almost certainly lead to war ; and war might mean the overthrow of Austria and an upset of the balance of power. Neither would their ideas for Italy's future coincide with his. Patriotic French republicans would not care for a strong north Italian kingdom on their frontier.[23] Still, if circumstances had allowed Palmerston to deal with the danger of French aggression in Italy by itself, his line of action would have been relatively clear : to employ persuasion in Paris so long as that availed, and to fortify his arguments by threats of supporting Austria if real pressure were needed. But the issue was not so simple as all that. He could not, even in appearance, align himself with Austria, as against the liberal elements in both France and Italy. His instincts, his record, and public sentiment among the vast majority of Englishmen, stood in the way. And Piedmont's position made his problem harder still. Charles Albert had no taste at all for French republicans, Italian republics, or the granting of territorial *pourboires* to Piedmont's great neighbour on the west. Immediately after the February revolution in Paris his great fear was of a French attack.[24] But he, too, had a public to think of. The liberals of all Italy expected him to lead in driving out the Austrians and setting up a united Italy of some sort. Thanks to their enthusiasm and to the panic of the old authorities, troops from every state in the peninsula were gathering to his flag. Not only would his reputation and popularity be lost, his very throne would be unsafe if he refused the task of helping the Lombards and Venetians to throw off Austrian rule. But in accepting the task he would accept war with Austria ; and reverses might easily force him to request French aid. Some of these eventualities became actualities at the end of March 1848, when, despite the warnings of Abercromby, the British minister at Turin,[25] the Piedmontese armies entered Lombardy. England, of course, declared neutrality; but it was certain that the Foreign Office would have to undertake diplomatic intervention of some sort.

No matter how the war might go, the danger would be very much the same. Whether the Austrians won or lost, it seemed too likely that France would send troops into Piedmont and Lombardy-Venetia, establish republics, appropriate Savoy and Nice, and, very possibly at least, provoke the whole of Germany to war. This prospect haunted Palmerston week after week, month after month. Month after month he laboured to keep France in check, now by what seemed a brotherly embrace, now by threats that brotherhood would give place to hostility, now by warnings of the power of Austria. Similar methods had to be employed with Charles Albert : above all, he had to be impressed with the dangers he would bring upon his state and throne by giving play in Italy to French cupidity and doctrinaire republicanism. And, finally, Palmerston had to deal with Austria. In some respects this was the hardest task of all. Naturally hostile to and suspicious of Palmerston and his policy, the Austrian government was made still more so by the news it received from Metternich in London, and the admonitions of the Tsar. It learned that the British court and most of British society shared the pro-Austrian sympathies of Palmerston's own ambassador at Vienna, the 'evergreen' Lord Ponsonby. Yet Austria had to be persuaded, if possible, that it would not pay her to provoke the French by proving too intransigent regarding her Italian provinces. Palmerston was even optimist enough to think that she could be persuaded of the advantages of having a strong buffer state in northern Italy under Charles Albert's rule. The manipulation of these three governments would in itself have taxed the capacities of any foreign minister. But Palmerston's task was rendered incalculably more difficult by the fact that he was constantly obstructed by his own sovereign.

Since his diplomacy in this whole matter has at last been traced most skilfully,[26] and since his relations with the Court rather than with continental governments were to shape his own career, his struggle with the Queen and Prince Albert claims particular notice. The difficulty with the Queen (for, whatever her submission to Prince Albert in foreign policy, it was with her he had to deal) was that she would not even try to understand his views. She saw clearly enough the faults in governing which had caused the overturn of so many courts and ministries; but, in so far as boundaries were concerned, she was insistent on the preservation of the *status quo ante*. She was impervious to Palmerston's argument that the establishment of a strong buffer state in northern Italy, with Piedmont for a nucleus, would lessen the probability of Franco-Austrian, and hence of general, wars. She was incapable of seeing that any changes in Italian boundaries might be advisable, or that the people of any of the states should have any choice of sovereigns. Her ideas belonged properly to the eighteenth century. Princes possessed titles to the territories and the peoples which they ruled, and any dispossession was sheer robbery. Years afterward, Prince Albert used the term in referring to the king of Piedmont's willingness to accept voluntary allegiance from the inhabitants of Lombardy.[27] The Queen, who must really have understood the Hanoverian title to the British crown, was shocked at the suggestion that the peoples of Parma and Modena should be allowed to decide whether they would have Charles Albert for their sovereign :

... the Queen was struck by the light way in which the claims of the Dukes of Parma and Modena are spoken of (as disposed of by the events), whilst their position and that of Austria are in every respect identical ... as soon as the war shall be terminated, the question of the political constitution of Italy (as a whole) will have to be decided. Why Charles Albert ought to get any additional territory the Queen cannot in the least see. . . .[28]

What eighteenth-century ruler could have bettered this ? Thus to criticise the Court is not to say that it was always wrong. There was at least one time when Palmerston would have been well advised to let Victoria and Albert have their way. For his judgment was sometimes at fault. He miscalculated the potential strength of the Austrian and Piedmontese forces ; and his calculations were probably affected by his sympathies. But if one wishes to decide whether the greater misunderstanding and partisanship lay with him or with the Queen, one has only to note the accusations hurled at him by the Court. The most constant aim of his diplomacy was to avoid French intervention in northern Italy. Yet Victoria remained convinced that he had entered into a conspiracy with low French republicans to despoil Austria of her lands, and that he stood ready, should necessity arise, to use French forces for the perpetration of this crime.[29] Though Russell and the cabinet almost invariably agreed with Palmerston, and seemed for a time at least to outstrip him in enthusiasm for the Italian cause, it was upon him alone that she always laid the blame.

Something of this was apparent even during the first critical juncture of the whole affair, which came in the last ten days of May 1848. The Austrian government, weakened by revolution at home, discouraged at finding that its troops in northern Italy had been driven out of Lombardy and confined to a small area defended by three of the fortresses of the famous Quadrilateral, requested the British government to mediate with Charles Albert. Its envoy, Baron Hummelauer, finally offered most favourable terms. Lombardy should be free to unite with Piedmont, as its people had voted to do ; and Venetia should be practically autonomous under Austrian sovereignty.[30] Palmerston seems to have been rather torn between discretion and desire. The Austrian offer did not provide for the strong Italian kingdom which he now had in mind. His hope, as he wrote King Leopold,[31] was that the peoples of Parma and Modena might be allowed to take Charles Albert for their sovereign, and that Venetia as well as Lombardy would be wrested from Austria by force of arms. But he did not entirely put aside the Hummelauer offer. It had probably come too late, he thought, to secure acceptance from the victorious Piedmontese ;[32] but as a basis for discussion it might be useful. But Russell and the cabinet seemed more zealous. Hummelauer wrote mournfully that the ministry ' had adopted *en masse* the point of view of the Italian revolutionists, and wished to give England direct influence over Italy through the creation of a great north Italian kingdom, to be formed out of Piedmont, Lombardy, Venetia, Parma and Modena, and placed under the rule of Charles Albert.'[33] And the cabinet did decide that mediation would be useless until Austria gave better terms. Palmerston's position seems to have been a shade ambiguous ; and the uncertainty deepens as one attempts to follow him. To Hummelauer he expressed regrets that his colleagues had gone so far, and his willingness that Austria should keep all of Venetia that lay eastward from the Adige and Mincio.[34] But, in view of a personal understanding which he reached with the Austrian envoy, and of a comment which he made concerning it, it seems difficult to believe he had been sincere. According to the understanding, and to an official note based upon it and ratified by the cabinet as of June 3, the British government would be ready to discuss mediation whenever Austria consented to retain only such parts of Venetia as might be agreed upon.[35] And Palmerston writing Russell, on June 8, wound up : ' This will of course be the whole.'[36] Perhaps he was not insincere ; for ten days had elapsed since the understanding had been reached, and fresh news may have given him fresh hope. But, however that was, he gambled on the war. Confident of Austria's entire defeat, he postponed mediation until she should be ready to give up all or nearly all Venetia. The Queen did not forget to remind him later of this fact.

She had full opportunity to rub it in; for, in so far as the Italian question was concerned, her foreign minister was entering on a year of deepening discouragement. This period was sharply punctuated by three events: the crushing defeat of Charles Albert's forces at Custozza, on July 25; the establishment of iron rule at Vienna through the accession to power of Prince Schwarzenberg, toward the end of November; and, finally, Piedmont's suicidal renewal of war in March 1849. The course of the negotiations which went on during this time between London, Paris, Vienna and Turin, cannot even be suggested here; but there is interest in seeing how Palmerston bore himself under some of the most trying circumstances of his public life. What made them especially trying was the fact that he was constantly handling three countries on the continent and fighting a rearguard action with the Court.

Between the end of May, when the cabinet decided that Hummelauer's peace proposals were inadequate, and the end of July, when the Italian army was virtually crushed, Victoria assumed an attitude that was offensive in more ways than one. At this time Palmerston was urging Austria to negotiate on the vague terms of the note of June 3, hoping for continued Italian victories that would make it impossible for her to retain much if any of Venetia, and attempting to secure acquiescence, both in Vienna and in Paris, in his plans for a strong and constitutional kingdom in northern Italy. It was apparently his hope of making England the guardian angel of this kingdom which especially irritated the Queen. As early as July 1, she wrote that she was 'ashamed' of his attempts to gain *'influence'* in Italy,—of a policy that had never done ' the *least good* . . . in Spain, Portugal and Greece.'[37] Palmerston, no courtier at any time, replied stiffly that he failed to find anything dishonourable in what he was doing; and went on to defend the diplomatic activities which she had attacked.[38] Angrier than ever, Victoria furnished him with the surprising information that the ' unfortunate combination ' of Queen Christina and Louis Philippe, which his patronage of the Spanish Progressives had brought about, was certainly ' the origin of all the present convulsions in Europe ' ![39] To his attempt to keep a friendly but restraining hand on France, she objected that he seemed ready to ' call upon the very power to judge the Italian dispute which ' it was ' the interest of Europe to keep out of it.'[40] She could only say that ' the establishment of an *entente cordiale with the French Republic*, for the purpose of driving the Austrians out of *their dominions* in Italy, would be a *disgrace* to this country.'[41] In vain Russell tried to explain matters, and to quiet her. She gave grudging assent to certain of his arguments, but always reverted to her attacks upon Palmerston and his policy.[42] And her attitude, if not her mistakes in facts and reasoning, prevailed among the British governing class. When news of the battle of Custozza reached London, Metternich wrote delightedly that he was overwhelmed with congratulatory visiting cards, and that Osborne was all gold and black.[43]

During the four months which elapsed between the battle of Custozza and the advent of Schwarzenberg, Victoria had to undergo the grief of seeing the Foreign Office working even more in concert with the French republic than it had before. With Piedmont sending envoys to beg French aid ; with the radical and chauvinistic elements at Paris showing irritation and uneasiness ; and with the obvious fact in view that English pressure on Austria would have to be reinforced if there were to be any chance of winning concessions for the Italians, Palmerston felt compelled to keep in closest touch with the French government. It was not realised that the time for giving diplomatic help to Italy had gone by. The cabinet now agreed to mediate jointly with France on the basis of Austria's relinquishment of Lombardy, and the gift of free institutions to Venetia. The Queen, albeit somewhat reluctantly, concurred. So did the French, despite their reluctance to see a stronger kingdom in northern Italy. Charles Albert, only too glad to have the assistance of two

QUEEN VICTORIA IN 1846

powerful friends, concluded an armistice with Austria on August 9.

So far so good. But Austria was not bound to any terms ; and her government received constant encouragement to play for time, and hope for full restitution of her possessions in the peninsula. Metternich, to whom the public opinion of any country was the opinion of the ruling class, wrote that England saw the Italian question far more from Austria's point of view than it did from Palmerston's.[44] *The Times* and the *Chronicle* (now utterly Peelite) substantiated his assurances. In parliament, Disraeli, most friendly now with Metternich,[45] denounced joint action with French Jacobins :

> It is the system that commences with ' fraternity ' and ends with assassination; it is the system that begins by preaching universal charity, and concludes by practising general spoliation.

And from Windsor and Osborne there went to Brussels, whence their purport at least was relayed to the Austrian capital, letters which warned the Austrian ministers against acceptance of the mediation which the Foreign Office urged on them.[46] ' It reminds me of the wolf in the lamb's skin,' wrote Victoria, when mediation was finally agreed upon.[47] And she added significantly, '*Nous verrons*, how matters will be arranged.' No wonder, then, that the Austrians held back for weeks, or that Palmerston fretted. He could relieve his feelings by writing privately to Ponsonby at Vienna that he would rather see the French in northern Italy than the Lombards forced back under the Austrian yoke ;[48] but he admitted to Russell that the intervention of a French army would never do :

> . . . it would of course turn its success to its own account, and would settle all matters as the French Government might chuse. We should be put upon the shelf and England would cut but a sorry figure in Europe.[49]

England was cutting none too brilliant a figure as it was. All the success her Foreign Office could achieve was to win Austria's acceptance, on September 7, of the mediation of the French and British governments. And this was hollow and fruitless from the first. The Austrians were now resolved to yield nothing; and the French once more resorted to a double game. In public they threatened armed intervention at Venice: in private they assured Austria that not even the cession of Lombardy would be required from her.[50] Yet Palmerston at least professed to be content in seeing what had really been the foremost of all his aims achieved. Lady Palmerston wrote proudly to Mrs. Huskisson:

> Palmerston believes that our joint mediation alone prevented the French from marching into Italy. This strengthened the hands of Cavagnac [sic] & enabled him to resist Lamoriciere & the war party. Mon^r de Beaumont [the republic's envoy at London] says that but for us, their Army of the Alps would now be there: and there is no saying how soon this would have lighted up a General War.[51]

Russell gave Palmerston as much credit as he gave himself;[52] but no sign of appreciation came from Osborne or Windsor.

The Queen's violent antipathy and invincible distrust would be difficult to understand were it not clear that Palmerston's foes, political and personal, had gained her ear. The exiles from the continent formed an influential coterie. The old trio from Paris, Louis Philippe, Guizot and the vindictive Princess Lieven, joined hands with Metternich. They joined hands, too, with Aberdeen, who admired and trusted them as of old; whose ideal of the kind of continental statesman needed at such times was that ruthless reactionary, Prince Schwarzenberg; and who found it as difficult as Victoria to see good in anything which the Foreign Office did. King Leopold, who had visited London early in the year, apparently with the object of exploiting the '*tendresse filiale*' of his dear niece, served as a link between the Ballplatz and Windsor.[53] Subjected to so many influences which reinforced her personal views, the Queen wrote constantly to Russell, repeating her charges of the preceding months and adding new ones as they occurred to her.[54] She, who from her soul detested the French republic and what she scornfully called the ' new entente,' was quick

ROYAL 'ABHORRENCE' OF THE ITALIAN CAUSE 435

to seize upon the fact that France disliked the idea of a stronger kingdom in northern Italy. And as for Palmerston's ' principle ' of *Italian Nationality and Independence from a foreign Yoke and Tyranny,*' she found it utterly detestable :

> It will be a calamity for ages to come if this principle is to become part of the international law, viz. ' that a people can at any time transfer their allegiance from the Sovereign of one State to that of another by universal suffrage (under momentary excitement). . . .'

Clarendon reported that she and the Prince expressed to him their ' abhorrence ' of Charles Albert, and their ' entire sympathy with all the political reactions now going on.'[55] Russell could no more manage them than he could his foreign minister. Piqued, perhaps, that in trying to placate her, he defended Palmerston, she suggested that Palmerston was tricking him.[56]

Hence, as the Foreign Office worked for compromise during the autumn of 1848, she contested every foot of ground. Refusing to believe that Palmerston had any object in promoting joint mediation with the French save that of gratifying his inconceivable ' partiality ' and ' personal *passion* ' by using French arms to expel the Austrians from Italy,[57] she worked for the submission of the whole question to a general conference of the Powers. Palmerston feared that such a conference would insist on taking up other troublesome problems, and that it would be dominated by the three great eastern courts. But he gave in when Russell declared himself in agreement with the Queen.[58] New disputes as to the location, the participants and the choice of a British representative arose. And when Palmerston, in January 1849, was ready to ' press all parties to send their envoys to Brussels,' he did so in full knowledge that the Austrians would not relinquish even Lombardy.[59] In the end, the whole project fell through ;[60] but not before Prince Schwarzenberg had been ruling for some months in the place of Metternich.

From Schwarzenberg's advent in November to the date of the last catastrophe, the prospects of the Italians grew more and more desperate ; while Palmerston, in his annoyance, partially disqualified himself for helping them.

Schwarzenberg was determined not to cede a foot of ground; and Nesselrode promised to support him, if necessary, against the French. As the winter passed, and the spring of 1849 opened, the Piedmontese lost their temper and their heads. In March, despite solemn warnings from the British government,[61] they recommenced the war. By the end of the month news reached London that their army had once more been crushed, and that their king had abdicated in despair. It arrived by chance just on the day of a royal drawing-room, ' at which everybody, the Queen included, complimented and wished joy to Colloredo (the Austrian envoy) except Palmerston.' Charles Greville, who recorded this, added a note two days later :

> I do not think anything Palmerston has done has excited so great a sensation, and exposed him to so much animadversion, as his behaviour to Colloredo at the Drawing-room. . . . Lord Lansdowne . . . was both shocked and surprised. The impolicy of this unmistakeable display of *animus* is the more striking, because we are now (through Ponsonby) entreating the Austrian Government to show moderation, and not to exact large contributions.[62]

Ten days later, Russell had to read his foreign secretary a lesson on the tone and contents of the despatches he was sending to Vienna.[63] He did not think that Palmerston would help the Italians by ' meddling ' in the peace negotiations, by taunting Austria with her misdeeds in Galicia, and by threatening her with the condemnation of the whole European press. What was more, it was not good policy to throw her into Russia's waiting arms, so that 'the advances of that Power into the heart of Europe' would be furthered by the British government's own acts. Palmerston was in disgrace and under surveillance when he undertook his final task in the affair, the task of helping to save the Piedmontese from having to sign an utterly disastrous peace.

What he accomplished is hard to estimate. Certainly the Austrian terms, at first intolerable in their severity, were much softened before the treaty was signed in August 1849. Palmerston, now grown perforce more temperate, was unremitting in his efforts to forward the softening process; and Russell credited him with doing much to secure reduction of the indemnity.⁶⁴ But France was working for reduction, too ; and Schwarzenberg at least permitted it to seem that it was to her pleas for moderation, not to Palmerston's, that he gave ear. Moreover, de Tocqueville, in charge of French foreign affairs when the negotiations reached their close, charged Palmerston with deserting both Piedmont and France at a time when the Austrians had presented a virtual ultimatum at Turin, and the French government was threatening them with war.⁶⁵ There is some evidence to substantiate the charge, quite beside the fact that the British cabinet and Court would never have allowed the Foreign Office to associate itself with the French threat.⁶⁶ But de Tocqueville, in winding up his indictment of the British government for encourging continental liberals, and then deserting them in time of need, added a notable complaint :

. . . these tactics succeeded remarkably well. The Piedmontese remained convinced that England alone had defended them. . . . She remained very popular in Turin and France very much suspected.⁶⁷

In point of fact, no less a person than Victor Emmanuel's chief minister, d'Azeglio, gave Palmerston chief credit for the moderation of Austria's demands.⁶⁸ Were the Piedmontese, who must have followed every move, so curiously deceived ; or was it that they preferred to give their confidence to the more straightforward and less self-seeking of their two champions ? Only in times of desperation had they reconciled themselves to the dangers of asking France to intervene ; and Palmerston, failing in so much else, could claim that he had done much to avert those dangers, at any rate. There was even much justification for the claim he made before the House of having saved Europe from a general war.⁶⁹

Meanwhile his disagreements with the Queen had grown still more pronounced, and extended into wider grounds. She was complaining now, not merely of his policies and their effects, but of his attitude toward herself. At the Foreign Office he opened her private letters from continental royalties: he kept her in ignorance of essential facts.⁷⁰ He frequently (and, as his papers show, deliberately) ⁷¹ sent off despatches to which she had not given her assent, or altered those to which she had. She had real reason for complaint ; but she was quite unfair in treating all his excuses as mere evidences of insincerity.[72] Telegraphic communication was in its infancy ; and the transmission of despatches by messengers (who were by no means constantly available) was at best a matter of days or weeks. But situations at foreign capitals could develop as rapidly as they do now. Hence the need for avoiding all delay was sometimes overmastering. It was hard enough to keep up speed in an office which sent out some thirty thousand despatches (each written and copied from one to five times in longhand) within a single year.[73] Hard enough without a queen who took her time. Victoria, burdened by court duties, taught by King Leopold from early youth never to be hasty in making up her mind, and now in the habit of discussing everything with Prince Albert in a conscientiously thorough German way, was apt to keep drafts much too long for even the most complaisant of her foreign ministers. And Palmerston, far from being complaisant, took little pains to be overly respectful or even courteous.

She was especially sensitive to his sending off despatches which she had not seen, because their form was apt to be so offensive to foreign governments. All his arrogance had come back again. It seemed, in fact, more pronounced than it had ever been before. Regrettable though this was, it is not entirely to be wondered at. Events, as he saw them, had demonstrated not only the bankruptcy of the Metternich system, not only the faults of Aberdeen's diplomacy, but the superiority of his own policy. Some of his enemies had been confounded, and not a few of his predictions justified. If the Court and society disapproved of him, the people of England as a whole were at his back. He was determined as ever to be the patron saint of constitutional liberalism. Witness a private letter that he sent at the beginning of April 1848 to his ambassador at St. Petersburg, Lord Bloomfield :

All seems quiet by the last accounts in Poland . . . but the state of Europe is full of uncertainty. . . . It would be a thousand pities if the Polish situation should set Germany & Russia at variance . . . Would it not be possible for the Emperor to be before hand with events, & place the crown of Poland upon the head of some member of his family. . . . If in addition to what I have suggested above the Emperor or the new king of Poland would give to the kingdom a good constitution . . . consisting of two chambers with free press independent judges and open courts . . . tranquillity would be for a long time established in that country . . .[74]

The suggestion was naïve and perfectly harmless. The Tsar and Nesselrode, if it ever reached them, were in a position to treat it with a smile. But another piece of well-intentioned interference, undertaken at about the same time, had produced unfortunate results.

In this case he had undertaken to admonish the Spanish government. At the middle of March 1848, Bulwer had been instructed by private letter to remind Isabella's ministers of the lesson to be drawn from the fate of Louis Philippe and Guizot, and the danger of 'endeavouring to govern a country in a manner opposed to the sentiments and opinions of the nation.' Instead :

> The Queen of Spain would act wisely if she were to strengthen her executive Government, by widening the bases on which the Administration reposes, and in calling to her councils some of the men in whom the Liberal party places confidence.[75]

Bulwer, without permission,[76] had communicated the letter to Isabella's first minister. Back had come a stinging retort. The Spanish government could not 'see without extreme surprise the extraordinary pretension of Lord Palmerston.' What would he say if he were told that the lessons of late events on the continent showed that the British government should be 'given up to the illustrious Peel, to the skilful man, who, after having conciliated the general opinion of his country, has known how to merit the sympathies and the esteem of all the governments of Europe'? Palmerston's letter had been handed back to Bulwer with a warning that any despatches of similar import would be returned without comment. Palmerston had not been at all abashed. Determining, as he had told Russell, to give the Spanish ministers 'a Roland for their Oliver,' he had reminded them in the most offensive manner possible that Isabella owed to England her very throne, that her ministers had never been backward in asking British help, and that, but for such help, they themselves would have been ' proscribed exiles in a foreign land.'[77] After two or three weeks of bickering, Bulwer had been given forty-eight hours to leave the country. This was allegedly on the ground that he had mixed in political plots against the government ; but it had generally been believed that his real offence had lain in acting as Palmerston's mouthpiece.

By June 1848 the Queen's annoyance with Palmerston had become so apparent that his wife felt it incumbent on her to warn him :

> I am sure the Queen is very angry with you ! ! ! I am afraid you contradict her notions too boldly. . . . I am sure it would be better if you *said* less to her—even if you *act* as you think best. . . . You always think you can convince people by Arguments, & she has not reflection or sense to feel the force of them. . . . I should . . . lead her on gently, by letting her believe you have both the same opinions in fact & the same wishes, but take sometimes different ways of carrying them out.[78]

But alas for good advice ! The record shows only new complaints, and, in September of that year, Victoria's first decided effort to get rid of him.[79] She could ' hardly go on with him,' she told Russell. Could not Clarendon be put into the Foreign Office, and Palmerston be made lord-lieutenant of Ireland in his place ? Russell, though meeting the demand with a gentleness that Lady Palmerston would have approved, thought not. If the offender's faults were great, so were his virtues, his power and his pride. An attempt to carry out Victoria's plan would drive him into opposition ; and if he crossed the House, England would probably undergo a change of ministry at a dangerous time. Victoria, apparently quite willing to take this risk but not to come into direct conflict with her premier, contented herself with threats of what she might do ' some day.' The hapless Russell sent Palmerston warnings of engaging friendliness, assuring him of their constant agreement 'in opinion,' and begging that he would explain the reasons for his actions ' before and not after, an important despatch is sent.'[80]

PALMERSTON'S REMOVAL DEMANDED 441

Unfortunately for the culprit, the Queen was soon able to adduce new evidence of his insolence to other Powers, and of its bad effects. During the late autumn of 1848, he gave vent to his disappointment and impatience concerning developments in Italy by adopting a most offensive tone toward Austria. When Radetzky, the Austrian conqueror of Milan, falsified the promises of his government by his harshness to the inhabitants, Palmerston sent to Vienna a despatch which any independent government would have found intolerable :

> You will represent to the Austrian Govt. that if Marshal Radetzky . . . had been perfectly free to resort to such measures as those announced in his proclamation, yet the moral feeling of mankind and every sentiment of generosity and justice would have revolted against a proceeding conceived in the spirit of the most odious oppression and enuntiated by doctrines which belong only to the disciples of communism, and which are subversive of the very foundations of social order . . . the Austrian Govt. cannot have forgotten, . . . the solemn and public engagements entered into . . . by the capitulation of Milan, by the Armistice . . . and by the proclamation issued by the Emperor himself. . . . The proclamation of Marshal Radetzky is a flagrant and a palpable violation of the engagements contained in those truce instruments. . . .[81]

Those words were penned in November 1848, just before Schwarzenberg came into power.

Schwarzenberg was one of the last men in Europe to put up with language of that sort. Already irritated by the British secretary's studied insolence, he was apparently driven to the final point of exasperation by Palmerston's action in sending him a copy of a proclamation issued by the Consulta of Lombardy—a document which was interpreted as recommending the assassination of Austrians whenever opportunity occurred.[82] In his rage he gave Palmerston such a taste of his own medicine as ' the devil's son ' probably never experienced before or afterward. It was contained in a letter addressed to Baron Werner, the Austrian under-secretary for foreign affairs, for communication to Ponsonby, the British ambassador.[83] Palmerston's language in accusing the Austrians of ' odious oppression,' Schwarzenberg wrote airily, constituted a novelty in diplomatic intercourse, but was comprehensible when one considered that all his predictions with respect to Italy had been falsified. As for any idea on the British minister's part that he would be allowed to interfere in problems which were solely Austria's concern, that was only one illusion the more. As the letter progressed he became still more personal:

... In truth, my dear Baron, Lord Palmerston is a little too much inclined to consider himself the arbiter of the destinies of Europe. For our part we are not in the least disposed to attribute to him, in our own affairs, the rôle of Providence. We never pressed on him our advice concerning the affairs of Ireland. ... I must frankly confess that we are tired of his eternal insinuations, of his tone now protective and pedantic, now insulting, but always unbecoming and we have decided that we shall no longer tolerate it. Lord Palmerston remarked one day to Baron Koller that if we wanted war, we should have it: and I told him that if he wants it he shall have it. I do not know whether Lord Palmerston applies to himself the phrase of Louis XIV, and thinks that L'Angleterre, *c'est lui*.

Meantime, Schwarzenberg went on, he was taking measures to support Austria's dignity. While archdukes had been sent to Berlin and St. Petersburg to announce the accession of Francis Joseph to the imperial throne, the same courtesy could not be extended to the British court. For the Austrian government could not 'expose an Archduke to contact with the inveterate enemy of Austria, with the avowed protector of the Emperor's rebellious subjects, in short with a man such as Lord Palmerston.' Moreover, the chargé at London had been forbidden to have any relations with him which were not purely official in character. Ponsonby, although he answered Schwarzenberg's letter in a protesting and reproachful tone,[84] must thoroughly have enjoyed sending a copy of it to Downing Street. Whether Palmerston replied in kind, it seems impossible to ascertain. Having relieved his feelings by comparing Schwarzenberg's epistle to 'the outpourings of an enraged woman of the town when arrested by a policeman in the act of picking a pocket,'[85] he ordered and secured the deletion of every trace of this correspondence from the embassy archives.[86] But if he hoped that the incident was buried, he hoped in

SCHWARZENBERG FEEDS THE FLAME

vain. The substance, and at least part of the text, of Schwarzenberg's letter was soon common property among the Metternich circle in London.[87] What is more, copies of it and of related letters were made by Ponsonby's orders, and surreptitiously communicated to the Prince Consort ten years afterwards.[88]

Schwarzenberg, in refusing to send an archduke to England, had taken what was probably as shrewd a step as could have been devised for increasing Palmerston's difficulties at home. That he should bring so public and so marked a slight upon the Court, not only enraged the Queen and all those elements in government and society which were hostile to his policies, but gave them an opportunity of which they made full use. Victoria signalised the hearty support which she and her late foreign minister were prepared to give to Austria, by sending Aberdeen to explain to the Austrian chargé that she quite understood and sympathised with Austria's motives in withholding from her the courtesy shown to Frederick William and Nicholas. It was a most unusual step; but other unusual things occurred at London and Windsor about this time; and most if not all of them were traceable to Palmerston. Among them might be included the terms he employed in parliament, in July 1849, to describe some of his domestic foes.[89] These, it appeared, were persons who, 'having passed their whole lives in adoring the Government of Austria, because they deemed it the great symbol of the opinions which they entertained, at last . . . transferred their allegiance to the Government of France, because they thought that in that Government they saw an almost equal degree of leaning to the arbitrary principle.' Of their conduct he would 'only' say that it was 'an example of antiquated imbecility.' No one doubted that his particular target was Aberdeen; nor was anyone ignorant of the fact that Aberdeen's attitude toward Austria and France was, and had been, identical with that of the Court.

But long before Palmerston had made this daring thrust: at about the time, in fact, when the details of his quarrel with Schwarzenberg were becoming known in

London, he got into still another scrape through his sympathy with the Sicilian insurgents. Generally speaking, his diplomatic activities in connection with the Sicilian revolt (at times as exacting and critical as those in which he engaged with regard to northern Italy) had been cautious and correct. He had set himself to find some arrangement which, in giving the people of Sicily relief from the conditions which had provoked them for so long, would preserve the *status quo* to the greatest possible extent. His first idea was that the island should obtain complete autonomy without any change of sovereign : his second that, although separated from Naples, it should accept for ruler a prince of the Neapolitan royal house. But all his efforts broke down against the obstinacy both of the King and of the revolutionists. The latter insisted upon independence ; and so worried was the British government lest a Sicilian republic should be set up, that, according to Palmerston at least, it promised to acknowledge Sicily as an independent kingdom under the duke of Genoa, and to give it some protection against the Neapolitans.[90] But whatever was done had to be done surreptitiously ; and in the end Palmerston was compelled to stand aside while Ferdinand II of Naples re-established the old rule with all the old abuses which it had entailed. No doubt his feeling of resentment at Ferdinand's refusal to follow good British advice was in part responsible for his startling indiscretion in ' the affair of the Sicilian arms.'

The suggestion of mysterious crime which this title conveys was not a little borne out by the circumstances. Delane of *The Times*, while out hunting one day with a man who contracted to supply arms to the War Office, heard casual mention of a shipment of artillery which had, with Palmerston's approval, been sent from government stores to the insurgents in Sicily.[91] After a little quiet investigation, *The Times*, in January 1849, charged the Foreign Office with violating its professed neutrality, and directly aiding rebels against a sovereign with whom England was on friendly terms. This statement was too bald. What Palmerston had really done was to assist the contractor in withdrawing from a government arsenal guns which he had recently delivered there, but which he preferred to sell to the revolutionary government in Sicily.[92] Save for the technicality that the cannon had for a short time been in an arsenal, Palmerston had done less for the Sicilians than had Grey's cabinet for the Spanish and Portuguese insurgents of the early 'thirties.

But there was another side to the affair, which the third Earl Grey, Russell's colonial secretary, and a strong pro-Sicilian, immediately pointed out.[93] Palmerston had approved the shipment of the arms subsequent to the date on which the government had announced its strict neutrality, and without the knowledge of the prime minister or any other member of the cabinet. He had even attempted to deceive his colleagues after the news of his indiscretion had leaked out. That he should act so independently Grey found only too typical. In repeated instances he had sent off despatches or taken important steps without seeking the approval of his fellow ministers. And Russell was entirely too passive. 'We have a right,' Grey wrote, 'to expect that the Prime Minister shall exercise that control which as a body we cannot.' In the affair of the Sicilian arms, the good faith and honour of the government were involved. If the opposition undertook to censure the Foreign Office, as it ought to do, he for one would be unable to take part in the defence. He ended by demanding that the decision of the cabinet should be communicated to the Queen. This was really quite superfluous.

Victoria, very much on the alert, had reason to hope that her day of reckoning with Palmerston had come. Russell condoned the offence, allegedly in view of what had earlier been done for the Portuguese and Spanish liberals, but perhaps also in consideration of his own and his cabinet's rather unneutral conduct to King Ferdinand. But he demanded that an apology be made to the Neapolitan government.[94] Palmerston, while admitting that 'perhaps it would have been better' if he 'had said *no* instead of *yes*,' refused to concur. He suggested that if the government was bent on confessing its sins to Ferdinand, it 'ought at least to make a clean breast of it.' And he pointed out that no apology had been asked.[95] Lord John referred matters to the cabinet ; and told his delighted sovereign that he was now ready to consider transferring Palmerston to Ireland, provided that he could at the same time offer him an English peerage and perhaps the Garter. 'All Ld. John seemed to fear was Ld. Palm's throwing his office up in a huff.'[96] But, when the cabinet met, it was apparent that Palmerston had no intention whatever of relinquishing his post. On Grey's hinting at a change, ' Ld. Palm silenced him by asking him bluntly " what is it you propose to do ? " ' The only decision made was that the Neapolitan sovereign should have an apology if he chose to ask for it.[97]

Once more Palmerston had evaded punishment. In vain the Queen and Prince begged that he be removed at once, or at least that ' a change of office at a future but *stated* time ' should be arranged.[98] In vain they added to all other possible pleas that Victoria ' felt it repugnant to her character to show a degree of respect and politeness which was at variance with her real feeling towards him.' Russell would promise nothing save to reconsider the question with Lansdowne. Worse still, Palmerston, attacked in both Houses, turned his reverse into a success. As Greville reported, disgustedly, ' he delivered a slashing, impudent speech, full of sarcasm, jokes, and clap-traps . . . expressed ultra-Liberal sentiments to please the Radicals, and he gathered shouts of laughter and applause as he dashed and rattled along.'[99] A few months later he explained to Broughton that the Queen's unfriendliness to his foreign policy did not 'signify a pin, after all.'[100]

By the spring of 1849, his misdeeds had been piling up for well-nigh a year, and were making his position decidedly precarious. In still other matters he had incurred disgrace. On hearing that Ponsonby was telling Schwarzenberg that the cabinet did not endorse his (Palmerston's) policy, and was employing as secretary a young man who wrote anti-Palmerstonian articles for *The Times*, Palmerston had written the aged and incorrigible ambassador letters ' not to be submitted to.'[101] Ponsonby enjoyed a great position among certain of the Whigs, and was in close touch with his nephew, and Prince Albert's secretary, Charles Grey.[102] There was trouble, too, in Greece, where the government was highly irritated by Sir Edmund (later Lord) Lyons, Palmerston's too Palmerstonian minister. The Greek government complained of his bullying and was anxious for his recall. According to Stockmar, the cabinet was growing very weary of this turmoil :

> During the last few weeks Palmerston's colleagues . . . wished to get rid of him, but had not courage enough. . . . However justifiable his policy may be *in abstracto*, he is altogether wrong *in concreto*. . . .[103]

He believed that Palmerston was at least momentarily penitent :

> For the last eight days, there have been signs, that, owing to the persuasions or threats of his colleagues, Palmerston has promised ' to become a good boy.' Lady Palmerston said yesterday, ' It is delightful—everyone keeps what he has got.' Palmerston has agreed at last to the removal of his most obnoxious agents. The Spanish Bulwer goes to America, Lyons to Switzerland, and the very gentle Wyse to Greece. It is, therefore, to be hoped, that we are now entering on a line of policy more worthy of England, and more useful to the world.

But more than a month later (*i.e.* in March 1849) he pointed out that the foreign secretary's position was still unenviable :

> At home and abroad he is accused and condemned, both in matters where he is really in fault, and in matters where he is blameless.[104]

But it was too early to estimate how Palmerston would emerge from the great mid-century upheaval in Europe. In Italy, the struggle between Charles Albert and Austria was just about to enter on its final phase ; in Hungary, the Magyars were putting up a desperate struggle against Austrian suzerainty ; in Schleswig-Holstein, Danes and Germans alternated between armistices and hostilities ; and at Frankfort the leaders of the German liberals were still attempting to work out a plan which would give their country something approximating to a national government. In each of these regions Palmerston's principles and policies were put to the test.

GUIDE TO CITATIONS

WHAT follows is merely an explanation of the abbreviations used for the citations of unpublished documents in the notes, together with a list of some of the publications also cited there. The presentation of even a selective bibliography is rendered impracticable by strict limitations of space, taken in conjunction with the extraordinary scope and length of Palmerston's activities. Moreover, the selection of such books as do appear in the list which follows has been made, in most instances, not according to their general value or general usefulness, but according to what suitable documentary material they contain. Since the list of materials which follows is not a bibliography, no classification has been indicated, except as between unpublished and published sources. The need for economising space has also led to the adoption of the following procedure:

(1) The use of unusual abbreviations (shown in square brackets) for the citation of certain books included in the list of publications.

(2) The omission from this list of nearly all books cited only once or only in adjacent notes. Full references to these books have been incorporated in the notes.

(3) A similar omission from the list, and citation only in the notes, of all articles and other matter appearing in periodicals.

UNPUBLISHED MATERIALS

Aberdeen MSS. Papers of the 4th Earl of Aberdeen. Deposited at the British Museum but not incorporated into the *Additional Manuscripts* at the time when they were consulted.

Bowood MSS. Family papers of the Marquess of Lansdowne. Preserved at Bowood Park. Transcripts generously furnished by Mr. Philip Guedalla.

Br. Mus., *Add MSS.* The vast and varied collection of 'additional' manuscripts in the British Museum includes the papers of numerous associates of Palmerston (such as Liverpool, Huskisson and Peel) and of other persons who corresponded with him or commented upon his activities. Space is lacking for any reference to particular collections, or for the citation of most of these manuscripts in any manner save by the numbers of the volumes and folios. The printed indices of the *Additional Manuscripts* will afford some information as to the nature of documents cited in the notes.

Clarendon MSS. Family papers of the Earl of Clarendon. Preserved at Pitt House. Only a portion of these were available for my inspection.

GUIDE TO CITATIONS

Howick MSS. Family papers of the Earl Grey. Preserved at Howick House.

Johnston Coll. The collection of Albert W. Johnston, Esq., of Greenwich, Connecticut. Contains about 150 letters from Palmerston to Adair, the British minister at Brussels, dated 1831–1835, also twenty-three letters to Adair from Bagot, the British minister at The Hague, dated 1832, also copies of three letters from Palmerston to King Leopold of Belgium, dated 1833.

P.R.O., F.O. The Foreign Office papers preserved at the Public Record Office. I have made use, not only of the diplomatic correspondence between the Foreign Office and various foreign governments, but of Palmerston's unofficial correspondence with Bloomfield in F.O. 356, and of the 'working' papers of the Foreign Office in F.O. 96. These 'working' papers comprise notes, memoranda and queries written by foreign secretaries, permanent under secretaries and other officials; and bear various notations by persons other than the writers. They include first drafts of despátches, instructions for preparing the same, and, in a few instances, drafts of communications to be made to the press. They are of great value in showing Palmerston's personal opinions, his decisions as to the sending of despatches not yet submitted to the Queen, and his connection with the newspapers. They were brought to my attention by Mr. C. S. B. Buckland.

P.R.O., G. and D. Of these 'Gifts and Deposits' at the Public Record Office I have cited two collections constantly: the Russell papers (G. and D. 22) and the Granville papers (G. and D. 29). Other collections were examined.

P.R.O., W.O. The War Office papers preserved at the Public Record Office. (Some of the Home Office papers were also examined, but were not found suitable for citation.)

Stevenson MSS. The papers of Andrew Stevenson, American minister to Great Britain, 1836–1841. Preserved at the Congressional Library, Washington.

Van Buren MSS. The papers of Martin Van Buren. Preserved at the Congressional Library, Washington.

Windsor MSS. The nature of these papers (cited, except as otherwise noted, only for the reign of Queen Victoria) is sufficiently indicated by *The Letters of Queen Victoria*. Only a fraction have been printed. They offer a wealth of information on Palmerston's relations with the Queen and the Prince Consort, with other courts, and with his associates. And they contain many expressions of opinion on his part not to be found elsewhere. The classification, partly according to origin, partly topical, and partly chronological, results in a good deal of overlapping between the different series.

PUBLICATIONS

[*Aberdeen Corr.*] *Correspondence of the fourth Earl of Aberdeen.* Privately printed. 10 vols. Not numbered. Cited by dates (sometimes overlapping) of contents.

Adams, Ephraim D. *Great Britain and the American Civil War.* 2 vols. London, 1925.

Airlie, Mabell, Countess of. *Lady Palmerston and her Times.* 2 vols. London, 1922.

[*Ann. Reg.*] *The Annual Register.* London, 1761 ff.

Apponyi, Comte Rodolphe. *Journal.* Ed. by Ernest Daudet. 4 vols. Paris, 1914.

Argyll, eighth Duke of. *Autobiography and Memoirs.* 2 vols. London, 1906.

Arnould, Sir J. *Memoir of Thomas, First Lord Denman.* 2 vols. London, 1873.

GUIDE TO CITATIONS

Ashley, Hon. Evelyn. *The Life and Correspondence of Henry John Temple, Viscount Palmerston.* 2 vols. London, 1879. [Virtually a condensation and rearrangement of the five volume work of Bulwer and Ashley (*infra*), which I have used in preference.]
Aspinall, Arthur. *Lord Brougham and the Whig Party.* Manchester, 1927.
Atkins, John Black. *The Life of Sir William Howard Russell.* 2 vols. London, 1911.
[B. and A.] Bulwer, Sir Henry Lytton (later Baron Dalling and Bulwer) and Ashley, Hon. Evelyn. *The Life of Henry John Temple, Viscount Palmerston.* 5 vols. London, 1870–1876.
Barante, Baron de (A. G. P. Brugière). *Souvenirs, 1782–1866.* 8 vols. Paris, 1890–1901.
Barrington, Emilie I. (Mrs. Russell Barrington). *The Servant of All. Pages from the ... Life of ... James Wilson.* 2 vols. London, 1927.
The Life of Walter Bagehot. London, 1914.
Barrot, C. H. O. *Mémoires posthumes de Odilon Barrot.* 4 vols. Paris, 1875–1876.
Baxter, James P. 3d. *The Introduction of the Ironclad Warship.* Cambridge, Mass., 1933.
Beust, Friedrich F., Count von. *Memoirs.* 2 vols. London, 1887.
Bloomfield, Georgiana, Baroness. *Reminiscences of Court and Diplomatic Life.* 2 vols. New York, 1883.
Bowman, William. *The Story of 'The Times.'* New York, 1931.
Bright, John. *Diaries.* Ed. R. A. J. Walling. London, 1930.
Brooks, Constance. *Antonio Panizzi.* Manchester, 1931.
Brougham and Vaux, Baron (Henry Brougham). *Life and Times.* Written by Himself. 3 vols. Edinburgh, 1871.
Broughton, Baron (J. C. Hobhouse). *Recollections of a Long Life.* 6 vols. London, 1910–11.
Buckingham and Chandos, second Duke of. *Memoirs of the Courts and Cabinets of William IV and Victoria.* 2 vols. London, 1861.
Bunsen, Baron (Christian). *Memoirs.* 2 vols. Philadelphia, 1869.
Burghclere, Lady Winifred, ed. *A Great Man's Friendship. Letters of the Duke of Wellington to Mary, Marchioness of Salisbury, 1850–1852.* London, 1927.
Burghersh, Baron (later eleventh Earl of Westmorland). *Correspondence.* Ed. Rachel Weigall. London, 1912.
Cambridge History of the British Empire. Ed. J. Holland Rose, A. P. Newton, E. A. Benians. Cambridge, 1929 ff.
Cambridge History of British Foreign Policy. Ed. Sir A. W. Ward and G. P. Gooch. 3 vols. Cambridge, 1922–1923.
Cambridge History of India. Cambridge, 1922 ff.
Cavendish, Lady Frederick. *Diary.* Ed. John Bailey. 2 vols. London, 1927.
Cavour, Camillo Benso, conte di. *Il Carteggio Cavour-Nigra dal 1858 al 1861.* 12 vols. Bologna, 1926–9.
Christie, O. F. *The Transition from Aristocracy, 1832–67.* London, 1927.
Clapham, J. H. *An Economic History of Modern Britain.* 2 vols. Cambridge, 1926, 1932.
Clode, Charles Matthew. *The Military Forces of the Crown.* 2 vols. London, 1869.
Colchester, Charles Abbot, first Baron. *Diary and Correspondence.* Ed. the second Lord Colchester. 3 vols. London, 1861.
Coleridge, John Duke, first Baron. *Life and Correspondence.* Ed. E. H. Coleridge. 2 vols. New York, 1904.

GUIDE TO CITATIONS 451

Cook, Sir Edward. *Delane of 'The Times.'* New York, 1916.
Corti, Dr. Egon Caesar. *Leopold I of Belgium.* New York, 1923.
Cowley, first Baron (Henry Wellesley). *Diary and Correspondence.* Ed. Col. F. A. Wellesley. London, 1930.
Cowley, first Earl (Henry R. C. Wellesley). *Secrets of the Second Empire.* New York, 1929. [Published in Great Britain as *The Paris Embassy during the Second Empire.*]
Crawley, C. W. *The Question of Greek Independence.* Cambridge, 1930.
Creevey, Thomas. *The Creevey Papers.* Ed. Sir H. Maxwell. London, 1923.
Croker, John Wilson. *Correspondence and Diaries.* Ed. L. J. Jennings. 2 vols. New York, 1884.
Czartoryski, Prince Adam. *Memoirs.* Ed. Adam Gielgud. 2 vols. London, 1888.
Dalhousie, Marquess of. *Private Letters.* Ed. J. G. A. Baird. Edinburgh, 1910.
Dallas, George Mifflin. *Letters from London, 1856–60.* 2 vols. London, 1870.
Dasent, Arthur Irwin. *Piccadilly.* London, 1920.
John Delane. 2 vols. New York, 1908.
Daudet, Ernest. *Une vie d'ambassadrice au siècle dernière, la princesse de Lieven.* Paris, 1904.
Davis, H. W. Carless. *The Age of Grey and Peel.* New York, 1929.
Day, William. *Reminiscences of the Turf.* London, 1886.
Denison, Rt. Hon. John Evelyn. *Notes from my Journal When Speaker of the House of Commons.* London, 1900.
Dictionary of National Biography.
Dino, Duchesse de. *Chronique de 1831 à 1862.* Ed. Princesse Radziwill. 4 vols. Paris, 1909.
Driault, Édouard. *La question d'Extrême-Orient.* Paris, 1908.
Du Bled, Victor. *Histoire de la monarchie de juillet de 1830 à 1848.* 2 vols. Paris, 1877–9.
Du Bois, W. E. Burghardt. *The Suppression of the African Slave Trade.* New York, 1904.
Dunham, Arthur Louis. *The Anglo-French Treaty of Commerce of 1860.* Ann Arbor, 1930.
Eardley-Wilmot, Sydney Marow. *Life of Vice-Admiral Edmund Lord Lyons.* London, 1898.
Ellenborough, first Baron. *A Political Diary.* Ed. Lord Colchester. 2 vols. London, 1881.
Elliot, Hon. Arthur D. *The Life of George Joachim Goschen, First Viscount Goschen, 1831–1907.* 2 vols. New York, 1911.
Elliot, H. S. R., ed. *Letters of John Stuart Mill.* 2 vols. London, 1910.
Empress Frederick of Germany. Letters. Ed. Sir F. Ponsonby. London, 1928.
Fagan, Louis, ed. *Letters of Prosper Mérimée to Panizzi.* 2 vols. London, 1881.
The Life and Correspondence of Sir Anthony Panizzi. 2 vols. Boston, 1881.
The Reform Club. London, 1887.
Fawcett, M. G. *Life of Sir William Molesworth.* London, 1901.
Ficquelmont, Karl Ludwig. *Lord Palmerston, l'Angle erre, et le continent.* 2 vols. Bruxelles, 1852–3.
Fitzmaurice, Lord Edmond. *The Life of the Second Earl Granville.* 2 vols. London, 1905.
Gardiner, A. G. *The Life of Sir William Harcourt.* 2 vols. New York, 1923.
Grant, James. *Random Recollections of the House of Commons.* London, 1837.
The Newspaper Press. 3 vols. London, 1871–2.

Granville, Harriet, Countess. Letters of, 1810–45. Ed. Hon. F. Leveson Gower. 2 vols. London, 1894.
[C. Greville, *Mem.*, I–VIII] Greville, Charles C. F. *Memoirs. A Journal of the Reigns of King George IV and King William IV.* [Part I, 1818–37. 3 vols. Ed. Henry Reeve. London, 1874.] *A Journal of the Reign of Queen Victoria.* [Part II, 1837–52. 3 vols. Ed. Henry Reeve. London, 1885.] *A Journal of the Reign of Queen Victoria.* [Part III, 1852–60. 2 vols. Ed. Henry Reeve. London, 1887.] [Cited as Vols. I–VIII.]
Greville, Charles C. F., and Reeve, Henry. The Letters of, 1836–65. Ed. A. H. Johnson. London, 1924.
[H. Greville, Diary] *Greville, Henry William. Leaves from the Diary of.* Ed. Viscountess Enfield. 4 vols. London, 1883–1905.
Grey, Charles, second Earl. Correspondence of, with William IV and with Sir Herbert Taylor. Ed. the third Earl Grey. 2 vols. London, 1867.
Guedalla, Philip. *Palmerston.* London, 1926.
    Gladstone and Palmerston. London, 1928.
Guizot, François. Mémoires. 8 vols. Paris, 1858–67.
Guyot, Raymond. *La première entente cordiale.* Paris, 1926.
Gwynn, Denis. *Cardinal Wiseman.* London, 1929.
Halévy, Élie. *Histoire du peuple anglais au XIXe siècle.* 3 vols. Paris, 1913–1923.
Hall, John R. *England and the Orleans Monarchy.* London, 1912.
Hansard's Parliamentary Debates. London, 1829 ff.
Hardinge, Sir Arthur. *Life of [the] Fourth Earl of Carnarvon.* 3 vols. London, 1925.
Haussonville, Comte de. *Histoire de la politique extérieure du gouvernement français,* 1830–48. 2 vols. Paris, 1850.
Hayward, Abraham. *Biographical and Critical Essays.* 5 vols. London, 1873–1874.
Hertslet, Sir Edward. *Recollections of the Old Foreign Office.* London, 1901.
    The Map of Europe by Treaty. 4 vols. London, 1875–91.
Hillebrand, Karl. *Geschichte Frankreichs,* 1830–71. 2 vols. Gotha, 1877–9.
[His. MSS. Comm.] *Reports of the Royal Commission on Historical Manuscripts.* London, 1870 ff.
Hodder, Edwin. *Life and Work of the Seventh Earl of Shaftesbury.* 3 vols. London, 1886.
Holyoake, George Jacob. *Sixty Years of an Agitator's Life.* 2 vols. London, 1892.
Hoskins, Halford Lancaster. *British Routes to India.* New York, 1928.
Huskisson, William. Papers. Ed. Lewis Melville. London, 1931.
Jekyll, Joseph. Correspondence with his sister-in-law, 1818–38. Ed. Hon. Algernon Bourke. London, 1894.
Jordan, Donaldson and Pratt, Edwin J. *Europe and the Civil War.* Boston, 1931.
Juste, Theodore. *Memoirs of Leopold I, King of the Belgians.* Trans. by Robert Black. 2 vols. London, 1868.
Kendrick, Nathaniel C. *Palmerston and His North Italian Policy.* Unpublished.
Kerry, Earl of, and Guedalla, Philip. *The Secret of the Coup d'État.* London, 1924.
Lacour-Gayet, G. *Talleyrand,* 1754–1838. 3 vols. Paris, 1931.
La Gorce, Pierre de. *Histoire du Second Empire.* 7 vols. Paris, 1894–1904.
Lane-Poole, Stanley. *The Life of Stratford Canning.* 2 vols. London, 1888.
Lavisse, Ernest. *Histoire de France contemporaine.* 10 vols. Paris, 1920–2.

GUIDE TO CITATIONS 453

Layard, Sir Henry. Autobiography and Letters. Ed. Hon. William N. Bruce. 2 vols. New York, 1903.
Leader, R. E., ed. *Life and Letters of John A. Roebuck.* London, 1897.
Le Marchant, Sir Denis. *Viscount Althorp.* London, 1876.
Lieven, Princess, and Grey, second Earl. Correspondence. Ed. Guy Le Strange. 3 vols. London, 1890.
Lieven, Princess. Letters, 1812–34. Ed. L. G. Robinson. London, 1902.
Lorne, Marquis of. *Viscount Palmerston.* London, 1892.
Lucas, Reginald. *Lord Glenesk and the 'Morning Post.'* New York, 1910.
Lyall, Sir Alfred. *The Life of the Marquis of Dufferin and Ava.* 2 vols. London, 1905.
Lyttelton, Sarah S., Baroness. Correspondence. London, 1912.
MacCarthy, Desmond, and Russell, Agatha. *Lady John Russell.* New York, 1911.
MacColl, Malcolm. *Memoirs and Correspondence.* Ed. G. W. E. Russell. London, 1914.
Malmesbury, first Earl of. Diaries and Correspondence. Ed. the third Earl of Malmesbury. 4 vols. London, 1844.
Letters. Ed. the third Earl of Malmesbury. 2 vols. London, 1870.
Malmesbury, third Earl of. *Memoirs of an Ex-Minister. An Autobiography.* 2 vols. London, 1884.
Martens, George F. von. *Receuil des traités* and *Nouveau receuil.* Gottingue, 1817–42.
Martin, B. Kingsley. *The Triumph of Lord Palmerston.* London, 1924.
Martin, Sir Theodore. *The Life of H.R.H. the Prince Consort.* 5 vols. New York, 1880–91.
Martineau, John. *The Life of Henry Pelham, Fifth Duke of Newcastle.* London, 1908.
Mathieson, William L. *Great Britain and the Slave Trade, 1839–65.* London, 1929.
Matter, Paul. *Cavour et l'unité italienne.* Paris, 1922.
Maxwell, Sir Herbert. *Life and Letters of Fourth Earl of Clarendon.* 2 vols. London, 1913.
Life and Times of Rt. Hon. William Henry Smith. 2 vols. Edinburgh, 1893.
Meath, twelfth Earl of. *Memories of the Nineteenth Century.* New York, 1923.
Melbourne, second Viscount. Papers. Ed. L. C. Sanders. London, 1889.
Metternich, Prince Clement. Mémoires. 8 vols. Paris, 1880–4.
Minto, first Earl. Life and Letters. Ed. Countess of Minto. 3 vols. London, 1874.
Monypenny, W. F., and Buckle, G. E. *Life of Disraeli.* 6 vols. New York, 1911–20.
Morier, Rt. Hon. Sir Robert. Memoirs and Letters. Ed. Mrs. Rosslyn Wemyss. 2 vols. London, 1911.
Morison, J. L. *The Eighth Earl of Elgin.* London, 1928.
Morley, John. *Life of Richard Cobden.* 2 vols. London, 1908.
Life of Gladstone. 3 vols. London, 1903.
Morse, Hosea Ballou. *The International Relations of the Chinese Empire.* 3 vols. London, 1910.
Motley, John Lothrop. Correspondence. Ed. G. W. Curtis. 2 vols. London, 1889.
Nesselrode, Comte Charles de. Lettres et papiers. Ed. Comte A. de Nesselrode. 11 vols. Paris, 1904–12.

New, Chester W. *Lord Durham.* Oxford, 1929.
Newman, Bertram. *Lord Melbourne.* London, 1930.
Newton, Lord. *Lord Lyons.* 2 vols. London, 1913.
Nolte, Frederick. *L'Europe militaire et diplomatique,* 1815–84. 4 vols. Paris, 1884.
Oldfield, Susan H. *Some Records of the Later Life of Countess Granville.* London, 1901.
Panmure, Baron [later eleventh Earl of Dalhousie]. *Panmure Papers.* Ed. Sir G. Douglas and Sir G. D. Ramsay. 2 vols. London, 1908.
Parker, Charles Stuart. *Life and Letters of Sir James Graham.* 2 vols. London, 1907.
  Sir Robert Peel. 3 vols. London, 1891–9.
Parliamentary Debates. Published by Cobbett and Hansard. London, 1804–1829.
Parliamentary Papers. *Diplomatic Correspondence, Reports of Commissions and Select Committees.* London, 1801 ff.
Pirenne, H. *Histoire de Belgique.* 7 vols. Bruxelles, 1922–32.
[Prince Consort, Letters.] *The Prince Consort and His Brother. Two Hundred New Letters.* Ed. Hector Bolitho. London, 1933.
Puryear, Vernon John. *England, Russia and the Straits Question,* 1844–56. Berkeley, California, 1932.
Raikes, Thomas. *Journal,* 1831–47. 4 vols. London, 1856–7.
  Correspondence with Duke of Wellington and others. Ed. Harriet Raikes. London, 1861.
Ramsay, A. A. W. *Sir Robert Peel.* London, 1928.
Reeve, Henry. *Memoirs.* Ed. J. K. Laughton. 2 vols. 2nd ed. London, 1898.
Reid, Stuart J. *Life and Letters of the First Earl of Durham.* 2 vols. London, 1906.
Reid, Sir Thomas W. *Life of Richard Monckton Milnes, First Lord Houghton.* 2 vols. New York, 1891.
Riker, T. W. *The Making of Roumania.* Oxford, 1931.
Robinson, Gertrude. *David Urquhart.* Oxford, 1920.
Romilly, S. H., ed. *Letters to 'Ivy' from the First Earl of Dudley.* London, 1905.
Russell, Lord John (later first Earl Russell). *Early Correspondence.* Ed. Hon. Rollo Russell. 2 vols. London, 1913.
  Later Correspondence. Ed. G. P. Gooch. 2 vols. London, 1925.
  Recollections and Suggestions. London, 1875.
Schiemann, Theodor. *Geschichte Russlands unter Kaiser Nikolaus I.* 4 vols. Berlin, 1904–19.
Scott, Sir George Gilbert. *Personal and Professional Recollections.* Ed. G. Gilbert Scott. London, 1879.
Sedgwick, Rev. Adam. *Life and Letters.* Ed. J. W. Clark and T. Hughes. 2 vols. Cambridge, 1890.
Simpson, F. A. *Louis Napoleon and the Recovery of France.* London, 1923.
Snell, F. J. *Palmerston's Borough.* London, 1894.
Soulsby, Hugh Graham. *The Right of Search and the Slave Trade in Anglo-American Relations,* 1814–62. Baltimore, 1933.
Sproxton, Charles. *Palmerston and the Hungarian Revolution.* Cambridge, 1919.
Stanley, Lady Augusta. *Letters,* 1849–63. New York, 1927.

GUIDE TO CITATIONS 455

Stanmore, first Baron [Gordon, Arthur Hamilton]. *The Earl of Aberdeen.* New York, 1893.
    Sidney Herbert. 2 vols. London, 1906.
State Papers, British and Foreign. London, 1841 ff.
Steefel, Lawrence D. *The Schleswig-Holstein Question.* Oxford, 1932.
Stern, Alfred. *Geschichte Europas seit den Verträgen von 1815 bis zum Frankfurter Frieden von 1871.* 10 vols. Stuttgart, 1894–1925.
St. Helier, Lady. *Memories of Fifty Years.* London, 1909.
Stockmar, Baron. *Memoirs.* English edition, ed. by F. Max Müller. 2 vols. London, 1873.
Swain, James Edgar. *The Struggle for the Control of the Mediterranean Prior to 1848.* Boston, 1933.
Sykes, Sir Percy. *A History of Persia.* 2 vols. 2nd ed. London, 1921.
Talleyrand, Prince Charles Maurice de. *Memoirs.* Ed. Duc de Broglie. 5 vols. New York, 1891–2.
Taylor, Sir Herbert. *The Taylor Papers.* Ed. Ernest Taylor. London, 1913.
Temperley, Harold W. V., ed. *The Unpublished Diary of the Princess Lieven.* London, 1925.
Thureau-Dangin, Paul. *Histoire de la monarchie de juillet.* 7 vols. Paris, 1911–14.
Tocqueville, Alexis de. *Recollections.* Ed. Comte de Tocqueville. Trans. London, 1896.
Torrens, W. M. *Memoirs of Viscount Melbourne.* 2 vols. London, 1878.
Trevelyan, George Macaulay. *The Life of John Bright.* Boston, 1914.
    Lord Grey of the Reform Bill. London, 1920.
Trevelyan, G. Otto. *The Life and Letters of Lord Macaulay.* 2 vols. New York, 1877.
Van Buren, Martin. *Autobiography.* Ed. John C. Fitzpatrick. [Annual Report of the American Historical Association for the year 1918. Vol. II.]
[*Q.V.L.*] Victoria, Queen. *Letters. A Selection from Her Majesty's Correspondence between the Years 1837 and 1861.* First Series. Ed. A. C. Benson and Viscount Esher. 3 vols. London, 1907. Second Series. *A Selection from Her Majesty's Correspondence between the Years 1862 and 1885.* Ed. G. E. Buckle. 3 vols. New York, 1926–8. [Referred to as Q.V.L.]
Vitzthum, Count. *Berlin und Wien.* Stuttgart, 1886.
    St. Petersburg and London. Ed. H. Reeve. Trans. by E. F. Taylor. 2 vols. London, 1887.
Walpole, Spencer. *Lord John Russell.* 2 vols. London, 1889.
Walrond, T., ed. *Letters and Journals of the eighth Earl of Elgin.* London, 1872.
Ward, Robert (afterwards Plumer). *Memoirs of the Political and Literary Life of.* 2 vols. London, 1850.
Wellesley Papers. *The Life and Correspondence of Richard Colley Wellesley, Marquess Wellesley, 1760–1842.* 2 vols. London, 1914.
Wellington, Arthur Wellesley, First Duke of. *Despatches, Correspondence, and Memoranda.* Ed. his son, Duke of Wellington. 8 vols. London, 1867–1880.
    Supplementary Despatches and Memoranda. Ed. his son, Duke of Wellington. 15 vols. London, 1858–72.
West, Sir Algernon. *Recollections.* 2 vols. London, 1899.
White, William. *The Inner Life of the House of Commons.* Ed. Justin McCarthy. 2 vols. London, 1897.
Whitehouse, H. Remsen. *The Life of Lamartine.* 2 vols. Boston, 1918.

Whitty, Edward Michael. *St. Stephen's in the 'Fifties.* London, 1906.
Wiegler, Paul. *William the First.* Ed. and trans. by Constance Vesey. Boston, 1929.
Williams, Hugh Noel. *The Life and Letters of Admiral Napier.* London, 1917.
Williams, W. E. *The Rise of Gladstone to the Leadership of the Liberal Party, 1859 to 1868.* Cambridge, 1934.
Wilson, David Alec. *Carlyle to Threescore and Ten.* London, 1929.
Wilson, P. W., ed. *The Greville Diary.* 2 vols. New York, 1927.
Wolf, Lucien. *Life of the First Marquess of Ripon.* 2 vols. London, 1921.
Wolff, Sir Henry Drummond. *Rambling Recollections.* 2 vols. London, 1908.

NOTES

In order to bring these notes within reasonable compass, I have adhered in nearly all instances to the following rules:

1. To confine the notes entirely to references, omitting everything of an explanatory nature.
2. To make citations only by the surnames of the authors or editors (except where confusion might occur), or by the contractions given in the accompanying lists of documents and of published works actually cited.
3. To give only the page numbers of publications and the volume and folio numbers of the Add. MSS. in the British Museum, even when citing documents of significant origin or date.
4. To group references for whole paragraphs, pages or sections where practicable.
5. To cite biographies of Palmerston only for important documents, or (in the case of Bulwer and Ashley) where the authors could themselves speak authoritatively.

CHAPTER I

[1] P. 2. Mr. Guedalla's excellent bibliography for the years preceding Palmerston's entrance into public life scarcely needs amplification; but a few additional references, offered topically, may be of service.

Antecedents: J. A. Temple, *The Temple Memoirs* (London, 1925), *passim*; J. Farington, *The Farington Diary* (London, 1923–8), II, 229; V, 221–2; A. L. Dasent, *St. James's Square* (London, 1895), 53–7, 225; F. Bickley, *Diaries of Lord Glenbervie* (London, 1932), I, 109; II, 92–3; *His. MSS. Com.*, 12th Rep., append., Pt. X, 308; *ibid.*, 14th Rep., append., Pt. IX, 250–1; *ibid.*, 15th Rep., append., Pt. VI, 684, Pt. VII, 260.

Place of birth: Br. Mus., *Add. MSS.*, 28511, ff. 256–7; *Ann. Reg.* for 1865, 199, 199 n.

School-days: P. M. Thornton, *Harrow School* (London, 1885), 361–2, 300–1; *Harrow Class Lists* (Harrow School Library); *Harrow School Song Book* (Harrow School Library).

Life at Edinburgh: Romilly, 4; Nemo, *Earl Russell and the Foreign Office* (London, 1863), 23; Francis Horner, *Mem. and Corr.* (Boston, 1853), I, 153–74; J. H. Hollander, *Adam Smith*, in *Journ. Pol. Econ.*, vol. XXXV, no. 2 (Apr. 1927), pp. 177 *et seq.*; *The Times*, Oct. 19, 1865.

Life at Cambridge: Bunsen, II, 91; Henry Gunning, *Reminiscences* (London, 1854), II, 187–9; *Hansard*, 3rd Ser., CXXXVII, 247–8.

[2] P. 8. Minto, III, 234–5.
[3] P. 10. Lorne, 6–7.
[4] P. 12. Le Marchant, 86–7; Creevey, 76–7; H. Gunning, *Poll for the election* (Cambridge, 1831), 3–4; Romilly, 34–5; Sedgwick, I, 88 n.; R. and S. Wilberforce, *Corr. of William Wilberforce* (London, 1840), II, 64–70, 73; R. and S. Wilberforce, *Life of William Wilberforce* (Philadelphia, 1841), II, 13; Lorne, 9.
[5] P. 13. R. and S. Wilberforce, *Corr. of William Wilberforce*, II, 68.
[6] P. 13. Byron, *Works* (ed. E. H. Coleridge, London, 1898–1901), I, 57.
[7] P. 14. B. and A., I, 17–8.
[8] P. 15. Croker, I, 17; B. and A., I, 369.
[9] P. 15. Lorne, 43.
[10] P. 15. Ashley, I, 42.
[11] P. 15. Sedgwick, I, 87–9; Walpole, *Russell*, I, 29; Gunning, *op. cit.*, 4; Malmesbury (first earl), *Diaries and Corres.*, IV, 390.
[12] P. 16. B. and A., I, 370.
[13] P. 16. *Parl. Deb.*, X, 300–1.
[14] P. 17. Ward, I, 341.
[15] P. 17. S. Walpole, *Spencer Perceval* (London, 1874), II, 42–9, 48 n.; Romilly, 81; Broughton, V, 204; Ward, I, 249–51, 274; Malmesbury (first earl), *Letters*, II, 155, 160, 162; B. and A., I, 88–100.
[16] P. 18. B. and A., I, 93.
[17] P. 18. Acceptance of War Office and refusal of cabinet rank: Ward, I, 276–9; Malmesbury (first earl), *Letters*, 162, 173; B. and A., I, 101–6.
[18] P. 18. B. and A., I, 101–2.
[19] P. 19. Mrs. Hugh Wyndham, *Corr. of Sarah, Lady Lyttelton* (London, 1912), 85.
[20] P. 19. Romilly, 185.
[21] P. 20. E., *The New Whig Guide* (London, 1819); Croker, I, 52.
[22] P. 21. B. and A., I, 35.
[23] P. 21. *Ibid.*, I, 74.
[24] P. 21. Ward, I, 341–3, 351, 363.
[25] P. 21. Parker, *Peel*, I, 169.
[26] P. 22. *His. MSS. Com., MSS. of Earl Bathurst* (1923), 182.
[27] P. 22. *Parl. Deb.*, XXIV, 971–6.
[28] P. 23. Ward, 404; *Parl. Deb.*, XV, 660; B. and A., I, 115.
[29] P. 23. B. and A., I, 371–2.
[30] P. 23. Lorne, 13; Br. Mus., *Add. MSS.* 40232, f. 222; *ibid.*, 40234, f. 1; *ibid.*, 40235, ff. 228, 289.
[31] P. 24. B. and A., I, 85–7.
[32] P. 24. Malmesbury (first earl), *Letters*, II, 204; Ward, 404; Gunning, *Poll for election* (Cambridge, 1826), 4; Sedgwick, I, 108–9.

CHAPTER II

[1] P. 26. Memorandum by Lord Palmerston, Aug. 16, 1811, B. and A., I, 384–417; Clode, I, 110, 135–9, 196–200; Stanmore, *Herbert*, I, 224–5; *Parl. Papers*, Report of Commission on Consolidation of Military Departments (1837), III, 6–27; *Parl. Papers*, Commissioners of Military Inquiry, 6th Rep. (1808), 277 et seq.
[2] P. 27. *Ibid.*

NOTES 459

[3] P. 28. *Parl. Deb.*, XIX, 193-4 ; XXXVI, 517-26 ; *Parl. Papers*, Select Committee on Finance, 2nd Rep. (1817), 23.
[4] P. 28. Br. Mus., *Add. MSS.* 35677, ff. 72, 78, 192, 195, 200.
[5] P. 28. Br. Mus., *Add. MSS.*, 36543, ff. 112-15.
[6] P. 28. P.R.O., W.O. 4 : 425.
[7] P. 28. B. and A., I, 104.
[8] P. 29. P.R.O., W.O. 4 : 212, 307, 387, 415, 425.
[9] P. 29. P.R.O., W.O. 4 : 387.
[10] P. 30. *Parl. Papers*, Report of Commission on Consolidation of Military Departments (1837), III, 6-27.
[11] P. 30. *Ibid.*
[12] P. 30. B. and A., I, 127 ; *Parl. Papers*, Commissioners of Military Inquiry, 6th Rep. (1808), append. no. 1.
[13] P. 30. *D.N.B.*; Sir H. E. Bunbury, *Narratives* (London, 1854), 45-6.
[14] P. 31. B. and A., I, 110, 110 n.
[15] P. 31. Charles Dupin, *View of . . . the Military Force of Great Britain* (London, 1822), I, 28-9 ; Directions issued by the secretary at War (Lord G. Leveson Gower, afterwards Earl Granville), May 4, 1809 ; War Office Library (folded into *Instructions for . . . Clerks in the War Office, vide* n. 23).
[16] P. 31. *Parl. Papers*, Commissioners of Military Inquiry, 6th Rep. (1808), append. no. 6 ; *Parl. Papers*, Select Committee on Finance, 2nd Rep. (1817), 39 ; *Parl. Papers*, Evidence taken by Commissioners in 1833 (bound with Report of Commission on Consolidation of Military Departments (1837)), III, 60 ; *Hansard*, 2nd Ser., I, 452.
[17] P. 31. 45 Geo. III, c. 47. The 'Commissioners of Military Inquiry' issued 19 reports, 1806-12.
[18] P. 32. Dupin, *op. cit.*, I, 28-9.
[19] P. 32. B. and A., I, 107-8.
[20] P. 32. *Parl. Papers*, Evidence taken by the Commissioners in 1833 (*vide* n. 16, *supra*), III, 59.
[21] P. 32. *Ibid.*
[22] P. 32. *Parl. Papers*, Select Committee on Finance, 6th Rep. (1818), append. no 6.
[23] P. 33. *Instructions for the Guidance of the Clerks in the War Office.* Printed 1815. Bound with copies of additional instructions, issued 1815-19, written and bearing signatures or initials of Palmerston and other War Office officials. War Office Library. See also Report of Select Committee on Finance, 2nd Rep. (1817), 39.
[24] P. 33. *Ibid.*, Additional instruction, Aug. 27, 1816.
[25] P. 33. *Ibid.*, Additional instruction, May 21, 1817.
[26] P. 33. Dupin, *op. cit.*, I, 24 ; Br. Mus., *Add. MSS.* 38264, f. 72.
[27] P. 33. *Parl. Papers*, Select Committee on Finance, 2nd Rep. (1817), 39. See also *Hansard*, 2nd Ser., I, 452. A special department for handling accounts in arrear was established in 1809. *Parl. Deb.*, XV, 607-13 ; *Hansard*, 2nd Ser., V, 85.
[28] P. 34. *Parl. Papers*, Report of Commission on Consolidation of Military Departments (1837), III, 59-72.
[29] P. 34. *Parl. Papers*, Select Committee on Finance, 2nd Rep. (1817), 41 ; *Hansard*, 2nd Ser., V, 86.
[30] P. 34. *Parl. Papers*, Report of Commission on Consolidation of Military Departments (1837), III, 59-72 ; *Parl. Papers*, Select Committee on Finance, 2nd Rep. (1817), 39-40 ; *ibid.*, 7th Rep. (1818), 4-5 ; *Hansard*, 2nd Ser., V, 86 ; VI, 1215-20 ; XVI, 580-1.

[31] P. 34. *Parl. Papers*, Evidence taken by the Commissioners in 1833 (*vide* n. 16, *supra*), 60.
[32] P. 34. B. and A., I, 128.
[33] P. 34. Broughton, IV, 247, 270, 287.
[34] P. 34. Br. Mus., *Add. MSS.* 27598 *passim* (102 folios); 38190, f. 167; 38194, ff. 1–16, 26; 38245, ff. 154–5, 194; 38361, ff. 3, 154–91, 196–232; Clode, I, 108; B. and A., I, 124–8; *Parl. Papers*, Commissioners of Military Inquiry, 6th Rep. (1808), 367–81; 50 Geo. III, c. 107.
[35] P. 36. B. and A., I, 384–417; Br. Mus., *Add. MSS.* 38361, ff. 154–91 (appendix with 350–400 notes referring to period 1688–1801).
[36] P. 37. B. and A., I, 417.
[37] P. 37. *Hansard*, 2nd Ser., IV, 1198; VI, 1184.
[38] P. 38. His. MSS. Com., *MSS. of Earl Bathurst*, 566.
[39] P. 38. Br. Mus., *Add. MSS.* 38194, ff. 87–9, 96–8; 38292, ff. 260–2; 38370, ff. 164–232.
[40] P. 39. Wellington, *Desp.*, 2nd Ser., IV, 91.
[41] P. 39. *Parl. Deb.*, XXX, 45–51.
[42] P. 39. *Parl. Deb.*, XXI, 1208, 1281–2; XXVII, 215–16; XXXI, 936–7; *Hansard*, 2nd Ser., XIV, 1303–4; XVI, 1139.
[43] P. 39. *Hansard*, 2nd Ser., VIII, 491–3.
[44] P. 39. Wellington, *Desp.*, 2nd Ser., III, 199 n.
[45] P. 39. *Hansard*, 2nd Ser., XII, 928–9; XIV, 1103–4; XVI, 574; J. W. Fortescue, *History of the British Army* (London, 1910–27), XI, 87–9.
[46] P. 40. *Hansard*, 2nd Ser., XVI, 574.
[47] P. 40. *Taylor Papers*, 304–5.
[48] P. 40. *Hansard*, 2nd Ser., XVIII, 629–30.
[49] P. 40. Br. Mus., *Add. MSS.* 40395, f. 230.
[50] P. 40. Fortescue, *op cit.*, XI, 88.
[51] P. 40. *Hansard*, 2nd Ser., XXI, 895–6; XXIV, 1163, 1178–9, 1183; XXVIII, 252–6; XXXII, 1071–2; Fortescue, *op. cit.*, XI, 90; Br. Mus., *Add. MSS.* 38194, ff. 27–9, 73; 38264, f. 69.
[52] P. 40. Broughton, IV, 262–3.
[53] P. 41. B. and A., I, 135.
[54] P. 41. *Taylor Papers*, 304–5.
[55] P. 41. *Parl. Papers*, Select Committee on Finance, 2nd Rep. (1817), 23; Parl. Deb. XXXVI, 517–21.
[56] P. 41. *Ibid.*
[57] P. 42. Guedalla, *Palmerston*, 94.
[58] P. 42. Br. Mus., *Add. MSS.* 38566, ff. 85–7.
[59] P. 42. *Ibid.*, 38270, ff. 235–6.
[60] P. 42. *Ibid.*, 38251, ff. 188, 249; 38252, f. 20; 38258, f. 136; 38260, ff. 77, 170; 38261, ff. 83–4; 38266, ff. 288–98.

CHAPTER III

[1] P. 45. Lady Granville, *Letters*, I, 232–4; Br. Mus., *Add. MSS.* 40369, f. 101; *ibid.*, 40371, f. 226.
[2] P. 45. William Day, *Reminiscences of the Turf* (London, 1886), 210–14; T. A. Cook, *History of the English Turf* (London, 1901–4), III, 498.
[3] P. 45. Br. Mus., *Add. MSS.* 38194, ff. 56–8.
[4] P. 46. *Ibid.*, 40256, f. 29.
[5] P. 46. B. and A., I, 158, 161, 174–7, 203.

NOTES

[6] P. 47. Henry Crabb Robinson, *Diary* (Boston, 1871), II, 62.
[7] P. 47. B. and A., I, 157, 162, 162 n.
[8] P. 47. Day, *op cit.*, 210, 217.
[9] P. 47. Palmerston, *Selections from Private Journals of Tours in France in 1815 and 1818* (London, 1871), *passim*.
[10] P. 48. *Hansard*, 2nd Ser., I, 454.
[11] P. 49. *Parl. Deb.*, XXXIII, 108.
[12] P. 49. *Hansard*, 2nd Ser., I, 108 r.
[13] P. 49. *Parl. Deb.*, XXXII, 866–73. See also *Hansard*, 2nd Ser., XII, 927.
[14] P. 50. B. and A., I, 144.
[15] P. 50. Malmesbury (first earl), *Letters*, II, 531.
[16] P. 50. Br. Mus., *Add. MSS.* 40269, f. 210 (quoted in Parker, *Peel*, I, 256).
[17] P. 50. *Parl. Deb.*, XXXVI, 295.
[18] P. 50. B. and A., I, 150, 372, 377; Lorne, 43.
[19] P. 50. *Huskisson Papers*, 130–5; Br. Mus., *Add. MSS.* 38194, f. 83; B. and A., I, 150, 372.
[20] P. 51. Croker, I, 212.
[21] P. 51. His. MSS. Com., *MSS. of Earl Bathurst*, 182.
[22] P. 52. *Hansard*, 2nd Ser., XIV, 918–19.
[23] P. 52. *Ibid.*, 2nd Ser., XI, 359.
[24] P. 53. *Ibid.*, VIII, 1453.
[25] P. 53. *Ibid.*, XIV, 1088.
[26] P. 53. Br. Mus., *Add. MSS.* 40355, f. 206.
[27] P. 53. *Ibid.*, 38194, f. 94.
[28] P. 54. Br. Mus., *Add. MSS.* 36461, ff. 389–90; Sedgwick, I, 268; *Ann. Reg.* for 1826, 169; His. MSS. Com., *MSS. of Earl Bathurst*, 598–9; E. M. Seymour, *The 'Pope' of Holland House* (London, 1906), 253; Gunning, *Poll for election* (Cambridge, 1826), 46.
[29] P. 54. B. and A., I, 167.
[30] P. 55. *Ibid.*, 171–2.
[31] P. 55. Airlie, I, 132.
[32] P. 55. B. and A., I, 172.
[33] P. 55. *Ibid.*, 170–1.
[34] P. 56. R. Weigall, *Corr. of Lord Burghersh* (London, 1912), 258.
[35] P. 56. *Memorandum* of Prince Albert on conversation with Wellington, dated Jan. 21, 1852, *Windsor MSS.* (Russell), A. 80; Temperley, *Lieven*, 164, 164 n.; B. and A., I, 180–93; Lorne, 40–43.
[36] P. 57. *Hansard*, 2nd Ser., XVII, 299–304, 845–53.
[37] P. 58. Quoted in C. H. B. F. P., II, 95–6.
[38] P. 59. Br. Mus., *Add. MSS.* 28511, ff. 256–7.
[39] P. 60. Temperley, *Lieven*, 165.
[40] P. 60. Wolf, *Ripon*, II (Append. I), pp. 331–4; *Huskisson Papers*, 225, 227–8; C. Greville, *Mem.*, I, 109; Aspinall, *Brougham*, 153–8, 283; *Journal of Sir Walter Scott* (New York, 1890), II, 30; Croker, I, 361–2.
[41] P. 61. B. and A., I, 198.
[42] P. 61. Raikes, *Journal*, IV, 291–2.
[43] P. 62. Airlie, I, 153.
[44] P. 62. Wellington, *Desp.*, 2nd Ser., IV, 186–7; Romilly, 331; Br. Mus., *Add. MSS.* 38754, ff. 124–39, 148–55, 166–8; Lady Granville, *Letters*, II, 5–7.
[45] P. 62. C. Greville, *Mem.*, I, 123.
[46] P. 62. Br. Mus., *Add. MSS.* 38754, ff. 152–5.
[47] P. 63. B. and A., I, 379–80. (*Cf. Hansard*, 2nd Ser., XVIII, 536–8.)
[48] P. 63. B. and A., I, 217–20.

[49] P. 64. Henry (Lord) Cockburn, *Memorials* (New York, 1856), 389; C. Greville, *Mem.*, I, 122, 125, 127; Airlie, I, 151-3.
[50] P. 64. Lady Granville, *Letters*, II, 10.
[51] P. 64. Ellenborough, I, 2-4, 18-20.
[52] P. 64. *Edinburgh Rev.*, XLVII, 258; Ellenborough, I, 24-9, 34-5; Lady Granville, *Letters*, II, 7; Broughton, III, 241.
[53] P. 64. Lieven, *Letters*, 125.
[54] P. 65. Ellenborough, I, 76.
[55] P. 65. Prince Albert, *Memorandum*, Feb. 24, 1851; *Windsor MSS.* (Russell), C. 46.
[56] P. 65. Stanmore, *Aberdeen*, 75. Ellenborough also took a hand at times. *Diary*, I, 100-1, 103.
[57] P. 65. Ellenborough, I, 41.
[58] P. 65. B. and A., I, 226.
[59] P. 65. C. W. Crawley, *Anglo-Russian Relations* in *Cam. His. Journ.*, vol. III, no. 1 (1929), 51.
[60] P. 66. Ellenborough, 52, 60, 103.
[61] P. 66. *Melbourne Papers*, 108.
[62] P. 66. B. and A., I, 206.
[63] P. 66. *Hansard*, 2nd Ser., XVIII, 64, 76; Broughton, III, 238.
[64] P. 67. B. and A., I, 246-9; Br. Mus., *Add. MSS.* 38756, f. 46 (printed in Wellington, *Desp.*, 2nd Ser., IV, 339-40); *Huskisson Papers*, 303-5.
[65] P. 67. B. and A., I, 246-7.
[66] P. 67. *Ibid.*, 223-4.
[67] P. 67. *Ibid.*, 227, 249.
[68] P. 67. *Ibid.*, 227.
[69] P. 68. *Ibid.*, 228.
[70] P. 68. Ellenborough, I, 63.
[71] P. 68. *Ibid.*, 62-3; B. and A., I, 236-9.
[72] P. 69. *Ibid.*, 242-3.
[73] P. 69. *Ibid.*, 250.
[74] P. 70. Croker, I, 377-9, 387-91; Ellenborough, I, 107, 110-29; Broughton, III, 269-71, 275-6, V, 203; Fitzmaurice, I, 110-11; Romilly, 336-9; Br. Mus., *Add. MSS.* 38756, ff. 125, 127, 146-9, 152-4, 163-4, 175-7, 187-9, 458-63, 466-70, 472-3, 476-8, 481; His. MSS. Com., *MSS. of Earl Bathurst*, 653; Colchester, *op. cit.*, III, 567; *Windsor MSS.* (Geo. IV), Letters from Wellington to the King, 1827-28; Wellington, *Desp.*, 2nd Ser., IV, 451-6; Lady Granville, *Letters*, II, 20-1; *Hansard*, 2nd Ser., XIX, 962.
[75] P. 70. Br. Mus., *Add. MSS.* 38756, ff. 247-9.
[76] P. 71. *Hansard*, 2nd Ser., XVIII, 778-81.
[77] P. 71. Ellenborough, I, 104.
[78] P. 71. *Hansard*, 2nd Ser., XIX, 722.
[79] P. 71. Ellenborough, I, 107.
[80] P. 71. Note 74, *supra*.
[81] P. 71. Creevey, 501.
[82] P. 72. *Hansard*, 2nd Ser., XVII, 1217.

CHAPTER IV

[1] P. 74. Broughton, III, 272.
[2] P. 74. C. Greville, *Mem.*, I, 255-6; Lieven, *Letters*, 135-6; B. and A., I, 282, 287-95.

NOTES

[3] P. 74. B. and A., I, 279.
[4] P. 74. A. Aspinall, *The Canningite Party*, in *Trans. of the Royal His. Soc.*, 4th Ser., XVII (1934), append., 224–6 ; B. and A., I, 278 ; Colchester, III, 567.
[5] P. 75. Raikes, *Private Corr.*, 45 ; Brougham, III, 38–9.
[6] P. 75. Broughton, III, 300. He admitted even to parliament some sympathy with the Association. *Hansard*, 2nd Ser., XX, 235.
[7] P. 75. *Hansard*, 2nd Ser., XIX, 1538.
[8] P. 76. Trevelyan, *Grey*, Append. C., 376–8.
[9] P. 76. B. and A., I, 315.
[10] P. 76. Napoleon's great general and diplomatist—at this time merely a member of the assembly, but soon to be Louis Philippe's foreign minister. He was a particularly ardent expansionist.
[11] P. 76. B. and A., I, 322–3, 331–2.
[12] P. 77. *Ibid.*, 326.
[13] P. 77. C. H. B. F. P., II, 122–3.
[14] P. 77. B. and A., I, 316–20.
[15] P. 77. Lieven, *Letters*, 132.
[16] P. 78. C. Greville, *Mem.*, I, 213–14.
[17] P. 78. C. Greville, *Mem.*, I, 180, 182.
[18] P. 78. C. W. Crawley, *Anglo-Russian Relations*, in *Cam. His. Journ.*, vol. III, no. 1 (1929), 51 ; Lieven, *Letters*, 136, 196.
[19] P. 78. C. Greville, *Mem.*, I, 171–2.
[20] P. 78. *Hansard*, 2nd Ser., XX, 1238–52.
[21] P. 80. *Ibid.*, 234–7.
[22] P. 80. *Ibid.*, 1352–4.
[23] P. 80. Diary of the third Earl Grey, March 18, 1829, *Howick MSS.* ; C. Greville, *Mem.*, I, 191 ; *Hansard*, 2nd Ser., XX, 1253, 1256 ; Robert Heron, *Notes* (Grantham, 1851), 178 ; Jekyll, 196.
[24] P. 80. *Hansard*, 2nd Ser., XXI, 1643–60.
[25] P. 84. Diary of the third Earl Grey, June 2, 1829, *Howick MSS.* ; C. Greville, *Mem.*, I, 211.
[26] P. 84. B. and A., I, 334.
[27] P. 84. *Ibid.*, 339.
[28] P. 84. Lorne, 57–62.
[29] P. 86. *Ibid.*, 61.
[30] P. 86. Airlie, I, 167–8.
[31] P. 86. *Ibid.*, 168–9.
[32] P. 86. Airlie, I, 166.
[33] P. 86. B. and A., I, 355.
[34] P. 87. *Ibid.*, 350–1.
[35] P. 88. *Hansard*, 2nd Ser., XXII, 139–41, 559–64.
[36] P. 88. C. Greville, *Mem.*, I, 278.
[37] P. 88. *Hansard*, 2nd Ser., XXII, 142–5 ; XXIII, 98–9.
[38] P. 88. Jekyll, 229.
[39] P. 88. *Hansard*, 2nd Ser., XXII, 334, 678, 726, 917, 1122, 1332.
[40] P. 88. Croker, I, 448–51.
[41] P. 89. Lieven, *Corr. with Grey*, I, 416–17, 421.
[42] P. 89. *Ann. Reg.* for 1830, 145.
[43] P. 89. *Ibid.*, 146.
[44] P. 90. Airlie, I, 173.
[45] P. 90. Parker, *Graham*, I, 85.
[46] P. 90. Airlie, I, 172–4.
[47] P. 91. Wellington, *Desp.*, 2nd Ser., VII, 106–8.

[48] P. 91. Lieven, *Letters*, 225; C. Greville, *Mem.*, II, 32, 94, 104; B. and A., I, 361.
[49] P. 91. Brougham, III, 36.
[50] P. 91. C. Greville, *Mem.*, II, 48; Lieven, *Corr. with Grey*, II, 91–2; Durham to Grey, Sept. 17, 1830, *Howick MSS.*; Creevey, 555; Lieven, *Letters*, 241–2; Brougham, III, 49–51; Aspinall, *Brougham*, 181–2.
[51] P. 91. Lieven, *Letters*, 244–5; C. Greville, *Mem.*, II, 93.
[52] P. 92. Aspinall, *Brougham*, 180–1.
[53] P. 92. Lieven, *Letters*, 249, 254–5; Wellington, *Desp.*, 2nd Ser., VII, 281, 328; Lieven, *Corr. with Grey*, II, 105, 108; B. and A., I, 381–2.
[54] P. 92. Aspinall, *Brougham*, 182–3.
[55] P. 92. B. and A., I, 362–3.
[56] P. 92. Lieven, *Letters*, 254.
[57] P. 92. Lieven, *Letters*, 241; Durham to Grey, Oct. 4, 1830, *Howick MSS.*
[58] P. 92. Aspinall, *Brougham*, 181; Durham to Grey, Oct. 4, 1830, *Howick MSS.*
[59] P. 93. *Ibid.*
[60] P. 93. Aspinall, *Brougham*, 183; Lieven, *Letters*, 262; C. Greville, *Mem.*, II, 64; B. and A., I, 363–4.
[61] P. 93. Lieven, *Letters*, 262–3.
[62] P. 93. Parker, *Peel*, II, 163–7.
[63] P. 93. B. and A., I, 364; Lieven, *Letters*, 267.
[64] P. 93. Broughton, IV, 60; Diary of the third Earl Grey, Nov. 7, 1830, *Howick MSS.*
[65] P. 94. Temperley, *Lieven*, 165–9, 169 n.; Lieven, *Letters*, 274–5; Trevelyan, *Grey*, 241, 243, 243 n., 378–9; Walpole, *Russell*, I, 159–60.
[66] P. 94. Lieven, *Letters*, 276.

CHAPTER V

[1] P. 96. Day, 217.
[2] P. 96. Lieven, *Corr. with Grey*, II, 484, 491; Creevey, 541, 610, 611, 618; Charles Grey to Lord Howick, Nov. 26, 1833, *Howick MSS.*; C. Greville, *Mem.*, III, 57.
[3] P. 97. Wilson, *Greville Diary*, I, 547; II, 86; Creevey, 649.
[4] P. 97. Dino, 46–7.
[5] P. 97. Jekyll, 302.
[6] P. 97. C. Greville, *Mem.*, III, 56–7, 136; Lieven, *Corr. with Grey*, III, 33.
[7] P. 97. Snell, 95.
[8] P. 98. B. and A., II, 43, 43 n., 44, 44 n.
[9] P. 99. Dino, 94.
[10] P. 99. Broughton, V, 67, 92; Lyttelton, 316.
[11] P. 99. Czartoryski, II, 318, 318 n., 319, 319 n.
[12] P. 100. Lieven, *Corr. with Grey*, II, 154; Trevelyan, *Grey*, 362–3.
[13] P. 100. C. Greville, *Mem.*, III, 56.
[14] P. 100. Lieven, *Corr. with Grey*, III, 100.
[15] P. 100. B. and A., II, 160.
[16] P. 100. Palmerston to Grey, July 15, 1834, *Howick MSS.*
[17] P. 101. Creevey, 628; Lord Grey to General Grey, Oct. 21, 1865, *Howick MSS.*
[18] P. 101. Corr. between Grey and Granville, 1831 (copies), *Howick MSS.*

NOTES

[19] P. 101. Brougham, III, 175–6.
[20] P. 101. Diary of the third Earl Grey, May 30, 1834, *Howick MSS*. (cf. B. and A., II, 195–6).
[21] P. 102. Dino, I, 175, 220–5.
[22] P. 103. *Hansard*, 3rd Ser., XIV, 1045.
[23] P. 103. *Ibid.*, 1067.
[24] P. 103. See my article on *Palmerston and Parliamentary Representation* in *Journ. Mod. His.*, vol. IV, No. 2 (June 1932), pp. 186–213.
[25] P. 104. Trevelyan, *Grey*, 275, 275 n.
[26] P. 104. Palmerston to Grey, Apr. 8, 1831, *Howick MSS*.
[27] P. 104. Palmerston to Lansdowne, undated, *Bowood MSS*. (partly quoted in Guedalla, *Palmerston*, 159).
[28] P. 104. B. and A., II, 48, 51.
[29] P. 104. Palmerston to Grey, Apr. 8, 1831, *Howick MSS*.
[30] P. 105. Palmerston to Lansdowne (*vide* n. 27, *supra*).
[31] P. 105. *Hansard*, 3rd Ser., II, 1318–30; Broughton, IV, 90.
[32] P. 105. Sedgwick, I, 374–6; H. Gunning, *Poll for election* (Cambridge, 1831), 51; Palmerston to Grey, Apr. 25, 1831, *Howick MSS*.; Br. Mus., *Add. MSS*. 36466, f. 315; Wellington, *Desp.*, 2nd Ser., VIII, 1; *Hansard*, 3rd Ser., III, 1183–4, 1205.
[33] P. 106. Palmerston to Grey, May 14, Oct. 9, Oct. 10, Oct. 11, 1831, *Howick MSS*.
[34] P. 106. Quoted in Ramsay, *Peel*, 162. See Broughton, IV, 174–6.
[35] P. 106. C. Greville, *Mem.*, II, 211–12, 217–18, 220–1, 225, 230, 238–40, 259; *Melbourne Papers*, 140–2; Wellington, *Desp.*, 2nd Ser., VIII, 124–5; Croker, I, 531; Lord J. Russell, *Early Corr.*, II, 27–8; Broughton, IV, 177.
[36] P. 106. C. Greville, *Mem.*, II, 217, 230; New, *Durham*, 160; Brougham, III, 116, 305; Trevelyan, *Grey*, 386; Davis, 232.
[37] P. 107. New, *Durham*, 168; Broughton, IV, 197–8.
[38] P. 107. Brougham, III, 126–7, 182; C. Greville, *Mem.*, II, 290.
[39] P. 107. C. Greville, *Mem.*, II, 294.
[40] P. 107. Palmerston to Sir Robert Adair, May 14, 1832, *Johnston Coll.*
[41] P. 110. *Hansard*, 3rd Ser., XI, 882.
[42] P. 110. Raikes, *Journ.*, I, 218.
[43] P. 112. For this duel and for the best commentary on Palmerston's foreign policy, 1830–1841, see C. K. Webster, *Palmerston, Metternich and the European System* in *Proc. of the Br. Acad.*, vol. XX (1934), pp. 3–36.
[44] P. 112. Crawley, *Greek Independence*, 208–11; Lane-Poole, I, 492–519.
[45] P. 112. Palmerston to Granville, June 3, 1831, P.R.O., G. and D. 29 : 14.
[46] P. 112. Palmerston to Heytesbury, Sept. 21, 1831 (no. 49), P.R.O., F.O. 65 : 190.
[47] P. 112. *Supra*, ch. III, note 65.
[48] P. 112. Trevelyan, *Grey*, 229–30, 230 n.
[49] P. 112. Lane-Poole, I, 494.
[50] P. 113. *Ibid.*, 518.
[51] P. 113. Crawley, *op. cit.*, 189–201.
[52] P. 113. Lord J. Russell, *Later Corr.*, II, 300–1; C.H.B.F.P., II, 589 n.
[53] P. 113. Lane-Poole, I, 518–19.
[54] P. 113. Palmerston to Granville, June 3, 1831, P.R.O., G. and D. 29: 14.
[55] P. 113. Martens, *Nouv. Rec.*, X, 550–66; *State Papers*, IX, 2–54, 1229–51; Palmerston to Heytesbury, March 15, 1832 (no. 39), F.O. 65 : 190; Talleyrand, III, 303; Raikes, *Journ.*, I, 29, 97; Nesselrode, VII, 170–1.
[56] P. 114. Crawley, *op. cit.*, 205–8.

[57] P. 114. C. H. B. F. P., II, 586–9.
[58] P. 114. Palmerston to Erskine, Sept. 18, 1832 (no. 21), P.R.O., F.O. 9 : 63.
[59] P. 114. *Ann. Reg.* for 1832, p. 400.
[60] P. 114. B. and A., II, 145–6.
[61] P. 114. Palmerston to Heytesbury, March 2, 1832 (no. 29), F.O. 65 : 190 ; Trevelyan, *Grey*, 355–6.
[62] P. 115. Palmerston's memorandum, March 30, 1834, P.R.O., F.O. 96 : 17.
[63] P. 115. Palmerston to Erskine, Apr. 22, 1834 (no. 5), F.O. 9 : 68. See also Palmerston to Bligh, Apr. 22, 1834 (no. 13), F.O. 65 : 212.
[64] P. 115. Palmerston to Erskine, May 13, July 11 and 15, Oct. 17, 1834 (nos. 10, 19, 20, 25), F.O. 9 : 68 ; Eardley-Wilmot, 79–81.

CHAPTER VI

[1] P. 116. Van Kalken, *Histoire de Belgique* (Brussels, 1920 ?), 499.
[2] P. 116. Palmerston to Russell, July 27, 1861, P.R.O., G. and D. 22 : 21.
[3] P. 117. C. H. B. F. P., II, ch. III ; Pirenne, VII, 3–40 ; Stern, IV, ch. ii ; R. Guyot, *La dernière négociation de Talleyrand* in *Rev. d'hist. mod. et contemp.*, II (1900–1), 573–94, III (1901–2), 237–81 ; duc de Broglie, *Le dernier bienfait de la Monarchie* (Paris, 1901) ; C. White, *Belgic Revolution* (London, 1836) ; W. E. Lingelbach, *Belgian Neutrality* in *Amer. His. Rev.*, vol. XXXIX, no. 1 (Oct. 1933), 48–72.
[4] P. 118. Aberdeen to Stuart de Rothesay, Oct. 15, 1830 (no. 58), P.R.O., F.O. 27 : 405 ; Aberdeen to Heytesbury, Oct. 17, 1830 (no. 32), F.O. 65 : 184.
[5] P. 118. Guyot, *loc. cit.*, 277, 580–1 ; Lacour-Gayet, III, 258.
[6] P. 118. Guyot, *loc. cit.*, 277–9.
[7] P. 119. White, *op. cit.*, II, 87–98 ; Guyot, *loc. cit.*, 580–1, 592–3, 277. *Cf.* Broglie, *op cit.*, 211–58. See also notes 22 and 51, *infra*.
[8] P. 119. Palmerston to Heytesbury, Dec. 31, 1830 (no. 2), P.R.O., F.O. 65 : 184.
[9] P. 119. *State Papers*, XIX, 784.
[10] P. 120. Broglie, *op cit.*, 153.
[11] P. 120. Talleyrand, III, 284–5, IV, 7.
[12] P. 120. *Ibid.*, III, 286.
[13] P. 120. Protocol XI, Martens; *Nouv. Rec.*, X, 158–60 ; *Hansard*, 3rd Ser., II, 701 ; XIV, 616; Palmerston to Granville, Jan. 21, 1831 (no. 17), P.R.O., F.O. 27 : 424.
[14] P. 121. Temperley, *Lieven*, 175–8 ; B. and A., II, 27–8 ; Talleyrand, IV, 54; Palmerston to Granville, Jan. 21, 1831 (no. 17), P.R.O., F.O. 27 : 424 ; Granville to Palmerston, Feb. 14, 1831 (no. 76), P.R.O., F.O. 27 : 427 ; Pirenne, VII, 15 n.
[15] P. 121. Palmerston to Heytesbury, Dec. 31, 1831 (no. 2), P.R.O., F.O. 65 : 184; Palmerston to Granville, Jan. 17, 1831 (no. 13), P.R.O., F.O. 27 : 424.
[16] P. 122. B. and A., II, 27–9.
[17] P. 122. *Ibid.*
[18] P. 122. Lingelbach, *loc. cit.* ; Guyot, *loc. cit.*, 593–4 ; Pirenne, VII, 8–9.
[19] P. 123. B. and A., II, 29–31.
[20] P. 123. Palmerston to Granville, Jan. 21, 1831 (no. 17), P.R.O., F.O. 27 : 424.
[21] P. 123. B. and A., II, 30–1.
[22] P. 124. Martens, *Nouv. Rec.*, X, 160.

NOTES

[23] P. 124. Lacour-Gayet, III, 267; Granville to Palmerston, Jan. 19, 1831 (no. 20), P.R.O., F.O., 27 : 426.

[24] P. 124. Same to same, Jan. 21, 22 (nos. 32, 33), P.R.O., F.O., 27 : 426; Broglie, *op. cit.*, 293–8; Guyot, *loc. cit.*, 594, 237–45. *Cf.* Lacour-Gayet, III, 261–3.

[25] P. 125. B. and A., II, 32–5.

[26] P. 125. *Ibid.*, 32–9, 40 n., 46; Talleyrand, IV, 28–47, 117; Guyot, *loc. cit.*, 241, 248–52; Palmerston to Granville, Feb. 8, 1831 (no. 24), P.R.O., F.O., 27 : 424; Granville to Palmerston, Feb. 11, 1831 (no. 66), P.R.O., F.O., 27 : 426; White, *op. cit.*, II, 89; Broglie, *op. cit.*, 279–93; Pirenne, VII, 12–19; Guizot, VIII, 206–7; *State Papers*, XVIII, 761–8, 774.

[27] P. 126. Palmerston to Granville, Feb. 1, 1831 (no. 18), P.R.O., F.O., 27 : 424; B. and A., II, 35–6, 35 n.

[28] P. 126. *Ibid.*, 36.

[29] P. 126. *Ibid.*, 36–7.

[30] P. 127. Note 26, *supra*.

[31] P. 127. B. and A., II, 38 n.

[32] P. 127. *Ibid.*, 41–2.

[33] P. 127. *Ibid.*, 39.

[34] P. 128. *Ibid.*, 40 n., 41 n., 42.

[35] P. 128. *Ibid.*, 40–1, 49–50, 60.

[36] P. 129. *Ibid.*, 43–4.

[37] P. 129. *Ibid.*, 65–6, 84; Guyot, *loc. cit.*, 255–7.

[38] P. 129. B. and A., II, 51–6, 57 n., 65–70, 74–6.

[39] P. 129. Especially Palmerston to Granville, May 24, 1831, P.R.O., G. and D., 29 : 14; B. and A., II, 61–3, 77–81, 88–9; Guyot, *loc. cit.*, 259–65; Pirenne, VII, 19–29; New, 188–89.

[40] P. 129. Wellington, *Desp.*, 2nd Ser., VII, 32–3, 407, 511–14; *Supp. Desp.*, IX, 447–9.

[41] P. 130. Wellington, *Desp.*, 2nd Ser., VII, 143–7.

[42] P. 130. Talleyrand, IV, 83, 159.

[43] P. 130. Hertslet, *Map of Europe*, II, 856–7.

[44] P. 131. Talleyrand, IV, 237–8, 246–9; B. and A., II, 70–4.

[45] P. 131. *Ibid.*, 92–3; Talleyrand, IV, 165, 246–9; Stockmar, I, 213.

[46] P. 131. *Ibid.*, 212; Palmerston to Adair, Aug. 27, 1831, *Johnston Coll.*; B. and A., II, 63–4, 70–4.

[47] P. 131. *Ibid.*, 70–3.

[48] P. 131. Palmerston to Adair, Aug. 19, 1831, *Johnston Coll.* See also Juste, I, 182–4.

[49] P. 131. Palmerston to Adair, Aug. 19, 1831, *Johnston Coll.*

[50] P. 131. B. and A., II, 96–8.

[51] P. 132. *Ibid.*, 98–100; *State Papers*, XVIII, 825; *Hansard*, 3rd Ser., VI, 587–8.

[52] P. 132. B. and A., II, 100–103; Palmerston to Adair, Aug. 13, 1831, *Johnston Coll.* See also Lacour-Gayet, III, 275.

[53] P. 132. Juste, I, 197; Palmerston to Adair, Aug. 26, 28, 1831, *Johnston Coll.*; B. and A., II, 18. See also n. 48, *supra*.

[54] P. 132. Palmerston to Adair, Aug. 13, 1831, *Johnston Coll.*

[55] P. 133. Talleyrand, IV, 172–3, 181.

[56] P. 133. *Ibid.*, 174–7, 184 n., 188–9, 239; Barante, IV, 342–3.

[57] P. 133. Palmerston to Adair, Aug. 28, 1831, *Johnston Coll.*

[58] P. 133. Same to same, Aug. 17, *Johnston Coll.*

[59] P. 133. Same to same, Aug. 19, *Johnston Coll.*

NOTES

[60] P. 133. Talleyrand, IV, 205–6, 235–7, 239–40, 258.
[61] P. 134. Palmerston to Adair, Aug. 13, 16, 17, 19, 23, 26, 27, 28, Sept. 1, 2, 4, 10, 15, 1831, *Johnston Coll.*
[62] P. 134. B. and A., II, 109–10.
[63] P. 135. *Ibid.*, 114–16.
[64] P. 135. Martens, XI, 323–332 ; Palmerston to Adair, Oct. 15 and 18, 1831, *Johnston Coll.*
[65] P. 135. Martens, XI, 334–5.
[66] P. 135. Hertslet, *Map of Europe*, II, 858–71.
[67] P. 135. Lorne, 67–8.
[68] P. 136. Talleyrand, IV, 246–9, 260 ; Stockmar, I, 224–33.
[69] P. 136. Palmerston to Adair, Aug. 23, 28, Nov. 16, 25, 28, Dec. 9, 15, 1831, *Johnston Coll.* See also Wellington, *Desp.*, 2nd Ser., VII, 509–14.
[70] P. 136. Palmerston to Adair, Aug. 19, 1831, *Johnston Coll.*
[71] P. 137. Hertslet, *Map of Europe*, II, 881–4 ; Stockmar, I, 216–17, 224 ; Palmerston to Adair, Nov. 16, 1831, *Johnston Coll.* ; Talleyrand, IV, 236 n.
[72] P. 137. *Ibid.*, 240–4 ; Stockmar, I, 217–21, 224–5.
[73] P. 137. Stockmar, I, 224.
[74] P. 137. Palmerston to Adair, Dec. 27, 1831, *Johnston Coll.* See also Stockmar, I, 227–8 ; Brougham, III, 300–1.
[75] P. 137. Juste, I, 235–6.
[76] P. 137. Stockmar, I, 232–3 ; Talleyrand, IV, 262–9 ; B. and A., II, 130 n.
[77] P. 138. *Supra*, note 3.
[78] P. 138. *Infra*, ch. X.

CHAPTER VII

[1] P. 139. *Supra*, ch. IV.
[2] P. 141. Palmerston's memorandum, Dec. 9, 1830, P.R.O., F.O. 96 : 17.
[3] P. 142. *Ibid.*, Feb. 23, 1832, F.O. 96 : 17.
[4] P. 142. Br. Mus., *Add. MSS.* 2343, *passim.*
[5] P. 142. Lord J. Russell, *Early Corr.*, II, 39.
[6] P. 142. Palmerston's memorandum, Aug. 6, 1832, P.R.O., F.O. 96 : 17 ; Hansard, 3rd Ser., XVIII, 305.
[7] P. 142. Fagan, *Reform Club*, 98.
[8] P. 142. Hansard, 3rd Ser., XI, 894. See also B. and A., II, 168–9.
[9] P. 143. Palmerston to Adair, Sept. 14, 1832, *Johnston Coll.*
[10] P. 143. Hansard, 3rd Ser., XI, 879, 894, 917.
[11] P. 143. *Ibid.*, XVIII, 436–9, 444.
[12] P. 143. *Ibid.*, 440.
[13] P. 143. B. and A., II, 153.
[14] P. 144. Lane-Poole, II, 26.
[15] P. 144. B. and A., II, 153.
[16] P. 144. Lord J. Russell, *Early Corr.*, II, 34 ; C. Greville, *Mem.*, III, 34 ; Raikes, *Journ.*, I, 37.
[17] P. 144. Palmerston to Granville, June 3, 10, 14, 1831, P.R.O., G. and D., 29 : 14 (printed in B. and A., II, 85–8) ; B. and A., II, 89, 92–3 ; Lieven, *Letters*, 310 ; Talleyrand, IV, 74, 149 ; Palmerston to Granville, Aug. 2, 1831, P.R.O., G. and D., 29 : 14.
[18] P. 145. Cowley (first baron), *Diary and Corr.*, 198–9 ; Guizot, IV, 57 ; Talleyrand, V, 65–6.

NOTES

[19] P. 145. *Ibid.*
[20] P. 145. *Ibid.*, 65–71, 83 ; Br. Mus., *Add. MSS.* 37297, ff. 383–4 ; B. and A., II, 145–6, 152–3.
[21] P. 146. Hall, 177–8.
[22] P. 146. Brougham, III, 208 ; Lieven, *Letters*, 356–8 ; Diary of the third Earl Grey, Jan. 14, 15, 16, 1834 ; Lord Howick to Grey, Jan. 17, 1834, Howick MSS.
[23] P. 146. Lieven, *Letters*, 364–5 ; Brougham, III, 221–6 ; Lord Howick to Grey, Jan. 17, 1834, and Lord Grey to Gen. Grey, October 21, 1865, Howick MSS.
[24] P. 147. B. and A., II, 180–1.
[25] P. 147. d'Haussonville, I, 128–31 ; Dino, I, 51 ; Talleyrand, V, 240–58.
[26] P. 148. *Ibid.*, 257–8. See also Dino, I, 96.
[27] P. 148. B. and A., II, 181.
[28] P. 148. *Cf.* C. Greville, *Mem.*, V, 422–3.
[29] P. 148. Metternich, *Mém.*, V, 255–6 ; Lieven-Grey, *Corr.*, II, 423.
[30] P. 148. B. and A., II, 186. *Cf.* Hillebrand, I, 577 n.
[31] P. 149. B. and A., II, 197.
[32] P. 149. Talleyrand, V, 298–311, 311 n.
[33] P. 149. *Ibid.*, 308–9.
[34] P. 149. Palmerston to Russell, Dec. 15, 1836, P.R.O., G. and D., 22 : 2.
[35] P. 150. *Hansard*, 3rd Ser., XXVIII, 1148–9.
[36] P. 151. P. de Barante, 'Les procédés diplomatiques de Palmerston,' in *Rev. d'hist. dipl.*, 45e année, no. 4 (1931), 413–29.
[37] P. 151. Palmerston to Cartwright, April 15, 1834 (no. 16), P.R.O., F.O., 30 : 48.
[38] P. 151. Palmerston to Cowley, June 19, 1831 (no. 17), P.R.O., F.O., 7 : 226 ; Brooks, 58.
[39] P. 152. J. H. Clapham, 'The Last Years of the Navigation Acts,' in *Eng. Hist. Rev.*, vol. XXV (1910), 487–90.
[40] P. 152. *Hansard*, 3rd Ser., XX, 700–1.
[41] P. 152. *E.g.* Palmerston to Erskine, Nov. 15, 1832 (no. 27), P.R.O., F.O., 9 : 63 ; Palmerston to Disbrowe, Nov. 20, 1832 (no. 6), F.O., 82 : 26.
[42] P. 153. *State Papers*, XIX, 299–308.
[43] P. 154. *Hansard*, 3rd Ser., XIV, 1038–45.
[44] P. 154. *Hansard*, 3rd Ser., XIV, 1045–9.
[45] P. 155. B. and A., II, Append. IV, 415–18.
[46] P. 156. Palmerston to Durham, July 3, 1832 ; Durham to Palmerston, July 27, Aug. 2, Sept. 8, 12 (nos. 5, 8, 18, 21), P.R.O., F.O., 65 : 200 ; New, 206–8.
[47] P. 156. Metternich, *Mém.*, V, 368–70.
[48] P. 157. *Ibid.*, 257, 383–97.
[49] P. 157. Cartwright to Palmerston, June 11, 1834 (no. 77), P.R.O., F.O., 30 : 52.
[50] P. 158. Palmerston to Cartwright, May 15, 1834 (no. 24), F.O., 30 : 48.
[51] P. 158. Same to same, May 20, 1834 (no. 25) ; Palmerston to Erskine, May 16 and 20, 1834 (nos. 11, 13), F.O., 9 : 68.
[52] P. 158. Cartwright to Palmerston, June 11, 21, July 1, 19, Sept. 29, Oct. 1, 1834 (nos. 77, 82, 87, 94, 109, 111), and Palmerston to Cartwright, July 13, Nov. 16, 1834 (nos. 30, 31, 39), F.O., 30 : 48, 52, 53.
[53] P. 159. Cartwright to Wellington, Dec. 1, 1834 (no. 135), F.O., 30 : 53.
[54] P. 159. Palmerston to Cartwright, Feb. 14, March 8, May 9, 1834 (nos. 5, 9, 21), F.O., 30 : 48.

[55] P. 159. *State Papers*, XXIII, 341-3.
[56] P. 160. Palmerston to Cowley, March 22, 1831 (no. 5), P.R.O., F.O., 7 : 226.
[57] P. 161. B. and A., II, 50-1.
[58] P. 161 *Ibid.*, 47-8.
[59] P. 161. For Taylor's opinion, Barante, IV, 321-2.
[60] P. 162. Palmerston to Granville, Jan. 14, 1831 (no. 9), P.R.O., F.O., 27 : 424 ; Granville to Palmerston, Jan. 21, 1831 (no. 28), F.O. 27 : 426 ; Talleyrand, IV, 70-1.
[61] P. 162. Palmerston to Cowley, Apr. 1, 1831 (no. 8), P.R.O., F.O., 7 : 226.
[62] P. 162. Talleyrand, IV, 70-1, 79-80 ; *Taylor Papers*, 331-4.
[63] P. 162. Palmerston's memorandum, March 24, 1831, P.R.O., F.O., 96 : 17.
[64] P. 163. Palmerston to Durham, July 3, and Durham to Palmerston, July 27, 1832, P.R.O., F.O., 65 : 200 ; Metternich, *Mém.*, V, 373-9 ; corr. between Seymour, Luetzow (Austrian representative at the conference), Metternich and Sir Fred. Lamb, *Annual Register* for 1832, pp. 379-87.
[65] P. 163. *Ibid.*
[66] P. 163. Metternich, *Mém.*, V, 299.
[67] P. 163. William IV to Grey, Sept. 17, 1831, *Howick MSS.* ; Broughton, IV, 220, 241 ; C. Greville, *Mem.*, III, 137.
[68] P. 163. Grey (second earl), *Corr. with William IV*, II, 356-7.
[69] P. 163. Talleyrand, IV, 286.
[70] P. 164. *Hansard*, 3rd Ser., XI, 911.
[71] P. 164. B. and A., II, 154-5.
[72] P. 164. *Ibid.*, 157, 167, 175-6, 183.

CHAPTER VIII

[1] P. 165. Palmerston to Russell, Feb. 26, 1863, P.R.O., G. and D., 22 : 22.
[2] P. 166. B. and A., II, 49.
[3] P. 166. B. and A., II, 79. See also Palmerston to Adair, Sept. 1 and 2, 1831, *Johnston Coll.*
[4] P. 167. Palmerston to Heytesbury, Dec. 31, 1830 (no. 2), P.R.O., F.O., 65 : 184 ; Palmerston to Granville, Jan. 17, 1831 (no. 12), F.O., 27 : 424 ; Talleyrand, IV, 73 ; B. and A., II, 60.
[5] P. 167. B. and A., II, 76.
[6] P. 167. *Ibid.*
[7] P. 167. *Hansard*, 3rd Ser., XIX, 435.
[8] P. 167. Palmerston to Talleyrand, July 22, 1831, P.R.O., F.O., 27 : 438. See also Cowley (first baron), *Diary and Corr.*, 193.
[9] P. 168. Czartoryski, II, 317.
[10] P. 168. *Hansard*, 3rd Ser., XIV, 1215 ; XIX, 437.
[11] P. 168. Lieven-Grey, *Corr.*, II, 131, 144, 146-8, 184, 268 ; *Lieven, Letters*, 290 ; Nesselrode, VII, 190-1.
[12] P. 169. Schiemann, III, Anlage II, 423, 427-8 ; Nesselrode, VII, 167-8 ; B. and A., II, 60-1 ; Lieven-Grey, *Corr.*, II, 269, 311-19 ; Czartoryski, II, 321-5, 328-30 ; Brougham, III, 115.
[13] P. 169. Czartoryski, II, 329.
[14] P. 169. *Ibid.*, 325-6, 330.
[15] P. 169. Lieven-Grey, *Corr.*, II, 318.
[16] P. 169. Palmerston to Cowley, June 19, 1831 (no. 16), P.R.O., F.O., 7 : 226.

NOTES 471

[17] P. 170. Palmerston to Heytesbury, Nov. 23, 1831 (no. 52), P.R.O., F.O., 65 : 190.
[18] P. 170. New, 212.
[19] P. 170. Palmerston to Heytesbury, March 22, 1831 (no. 11), Nov. 23, 1831 (no. 52), P.R.O., F.O., 65 : 190 ; same to same, March 12, 1832 (no. 35), F.O. 65 : 198 ; Palmerston to Durham, July 3, 1832 (no. 2), F.O. 65 : 200 ; B. and A., II, 127 n.
[20] P. 172. Lieven, *Letters*, 282, 287–8 ; Lieven-Grey, *Corr.*, II, 160.
[21] P. 172. Nesselrode, VII, 174–5.
[22] P. 172. Lieven, *Letters*, 326–7.
[23] P. 172. Reid, *Durham*, I, 301–3.
[24] P. 173. New, 202–13 ; Reid, *Durham*, I, 310–12 ; Lieven-Grey, *Corr.*, II, 374–5.
[25] P. 173. Raikes, *Journ.*, I, 71–4 ; Nesselrode, VII, 232–4.
[26] P. 173. Durham to Palmerston, Sept. 8 and 12, 1832 (nos. 18 and 21), P.R.O., F.O., 65 : 200.
[27] P. 173. New, 204–5.
[28] P. 174. Lieven-Grey, *Corr.*, II, 402 ; New, 213.
[29] P. 174. *Hansard*, 3rd Ser., XX, 901.
[30] P. 174. Lieven-Grey, *Corr.*, II, 358–60.
[31] P. 174. Daudet, *passim*.
[32] P. 174. Lieven, *Letters*, 303, 337.
[33] P. 174. New, 224–5 ; Reid, *Durham*, I, 315–16 ; Palmerston to Bligh, Oct. 27, Dec. 14, 1832, Jan. 1, Feb. 1, May 14, 1833, and Bligh to Palmerston, Oct. 27, Nov. 17, 27, 1832 (all copies of private letters or of extracts from private letters), P.R.O., F.O., 65 : 201, 65 : 206 ; Lieven-Grey, *Corr.*, II, 412, 434, 436, 445, 498 ; III, 25, 71, 214 ; Lieven, *Letters*, 350, 359–60, 370 ; Temperley, *Diary of Princess Lieven*, 183 n. ; Daudet, 180–2 ; Talleyrand, V, 70 ; 216–17 ; C. Greville, *Mem.*, I, 352, 357–8 ; III, 39, 87 ; Raikes, *Journ.*, I, 233–4 ; Dino, I, 83–6 ; Aberdeen, *Corr.*, 1832–44, pp. 13, 54–5 ; Buckingham, *Courts and Cabinets*, II, 124–5 ; Lane-Poole, II, 18–23, 50–1 ; B. and A., II, 199.
[34] P. 175. Lieven-Grey, *Corr.*, II, 412, 445–6 ; C. Greville, *Mem.*, II, 358.
[35] P. 175. Palmerston to Bligh, Dec. 14, 1832 (extract, copy), F.O., 65 : 201.
[36] P. 176. Same to same, May 14, 1833 (extract, copy), F.O., 65 : 206.
[37] P. 176. Same to same, Oct. 27, 1832 (extract, copy), F.O., 65 : 201.
[38] P. 176. *Supra*, note 36.
[39] P. 177. Lieven-Grey, *Corr.*, III, 25–6. *Cf.* Talleyrand, V, 216.
[40] P. 177. *Supra*, note 35.
[41] P. 177. C. Greville, *Mem.*, II, 358.
[42] P. 177. Lieven-Grey, *Corr.*, II, 403 ; C. Greville, *Mem.*, II, 324–5 ; Lieven, *Letters*, 331 ; Bligh to Palmerston, Oct. 22, 1832 (no. 4), P.R.O., F.O., 65 : 201.
[43] P. 177. Lieven-Grey, *Corr.*, II, 421–6.
[44] P. 178. Palmerston to Bligh, Jan. 15, 1833 (incomplete copy of private letter), P.R.O., G. and D., 29 : 17.
[45] P. 178. Lieven, *Letters*, 359–60, 360 n.
[46] P. 179. Hoskins, 155, 155 n. ; Swain, ch. VIII.
[47] P. 180. C. W. Crawley, 'Anglo-Russian Relations, 1815–1840,' in *Cam. His. Journ.*, vol. III, no. 1 (1929), 55–6, 55 n.
[48] P. 180. Talleyrand, V, 67.
[49] P. 180. *Ibid.*, 76–80.
[50] P. 180. Metternich, *Mém.*, V, 490, 495–8.
[51] P. 181. Barante, V, 48.

NOTES

[52] P. 181. Palmerston to Ponsonby (private), Feb. 17, 1833, *Howick MSS*. See also B. and A., II, 144–5, 154.
[53] P. 181. Sir J. Headlam-Morley, *Studies in Diplomatic History* (London, 1930), 54.
[54] P. 182. *Supra*, ch. V, note 43.
[55] P. 182. Hillebrand, I, 560.
[56] P. 183. C. H. B. F. P., II, 639.
[57] P. 183. *Hansard*, 3rd Ser., XIX, 439, 578–81.
[58] P. 183. *Ibid.*, XX, 900.
[59] P. 183. Hillebrand, I, 561.
[60] P. 184. Lieven, *Letters*, 341.
[61] P. 184. Palmerston to Bligh, Dec. 6, 1833 (no. 101), P.R.O., F.O., 65 : 206.
[62] P. 184. B. and A., II, 165, 165 n.
[63] P. 184. Text in Headlam-Morley, *op. cit.*, 227.
[64] P. 184. Raikes, *Journ.*, I, 189–90.
[65] P. 184. Palmerston to Bligh, Oct. 13, 1883 (no. 93), P.R.O., F.O., 65 : 206.
[66] P. 184. B. and A., II, 170.
[67] P. 184. *Ibid.*, 171 ; Diary of the third Earl Grey, Oct. 12, 1833, *Howick MSS*.
[68] P. 184. R. L. Baker, 'Palmerston on the Treaty of Unkiar Skelessi,' in *Eng. His. Rev.*, vol. XLIII (1928), p. 84 ; B. and A., II, 170.
[69] P. 184. C. Greville, *Mem.*, III, 45.
[70] P. 184. Brougham, III, 215.
[71] P. 184. C. Greville, *Mem.*, III, 56.
[72] P. 185. Palmerston to Bligh, Feb. 28, 1834 (no. 5), P.R.O., F.O., 65 : 212 ; Talleyrand, V, 212–15. See also Palmerston to Bloomfield, Feb. 13, 1834 (private), F.O., 356 : 29 ; B. and A., II, 176.
[73] P. 185. *Hansard*, 3rd Ser., XXII, 323–5.
[74] P. 185. Lieven, *Letters*, 368.
[75] P. 185. Text in R. L. Baker, *loc. cit.*, 86–9.
[76] P. 186. *Supra*, n. 72.
[77] P. 186. F. S. Rodkey, 'Lord Palmerston and the Rejuvenation of Turkey,' in *Journ. Mod. His.*, vol. I, no. 4, and vol. II, no. 2 (Dec. 1929 and June 1930), *passim*.
[78] P. 186. B. and A., II, 182.
[79] P. 186. Swain, ch. VIII, *passim*.
[80] P. 186. *Hansard*, 3rd Ser., XXII, 339–40.

CHAPTER IX

[1] P. 187. B. and A., II, 206–7.
[2] P. 187. Metternich, *Mém.*, V, 590, 643–4.
[3] P. 188. B. and A., II, 194–7.
[4] P. 188. *Hansard*, 3rd Ser., XXIV, 79.
[5] P. 189. B. and A., II, 147–8.
[6] P. 189. *Ibid.*, 201–6.
[7] P. 189. *Inter al.*, Aspinall, 201–2 ; Lord J. Russell, *Early Corr.*, II, 56–9, 63–5, 76 ; Broughton, V, 24–6, 26 n. ; C. Greville, *Mem.*, III, 143–5, 150–1, 160–9 ; Buckingham, *Courts and Cabinets*, II, 143–6 ; Croker, II, 43–7 ; Parker, *Peel*, II, 251–61 ; B. and A., II, 207–14.
[8] P. 190. *Ibid.*, 207–8.
[9] P. 190. *Ibid.*, 178.

NOTES

[10] P. 190. *Hansard*, 3rd Ser., XIV, 1204.
[11] P. 190. *Ibid.*, XVII, 1371; XXI, 1339–40.
[12] P. 190. B. and A., II, 211.
[13] P. 191. *Ibid.*, I, 365.
[14] P. 191. *Ibid.*, II, 151.
[15] P. 191. *Ibid.*, 185.
[16] P. 191. Brougham, III, 255.
[17] P. 191. *Hansard*, 3rd Ser., III, 1126–7; XXII, 756; Estimate of diplomatic salaries for 1831, P.R.O., F.O., 82: 24; Palmerston's memorandum, Aug. 27, 1831, P.R.O., F.O., 96: 17.
[18] P. 191. T. Martin, *Prince Consort*, II, 347–8.
[19] P. 191. *Supra*, ch. VI.
[20] P. 191. *Supra*, ch. VIII.
[21] P. 191. B. and A., II, 163–4, 172–3, 176–8.
[22] P. 191. *Ibid.*, 185.
[23] P. 192. *Ibid.*, 17.
[24] P. 192. *Hansard*, 3rd Ser., X, 159.
[25] P. 192. Talleyrand, IV, 292–3, 293 n.; *Hansard*, 3rd Ser., V, 798–9; XVIII, 431; Raikes, *Journ.*, I, 103; Aberdeen, *Corr.*, 1832–44, pp. 5–7, 14; *ibid.*, 1848–50, p. 232.
[26] P 192. Lieven-Grey, *Corr.*, II, 300, 327.
[27] P. 193. Palmerston to Granville, June 10, 1831, P.R.O., G. and D., 29: 14.
[28] P. 193. Nesselrode, VII, 154; *Morning Chronicle*, Sept. 11, 1830 (quoted in Swain, ch. VII).
[29] P. 193. Dino, I, 184; *Morning Post* (quoted, without date, in Raikes, *Journ.*, III, 263–6); Raikes, *Journ.*, I, 106.
[30] P. 193. Daudet, 185.
[31] P. 194. *Hansard*, 3rd Ser., X, 159.
[32] P. 194. Broughton, IV, 182–3.
[33] P. 194. Barante, V, 5.
[34] P. 194. Talleyrand, IV, 316.
[35] P. 194. Raikes, *Journ.*, I, 81–2.
[36] P. 194. Barante, V, 56–9; Talleyrand, V, 117–18; B. and A., II, 159.
[37] P. 194. *Ibid.*, 175.
[38] P. 194. Talleyrand, V, 205.
[39] P. 194. *Hansard*, 3rd Ser., XXI, 2.
[40] P. 194. *Infra*, X, note 12.
[41] P. 195. Talleyrand, V, 186–99, 209–10.
[42] P. 195. *Mem. of the Attempts which have been made since 1830 to accomplish Commercial Arrangements with France*, P.R.O., F.O., 97: 207; Guyot, *Première Entente Cordiale*, 105–15; Talleyrand, V, 73–6, 128–9, 133; Maxwell, *Clarendon*, I, 62–3; Clapham, *Economic History*, I, 247–50, 333, 479, 490–1; C. Greville, *Mem.*, II, 219; Raikes, *Journ.*, I, 205, 219.
[43] P. 196. De l'Alliance Anglo-Française in *Rev. des Deux Mondes*, 4th Ser., vol. XXV (1841), 472–3.
[44] P. 196. H. Greville, *Diary*, I, 43–4, 50; Raikes, *Journ.*, I, 162.
[45] P. 196. Talleyrand, IV, 191; Raikes, *Journ.*, I, 9, 218; Monypenny and Buckle, I, 204; Metternich, *Mém.*, V, 458; Jekyll, 307.
[46] P. 196. C. Greville, *Mem.*, III, 21. See also *ibid.*, 210–11.
[47] P. 196. Dino, I, 128; H. Greville, *Diary*, I, 17.
[48] P. 197. Dino, I, 213–15.
[49] P. 197. *E.g.* C. Greville, *Mem.*, III, 20, 56–7, 211; Raikes, *Journ.*, I, 165; Talleyrand, V, 87 n.

[50] P. 197. Lieven-Grey, *Corr.*, II, 447.
[51] P. 197. Talleyrand, III, 281–2. See also C. Greville, *Mem.*, II, 222.
[52] P. 198. Barante, V, 177–8.
[53] P. 198. Esterhazy, *Berichte*, 253, June 4, 27, 1831 (quoted by C. W. Crawley in *Cambridge His. Journ.*, vol. III, no. 1 (1929), p. 55 ; C. Greville, *Mem.*, III, 371.
[54] P. 198. Charles Grey to Lord Howick, Jan. 22, 1835, *Howick MSS.*
[55] P. 198. Brougham, III, 313.
[56] P. 198. C. Greville, *Mem.*, III, 210.
[57] P. 199. *Ibid.*, 360.
[58] P. 199. B. and A., II, 214–16.
[59] P. 199. Durham to Grey, Oct. 4, 1830, *Howick MSS.*
[60] P. 199. Jekyll, 256.
[61] P. 199. C. Greville, *Mem.*, II, 116–17 ; III, 71–2, 82, 211 ; Broughton, IV, 96.
[62] P. 199. Brougham, III, 182.
[63] P. 199. Grant, *Random Recollections*, 118–19.
[64] P. 199. B. and A., II, 148–9, 161–2.
[65] P. 200. *Hansard*, 3rd Ser., V, 930.
[66] P. 200. Lieven-Grey, *Corr.*, III, 54.
[67] P. 200. Palmerston's memorandum on 'The line for *The Times* to take about the acknowledgment of Maria,' undated, P.R.O., F.O., 96 : 17.
[68] P. 200. Brougham, III, 313.
[69] P. 200. *Ibid.*, 314.
[70] P. 200. C. Greville, *Mem.*, III, 136.
[71] P. 201. Hertslet, *Recollections*, 78.
[72] P. 201. Memorandum of J. Backhouse, March 28, 1833, P.R.O., F.O., 96 : 17.
[73] P. 201. Memorandum of J. Backhouse, Sept. 23, 1835, F.O., 96 : 18.
[74] P. 201. Palmerston's instruction for draft (initialled), May 23, 1831, P.R.O., F.O., 96 : 17.
[75] P. 201. Palmerston's memorandum, Jan. 16, 1831 ; Hertslet, *Recollections*, 78–82.
[76] P. 201. *Ibid.*, 77.
[77] P. 202. Palmerston's instructions for drafts (initialled), Sept. 22, 1835, P.R.O., F.O., 96 : 18 ; Apr. 26, 1837, F.O., 96 : 19 ; June 22, 1841 (two instructions), F.O., 96 : 20.
[78] P. 202. Palmerston's instructions for draft, Jan. 13, 1831, P.R.O., F.O., 96 : 17.
[79] P. 202. Dino, I, 161–2.
[80] P. 202. New, *Durham*, 213 ; Lane-Poole, I, 518 ; Br. Mus., *Add. MSS.* 37294, ff. 252–3.
[81] P. 203. Torrens, 113–14 ; B. and A., II, 216.
[82] P. 203. Davis, 233.
[83] P. 203. Creevey, 628.
[84] P. 203. Lord J. Russell, *Early Corr.*, II, 107–8 ; Torrens, 113–14 ; Raikes, *Journ.*, II, 75–6 ; Malmesbury (third earl), *Mem.*, I, 62 ; Aspinall, 212–13 ; Diary of the third Earl Grey, April 10, 14, 1835, *Howick MSS.* ; Lady Granville, *Letters*, II, 185 ; *Melbourne Papers*, 268 ; Lieven-Grey, *Corr.*, III, 100 ; Reid, *Durham*, II, 110–11 ; Lord Grey to Gen. Grey, Oct. 21, 1865, *Howick MSS.* ; *supra*, ch. V, note 43.
[85] P. 204. Lord J. Russell, *Early Corr.*, II, 107.
[86] P. 204. *Ibid.*, 71–2 ; B. and A., II, 213 ; C. Greville, *Mem.*, III, 197–8 ;

NOTES

Malmesbury (third earl), *Memoirs*, 57, 59–60 ; Raikes, *Journ.*, II, 11–15 ; Broughton, V, 31.
[87] P. 204. Snell, 30–2 ; Buckingham, II, 178–9.
[88] P. 206. Lord J. Russell, *Early Corr.*, II, 61.
[89] P. 207. Christie, 150.

CHAPTER X

[1] P. 209. Palmerston to Adair, Apr. 21, 1835, *Johnston Coll.* ; C. Greville, *Mem.*, III, 186 ; Lord J. Russell, *Early Corr.*, II, 73.
[2] P. 209. Raikes, *Journ.*, II, 35.
[3] P. 209. C. Greville, *Mem.*, III, 385 ; Cowley, *Diary and Corr.*, 200–1.
[4] P. 209. *Melbourne Papers*, 339.
[5] P. 210. Cowley, *Diary and Corr.*, 203 ; Thureau-Dangin, II, chs. viii–xii ; Lavisse, V, 112–23 ; Hillebrand, I, ch. vii–viii ; H. Greville, *Diary*, I, 98–9.
[6] P. 210. Raikes, *Journ.*, II, 364.
[7] P. 211. Hillebrand, I, 562–6.
[8] P. 211. Thureau-Dangin, II, 403–4 ; Hillebrand, I, 587 n. ; C. Greville, *Mem.*, III, 314 ; H. Greville, *Diary*, I, 88.
[9] P. 211. Thureau-Dangin, III, 278 ; Q.V.L., 1st Ser., I, 121–3 ; *supra*, ch. V, note 43.
[10] P. 211. Palmerston to Granville, March 12, 1839, P.R.O., G. and D., 29 : 14.
[11] P. 211. Same to same, March 21, 1839.
[12] P. 212. C. K. Webster, 'France and the United States, 1834–36,' in *Eng. His. Rev.*, XLII (1927), 58–78.
[13] P. 212. Palmerston to Grey, Jan. 23, 1836, *Howick MSS.* ; C. Greville, *Mem.*, III, 322–3.
[14] P. 212. B. and A., II, 242.
[15] P. 212. Monypenny and Buckle, I, 336.
[16] P. 212. Guyot, *Prem. Ent. Cord.*, 139–51.
[17] P. 212. Palmerston to Granville, Feb. 22, March 21, 1839, P.R.O., G. and D., 29 : 14.
[18] P. 213. Metternich, *Mém.*, V, 670–1.
[19] P. 213. Q.V.L., 1st Ser., I, 107 ; Aberdeen, *Corr.*, 1832–44, pp. 92–3 ; Hansard, 3rd Ser., XLIX, 623.
[20] P. 213. Metternich, *Mém.*, VI, 134–5.
[21] P. 213. Maxwell, *Clarendon*, chs. iv–vi ; *Ann. Reg.* for 1835 ; B. and A., II, 223–47.
[22] P. 214. Guizot, *Mém.*, IV, 112–13.
[23] P. 214. Thureau-Dangin, II, 394–9 ; III, 99–102.
[24] P. 214. Palmerston to Russell, Dec. 15, 1836, P.R.O., G. and D., 22 : 2.
[25] P. 214. Buckingham, II, 184–5 ; Palmerston to Alava, June 8, 1835 (copy), P.R.O., G. and D., 29 : 17 ; Aberdeen, *Corr.*, 1832–44, pp. 42–3 ; C. Greville, *Mem.*, III, 265.
[26] P. 215. *Hansard*, 3rd Ser., XXXI, 117 ; Aberdeen, *Corr.*, 1832–44, pp. 42–3.
[27] P. 215. *Hansard*, 3rd Ser., XXXI, 994–1005 ; XXXVII, 257–70.
[28] P. 215. Buckingham, II, 184–5 ; *Hansard*, 3rd Ser., XXXV, 962.
[29] P. 215. Palmerston to Adair, June 23, 1835, *Johnston Coll.*
[30] P. 215. Malmesbury (3rd earl), *Mem.*, I, 76.
[31] P. 216. *Ibid.*, 71, 76 ; Lieven-Grey, *Corr.*, III, 230 ; *Hansard*, 3rd Ser., XXXIX, 1332 ; XLIII, 1143.

[32] P. 216. C. Greville, *Mem.*, IV, 241.
[33] P. 216. B. and A., III, 15.
[34] P. 216. Palmerston's instructions for despatch, Sept. 2, 1841, P.R.O., F.O., 96 : 20.
[35] P. 216. C. Greville, *Mem.*, V, 422 ; Palmerston to Russell, Dec. 15, 1836, P.R.O., G. and D., 22 : 2 ; B. and A., II, 239–42 ; III, 14.
[36] P. 216. *Ibid.*, II, 236 ; C. Greville, *Mem.*, III, 321.
[37] P. 216. Grey to Howick, Dec. 12, 1836, *Howick MSS.* See also Lieven-Grey, *Corr.*, III, 312.
[38] P. 217. H. Greville, *Diary*, I, 97.
[39] P. 217. B. and A., II, 239–40.
[40] P. 217. Palmerston's instructions for despatches, Dec. 30, 1836, Aug. 9, 1837, P.R.O., F.O., 96 : 19.
[41] P. 217. B. and A., II, 243–4 ; Palmerston's instructions for despatch to Granville, Feb. 6, 1837, P.R.O., F.O., 96 : 19 ; C. Greville, *Mem.*, III, 385 ; H. Greville, *Diary*, I, 113 ; Malmesbury (3rd earl), *Mem.*, I, 72–3.
[42] P. 217. Q.V.L., 1st Ser., I, 107.
[43] P. 217. Barante, V, 531 n.
[44] P. 217. B. and A., II, 245.
[45] P. 217. Palmerston's drafts of despatches to Granville, June 9, 1836, March 5 and Nov. 20, 1839 ; to Villiers, Dec. 30, 1836 ; to Aston, Nov. 24, Dec. 17, 1840, June 27, 1841, P.R.O., F.O., 96 : 18–21 ; B. and A., III, 19 ; Q.V.L., 1st Ser. I, 121–3.
[46] P. 218. Palmerston's instructions for despatches to Howard, May 19 and 20, 1835, P.R.O., F.O., 96 : 18.
[47] P. 218. Q.V.L., 1st Ser., I, 169 ; Juste, II, 120–2.
[48] P. 218. *Ibid.*, 120–2, 149–51 ; *Ann. Reg.* for 1835–40.
[49] P. 218. Raikes, *Journ.*, III, 34.
[50] P. 218. *Ibid.*, 74 ; Juste, II, 149 ; H. Greville, *Diary*, I, 105.
[51] P. 219. *Hansard*, 3rd Ser., XXX, 266 ; XLIV, 129–30 ; Barante, V, 373 ; Raikes, *Journ.*, IV, 14–15.
[52] P. 219. H. Greville, *Diary*, I, 105.
[53] P. 219. Palmerston's instructions for despatch for Granville, Nov. 21, 1836, P.R.O., F.O., 96 : 17 ; B. and A., III, 22–3.
[54] P. 219. B. and A., III, 21.
[55] P. 219. *Ibid.*, 27.
[56] P. 219. d'Haussonville, I, 137–8 ; Barante, V, 420–1, 429–33, 502–3 ; *Hansard*, 3rd Ser., XXXV, 615–19, 1149.
[57] P. 220. Eardley-Wilmot, 82–3 ; Palmerston's draft of despatch to Granville, Jan. 31, 1839, P.R.O., F.O., 96 : 20. For Palmerston's desire to divide Russia and Austria, see draft of despatch to Sir Frederick Lamb, March 5, 1837, P.R.O., F.O., 96 : 19.
[58] P. 220. Palmerston to Victoria, Jan. 28, 1838, *Windsor MSS.*, A. 8.
[59] P. 221. *E.g.* drafts of despatches to Granville, July 9 and Dec. 21, 1837, P.R.O., F.O., 96 : 19.
[60] P. 221. Barante, VI, 91, 97, 100–1.
[61] P. 221. New, 281–2 ; Reid, *Durham*, II, 53 ; Eardley-Wilmot, 83–91 ; Barante, V, 244–5, 264–72, 350–2, 360–1 ; draft of despatch to Granville, May 22, 1838, P.R.O., F.O., 96 : 19.
[62] P. 221. Same to Lyons, Jan. 4, 1839, P.R.O., F.O., 96 : 20.
[63] P. 222. Same to Sir Frederick Lamb, Dec. 8, 1837, P.R.O., F.O., 96 : 19.
[64] P. 222. Barante, VI, 89.
[65] P. 222. Parker, *Peel*, II, 377–78.

NOTES 477

⁶⁶ P. 222. Draft of despatch to Bulwer, May 23, 1841, P.R.O., F.O., 96 : 20.
⁶⁷ P. 223. Palmerston to Adair, May 15, 1835, *Johnston Coll.*
⁶⁸ P. 223. Same to same, May 22 and June 14, 1835, *Johnston Coll.* ; same to same, Sept. 4, 1835 (no. 4), P.R.O., F.O., 64 : 199.
⁶⁹ P. 223. Palmerston to Adair, Sept. 1, 1835 (no. 3), P.R.O., F.O., 64 : 199. See also same to same, May 1, 1835, *Johnston Coll.*
⁷⁰ P. 224. Palmerston to Adair, May 22, 1835, *Johnston Coll.*
⁷¹ P. 224. Palmerston to Hamilton, Aug. 19, 1837 (no. 1), P.R.O., F.O. 64 : 209 ; Palmerston to Seymour, Aug. 4, 1837 (no. 14), F.O., 10 : 48.
⁷² P. 225. Hamilton to Palmerston, Sept. 6, 1837 (no. 7), F.O. 64 : 211.
⁷³ P. 225. *Ibid.*
⁷⁴ P. 226. Lamb to Palmerston, Sept. 22 and Oct. 21, 1837 (nos. 63 and 74), F.O., 7 : 265.
⁷⁵ P. 226. Palmerston to Lamb, Oct. 7, 1837 (no. 127), F.O., 7 : 263.
⁷⁶ P. 226. Letters of Victoria to Melbourne, 1837-9, *Windsor MSS.* C. 1 ; Palmerston to Victoria, Aug. 18, 1837, *Windsor MSS.* A. 8 ; Q.V.L., 1st Ser., I, 80, 85-6, 119, 136-8, 217, 252-3, 268-9 ; Broughton, V, 92, 96-100, 258-9 ; Wilson, *Greville*, II, 78 ; B. and A., II, 250-1, 289-90 ; Creevey, 666 ; Aberdeen, *Corr.*, 1832-44, pp. 124-5.
⁷⁷ P. 228. Corti, *Leopold*, 106 ; Q.V.L., 1st Ser., I, chs. IV-VI.
⁷⁸ P. 229. Palmerston to Victoria, March 15, 1838, *Windsor MSS.* A. 8.
⁷⁹ P. 229. Lord William Russell to Lord John Russell, May 16, 1838, P.R.O., G. and D., 22 : 3.
⁸⁰ P. 229. Q.V.L., 1st Ser., I, 144, 148-9, 152, 170-1.
⁸¹ P. 229. *Ibid.*, 149-51.
⁸² P. 230. Palmerston to Melbourne, Dec. 3, 1838 (copy), P.R.O., G. and D., 22 : 3 ; Melbourne to Victoria, Dec. 4, 1838, *Windsor MSS.* A. 1 ; Q.V.L., 1st Ser., I, 172-3.
⁸³ P. 230. Q.V.L., 1st Ser., I, 170-1 ; Juste, II, 158-9.
⁸⁴ P. 230. Melbourne to Victoria, Aug. 26, 1838, *Windsor MSS.* A. 1 ; Palmerston to Melbourne, Dec. 3, 1838 (copy), P.R.O., G. and D., 22 : 3.
⁸⁵ P. 230. *Hansard*, 3rd Ser., XLV, 142.
⁸⁶ P. 230. Q.V.L., 1st Ser., I, 254-5.
⁸⁷ P. 230. Lord J. Russell, *Early Corr.*, II, 239, 248.
⁸⁸ P. 230. Palmerston to Granville, Apr. 19, 1839, P.R.O., G. and D., 29 : 14.

CHAPTER XI

¹ P. 231. C.H.B.F.P., II, 234-9, 244-7 ; L. F. Hill, *Diplomatic Relations between the United States and Brazil* (Duke Univ. Press, 1932), ch. V ; DuBois, chs. IX, X ; Mathieson, 1-74 ; Commander A. H. Foote, U.S.N., *Africa and the American Flag* (New York, 1854), *passim.*
² P. 231. *Hansard*, 3rd Ser., LXXVI, 931.
³ P. 232. Lord Leveson to Granville, Apr. 3, 1840, P.R.O., G. and D., 29 : 6.
⁴ P. 232. *Hansard*, 3rd Ser., LVIII, 654-5.
⁵ P. 234. Martens, *Nouv. Rec.*, IX, 544-58.
⁶ P. 234. *State Papers*, XXIII, 343-74.
⁷ P. 234. Palmerston to Stevenson, Dec. 8, 1840, *Stevenson MSS.*
⁸ P. 234. *Hansard*, 3rd Ser., XXXIV, 1266 ; XXXVIII, 1827-9 ; XXXV, 939 ; XLII, 1144-52 ; L, 119-27 ; LVIII, 648-55.
⁹ P. 234. *Ibid.*, L, 123-4.

478 NOTES

[10] P. 234. *Ibid.*, XLII, 1150.
[11] P. 235. Q.V.L., 1st Ser., I, 146–7 ; Broughton, V, 135–6.
[12] P. 235. Palmerston to Granville, May 8, 1839, P.R.O., G. and D., 29 : 14 ; Palmerston to Victoria, June 18, 1839, *Windsor MSS.* A. 10 ; 2 and 3 Vic., ch. lxxiii.
[13] P. 235. Lord J. Russell, *Early Corr.*, II, 253–5.
[14] P. 235. H. T. Catterall, *Judicial Cases concerning American Slavery* (Carnegie Institution, Washington, 1926–), I, 47–9 ; Sir J. Arnould, *Memoir of Thomas, First Lord Denman* (London, 1873), II, 119–25.
[15] P. 235. E. D. Adams, *British Interests and Activities in Texas* (Baltimore, 1910), chs. I–III ; G. P. Garrison (ed.), *Texan Diplomatic Corr.* (Am. His. Assoc., Rep. for 1908, Washington, 1908–11), II, 808–947.
[16] P. 236. *Ibid.*, 815.
[17] P. 236. *Ibid.*, 922.
[18] P. 236. Hamilton to Andrew Stevenson, Nov. 7, 1840, *Stevenson MSS.*
[19] P. 236. Garrison, *op. cit.*, 929.
[20] P. 237. Martens, *Receuil, Table Générale* (1875), 162–217 ; *Hansard*, 3rd Ser., LVIII, 649–51.
[21] P. 237. *Ibid.*, 651.
[22] P. 237. Catterall, *op. cit.*, I, 44.
[23] P. 237. DuBois, 142–7, 158–67 ; Hill, *op. cit.*, 134–41.
[24] P. 237. *Ibid.*, 121–2, 127–9.
[25] P. 238. Garrison, *op. cit.*, 921–5.
[26] P. 238. Van Buren to Livingston, Oct. 14, 1831, *Van Buren MSS.*
[27] P. 238. Palmerston to Stevenson, Jan. 7, Dec. 11, 1837, Sept. 10, 1838 ; Stevenson to Forsyth, Dec. 20, 1839, *Stevenson MSS.*
[28] P. 239. Catterall, *op. cit.*, I, 44–5 ; Hill, *op. cit.*, 121–30 ; DuBois, 158–67 ; Capt. Tucker, R.N., to R. M. O'Ferrall, March 16, 1841 (copy), P.R.O., F.O., 115 : 77.
[29] P. 239. Stevenson to Webster, Aug. 31, 1841, *Stevenson MSS.*
[30] P. 239. Note 23, *supra* ; Hill, *op. cit.*, 122 ; Foote, *op. cit.*, *passim*.
[31] P. 239. Hill, *op. cit.*, 121.
[32] P. 239. Aberdeen to Stevenson, Oct. 13, 1841, *Stevenson MSS.*
[33] P. 240. Palmerston to Stevenson, Feb. 15, 24, Apr. 23, July 21, 31, Aug. 5, 17, Sept. 10, Dec. 8, 1840 ; Stevenson to Forsyth, Feb. 29, 1840 ; Stevenson to Palmerston, Nov. 13, 1840 ; Palmerston's memorandum, Feb. 26, 1840, *Stevenson MSS.*
[34] P. 240. Stevenson to Webster, Apr. 19, June 18, July 3, 13, 1841, *Stevenson MSS.*
[35] P. 240. Stevenson to Webster, Aug. 18 (2 letters) ; Palmerston to Stevenson, Aug. 5 (no. 142) and undated (no. 143), *Stevenson MSS.* ; Dubois, 160.
[36] P. 241. Palmerston to Stevenson, Aug. 27, 1841 (no. 150), *Stevenson MSS.*
[37] P. 241. Stevenson to Webster, May 18, 1841, *Stevenson MSS.* See also Palmerston to Fox, July 16, 1841, P.R.O., F.O., 115 : 77.
[38] P. 241. Leveson to the Secy. of the Admlty., May 18, 1841, P.R.O., F.O., 115 : 77.
[39] P. 241. Stevenson to Aberdeen, Sept. 10, 1841 ; Stevenson to Webster, Sept. 18, 1841 ; Aberdeen to Stevenson, Oct. 13, 1841 ; Stevenson to Webster, Oct. 22, 1841, *Stevenson MSS.*
[40] P. 241. Webster, *Diplomatic and Official Papers* (New York, 1848), 142–6 ; Van Buren, 528.
[41] P. 243. *Ibid.*, 465–6.
[42] P. 243. Van Buren to Jackson, Nov. 25, 1831, March 1 28, 1832 ;

NOTES 479

Van Buren's notes and drafts of proposed treaty on impressment, March 10 ?, 1832, *Van Buren MSS.*
[43] P. 243. Van Buren to Jackson, Sept. 28, 1831, *Van Buren MSS.*
[44] P. 243. Van Buren to Jackson, March 9 (?), 1832; Van Buren to Palmerston, May 31, 1832 (draft); Vail to Van Buren, March 14, 1836, *Van Buren MSS.*
[45] P. 244. Vaughan to Palmerston, Aug. 30, 1835; Bankhead to Palmerston, Nov. 28, 1835, P.R.O., F.O., 5 : 301 ; Bankhead to Palmerston, Jan. 13, 1836, F.O., 5 : 306.
[46] P. 244. Bankhead to Palmerston (with Palmerston's holograph endorsement), Feb. 21, 1836, F.O. 5 : 306.
[47] P. 244. Fox to Palmerston, June 11, 1836 (no. 10), F.O., 5 : 307.
[48] P. 244. Palmerston to Van Buren, Dec. 22, 1835, *Van Buren MSS.*
[49] P. 244. Van Buren to Palmerston, Jan. (?), 1836, *Van Buren MSS.*
[50] P. 245. *Hansard*, 3rd Ser., XXXVII, 195.
[51] P. 245. Vail to Van Buren, March 14, 1836, *Van Buren MSS.*
[52] P. 245. *Ibid.*
[53] P. 245. Especially Forsyth to Vaughan, Apr. 28, 1835 ; Vaughan to Wellington (no. 29), May 12, 1835, P.R.O., F.O., 5 : 300 ; Palmerston to Bankhead (no. 1), Oct. 30, 1835, F.O., 5 : 299.
[54] P. 245. *Ibid.*; Palmerston to Fox (no. 14), Nov. 19, 1837 ; same to same, same date, unofficial, F.O., 5 : 313.
[55] P. 246. J. B. McMaster, *History of the People of the United States* (New York, 1883–1913), VI, 446 ; J. D. Richardson, *Messages and Papers of the Presidents* (Washington, 1896–1900), III, 482–3 ; Stevenson to Van Buren, Dec. 12, 1838, with enclosed copy of Stevenson to Palmerston, Dec. 6, 1838 ; Palmerston to Stevenson, Dec. 8, 1838, *Stevenson MSS.*
[56] P. 247. *Hansard*, 3rd Ser., XL, 716–17.
[57] P. 247. Palmerston to Victoria, Apr. 4, 1839, *Windsor MSS.* A. 9.
[58] P. 247. Same to same, June 15, 1839, *Windsor MSS.* A. 10.
[59] P. 247. Palmerston to Stevenson, Jan. 11, 1840, *Stevenson MSS.*
[60] P. 247. *Ann. Reg.* for 1841, p. 312.
[61] P. 247. B. and A., III, 46.
[62] P. 247. Stevenson to Forsyth, March 9, 18, 1841 ; Stevenson to Webster, Apr. 7, 1841, *Stevenson MSS.* ; B. and A., III, 48–9 ; Q.V.L., 1st Ser., I, 327.
[63] P. 248. *Ibid.* ; Stevenson to Webster, May 18, 1841, *Stevenson MSS.*
[64] P. 248. Stevenson to Van Buren, Feb. 9, 1841, *Van Buren MSS.*; B. and A., III, 48–50.
[65] P. 248. *Ibid.* ; Palmerston to Fox, Aug. 18, 1841, F.O., 115 : 75.
[66] P. 248. *Ibid.* ; Stevenson to Webster, Aug. 18, 1841, *Stevenson MSS.*
[67] P. 248. Palmerston to Stevenson, Aug. 27, Sept. 2, 1841 ; Stevenson to Palmerston, Aug. 31, Sept. 2, 1841, *Stevenson MSS* ; Howick to Grey, March 15, 1841, *Howick MSS.* ; Raikes, *Journ.*, IV, 134–5.
[68] P. 249. Stevenson to Forsyth, March 21, 1839, *Stevenson MSS.*
[69] P. 250. *Hansard*, 3rd Ser., LXVIII, 629.
[70] P. 250. *Quarterly Rev.*, LXXI, 582.
[71] P. 250. C. Greville, *Mem.*, V, 102. See also Justin Winsor, *Narrative and Critical History of America* (Boston, 1886–1889), VII, 181.
[72] P. 250. Palmerston to Fox, Aug. 24, 1841, P.R.O., F.O., 115 : 75.
[73] P. 250. Palmerston to Fox, Aug. 24, 1841, P.R.O., F.O., 115 : 75.
[74] P. 250. W. F. Ganong, 'Evolution of the Boundaries of New Brunswick,' in *Proc. and Trans. of the Royal Society of Canada*, 2nd Ser., vol. VII (Montreal, 1901), 234, 265 ff. ; Lord E. Fitzmaurice, *Life of Shelburne* (London, 1876), III, 324 n.

NOTES

[75] P. 251. Palmerston to Stevenson, Apr. 3, 1839, *Stevenson MSS*.
[76] P. 251. Palmerston to Russell, Oct. 25, 1839, P R.O., G and D, 22 : 3.
[77] P. 251. Palmerston to Fox, Nov. 19, 1837, P.R.O., F.O., 5 : 313 ; Palmerston to Lansdowne, Apr. 25, 1840, *Bowood MSS*.
[78] P. 251. *Ibid*. ; B. and A., III, 37–8 ; *Melbourne Papers*, 458–9.
[79] P. 252. Palmerston to Granville, March 29, 1839, P.R.O., G. and D., 29 : 14.
[80] P. 252. Russell to Melbourne, Apr. 26, 1840, P.R.O., G. and D., 22 : 3 ; Stevenson to Forsyth, Feb. 18, 1840, *Stevenson MSS*.
[81] P. 252. Ganong, *op. cit.*, 343–4.
[82] P. 252. Palmerston to Stevenson, June 2, 1840, *Stevenson MSS* ; B. and A., III, 38 ; Palmerston to Lansdowne, Apr. 25, 1840, *Bowood MSS*.
[83] P. 252. *Melbourne Papers*, 458–9.
[84] P. 252. Palmerston to Stevenson, June 2, 1840 ; Stevenson to Forsyth, June 3, 1840, *Stevenson MSS*.
[85] P. 253. Palmerston to Fox, Aug. 24, 1841 (no. 23), F.O., 115 : 75.
[86] P. 253. Palmerston to Russell, Jan. 19, 1841, P.R.O., G. and D., 22 : 4.
[87] P. 254. Broughton, VI, 29.
[88] P. 254. Br. Mus., *Add. MSS*. 39949.
[89] P. 254. Stevenson to Webster, Aug. 18, Sept. 18, 1841, *Stevenson MSS*.
[90] P. 254. Stevenson to John Rutherford, Sept. 30, 1841, *Stevenson MSS*.
[91] P. 255. *Hansard*, 3rd Ser., LXVIII, 1203–4.
[92] P. 255. Melbourne to Victoria, Oct. 17, 1841, *Windsor MSS*, A. 4.

CHAPTER XII

[1] P. 257. C. Greville, *Mem.*, IV, 118.
[2] P. 257. *Ibid.*, 179. See also Charles Mackay, *Through the Long Day* (London, 1887), I, ch. ii.
[3] P. 257. Palmerston's memoranda, March 25, June 9, 1836, P.R.O. F.O., 96 : 18.
[4] P. 257. H. Greville, *Diary*, I, 136 ; C. Greville, *Mem.*, IV, 179.
[5] P. 257. *Ibid.*, 326 ; Reeve, I, 127 ; Greville-Reeve, *Letters*, 31 ; Parker, *Peel*, III, 387.
[6] P. 257. Palmerston's memorandum, Oct. 24, 1835, P.R.O., F.O., 96 : 18 (printed as a leading article in the *Globe*, Oct. 26, 1835) ; other memoranda in F.O. 96 : 18 and F.O. 96 : 20.
[7] P. 257. B. and A., III, 11–12, 14, 18, 24–8, 39, 42 ; Palmerston to Victoria, Aug. 18, 1837, June 17, 21, 24, 1838, Jan. 16, 1839, *Windsor MSS*. A. 8, 9 ; Palmerston to Russell, June 23, 1838, P.R.O., G. and D., 22 : 3 ; Melbourne to Victoria, Nov. 30, 1838, *Windsor MSS*., A. 1 ; Q.V.L., 1st Ser., I, 180, 186 ; Palmerston to Granville, Jan. 15, 1839, P.R.O., G. and D., 29 : 14 ; Broughton, V, 189 ; Ellice to Russell, Aug. 27, 1839 (?), P.R.O., G. and D., 22 : 3 ; C. Greville, *Mem.*, IV, 242–3 ; Leveson to Granville, March 12, 1841, P.R.O., G. and D., 29 : 6 ; *Hansard*, 3rd Ser., LXI, 269–70 ; Lady Lyttelton, *Corr.*, 311.
[8] P. 259. Lady Cowper to Mrs. Huskisson, Nov. 7, Dec. 26, 1839, Br. Mus., *Add. MSS*. 39949 ; Lady Granville, II, 296–7 ; Palmerston to Victoria, Dec. 15, 1839, *Windsor MSS*., A. 10 ; Lieven-Grey, *Corr.*, III, 307–8 ; Airlie, II, ch. xiv.
[9] P. 259. C. Greville, *Mem.*, II, 229 ; Hayward, 293–301 ; Airlie, *passim* ; Lady Lyttelton, *Corr.*, 316.
[10] P. 260. Airlie, II, 46.

NOTES

[11] P. 260. Hayward, 297; B. and A., III, 34; Airlie, II, 42–3; Lady Palmerston to Mrs. Huskisson, March 19, 1840; March 1, 1841, Br. Mus., *Add. MSS.* 39949, ff. 172–3, 176–7.
[12] P. 261. Lady Granville, *Letters*, II, 297.
[13] P. 261. Leveson to Granville, Feb. 8, March 13, 1840, P.R.O., G. and D., 29 : 6.
[14] P. 261. Same to same, March 23, 1840.
[15] P. 261. Same to same, Jan. 10, 1840. See also C. Greville, *Mem.*, IV, 178; V, 48, 73.
[16] P. 261. Same to same, March 20, 1840.
[17] P. 261. Hertslet, *Foreign Office*, 81–2.
[18] P. 262. *Ibid.*, 61.
[19] P. 262. Palmerston to Russell, Oct. 20, 1839, P.R.O., G. and D., 22 : 3.
[20] P. 262. C. Greville, *Mem.*, V, 73.
[21] P. 262. Lord J. Russell, *Early Corr.*, II, 108–9, 190–2; Bankhead to Strangways, Nov. 5, 1835, P.R.O., F.O., 5 : 301; Reid, *Durham*, II, 49, 62–5; New, 298; C. Greville, *Mem.*, III, 404–5; Newman, 19; Wilson, *Greville*, II, 86; Airlie, II, 34, 51–2; *Hansard*, 3rd Ser., XXXIX, 1109.
[22] P. 263. P.R.O., G. and D., 22 : 3.
[23] P. 264. Lord J. Russell, *Early Corr.*, II, 238–9.
[24] P. 264. Czartoryski, II, 341.
[25] P. 265. Hoskins, 272–6; C. W. Crawley, 'Anglo-Russian Relations, 1815–40,' in *Cam. His. Journ.*, vol. III, no. 1 (1929); Barante, V, 548–50.
[26] P. 266. Broughton, V, 178.
[27] P. 266. É. Driault, *La Question d'Extrême Orient* (Paris, 1908), 115.
[28] P. 266. Schiemann, III, 295–6; Palmerston to Ponsonby, May 22, 1838, *Howick MSS*.
[29] P. 266. Sykes, II, 355–6; Palmerston to Durham, Oct. 26, 1835 (no. 6), and Durham to Palmerston, Dec. 7, 1835 (no. 25), P.R.O., F.O., 65 : 218; Palmerston to Victoria, June 26, 1841, *Windsor MSS.* A. 10; Palmerston to Bloomfield, June 23, July 7, 1840, F.O., 356 : 29.
[30] P. 267. In particular, Palmerston to Adair, Lord W. Russell and Sir G. Hamilton, Feb. 16 to Aug. 3, 1836, P.R.O., F.O., 244 : 49; Adair, Lord W. Russell and Sir G. Hamilton to Palmerston, Feb. 24 to Aug. 3, 1836, F.O. 64 : 205, 206.
[31] P. 267. Fox to Palmerston, May 3, 1836 (copy), F.O., 244 : 49.
[32] P. 267. Hertslet, *Map*, I, 218–20.
[33] P. 267. Barante, V, 344–5.
[34] P. 268. *Ibid.*
[35] P. 268. B. and A., II, 248.
[36] P. 268. *Ibid.*
[37] P. 268. Palmerston to Lord W. Russell [also to Durham and Fox], Apr. 15, 1836 (no. 9), P.R.O., F.O., 244 : 49.
[38] P. 269. Lord W. Russell to Palmerston, Apr. 24, 26, May 1, 1836 (nos. 27, 28, 36), F.O., 64 : 205; Palmerston to Lord W. Russell, May 10, June 28 (nos. 15, 34), F.O., 244 : 49.
[39] P. 269. B. and A., III, 13.
[40] P. 269. Copies of Fox to Palmerston, May 3 (no. 15), July 2 (no. 22), 1836, Palmerston to Fox, June 22, 1836 (no. 24), and Metternich to Hummelauer, May 9, 1836; enclosed in Palmerston to Lord W. Russell, May 10, June 28, 1836 (nos. 15, 35), and same to Sir G. Hamilton, July 12, 1836 (no. 5), P.R.O., F.O., 244 : 49; Barante, V, 398–9.
[41] P. 270. *Ibid.*, 345, 379–80.

I.

[42] P. 270. *Ibid.*, 379–80, 415.
[43] P. 270. Copy of Palmerston to Durham, June 30, 1836 (no. 93), enclosed in Palmerston to Sir G. Hamilton, July 5, 1836 (no. 1), F.O., 244 : 49.
[44] P. 270. *Ibid.*
[45] P. 270. Schiemann, III, 461–3.
[46] P. 270. Instructions for drafts to Lamb, May 11, 1837, and March 21, 1838, P.R.O., F.O., 96 : 19.
[47] P. 270. *Hansard*, 3rd Ser., LV, 685.

CHAPTER XIII

[1] P. 272. Morley, *Gladstone*, I, 225.
[2] P. 272. Morse, chs. VIII–XI ; C.H.B.F.P., II, 217–19 ; Driault, *op. cit.*, 121.
[3] P. 274. *Hansard*, 3rd Ser., LIII, 670 ff. ; Broughton, V, 256.
[4] P. 275. Morse, 623.
[5] P. 275. *State Papers*, XXIX, 942–78 ; XXX, 4–90.
[6] P. 275. *Ibid.*, 942, 947, 949.
[7] P. 275. Morse, 622.
[8] P. 275. *Hansard*, 3rd Ser., LIII, 694.
[9] P. 276. *Ibid.*, LI, 113–14.
[10] P. 276. *Ibid.*, LIII, 719.
[11] P. 276. *Bishop Burnet's History of His Own Time* (Oxford, 1833), I, 148.
[12] P. 276. *Hansard*, 3rd Ser., LIII, 669–951 ; Broughton, V, 256–7.
[13] P. 276. Morley, *Gladstone*, I, 225.
[14] P. 277. Broughton, V, 257. See also B. and A., III, 37.
[15] P. 277. *Hansard*, 3rd Ser., LIII, 955 ; Leveson to Granville, March 31, 1840, P.R.O., G and D, 29 : 6 ; C. Greville, *Mem.*, IV, 283.
[16] P. 277. Broughton, V, 227–8.
[17] P. 277. *Melbourne Papers*, 456.
[18] P. 278. Morse, 626–30, 636–40.
[19] P. 278. Broughton, VI, 13 ; Q.V.L., 1st Ser., I, 327–8, 333–4 ; *Melbourne Papers*, 493 ; Palmerston to Lansdowne, Apr. (?) 12, 1841, *Bowood MSS.*
[20] P. 278. *State Papers*, XXX, 389–92, XXXI, 132–8.
[21] P. 279. B. and A., III, 13.
[22] P. 279. New, 289–91.
[23] P. 279. Reid, *Durham*, II, 44.
[24] P. 279. Thureau-Dangin, III, 56–8 ; Hillebrand, I, 606–8.
[25] P. 281. Aberdeen, *Corr.*, 1832–44, pp. 55–7.
[26] P. 281. Note 36, *infra*.
[27] P. 281. Backhouse's memorandum, Nov. 8, 1834, P.R.O., F.O., 96 : 17.
[28] P. 281. Apponyi, III, 213–14 ; Lady Cowper to Lord J. Russell, 'Tuesday,' P.R.O., G. and D., 22 : 2 ; Lady Cowper to Mrs. Huskisson, Jan. 5, 1836, Br. Mus., *Add. MSS.* 39949, ff. 160–4 ; Lieven-Grey, *Corr.*, III, 175–85 ; Cowley (first baron), *Diary and Corr.*, 203–5 ; Aberdeen, *Corr.*, 1832–44, pp. 55–7.
[29] P. 282. Note 36, *infra* ; *The Times*, July 26, 1838, Jan. 26, 30, 1839 ; C. Greville, *Mem.*, IV, 117–20, 158–9 ; Robinson, ch. II.
[30] P. 282. Aberdeen, *Corr.*, 1832–44, pp. 55–7.
[31] P. 282. New, 295 ; Barante, V, 528–9, 540–8 ; *Hansard*, 3rd Ser., XLIII, 903 ff. ; B. and A., II, 248–9.

NOTES 483

[32] P. 282. *Ibid.*
[33] P. 282. *Hansard*, 3rd Ser., XXXVII, 633; XLIII, 940-4; Palmerston's memorandum, Feb. 11, 1837 (?), P.R.O., F.O., 96 : 19.
[34] P. 282. Palmerston to Ponsonby, Apr. 11, 1837, *Howick MSS.*; Barante, V, 529; *Hansard*, 3rd Ser., XCVII, 86.
[35] P. 283. Raikes, *Journ.*, III, 140.
[36] P. 283. For parliamentary discussion of all these affairs, *Hansard*, 3rd Ser., XCVI, 295-311, 623-31, 1135-1239; XCVII, 66-122, 698; C, 1119. For Urquhart's contentions and for his correspondence with Ponsonby, the *Diplomatic Review*, especially for 1875-6.
[37] P. 283. Palmerston to Ponsonby, Jan. 31, 1837, *Howick MSS.*; B. and A., II, 248-9; Palmerston's instructions for despatch to Lamb, March 11, 1837, P.R.O., F.O., 96 : 19; Barante, VI, 18-19.
[38] P. 283. Palmerston's instructions for despatch to Lamb, Feb. 11, Aug. 7, 1837, P.R.O., F.O., 96 : 19; Barante, V, 540-3.
[39] P. 283. Palmerston to Ponsonby, March 26, Apr. 10, 11, 1837, *Howick MSS.*; C. Greville, *Mem.*, III, 405.
[40] P. 283. B. and A., II, 257-64, 273-5, 284-5, 288.
[41] P. 283. *Diplomatic Rev.*, *passim*; Robinson, 105-76; *Quarterly Rev.*, LXVII, 258 ff.; Holyoake, 77.
[42] P. 283. *Ibid.*
[43] P. 284. Halévy, III, 246-7.
[44] P. 284. *Inter al.*, H. G. Keene, *History of India* (Edinburgh, 1906), II, 140-5; J. W. Kaye, *War in Afghanistan* (London, 1878), 300-2; *Cam. His. of the Br. Emp.*, IV, ch. XXVIII; L. J. Trotter, *The Earl of Auckland* (Oxford, 1893), 40-66, 75, 134-6; C.H.B.F.P., II, 199-215; Sir A. Colvin, *John Russell Colvin* (Oxford, 1895), 82-9; Sykes, II, 324-55; Hoskins, 272-6.
[45] P. 284. *Hansard*, 3rd Ser., LXIV, 527.
[46] P. 285. Torrens, 274.
[47] P. 285. Palmerston to Victoria, Oct. 8, 1837, *Windsor MSS.* A. 8.
[48] P. 285. Kaye, *op. cit.*, 487-91.
[49] P. 285. Palmerston to Bligh, June 16, Aug. 5, 1834 (nos. 26, 37), P.R.O., F.O., 65 : 212.
[50] P. 286. Lord J. Russell, *Early Corr.*, II, 222-6.
[51] P. 286. *Ibid.*
[52] P. 287. C.H.B. F.P., II, 206-7; *Cam. His. of the Br. Emp.*, IV, 498.
[53] P. 288. Broughton, V, 231.
[54] P. 288. Czartoryski, II, 339-40; Lord J. Russell, *Early Corr.*, II, 238; Torrens, 274; *Hansard*, 3rd Ser., LXVII, 198.
[55] P. 288. *E.g.*, Sir George Macmunn, *Afghanistan* (London, 1929), 107; Trotter, *op. cit.*, 56; V. A. Smith, *Oxford His. of India* (Oxford, 1920), 674-5; C.H.B.F.P., II, 199-201; Sykes, 324-5.
[56] P. 288. Kaye, *op. cit.*, 301.
[57] P. 288. Keene, *op. cit.*, II, 140; Kaye, *op. cit.*, 302; Trotter, *op. cit.*, 45; Colvin, *op. cit.*, 82-9; Hoskins, 273-4; C. W. Crawley, 'Anglo-Russian Relations, 1815-40' in *Cam. His. Journ.*, vol. III, no. 1 (1929).
[58] P. 289. Keene, *op. cit.*, II, 141-2, 144-5; *Cam. His. of the Br. Emp.*, IV, 499; Trotter, *op. cit.*, 60, 134-6; Robinson, 142-6; *Hansard*, 3rd Ser., LXVII, 119-98, CLXII, 37-89.
[59] P. 289. *Ibid.*

CHAPTER XIV

[1] P. 291. Rodkey, 'Lord Palmerston's Policy for the Rejuvenation of Turkey,' in *Trans. of the Royal Hist. Soc.*, XII, 163-92.
[2] P. 291. B. and A., II, 298-9.
[3] P. 292. Guizot, IV, 331-5; Hoskins, 272; B. and A., II, 272, 281; Martens, *Nouv. Rec.*, XVI, 108-17.
[4] P. 292. Rodkey, *Lord Palmerston and a Concert of the Powers on the Eastern Question, 1833-38*, unpublished MSS.
[5] P. 292. *Ibid.*; Diary of the third Earl Grey, Dec. 23, 1835; Grey to Howick, Jan. 10, 1836, *Howick MSS*.
[6] P. 292. Palmerston to Russell, March 7, 1836, P.R.O., G. and D., 22 : 2.
[7] P. 293. *Supra*, note 4; B. and A., II, 266-88; Palmerston to Ponsonby, May 22, 1838, *Howick MSS.*; Palmerston to Lansdowne, June 17, 1838, *Bowood MSS.*; Barante, VI, 159-61; C. K. Webster, 'Palmerston, Metternich and the European System,' in *Proc. of the Br..Acad.*, XX (1934), 21-7.
[8] P. 295. Palmerston to Granville, May 27, 1839, P.R.O., G. and D., 29 : 14.
[9] P. 295. Same to same, June 10.
[10] P. 295. Same to same, May 27.
[11] P. 296. Palmerston to Beauvale, June 20, 1839 (copy), P.R.O., G and D, 29 : 14.
[12] P. 297. Palmerston to Granville, June 21, 1839, G. and D., 29 : 14.
[13] P. 297. *Hansard*, 3rd Ser., XLIX, 81.
[14] P. 297. B. and A., II, 295.
[15] P. 297. Palmerston to Granville, June 10, July 29, 1839; Palmerston to Beauvale, June 20, 1839 (copy), P.R.O., G. and D., 29 : 14; Guizot, IV, 335-9, 479-99; C.H.B.F.P., II, 171; Barante, VI, 287-9.
[16] P. 297. Palmerston to Granville, July 23, 1839, P.R.O., G. and D., 29 : 14.
[17] P. 297. Lavisse, V, 167.
[18] P. 298. Barante, VI, 330-6, 342-4; Q.V.L., 1st Ser., I, 241.
[19] P. 298. Metternich, VI, 370-1; Nesselrode, VIII, 36.
[20] P. 298. Barante, VI, 184-5.
[21] P. 298. *Ibid.*, 229.
[22] P. 298. Palmerston to Beauvale, June 20, 1839 (copy), P.R.O., G. and D., 29 : 14.
[23] P. 298. Reid, *Milnes*, I, 246.
[24] P. 299. B. and A., II, 291-318, III, 425-33; Guizot, IV, *passim*; Barante, VI, 313 ff., 342-4; Palmerston to Granville, Nov. 5, Dec. 6, 1839, P.R.O., G. and D., 19 : 14; Lavisse, V, 166-70; Lord J. Russell, *Early Corr.*, II, 265; C.H.B.F.P., II, 171-7; Nesselrode, VIII, 2-3, 8-9.
[25] P. 299. Palmerston to Victoria, Sept. 18, 1839, *Windsor MSS.*, A. 10; B. and A., II, 300-1.
[26] P. 300. Nesselrode, VII, 288-90.
[27] P. 300. Barante, VI, 386-9.
[28] P. 300. *Hansard*, 3rd Ser., LIII, 194.
[29] P. 300. H. Greville, *Diary*, I, 140-1.
[30] P. 300. For the French side, Barante, VI, 479-85; Lavisse, V, 169.
[31] P. 300. B. and A., III, 30-40; Lord William Russell to Lord J. Russell (with enclosure), May 1840, P.R.O., G. and D., 22 : 3; Barante, VI, 445-6, 446 n.
[32] P. 300. Broughton, V, 267.
[33] P. 300. *Ibid.*, 276-7; B. and A., III, 43, 425-33; Walpole, *Russell*, I, 346, 346 n.; Maxwell, *Clarendon*, I, 193-6; Torrens, 329-30; Lord J. Russell, *Later Corr.*, I, 9; C. Greville, *Mem.*, IV, 307-9.

NOTES

[34] P. 301. Barante, VI, 388-9 ; Nesselrode, VIII, 20.
[35] P. 301. Melbourne to Victoria, Jan. 5, 1840, *Windsor MSS.* A. 3.
[36] P. 301. Guizot, V, 134-6.
[37] P. 301. C. Greville, *Mem.*, IV, 251 ; Maxwell, *Clarendon*, I, 184-93.
[38] P. 301. Lord J. Russell, *Later Corr.*, I, 6 ; B. and A., II, 356-63.
[39] P. 301. Minute of cabinet, July 8, 1840, *Windsor MSS.* G. 1.
[40] P. 301. Hertslet, *Map*, II, 1008-15 ; B. and A., III, 40-5.
[41] P. 302. Apponyi, III, 411 ; Q.V.L., 1st Ser., I, 286-7 ; Raikes, *Corr.*, 140 ; Raikes, *Journ.*, IV, 41-2, 45 ; d'Haussonville, I, 167-8.
[42] P. 302. *Ibid.*, 172-5.
[43] P. 302. Guizot, V, 201-3.
[44] P. 302. B. and A., III, 431-3 ; Metternich, VI, 436.
[45] P. 302. *Ibid.*, 472-81 ; Guizot, V, 221-3 ; d'Haussonville, I, 167-8, 293.
[46] P. 302. Raikes, *Journ.*, IV, 31 ; Lavisse, V, 170-3 ; Apponyi, III, 461.
[47] P. 302. *Ibid.*, 411.
[48] P. 302. B. and A., II, 318-19.
[49] P. 302. Maxwell, *Clarendon*, I, 198.
[50] P. 302. *Ibid.*, 199 ; Hertslet, *Foreign Office*, 62-3.
[51] P. 302. Palmerston to Bloomfield, Aug. 4, 1840, P.R.O., F.O., 356 : 29.
[52] P. 302. *Melbourne Papers*, 463-4.
[53] P. 303. *Hansard*, 3rd Ser., LIV, 787 ; B. and A., II, 308-9, 316-21 ; Raikes, *Journ.*, IV, 31 ; Palmerston to Bloomfield, July 29, 1840 (Private), P.R.O., F.O., 356 : 29 ; Raikes, *Corr.*, 142 ; Barante, VI, 485-7.
[54] P. 303. *Ibid.*, 461-4 ; C. Greville, *Mem.*, IV, 302 ; *Melbourne Papers*, 469-72.
[55] P. 303. Lord J. Russell, *Later Corr.*, I, 5.
[56] P. 303. Croker, II, 164.
[57] P. 303. *Melbourne Papers*, 462.
[58] P. 304. B. and A., II, 327-8.
[59] P. 304. C. Greville, *Mem.*, IV, 302. *Cf.* B. and A., II, 308.
[60] P. 304. Russell to Melbourne, Sept. 15, 17, Oct. 2, 1840, P.R.O., G. and D., 22 : 3 ; Palmerston to Russell, Sept. 26, 1840, P.R.O., G. and D., 22 : 3 ; Melbourne to Victoria, Sept. 28, 1840, *Windsor MSS.* G. 1 ; Wilson, *Greville Diary*, II, 79 ; B. and A., II, 316, 323, 334, 355-63 ; III, 43 ; C. Greville, *Mem.*, IV, 297-304, 307-54 ; Walpole, *Russell*, I, 347-54 ; Guizot, V, 140, 191-3, 213-14 ; Lord J. Russell, *Later Corr.*, I, 13-22 ; Greville-Reeve, *Letters*, 3-7, 11-12 ; Ernest II, Duke of Saxe-Coburg-Gotha, *Memoirs* (London, 1888-90), I, 114-15 ; Maxwell, *Clarendon*, I, 184-93, 208-11 ; *Melbourne Papers*, 467-83 ; Broughton, V, 293, 297-8 ; Reeve, *Memoirs*, I, 120-31 ; Hodder, I, 318 ; Torrens, 329-30 ; Lieven-Grey, *Corr.*, III, 317 ; Q.V.L., 1st Ser., I, 286-95 ; Martin, *Prince Consort*, I, 88 n. ; Corti, *Leopold*, 122-4, 131-6.
[61] P. 307. d'Haussonville, I, 174.
[62] P. 307. B. and A., II, 324-31.
[63] P. 307. *Melbourne Papers*, 481.
[64] P. 307. B. and A., II, 323 n.
[65] P. 308. *Ibid.*, 343-4.
[66] P. 308. Note 60, *supra*.
[67] P. 308. Hodder, I, 317.
[68] P. 309. Maxwell, *Clarendon*, I, 211-12.
[69] P. 309. Hoskins, 289.
[70] P. 309. Maxwell, *Clarendon*, I, 211.
[71] P. 309. B. and A., II, 348.
[72] P. 309. Reeve, *Mem.*, I, 127 ; Lord J. Russell, *Later Corr.*, I, 17, 24, 27 ;

Walpole, *Russell*, I, 354; C. Greville, *Mem.*, IV, 326; Maxwell, *Clarendon*, I, 213; Greville-Reeve, *Letters*, 31.
[73] P. 309.   Melbourne to Victoria, Sept. 28, 1840, *Windsor MSS*. G. 1.
[74] P. 310.   C. Greville, *Mem.*, IV, 320–2.
[75] P. 311.   B. and A., II, 349–50; Palmerston to Granville, June 10, 1839, P.R.O., G. and D., 29 : 14.
[76] P. 311.   B. and A., II, 320.
[77] P. 311.   *Ibid.*, 330–3. See also Raikes, *Journ.*, IV, 33–4.
[78] P. 311.   B. and A., II, 318, 326–7; Lorne, 75–7.
[79] P. 311.   B. and A., II, 338.
[80] P. 312.   Williams, *Napier*, 209; Broughton, V, 298; C. Greville, *Mem.*, IV, 356.
[81] P. 312.   Maxwell, *Clarendon*, I, 212–13; Walpole, *Russell*, I, 354–8; *Melbourne Papers*, 460, 485; Greville-Reeve, *Letters*, 18–19, 28; C. Greville, *Mem.*, IV, 334–46; Q.V.L., 1st Ser., I, 299–310; Lord J. Russell, *Later Corr.*, I, 24–7; Burghersh, 281–90; Lord Leveson to Granville, Nov. 10, 1840, P.R.O., G. and D., 29 : 6.
[82] P. 312.   Greville-Reeve, *Letters*, 13–14.
[83] P. 313.   *Ibid.*
[84] P. 313.   Reeve, *Mem.*, I, 130; Raikes, *Journ.*, IV, 69.
[85] P. 313.   *Ibid.*, 109–10; Leveson to Granville, Nov. 10, 1840, P.R.O., G. and D., 29 : 6; Martin, *Prince Consort*, I, 195; *Melbourne Papers*, 486–7.
[86] P. 313.   *Ibid.*, 487–9. *Cf.* B. and A., II, 352.
[87] P. 313.   Williams, *Napier*, 209; Lieven-Grey, *Corr.*, III, 328; Leveson to Granville, Dec. 1, 1840, P.R.O., G. and D., 29 : 6; Airlie, II, 58; Grey to Brougham, Feb. 1, March 26, 1841, *Howick MSS.*
[88] P. 314.   Martin, *Prince Consort*, I, 76. *Cf.* B. and A., II, 305, 351.
[89] P. 314.   Leveson to Granville, Dec. 1, 1840, P.R.O., G. and D., 29 : 6; Greville-Reeve, *Letters*, 50, 50 n., 51.
[90] P. 314.   *Ann. Reg.* for 1840, 181.
[91] P. 314.   Raikes, *Journ.*, IV, 89; Hodder, I, 318; Lieven-Grey, *Corr.*, III, 324–6, 326 n., 328; Maxwell, *Clarendon*, I, 214; Corti, *Leopold*, 133–5; Walpole, *Russell*, I, 357–8; Lord J. Russell, *Later Corr.*, I, 24–30; *Melbourne Papers*, 485–92; Guizot, VI, 41–6; Reeve, I, 136–7, 137 n.; Q.V.L., 1st Ser., I, 298–317; Malmesbury (third earl), *Mem.*, I, 128; Greville-Reeve, *Letters*, 28–31; Burghersh, 281–3, 287–8; Grey to Brougham, March 26, 1841, *Howick MSS.*; C.H.B.F.P., II, 179; Walpole, *Russell*, I, 357–62; B. and A., II, 346–9, 363–6; Clarendon to Russell, Nov. 27, 1840, P.R.O., G.and D., 22 : 3; C. Greville, *Mem.*, IV, 335–47, 347 n., 347–50, 357.
[92] P. 315.   *Ibid.*, 353.
[93] P. 315.   Maxwell, *Clarendon*, I, 217.
[94] P. 315.   Metternich, VI, 490.
[95] P. 315.   Croker, II, 168; Walpole, *Russell*, I, 362; Reeve, I, 139–40; Greville-Reeve, *Letters*, 19–20, 25, 47; Lieven-Grey, *Corr.*, III, 328–30; C. Greville, *Mem.*, IV, 356–8, 371; Lady Granville, *Letters*, II, 342.
[96] P. 316.   Barante, VI, 536.
[97] P. 316.   C. Greville, *Mem.*, IV, 358.
[98] P. 316.   Guizot, VI, 412–13; *The Times*, July 3, 1841.
[99] P. 317.   Guizot, VI, 131–2.
[100] P. 318.   B. and A., II, 375–83.
[101] P. 318.   Lord J. Russell, *Later Corr.*, I, 7–8, 15; Raikes, *Journ.*, IV, 40; *Melbourne Papers*, 461; Croker, II, 159; C. Greville, *Mem.*, IV, 300, 300 n.; Hodder, I, 317.

NOTES

[102] P. 318. Disraeli, *Tancred* (London, 1881), 211–2.
[103] P. 318. Hodder, I, 315–16.
[104] P. 319. Leveson to Granville, Dec. 1, 8, 18, 1840, P.R.O., G. and D., 29 : 6 ; Monypenny and Buckle, II, 96 ; Broughton, V, 297–8 ; Maxwell, *Clarendon*, I, 200 ; C. Greville, *Mem.*, IV, 377–8, 386 ; Walpole, *Russell*, I, 359, 363. See also note 53, *supra*.
[105] P. 319. C. Greville, *Mem.*, IV, 304–5, 312 ; Corti, *Leopold*, 133–5 ; Q.V.L., 1st Ser., I, 294–317.
[106] P. 320. *Ibid.*, 315–17.
[107] P. 320. Victoria to Melbourne, Apr. 22, 1841, *Windsor MSS.* C. 4.

CHAPTER XV

[1] P. 322. Lord Leveson to Granville, March 5 [1841], P.R.O., G. and D., 29 : 6.
[2] P. 323. *Hansard*, 3rd Ser., LVIII, 639.
[3] P. 323. *Ibid.*, 641–63 ; Broughton, VI, 25 ; Martin, *Prince Consort*, I, 97–8.
[4] P. 324. Q.V.L., 1st Ser., I, 341, 347, 354 ; C. Greville, *Mem.*, V, 1–2, 5 ; *Melbourne Papers*, 419–20 ; Broughton, VI, 22–7.
[5] P. 325. *Ibid.*, 36.
[6] P. 325. Lady Palmerston to Mrs. Huskisson, Sept. 26 (?), Oct. 18, 1841, Br. Mus., *Add. MSS.* 39949, ff. 200–2, 219–22 ; Day, 210–17 ; Airlie, II, 69–70, 86–90 ; B. and A., III, 86–178 ; C. Greville, *Mem.*, V, 104–6, 217 ; Brougham to Grey, apparently 1843 or 1844, *Howick MSS.* ; Broughton, VI, 90, 148 ; T. A. Cook, *History of the English Turf* (London, 1901–4), III, 498–9.
[7] P. 326. B. and A., III, 127–9 ; Hodder, II, 18–21.
[8] P. 326. B. and A., III, 129.
[9] P. 327. Lord J. Russell, *Later Corr.*, I, 54.
[10] P. 327. C. Greville, *Mem.*, V, 236–7 ; *Hansard*, 3rd Ser., LXXIII, 1645–7.
[11] P. 327. B. and A., III, 87, 125, 139, 145–60, 177 ; Palmerston to Russell, Aug. 24, 1844, P.R.O., G. and D., 22 : 4 ; Barante, VII, 114 ; Raikes, *Journ.*, IV, 416 ; Cowley (first baron), *Diary and Corr.*, 280–1 ; Metternich, VII, 15–16.
[12] P. 328. B. and A., III, 101.
[13] P. 328. *Hansard*, 3rd Ser., LXV, 1276.
[14] P. 328. Q.V.L., 1st Ser., I, 255.
[15] P. 329. C. Greville, *Mem.*, IV, 364.
[16] P. 329. *Ibid.*, V, 74–5 ; Greville-Reeve, *Letters*, 43.
[17] P. 329. Aberdeen, *Corr.*, 1832–44, p. 201 ; Temperley, *Lieven*, 203.
[18] P. 330. Palmerston to Lansdowne, Nov. 4, 1842, *Bowood MSS.* See also C. Greville, *Mem.*, V, 104 ; *Hansard*, 3rd Ser., LXX, 1462 ; B. and A., III, 64, 135.
[19] P. 330. Lord J. Russell, *Later Corr.*, I, 58.
[20] P. 330. *Ibid.*, 61–2 ; C. Greville, *Mem.*, V, 130–1 ; Broughton, VI, 81.
[21] P. 331. Palmerston to Russell, Nov. 14, 1842, P.R.O., G. and D., 22 : 4. (Quoted, with some alterations, in B. and A., III, 113–18.) See also Broughton, VI, 81.
[22] P. 332. Palmerston to Russell, Oct. 25, 1842, P.R.O., G. and D., 22 : 4.
[23] P. 332. Mathieson, *Slave Trade*, 62–3.
[24] P. 332. Aberdeen, *Corr.*, 1832–44, p. 201 ; Q.V.L., 1st Ser., I, 473 ; *Edinburgh Rev.*, CCXXXVIII (July–Oct. 1923), 292 ; Soulsby, 115–17 ;

Greville-Reeve, *Letters*, 66–7, 70–1 ; B. and A., III, 96–8 ; *Hansard*, 3rd Ser., LX, 145–6 ; LXV, 1255 ; Raikes, *Journ.*, IV, 352–3 ; Minto to Russell, Oct. 21, 1844, P.R.O., G. and D., 22 : 4 ; d'Haussonville, II, ch. XVI.

[25] P. 332.   Soulsby, 106–10.
[26] P. 333.   *Ibid.*, ch. III.
[27] P. 333.   *Ibid.*, 81.
[28] P. 333.   *Ibid.*, 82.
[29] P. 333.   Palmerston to Russell, Sept. 24, 1842, P.R.O., G. and D., 22 : 4.
[30] P. 333.   Soulsby, 100–3.
[31] P. 333.   Palmerston to Russell, Sept. 24, 1842 ; Soulsby, 115–17.
[32] P. 333.   Lord J. Russell, *Later Corr.*, I, 59.
[33] P. 334.   C. Greville, *Mem.*, V, 125 ; Raikes, *Journ.*, IV, 237.
[34] P. 334.   Palmerston to Russell, Sept. 24, 1842, P.R.O., G. and D., 22 : 4.
[35] P. 334.   B. and A., III, 110.
[36] P. 334.   *Hansard*, 3rd Ser., LXVI, 127 ; LXVII, 1197. See also C. Greville, *Mem.*, V, 104.
[37] P. 334.   Palmerston to Russell, Sept. 8, 1841, P.R.O., G and D, 22 : 4 ; Q.V.L., 1st Ser., I, 470–1.
[38] P. 335.   Articles in the *Morning Chronicle* for Sept. 19, 20, 21, 22, 24, 26, 27, 30, and Oct. 3, 1842, reprinted anonymously as 'well understood' to be Palmerston's under the title *Lord Palmerston and the Treaty of Washington* (London ?). See also Greville-Reeve, *Letters*, 62–3 ; Howick to Grey, Sept. 20, 1842, *Howick MSS.* ; C. Greville, *Mem.*, V, 105, 109 ; Lord J. Russell, *Later Corr.*, I, 61–2.
[39] P. 335.   B. and A., III, 112.
[40] P. 335.   *Hansard*, 3rd Ser., LXVII, 1165.
[41] P. 335.   *Ibid.*, 1218.
[42] P. 335.   Parker, *Peel*, III, 387 ; Lord J. Russell, *Later Corr.*, I, 61–2 ; C. Greville, *Mem.*, V, 126, 152 ; Monypenny and Buckle, II, 160–1.
[43] P. 335.   *Hansard*, 3rd Ser., LXVII, 1283.
[44] P. 336.   Lord J. Russell, *Later Corr.*, I, 58 ; Greville-Reeve, *Letters*, 69 ; *Melbourne Papers*, 515 ; C. Greville, *Mem.*, V, 109.
[45] P. 336.   Howick to Charles Grey, March 23, 1843, *Howick MSS.*
[46] P. 336.   Raikes, *Journ.*, IV, 257–8.
[47] P. 336.   Broughton, VI, 78.
[48] P. 336.   Bulwer's memorandum, containing despatches of Aston, Bulwer, and Cowley to Aberdeen, Oct. 1841 to June 1843, P.R.O., F.O., 27 : 769 ; C. Greville, *Mem.*, V, 50, 73–5 ; Raikes, *Journ.*, IV, 242–4, 265–82, 299 ; Lord J. Russell, *Later Corr.*, I, 54–5 ; Lady Palmerston to Mrs. Huskisson, Nov. 2, 1841. Br. Mus., *Add. MSS.* 39949.
[49] P. 337.   Q.V.L., 1st Ser., I, 558.
[50] P. 337.   C. Greville, *Mem.*, V, 74–5.
[51] P. 337.   B. and A., III, 118.
[52] P. 338.   Barante, VII, 49–51 ; Raikes, *Journ.*, IV, 286, 288–9, 331 ; Martin, *Prince Consort*, I, 149–58 ; Q.V.L., 1st Ser., I, 613–14.
[53] P. 338.   Raikes, *Journ.*, IV, 288.
[54] P. 338.   Palmerston to Hobhouse, Aug. 21, 1843, Br. Mus. *Add. MSS.* 36471, f. 232.
[55] P. 338.   Barante, VII, 51.
[56] P. 339.   B. and A., III, 78.
[57] P. 339.   *Ibid.*, 55–60.
[58] P. 340.   Walpole, *Russell*, I, 367.
[59] P. 340.   *Hansard*, 3rd Ser., LVIII, 655.

NOTES

[60] P. 340. B. and A., III, 52.
[61] P. 340. *Hansard*, 3rd Ser., LX, 613–18 ; LXIV, 1072–6 ; LXV, 1237–8.
[62] P. 341. Cowley (first baron), *Diary and Corr.*, 280.
[63] P. 341. Lord J. Russell, *Later Corr.*, I, 74.
[64] P. 341. C. Greville, *Mem.*, V, 310, 318, 348.
[65] P. 342. *Hansard*, 3rd Ser., LXXXV, 259.
[66] P. 342. Palmerston's memorandum, Sept. 8, 1846, *Windsor MSS.*, I. 1.
[67] P. 342. Lord J. Russell, *Later Corr.*, I, 51.
[68] P. 343. *Hansard*, 3rd Ser., LXXXV, 264.
[69] P. 345. *Ibid.*, LXX, 1067.
[70] P. 345. Lord J. Russell, *Later Corr.*, I, 65–7, 79 ; Palmerston to Lansdowne, Nov. 13, 1843, *Bowood MSS.* ; Palmerston to Russell, Dec. 22, 1843, P.R.O., G. and D., 22 : 4.
[71] P. 345. *Hansard*, 3rd Ser., LXX, 279–91, 1064–74, 1460–1.
[72] P. 346. *Ibid.*, LXXIX, 1304.
[73] P. 346. *Ibid.*, LXX, 279–91, 1064–74 ; LXXIX, 1302.
[74] P. 346. Palmerston to Russell, June 22, 1843, P.R.O., G. and D., 22 : 4. See also Lord J. Russell, *Later Corr.*, I, 66–7.
[75] P. 347. C. Greville, *Mem.*, V, 230.
[76] P. 347. Lord J. Russell, *Later Corr.*, I, 67.
[77] P. 347. *Hansard*, 3rd Ser., LXX, 282.
[78] P. 347. Palmerston to Lansdowne, Nov. 13, 1843, *Bowood MSS.*
[79] P. 347. *Hansard*, 3rd Ser., LXX, 281–2.
[80] P. 348. B. and A., III, 166–70.

CHAPTER XVI

[1] P. 349. *E.g.* Macaulay ; F. Merk, 'British Party Politics and the Oregon Treaty,' in *Am. His. Rev.*, XXXVII, no. 4 (July 1932), 653–77.
[2] P. 349. Q.V.L., 1st Ser., II, 19.
[3] P. 349. Raikes, *Journ.*, IV, 372, 418–20 ; Malmesbury (3rd earl), *Mem.*, I, 155 ; Q.V.L., 1st Ser., II, 25–33.
[4] P. 350. *Ibid.*, I, 614.
[5] P. 351. *Ibid.*, I, 607–8, II, 37.
[6] P. 351. *Ibid.*, 52–3 ; Martin, *Prince Consort*, I, 252–3.
[7] P. 351. Lord J. Russell, *Later Corr.*, I, 51, 56.
[8] P. 351. *Hansard*, 3rd Ser., LXXVI, 947.
[9] P. 351. Ellice to Russell, Aug. 14, 1844, P.R.O., G. and D., 22 : 4.
[10] P. 352. C. Greville, *Mem.*, V, 254.
[11] P. 352. Raikes, *Journ.*, IV, 391–2 ; Q.V.L., 1st Ser., II, 12–13.
[12] P. 352. *Ibid.*, 24.
[13] P. 352. Swain, 129–33.
[14] P. 353. *Hansard*, 3rd Ser., LXXVI, 1870–6 ; LXXVII, 112–22.
[15] P. 353. *Ibid.*, LXXVI, 1240–6.
[16] P. 353. *Ibid.*, LXXVI, 922–73 ; LXXVIII, 1292–1300 ; LXXX, 206–14, 470–9 ; LXXXII, 142–78.
[17] P. 354. Palmerston's memorandum, Sept. 4, 1844, P.R.O., G. and D., 22 ; 4.
[18] P. 354. *Hansard*, 3rd Ser., LXXVI, 1870–6.
[19] P. 354. C. Greville, *Mem.*, V, 270.
[20] P. 355. Lord J. Russell, *Later Corr.*, I, 104–5 ; Trevelyan, *Macaulay*, II, 147–8.

NOTES

[21] P. 355. Grey to Charles Grey, Dec. (?) 1845; Diary of the third Earl Grey, Dec. 19, 1845, *Howick MSS.*; C. Greville, *Mem.*, V, 322; Greville-Reeve, *Letters*, 114–15; Grey to Russell, Dec. 19, 1845, P.R.O., G. and D., 22: 4; Merk, *loc. cit.*, 667–8; Lord J. Russell, *Later Corr.*, I, 97–8.

[22] P. 356. *Ibid.*, 96, 105–6; Grey to Charles Grey, Dec. (?) 1845; Diary of the third Earl Grey, Dec. 13–22, 1845, *Howick MSS.*; C. Greville, *Mem.*, V, 341–4; Fagan, *Panizzi*, I, 251–4.

[23] P. 356. Grey to Russell, Dec. 19, 1845, P.R.O., G. and D., 22: 4 (printed in part in Walpole, *Russell*, I, 414–16).

[24] P. 356. Diary of the third Earl Grey, Dec. 16, 1845, *Howick MSS.*; Walpole, *Russell*, I, 411–13.

[25] P. 357. Grey to Charles Grey, Dec. (?), 1845; Diary of the third Earl Grey, Dec. 18–22, 1845, *Howick MSS.*; C. Greville, *Mem.*, V, 341–3; Lord J. Russell, *Later Corr.*, I, 105–6.

[26] P. 357. *Ibid.*, 95, 98, 106–7; Diary of the third Earl Grey, Dec. 19, 1845, *Howick MSS.*; Greville-Reeve, *Letters*, 123–5; Q.V.L., 1st Ser., II, 70–1; Trevelyan, *Macaulay*, II, 149–51; Broughton, VI, 158; Walpole, *Russell*, I, 410–19; Parker, *Peel*, III, 284; C. Greville, *Mem.*, V., 330–1, 339.

[27] P. 357. Trevelyan, *Macaulay*, II, 150–1.

[28] P. 358. Greville-Reeve, *Letters*, 134.

[29] P. 358. C. Greville, *Mem.*, V, 344–5.

[30] P. 358. Arnould, II, 198–9; Lord J. Russell, *Later Corr.*, I, 100–2; Walpole, *Russell*, I, 417.

[31] P. 358. *Ibid.*; Diary of the third Earl Grey, Dec. 20, 1845, *Howick MSS.*; Lord J. Russell, *Later Corr.*, I, 97–102.

[32] P. 358. Diary of the third Earl Grey, Dec. 19, 1845, also Dec. 1845 to April 1846, *passim, Howick MSS.*; Minto to Russell, Jan. 1, 1846, P.R.O., G. and D., 22: 5. *Cf.* Palmerston to Russell, Jan. 5, 1846, P.R.O., G. and D., 22: 5; Lady Palmerston to Mrs. Huskisson, March 19, 1846, Br. Mus. *Add. MSS.* 39949; Fagan, *Panizzi*, I, 205–6, 251–4; Greville-Reeve, *Letters*, 124.

[33] P. 358. Walpole, *Russell*, I, 416–17; Lord J. Russell, *Later Corr.*, I, 96–7.

[34] P. 358. Fagan, *Panizzi*, I, 205–6.

[35] P. 358. Greville-Reeve, *Letters*, 126; Walpole, *Russell*, I, 416; C. Greville, *Mem.*, V, 332.

[36] P. 359. Lansdowne to Russell, Dec. 30, 1845, P.R.O., G. and D., 22: 4; Palmerston to Russell, Jan. 5, 1846, P.R.O., G. and D., 22: 5.

[37] P. 359. *Ibid.*

[38] P. 359. C. Greville, *Mem.*, V, 345, 345 n.; Greville-Reeve, *Letters*, 114–38, 136 n.

[39] P. 360. *Ibid.*, 131.

[40] P. 361. Monypenny and Buckle, II, 338–43.

[41] P. 361. Lord J. Russell, *Later Corr.*, I, 90–1.

[42] P. 361. Greville-Reeve, *Letters*, 121.

[43] P. 361. *Ibid.*, 123; Lord J. Russell, *Later Corr.*, I, 90.

[44] P. 362. Monypenny and Buckle, II, 343.

[45] P. 362. Greville-Reeve, *Letters*, 138 n.

[46] P. 362. *Ibid.*, 100–2, 101 n., 122; Lord J. Russell, *Later Corr.*, I, 91–2; C. Greville, *Mem.*, V, 267, 267 n., 270, 298–9; Q.V.L., 1st Ser., II, 82; Fagan, *Panizzi*, I, 246, 253–4; Aberdeen, *Corr.*, 1845–7, p. 152; Barante, VII, 166; Palmerston to Russell, Oct. 21, 1845, P.R.O., G. and D., 22: 4.

[47] P. 362. Tocqueville-Reeve, *Corr.*, in *Edinburgh Rev.*, CCXXXVIII (July-Oct., 1923), 293–4.

[48] P. 363. Notes 50 and 69, *infra*.

NOTES 491

[49] P. 363. C. Greville, *Mem.*, V, 344 ; Trevelyan, *Macaulay*, II, 146.
[50] P. 364. Airlie, II, 100–9.
[51] P. 365. *Ibid.*, 105–6.
[52] P. 365. Palmerston to Russell, Oct. 12, 21, 1845, P.R.O., G. and D., 22 : 4 ; Greville-Reeve, *Letters*, 122 ; Monypenny and Buckle, II, 340.
[53] P. 365. Lady Palmerston to Mrs. Huskisson, March 19, 1846, Br. Mus., *Add. MSS.* 39949.
[54] P. 366. C. Greville, *Mem.*, V, 388–9 ; Aberdeen, *Corr.*, 1845–7, pp. 152, 184–5.
[55] P. 366. *Ibid.*, 159.
[56] P. 366. *Ibid.*, 184–5.
[57] P. 366. B. and A., III, 191–3.
[58] P. 366. C. Greville, *Mem.*, V, 384.
[59] P. 367. Aberdeen, *Corr.*, 1845–7, pp. 151–2.
[60] P. 367. *Ibid.*, 155.
[61] P. 367. *Ibid.*, 151–86.
[62] P. 367. *Ibid.*, 153.
[63] P. 367. *Ibid.*, 160.
[64] P. 368. *Ibid.*, 185–6.
[65] P. 368. *Ibid.*, 179.
[66] P. 368. *Ibid.*
[67] P. 368. Monypenny and Buckle, II, 373 n.
[68] P. 369. *Ibid.*, 393.
[69] P. 369. *Ibid.*, 372–3, 376–7, 392–3 ; Lady Palmerston to Mrs. Huskisson, March 19, 1846, Br. Mus., *Add. MSS.* 39949 ; C. Greville, *Mem.*, V, 391–4.
[70] P. 369. Q.V.L., 1st Ser., II, 97.
[71] P. 369. Diary of the third Earl Grey, Apr. 3, 1845, *Howick MSS.*
[72] P. 369. Merk, *loc. cit.*, 656–9 ; Palmerston to Russell, Feb. 3, 1846, P.R.O., G. and D., 22 : 5.
[73] P. 369. Merk, *loc. cit.*, 658.
[74] P. 370. *Hansard*, 3rd Ser., LXXXVII, 1057.
[75] P. 370. Q.V.L., 1st Ser., II, 98.
[76] P. 370. Quoted in Christie, 144.
[77] P. 370. Q.V.L., 1st Ser., II, 102.
[78] P. 370. Lady Palmerston to Mrs. Huskisson, March 19, 1846, Br. Mus., *Add. MSS.* 39949.
[79] P. 370. Maxwell, *Clarendon*, I, 268–9 ; Diary of the third Earl Grey, June 25 to July 2, 1846, *Howick MSS.*
[80] P. 370. C. Greville, *Mem.*, V, 403.
[81] P. 371. *Ibid.*, 409–10.
[82] P. 371. *Ibid.*
[83] P. 371. Lord J. Russell, *Later Corr.*, I, 90 ; Greville-Reeve, *Letters*, 121.
[84] P. 371. Nesselrode, VIII, 327–8.

CHAPTER XVII

[1] P. 374. Stockmar, II, 159–60 ; Bulwer to Palmerston, Sept. 12, 1846 (copy), *Windsor MSS.* J. 45 ; Q.V.L., 1st Ser., II, 122 ; B. and A., III, 294 ; Prince Consort, *Letters*, 90–1 ; Hall, 387–8.
[2] P. 374. H. Greville, *Diary*, I, 172.
[3] P. 374. Stockmar, II, 159–60.

[4] P. 374. Guizot, VIII, 225–7, 250–5 ; Louis Philippe to the Queen of the Belgians, Sept. 14, 1846 (copy), *Windsor MSS.* J. 45.
[5] P. 375. Palmerston to Normanby, Sept. 22, 1846 ; Victoria to the Queen of the Belgians, Sept. 27, 1846 ; Aberdeen to Prince Albert, Oct. 9, 1846, *Windsor MSS.* J. 45 ; Guizot, VIII, 233–4 ; Bulwer to Palmerston, Sept. 12, 1846 (copy), *Windsor MSS.* J. 45. See also Q.V.L., 1st Ser., II, 123–4.
[6] P. 375. Prince Consort, *Letters*, 87–8.
[7] P. 375. Guizot to Jarnac, Oct. 5, 1846 (copy), *Windsor MSS.* J. 45 ; Guizot, VIII, 237–41 ; B. and A., III, 296–7 ; Normandy to Palmerston, Oct. 1, 1846, *Windsor MSS.* J. 45.
[8] P. 375. *Ibid.*; C. Greville, *Mem.*, VI, 53–4 ; Guizot, VIII, 250–5.
[9] P. 375. B. and A., III, 263.
[10] P. 375. Prince Consort, *Letters*, 87–8 ; Louis Philippe to the Queen of the Belgians, Sept. 14, 1846, *Windsor MSS.* J. 45 ; Guizot, VIII, 260–73.
[11] P. 376. Cowley, *Diary and Corr.*, 251 ; Victoria to the Queen of the Belgians, Sept. 27, 1846 ; Prince Albert's memorandum, undated, *Windsor MSS.* J. 45 ; Raikes, *Journ.*, IV, 440 ; B. and A., III, 308 ; Palmerston to Lansdowne, Jan. 14, 1847, *Bowood MSS.*
[12] P. 376. B. and A., III, 268–9 ; Q.V.L., 1st Ser., II, 115–16 ; Prince Consort, *Letters*, 90.
[13] P. 376. Guizot, VIII, 283–4.
[14] P. 376. Guizot to Louis Philippe, July 24, 1846, *Rev. Rétrospective* ; B. and A., III, 260–2.
[15] P. 376. Palmerston to Russell, Aug. 11, 1846, P.R.O., G. and D., 22 : 5 ; B. and A., III, 268–9.
[16] P. 376. B. and A., III, 263–6, 275.
[17] P. 376. Palmerston to Russell, Aug. 11, 1846, P.R.O., G. and D., 22 : 5.
[18] P. 376. B. and A., III, 265–6.
[19] P. 376. Q.V.L., 1st Ser., II, 106–7 ; B. and A., III, 258–81, 298–9.
[20] P. 377. B. and A., III, 291 ; Hall, 389–90.
[21] P. 377. *Supra*, note 19 ; Stockmar, II, 161–3 ; Palmerston to Russell, Aug. 22, 1846, P.R.O., G. and D., 22 : 5 ; Palmerston to Normanby, Sept. 22, 1846 ; Palmerston to Victoria, Sept. 25, 1846 ; Victoria to the Queen of the Belgians, Sept. 27, 1846 ; Palmerston to Normanby, Oct. (?), 1846, *Windsor MSS.* J. 45 ; *Cf.* Barante, VII, 196.
[22] P. 377. Walpole, *Russell*, II, 3 ; Saint-René Taillandier, *Le roi Léopold et la reine Victoria* (2 vols., Paris, 1878), II, 107.
[23] P. 377. *E.g.* B. and A., III, 229–32 ; Q.V.L., 1st Ser., II, 113–14.
[24] P. 377. *Ibid.*, 107.
[25] P. 377. Prince Consort, *Letters*, 89.
[26] P. 378. Stockmar, II, 161–8 ; B. and A., III, 275–6, 275 n.
[27] P. 378. *Ibid.*, 258–63.
[28] P. 378. Palmerston to Normanby, Sept. 22, 1846, *Windsor MSS.* J. 45.
[29] P. 378. B. and A., III, 263.
[30] P. 378. *Ibid.*, 275–6.
[31] P. 378. *Ibid.*, 262–3. *Cf.* Hall, 386.
[32] P. 378. Normanby to Palmerston, Oct. 1, 1846 ; Guizot to Jarnac, Oct. 5, 1846 (copy) ; Sir A. Malet to Palmerston, Oct. 5, 1846, *Windsor MSS.* J. 45 ; C. Greville, *Mem.*, VI, 30–1.
[33] P. 378. Guizot to Louis Philippe, July 24, 31, Aug. 8, 1846, *Rev. Rétrospective* ; Hall, 399.
[34] P. 379. Guizot to Louis Philippe, July 15, Aug. 8, 1846, *Rev. Rétrospective* ; C. Greville, *Mem.*, V, 409–10, VI, 22.

NOTES 493

[35] P. 379. Guizot, VIII, 297–9.
[36] P. 379. Ibid., 301–3.
[37] P. 379. E.g. Q.V.L., 1st Ser., II, 115–16.
[38] P. 379. Guizot to Louis Philippe, July 22, 1846, Rev. Rétrospective.
[39] P. 379. Guizot to Louis Philippe, July 19, 1846, Rev. Rétrospective. See also Guizot, VIII, 284–5.
[40] P. 379. Louis Philippe to Guizot, July 25, 1846, Rev. Rétrospective.
[41] P. 379. Guizot to Louis Philippe, July 24, 1846, Rev. Rétrospective; Guizot, VIII, 301.
[42] P. 380. Ibid., 285–7.
[43] P. 380. Ibid., 301.
[44] P. 380. Walpole, *Russell*, II, 6; cf. Guizot to Jarnac, Oct. 5, 1846 (copy); Normanby to Palmerston, Oct. 8, 1846; Russell to Jarnac, Oct. 26, 1846, *Windsor MSS.* J. 45; Guizot, VIII, 291.
[45] P. 380. Ibid., 305–7.
[46] P. 380. Bulwer to Palmerston, Oct. 4, 1846 (copy, extract), *Windsor MSS.* J. 45; Q.V.L., 1st Ser., II, 117–18.
[47] P. 380. E.g. B. and A., III, 283–4; Bulwer to Palmerston, Sept. 22, 23, 1846, *Windsor MSS.* J. 45.
[48] P. 380. Normanby to Palmerston, Oct. 8, 1846, *Windsor MSS.* J. 45.
[49] P. 380. Bresson to Guizot, July 12; Louis Philippe to Guizot, July 20, 24; Guizot to Louis Philippe, July 22, 1846, Rev. Rétrospective.
[50] P. 380. Guizot to Louis Philippe, July 25, 1846 (2 letters), Rev. Rétrospective.
[51] P. 380. For his plausible but very misleading defence, *Mém.*, VIII, ch. xlv.; Saint-René Taillandier, op. cit., II, 67–138. Cf. B. and A., III, 208–313.
[52] P. 381. E.g. Guizot to Jarnac, Oct. 5, 1846 (copy); Palmerston to Normanby, Oct. (?), 1846, *Windsor MSS.* J. 45.
[53] P. 381. B. and A., III, 271–2, 278–9; Q.V.L., 1st Ser., II, 116–17; C. Greville, *Mem.*, VI, 17; Palmerston to Russell, Aug. 28, 1846, P.R.O., G. and D., 22: 5; Palmerston to Normanby, Sept. 22, 1846; Normanby to Palmerston, Oct. 1, 23, 1846, *Windsor MSS.* J. 45; Palmerston to Lansdowne, Sept. 28, 1846, *Bowood MSS.* Cf. Guizot to Jarnac, Oct. 5, 1846 (copy), *Windsor MSS.* J. 45.
[54] P. 381. B. and A., III, 306. See also Normanby to Palmerston, Sept. 25, 1846 (2 letters), *Windsor MSS.* J. 45; Palmerston to Lansdowne, Sept. 28, 1846, *Bowood MSS.*; Lansdowne to Palmerston, 'Wednesday,' *Windsor MSS.* J. 45; C. Greville, *Mem.*, VI, 16–17.
[55] P. 381. Ibid., 17–21. Cf. Greville-Reeve, *Letters*, 151.
[56] P. 381. Stockmar, II, 157–8; Guizot, VIII, 287.
[57] P. 382. Q.V.L., 1st Ser., II, 123.
[58] P. 382. Russell to Victoria, Oct. 5, 1846, *Windsor MSS.* J. 45.
[59] P. 382. Greville-Reeve, *Letters*, 1·51; Dasent, *Delane*, I, 58.
[60] P. 382. Normanby to Russell, Sept. 3, 1846, P.R.O., G. and D., 22: 6.
[61] P. 382. C. Greville, *Mem.*, V, 425; B. and A., III, 305.
[62] P. 382. Aberdeen to Prince Albert, Oct. 9, 1846, *Windsor MSS.* J. 45. See also C. Greville, *Mem.*, VI, 53; Hall, 392.
[63] P. 382. Greville-Reeve, *Letters*, 150–3.
[64] P. 382. C. Greville, *Mem.*, V, 425–6, VI, 6–7, 11, 16–49; Fagan, *Panizzi*, I, 221.
[65] P. 382. Maxwell, *Clarendon*, I, 271; C. Greville, *Mem.*, VI, 5.
[66] P. 383. Walpole, *Russell*, II, 5–7.

NOTES

67 P. 383. Q.V.L., 1st Ser., II, 105, 118–19, 128.
68 P. 383. *Ibid.*, 119–20.
69 P. 383. Louis Philippe to the Queen of the Belgians, Sept. 14, 17, 1846; Victoria to the Queen of the Belgians, Sept. 27, 1846; Aberdeen to Prince Albert, Oct. 9, 1846, *Windsor MSS*. J. 45; B. and A., III, 299; Prince Consort, *Letters*, 90–1.
70 P. 384. King Leopold to Victoria, undated, *Windsor MSS*. J. 45.
71 P. 384. *E.g.* C. Greville, *Mem.*, V, 418; Greville-Reeve, *Letters*, 152.
72 P. 384. Guizot, VIII, 319.
73 P. 384. Q.V.L., 1st Ser., II, 119, 122–5.
74 P. 385. B. and A., III, 288–302; Palmerston to Lansdowne, Sept. 28, 1846, *Bowood MSS.*; Q.V.L., 1st Ser., II, 127; Palmerston to Normanby, Sept. 22, 1846, *Windsor MSS*. J. 45; Victoria to Russell, Sept. 21, 1846; various drafts of despatches to British envoys at Madrid, Berlin, Vienna and St. Petersburg; Henry Howard to Palmerston, Sept. 27, 1846, *Windsor MSS*. J. 45; draft of identical despatches to Berlin, Vienna and St. Petersburg, Sept. 28, 1846, P.R.O., F.O., 96 : 21.
75 P. 385. Russell to Victoria, Sept. 14, 1846, P.R.O., G. and D., 22 : 5.
76 P. 385. Isturiz to Bulwer, Sept. 29, 1846 (trans.), *Windsor MSS*. J. 45.
77 P. 386. Guizot, VIII, 324–8.
78 P. 386. Palmerston to Victoria, Oct. 21, 1846, *Windsor MSS*. J. 45.
79 P. 386. *Supra*, note 74; Palmerston to Bloomfield, Nov. 3, 1846, P.R.O., F.O., 356 : 29; Palmerston to Victoria, Oct. 21, 1846, *Windsor MSS*. J. 45.
80 P. 386. Metternich, VII, 162, 273; Nesselrode, VIII, 346; Henry Howard to Palmerston, Sept. 30, 1846; Sir Robert Gordon to Palmerston, Oct. 5, 1846 (2 letters); Normanby to Palmerston, Oct. 9, 1846, *Windsor MSS*. J. 45. See also note 74, *supra*.
81 P. 386. Normanby to Palmerston, Oct. 5, 1846 (copy), *Windsor MSS*. J. 45.
82 P. 386. B. and A., III, 344.
83 P. 387. Prince Consort, *Letters*, 96.
84 P. 387. H. Greville, *Diary*, I, 174.
85 P. 387. Lucas, *Glenesk*, 171.
86 P. 387. Barante, VII, 193.
87 P. 388. Greville-Reeve, *Letters*, 159; C. Greville, *Mem.*, VI, 14.
88 P. 388. Metternich, VII, 327.
89 P. 388. B. and A., III, 331–2. See also Palmerston to Lansdowne, Jan. 14, 1847, *Bowood MSS.*
90 P. 388. B. and A., III, 322–4.
91 P. 388. *Ibid.*, 342–4.
92 P. 389. *Ibid.*, 320–1.
93 P. 389. Czartoryski, II, 348–9.
94 P. 389. Nesselrode, VIII, 360.
95 P. 389. *Ibid.*, 339, 343.
96 P. 389. *Ibid.*
97 P. 389. Palmerston to Bloomfield, Nov. 23, 1846, P.R.O., F.O., 356 : 29.
98 P. 389. Nesselrode, VIII, 360.
99 P. 390. Palmerston to Russell, Jan. 17, 18, 1847, P.R.O., G. and D., 22 : 6; B. and A., III, 330, 339, 387–8. See also C. Greville, *Mem.*, VI, 14.
100 P. 390. C. Greville, *Mem.*, V, 429; H. Greville, *Diary*, I, 169; Raikes, *Journ.*, IV, 442–3.
101 P. 391. B. and A., III, 198–9, 314–18; Martin, *Prince Consort*, I, 312, 334–5; *Ann. Reg.* for 1846, 295–8; Palmerston to Russell, Feb. 10, 1847, P.R.O., G. and D., 22 : 6.

NOTES

495

¹⁰² P. 391. B. and A., III, 316, 347–8 ; Palmerston to Russell, March 15, 1847, *Windsor MSS.* J. 57.
¹⁰³ P. 391. Q.V.L., 1st Ser., II, 129, 132, 137–8, 140–1.
¹⁰⁴ P. 392. Palmerston to Russell, March 15, 1847, *Windsor MSS.* J. 57.
¹⁰⁵ P. 392. Q.V.L., 1st Ser., II, 140–1.
¹⁰⁶ P. 392. Partially quoted in Prince Albert to Palmerston, Jan. 28, 1847, *Windsor MSS.* J. 56.
¹⁰⁷ P. 393. B. and A., III, 332–6.
¹⁰⁸ P. 394. Prince Albert to Palmerston, Jan. 28, 1847, *Windsor MSS.* J. 56.
¹⁰⁹ P. 394. Russell to Palmerston, Jan. 28, 1847 (copy), and Palmerston to Victoria, Feb. 3, 1847, *Windsor MSS.* J. 56.
¹¹⁰ P. 394. B. and A., III, 337.
¹¹¹ P. 394. Palmerston to Russell, Feb. 10, 1847, P.R.O., G. and D., 22 : 6.
¹¹² P. 394. Russell's memorandum for the cabinet, Feb. 13, 1847 (copy), *Windsor MSS.* J. 56 ; Q.V.L., 1st Ser., II, 139.
¹¹³ P. 395. B. and A., III, 347.
¹¹⁴ P. 395. B. and A., III, 344–6, 357–74, 379–80 ; draft to Wylde, Feb. 8, 1847, P.R.O., F.O., 96 : 21 ; Walpole, *Russell*, II, 9–12 ; Prince Consort, *Letters*, 95–7 ; Russell to Victoria, May 2, 1847 ; Palmerston to Victoria, Apr. 4, May 3, 1847, and Palmerston to Seymour, Apr. 5, May 4, 1847 (nos. 58, 84, copies), *Windsor MSS.* J. 57.
¹¹⁵ P. 395. *Hansard*, 3rd Ser., XCIII, 1204–6.
¹¹⁶ P. 395. B. and A., III, 354.
¹¹⁷ P. 396. Russell's memorandum on Portugal, March 27, 1847, P.R.O., G. and D., 22 : 6.
¹¹⁸ P. 396. Prince Consort, *Letters*, 97.
¹¹⁹ P. 396. B. and A., III, 381–3 ; Russell to Victoria, May 21, 1847 ; (electric) telegram to the Admiralty, June 10, 1847, *Windsor MSS.* J. 58.
¹²⁰ P. 396. Prince Consort, *Letters*, 96.
¹²¹ P. 396. Malmesbury (3rd earl), *Mem.*, I, 194 ; Q.V.L., 1st Ser., II, 144.
¹²² P. 396. B. and A., III, 384. See also *ibid.*, 385–7 ; drafts July 27, 28, Aug. 5, 12, 1847, P.R.O., F.O., 96 : 21.
¹²³ P. 396. Palmerston to Victoria, Aug. 6, 1847, *Windsor MSS.* J. 59 ; Palmerston to Russell, Aug. 9, 1847, P.R.O., G. and D., 22 : 6.
¹²⁴ P. 397. *Hansard*, 3rd Ser., XCIII, 1212–13.
¹²⁵ P. 397. Numerous drafts to Seymour, Aug. 1847, to Aug. 1848, P.R.O., F.O., 96 : 21, 22 ; Palmerston to Russell, Apr. 24, 1851, P.R.O., G. and D., 22 : 9.
¹²⁶ P. 397. Q.V.L., 1st Ser., II, 213.

CHAPTER XVIII

¹ P. 398. Metternich, VII, 298.
² P. 398. Nesselrode, VIII, 362–3.
³ P. 398. C. Greville, *Mem.*, VI, 52, 57–8.
⁴ P. 399. Palmerston to Melbourne, Dec. 26, 1845, *Windsor MSS.* C. 44.
⁵ P. 399. C. Greville, *Mem.*, VI, 15–16.
⁶ P. 399. Palmerston to Russell, Oct. 21, 1845, P.R.O., G. and D., 22 : 4.
⁷ P. 399. *Hansard*, 3rd Ser., LXXXI, 520.
⁸ P. 399. Broughton, V, 168–9 ; *Melbourne Papers*, 384.
⁹ P. 399. Lord J. Russell, *Later Corr.*, I, ch. ix ; Parker, *Peel*, III, 201–3, 211 ; Cowley, *Diary and Corr.*, 309–10 ; Broughton, VI, 187, 199 ; Maxwell,

Clarendon, I, 287–8 ; Parker, *Graham*, II, 67 ; Walpole, *Russell*, II, 13–25 ; Hodder, II, 90–1.

[10] P. 400. Parker, *Peel*, III, 201–3, 211 ; Cowley, *Diary and Corr.*, 309–10.
[11] P. 400. *Hansard*, 3rd Ser., LXXXII, 1223–7.
[12] P. 400. Auckland to Russell, Sept. 8, 1846, P.R.O., G. and D , 22 : 6 ; C. Greville, *Mem.*, V, 433.
[13] P. 400. Broughton, VI, 201–2 ; Hodder, II, 91.
[14] P. 400. Broughton, VI, 187–9 ; B. and A.,III, 390–402 ; Lord J. Russell, *Later Corr.*, I, ch. ix ; *Hansard*, 3rd Ser., LXXXI, 525 ; LXXXII, 1223–6 ; Palmerston to Russell, Dec. 22, 1846, Aug. 14, 16, 1847, Jan. 14, 30, 1848 ; *Proposed Report to be asked for from Board of Ordnance* (Palmerston's handwriting), Dec. 1, 1847 ; Palmerston's memorandum, Dec. 31, 1847, P.R.O., G. and D., 22 : 5, 6, 7.
[15] P. 401. Palmerston's memorandum, Dec. 1846, P.R.O., G. and D., 22 : 5. Printed in B. and A., III, 390–402.
[16] P. 401. *Supra*, note 14.
[17] P. 401. *Hansard*, 3rd Ser., LXXVIII, 1291 ; LXXXII, 1223–7.
[18] P. 402. Lord J. Russell, *Later Corr.*, I, 250–2.
[19] P. 402. Walpole, *Russell*, II, 13–25 ; Broughton, VI, 201–2.
[20] P. 402. Dasent, *Delane*, I, 70.
[21] P. 402. Lord J. Russell, *Later Corr.*, I, 244.
[22] P. 402. Williams, *Napier*, 222.
[23] P. 403. Palmerston to Russell, Feb. 1, 1851, P.R.O., G. and D., 22 : 9.
[24] P. 403. Hillebrand, II, 654–79 ; D'Haussonville, 301–82 ; C.H.B.F.P. II, 296–7 ; Nolte, I, 215–39 ; du Bled, II, 627–40 ; Guizot, VIII, 416–517.
[25] P. 404. Ficquelmont, 151–2.
[26] P. 405. Q.V.L., 1st Ser., II, 161–3.
[27] P. 405. *Hansard*, 3rd Ser., CXII, 424–31.
[28] P. 406. Guizot, VIII, 467–517 ; correspondence (mainly copies) between Palmerston, Russell, Victoria, Jarnac and Ponsonby, *Windsor MSS.* I. 103.
[29] P. 406. *Supra*, note 27.
[30] P. 406. Mainly in F.O. 192 : 8 ; 100 : 51, 52, 53.
[31] P. 406. Palmerston to Robert Peel [see Camden Soc., 3rd Ser., vol. L, 161], Oct. 29, 1847 (no. 21), P.R.O., F.O., 192 : 8.
[32] P. 406. Nolte, I, 224–5.
[33] P. 406. Palmerston to Peel, Nov. 17, 1847, P.R.O., F.O. 100 : 51.
[34] P. 406. du Bled, II, 638.
[35] P. 406. Palmerston to Lansdowne, Nov. 10, 1847, *Bowood MSS.*
[36] P. 406. Guizot, VIII, 517.
[37] P. 407. Nesselrode, IX, 52–3.
[38] P. 407. Metternich, VII, 523.
[39] P. 407. Barante, VII, 259, 267.
[40] P. 407. Palmerston to Ponsonby, Dec. 1847, *Windsor MSS.* I. 103.
[41] P. 407. Beust, I, 44.
[42] P. 407. Bunsen, II, 91–2.
[43] P. 407. Palmerston to Clarendon, Jan. 28, 1849, *Clarendon MSS.*
[44] P. 408. Airlie, II, 119–20.
[45] P. 408. *Ibid.*, 120–1.
[46] P. 408. Lorne, 90–1.
[47] P. 408. Williams, *Napier*, 221.
[48] P. 409. Reeve, I, 230.
[49] P. 409. Lady Palmerston to Russell, Apr. 27, 1848 (?), P.R.O., G. and D., 22 : 7.

NOTES

[50] P. 409. Airlie, II, 131.
[51] P. 409. Hertslet, *Recollections*, 67–9.
[52] P. 409. Airlie, II, 116–17; Lady Palmerston to Mrs. Huskisson, Apr. 15, 1848, Br. Mus., *Add. MSS.* 39949, ff. 233–40.
[53] P. 410. Holyoake, *Sixty Years*, 80.
[54] P. 410. Palmerston to Clarendon, Nov. 13, 1847, *Clarendon MSS.*
[55] P. 410. Lord J. Russell, *Later Corr.*, I, 172–3.
[56] P. 410. William Petre [see Camden Soc., 3rd Ser., vol. L., 108] to Palmerston, Nov. 5, 1847; Minto to Palmerston, Nov. 19, 1847, *Windsor MSS.* D. 16; C. Greville, *Mem.*, VI, 108–9.
[57] P. 411. Lord J. Russell, *Later Corr.*, I, 224–5.
[58] P. 411. Palmerston to Clarendon, June 22, 1848, *Clarendon MSS.*
[59] P. 411. Same to same, Sept. 23, 1847, *Clarendon MSS.*
[60] P. 411. Draft to William Petre (?), Nov. 23, 1846, P.R.O., F.O., 96 : 21.
[61] P. 412. H. U. Addington to Russell, Sept. 11, 1847, P.R.O., G. and D., 22 : 6; Gwynn, 153–4.
[62] P. 412. Matter, *Cavour*, I, 310–11.
[63] P. 412. *Supra*, note 61.
[64] P. 412. *Infra*, note 68; C. Greville, *Mem.*, VI, 126.
[65] P. 412. Palmerston to Russell, Aug. 21, 1847, P.R.O., G. and D., 22 : 6.
[66] P. 412. B. and A., III, 194–7.
[67] P. 413. *Ibid.*
[68] P. 413. Palmerston to Russell, Aug. 21, 1847, P.R.O., G. and D., 22 : 6; Palmerston to Victoria, Aug. 31, 1847, *Windsor MSS.* J. 1. *Cf.* Walpole, *Russell*, II, 38–9.
[69] P. 414. Draft to Minto, Oct. 26, 1847, P.R.O., F.O., 96 : 21.
[70] P. 414. Draft to Abercromby, Oct. 26, 1847, P.R.O., F.O., 96 : 21; Matter *op. cit.*, I, 319–20.
[71] P. 414. Q.V.L., 1st Ser., II, 138–9; Corti, *Leopold*, 204–7.
[72] P. 415. Martin, *Prince Consort*, I, 348–53; Palmerston to Victoria, Aug. 31, 1847, *Windsor MSS.* J. 1; Q.V.L., 1st Ser., II, 150–1.
[73] P. 416. Minto to Palmerston, Nov. 19, Dec. 1, 1847, *Windsor MSS.* D. 16; Minto to Palmerston, Jan. 16, 1848 (copy); Minto to Russell, Jan. 2, 1848 (?), P.R.O., G. and D., 22 : 7; copy of circular from the Congregation of the Faith to Irish bishops, Jan. 3, 1848 (trans., copied from the *Evening Post*), *Windsor MSS.* D. 17.
[74] P. 486. C. Greville, *Mem.*, V, 217; Lord J. Russell, *Later Corr.*, I, 315–16; Palmerston to Clarendon, Nov. 13, 1847, *Clarendon MSS.*
[75] P. 417. Palmerston to Clarendon, March 9, 1848, *Clarendon MSS.*
[76] P. 417. *Hansard*, 3rd Ser., XCVI, 878–81.

CHAPTER XIX

[1] P. 422. *Ann. Reg.* for 1848, *Chronicle*, 31–3, 153; H. Greville, *Diary*, I, 234–5; Barante, VII, 306, 320, 334–6, 456; C. Greville, *Mem.*, VI, 137; Wiegler, 124–9; Metternich, VIII, 16–71, 153–228; Q.V.L., 1st Ser., II, 176 *et seq.*; Monypenny and Buckle, III, 176–7.
[2] P. 423. *Ibid.*, 178–9; Barante, VII, 335, 422; C. Greville, *Mem.*, VI, 186.
[3] P. 423. Metternich, VIII, 41.
[4] P. 423. *Ibid.*, 30.
[5] P. 423. *Ibid.*
[6] P. 423. Reeve, I, 197; C. Greville, *Mem.*, VI, 154.

[7] P. 423. Palmerston to Victoria, March 10, 1848, *Windsor MSS.* J. 49.
[8] P. 423. C. Greville, *Mem.*, VI, 157 ; H. Greville, *Diary*, I, 235 ; B. and A., IV, 88–9.
[9] P. 424. *Supra*, note 1.
[10] P. 424. Monypenny and Buckle, III, 192.
[11] P. 424. C. Greville, *Mem.*, VI, 157 ; H. Greville, *Diary*, I, 245.
[12] P. 424. Broughton, VI, 202.
[13] P. 424. *Ibid.*, 207.
[14] P. 424. B. and A., III, 357.
[15] P. 424. *Ibid.*, 351.
[16] P. 424. Palmerston to Clarendon, Apr. 22, 1848, *Clarendon MSS.*
[17] P. 424. Same to same, March 18, 1848.
[18] P. 425. Drafts to ambassadors at Berlin, Vienna and St. Petersburg, Feb. 29, 1848, P.R.O., F.O., 96 : 22 ; B. and A., IV, 83–5.
[19] P. 425. Palmerston to Clarendon, March 9, 1848, *Clarendon MSS.* (partly printed in B. and A., IV, 86–7).
[20] P. 425. Palmerston to Grey, March 29, 1848, *Howick MSS.*
[21] P. 425. *Hansard*, 3rd Ser., CII, 206–7 ; Lord J. Russell, *Later Corr.*, I, 295–300 ; Russell to Victoria, Aug. 12, 1848, *Windsor MSS.* J. 4 ; Palmerston to Russell, Dec. 19, 1848, P.R.O., G. and D., 22 : 7 ; Q.V.L., 1st Ser., II, 204, 224–5.
[22] P. 426. Bunsen to the King of Prussia, Feb. 27, 1848 (trans.), *Windsor MSS.* J. 67.
[23] P. 426. Brooks, 83.
[24] P. 427. Lord J. Russell, *Later Corr.*, I, 331–4. See also Brooks, 84–5 ; Whitehouse, 310:
[25] P. 427. Palmerston to Lansdowne, Apr. 3, 1848, *Bowood MSS.*
[26] P. 428. N. C. Kendrick, *Lord Palmerston and his North Italian Policy, 1848–1849*, unpublished. [I have not seen A. J. P. Taylor's *Italian Problem in European Diplomacy.*]
[27] P. 428. Vitzthum, *St. Petersburg and London*, I, 109.
[28] P. 429. Q.V.L., 1st Ser., II, 206–7.
[29] P. 429. *Ibid.*, 230.
[30] P. 430. Kendrick, *op. cit.*
[31] P. 430. B. and A., IV, 96–9.
[32] P. 430. *Ibid.*, 101–2.
[33] P. 430. Metternich, VIII, 450.
[34] P. 430. *Ibid.*, 451.
[35] P. 430. *Ibid.* ; Lord J. Russell, *Later Corr.*, I, 338.
[36] P. 430. *Ibid.*
[37] P. 431. Q.V.L., 1st Ser., II, 215–16.
[38] P. 431. Palmerston to Victoria, July 2, 1848, *Windsor MSS.* J. 3.
[39] P. 432. Q.V.L., 1st Ser., II, 216–17.
[40] P. 432. *Ibid.*, 220–1.
[41] P. 432. *Ibid.*, 221–2.
[42] P. 432. *E.g.* Russell to Victoria, Aug. 20, 1848, *Windsor MSS.* J. 4 ; Q.V.L., 1st Ser., II, 227–8.
[43] P. 432. Metternich, VIII, 477.
[44] P. 433. Nesselrode, IX, 175.
[45] P. 433. Monypenny and Buckle, III, 183–4.
[46] P. 433. *E.g.* Q.V.L., 1st Ser., II, 237–8.
[47] P. 433. *Ibid.*, 230–1.
[48] P. 433. B. and A., IV, 108.

NOTES 499

[49] P. 433. Lord J. Russell, *Later Corr.*, I, 340.
[50] P. 434. Kendrick, *op. cit.*
[51] P. 434. Lady Palmerston to Mrs. Huskisson, Sept. 11, 1848, Br. Mus., *Add. MSS.* 39949, ff. 246–9.
[52] P. 434. Russell to Victoria, Oct. 10, 1848, *Windsor MSS.* J. 5.
[53] P. 434. Corti, *Leopold*, 204–7.
[54] P. 434. Q.V.L., 1st Ser., II, 227–8, 235–6.
[55] P. 435. Wilson, *Greville*, II, 387–8.
[56] P. 435. Victoria to Russell, Oct. 14, 1848 (draft), *Windsor MSS.* J. 5.
[57] P. 435. Q.V.L., 1st Ser., II, 235–6.
[58] P. 435. *Ibid.*; Lord J. Russell, *Later Corr.*, I, 343; Russell to Victoria, Oct. 10, 1848, *Windsor MSS.* J. 5.
[59] P. 435. Lord J. Russell, *Later Corr.*, I, 347.
[60] P. 435. Nesselrode, IX, 186.
[61] P. 436. *E.g.* Palmerston to Abercromby, March 12, 19, 1849 (nos. 32, 40), P.R.O., F.O., 67 : 159.
[62] P. 436. C. Greville, *Mem.*, VI, 282–3.
[63] P. 436. Lord J. Russell, *Later Corr.*, I, 357–9.
[64] P. 437. *Ibid.*, 360–1.
[65] P. 437. Tocqueville, 353–9.
[66] P. 437. Palmerston to Normanby, July 26, 1849 (no. 357), P.R.O., F.O., 27 : 837.
[67] P. 437. Tocqueville, 359.
[68] P. 437. B. and A., IV, 118.
[69] P. 437. *Hansard*, 3rd Ser., CII, 209.
[70] P. 437. Q.V.L., 1st Ser., II, 227; C. Greville, *Mem.*, VI, 178–9; Martin, *Prince Consort*, II, 348.
[71] P. 437. *E.g.* P.R.O., F.O., 96 : 21, *passim.*
[72] P. 438. Q.V.L., 1st Ser., II, 230.
[73] P. 438. *Ibid.*, 263–4; Palmerston to Russell, June 28, 1849, P.R.O., G. and D., 22 : 7.
[74] P. 439. Palmerston to Bloomfield, Apr. 4, 1848, P.R.O., F.O., 356 : 29.
[75] P. 439. Martin, *Prince Consort*, II, 63; *Hansard*, 3rd Ser., XCIX, 393. See also draft to Bulwer, March 16, 1848, P.R.O., F.O., 96 : 22.
[76] P. 439. Airlie, II, 118; C. Greville, *Mem.*, VI, 170–1.
[77] P. 440. Palmerston to Russell, Apr. 21, 1848, P.R.O., G. and D., 22 : 7; draft to Bulwer, Apr. 18, 1848, F.O., 96 : 22; C. Greville, *Mem.*, VI, 169–70; Walpole, *Russell*, II, 43.
[78] P. 440. Airlie, II, 122.
[79] P. 440. Q.V.L., 1st Ser., II, 231–3.
[80] P. 440. Walpole, *Russell*, II, 46–7.
[81] P. 441. Palmerston to Ponsonby, Nov. (?), 1848 (copy), *Windsor MSS.* J. 6.
[82] P. 441. Gen. Grey to Prince Albert, Jan. 8, 1860, *Windsor MSS.* J. 24.
[83] P. 441. Schwarzenberg to Baron Werner, Dec. 4, 1848 (copy), *Windsor MSS.* J. 24.
[84] P. 442. Ponsonby to Werner, Dec. 7, 1848 (copy), *Windsor MSS.* J. 24.
[85] P. 442. Gen. Grey to Prince Albert, Jan. 8, 1860, *Windsor MSS.* J. 24.
[86] P. 442. *Ibid.*
[87] P. 443. Metternich, VIII, 45.
[88] P. 443. Gen. Grey to Prince Albert, Jan. 8, 1860, *Windsor MSS.* J. 24.
[89] P. 443. *Hansard*, 3rd Ser., CVII, 810.
[90] P. 444. Palmerston to Russell, Jan. 22, 1849 (copy), *Windsor MSS.* J. 7 (printed with important omissions in Walpole, *Russell*, II, 51–2).

[91] P. 444. Cook, *Delane*, 51-2 ; C. Greville, *Mem.*, VI, 272 n. ; Walpole, *Russell*, II, 50-1.
[92] P. 445. *Hansard*, 3rd Ser., CII, 1325 ; C. Greville, *Mem.*, VI, 272.
[93] P. 445. Earl Grey to Russell, Jan. 18, 23, 1849, *Howick MSS*.
[94] P. 445. Walpole, *Russell*, II, 51-2 ; Lord J. Russell, *Later Corr.*, I, 348-9.
[95] P. 445. *Supra*, note 90.
[96] P. 446. Q.V.L., 1st Ser., II, 250-2 ; Prince Albert's memorandum, Feb. 24, 1849, *Windsor MSS*. J. 7.
[97] P. 446. *Ibid.* ; C. Greville, *Mem.*, VI, 276. *Cf.* Walpole, *Russell*, II, 52.
[98] P. 446. Prince Albert's memorandum, Feb. 24, 1849.
[99] P. 446. C. Greville, *Mem.*, VI, 277.
[100] P. 446. Broughton, VI, 236.
[101] P. 446. Walpole, *Russell*, II, 53 ; Ponsonby to Russell, Dec. 4, 1849, enclosing Palmerston to Ponsonby, Oct. 19, Nov. 27, 1849 (extracts, copies) ; Palmerston to Russell, Dec. 6, 1849 ; Russell to Ponsonby, Jan. 29, 1850, P.R.O., G. and D., 22 : 8.
[102] P. 446. Ponsonby to Charles [Grey ?], Dec. 13, 1849, P.R.O., G. and D., 22 : 8.
[103] P. 447. Stockmar, II, 363-6.
[104] P. 447. *Ibid.*, 368.